THE MASTER MUSICIANS

TCHAIKOVSKY

Series edited by R. Larry Todd
Former series editor, the late Stanley Sadie

THE MASTER MUSICIANS

Titles Available in Paperback

Bach • Malcolm Boyd
Beethoven • Barry Cooper
Berlioz • Hugh MacDonald
Handel • Donald Burrows
Liszt • Derek Watson
Mahler • Michael Kennedy
Mendelssohn • Philip Radcliffe
Monteverdi • Denis Arnold
Puccini • Julian Budden
Schumann • Eric Frederick Jensen
Tchaikovsky • Edward Garden
Vivaldi • Michael Talbot

Titles Available in Hardcover

Mozart • Julian Rushton
Musorgsky • David Brown
Schoenberg • Malcolm MacDonald
Rossini • Richard Osborne
Verdi • Julian Budden

THE MASTER MUSICIANS

TCHAIKOVSKY

ROLAND JOHN WILEY

OXFORD UNIVERSITY PRESS
2009

OXFORD
UNIVERSITY PRESS

Oxford University Press, Inc., publishes works that further
Oxford University's objective of excellence
in research, scholarship, and education.

Oxford New York
Auckland Cape Town Dar es Salaam Hong Kong Karachi
Kuala Lumpur Madrid Melbourne Mexico City Nairobi
New Delhi Shanghai Taipei Toronto

With offices in
Argentina Austria Brazil Chile Czech Republic France Greece
Guatemala Hungary Italy Japan Poland Portugal Singapore
South Korea Switzerland Thailand Turkey Ukraine Vietnam

Published by Oxford University Press, Inc.
198 Madison Avenue, New York, New York 10016

www.oup.com

Library of Congress Cataloging-in-Publication Data
Wiley, Roland John.
Tchaikovsky / by Roland John Wiley.
p. cm. — (The master musicians)
Includes bibliographical references and index.
ISBN 978-0-19-536892-5
1. Tchaikovsky, Peter Ilich, 1840–1893. 2. Composers—Russia—Biography.
I. Title.
ML410.C4W52 2009
780.92—dc 222008032374
[B]

1 3 5 7 9 8 6 4 2

Printed in the United States of America
on acid-free paper

FOR MY WIFE

Contents

About Spelling and Citations in This Book

SOURCE CITATIONS ARE SET FORTH ACCORDING TO A METHOD PREferred in the social sciences, that is, by numbers which correspond to titles cited fully in the bibliography. A given entry is marked by punctuation in the following manner:

- the number representing the title of the work, separated by a semicolon from the next number title when several are being cited;
- after a comma, the page number, if cited;
- after the page number, a comma and the note number, if cited.

Citations of works in more than one volume dispense with internal punctuation unless a footnote is being cited. Thus, 255 II 147 refers to page 147 of volume II of the *Selected Articles* of G. A. Larosh [Laroche], which is published in five volumes (Leningrad, 1974–1978; source no. 255).

Much-cited sources are variously noted:

- Modest Tchaikovsky's biography, Chaykovskiy, *The Life of Pyotr Ilyich Tchaikovsky . . .* (Moscow, 1901–1903; source no. 75), is referred to as *The Life* in the main body of the text and cited in the following manner: 1997 (the year of the Russian reprint; source no. 76) + volume number (I, II, or III) + page number, thus, 1997 II 324 (volume II, page 324).
- The academic edition of Tchaikovsky's music in Chaykovskiy, *Collected Works* (Moscow, 1940–1990; source no. 89), is abbreviated CW, followed, if relevant, by volume and page. Some volumes have been divided and published in parts, each part designated by the volume number and an additional letter; CW 15-b is the second separately published unit of volume 15.
- The academic edition of Tchaikovsky's writings, the *Complete Works: Literary Works and Correspondence* (Moscow, 1953–1981; source no. 90), which includes his letters in volumes v–xvii, are cited as follows: volume number as lowercase roman numeral + arabic page number, thus, vii 235 (volume vii, page 235).

Some of these volumes are also divided into separately issued books marked "a" and "b," thus, xvi-b 175 (volume xvi-b, page 175).

- The compendium of Tchaikovsky's life, *The Days and Years of P. I. Tchaikovsky,* ed. Yakovlev et al. (Moscow, 1940; source no. 435), is abbreviated D&Y.
- The *Diaries of P. I. Tchaikovsky* (Moscow and Petrograd, 1923; source no. 81, are cited as Dnev (for *dnevnik,* or diary) with the relevant page number.

Newspapers are cited as follows: abbreviated initials + year in two digits + month in two digits + day in two digits, thus, MV980605 = *Moskovskie vedomosti* for 5 June 1898. Because many Russian dailies were but four pages long in the imperial period, with the first page containing headlines and the last containing advertisements and announcements, page numbers have not been specified on the assumption that someone reading the two inner pages will be able to find the article. Periodicals follow similar principles, adapted to their method of issue. RMG 1911/22–23, 504, for example, = *Russkaya muzïkal'naya* gazeta for the year 1911, the combined issue 22–23, column 504. Particulars of the citation of a periodical should be clear upon consultation with the original. Abbreviations used in the main body of the text are

BV	*Birzhevïe vedomosti* (Commercial News, St. Petersburg)
GM	*Gazette musicale* (Paris)
GO	*Golos* (The Voice, St. Petersburg)
JS	*Journal de St. Pétersbourg* (St. Petersburg)
LT	*Le temps* (Paris)
ME	*Le Ménestrel* (Paris)
MT	*Musical Times* (London)
MV	*Moskovskie vedomosti* (Moscow News, Moscow)
MW	*Musikalisches Wochenblatt* (Berlin)
NO	*Novosti i birzhevaya gazeta* (News and Commercial Gazette, St. Petersburg)
NV	*Novoe vremya* (The New Time, St. Petersburg)
NZ	*Neue Zeitschrift für Musik* (Leipzig)
PG	*Peterburgskaya gazeta* (Petersburg Gazette, St. Petersburg)
PL	*Peterburgskiy listok* (Petersburg Leaflet, St. Petersburg)
RMG	*Russkaya muzïkal'naya gazeta* (Russian Musical Gazette, St. Petersburg)
RO	*Russkoe obozrenie* (Russian Review, St. Petersburg)

RS	*Russkaya starina* (Russian Antiquity, St. Petersburg)
RV	*Russkie vedomosti* (Russian News, Moscow)
SM	*Signale für die musikalische Welt* (Leipzig)
SV	*Sanktpeterburgskie vedomosti* (St. Petersburg News, St. Petersburg)
VI	*Vsemirnaya illyustratsiya* (Universal Illustration, St. Petersburg)

Single dates refer to occurrences in Russia and are Old Style. Double dates indicate an occurrence outside of Russia and are given in Old Style and New Style, separated by a slash, as in 13/25 January. Old Style was 12 days behind New Style during Tchaikovsky's life.

Transliteration is mixed, which is to say inconsistent; decisions about it were motivated by some compromise between the pursuit of consistency and the desire to avoid oddity. Consistency was hemmed in by many considerations of so-called standard usage, beginning with the first and most central exception—spelling the composer's name with an initial *T*. The following general rule has been applied: to follow strict transliteration in bibliographic contexts (including titles within the main body of the text) and to follow more informal, usage-conditioned transliteration elsewhere, especially in the names of persons and theaters.

Preface

MORE THAN A HUNDRED YEARS AFTER HIS DEATH AND AFTER dozens of biographies, why another book about Tchaikovsky? There are at least three reasons: the continuing popularity of his music warrants periodic reassessment; changing political and cultural mores; and, not least, reconsideration of someone who has suffered at the hands of biographers. In the years around 1990–1993—anniversaries of his birth and death—it was clear that the easy comprehension of his work was fatal to understanding. "Tchaikovsky's music is not at all as simple and guileless as many propose," Gennady Shokhman wrote [344], and I. I. Skvortsova commented: "That of which one is fully aware, and therefore senses superficially, stands as a barrier to the deep layers of his thought" [361, 40]. Familiar data are outdated, including the academic edition of his music, which was published in Moscow and Leningrad from 1940 to 1990 and imaginatively edited to say the least. But flawed data reach back to the wellsprings of Tchaikovsky's biography. And that is where this story begins, with *The Life of Pyotr Ilyich Tchaikovsky* [75; 76], three volumes of materials assembled and elaborated by Tchaikovsky's brother Modest and definitively published in 1901–1903. Modest's work is fundamental to scholarship on Pyotr, yet, for all its author's authority as a sibling, it is not faultless. To alert the reader to problems in *The Life* is one aim of the present study.

Modest Tchaikovsky has been described as a whimpering sycophant, "a frustrated lover, a frustrated rival, a frustrated collaborator, and a frustrated biographer" [303, 233]. He was nevertheless a man of parts: a dramatist of six plays; a belletrist; a poet of short verses and a substantial "mystery," *Catherine of Siena;* a translator from Italian, French, and English into Russian (including Shakespeare's sonnets and *Richard II*) and of Chekhov from Russian into Italian; a journalist and occasional music critic; a librettist of opera for his brother and others and of ballet. He was, moreover, a recognized pedagogue of deaf mutes. In his brother's memory, Modest made a museum of Tchaikovsky's home at Klin, a town near Moscow; solicited, collected, and cataloged materials about the composer; arranged for the publication of his early music; and researched the family's history.

It is also clear that Modest fictionalized parts of *The Life* and omitted references to Pyotr's sexuality and awkward family circumstances. Perhaps to be excused for avoiding scandal and respecting the privacy of persons then still alive, he set an unfortunate precedent for the myopic investigation of Pyotr's life at the expense of serious engagement with his music. By making Pyotr's letters the substance of his biography, virtually without commentary after the composer's early years, he preempted many other voices and issues. Early critics lamented the elevation of Pyotr's letters to the status of biographical scripture. Nikolay Kashkin, the composer's friend and colleague from 1866, argued that Tchaikovsky's letters did not express the essence of his life, that they were contradictory and shielded the reader from the internal world of his feelings [MV020820]. He was but echoing the composer's own famous opinion: "It seems to me that letters are never fully sincere. I judge at least by myself. To whom and for whatever I write, I always take care for the impression the letter creates, not only on the correspondent, but also on some incidental reader in the future. Consequently, I pose" [Dnev 213–14].

For Kashkin, substituting letters for a vigorous, independent biography was due to the "fainthearted impartiality of his brother" [MV030316]. Worse still, Modest did not reveal the state of the letters he published in *The Life*—that he had modified them and that some had been mutilated and ransacked by family members. Within six weeks of Pyotr's death, his brother Anatoly wrote to Modest, "I wish that nobody besides you and me have contact with the surviving papers and letters until all of them which compromise his memory in any degree will be destroyed." Modest does not refer to originals with erasures, strike-throughs, hachures; those with portions cut away by scissors, torn away by hand, or blotted out with India ink [369, 119–20]. Another brother, Nikolay, visited Klin within two months of Pyotr's death (Modest was away), read letters about his adoptive son from the child's mother to Pyotr, took them with him, and proposed to Modest that any other such letters be destroyed [409, 14–15]. This mischief has confounded the perception of Tchaikovsky's life, especially those periods when no letter of Pyotr survives or when the letters significantly favor business addressees over family. Modest saved a few of Pyotr's intimate letters, but he was still his brother's most comprehensive censor.

A major problem with Tchaikovsky's letters is our continuing ignorance of their contents, as many are still held in private hands. In what we have, censorship has compounded the effect of tampering by family. Some editorial modifications were prudish—expunging profanity or Tchaikovsky's references to his wife as a "serpent." Censors also were flummoxed by expressions of affection in perfectly acceptable language, as when Tchaikovsky wrote to his sister (16 April 1868):

> I love you just as powerfully and strongly as before, and as ever! And can you seriously doubt this? . . . To show you that I love you, perhaps much more than you think, I shall tell you what I dream about [i.e., a quiet, peaceful life]. . . . To me there is no doubt that this future blessedness is unthinkable without *you*. [v 136]

Or to his brother Anatoly (11 December 1875): "But the less I write to you the more I love you, my dear and very best of all jurisprudence colleagues!" (this was censored in all expurgated editions). Or to his brother Modest (11 January 1876): "In general, keep in mind that I *love* you *very, very, very* much" [vi 16]. Or to his servant (27 October/8 November 1877): "I kiss you, my joy" (censored in all expurgated editions).

Soviet editors also took seriously what Tchaikovsky wrote in jest. One letter to his friend Ivan Klimenko, full of leg pulling, silliness, and wordplay, is reduced to three sentences in the academic edition, where Tchaikovsky reports learning that Klimenko was angry that he hadn't written. The following was expurgated:

> But can you really, most beloved woman in my harem, young and beautiful Klimena, doubt my love for a single moment[?] No, the silence is explained only by your voluptuous Sultan's laziness. . . .
>
> Strictly speaking, it isn't worth writing, since we shall soon see each other; but I took my pen in hand according to the indefatigable requirements of my divan, which, because of my removal to a new flat, having been upholstered with new material, is bogged down in longing for you and prays for your visit to Moscow to rest your tired limbs on its resilient shoulders, which have new springs. To its request I add my own. If you would provide us both no small pleasure, then stay with me and live with us as long as you see fit. I hope you will not compel me, that is the *Sultan* and my *Divan,* that is, *my government,* to turn our requests into a command, the disobedience of which will call for mortal punishment by impaling. [199, 60–61]

Tchaikovsky plays on words—on *divan* both as "sofa" and as "Turkish council of state" and, more cleverly, on the term *sidenie na kole,* which means "to impale" (the mock punishment), and puns on the meaning of "to sit" (i.e., at home), the punishment Klimenko will suffer if he declines the composer's invitation. One questions here the threat to public decency. The problem is that his words are plainly homoerotic [305, 139–40], and Tchaikovsky's censors, in their uncertainty as to what to suppress, have raised sensitivity to sexual innuendo to a greater degree of prominence than if they had done nothing at all. In fact, restored expurgations find Tchaikovsky urging Modest to fight his homoerotic inclinations, relating news of homosexual acquaintances, and recounting his own love affairs [369]. Elsewhere, he feminized masculine names—Klimena for Klimenko in the letter just cited—including his own, and he used women's names in reference to men. In a published letter to Modest, he signed himself "Your devoted and loving sister Petrolina" [v 288]. How could a Soviet censor, let alone the zealous Anatoly, see nothing compromising in this? In his own unfinished autobiography [306, 23–25], Modest identified with Pyotr and wrote about his own sexuality. Our realization now that Modest was laundering his public account while reserving his candid thoughts to a private one has further undermined the credibility of *The Life.*

Editors, then, have fallen about in confusion over what to do with Tchaikovsky's letters. Yet Tchaikovsky was personally sensitive to the exposure of his sexuality, and his siblings were obviously concerned about it. Soviet censors in the ultraconservative political environment before World War II were, ironically, the first to restore some original texts and to deal with the issue candidly, in both the composer's correspondence with his patron, Nadezhda von Meck, and the collection *Pis'ma k rodnïm* (Letters to Relatives) [88]. Editorial policies, in turn, have intersected on a historical plane with two other circumstances which have complicated the picture of Tchaikovsky's life.

First is the exceptional public discourse on Tchaikovsky's homosexuality. No other composer of his day, let alone his Russian contemporaries Musorgsky and Balakirev or other composers who may have been homosexual, has generated the commentary and speculation in print that Tchaikovsky has, so early after his death and so extensively, in respect to sexual orientation. It could hardly have been a secret to his contemporaries, who would have observed his bachelorhood and disastrous marriage. But one need not advocate the suppression of homosexuality in biography to appreciate the distorting lens through which Tchaikovsky's life has been viewed since then, including the virtual expunging of references to homosexuality in Soviet biography and its acknowledgment and a descent into amateur psychology in some Anglophone literature about him [e.g., 132, 4, 16; 60, 50]. From this last, his reputation stands in need of rehabilitation [173].

Second is the new wave of biography that deals candidly with Tchaikovsky's homosexuality and so reverses the tendencies of expurgation to which Tchaikovsky's letters have been subject [305; 161]. This effort implicitly acknowledges that discussing sexuality was a sensitive matter for Tchaikovsky and identifies in him a mode of utterance that is sometimes mannered (as in the examples cited above) but not limited to times of crisis. It necessarily involves interpretation, which affects its efficacy as evidence, and so far, the new biographies have maintained some distance from any engagement with Tchaikovsky's music. They are the opposite, in immediate impression, of literature which links homosexuality with style. The present volume has no issue with the decoding of Tchaikovsky's letters, acknowledging the need for subjectivity in such an enterprise, but the new biographies' focus on homosexuality, combined with their non-engagement with Tchaikovsky's art, leaves no response to the question of how the two may be related. What is heard and how it is heard reside in the ears of the listener, while the necessary link between homosexuality and the elements of musical composition is one of continuing dispute [e.g., 341].

The state of Tchaikovsky's letters—or the possibility that he did not address certain topics in his correspondence—has obscured his personal life. We know little about his sexual awakening; no evidence survives of a loving, mutual, sustained relationship with anyone. His attraction to his nephew Vladimir "Bob" Davïdov was unreciprocated, apart from being unthinkable in real terms, while other recipients of his affection are obscure; the personal letters Modest saved are mostly about passionate encounters unfulfilled [369, 127–34]. The unmutilated or destroyed correspondence would have to be immense if all mentions of a companion were expunged and 6,000 letters remained, with such references also remaining undetected in sources over which Modest and Anatoly had no control. Two biographies descend from the letters—a Western one lacking discipline and data and a Russian one shaped by Marxist proprieties—framed by imperial period sources and a new Russian, mostly revisionist, sometimes richly perceptive literature of recent years, more sensitive to Western context and devoted to bringing obscure and unpublished documents to light. These moderate the image of Tchaikovsky the homosexual with the Tchaikovsky of compassion, who fretted over family members, gave to those in need, read the Bible, paid students' fees, mentored colleagues, and wrote countless letters of recommendation. This is the Tchaikovsky who summoned his muse in the morning at 10, and so composed *The Queen of Spades* in 43 days and the Sixth Symphony in 24. This is Tchaikovsky the chain smoker, who suffered woeful illness but hated doctors, who in private declared himself a tsar in music but in public was too shy to take a graceful bow, who once on a windy day bought 10 pounds of cotton, too embarrassed to ask a shopkeeper how little was enough to plug his ears.

That music and biography are segregated in this study was a difficult choice, and the decision risks the appearance that the two are unrelated. This cannot be true, but the present state of knowledge about Tchaikovsky's life is no boon to illuminating the ways in which it interacted with his art, while the composer himself claimed that the artistic and the everyday were separate realms of activity. The premise that all of Tchaikovsky's music had immediate and profound motivation in his life cannot be sustained. Part of the reason is his facility: he could write a piano piece as Picasso could make a drawing, and he did, on sheer technique, leaving no distinctive biographical trace. Part of the reason is simple obscurity: he composed *Fatum,* the *Rococo Variations,* and the *Serenade for Strings* in times of his life so undocumented that the merest speculation on the relation between life and art is idle. Many pieces were motivated by commerce; others, such as the *Souvenir de Florence,* were manifestly about solving artistic challenges. At the same time, some of his music, on the basis of his own acknowledgment or else strongly implicit in its compositional behavior, speaks to particular issues of his life. Important here are his most famous and popular works: the operas *Evgeniy Onegin* and *The Queen of Spades,* the symphonies from no. 4 onward, and the ballets *The Sleeping Beauty* and *The Nutcracker.* The songs, more than any other subset of his repertoire, may also be linked to his life through the contents of the poems and his relationships to the dedicatees. The biographical implications of these works have all been referenced in analyses.

All told, the segregation of music from life is the better choice. Those interested in Tchaikovsky's music, as indicated at the outset of this preface, seek a fresh look at its sophistication and its place within the musical thought of his day. Musical creation was as much a part of Tchaikovsky's world as his personal life and warrants its own celebration. That celebration is necessarily technical to some degree and non-narrative in presentation, risking a greater sense of disjunction if the discussion is integrated with the biography than if it is kept separate. Moreover, the ability of a composition to transcend generations, whatever its genesis in life experience, is increasingly divorced from biography over time as it resonates with the concerns of new audiences.

Whatever its success in the concert hall, Tchaikovsky's music has not fared well in the literature. Its popularity has always been suspect, and nationality has always been an issue—whether, with a frail indigenous tradition, a Russian composer could keep company with international masters and establish an identity in different lands. Early on, his work was disdained by non-Russian academics, not least for its puzzling, presumably undisciplined nonconformity. In Russia, by the later 1930s, attitudes toward Tchaikovsky were again reverential after harsh critique a decade earlier. But complex problems arising from stultifying insularity, taboos against Western analytical terminology, lack of translation, limited circulation—not to mention world war—kept Russian insights from having much effect in the West. The study of the compositional process has come to Tchaikovsky's music only in this recent period [116; 403; 404; 424]. As a composer, Tchaikovsky followed no manifesto, avoided alliances, and formed no recipe for others to follow. His limited exposure to Western European masterworks was enough for him to assimilate their form and sense, yet not so controlling as to preclude a powerful individuality. Two aspects of his musical thinking may be anticipated here.

The Russian term *prelest'* is used in this study to connote that property of Tchaikovsky's music that is rooted in sheer attractiveness and enticing sound, a quality associated with Glinka, Musorgsky, Borodin, and other Russian composers of the nineteenth century. Its modern translation is "charm" or "fascination," but Vladimir Dal' in his monumental *Explanatory Dictionary of the Living Great Russian Language* (1880–1882) [III, 393], opened a sizable entry on the term with "what captivates [or seduces] in the highest degree; seduction, fascination," followed by more sinister connotations ("darkness," "seduction by the evil spirit"), moving subsequently to "beauty," "comeliness and good-lookingness, elegance"; "what captivates and charms the senses, or subdues mind and will to itself." This latter connotation is closest to the one intended in this volume. Whether Tchaikovsky composed with this term and its connotations in mind cannot be determined, as he did not use it that we know, though the concept, in his letters, is linked to inspiration on a given day and with his belief that only music sincerely felt has the power to move a listener. He seems aware of its presence and degree as a measure of the effectiveness and accessibility of his ideas.

In addition, *prelest'* is a useful term in the assessment of musical coherence in Tchaikovsky because it is of the moment, and as such affects the aesthetic of capital works, that is, whether he will construct a series of captivating moments briefly elaborated or forge a longer musical discourse in the Germanic tradition with musical ideas of this kind. The tension between "good-soundingness" and producing a cogent argument explains Tchaikovsky's but occasional conformity with Germanic formal patterns. At the same time, it wins adherents in audiences who listen instinctively.

The relationship of Tchaikovsky's music to Western European models is a window onto his musical thinking. To suggest that he somehow wished to emulate these models and couldn't is demeaning and unsupportable in the face of his manifest ingenuity. This does not mean that inspiration never faltered, that every composition is a masterwork and every experiment a success, least of all that Tchaikovsky rejected the Western European heritage, but simply that giving him some credit for autonomy and individual approaches to composition will rectify the tendency, over the decades, to reject his music as unassimilated—not quite up to standard—eccentric, and too personal. While Tchaikovsky may not deserve recognition as an innovator at the rank of Debussy or Schönberg, his best music, like theirs, builds new paradigms out of old. This experimentation, together with his love of sound, are contentions of the present volume which align with larger historical issues in Russian music having to do with the assimilation and individualization of foreign models, starting with Glinka, and with forming vocabularies of national identity in music.

Over the long preparation of this book, generous assistance has been provided by numerous institutions and individuals. These include the following grant-giving organizations: the International Research and Exchanges Board, the John Simon Guggenheim Foundation, and the National Endowment for the Humanities. I am indebted in various particulars to the Library of Congress, the New York Public Library, the Boston Public Library, the Newberry Library, the British Museum, the Library of the Academy of Sciences and the Saltïkov-Shchedrin Public Library in St. Petersburg, the Russian National Library in Moscow, with special thanks to the staff of its newspaper annex in Khimki, and the Tchaikovsky Home-Museum at Klin. Among university libraries, those of Harvard, Yale, Cornell, Stanford, the University of California at Berkeley, the University of Michigan, and Indiana University deserve special mention. The individuals, either whose efforts in supplying data or whose ideas and insights are reflected in the following text, comprise a list too numerous to mention, but must include John Milton Ward, Elizaveta Yakovlevna Surits of Moscow, Thomas Kohlhase of the Tschaikowsky-Gesellschaft in Tübingen, and generations of faculty colleagues and students. Special thanks are owed Natalia Challis of Ann Arbor for years of patient and wise counsel, not least in connection with questions of verbal prosody in the Sixth Symphony, and Inessa Sergeyevna Preobrazhenskaya and Valery Vladimirovich Gubin, now of fond memory but lately the chief archivist and director, respectively, of the Bakhrushin State Theater Museum in Moscow. For publication support, acknowledgment is happily made to the Office of the Vice President for Research and the College of Literature, Science, and the Arts Publication Subvention program, and to Dean Christopher Kendall and Associate Dean Mary Simoni of the School of Music, Theater, and Dance at the University of Michigan. Not least, my thanks go to my wife, Jitka, whose experience during the writing of this piece can most charitably be described as long-suffering.

THE MASTER MUSICIANS

TCHAIKOVSKY

Series edited by R. Larry Todd
Former series editor, the late Stanley Sadie

CHAPTER ONE

Tchaikovsky's Early Years

IN THE FIRST PARAGRAPH OF *THE LIFE OF PYOTR ILYICH TCHAIKOVSKY,* Modest remarked on his brother's ironic stance toward his family's gentrified status. As well he might, it having originated but two generations earlier with Pyotr Fyodorovich Tchaikovsky, the son of a Ukrainian Cossack known as Fyodor Afanasyevich Chaika, with whom the traceable genealogy of the composer's paternity begins [318]. Fyodor fought with Peter the Great at Poltava, dying of his wounds and leaving a widow and two orphans. His son Pyotr Fyodorovich served as a military doctor until 1774, then took up posts of civic responsibility in various towns in the Urals until his retirement from state service in 1789; he was seeking a judgeship in the town of Glazov four months before his death in 1818, at the age of 73. The status of gentry had been conferred on Pyotr Fyodorovich by decree of Catherine the Great in 1785. His wife, Anastasiya Stepanovna Posokhova, endured 20 pregnancies (according to Modest) from which nine children survived, most to a ripe maturity. Four of Pyotr Fyodorovich's sons were soldiers, some winning fame in battle, including Pyotr Petrovich, a veteran of 52 engagements [421].

Civil service was the profession of Pyotr Fyodorovich's youngest son, Ilya, the composer's father. He was sent to a factory in Izhevsk at the age of 13 to learn the principles of manufacture, and he became copyist to its supervisor, who, when reassigned to the Mining Cadet Corps in St. Petersburg, took Ilya with him [164, 5–6]. Ilya Petrovich graduated from the corps in 1817 with a silver medal. In 1827 he married Maria Karlovna Keiser, who bore him a daughter, Zinaida. Maria died in 1831. By 1833, Ilya, then 38, was courting Alexandra Andreyevna Assier, then 20, who would be the composer's mother and about whose lineage we have much data [154; 355]. She was of French extraction through her father, Hendrich Mikhaylovich Assier [421], who emigrated to Russia from Prussia [55], began Russian service in 1795, took Russian citizenship, and married in 1800. Trained in porcelain manufacture, Assier worked in Russia as a customs official and translator, retiring in 1830 a wealthy man [370, 10]. He taught at the Mining Cadet Corps, as did Ilya from 1828 to 1831 [GO800111]. On her mother's side, Alexandra descended from Orthodox clergy from Moscow and St. Petersburg [368, 236–39]. Three generations back, Tchaikovsky's ancestors ranged from France east to the Urals and from the Poltava region north to St. Petersburg. Any claim of his Polish origin [viii 229] has no basis.

Married on 1 October 1833, Ilya and Alexandra in 1836 had a daughter, Ekaterina, who died the next year; in 1838 the composer's elder brother, Nikolay, was born. By then, Ilya had been promoted to lieutenant colonel in the Corps of Mining Engineers and director of the Kamsko-Votkinsk factory, about 620 miles east-northeast of Moscow [164, 6], where the family had arrived in March 1837 [130, 36]. Close to Izhevsk, it was, for Ilya, much like going home. The factory flourished under his management, expanding into "sixteen important sections and studios with the most varied manufacture. Specialists at Votkinsk produced both the most precise watch springs and 200-horsepower steamboats (from 1847), razors and anchors, scissors and penknives, side-by-side with heavy plates for warships . . . and diverse other wares" [9, 12].

In 1837 Votkinsk had 10,000 inhabitants, its own police and administration, and a lively commerce in engineers and technicians. The director's house had a large social hall; the factory provided an orchestra, the nearby Cathedral of the Annunciation a choir, and the staff a respectable if diverse chamber ensemble [14, 9, 28, 40–44]. Ilya himself expanded the library at Votkinsk with books and musical instruments [117, 247–50] and purchased an orchestrion, a large music box which played a drum-like cylinder. Pyotr Ilyich Tchaikovsky was born there on 25 April (7 May N.S.) 1840, "with a kind of strange abscess on his left temple, which was operated on successfully soon after his birth" [71, 24]. His sister Alexandra (Sasha) followed late in 1841 and his brother Ippolit in 1843. Had Pyotr's gift been for mining and manufacture, living his entire life as a third-generation civil servant in the Urals would never have raised an eyebrow.

What was Tchaikovsky's childhood like? In an autobiography written in 1889, he disparaged it. His innate abilities as a child attracted no particular attention from his parents, and when he would come home from school on holiday (he did not attend until he was 12, four years after leaving Votkinsk), the house was completely lacking in atmosphere encouraging to his musical development [309 I 523]. In *The Life,* Modest took a similar tack, emphasizing rural mores, dullish elders, and antimusical circumstances:

> Pyotr Ilyich was born and lived in a place where there was no music whatever, besides amateurs of primitive gifts tinkling on the piano. Alexandra Andreyevna sang nicely, but her playing went no further than dances for the children. . . . The rest of Ilya Petrovich's householders could not even do this. Unfortunately even Fanny [Pyotr's governess] was no musician or even a music lover, such that the future composer's musical education fell to a soulless object—the so-called orchestrion. [1997 I 40–41]

The neglected child-genius made a better story than the belated professional who did not seek training until he was 21. Short of perceiving the immensity of his gift—which, as distinct from his precociousness, Pyotr himself took years to realize—Ilya and Alexandra did everything for him that good parents should. Ten years after Votkinsk, when formal music training was still unavailable in Russia, a professional musician in St. Petersburg saw no extraordinary talent in their son, and Tchaikovsky later admitted that upon graduation from the School of Jurisprudence (at the age of 19), he wavered between urges to compose and sentiments that gave him pause [309 I 524–25].

Other points in these canonic sources warrant challenge. Modest himself included more generous assessments of Votkinsk in an earlier draft of *The Life:*

> [I]t is impossible to imagine a nest more warm and gentle than that in which this little chick was born and spent his first seven years. Around him at this time was not one severe and unfair person or a single cloud of deprivation and woe. . . . His situation . . . gave full breadth to the development of all the noble

> and beautiful qualities of his spirit. . . . Fully satisfied with his situation, he could not wish for better. [71, 48–49]

That his parents were insensitive to Pyotr's gift is disputed. They were trained in the arts in anticipation of postings to remote areas and gave Pyotr music lessons in Votkinsk, Alapaevsk, and St. Petersburg. His first teacher, Maria Palchikova, was a musician of "firm knowledge" [1997 I 42] to whom Pyotr gave a pension when he encountered her later in life [on Palchikova, see 14, 25–30]. His allusion in the autobiography to playing Kalkbrenner's "La fée" as a child—a reference too specific to be imagined—speaks to his facility at that age. Dismissing the orchestrion, Modest gave no quarter to the impact on Pyotr of hearing Mozart for the first time, impressions played out in his lifelong affection for *Don Giovanni* and Italian opera. Although regretting his lack of information about the orchestrion, Modest possessed the letter in which Ilya Petrovich instructed Alexandra to spend 700 or 800 rubles—a huge sum in 1844—on its repair in St. Petersburg even if it meant making other sacrifices [9, 10–11]. Modest may even have remembered the instrument, which left the Tchaikovsky home in 1854 in Zinaida's dowry. She and her husband took it with them to Ufa in 1870; after they died, it passed to their son, thence to a tavernkeeper, a merchant, and the Ufa Temperance Society, where it was still to be found in 1911 [RMG 1911/22–23, 504].

Modest claimed to enjoy his siblings' recollections of Votkinsk but did not specify them in *The Life*. Eyewitness testimony of Tchaikovsky's childhood came from the one person who could still provide it when Modest took up his pen. This was Fanny Dürbach, the family governess between 1844 and 1848 [228], whom Modest interviewed in 1894 [72, 154]; of the Votkinsk Tchaikovskys, Pyotr is the only one she ever met again. An excellent teacher, credited with Pyotr's fluency in French and German at the age of six, Fanny described the children's routine:

> We lived our lives completely separate from the adults except during meals. Both studies and amusements were our own. We spent evenings before holidays by ourselves, upstairs, reading and conversing. In the summer we had a carriage, and took trips around the charming environs of Votkinsk. On weekdays from 6 o'clock in the morning the time was strictly allocated, and the day's program would be executed punctually. Since free hours, when the children could do anything they liked, were extremely limited, I insisted that they spend

> them in physical exercise, about which I was always wrangling with Pierre, who after lessons was drawn to the piano. . . . Left to himself, he went more for music, took up reading, or writing verse. [1997 I 27]

Dürbach saved Pyotr's compositions. Discounting a song, lost if ever written, by the four -year-old Pyotr and two-year-old Sasha, called "Our Mama in Petersburg," these date from 1847–1848 and comprise essays and poems in two copybooks and some loose sheets. Pyotr wrote mostly in French, on secular and metaphysical topics precocious for a seven-year-old. His work includes prayers and prayer-like poems, other religious topics (the fall from grace, the birth of Christ, the prodigal son), compassion ("Mort d'un oiseau"), philosophy ("La mort"), patriotism ("Sur ma Patrie"), and Joan of Arc [1997 I 30–40; 71, 32–41; 100]. Fanny valued Pyotr's literary talent, calling him "le petit Pouchkine." To Modest, these texts lacked significance for the musician.

Fanny is the source of famous anecdotes about Pyotr the child. He begged mercy for a kitten about to be drowned and interrupted his father with news of its rescue. Scolded for kissing the map of Russia while spitting on the rest of Europe, he answered that he had covered France, Fanny's homeland, with his hand [1997 I 25–26]. Cautious about Pyotr's love of music, she noted his nerves after free time at the piano and how, energetically tapping a pane of glass as if it were a keyboard, he broke it and cut his hand [1997 I 41–42]. Recalling the child in the knowledge of the man, she attempted to identify what made him extraordinary:

> Nothing particular, but decidedly in everything he did. In class one couldn't be more diligent and quick; at play no one devised merrier entertainments; during recreational reading no one listened more attentively, and at dusk before a holiday, when I gathered all my students around and asked each in turn to tell us something, no one indulged his imagination in a more charming way. [1997 I 24]

Topics that Fanny taught him sparked his interest later, including the exploits of Raymond Lully, Alexander the Great, and Joan of Arc and tales like "The Captain's Daughter" and *Undine* [117, 249].

Tchaikovsky repeatedly affirmed his affection for his parents. We know little about Alexandra [71, 22–24], who in photographs seems aloof, but Pyotr emulated much in Ilya [164, 58–78]. At the conservatory, he took up his father's instrument, the flute, and later opened a school for the children of Maydanovo, as his father had for the children of Votkinsk. They both loved theater and Italian opera and were amateur actors. They shared attitudes about hard work and responsibility. As Ilya loved rural life, preferring to be first in the country to being last in Rome [164, 63], Pyotr gravitated to rural places, long walks, weather changes, and gathering mushrooms. Both disdained rank or power. They conducted their personal affairs on the basis of sympathy, professional ones on the basis of merit. They were gentry but did not live for status.

Graduates of institutes in St. Petersburg, Tchaikovsky's parents educated their children as they had been educated. By 1846, Nikolay and Pyotr had been accepted, at the ages of eight and six, at the Mining Institute there [13, 15]. Why, then, did Ilya leave Votkinsk, a desirable posting? The reason was money. Even though the children's fees would be paid by the state, he would have to finance their domestic arrangements while maintaining his own considerable household. His correspondence with the Ministry of Finance showed his situation early in 1848 to be acute. In a letter of 20 January, his chief had made plain that Ilya was leaving civil service for better pay, a petition to increase it having been rejected. Ilya's own appeal of 22 March suggests that a further request had also been denied:

> The extremity of my present situation compels me to make bold to explain to Your Excellency that the Votkinsk works, before being placed under my supervision . . . produced only losses, but under my governance in the very same conditions . . . it achieved an annual profit, which comes to 447,000 rubles silver. Moreover, this important state institution, put in completely satisfactory order, was provided in all its parts with good and correct management. . . . I labored, expecting no reward, and held to the sacred rule that for God no prayer, and for tsar no service, is wasted. [164, 87]

He was denied again.

In *The Life,* Modest did not mention his father's financial troubles. Rather, the family left Votkinsk in pursuit of a lucrative prospect that Ilya confided to a friend, who took advantage of it first. The family lingered in Votkinsk until September: an aged aunt stayed there; Fanny Dürbach found another job; Anastasia Vasil'evna Popova, Ilya's niece known as "Sestritsa" (Little Sister), went to other relatives in Ufa.

Between 26 September and 9 October 1848, the Tchaikovskys journeyed to Moscow, where their stay was a nightmare: Ilya discovered the treachery against him and went to Petersburg, leaving his family to cope with uncertainty and a cholera epidemic. They joined him in November: Nikolay and Pyotr attended school at the Pension Schmelling, which took up their days and half their nights catching up with the rest of the class. Pyotr was also taking piano lessons from one Filippov and going to the opera and ballet. But the trials of autumn took their toll: in December Nikolay and Pyotr fell ill with the measles. Nikolay recovered; Pyotr worsened, recovering physically only in June 1849. By then, Ilya Petrovich was the manager of an iron works at Alapaevsk, not far from present-day Sverdlovsk.

Alapaevsk yielded to Votkinsk in natural beauty and amenities. Privately owned, there was "no society here besides the family of a doctor, and the manager's external situation yielded significantly in brilliance, offering neither the power nor the representation that accompanied state service in places of this type." In due course, the family adjusted. "The house turned out to be spacious and comfortable, the pay was excellent, and very soon after their arrival the Tchaikovskys settled in, trying in all details to restore the patriarchal way of life they were accustomed to at the Votkinsk factory" [1997 I 47]. Ilya hired back his principal advisors from Votkinsk. Sestritsa was recalled. When Alexandra's brother-in-law died, her sister Elizaveta Schobert came to Alapaevsk with children of Tchaikovsky's age.

Their situation challenged the family's ability to pass the time. Of two theatricals on record, one was a masquerade with the children in period and national costumes. The other was on Ilya's name-day, 20 July 1849, comprising *tableaux vivants,* fireworks, and a cachucha by Sasha, surely imitating Fanny Elssler (or possibly Marie Taglioni, its creator), who was performing this dance on the imperial stages to great acclaim. "In the evening we made *tableaux vivants,*" Tchaikovsky wrote, "the first was of the Turks, which Sasha and I represented, this *tableau* was very *joli,* after which there were Gypsies, where Pola assisted; but the Italians were truly admirable. Papa was enchanted with this *tableau*" [v 7; 147, 13–14].

Important issues at Alapaevsk were Alexandra's health and Tchaikovsky's education and state of mind. Three months after the family arrived, Alexandra was pregnant again. Pyotr wrote to Fanny, "Mama is not altogether well; she has asked to tell you that she loves you very much, but that she cannot write this time because she is indisposed" [v 7]. Modest noted that his mother grew thin at Alapaevsk, pining for Nikolay, who had stayed in St. Petersburg for school (1997 I 47). But it may have been something more. Twenty-five years after his mother's death, Tchaikovsky remarked that her final illness was "complicated by another disease" [viii 255].

Who should prepare Pyotr for entrance examinations? Fanny may have wanted to, but the task fell to Anastasia Petrovna Petrova [1997 I 52; 147]. Aunt Nastya was a recent graduate of the institute attached to the St. Petersburg Orphans' Home when, like Fanny, she made the long journey across Russia to the Tchaikovsky home. She arrived at Alapaevsk in November 1849 and quickly won the children's affections. Modest agreed that Petrova was "probably more suited" than Fanny to the demands of Russian students [1997 I 51]. She had about six months to prepare Pyotr, and did it well. "You ask me what I am studying," he wrote to Dürbach. "French grammar, Russian and German, geography, universal history, and also sacred history and arithmetic; I am translating, I am conversing in French, in Russian and in German and I often conjugate" [v 11].

Pyotr was moody at Alapaevsk, "unrecognizable," his mother wrote, "he has become lazy, he doesn't study at all and often distresses me to tears" [1997 I 48]. And later: "He has become impatient, and with every word you say to him not to his liking—tears in his eyes and a ready answer" [1997 I 51]. He had endured much. Nikolay was away, Ippolit and Sasha were still too young to be his pals. Bored, he wrote to Fanny that reading was his sole amusement, but having so few books made him reread the ones he had. Making matters worse were reports of Nikolay's success. The family missed him, while the luster of his accomplishment stifled Pyotr's local initiatives to compete. Offsetting distress was his consolation in music. Pyotr claimed he never left the piano, which cheered him when he was sad [1997 I 53]. Modest again troped the neglected genius: the child who arrived in Alapaevsk "brought within himself the light, invisible to others, of his true calling, which consoled him in difficult moments, and gave him the right to look ahead boldly" [1997 I 56]. From this time, as Tchaikovsky himself affirmed:

> [H]e began to compose, but composition went no further than improvisation. . . . [H]is parents, perhaps fearing that his nervous illness might return, or be-

> cause they did not foresee and did not want to see a specialist-musician in the future, turned away from every active participation in the matter of his artistic development. [1997 I 55]

To Modest, "the only thing in which Dürbach and Petrova were fully alike was their complete lack of knowledge of and indifference to music" [1997 I 52]. Yet an acquaintance of Petrova affirmed that she played the piano well and shared Pyotr's musical inclinations [441], while records from her time at the institute show that she received the highest grade in all subjects, including music [148, 42].

Was Tchaikovsky's interlude at Alapaevsk unrelieved dark and gloom? No. He had to adjust to disruption in his life as order was established in a new, remote place. The arrival of cohorts and a teacher improved his spirits. And there were memorable occasions. On 1 May 1850, Alexandra gave birth to Anatoly and Modest. Pyotr wrote to Dürbach: "I also want you to know, my dear Fanny, some news that can rejoice you a little: it is the birth of my brothers who are twins (the night of 1 May). I have already seen them several times; but each time I see them I believe that they are angels who have descended to earth" [v 11].

The family stood ready to enjoy life, as on a July day:

> I remember how we rode along the Old Man and Old Woman [a roadway for promenading with a remarkable echo], I remember the tent, I remember the boat, I remember the peasant chorus, I remember the Ekaterinburg orchestra, I remember the illuminations with the monogram, I remember the dances of Spiring and Aunt Lise, I remember Sasha, Malya, Polya and me sitting around good old P. P. Akhmatov, I remember all the guests, I remember dear Zinushka, dancing nicely with lovely Lidusha, I remember dear Sestritsa, I remember everything and finally I remember—having flown his little nest and bid farewell to all, never to return—Pyotr Tchaikovsky! [1997 I 65]

CHAPTER TWO

Childhood and Youth in St. Petersburg

For Pyotr to join Nikolay at the Mining Cadet Corps in St. Petersburg was still the plan in February 1850; when and why his parents decided on the School of Jurisprudence is unknown. In late summer, Alexandra left Alapaevsk to matriculate Pyotr, and so began the second poorly documented decade of his life. For the first two years, he wrote home; after that, St. Petersburg was home, and the letters ceased. Reminiscences of his classmates, solicited after his death, are anecdotal. Modest described his brother's life in school impressionistically, blending Pyotr's remembrances with his own assessment as a student there. The School of Jurisprudence produced distinguished jurists, hundreds of civil servants, and individuals like Tchaikovsky who excelled in nonlegal fields. It commanded the loyalty of its graduates, who lent their talents to its good name. Yet Modest, who took an extra year to graduate, was cynical: "Tutors and teachers passively, the fellowship [of students] actively, instilled contempt for virtue, disgust for work, [and] an ironic response to everything that did not lead to pleasure" [159, 62]. Biographers focused on psychosexuality have dwelled on the conditions in closed boarding schools, which condoned corporal punishment, hazing, and unsanctioned sexual activity beneath an ordered exterior. That Tchaikovsky's homosexuality originated in these circumstances is disputable; he and Modest considered it innate [88, 374; 306, 24].

The Tchaikovskys were in St. Petersburg by 22 August 1850. At month's end, Pyotr passed his entrance examinations and was admitted to the preparatory school. Much of September was spent settling in, including arrangements for Pyotr, like Nikolay, to spend holidays at the home of Ilya's friend Modest Vakar. As Alexandra's departure approached, Ilya reminded her that Pyotr would soon be deprived of his parents' endearments and that she should inspire him with courage [v 14]. That strategy failed. Pyotr (Modest claimed) considered her departure to be one of the most horrible moments of his life:

> It happened on the Central Turnpike, where in those days they saw people off who were leaving on the Moscow road. Besides the two boys, Zinaida's maternal uncle—Ilya Karlovich Keiser, who had to return to Petersburg with the children—was with the departure party. While going there Petya cried a little, but the end of the journey seemed far off, and treasuring each second he could look at his mother, he was comparatively calm. With the arrival at the place of departure he lost all self-possession. Pressing himself to his mother, he could not tear himself away from her. Neither endearment nor consolation nor the promise of an early return had any effect. He would hear nothing, see nothing, and was as if merged with the adored being. The poor child had to be wrested from Alexandra Andreyevna. He clutched at whatever he could, unwilling to let go of her. Finally it happened. She got into the carriage with her daughters. The horses started, whereupon, summoning his utmost strength, the lad broke away from Keiser's arms and rushed with a cry of mad despair after the tarantass, trying to seize the footboard, the mudguards, whatever he could, in the vain hope of stopping it. [1997 I 57–58]

We may wonder if this account, from someone who was not there, is overplayed. The circumstances clash with common sense. Nikolay brought Pyotr no solace? No thought was given to avoiding farewells on a public thoroughfare? "The dark shadow of this separation," Modest continued, "lay on the first years of his school life. Longing for his mother erased all other impressions, deadened all prior strivings, desires and meditations. He spent two years, as we shall see from his letters, in the unceasing expectation of a reunion with his parents. Nothing else occupied, stirred, or attracted him" [1997 I 58].

Nonsense. Modest could not begin to justify these claims in his subsequent account. In Pyotr's first letter home, about 21 October, he devoted but one phrase to missing his parents as he reports on the ballet (*Giselle* with Carlotta Grisi), looks forward to seeing Nikolay, and imagines his mother's homecoming [v 12–13]. He does not even mention the Central Turnpike. Tchaikovsky's letters do reveal other important details. On 23 November 1850, Pyotr's first line to his parents was, "I kiss you hard, my dear ones, on your hands and feet and your whole body" [v 15], a graphic turn of phrase in the boy that will continue in the man. He twice observed that his mother was ill. He thanked Petrova for preparing him so well for his examinations and asked his parents to greet Fanny in their next letter [v 15–16].

His life, however, was not carefree. In his first letter, Pyotr also reported staying with the Vakars for a week due to an outbreak of scarlet fever at the school. Allowing Pyotr to wait out the quarantine led to tragedy, in that he supposedly exposed Vakar's son Nikolay to the illness. Young Vakar died within a month, his family gamely attempting to conceal the cause. The other source of Tchaikovsky's unhappiness was his parents' postponement of a visit. In most of Pyotr's 40 letters home between 23 November 1850 and 28 March 1852, he expressed a wish to see them. First, their visit was to be in February 1851, then in June, then September, when Ilya Petrovich spent three weeks with his sons, then December, then January 1852, and finally May 1852, within days of final examinations at the preparatory school. In September Ilya's confrontation with the owners of Alapaevsk brought him to resign. As each deadline approached, Pyotr was filled with anticipation, bolstered by his belief that Alexandra would be coming too. That she stayed home did not "erase all other impressions" from his mind. Pyotr's friends, their families, and his principal teacher in the first year offered solace and hospitality in the diversions of happy homes on weekends and holidays, a ball at which he saw the emperor, and a splendid summer in 1851 in the country. On his father's name-day in 1851, he recalled the celebration at Alapaevsk the year before, but added that he had a very good time this summer [v 36].

Despite concerns about his youth, which threatened to keep him in the preparatory class another year, Tchaikovsky passed his entrance examinations for the School of Jurisprudence in May 1852. He was one of 60 applicants competing for 33 vacancies and the third youngest to enter; his grades placed him in the upper 10 percent of his class [71, 60–61].

Reunited, the family spent the summer of 1852 at a dacha outside St. Petersburg, joined by Pyotr's cousin Anna, daughter of Ilya's brother Pyotr Petrovich and his wife Elizaveta Petrovna (née von Berens). Known in the literature by her married name, Anna Merkling, she recalled him as "a skinny lad, nervous, very impressionable. He was always fawning over and pampering Alexandra Andreyevna. In general one noted his affectionate regard, especially for his mother. I recall him hanging on my arm when I would have liked it better if Alexander Chatelain [a suitor] were walking with me alone" [71, 61].

Modest marked a change in Pyotr after he entered the school. His belief in the immutability and sanctity of things vanished in an institution where bullying, mockery, and deceit were rife. He learned to avoid controversy, managed academically, and assumed the guise of a likeable bureaucrat, passing from class to class without retaking examinations. Only algebra, it appears, was a problem. "All would have been well were it not for mathematics," Modest wrote. Tchaikovsky's schoolmates recalled his attractive personality and endearing absentmindedness. "Petya was always without textbooks," Fyodor Maslov observed. When studying together in the summer gardens, they stowed their books in a tree trunk to avoid carrying them back and forth. Pyotr's may still be there. Ivan Turchaninov thought that disorderliness and a lack of punctuality distinguished Tchaikovsky, and yet, "Goodness, softness, responsiveness, and a kind of carelessness with respect to himself were features of his character from the very beginning." As for the school's discipline, he adapted to it with one exception. In 1854, he broke its strict prohibition against smoking; he became addicted early and irrevocably [1997 I 85–96].

Life at home was lively. Zinaida became engaged to Evgeny Olkhovsky in the spring of 1853 and married him early in 1854; Pyotr's cousin Lydia followed suit, becoming engaged to Evgeny's brother Nikolay. They moved back to the Urals. The defining event of 1854, however, was the death of Tchaikovsky's mother on 13 June, about which little is known. She died of cholera, but nothing explains why she (and Ilya) should have been at risk. Modest called it an event so dark that no one liked to remember it; he did not cite Ippolit's letter—still unpublished—of 4 December 1895 containing recollections [409, 15]. The only source he used was Pyotr's letter to Fanny two years later, whereas Alexandra's entire family was living in St. Petersburg when she died. That no one informed Fanny of it then is extraordinary. Pyotr's tone is sheepish; he reintroduces himself, cites the letter as proof that he still thinks about her, and includes his mother's death in a matter-of-fact account of the family's life since Votkinsk:

> Four months after Zina's departure Mama suddenly fell ill with cholera, and, while she was dangerously ill, thanks to the redoubled efforts of the doctors she recovered her health, but this was not for long, because after three or four days of convalescence she died without having had the time to bid farewell to those around her. While she did not have the power to speak the words clearly, it was nevertheless understood that she wanted absolution, and the priest with the Holy Sacraments arrived just in time, because after receiving absolution, she gave up her soul to God. On the day of Mama's burial Papa in turn fell ill with cholera, such that his death was expected from minute to minute—but thanks to God in a week he had recovered. [v 56–57]

Alexandra's passing reduced the household to a shambles. The eldest woman in it, Ilya's niece Lydia, was about to marry. Ilya again recalled Sestritsa, though she was capable only of supervising domestic chores, placed Sasha in the Smolny Institute and Ippolit in the Naval Corps. "In 1855, no trace remained of the previous family life of our home, not just because four children were in closed educational institutions, but chiefly because the expression of its spirit and direction died in the person of Alexandra Andreyevna" [1997 I 97]. Ilya invited his brother Pyotr Petrovich to join households. The old soldier brought some color back into Ilya's family, his strict Lutheran wife some order to its management, and his vivacious daughters high spirits to its routine. This arrangement lasted from the end of 1854 until the autumn of 1857 and involved merry summers for the children at a dacha in the imperial village of Peterhof. Some 30 years later, a concert of Johann Strauss, Jr., caused Anna Merkling to recall:

> I so vividly imagined myself at a ball or at home in a family dance, and you—one leg drawn back under the chair, at the piano, unhappy that again and again you were being asked to play dances, at just the time that you, coming home, positively declared that you would not play for anything! God, how vivid all this is before my eyes! Do you remember? And then there was Kolya, Kolya with his waltz took but three dance movements to pass from one corner of the sitting room to the other, and how I loved thus to be borne, and got frightfully angry when he, contrary to the waltz, polkaed to the stove and back using only one step. How young everyone was then! [294, 227]

While Pyotr surely grieved for his mother, the scarcity of documentation cautions against exaggerating the tragedy of her death. Whatever else, it seems to have spurred him to write his music down. Modest adduced only his ability to improvise, while Merkling marveled at "the expression of his childlike lyricism when he played alone, for himself, looking off into the distance and evidently aware of nothing around him. At such times it cost to make one's presence known and call attention to his piano improvisations when he thought that no one was listening" [1997 I 76]. "He often recalled that in school the thought of composition gave him no peace," Modest added, "but he felt that no one around him believed in his talent, and therefore he spoke about his dreams very rarely" [1997 I 117]. Pyotr's first surviving composition was written in 1854 and is marked 1 August [440]. The "Expromptum: Anastasia Valse par Pierre Tschaikovsky" was named for and dedicated to Anastasia Petrova, his governess. Modest knew nothing of it when he wrote *The Life,* though the manuscript, with an inscription by Petrova, was still extant in 1913 [RMG 1913/44 995–96], and a photograph of it was published in the Petersburg newspaper *Den'* (Day) on 21 October of that year [441]. Pavel Zaitsev, who annotated the publication but is otherwise unknown, described Petrova as a good musician having rare qualities of spirit, who loved to recall what Pyotr often said at the time: "I shall without fail be a great musician" [441].

The music is probably like Tchaikovsky's improvisations at the time. One hesitates to judge too harshly a work whose composer mislocates the note stems, or critique any particular of an imperfect reproduction. The piece nevertheless hints at the later composer: 14 bars of dominant preparation (in 6/8 time) anticipate the waltz proper in the dramatic manner of later waltzes, while the melody breathes that urge to extend, that energy of continuation we know from the mature composer. Here is the opening of the principal melody:

Ex. 1

(continued)

Ex. 1 *(continued)*

Tchaikovsky's shift from the home key to the seventh degree for the subsidiary theme, F to E-flat, anticipates comparable moves in his later work. Approaching the final cadence with dense chords anticipates the bigness of sound he will express more cogently in the orchestra. Before signing his name at the end, he wrote: "La fin couronne l'oeuvre (Proverbe français)."

It is one thing for a 14-year-old to write down a dance; it is another to begin an opera. Two letters from Pyotr to Viktor Ivanovich Olkhovsky, brother of the husbands of Zinaida and Lydia, probably date from the summer and autumn of 1854. In them, Tchaikovsky remarks on Olkhovsky's work as librettist, "which corresponds fully to my wishes; only there are too many arias and recitatives, and very few duets, trios, etc." [v 54–55]. The piece was a one-act farce, *Hyperbole* (named after the leading female character), set in a place called Dopotopia, with the stage representing "a location." One description in the letters refers to the phrase "Beard, o my little beardlet" with its folkish diminutive [163]. Olkhovsky's libretto survives, but no music for the project is extant [135, 76].

With Pyotr's compositional ambitions stirring, Ilya in 1855 retained an important pianist and teacher, Rudolf Kündinger, to give him private lessons, which lasted until 1858 [1997 I 111]. Kündinger recalled:

> If I could foresee who would come of the jurist of that time I would have kept a diary of our lessons, but unfortunately it must be said that then it never entered my head what kind of musician I was dealing with. . . . No doubt his abilities were outstanding: an amazing subtlety of ear, memory, excellent hands—but this gave no cause to foresee either the composer or even a brilliant performer. There was nothing phenomenal in him; often before and since Tchaikovsky I have met young people with such gifts. The only thing that somewhat caught my attention were his improvisations; in them one dimly sensed something extraordinary. Besides that, his flair for harmony at times astonished me. He was barely familiar with music theory, but when occasionally I showed him my compositions, several times he gave me advice about harmony. . . . Despite this, when Tchaikovsky's father once asked my opinion if it was worth it for his son to devote himself to music—I answered in the negative. Of course, the lamentable position of specialist musicians in Russia at that time played an important part in my answer. But I nevertheless remember—at the time I had no belief in Tchaikovsky's exceptional talent. [1997 I 111–12]

Kündinger's lessons, plus tutoring in music theory from his brother August [316, 36], ended in 1858 when Ilya lost his retirement capital in a bad investment. Impoverished, the family moved in with Elizaveta Schobert, who had lived with them in Alapaevsk. At the end of 1858, Ilya was appointed director of the Technological Institute in St. Petersburg.

Complementing Tchaikovsky's work with Kündinger was his study of Italian opera, begun in 1852 when another aunt, Ekaterina Alexeyeva, became his voice tutor, working on *Don Giovanni* and Rossini's *Semiramide.* As he turned 16, Pyotr got acquainted with Luigi Piccioli, a famous singing teacher and a colorful eccentric. In his 50s when he met Tchaikovsky, Piccioli dyed his hair, used cosmetics, and (according to wicked tongues) hid a mechanical device beneath his necktie to stretch his skin, emulating a facelift. He was ebullient and youthful, repelled by any thought of age, suffering, or death. He developed Tchaikovsky's knowledge of Italian opera and the Italian language.

With "My Genius, My Angel, My Friend," a song, we come to the last notated composition thought to be written by Tchaikovsky the student [facsimile in 75 I, between 128–29; 416, 31]. The words are by Fet:

Are you not here as a light shade,
My genius, my angel, my friend,
Do you speak to me calmly,
And calmly hover about?
And bestow timid inspiration
And treat my sweet ailment,
And bring peaceful slumber
My genius, my angel, my friend[?]

Its greater sophistication suggests that the song is later than the "Anastasia Waltz" (despite Modest's suggestion that Pyotr wrote it in 1854 in memory of his mother). Tchaikovsky was learning to compose by emulation, perhaps using Glinka's venerable "I remember the wonderful moment" or "Doubt."The hypnotic pulse in the piano, the soft dynamic, and the motto-like repetition of the opening motif express the sense of the text, especially "And bring peaceful slumber" followed by a repetition of "My genius, my angel, my friend" in falling phrases, as if the singer were drifting off to sleep. The pitch G, a frequent point of arrival in the vocal line, may refer to the beloved's pervasive presence [for Tchaikovsky's songs, see 10; 287; 377].

Modest's treatment of Pyotr's personal development is obscure. When discussing Pyotr's school friends, he could not describe Alexey Apukhtin as immediately attracted to Pyotr, having an immense influence on his life in the school, and being his best friend after graduation without leaving a pointed implication, since Apukhtin, a gifted poet, was openly homosexual. He may have intended this and similar references, as to Prince Vladimir Petrovich Meshchersky, an advisor to high officials and editor of an important periodical, to speak for themselves. By abstaining from elaboration, however, he prompted the later scrutiny of all Tchaikovsky's friendships for sexual connections, while most of the surviving evidence points to celibacy. Claiming that his affection for fellow student Sergey Kireyev, which Pyotr himself described as joy entangled with bitterness [369, 121], was "the strongest, most durable and purest amorous infatuation of his entire life," Modest added that it was courtly, "without the slightest sensual design or intention." Describing a new friend in Vienna years later, Pyotr still awaited "the real thing," and in his passion for his former student Josef Kotek he would deem physical consummation far from his desires. Yet, on his own authority, Modest remarked that "Pyotr experienced many involvements of a different character, yielding to them unrestrainedly, and with the full fervor of his passionate and sensuous nature" [306, 23].

In seven years at the School of Jurisprudence, Tchaikovsky surely took his sexual rites of passage. Special friendships probably occurred but cannot be verified. His adolescent development would appear to have engaged in a number of distinctions—between emotional and physical communion—in which social dictates, artistic ability, human sympathy broadly construed, and even fascination with women may have come into play. The impact of his homosexuality, never inconsequential and occasionally severe, still does not support the popular notion that his life was devastated by it.

Modest was also glib in declaring his brother's stay at the school "an episode only obliquely affecting the principal direction of his life" [1997 I 78]. Pyotr's studies—Latin, other languages, physics and mathematics, logic and psychology, advanced topics in the law—were too demanding to be irrelevant. No institution of higher learning in music was available to him, nor was he was committed to music, coming to it gradually from 1854 to 1863. Modest disparaged Pyotr's study of choral singing at the school with Gavriil Lomakin [1997 I 110], a recognized authority, even though seven years of rehearsal, singing solos, conducting, and thinking about Orthodox polyphony must have provided some benefit to the person who would later reform that repertoire. This exposure—attending performances and studying with Alexeyeva, Kündinger, and Piccioli—comprised respectable musical training for St. Petersburg in the 1850s.

Tchaikovsky's second decade was a time of greater complexity and accomplishment than can be defined by single issues. The word *adjustment,* so ordinary and unsensational, explains his engagement with life's realities: separation from his family, the death of Nikolay Vakar, and intense competition at the age of 10; resolving issues of sociability and determining who he was in personal relationships; confronting the loss of a beloved parent; and, not least, the continuing tension between his formal training and an instinctively desired alternative career. That Tchaikovsky met these challenges with aplomb is easily overlooked in the quest for details of increasingly doubtful relevance to our reasons for cherishing him.

 CHAPTER THREE 

Civil Service (1859–1863)

TCHAIKOVSKY GRADUATED FROM THE SCHOOL OF JURISPRUDENCE on 13 May 1859 and was posted to the Ministry of Justice five days later. Modest's remark that nothing began and nothing ended with graduation nicely conveys that Pyotr's career had not really been decided. With Nikolay about to leave home, Lydia and Zinaida long married, and Sasha and Ippolit about to complete their educations, Pyotr may have needed the settling effect of a job. Moreover, he owed four years to the Ministry of Justice in return for his education [136, 84].

He worked hard. In his first two years he handled some 265 cases, reviewing complaints at a petitions desk—from serfs, gentry, merchants, and others all over Russia. Vladimir Gerard recalled that Tchaikovsky did not stand out as a bureaucrat [316, 31]; Modest played down his brother's civil service and let stand the "legendary" anecdote in which Pyotr, distracted, started munching on an official document which then had to be redrafted [1997 I 103]. His superiors thought otherwise. Hardly six months into his first posting, a supervisor wrote, "Titular Counsellor Tchaikovsky, who finished his studies in 1859, has attracted particular attention by his constant diligence and exact fulfilling of obligations" [316, 430, n. 4]. He was promoted twice in the first nine months. In 1862, he was working so hard to become "head of desk" that he brought work home and stayed back when the rest of the family went on holiday. An evaluation that year found him "constantly occupied with the proper diligence" [136, 86]. But when Fyodor Maslov was promoted ahead of him, Tchaikovsky soured on jurisprudence.

As he turned away, he faced obstacles familiar to anyone who has ever pursued music professionally: a dread of failure, doubts about his resolve, and a reluctance to alienate a loving family. Tchaikovsky's transition from law to music may be summarized from letters to his sister Sasha between March 1861 and April 1863. She was far away and pining for her old life, as she had married Lev Davïdov in November 1860 and moved to his estate at Kamenka in the Ukraine. There were other changes at home: Nikolay was posted to the country; Ippolit was on a cruise; Anatoly and Modest were in the School of Jurisprudence. Pyotr took an interest in the twins, re-orphaned by Sasha's departure and neglected by a bad tutor. Between them, a "three-way unity" developed, which would be broken only by death [1997 I 126].

Writing to Sasha on 10 March 1861, Pyotr consoled her and pondered his summer plans. A musical career for him had been discussed after dinner that night:

> Papa claims that it is still not too late to become an artist. If that were so, it would be excellent; but the fact is, if there is talent in me it is now probably impossible to develop. They have made me a bureaucrat—and a poor one at that; I try as much as possible to improve myself, take my service work ever more seriously—and suddenly study general bass at the same time? [v 61]

Despite Kündinger's assessment, Ilya continued to consider a career in music for his son—but how might he be prepared? Haphazard training had been the rule for Russian composers, who wrote operas for a company degraded by comparison with the Imperial Italian Opera and concert music with no regular concert life in their midst. The year 1858 had marked the return to the city of an artist who would change all this. Not yet 30, a celebrated pianist, prolific composer, and outstanding pedagogue, Anton Rubinstein in 1859 created the Russian Musical Society in St. Petersburg, dedicated to giving regular, high-quality concerts. By 1865, it had branches in Moscow, Kiev, Kharkov, and Saratov. Within a month of his first concert in St. Petersburg, Rubinstein proposed to offer music classes under the society's auspices. Thus, Tchaikovsky studied general bass in the autumn of 1861, after touring Western Europe as a translator during the summer. Nikolay Kashkin recalled his immediate motive:

> Among Tchaikovsky's relatives and genteel comrades was a guards officer, a great music lover, conspicuous in society for his musical talent. . . . Once the

> young officer, meeting him in society, said he could move in three chords from whatever key one chose to whatever other: the task was quickly done and immediately executed—then another time, and a third—with the same result. The astonished Pyotr Ilyich asked how this was done, and was told that it was impossible to explain in a few words, but one could study it in a music theory class started by the Musical Society. [MV020111]

Tchaikovsky's first theory teacher, Nikolay Ivanovich Zaremba, was eloquent, well trained (by Adolf Bernhard Marx in Berlin), and prepared. He was unusual in his appreciation of Beethoven's late music, although Schumann and Berlioz were unknown to him. He disdained Mozart, yet was among the first to appreciate Tchaikovsky's talent [1997 I 148–51].

By the time Pyotr wrote Sasha on 23 October 1861, things were going badly at work but music was going extremely well. "Perhaps in three years or so you will be listening to my operas and singing my arias," he quipped [v 70]. On 4 December, music continued strong. He was ill advised not to test his fortunes in it—except for his laziness, spending, and lack of character. By 10 September 1862, he had abandoned the *monde* and turned ascetic, dining at home, playing cards, or taking his father to the Russian theater. Ilya had suffered another setback. When he lost his fortune, he had sued for recovery; this failing, he abandoned an appeal to avoid further expense. At this point, Pyotr was soon to enter Rubinstein's conservatory. He wrote to Sasha that day:

> Last year, as you know, I studied the theory of music very hard, and now am absolutely convinced that sooner or later I shall give up government service for music. Don't think that I imagine becoming a great artist—I simply want to do that to which I am called. . . . Of course, I shall not leave the service until I am absolutely sure that I am an artist and not a bureaucrat. [v 74]

On 11 April 1863, Tchaikovsky asked to be struck from the rolls of the Ministry of Justice "for domestic reasons" [136, 86–87]. He was transferred to the Moscow Archive of the Ministry and freed of the responsibility to come to work every day. But in May 1867, the ministry would propose that he retire due to nonperformance of his duties. When his supervisor complained that he had not appeared in months, the composer did retire, effective September 1867 [136, 87–88]. His domestic reasons were real. Ilya's debts, paid from a pension far smaller than his salary, had forced him into a peripatetic life, staying with his children to defray expenses and reducing Pyotr to near-indigence. He too lived away in the summer in 1863 (at Apukhtin's family estate, much of the time without Apukhtin), and in St. Petersburg, Tchaikovsky was obliged to give lessons and to accompany. Modest claimed that Pyotr thrived on the hardship, maintained a good humor, and rarely in his life was so bright and bold [1997 I 146]. On 15 April 1863, Pyotr wrote to Sasha:

> I see today from your letter to Papa that you are taking a lively part in my situation and look with mistrust upon the decisive step I have taken on the path of life. For that reason I want to explain to you in detail what I intend to do and what I hope. You, I think, will not deny in me an aptitude for music, but also that it is the only thing for which I have an aptitude; if that is the case, then you understand that I must sacrifice everything to develop and form what God gave me in the womb. With this aim I began to study the theory of music seriously; as long as this did not in any way interrupt studying and the civil service, I remained at the Ministry, but since my studies have grown more serious and difficult, I must of course choose one or the other. To work conscientiously during my study of music is impossible; to receive a salary for my entire life under false pretenses cannot be, and I cannot permit it. Consequently, only one choice is left: to leave the civil service (all the more as I can never return to it). . . . Do not conclude from this that I intend to accrue debts or to ask money of Papa, whose present situation is far from brilliant, in place of my salary. Of course, I will not benefit much materially, but in the first place, I hope next season to get a position at the conservatory (a professor's assistant [i.e., a "*répétiteur* in theory," at 440 rubles per year; 368, 242]); in the second, I have already acquired several lessons to give next year; and (3)—and most important—since I have completely repudiated worldly pleasures, fancy clothes, etc., my expenses will be reduced to extraordinarily small amounts. After all this you are probably asking: what will finally come of me when I finish studying? Of one thing only am I certain: that an excellent musician will come of me, and that I shall always have my daily bread. [v 77]

In *The Life,* Modest made much of Pyotr's socializing after graduation. The French theater stood above all other entertainments, followed by the ballet (he preferred fantastic stories with lavish transformations and learned the terminology of the *danse d'école*), and amateur productions as an actor, where he polished a talent for mime and comedy [1997 I 104–7]. This social whirl reached its apex early in 1861, manifested in a short temper and a disdain for family [1997 I 109]. Then, Pyotr abandoned the *monde.* Whether the cause was "a surfeit of the idle life, under the influence of some occurrence not immediately known to us, or whether it was prepared gradually and slowly—one cannot say, because Pyotr Ilyich at that time experienced these painful moments alone, unseen by others. He reappeared again only when the turning point was past" [1997 I 121]. This explanation of Pyotr's transformation was neither incredible nor fully accurate, as we learn from Modest's autobiography: Pyotr and Apukhtin were notorious in St. Petersburg as homosexuals. Gossip caused Pyotr to confront public attitudes about homosexuality; indignant and contemptuous, he began to avoid company and situations harmful to his reputation and self-esteem. Even though he considered such attitudes unjust, he succumbed to them, and the self-criticism that followed left him so dissatisfied with himself that he was transformed into a dedicated son and brother—and into a musician [306, 24].

A loose end of composition from this time, the song *Mezza notte,* is variously an orphan. The composer never claimed it; no autograph survives; it was discovered only in 1926 in his publisher's archives. It was originally issued under Tchaikovsky's name sometime in the 1860s in an undated issue of Leibrock's *Musée musicale.* The poem describes an impatient lover, the beloved's timid greeting, and love's profit from the darkness. The music is unsophisticated, even incomprehensible coming from someone who might already have written "My Genius, My Angel, My Friend." Incorrect stresses and sloppy text underlay discourage an attribution to Tchaikovsky. Nor is there any sign of Italian cantilena or sensitivity to the passionate shadings of the text. The repeated attacks on high A, one at *subito piano,* are ungrateful to the voice.

For Tchaikovsky, the years 1859–1863 were at once propitious and unsettling. The St. Petersburg Conservatory came into being precisely when he needed it. Out of family dislocations came lasting affinities with Sasha, Modest, and Anatoly, while Ilya deserves special praise. "One had to have seen father's sorrow," Ippolit wrote. "At that time musical artists were perceived as comedians, and our intelligent, enlightened father for a long time could not be reconciled with this, until Pyotr Ilyich, having abandoned the law, became a professor at the conservatory" [136, 83]. He understood his son's compulsion, but was not finished speaking his mind.

CHAPTER FOUR

Tchaikovsky at the St. Petersburg Conservatory

It was one thing for Anton Rubinstein to organize the Russian Musical Society; it was another to open a conservatory [451], which focused attention on the contentious issue of how Russian musicians should be trained. To Rubinstein's opponents, musicians must be self-taught, as foreign pedagogy would depersonalize and German discipline stifle precisely the Russian qualities they wished to nurture. To Rubinstein good pedagogy was unrelated to nationality, whereas dilettantism was the negation of competence. The social outcome of his position was radical: the title of "free artist," which recognized conservatory graduates as members of a profession, like doctors or soldiers.

The St. Petersburg Conservatory opened on 8 September 1862—Russia's thousandth birthday. After exhorting students the day before to eschew absenteeism, Rubinstein at 9 o'clock on the first morning was alone at his post—no teacher and no student other than Alexander Ivanovich Rubets, a singer, folklorist, and future professor, who recalled 50 years later:

> Two months passed from the day the conservatory opened before order began to be established. At the outset there were all manner of curiosities: students were late for their lessons, especially the women. Accustomed to being unpunctual at home, they thought they would receive a lesson whenever they arrived. . . . Rubinstein told them that if they all arrived when they felt like it, nothing would come of it but nonsense and disorder. [NV120827]

Tchaikovsky had petitioned to enroll in the "music school" on 22 August 1862 [D&Y 30; 416, 30]. For knowledge of his years there, we are indebted to Hermann Laroche, the composer's best friend at the time [103], who wrote this part of *The Life.* Laroche was the Fanny Dürbach of Pyotr's 20s; without the two of them, our knowledge of Tchaikovsky before the age of 26 would be limited to his youthful letters and brief reminiscences.

What was Tchaikovsky like at 22? Worldly, clean-shaven despite current fashion, dressed in a suit from an expensive tailor but not quite new,

> with enchantingly simple, and, as they struck me then, cold manners. He had a host of acquaintances, and when we walked down the Nevsky there was no end to the doffing of hats. Elegant people mostly (but not exclusively) exchanged bows with him. Of languages he knew French and some Italian; he liked to flaunt his ignorance of German, saying, for example, "Er ist an der Sehnsucht gestorben" [He is dying of yearning] (wishing to say "He is dying of consumption") . . . at which Germans in his company would invariably take delight. [255 II 178]

What of his readiness for study? He excelled in a mandatory "piano class for theorists" taught by Anton Gerke, who in his red peruke resembled Monsieur Triquet and over whose manner Tchaikovsky and Laroche made merry:

> [H]e played not only "completely adequately for a theorist," but generally he could play pieces of first-class difficulty very well, deftly, with panache. To my taste at the time his playing was rather coarse, insufficiently warm and heartfelt. . . . The fact is that Pyotr Ilyich feared sentimentality like fire, and so in playing the piano avoided superfluous emphasis, and laughed at the phrase "to play with soul." . . . [T]he musical feeling within him was constrained by a certain *chastity,* and fear of vulgarity kept him from moving to the opposite extreme. [255 II 167–68]

Tchaikovsky was a good singer. His baritone was not large but was pleasant and unerring in pitch, enabling Laroche to accompany him in "La ci darem la mano" in keys other than the A major in which Mozart wrote and Pyotr sang. In general, however, his knowledge of repertoire was, "for a 22-year-old man who had decided to dedicate himself to composition, frighteningly slight" [255 II 178]. He knew *Don Giovanni, A Life for the Tsar, Der Freischütz,* Serov's *Judith,* Overtures of Meyerbeer's *Struensee* and

Litolff's *Robespierre* and *Die Girondisten;* and, from playing four hands, Beethoven's Ninth, Schumann's *Rhenish* and Rubinstein's *Ocean* symphonies, Schumann's *Genoveva* and *Paradise and the Peri,* and Wagner's *Lohengrin.* He did not like earlier music except for Mozart and some Haydn [178, 19]. Among adjunct preparations, "[l]iterature occupied a much larger place in his life than that of a typical educated person: it was after music his principal, most essential interest." Tchaikovsky was a man of letters, whose tastes ran from Pushkin's period back into the eighteenth century [209, 165]. When the composer's correspondence is published, "how much a person living in a world of chords and rhythms would write more clearly, cleanly, logically and elegantly than most of our contemporary professional artisans of letters will be revealed" [255 II 182; on Tchaikovsky as writer, see 300].

What did he study? Piano for a time, flute with Cesare Ciardi, organ with Heinrich Stiehl, counterpoint and form with Zaremba, instrumentation and free composition with Anton Rubinstein. He sang in the chorus, which in two seasons performed works from Lotti's "Crucifixus" to Lully to Bach's *St. Matthew Passion* to Beethoven and Schumann [368, 241]. As a theory student, he had to conduct, which prompted a strange performance anxiety. "Standing on the stage awoke in him such a nervous fright that it seemed the whole time that *his head would come off from his shoulders,*" Laroche reported. "In anticipation of such a catastrophe, holding the baton in his right hand, he firmly held his chin with the left" [1997 I 162–63].

The heart of Tchaikovsky's training was his study with Anton Rubinstein: "The Director of the Conservatory inspired us . . . with unbounded love mixed with considerable fright. . . . [H]is gloomy mien, irascibility and agitation, joined with the fascination of a name famous in Europe, nevertheless acted on us in an extraordinarily inspiring way" [1997 I 154]:

> To the extent that everything in Zaremba was guided by system, each word, so to speak, in its proper place, so in Rubinstein a lovable disorder reigned . . . everything depending on the inspiration of the moment. . . . Enormous practical knowledge, a huge range of interests, compositional experience unlikely for a thirty-year-old man, gave an authority to his words we could not help but sense. The very paradoxes which poured out of him and which now irritated us, now made us laugh, bore the stamp of a genius-like nature and a thinking artist. [1997 I 155]

"His lectures were of tremendous benefit," Rubets remarked, "and when he illustrated his thoughts and explanations at the piano there was general delight; they were magical. We rejoiced when he praised our compositions" [NV120827].

Rubinstein insisted that creativity without discipline was a waste of talent, and he showed how discipline could be achieved:

> He always went on about the harm of timidity, . . . advised us not to stop at a place that was giving us trouble, but to pass on and move forward, training us to write in sketches, with allusions, in one form or another, without a piano: if inspiration leaves during improvisation at the piano, progress will inevitably move slowly, and in general nothing will come of it. [NV120827]

He demystified composition. Tchaikovsky later wrote: "As a teacher he was incomparable. He got down to work without pompous remarks and lengthy digression, and always kept strictly to business" [xvi-b 102]. He admitted a profound respect for Rubinstein, but esteem never developed into warmth:

> Rubinstein produced a magical effect on Tchaikovsky, who not without humor observed flaws of logic and grammar in his lectures, [and] not without chagrin looked upon the mass of insipid compositions with which Rubinstein, as it were, erased the memory of his several masterpieces. But neither the professor's strangeness nor the ever more evident defects of the composer could weaken in Pyotr Ilyich's soul the enchantment he experienced from the man[,] although intimate or simply friendly relations with Anton Rubinstein (of the kind Tchaikovsky enjoyed with his brother Nikolay) there never were. [1997 I 156]

For his part, "Rubinstein loved Tchaikovsky, took pride in him, advanced him in every way and took pains with him" [Rubets in NV120903], even paying his fees the first year [368, 241]. "Observing his student's exceptional zeal, and perhaps judging compositional effort by the enormous ease with which he himself worked, Rubinstein became ever less shy with the size of his assignments," Laroche wrote. "But as the professor's demands increased, the student's love of work grew more desperate. . . . Pyotr Ilyich sat up entire nights, and mornings dragged his just-finished score, the ink barely dry, to his insatiable professor" [1997 I 156].

Rubinstein fostered Tchaikovsky's talent without demanding allegiance. Like him, Tchaikovsky would command the respect of artists, shun controversy and polemic, and espouse an international outlook. He avoided manifestos, labels, and restrictions. Rubets was doubtless correct, noting that sometime in those first conservatory years, Tchaikovsky reached a turning point in his soul [NV120827]. For this, Anton Rubinstein may be thanked.

Tchaikovsky's conservatory compositions fill over 700 pages in modern print [417]. He also wrote much that was lost, of which the following can be identified:

a. An oratorio. Laroche refers to it in a letter complaining of Tchaikovsky's noisy passages for brass in all his early works, including this one [1997 I 210].
b. Fantasia for piano on the song "By the River, By the Bridge" [1997 I 153]. One page written in 1862, a send-up of Anton Gerke's pianism is reflected in the rubric, *senza gherkando,* which meant *ritardandi* and *accelerandi* in the wrong places.
c. An orchestration of Beethoven's *Tempest* Sonata [1997 I 155], possibly just the first movement. Tchaikovsky scored it in four different ways, one for English horn and other rarities, which brought a rebuke from Rubinstein.
d. A setting of the Fountain Scene from Pushkin's *Boris Godunov* [1997 I 189]. Assigned in connection with writing for the harp, this is a large, orchestrated piece, with "inspiration and flights of fancy despite its Italianisms" [Rubets in NV120827].
e. A setting of Zhukovsky's dramatic poem "The Midnight Review" [NV 120827] so pleased Rubinstein that he interrupted Zaremba's class for his students to hear it; unrelated to Glinka's famous setting, Tchaikovsky's accompaniment of each strophe was varied and complex.
f. "The Romans in the Coliseum" [1997 I 189, 210]. Apparently an orchestral work; Laroche called it "wretched vulgarity."
g. Characteristic Dances for orchestra, revised for *The Voevoda;* the original is lost.

Fourteen student exercises [CW 58] include a trio for strings and a quartet for horns tuned to different pitches. Some are short, complete movements; some imitate famous composers or anticipate Tchaikovsky's later music. Some are innovative in pattern, such as no. 12, an introduction and allegro divided into strophes (segments of music with similar beginnings which form a pattern when juxtaposed). The most striking is a miniature concerto grosso with four statements of a ritornello framing episodes of different texture and sonority (no. 10). Everywhere, facility is taking shape—imitation, characteristic orchestral sounds, syncopated and dissonant prolongations, reprises varied by references to a prior section, lengthy introductions.

Four student orchestrations survive [CW 58 and 59]: the Scherzo from Weber's Second Piano Sonata, the first-movement exposition of Beethoven's *Kreutzer* Sonata, and part of Johann Gungl's waltz, "Le retour." Gungl conducted popular concerts at the Pavlovsk Railway Station from 1845 to 1848, as did Johann Strauss, Jr., from 1856 to 1865 [NV120618; RMG 1912/23–24, 516]. "Le retour" may be linked to Strauss's performance of Pyotr's Characteristic Dances there on 30 August 1865 [249], his first publicly performed composition. The fourth orchestration is of the last variation and finale of Schumann's *Symphonic Études.* Laroche's remarks in the manuscript (e.g., "I did not hear the bassoons") suggest an early performance [417, 140].

Tchaikovsky's Variations in A Minor for Piano were lost, rediscovered in 1908, published in 1909 [RMG 1909/41 cols. 909–10; CW 51a, 3–24], then lost again. Music labeled "Variation 5" was found at the end of the manuscript; with a fifth variation already in place, it was made a ninth variation. Vaydman describes an earlier version of the theme as distinctively Schumannesque [424, 50], unlike the foursquare theme we have:

Ex. 2

Here, in some alteration which transforms an unmistakable allusion into a merely recognizable one, we encounter a staple of Tchaikovsky's thinking. It is not style play as jest (e.g., aping Mendelssohn in act II of *The Sleeping Beauty* when the balletmaster asked for a reference to *A Midsummer Night's Dream*), but rather an intentionally generalized allusion where a more direct one would be too obvious and distracting. In his theme, Tchaikovsky retains a Schumannesque shape and periodicity without closer stylistic mimesis: after a pair of almost inane phrases, he proceeds to more particularly Schumannesque melodic and tonal nuances in bars 5–8. Typically, his allusions are one or two details removed from the model. These Variations are also paradigmatic of Tchaikovsky's formal method in this genre: variations just after the theme faithful to it in melody or chord, followed by fanciful variations. Before the final variation, the theme returns.

Tchaikovsky the student made two choruses of Nikolay Platonovich Ogaryov's poem "Before Sleep Comes" (also called "At Bedtime"; tr. 389, 17), one unaccompanied, one with orchestra. Night calls the weary to rest, before which a prayer is said: for peace, that the child's dream, the beggar's couch, and the gentle tears of love be blessed; that sin be forgiven and all of God's sad creatures be consoled. The vocal parts are the same in both settings—and expert: textural variety, effective part writing, exclamations, sudden contrasts of volume. The minor key, drooping rhythmic effects, mildly unsettled text underlay, and passing dissonance set the mood before the prayer, with litany-like appeals and recitation in the major. Tchaikovsky highlights words, rising on "quiet tears of *love,*" and marking "intense suffering" with a dissonance. On the exclamation "It is time!" he pairs the choral parts, producing an effect suggestive of physical weariness. We see here the rudiments of his individual choral style [261; 395].

The Overture in F is usually dated to the autumn of 1865, in time for Tchaikovsky's conducting debut in November. Its artless expression and textbook structure suggest a class assignment: simple themes, clear cadences, classical proportions, deft if unexceptional scoring. It shows him in perfect command of sonata-allegro, but at the expense of imagination.

Tchaikovsky's muse advanced in daring compositions from his last 18 months at the conservatory. Unable to visit Kamenka in the summer of 1864, he went to Trostinets, the estate of Prince Alexey Vasilievich Golitsïn, where he translated Gevaert's *Traité général d'instrumentation* and composed an Overture on Alexander Ostrovsky's play *The Storm* [255 II 286], posthumously published as op. 76. In the play, Katerina, unhappy in marriage, is driven to an illicit affair and ultimately to death, her mother-in-law's nagging increasing her desire to escape. Modest wrote that Pyotr wanted to write an opera on this play, but no other evidence supports this. A scribbled program for *The Storm* on the manuscript of the *Symphonic Études* [60, 75] is insufficiently aligned with the music to explain it.

An introduction, *Andante misterioso,* punctuated by sudden loud chords, yields to a folk melody (no. 11 of Rimsky-Korsakov's collection). The Allegro is symmetrical, the first section comparable in musical content with the third, each containing a dotted motif, a *tutti* outburst, and a contrasting lyrical theme. The middle section (from 166) juxtaposes themes abruptly and leads to a fugue on the dotted motif, scattered contrapuntally among other musical ideas. Associations can be assigned to the themes:

- the *Andante misterioso:* the atmosphere of the play—uneasiness and malaise
- the folk tune: the heroine Katerina
- the dotted motif: Katerina's mother-in-law (affirmed by Tchaikovsky [1997 I 176])
- the *tutti* and related themes: the storm
- the contrasting lyrical theme: the beauty of nature

Finding fault with *The Storm,* unplayed and unpublished in Tchaikovsky's lifetime, is a staple of criticism. Laroche called it "a museum of anti-musical curiosities" [1997 I 189]; a later reviewer called it a work "carefully hidden by its composer" before its posthumous publication [NV120812]. Understanding is at risk if one misperceives the music as a sonata-allegro in light of Tchaikovsky's many exceptions: frequent and striking juxtapositions of theme; new, unreprised themes throughout; disregard for the preparation of structural cadences; and the harsh abruptness of the ending. These suggest another strategy: following Ostrovsky. In Overture and play, the beauty-of-nature theme is detached from the others, nature's beauty being extolled by a secondary character apart from the central tragedy; this theme grows shorter as references to nature in the play diminish. The silent text of the folk melody describes Ostrovsky's heroine: a young woman anxiously wandering the meadows and the swamps. The fugue on the mother-in-law's theme metaphorizes her nagging. The abrupt ending of the Overture, where peroration might be expected, closely follows the play, as the curtain suddenly drops, Puccini-like, after

Katerina's husband, horrified, discovers her corpse before anyone else has time to react.

As an assignment for Anton Rubinstein, *The Storm* was heretical, not least for requiring three trombones, tuba, English horn, harp, tremolo in divided violins, large drum, cymbals, snare drums, and tam-tam. When the time came to submit the piece, Tchaikovsky claimed he was ill and posted it to Laroche to present in his stead. "Never in my life did I receive such a reprimand for my own misdeeds as I was now obliged to hear on behalf of another," Laroche recalled [1997 I 158]. *The Storm* merged the Western theater overture and its freedoms with the direct stimulus of Ostrovsky's narrative. It was not misshapen juvenilia, but experiment.

The Sonata in C-sharp Minor for Piano, conventional in pattern but unusual in expression, was published in 1900 as op. 80, edited by Sergey Taneyev, who finished a few bars in the slow movement. One might attribute its motleyness to Rubinstein's advice to proceed rapidly when inspiration falters. Or it could be a message to Zaremba, perfect in form but crude in theme, as if Tchaikovsky were daring his teacher to look beyond pattern to distinguish good taste from bad. The beginning, *allegro con fuoco,* combines a *piano* dynamic with accented chords to be played *marcato,* creating a sense of caricature:

Ex. 3

By the time the exposition is over, a pastiche has taken shape: the opening alludes to Beethoven (Violin Concerto mvt. I, 260ff.), then follows a Gypsy tune at 36 and the second of Schumann's *Kreisleriana* at 69. The formal clarity and Tchaikovsky's deferral of any effort to temper these allusions support this hypothesis. The slow movement is a rondo contrasting lyrical and dotted themes, the second intensifying, then spilling over into the reprises of the first. The opening is notably sparse; Tchaikovsky separates the two statements of the theme with a virtuoso flourish at *presto,* juxtapositions worthy of late Beethoven.

The Scherzo is engaging as a theme, a texture, and an image:

Ex. 4

It eschews predictable form, playing off internal repetitions against conventional expectations, and forges a distinctly Beethovenian bridge to the finale. A rhythmic element in the theme suggests Tchaikovsky's sensitivity to words. Alexander Dolzhansky explained of the opening motif: "Its triply-compounded dactylic structure replicates the rhythm of the numerous diminutive, caressing, tender, heartfelt, mournful, sentimental Russian words, so characteristic of Russian folk poetry and prose" [107, 34].

The finale spins out a sonata-allegro pattern—Rubinstein's frothiness without his pianism—and hints that, if the Sonata were written for a class, it was probably Zaremba's.

The historical assessment of the Sonata rests on its allusions, especially Beethoven burlesqued while Schumann is lovingly extended. From this, analogies emerge: old-new, Beethoven-Schumann, Zaremba-Tchaikovsky. If the Sonata was a jest, posterity's pious response to it suggests that the composer's wit ranged well ahead of ours, or that he lacked a gift for musical humor.

Tchaikovsky spent the summer of 1865 at Kamenka, where he drafted a String Quartet movement in B-flat and an Overture in C Minor. The Allegro of the Quartet quotes a song that women were singing in the garden at Kamenka [399, 87], but the éminence grise behind the work is again Beethoven. The narrow melodic compass and rhythm of the *Adagio misterioso* suggest something churchly (the resemblance of this melody to the middle of Chopin's *Nocturne,* op. 37/1, surely being fortuitous), a strange but essential effect if the following eight bars are to make their point: an allusion, a note or two offset, to the opening of Beethoven's String Quartet, op. 130:

Ex. 5 Tchaikovsky

Ex. 6 Beethoven

Eliding introduction with Allegro recalls the join between movements III and IV of the first "Razumovsky," where Beethoven also quoted a Russian folk song. Subtler aspects of Beethoven link the second area theme with the *Adagio misterioso,* such as the melody circling around a single note with a turn at the end:

Ex. 8a

Ex. 8b

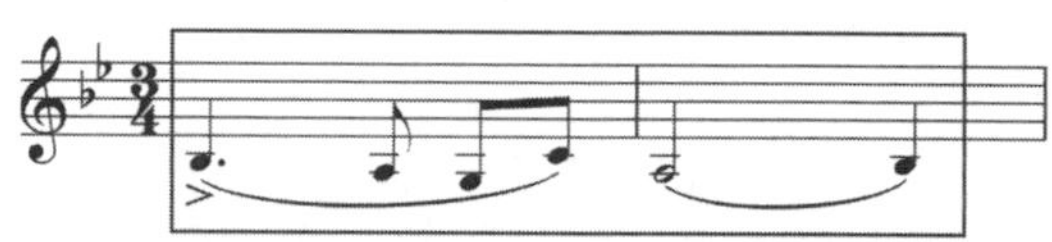

In the development, after reviewing the first and second themes, Tchaikovsky recalls movement I of the *Eroica* by setting a dominant pedal, which is broken off before resolving (bars 212, 220). This augurs treachery when the bass slips from F to F-sharp to G and back again (bars 220–46), Tchaikovsky transposing the second area to F-sharp in another mutation of Beethoven—the key scheme of the exposition in op. 130, from B-flat to G-flat—here relocated to the recapitulation. Whereas Beethoven introduced anomalies early to be resolved by the end, Tchaikovsky eschews anomaly just to introduce one where closure is expected. This forces him to affirm the home key only after the recapitulation, by repeating the entire *Adagio misterioso.* After the String Quartet was performed on 30 October 1865 at the conservatory, he revised it into the *Scherzo à la russe* for piano, op. 1, no. 1 (1867), which Laroche declared "a very coarse adaptation" of the original [255 II 172]. The introduction, now much faster, was placed in the middle, the formal strategy was simplified, and all allusions to Beethoven were removed, suggesting a linkage between allusion and performance medium in the original.

The Overture in C Minor, unscored until after Tchaikovsky moved to Moscow, was triply rejected—by Nikolay and Anton Rubinstein and by the opera conductor Konstantin Lyadov. The autograph, thought lost, was discovered in 1922 among Sergey Taneyev's papers [301, 103]; it was first performed in 1931 and first published in 1952. Long after it was composed, Tchaikovsky referred to it as a "strange abomination." After the introduction, borrowed from *The Storm,* the long sonata-allegro in three theme/key areas reprises the introduction at the end of the development and again after the recapitulation, with a coda only after that. The themes are more eloquent than those of the Overture in F, the key relationships more distinctive (the exposition from C minor to G-flat major), and the rhetoric more individual, with massive shifts of momentum in the post-recapitulation, slowdowns mirthful in relation to the hurried close. Discursive, willful, and extravagant, the Overture seems over-argued.

Tchaikovsky's conservatory compositions reveal an increasing independence of thought. His music veers toward the word and balances musical architecture with unabashed beauty for its own sake, as connoted by the term *prelest'*—the charming, the fascinating, even the seductive. This conscious pursuit of effective sound constitutes a Russian element deeper than hackneyed determinants of nationality, enhancing it in pieces where no phrase of folk song ever sounds.

In September 1865, Nikolay Rubinstein, Anton's brother, visited St. Petersburg to recruit a theory teacher for his music classes in Moscow. Alexander Serov had accepted and withdrawn, whereupon Tchaikovsky was approached. He balked at the miserly pay, then accepted the job [1997 I 184] and Nikolay's invitation to reside in his quarters [187, 9]. By November, he had finished the String Quartet in B-flat and the Overture in F. All that remained was to graduate.

After observing graduation at the Paris Conservatory in 1865, Anton Rubinstein rejected the universal preparation of the same piece as a finishing exercise in favor of examinations particular to the student [26 I 265]. Tchaikovsky's was extraordinary: to compose a cantata on the text of Schiller's ode *An der Freude,* a text familiar from Beethoven's Ninth Symphony.

He set a new translation, quite literal, at times inelegant, and eschewed in performances of the Ninth [96, 343]. Scored for four-part chorus, vocal soloists, and orchestra with enriched brass and percussion, it was to be a test of orchestration, choral writing, and fugue.

The cantata was unpublished in his lifetime and first issued in the *Collected Works* [CW 27]. Using many biblical and liturgical words, the translators infused the new version with a religious mood, which Tchaikovsky, in another subtle appropriation of words, catches in his orchestral first movement. The rhythm of his opening melody embeds the verbal rhythm of Angel Gabriel's announcement to Mary of the birth of Christ from Luke 1:28:

Ex. 9

Andante

[Ra - duy - sya, bla - go - dat - na - ya Ma - ri - ya]
[Rejoice, Mary, who art highly favored...]

This allusion does not affect the sense of the movement, which follows Schiller's poem from a nondescript beginning to a sublime ending. After the first movement, Tchaikovsky withholds the restatement of this theme until the upbeat to the last (V, 67–72), where the text refers to all-embracing brotherhood and God abiding beyond the arch of stars. The soloists sing the first two lines, the chorus all of the second movement:

Joy! Adornment of the world!
Daughter native to the heavens!
We, having partaken of ecstasy's sweetness,
Enter into thy sacred temple.
Thou callest into love's extended arms
The children of hostile vanity,
There all people are again brothers
Where thou touchest them with thy wing.

Tchaikovsky's response to these ecstatic words is a bland melody for the chorus. In the third movement, the soloists sing:

Abide with us, who received the grace,
The desired companion of friendship,
Who even a single chosen soul
Can call his own.
Who knows how, with sweet joy
Beats impassioned, heart upon heart.

This is followed by the chorus, which sings the last couplet:

Whoever these blessings has not known, furtively,
With lamenting withdraw from us!

The introduction for winds, a timbral code for Elysium, is the first of many eighteenth-century touches in the cantata. As the voices wax more Italianate, the flutes and clarinets play a fluttering figure, the "sweet joy" of heart beating upon heart. At the end, the orchestra falls silent, and the chorus waxes madrigalesque (sighing figures on "lamenting," soft recitation and pauses on "furtively"), recalling Marenzio, or the Orthodox Good Friday service. Movement IV is brief:

All living creation
Drinks joy amidst nature.
All, the good and the evil,
Walk along her path.

The chorus variously declaims this text over an eighteenth-century *agitato Affekt* in the orchestra. The tenor soloist leads the chorus in the last, awkward section of the verse:

Dream, wine, kindness, compassion
Of a friend she gives to us.
The worm breathes with animal lust,
The Cherub flies towards the Creator.

The last line excites an enthusiastic, Haydnesque response (cf. "The Heavens Are Telling") before trailing off into silence as the cherub soars beyond the reach of our perception.

Movement V is an interlude which resolves into the finale. The chorus begins:

The steadfast spirit we shall follow even in sufferings!
We shall dry the tears of innocence.

Truth shall be dispensed in heaven.
Perdition to the offspring of the lie.

The bass soloist continues, with the chorus affirming the last line:

As the heavenly bodies fly,
So too along the distant course
Each of us, brothers, in whom there is strength,
Flies into battle like a hero!

Tonal instability and gentle dissonance prevail in phrases with furtive, unsustained crescendos leading to the final line, before the restatement of the cantata's opening theme.

The finale is a mock double fugue, more facile than inspired. The exposition, followed by declamatory shouts and episodes, takes up the first two lines:

To all arms extended,
Peoples, we embrace thee!

The final couplet, introduced by the soloists, is then elaborated by the chorus:

There, above the starry vault, brothers,
Must be a Father to us!

The beginning of this movement is skillful and effectively timed. The first 151 bars, however, serve only to introduce a further orgy of counterpoint, to wearisome overall effect.

Tchaikovsky's "To Joy" was performed on 29 December 1865 before the direction of the Russian Musical Society, three conductors of the Imperial Theaters, and Nikolay Bakhmetev, Director of the Imperial Court Chapel. The committee reported all examinees present [96, 344], though Modest claimed that Pyotr absented himself to avoid public interrogation. Tchaikovsky was one of two silver medalists among six graduates [1997 I 187], but his diploma [416, 40] was not issued until 30 March 1870 [368, 242]. Rubinstein agreed to conduct "To Joy" at a concert of the Russian Musical Society but stipulated changes; Serov and César Cui came out against it in the press. Tchaikovsky found Cui's review especially hurtful [D&Y 600], which initiated an ambivalent lifelong relationship with the Petersburg critic.

On 30 December 1865, Ilya, staying with Zinaida in the Urals, wrote to his son:

> My Dear Petya!
>
> I thank you for the pleasant letter, but I nevertheless have the right, my pet, to say that my heart is sore over you. Now, praise God, you have, in accordance with your own wishes, finished your musical education, and what will it give you: you say they propose for you to be a teacher, perhaps they will name you a professor of the theory of music with a miserly salary! Are you really deserving of this? You have a good head, an excellent education, a magnificent character—do they deserve that? . . . Your passion for music is praiseworthy, but my friend this is a slippery path, the reward for work of genius comes much, much later. . . . I nevertheless have advised you to hold to jurisprudence, although it doesn't pay a large salary. . . . You, however, have a tsar in your own head; I but wish to see you happy, healthy and satisfied. . . . May the Lord God bless you with happiness in the New Year.
>
> Father [414, 20–21]

In *The Life,* Modest made no mention of Ilya's letter but cited another unbidden assessment from the same time:

> I am desperate to acknowledge, as a critic, that you *are the greatest musical talent in contemporary Russia.* More powerful and original than Balakirev, loftier and more creative than Serov, immeasurably better formed than Rimsky-Korsakov, *I see in you the greatest—or, better said—the only hope of our musical future. . . . Your work will begin, perhaps, only in five years: but these mature, classical compositions will surpass everything we have had since Glinka.* [1997 I 188–89]

Given the state of Russian music at the time, Laroche's words were more prophetic than Schumann's, coming at the end of that critic's career, about the young Brahms.

CHAPTER FIVE

Tchaikovsky's First Years in Moscow

TCHAIKOVSKY ARRIVED IN MOSCOW ON 6 JANUARY 1866 AND met his new colleagues the next day. His boss, Nikolay Grigorievich Rubinstein, was a superior musician, trained under Theodor Kullak and Siegfried Dehn, and an organizer of enterprises, of which the Moscow branch of the Russian Musical Society and the Moscow Conservatory were the most important. A strong leader, he was dedicated to music and recruited a cadre of devoted lieutenants. Karl Karlovich Albrecht, cellist and choral conductor, would become the Inspector of the Moscow Conservatory and Tchaikovsky's close friend. Pyotr Ivanovich Jurgenson, who would later be Tchaikovsky's principal publisher, was an Estonian who apprenticed with various Russian music companies before Rubinstein, in 1861, assisted him in starting his own. Nikolay Dmitrievich Kashkin—pianist, critic, historian—was Tchaikovsky's staunchest ally in the press and a leading memoirist of musical activity in Moscow [e.g., 179; 181; 184; 185]. On 11 January Tchaikovsky's course was advertised [416, 49], with a trial lecture on the 13th and classes to begin the next day. It met Tuesdays and Fridays at 11:00 a.m., and cost three rubles a month. He was flustered at his first lecture, but it turned out well [v 92].

Another Rubinstein project, a social club called the Artistic Circle, offered food and drink, entertainment and conversation [329]. Of an evening, artists of the Italian opera or a guest from the provinces might perform, or Rubinstein and Josef Wieniawski, at two pianos, might improvise quadrilles for dancing [MV990212]. Here Tchaikovsky met Alexander

Ostrovsky, on whose *A Dream on the Volga* he would write his first opera, and Count Vladimir Sollogub, on whose *Undine* he would write his second. The Artistic Circle shared a building with the home of author Konstantin Tarnovsky [v 114]. At one point, Tchaikovsky noted a fascination for Mufka, one of Tarnovsky's nieces, though he denied loving her.

Tchaikovsky's subordination to Rubinstein, who was but five years his senior, made for stormy relations [150]; Tchaikovsky declared Rubinstein "excessive in his sovereign control" while Rubinstein found Tchaikovsky insufficiently humble [1997 I 194]. Compulsive about boarders, Rubinstein, when Tchaikovsky moved in, had a violinist living in the house, the irritation of whose practicing was aggravated by Rubinstein's new servant, the lame, wretched, and garrulous Agafon [MV020514]. After a few days, Tchaikovsky worried to the twins that the scratching of his pen might keep his host awake [v 91]. In fact, this living arrangement denied Tchaikovsky repose.

Getting his music performed was a priority. Within a week he was orchestrating the Overture in C Minor, "and to my horror it is coming out inordinately long" [v 91]. After it was rejected, Tchaikovsky agreed to revise the Overture in F, which was performed on 4 March 1866 at Tchaikovsky's debut as a professional composer. The press was silent, though Kashkin recalled that the Overture attracted the notice of musicians. To Laroche, it was an improvement on the first version in integrity and formal proportions [187, 13–14]. Tchaikovsky wrote to Sasha:

> Still more flattering to my self-esteem was the ovation given me at Rubinstein's dinner after the concert. I was last to arrive, and when I entered prolonged applause broke out, at which I bowed awkwardly to all sides and blushed. . . . This is in effect my first public success, and therefore eminently pleasant to me (one more detail: at rehearsal the musicians applauded me). I will not hide that this circumstance added many charms to Moscow in my eyes. [v 104]

Fresh composition ensued. Tchaikovsky started the First Symphony, probably in March [1997 I 253], though the earliest surviving mention was on 25 April to Anatoly: his nerves were delicate because the symphony was not going well [v 109]. On 7 June he wrote to Sasha: "I have already begun to orchestrate the symphony; I am in perfect health; only the last few days I have not slept all night, for I was working a long time, and then attacks tormented me" [v 113]. At the end of July, he was "a step away from madness" with attendant hallucinations and physical numbness in his extremities. As a result, he did not finish the symphony for a time, and he never again composed at night [1997 I 230].

Working at night, let alone the attentions of heterosexual women, cannot have been the sole causes of Tchaikovsky's distress in his early Moscow days [161, 55]. There was much at stake: justifying his profession to his father; bolstering his confidence and self-esteem after Cui's critique of his graduation cantata on 24 March. Not least was the historical burden. "Tchaikovsky *as a symphonist* had no direct predecessors in Russian music" [449, 50], a problem magnified by his Germanic teachers in St. Petersburg. Zaremba and Anton Rubinstein approved only the middle movements of the First after revision, and a critic of the concert there on 11 February 1867 found them remarkable, in the highest degree melodious and magnificently scored [50, 61]. Nikolay Rubinstein had conducted the Scherzo in Moscow on 10 December 1866, and would conduct the entire work in February 1868. Tchaikovsky revised the First again in 1874; he later called it an indulgence of his youth, as it was too great a task too early.

On 1 September 1866, the Moscow Conservatory opened. Tchaikovsky spoke at the inauguration and played the Overture to Glinka's *Ruslan and Lyudmila* at the piano prior to the scheduled concert, making it the first music heard in the new institution. The doubling of his salary boosted his spirits, though it was still insufficient to live alone. His circle of friends now included Vladimir Petrovich Begichev, a dramatist and the Intendant of the Moscow Theaters, whose wife, Maria Shilovskaya, a charming woman with a stormy past [1997 I 239], maintained one of Moscow's brilliant salons. She was the mother of Konstantin and Vladimir Shilovsky; Konstantin would help write the libretto of *Evgeniy Onegin,* and Vladimir would become the composer's student and more in a friendship at times contentious and frustrating [e.g., 306, 96–97].

Tchaikovsky interrupted work on the First Symphony to write, at Nikolay Rubinstein's request, the *Ouverture triomphale sur l'hyme national Danois* to mark the Moscow visit of the future Alexander III and his bride, Princess Dagmar of Denmark. The robust, 13-minute piece is dated 12 November 1866. It seems never to have been played before the imperial couple; three months before their visit, Rubinstein conducted it at a charity concert. We can only guess how the *Ouverture triomphale* (or the First

Symphony) might have been received had the music been available. The piano arrangement, score, and parts were issued 12, 26, and 28 years after composition.

1867

The first half of 1867 is poorly documented, no letter of Tchaikovsky surviving before May. The *Danish Overture* was performed on 29 January, the incidental music to Ostrovsky's play *The False Dmitry and Vasily Shuisky* the next day (two short pieces requested late in 1866), two movements of the First Symphony in St. Petersburg on 11 February, and the *Scherzo à la russe* played by Nikolay Rubinstein on 31 March. Early in the year, Tchaikovsky and Ostrovsky agreed to collaborate on an opera. Tchaikovsky received act I of *The Voevoda* on 5 March, began work three days later, then lost the libretto in April. Ostrovsky began to rewrite it in June but stopped after two weeks.

The summer began with a mishap that made plain Tchaikovsky's inability to handle money. Having promised Anatoly a holiday in Finland, the two departed with insufficient funds and were forced to seek refuge with Sasha's mother-in-law and her daughters in Hapsal, Estonia. There, after money from Sasha and a substantial sum from Moscow were received [v 119], Tchaikovsky composed the *Souvenir de Hapsal* and revised his Characteristic Dances of 1865 as the Dances of the Serving Maidens in *The Voevoda*—obviously still in possession of the earlier score. He wrote to Ostrovsky in June with a new plan for act II; in September, he wrote again, begging the librettist to finish, as he still lacked part of act II and all of act III. No further communication between them on this topic survives; Tchaikovsky finished the libretto himself.

The social whirl of Hapsal interfered with Pyotr's composition and made him complain to Sasha of "misanthropy," or powerful attacks of hatred for people [v 120]. Modest cited this letter without explaining that Vera Vasilievna Davïdova, Sasha's sister-in-law, had eyes for Pyotr. How much her feelings were puppy-love, fascination with artistic genius, or the desire for another union of siblings from the two families can only be guessed. But Vera confided in Sasha, who chided Pyotr for raising her hopes; in fact, he had dedicated the *Souvenir de Hapsal* to Vera and hinted at living out their lives together in idyllic solitude. When he learned of Vera's confidences, he offered Sasha a variety of explanations, including "misanthropy." Vera was a beloved family member, yet two months later he called her an actress without strong feelings for him and stated that he would cease visits to St. Petersburg if going there made the family anxious [v 126].

In August, he returned to Moscow and many distractions. Rubinstein moved into new quarters where Pyotr would have a separate room. In September, he retired from the civil service at the rank of court counselor (the civil equivalent of lieutenant colonel). In October, he encountered Sergey Kireyev, for whom his earlier feelings were not rekindled [v 127]. By the end of November, the Dances of the Serving Maidens from *The Voevoda* were ready, which were conducted by Nikolay Rubinstein on 2 December; then came a request to play the Dances in St. Petersburg and news that Hector Berlioz would be giving two concerts in Moscow that month. Tchaikovsky honored Berlioz with a speech. In mid-December, he wrote a recitative and couplet, now lost, for an amateur staging of a play [1997 I 264]; he probably arranged Alexander Dargomïzhsky's *Kazachok* for piano in 1867 [CW 60 XI, 3–13]. At year's end, his friend Ivan Klimenko, among the first to appreciate Tchaikovsky's significance to Russian music, moved to Moscow.

1868

In 1868, Tchaikovsky finished *The Voevoda,* dealt with Vera Davïdova's continuing attentions, and entered into a complex relationship with Mily Balakirev and his colleagues, who were known as the Mighty Handful. In the summer, he traveled as Vladimir Shilovsky's music tutor. He composed the piano pieces opp. 4 and 5, a potpourri on *The Voevoda,* and the tone poem *Fatum;* arranged the first 25 of 50 Russian folk songs he would publish; and translated Schumann's *House Rules and Maxims for Young Musicians* and *Foreword to [the Études,] op. 3* for an edition of that composer's piano music [iii-b, 363–76]. His acquaintance with another traveling companion, the actor Konstantin Nikolaevich de Lazari, ripened into friendship. On 10 September, the Director of Imperial Theaters, Stepan Gedeónov, ordered rehearsals of *The Voevoda* to begin and the production to be ready in a month. In 15 days, Tchaikovsky withdrew the opera until after the Italian season, the demands of which on time and rehearsal space left the Russian company too little time to prepare, and the production was moved to January 1869. He maintained cordial relations with Ostrovsky; by October, they were discussing but never seriously pursued an opera about Alexander the Great.

Tchaikovsky's rejections of Vera Davïdova to Sasha on 16 April and 24 September imply her continuing pursuit. He declared himself an unfit spouse, too lazy to be responsible for a wife and children [v 136]. Vera's attentions may have had some connection to Pyotr's relationship with the Belgian mezzo-soprano Désirée Artôt, who first appeared with the Italian opera in Moscow in March. By September, he was calling Artôt "a magnificent individual" and "kind, intelligent and good" [v 145]. Many questioned the Artôt-Tchaikovsky affair. Laroche noted her plainness and declining artistic gift, while Nikolay Rubinstein mocked the thought of their marriage. De Lazari claimed that Artôt's mother disapproved of the match, said that Tchaikovsky had a rival, and implied that the couple had pondered having children [306, 88–91]. The affair reached its zenith near the end of 1868, when Pyotr wrote to his father of possible marriage, obstacles, and the clash of interests. A few weeks later, Artôt married the tenor Manuel de Padilla, Tchaikovsky receiving notice in an unsigned telegram on her wedding day. His intentions, according to one theory, had irritated her admirers in Moscow, who used all their persuasion to prevent the marriage [MV020514]. His jocular response—possibly relief—suggests a strategy to use Artôt to discourage Vera Davïdova. The anecdote of Tchaikovsky crying beneath his opera glasses at a later Artôt performance is suspect once we know Vera was present [187, 78–79; v 192]. Yet his affection for Artôt was to some degree serious, judging by the dedication of the *Romance,* op. 5, and internal evidence from the op. 6 songs and the First Piano Concerto [60, 197–200]. The tone poem, *Fatum,* may also be relevant. On 25 September, the day after denying his love for Vera, Tchaikovsky informed Anatoly that he was writing *Fatum,* and he was orchestrating it in mid-December. He would use the middle theme of *Fatum* again in *The Oprichnik* (no. 16 at 237), as Natalia and Andrey fatefully affirm their love —shortly before Andrey is executed.

Tchaikovsky's first involvement with Mily Balakirev developed from the latter's wish to perform the Dances of the Serving Maidens in St. Petersburg. Tchaikovsky felt ambivalent toward Balakirev—for opposing Anton Rubinstein and for mentoring composers he did not admire. Chafed by the ultraliberal tendencies of the Mighty Handful, Pyotr kept his distance and scorned their naïve, sometimes coarse works (especially Musorgsky's)

[1997 I 268]. On the other hand, he respected Balakirev's efforts to advance Russian music and subsequently befriended Rimsky-Korsakov and Borodin. Relations with Balakirev improved when Nikolay Rubinstein sought to increase the performance of new pieces from St. Petersburg, minimize factional differences, and make opportunities for composers from one city in the other. This rapprochement had begun by December 1867 when Rubinstein conducted Rimsky-Korsakov's *Serbian Fantasia* in Moscow, a local critic attacked the piece, and Tchaikovsky was enlisted to respond. Any philosophical affinity with the Mighty Handful was, however, largely illusory, the nationalists misconstruing improved collegiality as kinship. Tchaikovsky's Dances of the Serving Maidens were performed in the exchange of repertoires between the cities. On 19 February, he conducted them himself, coping with his old fear that his head would fall off. The experience so terrified him that he laid down his baton for several years.

1869

Rubinstein, who conducted the first performance of *Fatum* on 15 February, wanted an explanation of its title, whereas Tchaikovsky's friend Klimenko urged that the title be suppressed [1997 I 296; 199, 70]. Another friend, without hearing the piece, proposed a verse by K. N. Batyushkov as a suitable program [423, 353; 60, 165], to which Tchaikovsky agreed. He dedicated *Fatum* to Balakirev, who conducted it on 17 March and again a year later but complained of signs of haste and obvious joins [22, 26–31]. Cui praised its form but observed that "the darkness of the beginning, the beauty of the Andante and the caricature-like jesting of the Allegro cannot be reconciled" [D&Y 60–61]. Balakirev's criticism paved the way for Tchaikovsky to write something more to his liking. This would be *Romeo and Juliet,* begun in October. After *Fatum,* Tchaikovsky's attention passed to the staging of *The Voevoda* and to composing *Undine,* which was finished by the end of summer. Among smaller projects were four-hands arrangements of another 25 folk songs, a reduction of Anton Rubinstein's *Ivan the Terrible,* and the songs, op. 6. Ippolit's wedding in June focused his attention on family matters. For a time, he tried to secure a post in Moscow for Anatoly, who had graduated from the School of Jurisprudence in May.

The history of Tchaikovsky's first opera has been reduced to a formula: he tried, it failed, he burned the score. In rehearsal, he discovered defects too late to correct them and was surprised by the technical limitations of experienced artists [187, 51–60]. Laroche observed precisely devised instrumentation, soft and elegant lines, warm and feminine-tender feeling in the music, but when the drama did not call for these qualities, the music drifted into coldness and artificiality, making energetic and passionate places strained and unbeautiful. He found the orchestra too loud and the scoring indifferent to the voice; the Russian element was distinctive, but when it was absent Tchaikovsky's kinship with Italian and German models was made plain [255 II 23–26]. Pyotr subsequently affirmed most of Laroche's critique, but at the time his "extreme wrath struck us [Tchaikovsky's intimate circle in Moscow] as exaggerated" [MV020514]. Tchaikovsky had shown Laroche his music for *The Voevoda* and enlisted his assistance in harmonizing folk songs [184, xxxix]; to be treated so harshly after this triggered a sense of betrayal. "If only you knew the circumstances leading up to the composition of that article," he wrote to Anatoly [v 156]. A two-year rupture in his and Laroche's friendship ensued.

Despite 12 orchestral rehearsals [238, 129], *The Voevoda* might have been given more than five times if it had enjoyed stronger musical direction, bigger outlays on production, and had been performed by itself, without separate ballets on the same evening. We have only fleeting glimpses of it—from an illustrated newspaper [VI690524] and the recollection of one of the artists:

> [A] little house standing in the middle of the stage; its architecture was neither Swiss nor Russian; a balcony was located beneath the wing, and when the Voevoda (sung by an Italian ignorant of Russian), pursuing his beloved in a passionate outburst, climbed the staircase to the balcony, his waist was higher than the wing of the little house. [284, 322]

Tchaikovsky took 15 calls and received a laurel wreath at the first performance.

The Voevoda revealed three idiosyncrasies in the composer: he realized major faults in his operas only in production, he responded to the failure of one opera by taking up another, and he favored balanced patterns in his operatic music—submission to old forms, as he described it—overruling any unencumbered musical response to a dramatic situation. In January 1869, he reported to Anatoly that rehearsals were going badly and alerted him to a new operatic project; Pyotr was applying himself to *Undine* "with great fervor" [v 153, 156].

De la Motte Fouqué's story of a water spirit who falls in love with a mortal man to gain a soul, is betrayed by him, and returns to her natural element was famous in Vasily Zhukovsky's verse translation, a copy of which was in the library at Votkinsk. Tchaikovsky loved *Undine:* he would later contemplate another opera and a ballet by this title, and he composed variants of it in *The Snow Maiden* and *Swan Lake.* Count Sollogub's libretto for *Undine* had been set by Alexey Lvov in 1848, was revived in 1862, and was composed by Tchaikovsky in 1869 between January and July. By mid-April, he had inquired about staging and was informed that if the score were received in St. Petersburg by September, *Undine* would be performed in November [v 161]. He finished it in July and sent it to St. Petersburg in August. Only in mid-November did the Petersburg direction realize that the score had been left untouched. This news came on the heels of a rumor, described to Sasha on 15 November, that there had been a read-through of the opera.

Tchaikovsky had written to Balakirev on 2 October regarding *Romeo and Juliet,* "I have been waiting for inspiration to condescend to visit me. . . . But imagine, I am utterly played out, not one little musical idea, however tolerable, has crawled into my head" [v 174]. Balakirev responded like an angry parent, and by month's end Tchaikovsky reported *Romeo* nearly finished, based on Balakirev's formal plan: an introduction depicting Friar Laurence, an Allegro depicting the animosity of the families, and a second theme representing love. Tchaikovsky sent his themes to Balakirev, who mocked them [22, 48–50]. The introduction sounded like a Haydn quartet, whereas Friar Laurence needed something in the manner of a Liszt chorale; the animosity theme was not a theme but a very beautiful introduction to one; the love theme was "very beautiful, although a little putrid"—when he played it, he pictured Artôt-Padilla stroking Tchaikovsky's tummy in his bath with the lather of perfumed soap—though the second part of the theme was charming. Tchaikovsky agreed to revise, but only in the new year.

The day after Tchaikovsky sent his themes for *Romeo* to Balakirev, he queried Modest about Modest's own Overture to *Romeo and Juliet,* written to the following musical plan:

> First the enmity of the two families, represented by *ff* and *Presto,* then little-by-little from all manner of noise and nonsense emerges a divine hymn of love (*pp*), trumpets and violoncelli represent love and the character Romeo, and the

> violins and flutes—Juliet. At last this hymn develops to the point of terrifying passionateness and takes on a sinister tone, the whole time being interrupted by the first theme of the conflict, but at once—suddenly from a frightful *ff*—a pause and then a sombre phrase, which ends in quiet, reconciling chords. Not bad, is it? [v 190, n. 3]

Odder still was Tchaikovsky's remark to Modest the day before the first performance of *Romeo,* "in the composition of which I am so obliged to you" [v 207].

By 19 December, Tchaikovsky had been drawn to another opera subject, *Mandragora* by Sergey Rachinsky, the botany professor at Moscow University who had proposed the program for *Fatum.* A knight is sent in quest of Mandragora, a magic root. It turns into an enchanted maiden with whom he falls in love. When he subsequently falls in love with someone else, Mandragora reverts to a flower [1997 I 313]. Kashkin discouraged Tchaikovsky, arguing that *Mandragora* was better suited for ballet (a similar story, *The Fern,* had been choreographed by Sergey Sokolov in Moscow in 1867), but not before Pyotr had composed an elaborate Chorus of Flowers and Insects for it.

Tchaikovsky has achieved notoriety for burning three important works of 1869, *The Voevoda, Fatum,* and *Undine.* He did not do this for several years, possibly well past 1875, his motive not so much rejection as to obscure the origins of music used again.

1870

Early in the year, Tchaikovsky rejected another scenario by Rachinsky, on *Raymond Lully*—both it and *Mandragora,* apparently, impulsive responses to the neglect of *Undine*—in favor of Ivan Lazhechnikov's play *The Oprichnik,* on which he began work. He composed the piano pieces opp. 7–9 and revised *Romeo and Juliet* during the summer. In October, he agreed to compose a ballet on the story of Cinderella [scenario in 362, 297–303], to be ready in December. After he reported this to Modest and Anatoly, the project dropped from view [v 234–35]. He wrote the songs "To forget so soon" (Apukhtin) and "Zemfira's Song" (Pushkin) and, in December, an ensemble for women's voices, "Nature and Love," to his own text.

Nikolay Rubinstein conducted *Romeo and Juliet* in Moscow on 4 March and upstaged Tchaikovsky's music, his rudeness toward a student having become a cause célèbre. After one court dismissed the complaint, an appeal found Rubinstein culpable, which decision rallied the conservatory professors to threaten their resignations should the appeal be affirmed. An article on the day of the concert sparked a demonstration in the hall that evening [187, 64–66; MV990806]. On 16 March, three excerpts from *Undine* were performed in Moscow, again with Rubinstein's participation, together with the Adagio from the First Symphony [187, 73–74]. This occasion seems to acknowledge and anticipate the official cancellation, in St. Petersburg in May, of *Undine,* which a committee of conductors found unworthy of the Maryinsky stage [1997 I 320–21].

Since March, Vladimir Shilovsky, who was ill, had been pressing Tchaikovsky to join him in Western Europe. In April, he agreed and arrived in May. They went to Soden, a gloomy place filled with consumptives, whence Tchaikovsky went to Mannheim for a Beethoven festival to hear the *Missa Solemnis* [v 276], "a work of greatest genius," and to Wiesbaden to visit the gaming-addicted Nikolay Rubinstein. If these weren't sufficient distractions, the Franco-Prussian War broke out, clogging routes leaving Germany and filling Switzerland with foreigners. Tchaikovsky found his way to Interlaken and returned to St. Petersburg late in August.

Modest graduated from the School of Jurisprudence in May. Pyotr had been urging him to study, fretted over his cutting classes, and encouraged certain friendships over others. In mid-February, he railed against masturbation and before that had urged Modest to fight his homoerotic inclinations: "If there is the least possibility, try not to be a *bugger.* That would be very sad. At your age you can still force yourself to love the fairer sex; try it once, perhaps it will work" [369, 121]. Modest's perpetual lack of money also worried Pyotr. In September, he was incensed when Modest wheedled 500 rubles from Ilya and squandered it on drink and billiards [v 230]. At year's end, Tchaikovsky was still irritated with Modest because he had few means, could not live without superfluities, didn't fulfill his service obligations—but was hardly short on pride [v 245].

On 6 September, Tchaikovsky reported the revision of *Romeo and Juliet* to Balakirev. The introduction was new, the middle section almost so, and the second statement of the second theme reorchestrated [v 230–31]. All told, Balakirev's influence on Tchaikovsky's *Romeo* involved following his keys and program and making the revisions, the last motivated by Tchaikovsky's own conviction as well. In other respects, Balakirev wanted a particular key and character in the introduction, and Tchaikovsky gave him neither. Balakirev found fault with the Allegro theme, and Tchaikovsky kept it anyway. Nor would he delay publication to accommodate further revision.

By 1870, Tchaikovsky's dependence on critique from St. Petersburg was over. He had no further need of Anton Rubinstein's approbation and required nobody's tutelage. He had become a Muscovite. The reception of his music in Moscow was good; he enjoyed certainty of publication and the support of Nikolay Rubinstein. The Russian Musical Society in Moscow had rewarded him with a stipend for *Romeo and Juliet,* the first of many special awards. In November 1870, he wrote that he was becoming more and more attached to Moscow and could live there happily if only he had more money [v 243]. To put the years 1866–1870 in perspective, we need but recall Laroche's words: "Your work will begin, perhaps, only in five years: but these mature, classical compositions will surpass everything we have had since Glinka." [1997 I 189]. Tchaikovsky's work on *Romeo and Juliet* had begun in the fifth year after his graduation. It was his first piece to be published and played outside Russia, when Hans Richter conducted it with the Vienna Philharmonic Orchestra; it was his first work to enter the continuing repertoire.

CHAPTER SIX

Music of the First Five Years

MUCH THAT TCHAIKOVSKY COMPOSED IN HIS FIRST FIVE YEARS of professional life was destroyed, has been retrieved from orchestral parts, is seldom played, or is familiar in revisions made after 1870 [50; 238]. Self-borrowing—a device he used throughout his life [217, 185–91]—is especially prominent in his early compositions, as are routine chores stemming from his increasing stature or need for money, such as orchestrations and arrangements of other composers' music.

The first music he produced in Moscow was a new version of his Overture in F, made in February and performed in March. To the orchestra he added three horns, a trumpet, and three trombones, and he added 310 bars to the score. Four statements of the introduction theme made that section fulsome; in the Sonata proper, the transition and development were expanded and the introduction theme reprised with the recapitulation. The 33-bar coda of the first version was transformed: Tchaikovsky stopped at the end of the recapitulation, wrote a fugue of 44 bars, then 104 bars of *maestoso* on a new theme, and then a closing of some 20 bars recalling the first theme of the Allegro. This hyperbole surpassed any reasonable measure of thematic elaboration to distort the formal pattern. His unclassical emphasis and unexpected reprise were idiosyncratic, as were the stopping and restarting of a large ensemble in mid-discourse. Nikolay Rubinstein may have insisted on additional changes, which are reflected on surviving orchestral parts [238, 133].

Sometime in March 1866, when the Overture received its first performance, Tchaikovsky began his First Symphony, op. 13 in G minor, *Winter Reveries.* Late in 1866, he revised passages he had shown to his former teachers for critique and made other changes before the first performance in 1868. We know details of this early version by sheer luck [217, 174–76; 238, 134–36; 450]. In 1886, Mikhail Ippolitov-Ivanov requested the score from Jurgenson. He probably received orchestral parts made in 1866 [238, 134–35] and a copy of the first published edition (which was based on further revision in 1874) with passages from the earlier version pasted onto its pages. Tchaikovsky was furious to learn of this [xiii 319–20], but the copy showed his changes: a new second theme for the first movement, two 4-bar phrases cut in the second, and short passages cut just prior to the Allegro in the finale [CW 15-a, 169–85]. Reception was stunted by the error-ridden 1875 score and by the delay in printed orchestral parts until 22 years after composition.

The relevance of the titles—of the symphony and the first two movements—is uncertain. Tchaikovsky remarked in 1878 that one of Meck's paintings could be "an illustration of the first movement" [86 I 448; 282, 12–32], and in fact, the atmospheric opening theme is a splendid metaphor of "winter reveries":

Ex. 10

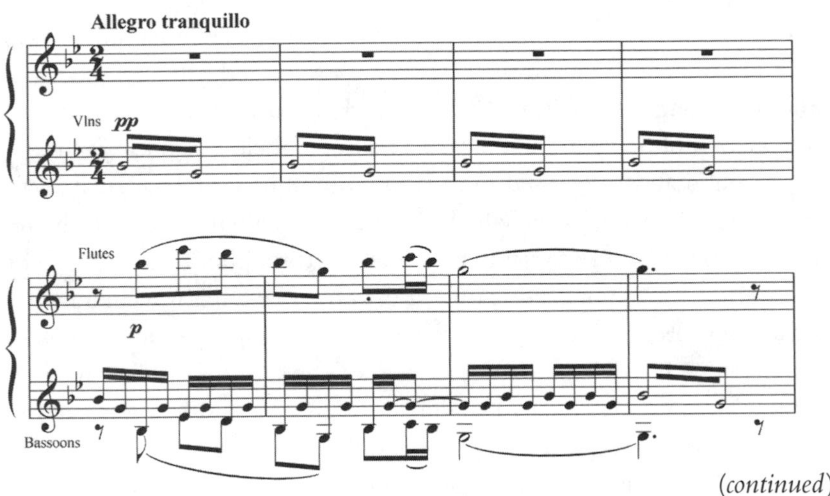

(continued)

Ex. 10 *(continued)*

The opening melody of the slow movement fits the Russian prosody of its title, "Gloomy Land, Misty Land" (see example 11); the Scherzo, with its resonance of winter, and the folk song finale, though untitled, are amenable to a program [8, 132].

The structure of the symphony recalls that of Schumann's Fourth, which (Modest wrote) Tchaikovsky played often during the summer of 1866: a hybridized pattern in the outer movements while the inner ones yield to beauty and attractiveness [on Tchaikovsky and Schumann, see 66; 246]. After long introductions in many earlier works, Tchaikovsky began the First Symphony with the Allegro. The initial melody's shifting phrases, relaxed pulse and meter, and unusual pitch emphasis and cadence await clarification in bar 14, after which these features attenuate as the theme proceeds into formula, figuring prominently throughout the movement but returning to its initial guise only at the end. The result is what Susanne Dammann calls "expressive excess in the form of disparate motivic details that threatened to explode the framework of the sonata form Tchaikovsky nonetheless was unwilling to abandon" [92, 205]. A transition between the first and second areas is eccentric tonally, darting away from and back to the home key, including visits to B-flat and B at 68 and 84. Pauses between the transition and the second theme, and between the second theme and closing, seem to mock Germanic continuity, the most prominent break coming in the middle of the development (at 383) before the deliberate retransition, where the horns anticipate the "fate" fanfare of the Fourth Symphony.

Movements II and III contain borrowed music: the nature theme from *The Storm,* which frames the slow movement, and the Scherzo from the C-sharp Minor Sonata for Piano, now in C minor. The slow movement, with folkish touches (rising melodic octave at cadences, allusion to changing background variation, blending of the home key and its relative), is spun out phrase by phrase to a climax before the introduction returns as an epilogue. The opening four notes touch melodically on C-flat and B-flat:

Ex. 11

These echo tonal destinations in the transition of movement I; later, in the Andante, the more distant C-flat becomes the first important modulation outside the home key (enharmonic B at 54). The Scherzo in C minor fulfills the plagal hints of the melody at the beginning of movement I and the mingling of this key with E-flat in the Andante. Key thus unifies, just as the folkish verbal rhythms observed in the Scherzo theme provide individuality (above, p. 36). The Trio is Tchaikovsky's first orchestral waltz.

In the finale, Schumann's Fourth is recalled in the *accellerando* between the opening theme and the Allegro; Tchaikovsky pauses in mid-development again, as he did in the first movement, enhancing the parallel with elements of the rhythmic, tonal, and timbral world taken from movement I. Folkish references find their apotheosis here: the introduction is a folk theme treated in changing background (anticipating the opening movement of the Second Symphony), which returns as the second theme of the Sonata exposition—in B minor, echoing earlier occurrences of that key—and again, after the retransition, in a triumphal variant (at bar 431).

The First Symphony illustrates Tchaikovsky's characteristic interplay of conformity and independence, making his music at once original and responsive to tradition [92, 204].

Tchaikovsky composed the *Ouverture solennelle sur l'hymne national danois,* op. 15, from 10 September to 12 November 1866. The scant literature about it centers around a brief assessment published in the St. Petersburg newspaper *Golos* on 12 April 1867, about 10 days before the imperial couple were to arrive in Moscow and some two months after the first performance:

> In the original announcement a performance of Mr. Tchaikovsky's overture was promised. . . . Mr. Tchaikovsky's overture, written on the conjoined themes of the Russian and Danish national hymns, was not permitted for performance because the talented young composer got it into his head, for unknown reasons, to set forth our Russian national hymn in the minor tonality, which completely changes the character of this universally known melody. [108, 333]

This problem may explain Tchaikovsky's remarks to Jurgenson in 1892: "[I] once dedicated the *Danish Overture* to the heir apparent. . . . [B]ut in any case we *cannot* trouble over permission to print the dedication," for reasons he would report in person [xvi-b 92].

Meyerbeer had used the Danish hymn in his Overture to *Struensee,* which Tchaikovsky admired as a student. His procedure is clichéd: hints of the melody at the beginning proceed to a coherent statement and ever more flamboyant locutions. Tchaikovsky added the Russian anthem and cast the piece as an introduction and sonata-allegro, stating the Danish hymn triumphantly in a long post-recapitulation. The introduction also contains a brief Slavic intonation (at 29), a paraphrase of the Russian anthem (at 73), and the Danish hymn set as a funeral march (at 107). In the recapitulation, Tchaikovsky moves directly from the first area to the post-recapitulation, where the two hymns are juxtaposed and then combined contrapuntally (at 450, 467) before he concludes with the Danish hymn alone. The Russian hymn, excluded from the exposition and recapitulation, is melodically altered and harmonized in the minor. Especially striking are its statements in the introduction, where the initial note is dissonant to the harmony. There is no topical justification for these changes nor for the funeral march on the Danish melody. Yet Tchaikovsky, let alone Rubinstein, would surely have avoided any lapse of musical diplomacy.

In January 1867, Tchaikovsky wrote an introduction and a mazurka as incidental music to Alexander Ostrovsky's play *The False Dmitry and Vasily Shuisky.* The introduction was lost, then found and published in 1955 [143, 414–28; CW 14, 3–7]. He arranged the mazurka for piano (omitting a repetition of the Trio) in the summer of 1867, writing it out in an album belonging to Vera Davïdova [412]. For the principal theme of the introduction, he used the first 12 bars of his Variations in A Minor. Judging from his annotations in a copy of N. Ustryalov's *Reports of Contemporaries of the False Dmitry* (St. Petersburg, 1859), which described musical practices of Dmitry's time [143, 265–66], he may have been seeking a degree of historical authenticity in this music. The unexpected *tutti* that closes the introduction with prominent brass and drum may refer to ceremonial outdoor music cited in Ustryalov, just as his description of a mysterious instrument which plays and hums on one note may be related to the main theme of the mazurka, which centers around the single pitch of D.

Tchaikovsky wrote piano music in 1867, mostly charming miniatures or lyric effusions which helped to establish his reputation without occupying a distinctive niche in his larger repertoire or that of the instrument [5, 11–43; 133; 281, 66–92]. Of the *Two Pieces,* op. 1, finished in 1867 but begun earlier, the *Scherzo à la russe* (at first called a capriccio, an arrangement of the String Quartet in B-flat), focuses on virtuosity. The principal tune is *russe* but short, on which Tchaikovsky composed mock variations to humorous effect. After the middle section of quicksilver modulations, it returns, embellished; octaves are prominent, especially in the left hand; a drooping *quasi adagio* serves as the upbeat for a toccata-like *presto* which races to the final cadence. Laroche questioned the tune's suitability for a virtuoso piece and faulted the middle section for poor invention [255 II 43]. Op. 1, no. 2, the *Impromptu,* in E-flat minor, is another student work. According to Kashkin, Tchaikovsky did not submit it for publication, but allowed it when the printers set it by mistake [187, 41].

Three short pieces make up the *Souvenir de Hapsal,* op. 2, from the summer of 1867. Only the first, "Ruins of a Castle," gives any sense of Hapsal, in the mysterious bass in open fifths, played against the *Marche solennelle* in the right hand. Fanfares clash in the middle section—a call to arms that vanishes with the reprise. No. 2, a scherzo, draws on a student piano sonata [CW 58, 205–10]. The third piece, "Chant sans paroles," was Tchaikovsky's first popular success. The melody, the long pedal point at the close, and the supporting chords, all of homey and sentimental cast, proved irresistible; it was variously arranged.

The *Valse-caprice,* op. 4, was composed for Anton Door, possibly in October 1868. This first of Tchaikovsky's dozen waltzes for piano is hardly a miniature at nine minutes. Caprice resides in the many unexpected turns of chord, figuration, and key, as well as in the charming intonations of the music box before the hackneyed bravura ending. Only sensitive playing will offset long-windedness and the impression of taking cleverness to extremes. Better can be said of the *Romance,* op. 5, laid out like a Chopin nocturne, the main section emulating Italianate cantabile (with ornamentation more violinistic than vocal) set upon a simple accompaniment, with a distinctive contrast in the middle section. Related by their initial fall of a melodic fifth, the two sections—operatic melody and Russian dance—may depict Artôt, the work's dedicatee, and Tchaikovsky. The *Romance* and the *Valse-caprice* are Tchaikovsky's earliest surviving autographs.

Sometime in the autumn of 1868, Tchaikovsky turned to *Fatum* (published posthumously as op. 77), perhaps his most enigmatic work in terms of its meaning. As music alone, *Fatum* might have cohered via a conventional formal pattern, but Tchaikovsky preferred two large strophes of three themes apiece: a *tutti* flourish of 15 bars that hints at folk idiom with its partial scale, a lyric theme elaborated for about 100 bars, and an agitated, trepak-like theme extended for another 100 bars with a dactylic countermotif. Lacking a coherent explanation of its title, *Fatum* simply repeats this unruly sequence of ideas. Having found the piece satisfactory for his own reasons, Tchaikovsky may have provided a title after the unusual structure gave him pause, illuminating nothing but diverting the listener's attention from the curious pattern; then, he suppressed the piece rather than make a bad situation worse with further tampering.

The first of two installments of *Fifty Russian Folk Songs* in Tchaikovsky's arrangement for piano, four hands, was issued in December 1868. It included 23 songs from *100 Russian Folk Songs* (1860) by Konstantin Petrovich Villebois, with no. 24 notated by Tchaikovsky and no. 23 by Ostrovsky; the second installment (issued in the autumn of 1869) reworked 24 songs from Balakirev's *Collection of Russian Folk Melodies* (1866), to which

Tchaikovsky added no. 47, notated by himself. In exceptions to typical practice, he omitted the text and classification of the songs, revised them where Villebois had violated principles of diatonicism or modality, and changed the format of the arrangements. Villebois and Balakirev (and, later, Rimsky-Korsakov) typically included one statement of the tune and underlaid it with a sparse accompaniment; Tchaikovsky's settings are polyphonic elaborations of the tunes, without text. He had already used some of these tunes in *The Storm* and *The Voevoda* and would use many later: no. 6 (Symphony no. 2); nos. 10, 17, 32, and 34 (dances in *The Oprichnik*); nos. 14, 26, and part of 31 (*The Snow Maiden*), nos. 28 and 42 (*Serenade for Strings*), no. 48 (*1812*), and no. 47 (First String Quartet). [On Tchaikovsky and folk song generally, see 118; 319.]

Tchaikovsky composed the first version of the *Romeo and Juliet* fantasia-overture between 25 September and 15 November 1869, but it was published only in 1950 [CW 23, 3–86]. The second version, from the summer of 1870, was published, score and four-hands reduction, by Bote & Bock in Berlin in 1871 and later by Bessel in St. Petersburg [music unique to this version in CW 23, 199–223]. The standard revision dates from 1880. All share the animosity theme of the Allegro and the love theme. The introduction of the first version is not obviously suggestive of Friar Laurence, an ambiguity compounded by its recurrence in the funeral march at the end. Tchaikovsky thought better of this and of other first thoughts: he removed the furtive appearances of the love theme in the introduction and development, opting for more effective statements in the exposition and recapitulation; he relocated the fugato on the animosity theme to the interior of the development, where it was more effective than at the beginning; and he wrote the new, chorale-like introduction, substituting this melody for its predecessor throughout except for the funeral march, where he reprised the love theme. The extent of each revision coincides with the amount of new music: 342 new bars in the second version, 34 new bars in the third.

Romeo and Juliet is an advance over *Fatum,* the cogent synthesis of a famous play. Tchaikovsky's vivid themes befit a tone poem, including the clash of swords to show animosity and the sighs of the famous love music. This graphic element was enhanced in revision by the intonations of lament in the second theme of the introduction, the *stringendo* before the Allegro, and by the new funeral march at the end. In the revision, the development improvises without losing its narrative sense: outbursts of the animosity theme are contained by the Friar Laurence theme. The effect is calm but edgy before fresh outbursts of animosity (at 320) and the friar's fierce objection (at 335). This is the high point of intensity so far, surpassed only by the love theme in the recapitulation. This sequence—outbursts of hostility, Laurence's attempts to contain them, and the implication that they are surpassed by love—point more to Tchaikovsky's reading of Shakespeare than to Balakirev's and to stronger invention.

The *Six Romances,* op. 6, were composed just after *Romeo and Juliet*—between 15 November and 17 December 1869. In the autograph, titles and authors are listed together on the dust cover but not at the beginning of each song, suggesting a cyclical conception [424, 75]. We do not know what brought Tchaikovsky to compose them, but on 15 November 1869 Désirée Artôt, Tchaikovsky's "former bride," for whom he still felt "an inexplicable sympathy," had arrived in Moscow, and he claimed he had to see her [v 184, 182]. The *Six Romances* make sense as an address to her: Do not believe . . . that I no longer love you, . . . There were days of bright happiness that are no more . . . , It is both painful and sweet, . . . You are still dear to me, . . . Did you forget me? . . . Only one longing for reunion will grasp how I have suffered.

In no. 1, "Do not believe, my friend," to a text by Alexey Tolstoy, the singer should not believe the lover's denial just as the earth should not believe the ebbing of the sea. The assurance of return is expressed in the introduction by a simple metaphor—the dominant pedal resolving to the tonic, whereupon the dominant pitch and chord, like the tide, are reset. The tonic is reached as the voice comes in, implying the return of love, which is affirmed by the reprise of the opening in interludes. The understated relationship of the broken chords and the verbal reference above them to "the waves rush back noisily" is typical of Tchaikovsky's generalized response to words. The fanfare, double *forte,* before the reprise of the opening verse, anticipates similar chords in no. 6.

Willows incline over a grave as lovers ponder lost happiness in no. 2, Pleshcheyev's translation of Hartmann's "Not a word, o my friend." Their sorrow intensifies in the middle when Tchaikovsky restates the piano introduction, which distinguishes past from present in the two-note groups of the voice set against three-note groups in the piano. Much of the rest is recitative-like, except a descending figure in the accompaniment, pointing to the drooping willows.

In "It is both painful and sweet" (no. 3, by Rostopchina), pain and sweetness commingle at the outset of love, when one is speechless while trying to make an avowal and when the words flow but one is alone. Agitation and nervousness guide the expression and structure, which begins strophic and ends reprise, the shift from one to the other marked by extending the second stanza beyond its expected limits. Brief changes in tempo and dynamic belie nervousness, as does the false start in the opening vocal phrase, which proceeds only on repetition.

No. 4, Alexey Tolstoy's "A tear quivers in your jealous gaze," is an assurance of union after death from one lover to another at the moment of parting. The vocal cantilena recalls Borodin, with tremolo-like accompaniment and touches of pathos in the harmony, and anticipates Prince Gremin in *Evgeniy Onegin* in its key, tessitura, and nobility of style. The piece affirms the wellsprings of Tchaikovsky's operatic style in song. The opening dotted figure is relatable to a falling tear, the grand descent in the piano near the end of each strophe to the spaciousness of a love "as wide as the sea."

The question "Why?" in no. 5 is hyperbole typical of Heine: why is the rose faded, the birdsong sad, the sun cold, and the singer gloomy? As the words intensify, the music grows in range, texture, chromatic inflection, syncopation, and volume to the point that when the text turns personal ("Why am I gloomier?"), voice and piano are at a shout. By then, the verse is finished, leaving but a few postludial measures in the piano to absorb the impact of the buildup.

No. 6, "No, only one who has known," is set to Lev Mey's translation of Mignon's song, celebrated in English as "None but the lonely heart." Mey maintained Goethe's meter and stress; Tchaikovsky preserved a simple melody and accompaniment in what was already a song in Goethe, the piano introducing the voice at each new stanza save the last. Here (after the fanfare at 43 that echoes song 1), Mignon's most intense suffering ("My breast is afire") is conveyed by the vocal line overreaching its expected destination, forming a dissonance with the piano. This is a marked contrast with the earlier stanzas, together with the new counterpoint of voice and piano, which here reprises the introduction before the voice enters. It is as if Mignon's fictive accompanist had thought to end the song and was caught unaware by her unexpected burst of feeling.

Two other romances date from this period. On a text from Pushkin's *The Gypsies,* "Zemfira's Song" survives in autograph as a song and in copy as a *scena,* or part of a play [CW 44, 5–7], with a repeat of the first couplet, several additional bars of music, and Aleko's spoken responses to Zemfira's taunts. It was first thought to date from the 1860s; Vaydman places it about a decade later [424, 37]. In a swaggering melody with percussive dotted rhythm, Zemfira dares Aleko to cut or burn her for taking another lover, as Tchaikovsky attempts a pseudo-Gypsy idiom, then sets Zemfira's brazen "I hate you, I despise you / I love another, I'm dying of love" with a chord progression of singular audacity.

"To forget so soon" was finished before 26 October 1870. The iteration of Apukhtin's title phrase makes the recital of the lover's forgetfulness a tirade at odds with the nuanced music. When the voice enters, Tchaikovsky gives the phrase a sturdy, confident extension, unlike the sob-like effect of the opening, then modulates, returns, and varies melodic contour to differentiate line and stanza. For the reference to love and vows near the end—the gravest transgressions against memory—he reserves an angry Allegro in the minor, smoothed over in the postlude.

Tchaikovsky's remaining piano pieces from this period have largely dropped from view. The *Valse-scherzo,* op. 7, dedicated to Sasha Davïdova, is an epigone of the *Valse-caprice,* op. 4. It tries too hard for a result so modest, failing to convey the scherzo as well as op. 4 conveyed the caprice. Playing off the upbeat in regular note values against the upbeat in grace notes grows old quickly, and the Trio is simply plodding. The *Capriccio,* op. 8, retreats from a standard so undistinguished. As an exercise for the wrists, it recalls Anton Rubinstein's *Staccato* étude, op. 23, no. 2, deferring to its dedicatee, Karl Klindworth. Again, conscious interpretation is critical to avoid the exposé of music so ungrateful in its difficulty and in places even ugly. Here, Tchaikovsky curtailed his appetite for extension with virtuoso demands—the pervasive sixteenths, the *expressivo* in the middle register with figuration on either side, cross-hand work, and octaves.

The *Three Pieces,* op. 9, are pleasing in their variety but press their suit too forcefully. The "Rêverie" overstays its welcome when Tchaikovsky squeezes its slight motifs beyond the limits of their interest. The boisterous "Polka de Salon" parlays a more interesting theme into rhythmic witticisms—a polka without downbeats in the first episode—which become trite when trotted across the stage again. The "Mazurka de Salon" is arranged from the *False Dmitry* music, its seductive principal theme relieving the *ennui* of subordinate episodes and a long Trio.

None of Tchaikovsky's three operas from this period survives complete. *The Voevoda,* on which he worked from March 1867 to the summer of 1868, awaited staging until January 1869; *Undine,* composed between January and July of that year, was rejected by the Imperial Theaters in St. Petersburg and survives in the fragments performed in Moscow in 1870; *Mandragora,* he abandoned but not before composing a chorus for it at year's end 1869.

The action of *The Voevoda* may be summarized from the published libretto of the work, which passed the Moscow censor on 18 January 1869:

Act I. Praskoviya, Vlas Dyuzhoy's daughter, is betrothed to Nechay Shaligin, the Voevoda, while her sister Marya is secretly in love with Bastryukov, his enemy; the Voevoda disturbs their tryst. In a matchmaking scene, the Voevoda sees Marya for the first time and chooses her over Praskoviya, whereupon Bastryukov decides to abduct Marya. At his signal, she comes to him, but they are foiled by Vlas and the Voevoda, who restrain Marya but fail to subdue Bastryukov and his men.

Act II. Bastryukov is pining for Marya when Dubrovin arrives; he has suffered the Voevoda to kidnap his wife and himself to be persecuted. They plan a double abduction for the next night, when the Voevoda will be away on a pilgrimage. In the women's quarters, Marya sings of a captive young woman desiring freedom; Dubrovin's wife, Olyona, enters and tells Marya of the plan. The other women return and perform a dance-song.

Act III. The two couples are reunited and sing an apostrophe to the night. Dubrovin and Olyona exchange assurances. As they sing of the night again, they are interrupted by the Voevoda, who has returned early. Dubrovin threatens him and is disarmed. The lovers decide to die rather than part again. The Voevoda orders the men held and leads Marya to the women's quarters. As she attempts to break free, fanfares announce the arrival of a new *voevoda,* who puts matters right amid general rejoicing.

A reconstruction by Sergey Popov, completed by 1933, is apparently lost. The reconstruction in the *Collected Works* [CW 1] is flawed, in part by a new final chorus texted by Sergey Gorodetsky, who did not let stand Tchaikovsky's apostrophe to God and tsar. The 1869 libretto, itself sloppily printed, was disregarded in that restorers added text, changed the characters to whom text was assigned, expanded solo numbers into ensembles, and changed modes of address. Vissarion Shebalin gratuitously extended music that Tchaikovsky had extended quite enough. In addition, editorial restoration was complicated by the lack of surviving vocal parts for the Voevoda, Marya, Olyona, Nedviga, and three secondary characters [viii 444–45; 108, 12–15; 302, 29–30].

Tchaikovsky recycled earlier music: the tenor aria from the ode "To Joy" for the duet of Marya and Bastryukov in act I; the beginning of *The Storm* for the introduction of act II; the fifth of the piano Variations in A Minor for the Moderato which follows it; themes from the Overture in C (bars 178, 234) in act I when the Voevoda first sees Marya; and the Characteristic Dances of 1865 for the Dances of the Serving Maidens in act II. New in *The Voevoda* was music more familiar in later works: the Entr'acte before act IV of *Swan Lake* is partly in act II, no. 7, and partly in the Entr'acte before act III; the opening of the *Swan Lake* finale is in no. 2 of act III; and a lyric theme in *1812* (164) is from act II, no. 8. Perhaps the most striking familiar music in *Voevoda* is the melody Musorgsky used in Marina's aria in act III of *Boris Godunov* (at 72 in Rimsky-Korsakov's edition), here in a 4/4 variant for the chorus of servants (act II, no. 1) and again in nos. 1 and 10 of act III. This tune was used again in *The Oprichnik*.

Within numbers, he showed exemplary care in the smooth shifts between soloists and chorus and recitative, and finesse in the handling of the orchestra—big sounds countered by the effective cello solo in no. 1 of act III and in many other shadings of color, especially in the winds, which would become a staple of his operatic writing. There is much compelling music: the opening chorus with its piquant dissonance; the Entr'acte and Dances of the Serving Maidens, responding in sound to the evocative stage picture, as the maidens enter "covered in veils" while Marya and Nedviga lie asleep; Marya's "Nightingale Song," the big folk number in the manner of Senta's ballad, in which she sings metaphorically of the present moment in the opera; and the ravishing apostrophe to night in act III. At the same time, the composer overrides dramatic nuance, appending superfluous reprises to almost every number. These are facile but lack good sense. The orchestra does not overwhelm the voice, as Laroche remarked, so much as fluency overwhelms the drama.

The Voevoda suffered from its libretto. Ostrovsky's charming detail was lost in the adaptation, leaving a dull and conventional narrative. His folkish words and seventeenth-century usages gave way, in Tchaikovsky the librettist, to phrases famous in later pieces. Marya and Olyona anticipate Lensky when they sing "Come soon, desired friend," whereas Bastryukov's remark to Dubrovin just before the abduction, that "happiness is so close," will be astringently reinterpreted by Onegin and Tatyana. Ostrovsky called his play a comedy, but the opera hardly conveyed this. Among colorful ethnic types, only the rickety old nurse, Nedviga (literally, cannot move), and the Voevoda's jester survived the adaptation. Tchaikovsky responded to them characteristically and treated Dyuzhoy as a buffo bass in no. 7 of act I, but omitting the hermit, the pilgrimage, and the Voevoda's dream in the libretto increased the Voevoda's menacing aspect, which Tchaikovsky did little to alleviate. It is as if the music did not strike the right generic stance, a problem that will recur. Tension between genre and expression underlay Laroche's criticism that Tchaikovsky was unable to conform to word and situation.

Laroche found *The Voevoda* wanting in Russian style. This claim disregards the challenge of how to match the intensely Russian element from Ostrovsky with an operatic legacy still rooted in Western devices, as well as claims of Tchaikovsky's contemporaries and later scholars who heard Russian intonations in it [1, 16–18; 306, 95–96]. Clashes of idiom occurred in the act I finale, where the Voevoda's interruption of the lovers prompted an extended, unabashedly Western ensemble of consternation, within which Bastryukov's sudden Adagio interpolation shifts into a folk idiom when he would wash away his sorrow in the Mother Volga. Tchaikovsky's indulgences in canon between Vlas and Nastasya in the midst of offering mead to the Voevoda and again in the act I finale (at bar 163) seem to be unnecessary provocations of Western-Russian disparity. The long opening scene, Marya's "Nightingale Song," and all the dances are folkish. Elsewhere, Tchaikovsky's chord and melody emulate folk accents, as in Olyona's music and Bastryukov's act I aria, Western operatic in its breadth yet based on a pentatonic scale. The result is a nod to grand opera without fully yielding to it, as Borodin in Vladimir's cavatina in *Prince Igor* or Glinka in Sobinin's opening scene in *A Life for the Tsar.* Laroche may have perceived as Western Tchaikovsky's halfhearted effort at reminiscence motifs, assigned to Bastryukov's retainer, Rezvïy, and a march for Bastryukov himself, derived from his aria at the beginning of act II.

The composer made a potpourri for piano from the opera, which was published under the pseudonym H. Kramer [CW 51-b 197–215].

Undine was set not to the separately published libretto of 1862 (presumably, a reprint of the version set by Alexey Lvov in 1848), but to the version in Count Sollogub's *Collected Works,* from which it differs in many details.

Act I. Night is falling. The fisherman Goldman and his wife are distressed that Undine has not returned. The knight Huldbrand knocks at the door, seeking refuge. He had nearly perished, accosted by a water spirit, when a luminous vision lifted him from the raging stream. It was Undine, who now arrives, singing of the waters, which warn her against mortal love. Goldman explains how Undine appeared one day years after their real daughter had drowned. Huldbrand is smitten; when Undine returns, he curses his fiancée and declares his love for Undine. A water spirit warns her, but Undine pledges her love to the knight. As he embraces her, she gains a soul. They depart for his castle as a storm strikes the village. In the distance, Huldbrand battles with a waterfall as the curtain falls.

Act II. The Duke, whose daughter Bertalda is Huldbrand's scorned bride, seeks revenge. He has invited Huldbrand and Undine to a feast in her honor, where Goldman and his wife, to whom Undine promises a gift, are in the crowd. Huldbrand and Bertalda reconcile after he claims his love for Undine was a spell. Undine interrupts them; he cannot choose between them. Undine sings a ballad in which she discloses her gift: Bertalda is the daughter of Goldman and his wife. Bertalda rejects them, and they curse her. Huldbrand and Bertalda accuse Undine of jealousy; he rejects Undine, who vanishes into the river.

Act III. Huldbrand is contrite over Undine's death. His wedding procession is twice stopped by a vision of her attempting to prevent the marriage. The wedding party disperses. A confidant brings news of a miracle: a well has sprung up in a fountain, whence Undine has reappeared. Huldbrand rushes to her and she kisses him with the kiss of death; he appeals to their happy days, then welcomes union with her in death.

Sollogub made changes in the original story. Recast, the plot—lacking tension and credibility as the hopelessly variable Huldbrand consorts with

Undine and Bertalda, who are both steadfast to the point of caricature—defied even operatic logic. Dramatic weakness was compounded by verbal devices: the text of one character was assigned verbatim to another, while individuals expressing different emotions in ensembles were assigned nearly identical words. Such artifice suggested an idiosyncratic view of craft, made worse by dreadful clichés of language, especially the ubiquitous expressions of fright.

Tchaikovsky recycled parts of *Undine:* the orchestral introduction and Undine's song from act I was used in *The Snow Maiden* (the act I finale, depicting the storm that strikes the village [CW 2, 344–90]); the wedding march became movement II of the Second Symphony; and a duet of Huldbrand and Undine (reconstructed and recorded [390]) was rewritten as a *pas d'action* in *Swan Lake.* Mining the opera for these different purposes suggests that Tchaikovsky still possessed the score as late as 1875.

The "Chorus of Flowers and Insects" from *Mandragora* so impressed Balakirev that he urged Tchaikovsky to expand it into a cantata, to be called "Night":

> Quietly whispers the clear air with a silvery breeze,
> The peaceful light of the golden moon lights the scented forest.
> High above the tsarina of night glimmers in the blue heavens.
> Like sparkling eyes the stars are glimpsed in the streams.
> Our time flows by quickly and the earthly sphere is ravishing.
> Let us now take untroubled the pleasures of this golden night.

The music has antecedents in Weber (*Oberon*), Mendelssohn (*A Midsummer Night's Dream*), and especially Berlioz (recently deceased at the time of composition), especially the "Chorus of Gnomes and Sylphs" from *La damnation de Faust.* The last may have been Tchaikovsky's model in the choral texture, where a principal line (sung in Tchaikovsky by children) is punctuated by outbursts of rapid declamation, and the orchestra divides into choirs which create a collage-like texture of gossamer figures depictive of the setting. In Berlioz, the sylphs enchant Faust as Mephistopheles sings him to sleep. Tchaikovsky describes the air and forest, the moonlight and stars—and reminds us that our time is fleeting.

 CHAPTER SEVEN 

Before the Fall (1871–1877)

TO ALL APPEARANCES, TCHAIKOVSKY'S LIFE BEFORE 1877 IS MOSTLY flat terrain. Years later, he described a "constant correspondence with his sister, four brothers, several cousins, and a number of friends" [xiii 407–8], yet from 1871 to 1874, for months at a time, no letter of his survives, suggesting, together with the image of Tchaikovsky the melancholic in these years, some concealment of his private life. Modest described his brother's problem as an illness, a "moral ailment" (*moral'nïy nedug*) comprising increasingly harsh symptoms of loneliness and discontent—"a fierce desire to break free from any fetters to his creative activity"—starting in about 1872, reaching a high point in 1874–1875, and leading to his marriage in 1877:

> As ill people, who do not understand the essence of their ailments, create in their imagination illusory determinations of it and seek treatment where in fact it is not, so Pyotr Ilyich considers one of the principal causes of his melancholy a "deficiency of people close to him in Moscow," and sees his recovery in "the possibility of having a 'loving person' around him," who would deliver him from the "solitude" which particularly tormented him. I must stress this delusion here first, because with the increase of his ailment it came to take on the significance of a point of insanity which led Pyotr Ilyich to the mindless deed which nearly destroyed him in the end, and second, to point out the causes of its origin and increase in the sick man's imagination. [1997 I 433–35]

Tchaikovsky's discontent was partly rooted in his job. He did not like to teach and belittled his teaching, "[b]ut his irreproachable conscientiousness, intelligence and knowledge of the field forced him to be a good teacher, especially of the more talented students, to whom he could explain directly with examples from his musical memory" [187, 12]:

> Tchaikovsky entered the hall with a rapid gait, a little embarrassed, a little annoyed, as if vexed at the inevitability of imminent boredom. The banal conduct of the theory class got on his nerves, with its desks and the old, battered yellow piano and trampled, discolored keyboard, with the chalkboard, black with red lines. Standing at the chalkboard, Tchaikovsky would write out our assignments and examples. I recall the fastidious gesture with which, having put down the chalk and the grey canvas towel, he would wipe his fingers with his [hand]kerchief. The slow comprehension of most women students vexed him, [and] the blunt, superficial response to the essence of art from these future graduates, who dreamed only of the concert platform and believed that the public, applauding their playing, would have no interest in their theoretical knowledge. Shrugging his shoulders, Tchaikovsky had to listen through the banging-out of sequences and modulations on the awful-sounding piano, patiently noting with a red pencil the forbidden fifths and octaves. . . . Pacing around the class, he would dictate to us, slowly and very distinctly, and we would take it down. . . . Tchaikovsky's way of exposition, his observations, explanations and corrections were remarkably clear, concise, and easy to comprehend. [RMG 1916/49, cols. 940–41]

Some found him careless and thought it unfair that he lavished much attention on some students and little on others [316, 77]. Whatever the truth in this, he wrote two books that helped to standardize the teaching of music in Russia in light of the ad hoc Germanic pedagogy of his colleagues [129]: *A Guide to the Practical Study of Harmony* (1872) and *A Short Manual of Harmony, Adapted to the Study of Sacred Musical Works in Russia* (1875). In 1871, he published a translation of Johann Christian Lobe's *Katechismus der Musik* (1870).

Professional considerations beyond teaching, from discontent to fame, were prompting Tchaikovsky to radical change. In October 1870, Nikolay Rubinstein's rapprochement with St. Petersburg broke down after his mysterious withdrawal as a soloist from a concert conducted by Balakirev, whose ascendency in St. Petersburg had peaked [22, 61]. A year later, Tchaikovsky declared, "To the extent my work has become loathsome, to the extent I am weary and put out, I would be happy for any change whatever" [v 265]. Still ostensibly friendly, his relations with the Mighty Handful became more volatile. The Second Symphony and *The Tempest* enhanced his stature with them, while his wariness of César Cui burst into hostility after Pyotr started writing criticism, declaring Cui a composer *manqué* making a living by faulting music he could not write himself. Newspaper reports, in turn, also revealed to Tchaikovsky that his fame abroad was increasing. After Eduard Hanslick's notorious critique of *Romeo and Juliet* in Vienna in 1876 and Camille Benoit's friendly survey in the *Revue et gazette musicale* in 1877, reports of Tchaikovsky's music abroad were no longer rare. Celebrity was urging him toward liberation.

In the 1870s, he undertook a long mediation between his publishers Jurgenson and Vasily Bessel, his classmate at the St. Petersburg Conservatory who had published *Romeo and Juliet* in Russia and would bring out *The Oprichnik,* the Second Symphony, some songs, and piano pieces. Both men were proprietary, taking offense when Tchaikovsky gave the other a new piece. Jurgenson ultimately won the composer's approval less because of his efficiency as a publisher than for his willingness to meet Tchaikovsky's financial needs and to distribute his music abroad, together with the composer's weariness of Bessel's business conduct.

His sense of isolation in Moscow was acute after Nikolay Rubinstein's magisterially wrongheaded critique of the First Piano Concerto late in 1874. That incident may have fixed his intention to leave the conservatory and shifted his perspective from local to international. He gave the concerto to Bülow, who took it to America, where Tchaikovsky would find his music more often and better performed than in his homeland. For now, capitalizing on his fame must have seemed irresistible, the inability to do so producing the misery that Modest observed that winter. When Pyotr's marriage crisis passed, his intoxication with Western Europe never diminished and was overcome for practical purposes only in 1885.

1871

At the end of 1870, Tchaikovsky was content in Moscow. He was making new friends, such as Nikolay Bochechkarov—a gossipy older man in touch with the homosexual community—and reviving others, such as Nikolay

Kondratiev, whom he had met in 1864. Through Kondratiev, Tchaikovsky also met Sergey Ivanovich Donaurov, a song composer, savant of painting [1997 I 334–35], and the composer's traveling companion for a time. Early in 1871, Ivan Klimenko was living with Tchaikovsky. Yet of impassioned relationships, there is no confirmation. Among family, he mourned the death of his uncle Pyotr Petrovich and offered financial support to Sasha, who had taken in Sestritsa. Thirty-three years Pyotr's senior, Sestritsa would remain at Kamenka until her death, a year after his. He continued to mentor the twins, reluctant to see Anatoly posted outside Moscow [v 251, 253] and railing against Modest's debauchery in Simbirsk [v 253–54; 291]. No letter from Pyotr to Modest survives from 1871—a suspicious lapse. Except for a note to Klimenko, no letter of Tchaikovsky survives between mid-February and mid-May 1871, nor from June to August, except one letter to Jurgenson on 15 July.

Tchaikovsky was composing for the concert he would give in March and continued work on *The Oprichnik*. Of uncertain date is an arrangement of the finale of Weber's Piano Sonata in C, op. 24. Described as for the left hand, it is actually played with both. Tchaikovsky fashioned a new right-hand part after shifting Weber's to the left hand [CW 60 xi; 96, 492].

The silence imposed by the dearth of letters was broken on 16 March at Tchaikovsky's benefit concert. Besides the First String Quartet, composed in February, and the chorus "Nature and Love" from December 1870, three songs, a duet from *The Voevoda,* and two pieces from op. 9 were performed. Of the two new pieces, Laroche found "Nature and Love" ordinary if well made, and wrote of the Quartet:

> This work is distinguished by that charm [*prelest'*] of succulent melodies, beautifully and interestingly harmonized, by that noble tone, devoid of the commonplace, by that somewhat feminine softness that we are used to encounter in this gifted composer; needless to say there are beautiful effects of sonority in it . . . but beyond all these qualities I found in his new quartet such a command of form . . . as found in none of his prior compositions. . . . All the more precious for criticism are those rare compositions in which interest of content is joined with maturity of form. [255 II 33]

Tchaikovsky adopted a distinctive pattern of summer travel in this period. Every year, he visited Kondratiev at Nizï, Vladimir Shilovsky at Usovo, and possibly the Davïdovs at Kamenka. In these places, he would write the

Second and Third Symphonies, *Swan Lake,* and *Vakula the Smith.* Family lore records a house production of a ballet called "The Lake of Swans" in the summer of 1871. One account, from someone born five years later, claimed that the "swan theme" familiar from the later ballet was used in it, a while a second informant, alive at the time, attributed this production to 1867—the summer that Tchaikovsky was stranded at Hapsal [95, 26; 362, 89].

In the autumn of 1871, Tchaikovsky moved out of Nikolay Rubinstein's quarters. While he could not "sufficiently delight" at living separately [v 262], he filled his home with people. He took a servant, Mikhail Sofronov (brother of Aleksey, called Alyosha, who would remain with Tchaikovsky and become his legatee), developed a friendship with Nikolay Bochechkarov, and housed other friends who visited Moscow. His sultan letter to Klimenko (above, p. xv) was written soon after the move. That his new situation was insufficient to assuage the composer's loneliness is implicit in a letter of 28 September to his brother Nikolay, urging him to give Eduard Zak leave to come to Moscow:

> Since you (to my greatest pleasure) wish to relieve Zak of trips during the winter, you might find it possible and useful for him to grant him a short leave to Moscow soon. I consider this necessary for him to be revived in a milieu rather more elevated than the one that surrounds him now. I am afraid that he might get coarse and be choked off from instincts toward intellectual perfection.
>
> I ask you, my pet, if you find any basis in my opinion—to permit and even command him to travel to Moscow; you would bring me great pleasure in doing this.
>
> I have had a powerful yearning for him and fear for his future: . . . it is absolutely necessary for me to see him. For God's sake, arrange it. [v 262]

We do not know the outcome of Tchaikovsky's request, and his relationship to Zak is mysterious. Modest did not mention Zak in *The Life.* Pyotr referred to him in passing but twice more [v 319, 325]. Vaydman suggests that they got acquainted in 1867–1868, when Zak entered the Moscow Conservatory; he would have studied with Tchaikovsky during the next academic year. In a letter from 1869 or 1870, Zak, then 15 or 16, addressed Tchaikovsky in the familiar second person. By 1871–1872, he was working for the Konotop Railway, which was administered by Nikolay. On 2 November 1873, at the age of 19, Zak shot himself. His mother knew enough to write Tchaikovsky: "[as you are] the only person who can know the reason that compelled him to make an attempt on his life, I most humbly ask you, write to me what you know about this incident, what spurred this action. I ask you and beg you as an unfortunate mother, write to me where he is buried and place a cross on his grave" [408, 177].

The sense of a historical record obscured persists in documents from the autumn of 1871. In September, Tchaikovsky referred to a crisis in Modest which threatened to change him if he did not cease his disgraceful behavior [v 258]. By December, the focus had shifted to Anatoly's venereal disease with a gesture of fraternal solidarity: "Whatever chancre you have, it doesn't surprise me in the least, since for whom was this never the case? (Just remember what a chancre *Gulda* gave me at Fürst's in Petersburg!) And so, there is nothing more innocent than this mark of an order, accessible to everyone" [369, 126]. We don't know who Gulda was; if a woman, Tchaikovsky's sexual appetites may have been more varied than we have assumed.

On 5 November, Tchaikovsky attended his first concert as a professional critic [on Tchaikovsky as critic, see NV980223; NV981026; 146; 396]. He reviewed the introduction to *Lohengrin,* Liszt's First Piano Concerto, Raff's *Die Liebesfee,* and Beethoven's Eighth Symphony. He noted the delights of Italian opera and the abasement of Russian opera, the latter a recurrent motif of his criticism. After four articles in some five weeks in a Sunday newspaper, *Sovremennaya letopis'* (Contemporary Chronicle), he stopped until the autumn of 1872, when he began again, this time on a regular, extended basis, for the *Russkie vedomosti* (Russian News).

In mid-December, Tchaikovsky was commissioned to write a cantata for an exhibition in May marking the 200th anniversary of the birth of Peter the Great. He then left for Nice to visit Vladimir Shilovsky. At some point in 1871, Tchaikovsky may have first met his future wife, who, in a letter of 1886, referred to their first meeting 15 years before.

1872

For most of January he stayed in Nice, where he wrote the Piano Pieces, op. 10. Concern over Anatoly's illness pressed him on 31 January to urge his brother to come to Moscow for treatment [v 273–74]. Then, silence again, no letter surviving from 4 February to 4 May 1872, and nothing to the twins between 31 January and 10 June. In February, the revised *Romeo and Juliet* was performed twice; even Cui praised it [D&Y 79]. On 4 May, Tchaikovsky sent *The Oprichnik* to St. Petersburg; on the 27th, he gave Bessel various rights to this opera in return for publishing a piano-vocal score in time for the premiere and seeing the work through production [D&Y 80]. In memoirs, Bessel named his connections in the theater, participation in operatic productions, and record of publication of Russian operas as the reasons Tchaikovsky turned to him with *The Oprichnik* [NV961007].

The exhibition cantata occupied Tchaikovsky between February and April. Laroche had warned him that Yakov Polonsky's text was antimusical. Replete with bright images, some sanguine, some banal, it passed from the world of ancient epics to the time of Peter. Modest quoted a report of the first performance on 31 May:

> [It] took place at two o'clock in the afternoon at the exhibition beneath an awning at Trinity Bridge. . . . A small part of the audience was seated in chairs placed around the platform; the rest, located in the garden, could not, it is said, hear a single sound. For those sitting upstairs much was also lost to attenuation of the sound, unrestrained by any walls, as a result of which the public could not form an understanding of this work, which, judging by certain excerpts and the reports of those who heard it at rehearsal, must be remarkably beautiful. [1997 I 352–53]

To promote folk music at the exhibition, Nikolay Rubinstein had proposed that Laroche, Tchaikovsky, and Kashkin notate songs and epic poems in the field during the summer of 1871 and then invite the best singers to Moscow [187, 80–81]. When this project was deemed too expensive, Rubinstein withdrew from the committee, and Tchaikovsky, as if in compensation, edited *65 Russian Folk Songs* (collected and arranged by Vasily Prokunin, published in 1872 and 1873) and the first volume of Maria Mamontova's *Children's Songs on Russian and Ukrainian Melodies* (the second volume [CW 61, 207–23] was unpublished during Tchaikovsky's lifetime).

Two days after the cantata was performed, Tchaikovsky was en route to Kamenka, where he worked on the Second Symphony until late June. From there, between Nizï and Usovo, he rented a private carriage, proceeded with Modest to the next stop, drank too much, and flew into a rage when informed there were no horses to continue. The stationkeeper declared himself unobliged to deal with inconsequential people, whereupon

Tchaikovsky signed the complaint book "Kammer-Junker Prince Volkonsky" (a venerable Russian surname), horses were found, and the trip proceeded. At the next stop, Tchaikovsky realized he had left his money and papers behind. Mortified, he sent a carriage, but the stationkeeper would give them only to "Prince Volkonsky." He returned, relieved that his cover had been maintained. An unexpected irony was the stationkeeper's own surname: Tchaikovsky [1997 I 354–56].

Between 5 September and 2 November, the correspondence lapses again. During this time, Tchaikovsky was finishing the Second Symphony, writing reviews, and meeting in St. Petersburg with the committee adjudicating *The Oprichnik.* From his concert reviews, one senses irritation. When he chides Moscow for accepting the Italian opera's low standards [83, 54, 72], he is accusing the city of insularity. When he finds Brahms's music overrated [83, 58–60], he is belittling European celebrity. When he critiques Schumann's orchestration (which led to an unrealized ambition to rescore Schumann's symphonies [83, 59–60, 66; D&Y 73]), he is declaring the mainstream less than perfect. Mocking a critic in Meshchersky's journal *Grazhdanin* (Citizen), who borrowed from his reviews [83, 48–49], he is hinting at the bankruptcy of Russian criticism. This testiness peaked in a review of Glinka's *Ruslan and Lyudmila* on 17 September. He took sides with Glinka's other opera, *A Life for the Tsar,* claimed that César Cui's approval of *Ruslan* had no basis in philosophical principle or beguiling aesthetic, and declared Beethoven to be the greatest composer, with whom Glinka could stand on the basis of creative genius but not in the poverty of Russia's musical environment [83, 32–35].

His public irritability showed a private side in November. A letter to Modest on the 2nd is remarkable for being published with its homosexual mannerisms, including a reference to Bochechkarov using the feminine *staraya L'vovna* and the closing, "Your devoted and loving sister Petrolina" [v 288]. (Modest restored the masculine in the first and omitted the second [1997 I 369].) On 22 November, Pyotr seemed to be appeasing his father:

> As regards my marrying I tell you that sometimes it pops into my head to find a housemate just as plump and kind-hearted as your good wife—but then I fear I might repent of it later. I am making a completely respectable sum (about 3,000 rubles a year), but since I am disorderly I constantly find myself

> in difficult straits. For one person it is nothing; but what if there is a wife and children? [v 290–91]

The verbal feminine forms persist in Tchaikovsky's last substantive letter of 1872, to Modest on 10 December. He thanks "amiable Modestina" for concern about his depression, which he denies: "There is no particular depression, though anguish and misanthropy sometimes take possession of me, as has happened before. This is in part because of my nerves, which sometimes fall apart without evident cause, in part because of the not especially consoling state of my compositional work." He closes, "Farewell, amiable sister, I kiss you. Petrolina" [v 293–94].

Professional setbacks could not have been responsible for his mood. He had finished the Second Symphony in November. The evening that *The Oprichnik* was approved for production, he played the finale of the symphony for the Mighty Handful, to great acclaim. In Moscow on 30 December, he received suggestions from Vladimir Stasov about subjects for a tone poem: Scott's *Ivanhoe,* Gogol's *Taras Bulba,* and Shakespeare's *The Tempest.*

On 2 December, Tchaikovsky's nephew Vladimir Lvovich Davïdov was born; he would be known as "Bob" and one day would command his uncle's affections [371].

The absence of letters for nearly half of 1872, the hostile accents of Tchaikovsky's criticism, and his letters from late in the year point to something not quite right.

1873

For most composers, writing music for the country's leading playwright, an important tone poem, and two collections of piano pieces would constitute a good year. For Tchaikovsky, however, 1873 was middling. Juggling several projects from January to May, in the summer he went to Europe, then returned to his autumn routine—teaching, reviewing, moving to a new flat. He was preparing *The Oprichnik* for the stage and contemplating his next opera, *Vakula the Smith.* His surviving letters are mostly to people outside the family; except for a jest to Modest and Sasha (on 27 April, in broken English), no letter to Modest survives between 13 February and 28 November. There were also physical setbacks: a severed artery in April, various symptoms in June for which doctors found no cause, a bout of quinsy and a boil in his mouth in October. Bessel's piano-vocal score of *The Oprichnik* was too flawed for singers to use, as was his print of Tchaikovsky's op. 16 songs; all copies were sequestered. Bessel, moreover, exploited the composer's idle chatter, acting decisively on his merest assent to publish.

On 15 January Tchaikovsky responded to Stasov, choosing *The Tempest.* On 26 January, the premiere of the Second Symphony pleased everyone. Laroche ranked it with the best European music [255 II 34]; he found something Mozartian in Tchaikovsky's command of theme but said the composer had invoked Beethoven more emphatically, in the merriment that the folk songs conveyed, the shift of gravity from the first movement to the finale, and his substitution of an *Andantino marziale* for the customary Adagio. Laroche hoped that early publication would alert the Germans to a Russian composer prepared to compete with them [255 II 37–38].

For Tchaikovsky, Beethoven was in the air. He was reviewing the Quartets, op. 59, no. 2, and op. 135 ("the swan song of a dying genius"), and would emulate Beethoven in his own Second String Quartet, finished early in 1874. He agreed to write a biography, "Beethoven and His Time," for the Petersburg journal *Grazhdanin* [79]. In 17 chapters between 11 February and 12 March, he traced Beethoven's life through his first years in Vienna. Tchaikovsky never personally commanded such massive data about Beethoven; rather, he abridged Alexander Wheelock Thayer's *Ludwig van Beethovens Leben.* His fourth installment, despite an encouraging "to be continued," brought the charade to an end. Perhaps he sensed the irony of mocking an anonymous author who had borrowed unacknowledged from him the year before [83, 48–49], as he now borrowed unacknowledged, in the same journal, from an obscure American biographer. Or perhaps he was answering the call to write music for Ostrovsky's *The Snow Maiden.*

Snow Maiden is the daughter of Spring and Frost; the latter frustrates the return of Yarilo (the sun). Like Undine, she experiences love and dies. Kashkin explained:

> In 1873 . . . the Bolshoy Theater remained the only venue where all three companies could work: drama, opera and ballet. It occurred to V. P. Begichev, the inspector of the repertoire, to stage a kind of *féerie* in the Bolshoy Theater

> in which all three troupes would take part. A. N. Ostrovsky was asked to write such a play, who gladly agreed and chose the story of *The Snow Maiden,* and commissioned the music from P. I. Tchaikovsky. . . . In 1873, it seems, spring was quite early, so that writing music to this "springtime tale" coincided with spring itself. [187, 85]

Tchaikovsky finished *The Snow Maiden* on 25 March 1873, barely three weeks after the commission, within a month of rehearsals and before Ostrovsky had finished the play. A work of such good intentions might have fared better. Part of the audience left before the end of the first performance; a call for "Author!" was drowned in whistling [326, 44–49]. Critics found it unstageworthy. When music from *The Snow Maiden* was published, Laroche praised it but Cui was offensive and personal—banal thoughts; worn-out harmonies; no finish, taste, or elegance; only the practiced hand of a ballet composer [108, 266].

The Cui-Tchaikovsky exchange grew heated in 1873. On 2 February, Tchaikovsky labeled him the spokesman for a circle of musicians who rejected everything but themselves. He compared Cui's judgments to those of an earlier age that found Beethoven, Mozart, and Raphael no better than a chef or a gardener. This led to an exchange of insults [83, 119–22].

In the summer, Tchaikovsky traveled to Western Europe, began a diary, and composed *The Tempest.* The European trip began in northern Germany, proceeded down the Rhine and into Italy (Turin, Lake Como), then on to Paris. His diary runs from 11 June to 18 July 1873 [Dnev 3–8]. According to Modest, Pyotr kept diaries to reconstruct the past when life had transformed reality, never showed them to anybody, made Modest promise to burn them after his death, and then burned some of them himself [1997 I 382]. The surviving ones hint at extraordinary issues, sometimes indirectly; in the 1873 diary, for example, several pages have been torn away that would have covered a period with no surviving letters. Some thought of dissemination explains Tchaikovsky's editorial marks in the diaries he kept [409, 37].

Near the beginning of August, he arrived at Usovo and wrote *The Tempest* from the 10th to the 17th. Shilovsky was in Moscow. Five years later, Tchaikovsky recalled:

> Thus I found myself completely alone in a charming oasis within the steppe. I cannot describe to you how much I found myself in a state of bliss these two

> weeks. I was in some blessed, exalted state of mind, wandering alone daytimes around the forest, towards evening along the immense steppe, and sitting nights at the open window, listening to [the] solemn quiet of a faraway place, broken from time to time by some ill-defined nocturnal sounds. In these two weeks, without the least effort, as if being moved along by some supernatural power, I drafted all of *The Tempest.* [vii 232]

In the autumn, Tchaikovsky was again caught up in the *zhiteyskoe morye* —the sea of life. He was arranging the Second Symphony and scoring *The Tempest.* He attended two review performances by 14 September. In October he completed the op. 19 piano pieces and continued work on *The Oprichnik.* On 2 November Zak committed suicide; on the 7th Cui condemned the music of *The Snow Maiden.* Early in November he moved again. By the 28th, he was feeling downhearted: "Only this year have I assured myself that in essence I am quite alone here. I have many friends, but of the kind with whom you unburden your heart, such as Kondratiev, absolutely none" [v 335]. Nikolay Rubinstein conducted the first performance of *The Tempest* on 7 December, which passed without substantial response. On the 16th Nápravnik asked him to revise *The Oprichnik,* which was too repetitious and heavily scored. After two months, he returned to criticism, rebuking his audience for its undiscriminating taste. Yet his own music was reaching a wider public. A romance, "Take my heart away," had appeared in the popular journal *Nouvelliste;* three more songs and a dozen piano pieces would follow in the next three years.

1874

Criticism defined the first half of 1874, followed by work on *Vakula the Smith* in the summer. In the autumn Tchaikovsky reviewed, attended the first production of *The Oprichnik* in Kiev, and composed the First Piano Concerto. His letters are still mostly about business; again, there are silences in letters to Modest (June–October) and Anatoly (April–November).

The first remarkable event that year was Tchaikovsky's broadside against Cui on 16 January. Digressing from a review of *Don Giovanni,* he attacked Dargomïzhsky's *The Stone Guest* (which Cui had co-edited), which caused "deadly melancholy in the listener, who seeks in art not that narrowly construed truth by which a real apple is better than a drawn one, but rather a lofty artistic truth which springs from the secret depths of humankind's creative power" [83, 163]. He reveled in his own superiority to Cui:

> [For many years, he] has astounded the reading public as much by the sharpness of his judgements and reviews and the absence in them of any principle, as by the smug ignorance with which, at one stroke of the pen, he reduces the authorities of centuries to dust, installing in their place composer-friends from his own circle. As a composer Mr. Cui made his debut in St. Petersburg with his opera *William Ratcliffe,* which failed and quickly fell out of the repertoire. In addition, Mr. Cui has written several songs, which have sustained an obscure existence on the shelves of music shops, whence they have almost never been dragged into the light of day. Given their utter musical insignificance, offering nothing more than idle decantation from the empty to the emptier, they are written with the wholly comical pretense of soulfulness and passion. [83, 166]

Two days after this review, Tchaikovsky finished his Second String Quartet, which was performed privately in February for Anton Rubinstein, who listened with a somber, dissatisfied look and claimed it was not in the chamber style and that he did not understand it [187, 84]. Did pique then bring Tchaikovsky to observe that Rubinstein's music has "no forward movement, no perfection and development" and that his best works were from his early period [83, 183]?

By 24 January, Tchaikovsky had made changes in *The Oprichnik,* which would occupy him until the first performance on 12 April. To Anatoly, he wrote in passing of Vladimir Shilovsky's marriage to a rich young woman "who will be amazed when she finds out" [88, 201]. Shilovsky was joining the ranks of Tchaikovsky's homosexual friends who married. The six weeks before the premiere of *The Oprichnik* were fraught. On 18 February he was incredulous that Bessel could think rehearsals were possible without accurate music, and he offered to help revise the faulty copies [v 343–44]. That offer was idle, as between then and 15 March he would review nine Lenten concerts in Moscow, including the first public performance of his Second String Quartet on 10 March and a recital by Hans von Bülow on the 13th. The first conductor of *Tristan und Isolde,* a son-in-law of Franz Liszt and later advocate of Johannes Brahms, who had performed in Russia a decade earlier without much impact, Bülow now elicited Tchaikovsky's hyperbole:

> Everything Mr. Bülow performed was played with equal mastery, taste, and the astonishing ability to transmit the spirit and mood of a piece objectively. . . . Before all else the listener is struck by Mr. Bülow's unprecedented development of technique. The purity of his playing is absolute, irreproachable, unconditional. [83, 185]

Around 20 March, Tchaikovsky went to St. Petersburg for rehearsals of *The Oprichnik,* and by the 25th he was advising his friends to stay home. At first everything went well; then the mezzo-soprano who sang Basmanov, the hero Andrey's friend, fell ill, and Tchaikovsky had to arrange her part for a bad tenor. The more he saw, the worse he felt [1997 I 400–1]. Four days before the first performance, he sold his performance fees to Bessel for 1,000 silver rubles [158, 58–59]. It was a gamble. Had the opera succeeded, he would have earned more. Bessel called the premiere a triumph for Tchaikovsky, who after the performance was given the first Kondratiev Prize—300 rubles—for the encouragement of Russian composers, and Bessel claimed that the opera played to full houses six times in 16 days, including two benefit performances at increased ticket prices [41, 34–37]. Modest used a different measure:

> Ilya Petrovich and his family were sitting in a box in the second tier. The old man was radiant with happiness. Nevertheless to my question, "Which in your opinion is better—this, or as a civil servant to receive the Order of St. Anne, First Class?"—he answered: "The St. Anne's star is still better." It was one of those rare occasions when Ilya Petrovich revealed that in the depth of his soul a regret still lurked that Pyotr Ilyich was not a bureaucrat. [1997 I 402]

The *oprichniks* were agents of Ivan the Terrible who were notorious for the license with which they pursued the tsar's ends. Andrey joins them to win his sweetheart, Natalia, who is betrothed to another, and to seek vengeance for his father's ruin. No one approves his decision; even Andrey is uncertain, seeking release from his vows after he makes them. At his and Natalia's wedding, Ivan the Terrible asks to see her alone. When Andrey challenges this, he is beheaded for insubordination. The invocation of ancient Russian mores places this work among many historical plays and operas of the 1860s and 1870s. But the historical trappings of *The Oprichnik* are illusory; the libretto emulates the theatricalized history of French grand opera [382, 86], focusing on Andrey's indecision, the distress of his mother and his bride, and the skullduggery of his enemies.

To Laroche, the libretto lacked psychological truth [255 II 63]. In act I, Andrey arrives at Natalia's garden in a crowd (in the play he came alone, Romeo-like), and the lovers do not meet. Tchaikovsky failed to vivify his characters' emotions, avoiding terse statements such as Rigoletto's terrified "Le maledizione!" Elaboration blunted effect, as it had in *The Voevoda.* Laroche argued that Andrey's oath to become an *oprichnik* "should be uttered in an outburst of recitative; Mr. Tchaikovsky set it to an extended, broad melody in a slow tempo in the character of an *amoroso*" [255 II 59]. Cui concurred, citing the passage where the girls ask for a story: "It is clear that these eight verses can serve only for an insignificant passing recitative. Yet Mr. Tchaikovsky builds a separate number on them, indeed with two more themes, and repetition of themes, necessarily with endless word repetition" [SV740423].

A Russian topic called for *couleur locale,* which Tchaikovsky provided, but what of the rest? As they had with *The Voevoda,* even favorable reviewers [376] had difficulty coming to terms with the lyrical music, some describing it as "Italianism." This claim—perhaps in response to Musorgsky's *Boris Godunov,* recently staged—lay at the heart of Cui's notice, which contained a handful of perfunctory compliments in 4,000 words of bile [condensed in 108, 43–45]. He aired personal grudges but also identified real problems. Lacking identity as a stylist made Tchaikovsky derivative (from *Il Trovatore, Les Huguenots, Le Comte Ory,* and others); he also failed as a librettist ("the wretched lack of substance in this libretto, . . . the absence of character in the dramatis personae, the extremity of their marionette-like quality"). His judgment had lapsed; he demanded sustained high tessituras from the singers and cluttered the vocal line with orchestral textures, wretched declamation, and striving for cheap effect. Worst of all, *The Oprichnik* suffered from an almost unparalleled deficiency of style:

> [It is] a bankrupt opera: its music is bereft of ideas and weak almost throughout. In it there is not one sustained, happy inspiration; everything is grey, dull, monotonous, boring, and the excellent, talented and painstaking instrumentation does not save it. . . . Mr. Tchaikovsky's vulgar Italianate cantilena, assigned to the principal characters, is false, feigned fervor, intrepidity which he will

> muddy into feeble and trivial candor, with which he reveals a lack of taste, excites profound regret, and from time to time even alienates.

At the same time that Tchaikovsky had faulted melodic recitative in *The Stone Guest,* he could not compose well in recitative and closed aria, the "old forms" which he advocated. This was Cui's revenge: motley style and bad vocal writing (citing the St. Petersburg Conservatory's unvocal graduation cantatas). "*The Oprichnik* is a mongrel," he concluded, "without individuality, without personality, without conviction" [SV740423].

Tchaikovsky's jousting with Cui reached its apex with this article. Cui was never Tchaikovsky's advocate and easily slipped into derision. By the autumn of 1874, however, his tone had softened, though the reason is not clear.

Two days after the premiere of *The Oprichnik,* Tchaikovsky left for Italy to review Glinka's *A Life for the Tsar* in Milan, just to have it postponed. Had he stayed he would have met Bülow, whose own review digressed on the present state of music in Russia:

> We know at present only one who like Glinka is untiringly "striving to be noticed." . . . It is the youthful composition professor at the imperial conservatory in Moscow, Mr. Tchaikovsky. A beautiful string quartet has already taken root in many German cities, many of his piano compositions [and] two symphonies deserve the same attention, and most of all the uncommonly interesting Overture to "Romeo and Juliet." . . . By virtue of his versatility, this composer will be protected from the danger of disregard abroad, as happened to Glinka, who had to settle for glory in his homeland. [65]

A purge for melancholy, a repudiation of his critics, a call to heed his international reputation, and a warning to those who would take him for granted, Bülow's words delighted Tchaikovsky more than any printed notice had ever done before [v 357]. Together with pianist and conductor Karl Klindworth, Bülow would become one of Tchaikovsky's most influential advocates abroad, especially in Germany [48; 233].

At Nizï and Usovo in the summer of 1874, Tchaikovsky wrote *Vakula the Smith,* an opera based on Nikolay Gogol's story "Christmas Eve," to a libretto by Yakov Polonsky, written for the late Alexander Serov. It was for a competition sponsored by the Russian Musical Society in memory of the Grand Duchess Elena Pavlova, sister of Nikolay I and an important patroness of the arts. Tchaikovsky's views on the competition's regulations were solicited, and on 7 March 1873 he wrote to Prince Dmitry Alexandrovich Obolensky, vice president of the Russian Musical Society, asking: should it be a conventional number opera or a modern Russian opera, striving excessively for realism, which produces artistic "nonsense"? Fair judgment would be impossible if the judges' opinions were predisposed [v 308–9]. This question was never answered.

In the autumn, several events bolstered his self-image. On 25 September, Vladimir Stasov asked him for the original scores of *Romeo and Juliet,* the Second Symphony, and *The Tempest,* for deposit in the St. Petersburg Public Library "together with musical autographs of the rest of the new Russian school" [v 368]. Tchaikovsky declined, but the fact that his scores had achieved historical status was surely a compliment. Stasov wrote again in November, asking him for details of his official service and conservatory studies and a list of compositions. On 22 October in Moscow (noted on the autograph), the composer orchestrated Liszt's romance "Es war ein König in Thule" for the singer Ivan Melnikov [CW 59, 305–18], apparently the result of a friendship initiated during rehearsals for *Oprichnik* in the spring [301, 103]. He finished *Vakula* and reported to Bessel that the submission deadline for it was seven months later than he thought. He had inquired of Nápravnik and the chief opera *régisseur* in St. Petersburg about a staging outside the competition, an indiscretion for which he later apologized, and regretted that word of it reached the higher powers. He was unchastened, however, and allowed Nikolay Rubinstein, a judge of the competition, to conduct the Overture to *Vakula,* called the Overture "to an unfinished opera," at a concert on 22 November.

On 29 October, Tchaikovsky noted to Modest the tentative beginning of a piano concerto [v 372]. In three weeks he was immersed in it, laboring especially over the solo part [v 379]. On 28 November, he heard Henri Litolff's Fourth Concerto symphonique, in which he observed the successful confrontation of orchestra and soloist, such that the piano "was not playing a pre-eminent role, but would wrestle with its mighty competitor" [83, 224]. We hear no more of the concerto for a time, as Tchaikovsky went to Kiev early in December for the first performance there of *The Oprichnik* on the 9th. He liked the production and praised the artists, including Fyodor Stravinsky, Igor's father [83, 232].

By 21 December he had finished the two-piano arrangement of the concerto, and sought Nikolay Rubinstein's critique on Christmas Eve:

> I played the first movement. Not a word, not a single remark! If only you knew how stupid and unbearable it is when a person presents his friend a dish of his own devising, and the latter eats and remains silent! Then say something, even curse it in a friendly way, but for God's sake, just one sympathetic word, even if not praise! . . . I needed observations on the matter of virtuoso piano technique. R[ubinstein's] eloquent silence was full of import. It was as if he said to me: "My friend, can I really say something about details when the whole is so objectionable?!" I armed myself with patience and played through to the end. Again silence. I stood up and asked: "So, what then?" At that point words gushed from N[ikolay] G[rigorievich], calm at first, then shifting ever more into the tone of Zeus the Thunderer. It turned out that my concerto was altogether unsuitable, to play it was impossible, that passages were so trite, awkward and clumsy that they could not be corrected, that as a composition it was bad, vulgar, that I had stolen this from that place, and this from another, that there were only two or three pages that could stay, while the rest had either to be thrown out or completely rewritten. "Such, for ex[ample], this! What does it mean? (playing the passage in caricature as he spoke). And this! It's impossible!" etc., etc. I cannot convey to you the main thing, the *tone* in which he said all this. In a word, a passerby could have thought I was a maniac, an ungifted and unthinking scribbler who had come to a famous musician to pester him with nonsense. [Nikolay] Hubert, noting that I was stubbornly silent, amazed and struck at such a rebuke being made to a person who had already written much and who taught a course in *free composition* at the Conservatory, at such a scornfully categorical verdict being passed as would be forbidden to pass on any able student, unthinking began to elucidate N[ikolay] G[rigorievich's] judgment. [vii 64–65]

This commanding testimony has swept all else aside, including negative critique in the press by Nikolay Solovyov ("a first pancake, which turned out lumpy" [281, 161, n. 2]) and Laroche ("eminently second-tier" [255 II 78]). Tchaikovsky made no such vivid account in the immediate wake of the incident. By January 1878, when he wrote it, he was urging Meck's support if he left the conservatory. It was evidence of the arbitrariness of those on whom his livelihood depended.

1875

For the first time in five years, surviving correspondence shows Tchaikovsky referring to personal matters. Nothing more persuasively suggests the destruction of his earlier letters than this sudden manifestation of candor. On 6 January, he complained to Modest of shattered nerves [v 388–89], to Anatoly on the 9th of terrible woes:

> I live in Moscow, strictly speaking, somewhat like an orphan. On weekends, for this reason, a terrible depression comes over me. It is boring at the Davïdovs; I am not that close to my conservatory pals and their wives. In a word, I would like very much to be in Peter[sburg], but lack the money. Moreover, there is no one here I could truly call a *friend* (such as Laroche was, or as Kondratiev is now), but I still suffer greatly from the blow to my compositional self-esteem by none other than Rubinstein.

He questioned Rubinstein's friendship, promised to tell Anatoly about the concerto incident, complained about the critics in St. Petersburg, and then:

> I am very, very lonely here, and if it were not for constant work, I would simply burst with melancholy. Yes it is true that cursed buggermania forms an impassable gulf between me and most people. It imparts to my character an estrangement, fear of people, shyness, immoderate bashfulness, mistrust, in a word, a thousand traits from which I am getting ever more unsociable. Imagine that often, and for hours at a time, I think about a monastery or something of the kind. [v 389–90; 369, 122]

Tchaikovsky had scored the new concerto by 9 February and sent it in May to Bülow, who was delighted:

> [Y]our op. 23 strikes me as the most brilliant, the most accomplished manifestation yet of that creative ability with which you have enriched the musical world. The ideas are so original without ever being affected, so noble, vigorous, interesting in detail without detriment, in their abundance, to clarity and unity in the overall conception. The form is so mature, so full of "style"—intention and execution blend so harmoniously—that I would weary you, listing all the qualities that make me congratulate the composer and all those called upon to take delight in it, actively or "receptively." It is, finally, a veritable jewel, and you deserve the recognition of all pianists. [6, 50, 197]

The composer did not read this until June. In the meantime, Rubinstein's tirade may have diminished Tchaikovsky's Muscovite chauvinism in reviews and moderated his harsh line toward the Mighty Handful. He grew closer to Rimsky-Korsakov in 1875, whose Third Symphony he faulted without rancor. He praised Balakirev's Overture *1000 Years* and reviewed another performance of Glinka's *Ruslan and Lyudmila* without sermonizing. He cited Cui without attacking him [83, 260].

In April, whence no letter survives, Tchaikovsky completed the songs of opp. 27 and 28 and attended rehearsals of *The Oprichnik* in Moscow. He was not optimistic about his opera's prospects. The first performance there was on 4 May; eight days later, the composer wrote: "I was present at many rehearsals of *The Oprichnik,* and with stoic courage I endured the systematic disfigurement of this ill-starred opera, already ugly before this. The performance of *The Oprichnik* last Sunday, however, did not conform to my expectations in the sense that I was expecting much worse still" [v 403].

In May, he also was overseeing the submission copy of *Vakula the Smith;* twice before the adjudication, he emphasized to Rimsky-Korsakov, one of the judges, his embarrassment if he lost [v 404, 412]. That month, Sergey Ivanovich Taneyev, later an important colleague, graduated from the conservatory, and Tchaikovsky was commissioned to write a ballet called *The Lake of Swans.* He spent much of June composing the Third Symphony and received another letter from Bülow: "I am proud of the honor bestowed on me by the dedication of this capital work, delightful in all respects" [v 409, n. 1 to no. 407]. Tchaikovsky instructed Jurgenson to have the parts and score of the First Piano Concerto in London before 1 September, so Bülow could take them to the United States. From 18 July to mid-August, he finished the Third Symphony and composed two acts of *Swan Lake.* The ballet was another work of obscure genesis. Kashkin recalled long consultations with balletmaster Julius Reisinger [187, 101], and stage machinist Karl Valts that Tchaikovsky had no one to advise him on details of the music [402, 108]. Through much of 1876, when *Swan Lake* was in rehearsal and Tchaikovsky was in Moscow, there is no sign of his involvement. The score—its rubrics, sequence of numbers, and format—permits the balletmaster to repeat or delete sections at will, which may explain why Tchaikovsky's one reference to rehearsals emphasized the comical look of the proceedings, not the mutilation of his score. On 5 October

Rimsky-Korsakov informed Tchaikovsky that he would surely win the competition with *Vakula,* and on the 16th he did. Three days before this, Bülow had played the first performance of the First Piano Concerto in the Boston Music Hall. Critics did not like it [123, 248], though he had to repeat the finale at every performance. At the end of the month, Tchaikovsky went to St. Petersburg for the first Russian performance of the concerto, with Gustav Kross as the pianist and Nápravnik conducting. Taneyev played it in Moscow on 21 November.

With his Piano Concerto launched on two continents, the Third Symphony performed (on 7 November, under Nikolay Rubinstein), and *Vakula* guaranteed a production, Tchaikovsky could pursue fresh challenges. *Swan Lake* was incomplete. Karl Klindworth, a Wagnerite and professor of piano at the conservatory, was acquainting prospective attendees at the first Bayreuth Festival with *The Nibelung's Ring.* In November, after printing four of Tchaikovsky's songs, Nikolay Matveyevich Bernard, publisher of *Nouvelliste,* asked him to write 12 piano pieces for publication in each month of 1876. The collection would be known in English as *The Seasons* (*Les saisons*).

In his last months as a music critic, Tchaikovsky's disenchantment was manifest. Two years earlier, he had rued the disregard of his words; now, they were drawing too feisty a response:

> Every day, every hour, in unpleasant conversations, anonymous letters, of which some contain nothing but abusive language unsuitable for publication—I reap the bitter fruit of my essayist's zeal. I have endured especially powerful attacks when my review of some fashionable idol of the crowd went against public opinion. [83, 284]

For criticizing soprano Christine Nilsson, Tchaikovsky was called an insane profaner, an impertinent hack, a vulgar liar. When his views on another popular singer were disputed, he ended his regular career as a critic. Doing so may have masked another motivation: to withdraw support for Nikolay Rubinstein and the projects he espoused.

Camille St.-Saëns made his Russian debut as a composer, pianist, and conductor in Moscow on 28 November 1875 and as a chamber musician three days later. Tchaikovsky praised these concerts. Modest recalled a striking adjunct to their friendship:

> [B]oth of them in their youth were drawn to ballet and imitated dancers excellently. And so once, at the conservatory, boasting to each other about their

> art, on the stage of the conservatory hall they performed complete a little ballet, "Galatea and Pygmalion." The 40-year-old St.-Saëns was Galatea, and played the role of the statue with extraordinary application, and the 35-year-old Tchaikovsky was Pygmalion. N. G. Rubinstein substituted for an orchestra. Unfortunately, besides the three performers, no one else was in the auditorium during this curious presentation. [1997 I 447]

Of greater import for Pyotr's future was a new job for Modest, a change "which passed not without significance for Pyotr Ilyich" [1997 I 450]. In December 1875, Modest left the civil service to undertake the education of a deaf mute child of seven, Nikolay "Kolya" Konradi. This required special training under Jacques Gugentobler. On 20 December, Modest and Pyotr left for Lyon, spending 10 days with Sasha in Geneva.

1876

On New Year's Day (O.S.) Bülow, who after Boston had played the First Piano Concerto in New York and Philadelphia, reported the success of Tchaikovsky's First String Quartet and declared him one of the five outstanding musical personalities of the time [6, 198]. This compliment surely pleased Tchaikovsky, if not the other four personalities: Brahms, Raff, Rheinberger, and St.-Saëns. In a letter to Klindworth, Bülow criticized Jurgenson who, "if he weren't such a damned jackass," would make Tchaikovsky's music available in America [48, 359].

The year 1876 would be rich in compositions—*Swan Lake,* the Third String Quartet, *Francesca da Rimini,* the Serbo-Russian March, and the *Variations on a Rococo Theme*—but the personal ledger was mixed. In a matter of weeks after Tchaikovsky had met Modest's new student, his adoration had grown so overwhelming that by August he was counseling Modest to marry as an antidote to his natural tendencies, and announced his intention to do precisely that himself.

Tchaikovsky began the Third String Quartet early in January. Forbidden by his doctors to work, he composed it in his head and played it in Moscow before a note had been committed to paper [MV000606]. On 8/20 January, he heard *Carmen* for the first time, bolstering his esteem for modern French music. When he returned to St. Petersburg in mid-January, rehearsals were under way of his Third Symphony, which Nápravnik conducted on the 24th. He declined an opportunity offered at this time to go abroad on a Russian type of Prix de Rome. On 10 February, he wrote to his former colleague Anton Door, now in Vienna, that a performance of one of his orchestral works there would be "the happiest event" of his life [vi 23]. It was made so: Hans Richter conducted *Romeo and Juliet* on 14/26 November [xvii 222], then Jules Pasdeloup did the same two weeks later in Paris. Meanwhile, he worked on *Swan Lake.* By 23 March, rehearsals were under way; the sight of dancers performing his music reduced to solo violin amused him [vi 33], but the score was still not ready; he left for Konstantin Shilovsky's estate on 29 March and finished it within a fortnight. In March he was also considering opera projects: *Efraim,* to a libretto Konstantin Shilovsky had written in 1874, and *Francesca da Rimini,* to a libretto by Konstantin Zvantsev, which Tchaikovsky abandoned when he learned that Zvantsev expected him to compose in accordance with Wagner's reform theories [187, 106–7].

The summer was a miscellany. On 5 May, *The Marriage of Figaro* was performed by conservatory students in Tchaikovsky's translation, and on the 16th, in St. Petersburg, the first of a four-installment critique of *Vakula the Smith* was published, six months before the premiere. At the end of May, the violinist Josef Kotek, of whom Tchaikovsky was growing fond, graduated from the Moscow Conservatory. On 27 July/8 August, on a train to Paris, Tchaikovsky read Dante's *Inferno* and considered writing a tone poem on it. From 31 July to 5 August (N.S.), he attended the first performance of *The Nibelung's Ring* at Bayreuth, reporting for his Moscow newspaper and discovering that he was better known in Germany than he had thought. The production impressed him, but not the music; he thought *Das Rheingold* "unlikely nonsense, through which, from time to time, sparkle unusually beautiful and astonishing details" [vi 64].

On 17 September Tchaikovsky declared to Modest that he had stopped composing. This was eight days before he finished the Serbo-Russian March, also called the Slavonic March or *Marche slave.* It was conducted on 5 November by Nikolay Rubinstein before an audience fired by Russia's declaration of war against Turkey. From a document preserved at Klin identified only as by "one of those taking part in the concert," we read:

> The commotion and roar raised in the auditorium after this [performance] beggar description. The entire audience came to its feet, many jumped up on their chairs, one after another; to cries of "Bravo" were mixed cries of "Hurrah!" The March had to be repeated, after which the same tempest was raised

> anew. Because it was impossible to extend censorship to musical works, Tchaikovsky managed to do what seemed impossible at the time—to stage an imposing public demonstration. It was one of the most thrilling moments of 1876. Many in the hall were weeping. [108, 364]

Rehearsals of *Vakula the Smith* had begun in late summer. Tchaikovsky scarcely attended; there were no requests for changes, nor advice to friends to stay away. In November, he agreed to be in Petersburg "Tuesday" [vi 87], the 16th, eight days before the premiere. Vakula's mother, the witch Solokha, conspires with the devil to raise a blizzard on Christmas Eve. This brings a number of suitors to pay her court, each hiding in a coal sack when the next unexpectedly knocks at the door. Meanwhile, Vakula loves the beautiful if vain Oxana, who will marry him if he acquires for her the beautiful slippers worn by the tsaritsa. Vakula tricks the devil into flying him to St. Petersburg, where he obtains the slippers.

The premiere of *Vakula* on 24 November 1876 was a success, "[j]udging by the number of calls with which the esteemed composer was favored" [PG761126]. Seated next to librettist Polonsky, Kashkin recalled:

> Despite the brilliance of the first performance of *Vakula the Smith* the public sensed a certain perplexity, which one could especially notice listening to conversations in the foyer during intervals. . . . Yakov Petrovich was genuinely excited by much in the music, but said that it had not come out exactly as he had expected.
>
> . . . [He] was expecting something in the manner of an Italian *opera buffa,* a light, mirthful opera, and Tchaikovsky wrote a grand lyric comedy. In addition, knowing Ukrainian songs not from urban amateurs but directly from the mouths of the folk, Tchaikovsky carefully avoided the sentimental coloration inherent in most Ukrainian songs that circulate here in the cities. With the generally magnificent musical portrayal of the opera's characters, he gave the women's part[s] a more tender shading, lightly recalling (but no more) this well-known Ukrainian genre. As for the men's parts and the opera's folk scenes, the themes are marked by a robust simplicity, matching the character of a robust people. [188]

Critique of *Vakula* focused on its shape, style, and dramatic effect. Tchaikovsky did not convey Gogol's satirical edge, the rapier-like twists that undermined the chatty surface of a passage with hypocrisy-deflating reality, or by which he pulled his reader's leg with hyperboles of absurdity offered up as perfectly normal. Laroche complimented Polonsky on preserving Gogol's expressions, but found the libretto lacking in "effective act conclusions . . . and thus the music, in its turn, is not concluded with powerful finales" [255 II 87]. He also reiterated Tchaikovsky's central problem—musical beauty without dramatic life:

> Time and again in the new opera you sense how the composer's invention outstrips the requirements of character and situation, how it distracts him, makes him write a phrase longer or shorter, louder or softer, faster or slower, in greater or lesser relief than appropriate to the person or situation. The composer's lack of stage flair is chilling, though at the same time one continues to sense the beauty of the musical thoughts and their development, irrespective of the drama. [255 II 89]

Gogol's language aside, the lyric-operatic appeal of the story rested with the lovers, justifying Tchaikovsky's wish to know whether speech-like delivery or traditional form was expected. As it was, "Mr. Tchaikovsky transgressed mostly . . . by taking the fate and feelings of his characters too much to heart, making his music too warm, one could say too tragic for what takes place; that lyrical enthusiasm throbs over the limit at every turn and keeps the spectator from laughing at the amusing figures represented onstage" [255 II 93].

For all this, *Vakula* improved on *The Oprichnik:* there were no wholesale borrowings, no excessive repetition, mechanical reminiscence motifs, or semi-digested quotations from other works. Idiom was deft and sure, from the portrayal of the simple folk to the panache of the Winter Palace. Orchestral wizardry, from the devil's storm to the resplendent polonaise, was the equal of anything else he ever wrote. Two weeks after the first performance, *Vakula* was exciting powerful interest and bringing full houses at raised ticket prices. In its fourth performance, its receipts had exceeded those of seven or eight performances of Cui's *Angelo* [PG761209]. It was performed 18 times in three years [108, 62]. Perhaps in response to what he considered defects in *Vakula,* Tchaikovsky engaged Stasov to write a libretto on *Othello.*

By 15 December, Tchaikovsky was composing the *Variations on a Rococo Theme,* though the silence that descended upon this work makes it difficult to connect the facts: he declared in March 1875 that the virtuoso flowering of the cello was approaching its last stage of decline [83, 265]; he accepted specialist advice soon after his bitter experience with Nikolay Rubinstein; he permitted Wilhelm Fitzenhagen, professor of cello at the Moscow Conservatory, to send the *Variations* and the *Valse-scherzo,* op. 34, to Leuckhardt in Germany for publication, then offered them to Jurgenson free of charge [vii 71]; and he granted Fitzenhagen, who had already suggested changes in the Second String Quartet [238, 130], editorial license amounting to mutilation. These curiosities may have warranted silence (there being sufficient embarrassment to go around), except to heap blame on Fitzenhagen in such few references to the *Variations* as we have. Sending the music to Leipzig was "Seine Hochwohlgeborene Fitzenhagenische Dummheit" (Fitzenhagen Esquire's Foolishness) [vii 71], while Jurgenson fumed: "Lord! Tchaikovsky *revu et corrigé par* Fitzenhagen!" [87 I, 35]. At the same time, it is hardly credible that Fitzenhagen would send the *Variations* abroad on his own authority, or that Tchaikovsky would give the cellist a new piece and control over it without understandings in place. Between the lines, one reads the composer's desire, more pressing now than in 1874, to seek his fortune abroad.

In mid-December came two remarkable experiences. At a soiree for Count Leo Tolstoy, the honored guest broke down in tears as the *Andante cantabile* from the First String Quartet was played. In subsequent communications, Tchaikovsky learned that a great writer did not necessarily make a great musician. When Tolstoy sent him some folk songs, Tchaikovsky had to reply that they were corrupt [vi 100]. More disenchanting was the writer's dismissal of Beethoven, at which point Tchaikovsky concluded that Tolstoy was a paradox, if direct and good in his way [252, 114–20]. The date 18 December 1876 marks Tchaikovsky's first surviving letter from Nadezhda Filaretovna von Meck, the widow of a recently deceased railroad magnate. It was in connection with a prior request for a simple arrangement of music. A mere note, it portended nothing of the correspondence to come. On Christmas Day 1876, Tchaikovsky wrote to conductor Édouard Colonne, investigating the possibility of a concert of his works in Paris, but nothing came of it [vi 102; 235, 4–6].

Tchaikovsky's personal life in 1876 forms a counterpoint to his professional life in that his desire to acquire fame abroad was linked with his discontent at home. But there were other distractions. In February, the petulant Vladimir Shilovsky went to St. Petersburg after a "disgusting dramatic scene of jealousy and inestimable love" [88, 230]. A "marvelous performance" by Désirée Artôt as Amneris in *Aïda* delighted Tchaikovsky [vi 24]. By the end of April, he was complaining about his health. Typhus was suspected of a lingering cold with paroxysms of fever. His doctor prescribed treatment at Vichy, an imperative hampered by lack of money [vi 39–40]. By 4 June, when he arrived "completely ill" at Kamenka, Tchaikovsky's attacks of fever kept him from composing. In a few days, he was feeling better.

The summer of 1876 produced a rare look, amid documents that projected so chaste a life in general, at Tchaikovsky's response to the blandishments of passion. It came in heavily censored letters, mostly to Modest. On 23 June/5 July, Pyotr wrote from Vienna, awaiting Sasha, who had been delayed. He would go to the Cirque Carré, where if he met someone, he would stay. He did, and an impetuous flirtation ensued; he described his friend in the feminine:

> We spent the evening together, in the cirque and in the Prater. Yesterday we did not part company, that is, we took an excursion far out of town. This morning she was with me, then we went shopping and I *equipped* her from head to toe; we spent the evening again together and only just now have parted company. . . . The fact is that my beauty is a *gymnasium student,* and must finish her examinations on Monday the 10th; for me to leave here before then is impossible, for she *wants* to go with me as far as *Munich.* For that reason I cannot deny myself the bliss, as up to now *the real thing* has not happened (that is, a whole night spent together in bed). And so I shall leave here with *her* on Monday evening; on Tuesday morning we shall be in *Munich,* where we shall spend the day and night, consequently only on *Wednesday* will I leave Munich direct for Lyon, where I hope to embrace you. [369, 128]

This encounter paled before what happened next. Four days after this letter he met Kolya Konradi, and four days later still he arrived at Vichy, stricken with melancholy at its puritanical regimens and the frustrating nearness of companionship. His feelings for Kolya escalated rapidly, reflected in the number of expurgated passages in his letters. A week after meeting Kolya, Tchaikovsky described him as "one of the beings closest to my heart in the world" [88, 243]. On 7/19 July, he wrote that he would come to Lyon and kiss his dear Kolya "whom I love, 1,000,000 times" [294, 258]. On 27 July/8 August, en route to Bayreuth, Pyotr wrote of his adoration of Kolya [88, 249]. After a week at Verbovka, his passion had increased: "Modya, kiss this divine child on his little hand, his little nose, but especially on his wonderful, lovely eyes! You don't know how much I adore him. There is not a minute when I don't think about him" [88, 252]. A few lines later, he struck a different, astounding note:

> I am now experiencing a very critical moment in my life. . . . *I have decided to marry.* This is inevitable. I must do it, not only for myself, but also for *you,* and for Tolya, and for Sasha, and for everyone I love. For *you* in particular! But you, Modya, need to think well on this. Buggermania and pedagogy cannot coexist. [369, 121]

On 10 September, he wrote again:

> [F]rom today forward I seriously intend to enter into legal matrimony with someone or another. I find that our *inclination* is for us the greatest and most unconquerable barrier to happiness, and we must struggle against it with all our powers. I love you very much, and very much love Kolya, and I quite desire that you two not part company, for your common good, but the condition sine qua non for the stability of your relationship is that you would not be *that* which you have been up to now. This is necessary not for *q'en dirat'on* but for you yourself, for your spiritual tranquility. A person who, parting company with *his own* child (for he may be called your own), falls into the embrace of the first scum that comes along, cannot be the teacher that you want to and must be. . . . You say that at your age it is difficult to overcome passion; to this I answer that at your age it is easier to channel your tastes in another direction. Here your religious belief must, I propose, be a firm support.
>
> As for me, I shall do everything possible to be married this year, and if I cannot be so bold, in any event I shall forever cast off my habits. [369, 128–29]

Throughout September, Tchaikovsky elaborated his plan to marry and his feelings for Kolya, the first clearly defending against the second. If anyone, Modest understood the futility of his brother's plan, which was expressed in a letter we lack, though we may infer Modest's reasons from Pyotr's reply to it. Pyotr will turn out like Kondratiev and others—homosexual and married—and one should spit on what people say. But Tchaikovsky was concerned about precisely that, especially from people like Sasha, who knew him before suspecting that his reputation was lost. "Do you really think that this awareness, that I am *pitied* and *forgiven* does not weigh heavily on me, when in effect I am not guilty of anything! And do you not really think that I find killing the thought that people who love me must sometimes be *ashamed* of me!" He would marry to stifle the gossip which hurt his loved ones [88, 259]. Tchaikovsky's next remark, however, took the luster off his resolve:

> I am so inveterate in my habits and tastes that to cast them off immediately, like an old glove, is impossible. Moreover, mine is far from an iron character, and after my letters to you I have given way to my natural tendencies some three times. Imagine! A few days ago I even went to the country to *Bulatov,* whose house is no more than a pederastic bordello. It was bad enough that I was there, but *I fell in love* like a cat with his coachman!!! So you are utterly correct in your letter, that it is impossible to restrain oneself from one's weaknesses, whatever one vows. [369, 121]

With this, but for occasional echoes, Kolya and Tchaikovsky's marriage as issues fall silent in the public record. On 6 October, he told Sasha that he wanted to take the current academic year to get used to the idea of marriage [vi 78]. By 8 November, his attitude about marriage had become more abstract and philosophical, attributable to nervous sensitivity, his bachelor's existence, the complete absence of self-sacrifice in life. He claimed to lack any usefulness to people: "If today I dropped off the face of the earth, Russian music might perhaps be a little the worse, but no one would be chagrined by it. In short, I lead a bachelor's egotistical life" [vi 85].

1877

Until late April, Tchaikovsky sparred with Stasov over an opera on *Othello* before giving it up; in February and March, he composed the *Valse-scherzo,* op. 34, and a funeral march (lost) on motifs from *The Oprichnik* for Meck; he also arranged the "Humoresque," op. 10, no. 2, and the *Andante funebre* from the Third String Quartet for violin and piano. Over the winter, he began the Fourth Symphony, and in June began *Evgeniy Onegin,* after the singer Elizaveta Lavrovskaya suggested it early in May [vi 135–36]. On 13 February, he conducted *Marche slave* at the Bolshoy; a week later came a premiere of greater import than anyone could have imagined.

Swan Lake began its life inauspiciously. The printed libretto cites no scenarist or literary source. No performance score or rehearsal material survives. Tchaikovsky took curtain calls at the premiere, but never recorded his impressions. Ballet in Moscow at this time was the most degraded of the state companies and would be subject in a few years to an administrative "reform" which would nearly kill it. The rarity of a new ballet in Moscow, the assignment of the company's second ballerina to this one, and allowing such a complex score only two orchestral rehearsals [RV770303] speak further to official disregard.

The basic story is that Prince Siegfried has fallen in love with the swan queen Odette just after his mother commanded him to marry. At a ball put on to choose a bride, Siegfried mistakes the daughter of the evil genie Rothbart for his beloved. He swears fidelity to her and thus betrays Odette, whom he rushes to the lake to find. "Thunderclaps resound," wrote one reviewer:

> [L]ightning flashes; the lake overflows its banks and envelops the lovers. Then the furious elements calm, the moon floats out from behind the clouds, and a band of swans flies on the barely swelling waves of the lake. . . . Mr. Valts's "miracles" are especially remarkable: the flood, lightning, the stormy lake, the breaking-up of trees—in act IV, where, among the whirling waves on the debris of a tree are to be found the "foundering" Odette and Siegfried. [VI770423]

According to the reviews, mostly by drama critics, music critics, and gossip columnists, the choreography (the component they least understood) was distinguished "neither by character nor novelty" [PG770224]. It is not clear if a complaint in the *St. Petersburg News* about the music was in fact the fault of Julius Reisinger's dances or lack of rehearsal: "in some places, soloists and corps de ballet are positively at odds with the orchestra, and you see that it could not be otherwise: the melody is too . . . how can I say it? Too confused, too capricious—in a word, it was not written 'balletically'" [SV770223]. Whatever else he accomplished, Tchaikovsky had turned watchers into listeners. Besides listing favorite numbers (the Hungarian Dance) and making grand if amateurish pronouncements, critics addressed the composer's handling of balletic style. This was a manner of composition dismissed by serious musicians, the province of hacks who kept the rhythm clear and texture thin to accommodate a ballerina's imperfect ear. It involved a mastery elusive to words: *musique dansante,* the ability of music to support, complement, vivify, even enliven the physical movement matched to it. Rhythmic punctuation and texture were subordinate to line, which offered an elegant analogy between sight and sound, rendering inconsequential the particular interest of music as music. Kashkin wrote:

> Mr. Tchaikovsky has not striven for the role of reformer in ballet music. . . . The difference resides in the mastery of technique, the elegance of the harmonies, melodic inventiveness, and so forth, in things which comprise the attributes of Mr. Tchaikovsky's talent. . . . [T]here is almost no example of such a significant artist dedicating his talent to this genre of composition, the unfavorable conditions of which present too many inconveniences for a musician. [RV770225]

Some 18 months later, Laroche was concerned that *Swan Lake* was "too grandiloquent for ballet," but "[m]elodies, one more plastic, singing and attractive than the last, poured forth as from a horn of plenty; waltz rhythm, which predominates among the danced numbers, finds such varied, graceful and winning designs that never did the melodic invention of the gifted, many-faceted composer stand the test more resplendently" [GO780914].

Kashkin summarized the ballet's fate in the theater:

> During the staging of the ballet several numbers were omitted as unsuitable for dancing, or replaced by interpolations from other ballets, besides which the balletmaster insisted on the need for a Russian Dance, the inclusion of which was very thinly motivated, although the composer yielded. . . . The substitution of original numbers with interpolations was carried to ever greater lengths, and by the end wholly a third of the music of *Swan Lake* was replaced by substitutions from other ballets, what's more, the most mediocre ones. [187, 103]

Tchaikovsky claimed not to sanction others' music in *Swan Lake* [431, 58–59]; the interpolations were surely by specialist composers. *Swan Lake* was last seen in Moscow in 1883 after 41 performances—twice the number of the surviving "traditional version" in a similar time frame. Yet history has deemed it a failure, along with *The Oprichnik* and its four productions and *Vakula* with its 18 performances. Immortality cannot be the only indemnity against failure.

Complicating Tchaikovsky's desire to break away from Moscow were the marital aspirations over which he had agonized in the autumn and the realities which had discouraged him since. He reported one such reality to Modest on 19 January—his love for Josef Kotek:

> I have known him for six years already. I always liked him, and several times have fallen in love with him a little. These were the running starts of my love. Now I have made a true start and have fallen in love with him most definitely. I cannot say that my love was altogether pure. When he caresses me with his hand, when he lies with his head inclined on my breast, and I run my hand through his hair and secretly kiss it, when for hours on end I hold his hand in mine and grow faint in my battle with impulse to fall at his feet and to kiss them—these little feet—passion rages within me with such unimaginable strength, my voice trembles like that of a youth, and I talk nonsense. Yet I am far from the desire for a physical bond. I feel that if this happened, I would cool towards him. It would be unpleasant for me if this marvelous *youth* debased himself to copulation with an aging and fat-bellied man. How disgusting that would be and how I myself would be repelled by it! It isn't necessary. [369, 129]

Nikolay Rubinstein conducted the first performance of *Francesca da Rimini* in Moscow on 25 February. Tchaikovsky had quoted Dante's "Nessun maggior dolore, che ricordarsi del tempo felice nella miseria" (Nothing is sadder than to recall times of happiness in misery) in letters—to Modest in 1876, announcing his interest in composing the work; later to Taneyev, Bob Davïdov, and Meck; and above a troparion in an Orthodox chant book [96, 469]. The composition of *Francesca* spanned his fascination for Kolya Konradi, his decision to marry, and his affair with Kotek; his program refers to "the souls of people whose reason was obscured in life by love's passion" and "the bonds of forced marriage." The intense love music suggests his approval of Francesca's following her instinct and transgressing against society's rules.

By 25 February 1877, events that would change Tchaikovsky's life had commenced.

 CHAPTER EIGHT 

The Music of 1871–1877

THE FOCAL POINT OF TCHAIKOVSKY'S COMPOSITION AT THE OUTset of this period was his benefit concert on 16 March 1871, at which two new works were performed. Written for voice students of the Moscow Conservatory, "Nature and Love" [tr. 389, 17] was scored for alto and two soprano soloists and women's chorus. Extolling the delights of moonlight, the fragrant air, and the sparkling stars, nature and love provide respite from life's disquiet. The simple layout of the soloists, the phrase repetition, and the avoidance of complexity show the work's ancestry in Schubertian *Hausmusik* for small vocal ensemble. Here, in contrast to the *Mandragora* chorus, there is no word-painting.

If Tchaikovsky's challenge in chamber music was to Russify the Western European heritage of skillful construction, diverse textures fluently deployed, and clarity of formal pattern, he caught his stride immediately in the String Quartet, no. 1, op. 11. While the full, invariable *facture* and the simple melody, embedded in the syncopations of the 9/8 time, are his, the sense of the music is classical, including the proportions and contrasts of the sonata and the distinctive mode change in bars 5–6. If Mozart would begin a transition in the 16th bar and move smartly to the new key, so does Tchaikovsky, precisely and elegantly. If a second theme would be more expansive and lyrical than a first, so is Tchaikovsky's, its headmotif subtly forecasting the opening of the next movement. And everything is linked by the initial syncopation. The development is romantic in its sequences and repeated sections but classical in texture and process, spinning out ideas from the exposition (the mode change at 61, the new guises of syncopation). The recapitulation is Schubertian in its fresh ornamentation but Tchaikovskian in borrowing the ornament from the development (at bar 62). Only in the coda does he tilt toward orchestral extravagance.

The slow movement quotes the tune "Vanya was sitting on the divan, smoking a pipe with tobacco," no. 47 of Tchaikovsky's *Fifty Russian Folk Songs.* As would Brahms on occasion, Tchaikovsky graced the original with his own continuation. The key, B-flat major, borrows from the minor scale of the home key, echoing the mode change early in the first movement and forecasting moves to D-flat major and on to B-flat minor in the second theme. The pattern is ABAB, where the second B is structurally a reprise but poetically an epilogue. The single pitch linking the first and second sections (at bar 50) echoes the syncopations of movement I.

The vigorous Scherzo is classical in pattern, the Trio an ABAB in the key of B-flat. While the Scherzo returns to the syncopation of movement I, the Trio starts out with an arhythmic bass, a distinctive contrast for the entire work. The finale may be acknowledging Beethoven's first "Razumovsky" in its double start (first in chamber scoring, then orchestrally, at 51), recalling Beethoven's jest at restarting in the Scherzo. Ambiguity of key (at 79), big dimensions, a long post-recapitulation, shifting the center of gravity to the finale—all evoke Beethoven.

This work spread Tchaikovsky's fame, most of the first printing being sent abroad [1997 I 414–15]. By the later 1870s it was popular, and the slow movement was available in various arrangements.

Tchaikovsky's presence in Nice at the end of 1871, when he composed the *Deux morceaux,* op. 10, may account for their French suavity (Modest claimed that the second theme of the "Humoresque" was a folk song from that area). The "Nocturne" also recalled Schumann in its opening idea (beginning in midphrase on the third inversion of the dominant seventh) and the overlapping of the hands. It illustrated Tchaikovsky's elegant elaboration of motif, especially in the bridge from the first theme to the second (18–23) and in the reprise of the cantabile (at 43). The infectious rhythm of the "Humoresque," made ambiguous by the hands' competition for the strong beat, to say nothing of drifting toward the wrong key (E minor instead of G major), was perfectly timed. Any more than 8 bars would irritate

—so in bar 9 Tchaikovsky aligned the rhythm in the rollicking tune which Stravinsky so loved in *Le baiser de la fée,* which propels the music forward with its impish recurrence.

Composed in February–March 1872, the Cantata on the 200th Anniversary of the Birth of Peter the Great was filled with Polonsky's vivid images [1997 I 356–59], modified by A. (Alexander?) Mashistov in the *Collected Works* [CW 27 and 33], following another version of the text by Sergey Gorodetsky [CW 27, xii]. The imperial national anthem was removed to an appendix.

The opening established an epic-heroic atmosphere, set in call-and-response:

As through the hazy, nighttime vault of heaven,
Gleams the round dance of distant stars,
So in the murky depth of ancient years
Flickers the epic poems' restless world.

The narrative proceeded from ancient years to Peter's time. First came the building of Moscow, a kernel "trampled by the Horde—a countless host," which broke through to the light, followed by Ivan the Terrible and the deeds of boyars, "the stench of torture, the ashes of the burned." Peter was apostrophized, "laborer and tsar, navigator, metalsmith and carpenter, studying he taught, and with a boldness born of God began the people's work." But Peter died, "[a]nd towards the light from darkness we meekly find our way." The poem ended with an appeal:

That the path to happiness for us be direct,
Bless the people's labor, anointed of God,
Let the world exult, let freedom ever reign!

Like Tchaikovsky's ode "To Joy," composed for similar reasons on short notice to awkward texts, this cantata prompted a workmanlike response. He used the introduction to movement IV of his First Symphony to express "As through the hazy, nighttime vault of heaven." After 100 bars, a new theme, used again in movement IV of the Third Symphony, may refer to the "epic poems' restless world." Nowhere else does Tchaikovsky indulge such colorful responses. The conductor's charge to keep the chorus simple and the conditions of outdoor performance may explain the persistent four-part homophony. Tchaikovsky spread too few ideas over too much music and rose above expediency but once, in a massive a cappella shout (at 671) that initiates the finale. A fugue on the words "Moscow rose up with golden crown. . . . Again war, and blood in rivers flows" provides contrast of texture but is otherwise a haphazard assignment of music to text.

Of the long-gestated *The Oprichnik* (January 1870–April 1872), Bessel published the piano-vocal score in 1874 (plates 400–427) and the full score (plate 3965, 475 pages with 3 pages of corrections) with a St. Petersburg censor's date of 16 October 1896. The opera was dedicated to Grand Duke Konstantin Nikolaevich. Here is a scenario attributed to the composer [41, 32–33].

Act I. In a garden, Prince Zhemchuzhny converses with old Mitkov, to whom his daughter Natalia is betrothed. They exit; Natalia enters with her nurse and girlfriends. She sings, the girls ask the nurse for a love story, and they move into the garden. Basmanov and Andrey Morozov break into the garden with a crowd of *oprichniks.* Basmanov urges Andrey to join them, to which he agrees if he can see Natalia first. Basmanov advises him instead to bid farewell to his mother and then go directly to the tsar. Fired by revenge (for treachery against his father), Andrey agrees. Natalia runs out to meet him, her mood melancholy. Her girlfriends divert her with dancing.

Act II. Boyarïnya Morozova (Andrey's mother) bemoans the intrigues of Zhemchuzhny, her late husband's enemy. Andrey comes to bid farewell (in the libretto, he brings her money), but says nothing to her about becoming an *oprichnik,* which would disgrace her ancient line, but says that he is seeking judgment against Zhemchuzhny. Mother and son part tenderly. In scene 2, at the tsar's special settlement, *oprichniks* sing a religious chorus offstage, then enter. Basmanov announces a new candidate, whom the tsar commands them to accept. Prince Vyazminsky, an oprichnik commander, is unhappy that it is the son of Boyar Morozov, with whom he was in dispute. Andrey declares his readiness to serve. Vyazminsky reads the vow: Andrey must renounce everything dear to him—his father's memory, his mother, his bride. His hesitation over this pleases Vyazminsky, who foresees him breaking his word. Andrey vows; the *oprichniks* glorify the tsar.

Act III. In a square in Moscow, a crowd of youths taunt Morozova as a member of the *oprichniks.* Perplexed, she tries to withdraw as Natalia rushes in, escaping her father, who would give her forcibly to Mitkov. Morozova is begging his forbearance when Zhemchuzhny seizes Natalia. The *oprichniks* arrive to general horror. At first, Morozova does not recognize Andrey; he begs her forgiveness; he joined to wreak vengeance on Zhemchuzhny and restore prosperity and tranquility to her. Disgraced, she curses him. Basmanov advises her to beg the tsar for Andrey's release from his vow. Finale.

Act IV. A wedding feast in the tsar's settlement. Dances. The tsar has released Andrey from his vow, but he will remain the tsar's faithful servant. Basmanov reminds him that his vow lasts until midnight. Natalia, sensing danger, warns Andrey; he calms her. Vyazminsky brings her the tsar's invitation to visit—without Andrey. Basmanov assures Andrey that it is a test of his vow but Andrey, in a burst of jealousy, goes with her. The tsar's chambers open. Basmanov rushes to intercede, but too late: for breaking his vow, the tsar orders Andrey's execution. Vyazminsky, gloating, leads Morozova to the window at the moment her son approaches the executioner. She cries out and falls in a faint (in the libretto, she dies).

Tchaikovsky wrote the libretto himself [tr. in 384, 54–84; 388]. Assessing it as an experiment gives him the benefit of the doubt in response to obvious complaints and acknowledges that his approach to opera in general, often claimed to be naïve and defective, may in fact have been iconoclastic, comparable in this respect to his advanced student compositions. Unusual in *The Oprichnik* was the inclusion of so much self-borrowing: of the 998 bars in act I, 668 were from *The Voevoda,* 371 with the same text or nearly so [423, 39–40]. These borrowings delayed the plot and placed excessive emphasis on *couleur locale,* Tchaikovsky making no dramatic issue of Natalia's gloomy "Nightingale Song" in relation to the odious matchmaking just ended. In the conventional view, he squandered act I: the action set no premise or forecast, and the principal love interest was frustrated. In the experimental view, he showed by this that the lovers had no future, presenting Andrey as an antihero who was emotionally and spiritually closer to his mother than to his bride. Andrey and Natalia did not enjoy an intimate exchange anywhere in the opera, and in act IV, their first opportunity to sing together, Natalia expressed ill presentiments to music that may have been topical to Tchaikovsky: the lyrical theme from *Fatum* (no. 16, bars 237–65). Meanwhile, he wrote two heated duets for Andrey and his mother (nos. 8 and 13, bars 37–226), and when Andrey is executed his mother, not his bride, is forced to watch. The introduction hints at this, using associative motifs of Andrey, the *oprichniks,* and Morozova, but not Natalia.

In the conventional view, these faults showed Tchaikovsky's ineptitude for drama. His borrowing can be inappropriate, as in no. 4, when the breaking into Natalia's garden is accompanied by music of jocular expression. Andrey ponders joining the *oprichniks* as they extol their ways, and suffers the indignity of abandoning his beloved to borrowed music as he blusters about vengeance and love. In the experimental view, this is appropriate to someone who deceives his mother, suffers terminal hesitation, and takes pleasure in using status to effect revenge. The discontinuity between the new and borrowed music identified Natalia in act I. Her "Nightingale Song" prepared her arioso at the beginning of no. 6 which was, in broad strokes, where Tchaikovsky began new composition, and showed her, in ravishing music, to be strong in passion—the opposite of the emotionally mincing Andrey. Did Tchaikovsky not notice this disjunction of style? Or was it proper characterization, whereby Natalia will prove to be as insightful as Andrey is equivocal?

The Oprichnik was criticized for its *longeurs,* extension being so facile in Tchaikovsky that indulging it bespoke a want of control. Moreover, the grand ensemble of Meyerbeer was his legacy. The townsfolk's alarm over the *oprichniks* at the end of act III, comparable to scenes of religious disturbance in Meyerbeer, encouraged this linkage, as did the anointing of an elect with a ritual of drawn swords, the cynical denouement, and Tchaikovsky's blunt treatment of associative themes. Viewed as an experiment, this was a planned overreaching of French models, as it was for Musorgsky in *Boris Godunov:* to disdain the worldly and uphold the spiritual, for example, the Coronation Scene in relation to Pimen's cell, or the polonaise in relation to Boris's death. The *oprichniks* were vanity (Cui rightly observed the hypocrisy of their singing in a churchly style); the only character who yielded to them (other than the amoral Basmanov) was Andrey. In the experimental view, the opera was not about the *oprichniks* and Andrey's revenge. Andrey was a cipher. The women—Natalia in love and insight, and Morozova, who realized that her soul was ungodly—were stronger. It was a parable on the sins of pride and avarice. Despite likenesses to *Il Trovatore* (when the Count di Luna makes Azucena observe the freshly executed Manrico), the sense was closer to *Aïda:* as the worldly power of the *oprichniks* means nothing to Morozova, so the regalia of the Pharaoh's kingdom mean nothing to Amneris as the final curtain falls. The loud and overextended act finales cast aspersions on that which glittered.

The obvious view attributes Tchaikovsky's departures from convention to ignorance, lack of discipline, or imperfect assimilation. Analyzing *The Oprichnik* as an experiment does not excuse his faults nor exempt him from the need to make his message clear. But it does outline a theory of opera less defined by composition (associative motifs, arioso action scenes, big centerpiece numbers, Russian genre painting, vivacious dances, elaborate act finales), than by philosophy and character type: strong, misunderstood women; weak, insensitive, sometimes villainous men, thicker than the women; their tragic interactions, marked by blind impulses or senseless social dictates; and an emphasis on spiritual values in contrast to the worldly. It distinguishes Russian opera from Western: unruffled discontinuities of time and place and (to borrow Stravinsky's phrase) a moratorium on value judgments.

The first version of the Second Symphony in C Minor, op. 17, was published by Bessel in a four-hands arrangement, the autograph of which survives (CW 47). The original score was unpublished until the *Collected Works* [CW 17], Tchaikovsky having destroyed it at the time of revision [ix 265]. It was restored from orchestral parts in imperial times by the librarian of the Moscow Conservatory, Ivan Romanovich Shorning, whose work was lost, found again in 1949, and edited by S. S. Bogatïrev [217, 178–79; 399, 257, n. 77]. From extant orchestral parts, we know of revisions and the timings of one early performance: 17, 7, 4, and 11.5 minutes [238, 129]. In 1879, Tchaikovsky rewrote the first movement's Allegro, omitted short repeats in and rescored parts of the second, and made a large cut in the finale. The autograph of this version is also lost.

The symphony came at a time of his preoccupation with folk song (June–November 1872), and it was the first of several works with Ukrainian connections: the operas *Vakula the Smith* and *Mazepa* and the First Piano Concerto. The subtitle *Little Russian* traces to Kashkin, who wrote that Tchaikovsky declared the opening theme to be a Ukrainian variant of the tune "Down along the Volga, Mother Volga" [187, 94], though it does not match published songs of that name. "The Crane," used in the finale, is indisputably Ukrainian, the only tune Tchaikovsky identified in the surviving autograph. The Trio of the second movement is based on no. 6 of his *Fifty Russian Folk Songs,* and the Trio of the third is recognizably close to another Ukrainian song [399, 271].

Tchaikovsky integrates folk song into sonata-allegro in the outer movements, which poses a problem not of making a pattern of key and theme, but of developing a sense of discourse when the conventional treatment of folk song—changing background variation—was static and decorative. In the movement I introduction, he emphasizes the song, the clear harmony of which establishes the key at the beginning of the symphony:

Ex. 12

The second of two changing background variations which ensue flows into five bars of interlude based on one of its motifs. This signals Tchaikovsky's procedure in the movement: shifting between folk and motivic discourse.

The exposition proceeds independently of the introduction theme through the first area, but it returns at the closing, thence to nearly continuous elaboration in the development. The recapitulation is marked by the near-omission of the first area, a strategy revisited in movement I of the Fourth Symphony. From bar 293, Tchaikovsky reprises the exposition in a different sequence (bars 96–116, then 79–83, a new 10-bar bridge, then 115–90), followed by a lengthy coda (at 405) which invokes the same fateful horn calls heard in the First Symphony, to be heard again in the Fourth Symphony, the First Suite, and *The Sleeping Beauty.*

The March, borrowed from *Undine,* and the Scherzo do not raise issues of discourse, but the massive finale echoes movement I in its structure. Tchaikovsky announces "The Crane" in the magisterial introduction and adorns it with an abundance of changing background in the first area, then silences it before the second area. Too addictive to abandon, the tune returns at the closing and is further elaborated in the development. In the finale, he makes a complete recapitulation of the first area (compensating for the omission of this section in movement I), adding a long post-recapitulation, which brings the entire movement to over 1,000 bars.

To Laroche, Tchaikovsky's treatment of theme was the winning feature of the work, and he cited Beethoven's Seventh and Eighth Symphonies as precedents for the lively mood of the finale [255 II 36]. To this could be added references to the opening of the finale of Beethoven's First Symphony at the beginning of Tchaikovsky's, and to the "mystery chords" of the first "Razumovsky" in Tchaikovsky's finale at the beginning of the development (bars 313–24).

Upon hearing the Second Symphony, Tchaikovsky was unhappy with the first two movements and wanted to change details of the orchestration [v 300]. When in November 1879 he repossessed his score, he revised it in spite of the work's success. Kashkin and Laroche preferred the first version; the finale had delighted the Mighty Handful; the symphony had twice been performed in Moscow in the same season. And yet, as Tchaikovsky explained, "If the epithet impossible ever applied to anything, it was to this first movement in its former version. My God! How difficult, noisy, disconnected, confused it was! The andante is unchanged. The scherzo radically reworked. The finale has a huge cut" [ix, 15–16]. "It came out a new composition," he wrote to Bessel, "perhaps it is not a masterpiece, but it is incomparably more mature, more perfect and better than the first version" [viii 477].

The first theme of the original Allegro lacked tonic emphasis and cadential direction, obscuring formal articulation, and was followed by a *tutti* outburst that disrupted the train of thought. The new Allegro theme is tonally clear and folk-like, arriving at the second area in 33 bars instead of 64. But concision entailed risk: the streamlined first movement was now too light for the introduction, especially after Tchaikovsky omitted many references to it in the Allegro. Critical response to the 1879 version was less favorable than to the first version, raising complaints about length (although the piece was shorter) and the impression of an unpleasant miscellany.

On 6 December 1872, Tchaikovsky honored his director and mentor with the performance of *Serenade for the Name-Day of N. G. Rubinstein,* 50 bars for small orchestra surely composed not long before. A simple binary elaborates the melody stated by the lower strings in the first four bars, which returns triumphantly at bar 33. If there is a message here outside the music's social function, it resides in the part writing and the relationship of upper voice to bass—the kind of music that one good theory teacher writes for another.

Tchaikovsky dedicated the *Six Romances,* op. 16 (believed also to date from December 1872) to his friends. Song 1, a lullaby, is appropriate for a new bride, Natalia Rimskaya-Korsakova, and song 5 jests on the composer's relationship with Nikolay Rubinstein. Others express some duality—motion and stillness in song 2, happiness and anguish in song 3, Orthodox context and the Roman plainchant in song 6 [377, 47]. The merest veil of unity from song to song obtains in Tchaikovsky's prominent semitonal melodic sighs, which lead into the first notes of song 6.

In no. 1, Maykov's evocative "Cradle Song," the singer has summoned the wind, sun, and eagle as the child's nurse; but the eagle has flown, the sun set, and the wind raced home. The wind's mother asks where it has been; not battling the stars or driving the waves, it answers, but rocking a cradle. Tchaikovsky deploys the text over two strains of music. The first has a constant rocking figure in the piano, its Wolf-like descending chromatic figure distantly anxious. The second is more folk-like, omits the rocking figure, and carries the quoted text.

In Grekov's "Wait!" (no. 2), the singer appeals to the lover to pause in the onrush of life to enjoy the beautiful night. The opening motif in the piano is noticeably deliberate, as if attempting to slow time. The voice sings over it, yielding to the night with a surprising modulation and a beguiling new tune—it is night's seductiveness. By the end, the title's admonition has lost philosophical gravity, to become the urgings of a lover.

Fet's "Accept this once" (no. 3) is a hyperbole; the singer interrupts the "beautiful creature's" train of thought to unburden. Melancholic at the moment of separation, he treasures the anguish; he hymns the beauty, blessed in every new torment, foreseeing its triumph. The dissonant opening forecasts anxiety, an upbeat to the agitation accompanying the words. As the song progresses, norms are breached: strophic phrases are modified; conventional arpeggiation begins to form a linear counterpoint with the voice. The poem's urgency leads to a high tessitura and elided phrases before releasing the piano to a burst of energy at the voice's cadence.

No. 4, "O Sing That Song," addresses someone who sang for the singer in the past. That song was sad, this one less so, though it does have appropriate inflections of torment, anguish, tears, and the singer "broken with grief." Tchaikovsky jests with trying to remember: the introduction gives the "song," but the singer remains silent, as if summoning memory. Tune and voice join forces at the moment memory is revealed (bar 105), where the accompaniment, magisterial, imparts breadth and resonance to remembrance.

Tchaikovsky's "So what then?" (no. 5) reviews his relationship with Nikolay Rubinstein, whose "bright, angelic" image stays with him day and night. Tears, reveries, and terrible, frightening dreams are all filled with his image: "torture me but love me!" After the introduction, anxious but for a moment, the accompaniment is flippant, the stuff of restaurant singers, while the voice, in mincing phrases, mocks the seriousness of the words.

The *Dies irae* is named as the subtitle of the "New Greek Song" (no. 6) and is quoted in almost every bar, hinting at some topicality. (The dedicatee, Konstantin Albrecht, converted to Orthodoxy but not until the summer of 1876.) The Catholic tune sounds oddest in the distinctly Orthodox moment when the women ask if there are "God's church and golden icons" in the world. Atypically, Tchaikovsky paints the words: the precipitous drop in the piano's registration at "beneath the earth" and the wailing figure which accompanies "the girls are moaning, the women are weeping." The waltz-like *Dies irae* in running sixteenth notes at "do young girls weave, sitting at machines?" is a bizarre echo of "Gretchen am Spinnrade."

In 1873 and 1875, Tchaikovsky wrote four songs for publication in Nikolay Bernard's music journal, *Nouvelliste.* "Take my heart away" (Fet, 1873) creates a tension between the rapturous, near-Baudelairean verses ("Take my heart away into the resounding distance, / Where gently, like a smile, there is sorrow / And ever higher I begin to rush along the silvery path / Like a quivering shadow behind the wing") and the musical setting. The agitated accompaniment and vocal delivery are so rapid as to forgo *volupté,* coupled with awkward chromatic turns. In "The blue eyes of spring," to Mikhailov's translation of Heine, the twittering effect of the opening piano figure catches the fanciful clairvoyance whereby the nightingales divine the poet's thoughts and broadcast them to the entire grove. It contrasts with the Cherubino-like march in the voice: our lad is picking flowers for his heartthrob. "I should like in a single word," in Lev Mey's translation (1875), is the Heine of "Ich grolle nicht," the angry lover pouring out his sorrow and sending it to the beloved through the winds. Where Schumann's accompaniment was measured, Tchaikovsky's is spontaneous in rushing sixteenth notes. The dissonant, 2-bar chord at the beginning surely represents the "single word"; in the third verse, in reference to the beloved's dream, the expression becomes tender for a moment, hinting at the poet's celebrated irony. That lovers regret not having long to be together, to dream and flourish, finds a lyric response in "We have not far to walk" by Grekov (1875). The introduction is a motto for the song, its affective dissonances hinting at regret but resolving immediately, forming upbeats to consonance. The understated piano leaves the voice with tempered, broad phrases to convey the lovers' resignation. In the middle verse, Tchaikovsky marks the words "dreams" and "fleeting" in the piano with immediate echoes of the vocal part.

Tchaikovsky's principal theater work in 1873, composed in March and April, was music to a new play by Alexander Ostrovsky, *The Snow Maiden*. Here is a synopsis:

Prologue on Red Mountain near the capital of the Berendeys in prehistoric times; midnight at the beginning of spring. Overture (no. 1). The Beauty of Spring describes the desolate land, for which she is partly responsible: 16 years ago, Snow Maiden was born of her union with Granddad Frost; since then, he has been prolonging winters to protect her. Spring invites the birds to dance and sing (no. 2), whereas Frost delights in making things cold (no. 3). Spring would send Snow Maiden out among people, perhaps to fall in love, but Frost fears Yarilo, the sun, who has threatened to destroy Snow Maiden if ever she feels the fire of love. They decide to give her to the childless Bobïl. Snow Maiden is delighted, especially at the songs of the shepherd Lel, though Frost warns her about Lel, who is "pierced through with sunlight." Spring offers help in time of need; Frost calls forest spirits to watch over her. Some Berendeys pass by, bidding farewell to *máslenitsa* (carnival; nos. 4, 5a); Bobïl discovers Snow Maiden.

Act I. Snow Maiden is at her spinning wheel when a messenger reports the tsar's command to greet the sun on the morrow. Bobïl chides Snow Maiden's industry; she does not know love. Lel sings (nos. 6–7) in return for a flower from her. When other girls call him, he goes to them; he throws away her flower, and her heart is pained. Kupava enters, joyful over her betrothal to the merchant Mizgir. Mizgir enters and forsakes Kupava for Snow Maiden, who resists, then yields at Bobïl's urging. Kupava sorrows.

Act II. The court of the tsar of the Berendeys. An entr'acte (no. 8). Blind *gusli* players sing to the tsar (no. 9). The tsar thinks that Yarilo disfavors them, perhaps because his people have forsaken beauty and are envious and indifferent. He would celebrate a wedding on Yarilo's Day (no. 10). Kupava enters and tells her story; the tsar orders Mizgir's arrest; the people hail the tsar (no. 11). Mizgir admits his crime and is banished. Snow Maiden enters, and the tsar, amazed at her beauty, asks her to choose a fiancé; she cannot. He asks his wife to intervene; she chooses Lel, who promises that Snow Maiden will know the sun's warmth. Mizgir asks for his punishment to be rescinded if he wins Snow Maiden's heart that day.

Act III. A clearing in the forest. Young Berendeys are dancing (no. 12). The tsar orders the *skomorokhi* (vagabond entertainers) to dance (no. 13), then Lel to sing (no. 14a–b). In return for his song, he may choose a girl from whom to receive a kiss; Snow Maiden asks to be chosen, but he chooses Kupava. Crying, Snow Maiden runs into the forest. A straggler, Brusilo, sings a silly song (no. 15). Lel confronts her; she wants him to choose her, but she still does not know love. He leaves and Mizgir enters, pressing his suit. He and Snow Maiden argue, whereupon forest spirits foil him (no. 16). Lel has rejoined Snow Maiden when Kupava enters and declares her love for him. He rejects Snow Maiden again. Despairing, she invokes her mother.

Act IV. Dawn. An entr'acte (no. 17a). Snow Maiden asks her mother to know love. Spring wraps her daughter in flowers (no. 17b), transfigured in the experience of love, apostrophizes her, and withdraws. Snow Maiden wanders into the forest, meets and embraces Mizgir, but warns they must conceal their love from the sun. The people move across the mountain (no. 18, March) and sing with the sun's first rays (no. 18, Chorus). The tsar asks a blessing on the loving couples, but Yarilo seems angry; his mountain is covered with clouds. Mizgir approaches with Snow Maiden. Sunlight shines on her, and she dies. The tsar ponders what has happened and bids Lel to sing (no. 19). The clouds disperse; Yarilo appears on the mountain in the guise of a young man. The tsar orders feasting.

This lengthy piece was provided a surfeit of music exaggerated by internal repetition; some verses were omitted in the published score (e.g., nos. 9 and 12). Twelve of the 19 numbers were borrowed, including, from *Undine,* the Overture and Lel's first song. In that song, words and music are not in balance: lavish sound and operatic word repetition clash at Lel's character-accurate nonsense refrain, "Lado moyu lado," for a dozen bars at a time. When the orchestral textures are less imposing, as in Lel's song in act III (no. 14), the result is more effective. Just as folk songs, which may be short, do not always submit to grand theatrical treatment, miniature strophes set within larger ones add to the impression of unwarranted extension.

Between August and October 1873, Tchaikovsky composed *The Tempest,* op. 18, to a program by Vladimir Stasov, which was set out in Stasov's letter of 30 December 1872:

> [F]irst *the sea,* the desert island, the majestic and severe figure of the magician *Prospero,* and immediately grace and femininity itself, *Miranda,* like a primitive Eve who still has never seen a man (except for Prospero) and is amazed at the sight of the handsome youth *Ferdinand,* cast ashore by the tempest. They fall in love, . . . Miranda only little by little is enlivened, and from a state of childlike innocence is transformed into an enamored young woman; in the second half of the overture she and Ferdinand would already be borne away in the full sail of passion, embraced by the *fire of love.* . . . [A]round these three principal characters would be grouped, in the middle part of the overture: the half-beast *Caliban* and the magical spirit *Ariel* with his choruses of elves. The end of the overture would represent how Prospero relinquishes his magic, and having cast off the power of charms, blesses the young couple to be joined by the bonds of marriage and returned to society. [401, 100]

The score contains no rubrics. The following alignment of music and program is by Nathan Platte [296; see also 399, 297–308]; Tchaikovsky's synopsis from the score is italicized:

The sea (1–82). *The magician Prospero sends his obedient Ariel to raise a storm, the victim of which is to be the boat carrying Ferdinand.* Prospero calls Ariel (11), who answers his call (16–17); intimation of the boat (fanfare at 18).

The boat approaches (83–142) from a distance, with annunciatory fanfares (79–86), which are continued during the chorale theme, representing the boat's passengers, first in A-flat (91), then B (104), then majestically in E (121).

The storm (143–225) features Prospero's call (155–202), the initiator of the tempest.

The magic island (226–64).
The first timid surges of Miranda's and Ferdinand's love (265–343).
Ariel (344–73).
Caliban (374–459). Prospero's theme is reprised (438) as Prospero berates Caliban.
The enamored pair yield to the triumphant fascination of passion (460–553).
Triumphant reunion, reconciliation, and setting sail (554–83). Chorale in A-flat (572).
Prospero throws off his power as a magician and leaves the island (584–631).

Tchaikovsky asked, does *The Tempest* need a tempest? Stasov said it did, and his answers to further questions brought the composer to heed his own prerogatives. This meant (assuming the present rationale is accurate) referring to the boat carrying Ferdinand, without whom the love interest would be impossible and Prospero would have no cause to quit the island, and resolving the clash between Prospero and the Italian nobles, represented by tension between the home key, F minor, and the key of the arrival of the ship. The most elaborate presentation of the nobles' theme (at bar 121) brings the music to E major—a semitone below the home key, which triads pivot enharmonically between the pitches A-flat and G-sharp (a device used again at the opening of the Fourth Symphony). The narrative element needed to resolve this tension is the love of Miranda and Ferdinand. The love music enters the score in G-flat and B-flat (265–343) but rises up, after sections describing Ariel and Caliban, to A-flat and C major (460–553), thus affirming in keys—F, A-flat, C—the F-minor triad at the beginning. The lovers thereby become symbolically aligned with Prospero, and the "dissonant" E major is expunged [296].

The Tempest is more subdued in its pictorialism than is *Romeo,* let alone *Francesca.* A painterly aspect, perhaps inspired by nature (above, pp. 82–83), makes the cold sea music, the vivid storm, and the warm love music more directly analogous to color than if these ideas, like the battle and love music in *Romeo and Juliet,* interacted narratively. Hence the possible influence of *The Tempest* on Rachmaninov's *The Isle of the Dead,* with its parallel of crossing the sea to a magic island, based not on a play but on a seascape.

The autograph of the *Six morceaux* for piano, op. 19, completed by 27 October 1873, is more carefully notated for performers than were Tchaikovsky's earlier piano works [424, 66], though it is less detailed than the printed editions, an original and a second "reviewed and corrected by the composer." Suggestions by Hans von Bülow may account for differences between the printed versions [xvii 231, n. 4], though the copy Bülow sent to Tchaikovsky is lost. Opus 19 lacks collective identity and its dedicatees are a miscellany: the composer's friends Nikolay Kondratiev and Hermann Laroche (nos. 1 and 6), and the rest pianists, including Annette Avramova and Eduard Langer, the composer's colleagues at the Moscow Conservatory.

In op. 19, Tchaikovsky intensified technique and refined his personal idiom: octave work, pervasive syncopation, textures sometimes dense with secondary voices, a distinctive cantabile in the middle register for the left hand (no. 1, no. 4 reprise), and a toccata-like manner (middle of no. 5). Attractive ideas were placed over rhythmicized pedal points (nos. 1 and 2, variation 12 of no. 6), the steadily climbing chromatic line passing through the texture (end of no. 4). A sense of being written for the player's private satisfaction derives from the pianism and also from the occasional allusion to other composers, as if the pieces are musician-to-musician jests (the varied reprise in no. 4 à la Schubert, the Chopinesque touches in the reprise of no. 5, the Schumannesque theme of no. 6, the Mendelssohnian or Rubinsteinesque 4th variation of no. 6, the overtly identified Schumannesque portion of the 11th, "symphonic" variation).

No. 6, the Theme and Variations, has been published and played separately. Tchaikovsky orchestrated no. 4 for cello and small orchestra, probably in 1888. Stravinsky borrowed generously from nos. 2, 3, and 4 of op. 19 in *Le baiser de la fée.*

The sameness of theme in *Six morceaux pour le piano, composés sur un seul thème* (October–November 1873) is intervallic and not always easy to hear, the music in general somber, dense, introspective, tortured, in moments willful. Chopin lurks in the genres—prelude, impromptu, funeral march, mazurka, scherzo—but not the style, least of all the Bachian textures of the Fugue à 4 voix, which could almost fit into *The Well-Tempered Clavier.* For Tchaikovsky to speak in a voice so alien was exceptional.

By its brevity, the Schumannesque Impromptu prepares for the Marche funebre, the longest, weightiest movement of op. 21, which anticipates the funereal in late Liszt. When A-flat minor shifts to B major for a contrasting melody, the effect is vision-like at first (it uses the same two keys as in the funeral-march section of the Fourth Symphony, movement I), but the music gradually becomes frenzied and culminates in a quotation of the *Dies irae* (at bars 52–85). Tchaikovsky wrote this strangest of mazurkas first, easily as somber as Chopin's op. 68, no. 4, but without that work's glimpses of sweetness and protracted where Chopin was laconic. It apes the Funeral March in keys, but the continuously complex rhythm, perpetually offsetting the meter, seems to be reacting to the clarity of pulse in the Funeral March. The Scherzo, which echoes the *Souvenir de Hapsal* in its motif, is a furtive recall of happier times before proceeding to violence.

Op. 21 is linked with the death of Eduard Zak, though it is unclear how much Tchaikovsky had composed before that "tragic catastrophe" [v 333].

The String Quartet no. 2 is a striking work about which little is known. Corrections in manuscript parts, including a rewritten passage in the Andante, originate with Wilhelm Fitzenhagen, cellist in the quartet of the Moscow Russian Musical Society [238, 130]. A Beethovenian approach to key and working out produces unusual effects, especially in the first movement, while pattern and contrasts of theme and texture affirm Tchaikovsky's allegiance to Western form. Folk intonations speak to his individuality. Impassioned extensions and asperities echo op. 21. The opening of movement I is typical of his unusual sound in this work:

Ex. 13

Nowhere is the home key a destination, and passing keys lack affirmation. The introduction pivots into the exposition (at bar 19) from G minor, after a recitative-like outpouring in the first violin (13–18). The exposition begins without strong key definition, arriving at the transition (42) before a cadence in the home key, then drifts again to G (51–56). This prepares the second area, with its diatonic, folkish tune in C, articulated by its dominant:

Ex. 14

At the cadence (73), orchestral scoring, with wide arpeggios, tremolo, and multiple stops, hints at a folk ensemble in full swing. Modest wrote: "The new quartet . . . was begun at the very end of December, [or] at the beginning of January. I recall that in my stay at that time during *svyatki* in Moscow, I heard how he elaborated the first theme of the first allegro" [1997 I 399]. At *svyatki,* or Christmastide, which was marked by the custom of neighbors in costume (*ryazhenïe*) paying calls, we may have a hint of the music's sense. The costume is more ritual than ruse, the visits an occasion for sharing cheer. Tolstoy used this custom for the touching moment in *War and Peace* when Sonya, still in her false moustache, and Nikolay, still dressed as a boyar's wife, steal their first kiss. *Svyatki* return in *The Seasons, ryazhenïe* in *The Nutcracker.*

The festive element in movement I is offset by Tchaikovsky's elaborative tendency, producing a duality of jest and seriousness. This continues in the Scherzo, which reconsiders the Scherzo from Beethoven's op. 74 but touts a certain oddity in the persistent 3-bar phrases, grouped in 6/8 and 9/8. The opening does not portend a relaxation of complexity; at 32–57, the initial motif becomes more insistent and dissonant, qualities that persist in the Trio and recall the preceding movement. Movement III, anticipated by the increasing seriousness of the Scherzo, is the center of emotional gravity in the Quartet. The astringent beginning, the ritornello of a rounded pattern, and the lamenting theme in falling fourths recall op. 21; the manic insistence of motif (e.g., 74–81) echoes the Scherzo. The finale, like those of Beethoven's opp. 131 and 132—clear, resolving, unambiguous—is also a compositional summary: the complex rondo and the falling fourth in the A theme echo movement III; the B theme (at 24) in D-flat returns in A major (101), the principal keys of the Scherzo and Trio; the shift into homophony and fast note values at the beginning of the C section echo the identical shift in movement I (62 in mvt. I, 64 in mvt. IV). The "wrong scale" introduction persists into the movement proper, while the high spirits of the musical ideas shift to the serious with the fugue (at 129), evidence of a Germanic impulse to elaborate that Tchaikovsky will revisit in the Third Quartet.

Vakula the Smith, after Gogol, came to Tchaikovsky quickly in the summer of 1874. The action is summarized here from the published libretto of 1871, which was probably used in the competition (as the title page does not refer to a composer) and passed the censor on 3 May 1872 [299]:

Act I. A moonlit winter night (Christmas Eve) in the village of Dikanka, of which the witch Solokha extols the beauties: if only there were a little blizzard, she would invite someone in. The devil accosts her. Solokha, teasing, runs into her cottage. The devil is here because Solokha's son, Vakula, painted an unflattering picture of him at which the other devils in hell made merry. He wants revenge; he will foil Vakula's visit to Oxana with a blizzard that will keep her father, Chub the Cossack, at home. Solokha flies out of her chimney on her broom; the devil conjures up a storm and follows her. The moon is obscured. Chub and Panas, the mayor of Dikanka, emerge and notice the moon is gone. They are going back inside when they are tempted by the thought of mulled wine at the tavern. Oxana, dressed for caroling, observes the storm. She worries that she is too plain to find a man, then consults her mirror and finds herself just as beautiful as people say. Vakula enters and declares his love. Chub returns; Vakula does not recognize him and throws him out. Oxana sends Vakula away; she would cry, but is seized with laughter.

Act II. Solokha curses the devil for colliding with her coming down the chimney. He begins to flirt. She proposes a dance; strange creatures emerge from the stove and the crannies and begin to play music. A knock at the door disturbs the dance; the devil hides in a sack. Panas enters and is about to settle in when comes another knock. He too hides in a sack. Now, the schoolteacher makes advances; when interrupted by another knock, he takes similar refuge. Next it is Chub, whose arrival pleases Solokha. She is plying him with vodka when yet another knock interrupts. It is Vakula, and Chub crawls in with the schoolteacher. The pensive Vakula picks up the sacks to clear them away before the Christmas holiday but is shocked by their weight—a sign of the debilitating effects of his grief and passion.

The scene returns to the beginning of act I. A chorus approaches. Greetings sound from various cottages. Young men sing outside Oxana's window; she comes out and mixes with the crowd. She notices one girl's fancy embroidered slippers (*cherevichki*). She complains that no one gives her such gifts, and Vakula volunteers to do so; if he brings her a pair of *cherevichki* that the tsaritsa herself has worn, she will marry him on the spot. He ponders his love as she taunts him about the slippers. Suffering, he resolves to take his own life. The crowd espies the sacks he left behind and discovers their contents.

Act III. That night at a river bank, water spirits complain of the cold and a wood goblin chides them. He sees Vakula approach and warns that the lad might drown himself. But the devil accosts Vakula, having jumped out of the sack he was carrying; Vakula will drown or forfeit his soul in return for Oxana. Vakula chooses the latter. He reaches for a nail to sign his name in blood, and nails the devil to the ground instead. In return for letting him go, Vakula gets his wish—a trip to St. Petersburg. He climbs onto the devil's back and they fly off. In an entrance hall, Vakula meets some Cossacks going to the tsaritsa. A minuet. She enters; Vakula makes his request, and the tsaritsa commands that a pair of gold *cherevichki* be given to him. She calls for dances, then withdraws. Russian and Cossack dances. Vakula and the devil fly home.

A bright morning. Solokha is lamenting Vakula's disappearance. Even Oxana sorrows. Bells ring, and people disperse from church; Chub invites them to his home. Some men see Vakula in the distance; he is joyfully welcomed. Solokha regrets having troubled to lament. Vakula presents Chub with gifts from St. Petersburg. He asks for Oxana's hand, and the matchmakers are summoned. Oxana enters. Vakula gives her the *cherevichki*. She all but admits to loving him anyway. Chub blesses the marriage. Celebrations.

The 1871 libretto differs from Jurgenson's piano-vocal score of Tchaikovsky's opera, not least in omitting the tsaritsa, whose lines are transferred or adapted to the anonymous His Excellency. Differences between the *Collected Works* [CW 35] and what appears to be Tchaikovsky's submission copy for the competition also point to significant changes [352, 118]. Revision deepened Vakula's character. In the 1871 text, when he is about to carry out the sacks, he complains of spent passion and withering away. In the 1876 version, this was intensified:

> Ah, even my family home has grown hateful to me,
> It would be better to die than to suffer so!
> All day long I pine away, and there is no sleep at night,
> Passion is spent, I am withering away!

Why are you draining me, sorrow, anguish,
Why, serpent in the grass, do you suck my heart,
Why are you poisoning my soul?

In the 1871 libretto, Vakula agrees to find the *cherevichki,* then despairs with lines omitted in 1876:

If I were a drunkard,
I would take my sorrow to the Jewess [who runs the tavern]
I would hide myself from the whole world
In the tavern.

Presently, he pours out his feelings after Oxana mocks him again. Instead of "Go into the church for me / And mourn my sinful end," we read, "Brothers, mourn my sinful end / It is easier for me to damn my soul than to suffer thus and to love thus!" whereupon the townsfolk remind him that suicide is a sin. There are many similar changes between the two librettos.

Librettist Polonsky may have assumed that a funny story would make a funny opera, but the lovers are not especially comical, and they are striking for their lack of mutuality compared to famous *buffa* predecessors. While their seriousness was a problem, so were excessive conversation in general and the scarcity of dramatic climax. Tchaikovsky knew that the words must be delivered briskly if there were to be any hope of Gogolesque effect, but he abandoned any such aspiration. Despite declamatory touches, his lyrical arioso rarely conveys witticism or compelling emotion, save a few passages where the lovers break out in aria. Elsewhere, he made the best of spectacle, including the polonaise, missing in the 1871 libretto. Solokha's "little snowstorm" at the beginning of the opera is resplendent. The gopak, the caroling choruses, and the dances are picturesque but lack dramatic import. In details, *Vakula* breathes the air of later operas: when the master of ceremonies announces the entertainment, the imperial trappings and eighteenth-century manner anticipate *The Queen of Spades;* the cannon fire from the fortress at the ritual greeting of the tsaritsa, here at a distance, will be at closer range in *1812*.

The problems of *Vakula* lingered in self-critique. Seeing it in 1878, Tchaikovsky rebuked himself for "unforgiveable mistakes" [vii 440]. After Anatoly saw it in 1879, Pyotr added to his list the "lack of a sense of measure in orchestral effects," giving the listener no relief. It was *prelest'* immoderately applied, without due regard for cogent theatrical effect. These were traces of his previous, false operatic manner, which, corrected, would be marked by "breadth, simplicity and a certain decorativeness." *Vakula* was not operatic, but symphonic or even chamber-like. He nevertheless placed it in the front rank of his works [viii 391].

Tchaikovsky probably did not (as he claimed) publish the First Piano Concerto unchanged from what he played for Nikolay Rubinstein on Christmas Eve 1874. By the time he described that occasion, at least Bülow and Edward Dannreuther had advised him about revisions [6, 199; 123; 254]; in October 1878, Jurgenson could still ask, before publishing the full score, how to proceed with the piano part in view of changes [87 I 52]. The first edition, for two pianos (1875), is based on the only source for the solo part in Tchaikovsky's hand; the second edition, the first in score (1879), apparently incorporated Dannreuther's suggestions, "trés sages et trés practiques" [vi 32]; and the third (1889), made in consultation with Alexander Siloti [230, 168–71; 251, 89–96], incorporated more changes and corrections. Jurgenson issued at least a sixth edition, "revue et corrigée par l'auteur." The *Collected Works* [CW 28] provides two versions of the solo part, from the first edition in regular print and from the second, placed above it in smaller notes.

What were Tchaikovsky's models? The answer is complicated by the volatility of concerto conventions and the composer's ability to obscure an influence. The layout—complex first movement, lyric interlude, and short, rousing finale—recalls Schumann and Chopin. Equality of soloist and accompaniment in Litolff's *concertos symphoniques* may have inspired its imposing orchestral presence, and inspiration may also be found in the demanding technique and structural idiosyncrasies of Anton Rubinstein [150, 32–36]. It displays particular affinities with Rubinstein's Fourth (1864) in the sonata-allegro pattern in movement I, where the second area comprises two themes juxtaposed (bars 184, 204), then elaborated separately, in the cadenza in G-flat between the recapitulation and the close, and in the articulation of the whole as a succession of dynamic waves [279, 419–20], though Tchaikovsky's enactment of these devices is much bolder than his teacher's. A short leap of faith finds his concerto an answer to Rubinstein's Fourth, given the similarity of Rubinstein's opening theme (with prominent diminished fourth) to several in Tchaikovsky's concerto, the rapid octave writing in both, and Tchaikovsky's "correction" of Rubinstein's protracted reluctance to end the finale. This possibility accords with his irritation over Rubinstein's response to the Second String Quartet. In Tchaikovsky, a new theme, inchoate in the development cadenza, presently emerges to a state of clarity in the orchestra. Its stepwise descent at a tritone's distance from the home key echoes Beethoven's Fourth Concerto:

Ex. 15

Ex. 16

There is much original thinking as well. That the opening melody does not recur after the introduction is irrelevant, as it predicts the key of further cantabile melodies in its tonic or dominant and serves as an emblem of magnificence. It separates home key from singing melody, a distinction resolved only in the last presentation of the lyric theme in the finale. The cadenza in the middle of the introduction forecasts Tchaikovsky's unexpected cadenzas later, which together with the long spans, the two-themed second area, and powerful interior articulations within the movement produce a complex variant of sonata-allegro procedure:

Introduction, 1–106
Exposition, 107–291
  First area, theme 1 (B-flat minor), 107–69
    Transition, 168–83
  Second area (A-flat major), 184–291
    Presentation (A-flat major) of theme 2a (184–203), then theme 2b (204–17)
    Elaboration of theme 2a (A-flat to C minor, 218–66) and theme 2b (A-flat, 267–91)
Development, 292–450
  Elaboration of theme 2b, 292–345

Cadenza, 346–83

New (Beethovenian) theme insinuated at 369

Elaboration of the new theme (first at 388) over pedal point on B, 384–416

Elaboration of theme 2b and theme 1, serving as a retransition, 416–42

Recapitulation (abbreviated), 443 (cf. 160)–602

First area, theme 1 (B-flat minor), 443–70

Second area (B-flat major), 471–537

Elaboration of theme 2a, 471–512

Sets dominant pedal point in B-flat, 513–22, leading to

Deceptive cadence to G-flat major, 523–37

Cadenza in G-flat (flat VI to V in B-flat) recalls theme in development, 538–602

Restates theme 2b, 563; to dominant of B-flat at *quasi adagio*

Cadential closing (B-flat), 603 (*tempo I,* rehearsal 32)–657

Restates theme 2b

Theme 2b is emphasized in the development to the exclusion of theme 2a (which is hinted at in both cadenzas), the latter then banished in the recapitulation and restricted thereafter to brief statements in the cadenza and the closing. Similar individuality in the distribution of themes will inform the Violin Concerto and the Second Piano Concerto.

After the lovely cantabile of movement II, the swirling waltz seems anomalous—in an unrelated key, withheld from the soloist—until one senses its analogy with the new theme in the development of movement I. In both passages, an unexpected theme emerges from the midst of improvisation. Comparable analogy is responsible for the distinctive reminiscence of first movement themes in the middle section of the third (cf. mvt. I Allegro at 101).

Each movement quotes a borrowed theme: a Ukrainian song for the Allegro theme in movement I (at bar 107) and the opening melody of the finale (exhaustively scrutinized in 447), and a French chansonette for the waltz in movement II. Tchaikovsky did not call attention to them as such, nor to the Balakirevian key choices (B-flat minor and D-flat major), nor to the embedded musical anagrams of himself and Désirée Artôt in his themes, based on Germanic pitch names [60, 198–200]. These devices illustrate his tendency to imbue his music with meanings, laid bare upon scrutiny.

The *Sérénade mélancolique* for violin and orchestra came on the heels of the First Piano Concerto and shares certain features with it. Tchaikovsky dedicated this work to Leopold Auer, whom he met in 1875 and who took it up, as he did the Violin Concerto, after initial misgivings. The easy flow between B-flat minor and D-flat major in the first section, linked in the second with a striking movement to E major for a new theme with descending tetrachord in its headmotif, all echo the First Piano Concerto. The *Sérénade* demands superb cantabile in the opening melody with its throaty low register and distantly Gypsy contour, then in a new theme at a higher register and different key. The middle section offers two new themes in contrasting keys and is thematically rounded, but with only a modest contrast in tempo. The curtailment of rhetoric allows the soloist to engage freely the musical challenge of the moment: registration, melodic fluency, and increasingly long-breathed, ecstatic expression.

Before 11 April 1875, Tchaikovsky produced three sheaves of songs. The *Six Romances,* op. 25, probably from February–March, are dedicated to singers, including four of the principals in *The Oprichnik.* The dark sentiments of the first three, the vision of a bird escaping westward to freedom in the fourth, the ungratified pursuit of ideal passion in the fifth, even the jestful admonition to stay away from the tsar's tavern in the sixth—may all reflect Tchaikovsky's dissatisfaction with Moscow at the time of composition.

In "Reconciliation" (no. 1), the singer must cope with a hopeless present and escape in dreams, undeluded by pleasant memories of the past. Much of the vocal part conveys dignified self-control. On the words "Let not hope and false dream disturb your sleep and calm," however, the voice gives meaning to the introduction and postlude with angry outbursts based on it.

Fyodor Tyutchev's "As over burning embers" (no. 2) likens the unremarkable ebbing of life to a scroll burning in smoldering coals. The terrible monotony of this torments the soul; if only life would once more burst out in bright flame. Tchaikovsky embeds the vocal melody in the middle of the piano texture of the introduction—life hidden amid the embers—before yielding to a Musorgskian lassitude on "And thus, sadly, my life smolders." When resolve comes, the opening music returns transformed, the vocal part invigorated against a falling line in the piano, then the long postlude which represents the one bright flame.

"Mignon's Song," Tyutchev's translation of "Kennst du das Land?" in no. 3, preserves Goethe's rhythm, but the reversal of Goethe's second and third verses and the repetition of the first verse at the end transform his problematical close amid the "ancient brood of dragons" into a safe arrival at the columned house. Mignon's questions are more childlike than mysterious, her invitation to go forth more congenial than anxious. Tchaikovsky's introduction anticipates the melody of her questions; he hints at her enthusiasm by compressing phrases to suggest breathlessness (as at bar 13). He portrays the journey in offbeat rhythms and more complex textures, the blissful arrival with ethereal, harp-like arpeggios.

No. 4, "The Canary," asks whether it is better to be free or imprisoned in luxury. The sultana would know the world outside her harem, but the little bird declines—the harem is too crowded for its song, its words too foreign, for the song has a sister, which is called "freedom." Tchaikovsky floods voice and piano with clichés appropriate to a harem—augmented seconds, strumming effects, and arabesques.

Lev Mey's "I never spoke to her" (no. 5) treats the unattainable beloved as the singer's "ideal, delight, and torture." The first strophe (1–22) addresses his experiences in reality and dream, the second (22–40) the beloved's transformative effects, and the brief peroration is an apostrophe. Independent phrases in the piano hint at immediate meanings (e.g., the staccato at 15 in response to "ran away further" in 14). Tchaikovsky's descending figures in the accompaniment surpass the details and hint at irresolution and the unattainable.

"As they kept saying: 'Fool'" (no. 6) is a theatrical sketch, akin to Musorgsky's or Dargomïzhsky's vignettes of village life. The tipster is advised to drink water, not wine, and to visit the river to gain wisdom and sobriety. If the river can drown the "serpent melancholy," he will do this. Together with swaggering motifs and a folkish cast, outbursts in the accompaniment suggest mime, as if the singer were dancing or gesturing.

Op. 27, the next group of songs, comprises genre pictures; songs 4–6 are translations from Ukrainian and Polish. No. 1 resets Ogaryov's "At Bedtime" (above, p. 33) into a recitative-like opening invoking both rest at the end of the day and prayer, a hybrid of aria and hymn laid out in strophes, one asking blessings and the next forgiveness of sin. Except for word painting (the drooping line at 7–8 connoting weariness at the end of the day) and a distinctive motif at the close (bars 57–59), the prayer is carried by the strong vocal line, fervent in its nearly continuous delivery of the verses. Within B-flat minor, Tchaikovsky makes striking chord inflections on E (at "tears of silent love") and D (at "if only by a dream").

In "Look, the cloud there!" (no. 2), Grekov contrasts a bright cloud, radiant and beautiful, likened to the beloved, with a solitary storm cloud, dark and threatening, likened to the singer. Tchaikovsky sets the first and third verses darkly, with a cautious, constricted accompaniment oddly suited to the silver cloud in the pure sky. The second and fourth verses, which liken the clouds to people, are appropriately more expansive, but do not deliver the song from a certain strangeness of effect in the low tessitura at the vocal cadence.

Tchaikovsky built Fet's childlike "Do not leave me!" in no. 3 around simple metaphors of continuity—the constant, flowing accompaniment spurred on by gentle dissonances. The music quickens and modulates in the second verse, "Closer to one another than we . . . cannot be," and the piano adopts a palpitating rhythm. But in the third, with its hint of doubt ("Even if you came before me / your head inclining sadly"), he eschews a descriptive response in favor of the prevailing sentiment, "I am so joyful with you."

In Mey's "Evening" (no. 4), after Shevchenko, a mother who wishes to speak with her daughter falls asleep while putting the other children to bed. Tchaikovsky paints the buzzing beetles (at bar 3), portrays the chatter of the girls coming home (11–14) and the busy activity of dinner (15–19), then slows the rhythm and droops the voice to convey the mother dropping off (28–29). At the end, the girls' talking and the nightingale's trill show how the night silence was broken.

"Did my mother bear me for great sorrow?" (no. 5) is about a young woman pressured to marry whose beloved has gone off to the army. The song is marked *tempo di mazurka,* possibly in deference to Mickiewicz, possibly because mazurkas were traditionally sung and often dealt with the tribulations of love. The first line is subdued ("Did my mother bear me for great sorrow?"), but the second ("Or did a witch put a curse on my family nest?") is more insistent. A gentle folkishness informs the text in frequent pedal points and drones; a dance-like element attaches to the passages where the piano adopts flowing, consistent movement (e.g., 41–48).

No. 6, "My little favorite," unfolds in a rush of delighted words, at the prospect first of listening to and then of kissing the beloved. Tchaikovsky returns to *tempo di mazurka,* a folkish element easily lost without observing the phrasing precisely, as the voice unfolds in spans of 12 and of 23 bars. The song exists in two versions; in the first, the introduction is eight bars instead of four, and Tchaikovsky fashions the second verse to different, more operatic music, then reprises the first verse. In the second version, the voice part is strophic—the piano smartly rewritten—enhancing a sense of folkishness.

The dedicatees of op. 28 include the first Granddad Frost and Lel in *The Snow Maiden* and singers of *The Oprichnik* in Kiev. Here, as in op. 25, a short leap of imagination links each song to Tchaikovsky's own situation.

The singer refuses to identify the beloved in no. 1, "No, never shall I tell," because his passion is too great, a resolve challenged by outpourings of expression in the voice (operatic gestures at 13–14, 37) and constant echoing in the piano as a metaphor for intense feeling—the singer's thoughts unconstrained by the responsibilities of speech. In the middle, reference to hiding the agonies of love calls forth a more agitated accompaniment. Feeling is heightened further by fermatas in the reprise.

In "The Little Corals" (no. 2), a young Cossack goes off to battle. His sweetheart prays for his safe return and asks him for a string of coral beads. The battle is won; the corals appear as by divine intervention; the youth returns but the girl has died; he hangs the corals on the frame of an icon. In Tchaikovsky's setting, fanfares describe battle, an aggressive *Allegro con fuoco* is the lad racing back to his village. Declamation in the voice peaks when he learns of her death. Meanwhile, the opening motif in the piano, in reference to the little corals, works its way through the texture like a riff played on some folk instrument.

In no. 3, Mey's "Why?" the singer's dream of the distant beauty vanishes. Tchaikovsky divides the song into the prelude and postlude, emphasizing the home key and the central section bearing text, more chromatic in language and eschewing tonic cadence. The singer describes the dream, his emotions intensify at the ends of the verses, and the expression bursts out in irregular scansion, long-held high notes of operatic effect, or emphatic commentary in the piano. The postlude signals a return to the present, the singer stunned and angered.

In "He loved me so" (no. 4), a woman did not reciprocate love yet felt a "strange concern" in the beloved's presence—blushing and trying to please. She agreed to a tryst and then lost courage, pained and weeping. Simple devices convey the ambivalence: continuous dissonant chordal movement; contrapuntal interludes which suggest that the singer's unspoken thoughts are more complex than her spoken ones; and distinctive turns of vocal phrase, such as the rising line to cadence which spans a tritone melodically and comes to rest on a dissonance (at bars 8, 21, 42). By the end, the singer's emphatic repetition of "He loved me so" betrays regret.

Apukhtin's "Neither response, nor word, nor greeting" (no. 5) finds the singer's heart burdened that the past might vanish in anger and longing. The droning phrases of the introduction represent the longing and anger, the singer at the high point disallowing silence, shouting references to a forgotten song or a fallen star as if doing so will keep the past alive. Yet the droning phrases return; the world still separates the singer from the person being addressed.

In "The Fearful Moment" (no. 6), the beloved listens without emotion, making the singer, who is hoping for a decisive word, anxious and embarrassed. His declaration makes the beloved sigh and tremble and weep. Is it pity? He awaits a verdict. The first five notes of the introduction, recalling the opening of Schumann's *Dichterliebe,* form a mantra—of impatience or doubt—referring to "the fearful moment." Within the verses, frequent leaps and changes of direction in the voice convey anxiousness, offset by countermelodies in the right hand, conjunct and regular, as if some impulse within the singer were trying to maintain control.

Tchaikovsky's Third Symphony, from the summer of 1875, is the first for which an autograph score survives and the first he did not rewrite. A dedication to Vladimir Shilovsky is omitted in most editions [424, 77]. Errors in the printed score frustrated performance, about which Balakirev complained to Jurgenson as late as 1898 [23, 134]. The nickname "Polish," after the polonaise, is not Tchaikovsky's. Of all his symphonies, this one is the least conformative to preset schemes and may produce an impression of strangeness, especially of genre. It is not folkish, nor classical, nor Berliozian/Lisztian, nor particularly Tchaikovskian in light of his other symphonies.

Changing backgrounds on a tune, the introduction of the Third echoes that of the Second. This device typically employs a folk melody; here, it is a composed *tempo di marcia funebre.* The first area embeds a reprise (the opening theme returns at bar 127 after a contrasting theme at 95), moves on to an interim second area in B minor (143) and a closing in A major, a pattern echoed in movement I of the Fourth. Some of Tchaikovsky's themes suggest folk music: the short, jerky Allegro theme, the rhythmic modification of the folkish motif of the second area (143–46), and the balalaika sonority in pizzicato strings throughout the closing.

The five-movement format recalls the divertimento and makes us wonder if Tchaikovsky is alluding to the eighteenth century. He withholds the full resources of his large orchestra from time to time, mimicking a concerto grosso, the winds as concertino to the ripieno of the strings (mvt. I at 143; the principal waltz theme and Trio of mvt. II; the Trio of mvt. IV). The finale points out the distinction between divertimento and symphony. Integrated logic was not typical of the last movement of a divertimento, and Tchaikovsky addresses this problem by fortifying the polonaise with an uncharacteristic fugue and a grand reprise of the second theme (at 255), in the manner of a recapitulation. The result, more pretentious than a divertimento, less grand than a symphony, leaves the work's genre identity suspended in the breach.

A third query lies in the proximity of the Third Symphony to Tchaikovsky's suites. That the movements unfold without compelling internal logic enhances the suite-like element, freedom and beauty being their motivation. "Landscape or characteristic genre images predominate," wrote Keldïsh, "without wholeness of intensely developing dramatic thought" [193, 27]. The lovely peroration of movement III (at bar 68), a lyrical outpouring missing in the Second Symphony, is the expressive center of the entire work. Is the symphony a discourse or the play of sound? It revels in the moment.

Tchaikovsky redefines unity here with subtle connections and by altering local symmetries. The ABA of the movement I exposition is reduced to AB in the recapitulation; the ABA at the beginning of movement II is expanded to ABAB in the reprise. To compensate for this, he offers subtle cross-movement affirmations of theme. Among other examples, the triplet accompaniment in bar 10 of movement I recurs in the Trio of movement II, the bassoon solo of movement III, and variously in the finale (at bars 66, 120, and 245). The movement I introduction at 23 anticipates the theme of the movement IV Trio (204–6). These subtleties ensure that the Third does not lapse into miscellany, although the totality of connectives produces an eclectic unity far less monolithic than Beethoven's.

The historical significance of the Third may lie in its influence on a later composer: Gustav Mahler. In 1922, Boris Asafiev observed likenesses between Mahler and Tchaikovsky, and in 1941 Ivan Sollertinsky developed a typology of symphony in which Mahler and Tchaikovsky were distinguished from Beethoven by affinities of *Weltschmerz,* musical semantics, the treatment of melody, processes of elaboration, and occasionally the use of themes close enough to seem appropriated [28; 29]. Of however much Tchaikovsky that Mahler knew, there is no evidence that he knew the Third, yet easily imagined is his approval of its five-movement plan, suggestive musical ideas, and subtle thematic links between movements—which create the sense that one has heard something before without recalling where. In the slow movement, when the bassoon passes its melody to the oboe suddenly interrupted by the intrusive motif in thirds (bars 17–21), one may experience a shock of recognition, this undistinguished melodic fragment emerging from the musical void somewhere anterior to Mahler's primordial *Naturlaut.*

Tchaikovsky began his first complete ballet in August 1875 and finished it in April 1876. The following synopsis of *Swan Lake* is based on the libretto published in 1877, which passed the censor on 12 February; the text had already been published on 19 October 1876 in issue 100 of the Moscow newspaper *Teatral'naya gazeta.*

Act I. Prince Siegfried is celebrating his coming of age. Wine is flowing; his tutor, Wolfgang, flirts. Dances. A messenger announces the Princess, Siegfried's mother, who declares that he must marry and choose a bride the next day. She departs, and the party resumes. Night falls; a final dance. A flock of swans flies overhead; Siegfried and his friend Benno take up the hunt.

Act II. A mountainous locale near a lake; moonlight. A band of swans glides in the direction of a chapel ruin on the shore. Siegfried and Benno enter. Siegfried sees the swans, but they vanish when he takes aim. The men approach the mysteriously lit ruin, where they encounter Odette. She is the swan Siegfried just tried to kill; she is enchanted, transformed into a swan by day. Her grandfather, who lives nearby, protects her from the hatred of her stepmother, who at the lakeside takes the form of an owl. Until she marries, Odette's crown also protects her. Siegfried begs forgiveness. Odette's companions appear. Dances. Siegfried and Odette fall in love. Odette warns of her stepmother's wiles, but Siegfried swears to remain faithful to Odette the next day when he must choose a bride. They bid farewell. Dawn.

Act III. A magnificent ball. Guests arrive, then the Princess and Siegfried. Dances. Fanfares mark the arrival of new guests, the daughter of each family dancing with one of the cavaliers. After several such entrances the

Princess asks Siegfried his choice. He has none. Fanfares announce von Rothbart and his daughter Odile. Siegfried is taken with Odile's likeness to Odette, which Benno does not affirm; enchanted, Siegfried chooses her. As Rothbart gives Siegfried Odile's hand, the stage darkens; Rothbart turns into a demon, a window flies open, and a swan wearing a crown is seen. Siegfried flees.

Act IV. At the lakeside, Odette rejoins her companions and laments that she loves Siegfried even though he broke his vow. He arrives, and Odette agrees to see him one last time. A storm rises. Siegfried begs her forgiveness, but their situation is hopeless. As she attempts to retreat to the ruins, he takes her crown and throws it into the lake. Dying, Odette falls into Siegfried's arms, and they vanish in the waters. The storm quiets, the moon comes out, a band of white swans appears on the tranquil lake.

Ballet inspired by music is a twentieth-century conceit which obscures the genre's limited musical expression in earlier eras. Before Tchaikovsky, ballet comprised solo dance, ensemble dance, and music, not dance-sensitive, to accompany spectacle; of these, only the last had pretensions to portraying stage action. Solo dances were short and thin-textured, amenable to nuance in performance. An obbligato instrument often took the melody; this was typically a violin in a slow dance for the ballerina. Ensemble dances, especially of distinctive nationality, were dashing in sound but regular in rhythm to facilitate unison movement. As Kashkin noted (above, p. 102), Tchaikovsky preserved and enriched these distinctions.

Swan Lake calls for a sizable orchestra, a few instruments larger than Ludwig Minkus's for *La Bayadère,* first performed in St. Petersburg four weeks before *Swan Lake*'s premiere, and five more than the pit orchestra of *Tristan und Isolde.* Tchaikovsky orchestrated more artfully than Minkus, bolstering melody in solo dance with sound, as illustrated by the *pas de trois* (no. 4). The Andante sostenuto opens with a duet of oboe and bassoon (in canon, no less), which yields to strings and horns (at 25). Then the *allegro semplice* rises above the prevailing polka rhythm with color, leading off with the clarinet, passing to the flute and to the bassoon, then back to the clarinet and flute. Such elegant touches are too numerous to count in *Swan Lake.* Tchaikovsky's timbral variety transformed how audiences listened to ballet. If his sonorities are a tour de force, so is his skill in *musique dansante.* In no. 13/V, a *pas d'action* adapted from his opera *Undine,* he begins with a harp cadenza and maintains a sparse texture in the main sections, giving the principal melody to a violin soloist following a conductor whose beat, in turn, conforms to the dancers' movements. Style and texture suggest that the main sections were danced by soloists, passages in regular rhythm (*più mosso*) by the ensemble. The clear but lilting rhythm is *dansante* in the latter, while in the solo passages it resides in melodic details, rhythmic flexibility, and the propensity to be fitted to bodily movement.

Coherence in *Swan Lake* surpassed that of specialist ballet and was concentrated in the narrative music. The introduction sets out a sonority (the oboe, associated with Odette) and a rhythm (of the so-called swan theme) that are both meaningful to the composition at large. The oboe returns at Odette's first appearance onstage (at bar 48 of no. 11) and her last (at 27 of no. 29). At the end of act I (no. 9, finale), we first hear the swan theme, with its distinctive rhythm, as a flock of swans flies overhead. The evocation of atmosphere was unprecedented in specialist ballet music:

Ex. 17

This theme recurs, varied, in every act. Local coherence runs through no. 13, the Dances of the Swans, of act II, where the initial waltz occurs three times, forming a ritornello. The third presentation follows and is affected by the *pas d'action* in its key (pulling it down from A major to A-flat major) and rhythm (the motif of the *più mosso,* here to nervous effect). The melody of Odette's solo in no. 13/II recurs in the interludes of the love duet, though the meaning of this allusion is obscure without knowledge of the stage action. Tonality in *Swan Lake* is associative, with the swans at one extreme of a tritone (B minor) and the evil genie at the other (F minor). E major in its association with Odette and G-flat major (the enharmonic dominant of B minor) as the key of her *pas d'action* with Siegfried thus fall—metaphorically—within the gravitational pull of the swans. That these relationships organize complex music is more relevant than the fact that they may not be obvious to the ear.

Before 17 December 1875, Tchaikovsky wrote a celebratory Chorus for the Jubilee of O. A. Petrov, a venerable bass singer of the Imperial Russian Opera, to the following text:

> Touching the heart of man, giving pleasure unalloyed,
> Your voice, a half-century unsilenced, is the singer-bogatïr's magic gift!
> Weaken not in the yoke of advanced years! Thousands upon thousands
> Of loving hearts, deeply touched, give thanks, singer, to you!
> Embodying Russian art in the sound of life, passion, beauty,
> You bring work, love and creativity to its altar!

This is a *slava,* or ritual greeting, in call-and-response format, preceded by fanfares embedded in a 13-bar orchestral introduction. Clear melodic lines based on the opening verse project the words cleanly. Choral responses mimic a tenor soloist.

The String Quartet no. 3, in E-flat minor, from January–February 1876, like the Second, features expanded formal patterns, Beethovenian progress from problematical first movement to streamlined finale, with added extramusical significance emerging from the memorial dedication to Ferdinand Laub, Tchaikovsky's colleague at the Moscow Conservatory. If we discount the parts of the 629-bar first movement devoted to lament and peroration—the introduction, extended transition analogy, and post-recapitulation—the length and proportion of the subsections are nearly Mozartian. The rarified effect of the opening phrases in contrary motion, the distinctive headmotif of the theme that follows (at 9–10), the unabashed funeral march (at 21), and the accented intrusion of duple time (at 37)—all in the introduction—provide the much-transformed motivic stuff of the *Allegro moderato.* Making the recapitulation arch-like by return of the funeral march, Tchaikovsky reshaped the classical pattern and emphasized memorial expression.

After this, the wispy second movement almost lacks identity; it lightens the mood before the gravity of the third. The rapidly unfolding textures recall the First Piano Concerto (mvt. II, introduction to the middle section). Are the *sforzandi* at the end of the phrase—ad hoc, not on point tonally—another recollection of the so-called mystery chords in Beethoven's first "Razumovsky"? The key of movement II—B-flat—echoes the opening of movement I and is the key of the Scherzo in Beethoven's op. 59, no. 1. Movements III and IV of this work parallel the Second Quartet in structure—both are complex rondos—and in the progression from high seriousness to robust convention. The slow movement is explicit in its deathly accents, including a nearly operatic funeral march with a distinctive Scotch snap on the last half of the bar:

Ex. 18

The most graphic funereal expression in the Quartet comes with the second theme (at 28), where the organum-like perfect intervals emulate a choir and the second violin mimics a priest's recitation tone. These ancient and mysterious accents were too strong for the rondo pattern: Tchaikovsky immediately lightens the expressive weight in the middle section (first at 40–41) and excuses this churchly music from reprise until the end of the movement (at 114).

The emphatically duple finale relieves the triple rhythms of the other movements. The main themes are folkish, until the second part of the C section (at 142). This new motif is elaborated throughout the middle of the movement and returns at the end in a classic Beethovenian manner. The music slows to a *quasi andante* (at 314), then a fermata, then on to a Beethovenian jest, increased in tempo to a *vivace.* To finish thus is difficult to imagine in the absence of Beethoven's op. 95 or the *Waldstein* Sonata.

The Seasons: 12 Character Pieces, op. 37b, were composed between December 1875 and May 1876 and were published, one each month, in the music journal *Nouvelliste* from January to December 1876, headed by titles (suggested by the editor) and epigraphs from celebrated poets. They were collected in a single edition by the end of 1876, and Jurgenson republished them in 1885. Tchaikovsky received the titles after composing (all were printed in *Nouvelliste* before the first music), so his expression may be unrelated to the poetry.

In *The Seasons,* he favored more direct language than in opp. 19 and 21. Lyric melodies and dance rhythms predominate. Structures are thematically rounded but open to complex, mosaic-like patterns. He favored varied reprise, indulged coloristic sonorities, and standardized texture, including a contrapuntal elaboration whereby motifs exchange hands, move to middle or low registers immediately following the melodic voice, or middle voices form a counterpoint in longer notes or contrasting motifs as a grace to the *facture.* This produces a broken style, a many-layered counterpoint without continuous individual voices.

Expression is most direct in September, "The Hunt," which is built on the motif of hunting horns. In February, "Máslenitsa"—the carnival or so-called Shrovetide Fair—Tchaikovsky caught the variegated roistering of the fairgrounds in gesture, phrase, and rhythm, often dance-like and abrupt, sometimes clowning in melodic inversion. In July, "The Reaper's Song," the energetic theme at 14, across the beat, has a sense of repeated labor. August, "The Harvest," is subtler: frenetic rhythm symbolizes the activity of harvesters, followed by a theme suggestive of rest. The accented pitches of November, "Troika," recall sleigh bells, later motifs the clatter of horses' hooves. In December, "Noël," a sentimental waltz conjures up the image of a young girl dancing with her uncle or grandfather, while

October, "Autumn Song," resonates with Alexey Tolstoy's words about a crumbling garden and yellowed leaves tossed in the wind.

The rest are more indirect. March, "The Song of the Lark," despite an epigraph extolling fields full of flowers and waves of light, yields to Tchaikovsky's darker mood, and in June, "Barcarolle," nothing about the gloomy principal theme hints at a Venetian gondolier's song. In April, "Snowdrop," Tchaikovsky alludes to Mendelssohn, and he refers to Schumann in May, "May Nights," without obvious motivation. January, "By the Hearth," is accompanied by lines from Pushkin:

And the little corner of peaceful comfort
The night has clothed in twilight,
The little fire sputters in the hearth,
And the candle is burnt down.

Taking the first 10 bars as symbolic of the corner by the hearth, its various continuations represent the reverie at twilight with the fire nearly out, and they return periodically to revive awareness with the opening theme. Telling is the motif first at *meno mosso,* brief and defined, which fades into arpeggios only to return like a thought that will not go away.

The celebrated *Marche slave,* op. 31, from September 1876, has been altered in the *Collected Works* [CW 24, 149; bars 123–24 of the piece; and 171–73; bars 202–10], omitting Tchaikovsky's quotation of the imperial national hymn, which has been banished to an appendix [CW 24, 329–36]. In the composer's day, it soon became a concert work: it is compact and exudes atmosphere from somber beginning to victorious end. It is based on three Serbian folk songs (at bars 5, 86, 102), cast into two strophes by the imperial Russian hymn, which effectively divides the piece.

Tchaikovsky was at his best in this orchestration. The second Serbian theme stands out for the effectiveness of the sound: first, clarinets and bassoons on a cushion of low strings in repeated notes, then trumpets and trombones, then flutes and piccolo, with the horns coming in jauntily on offbeats. Tchaikovsky's handling of loudness is most effective when it joins forces with clear texture, as at 66, where winds and strings play the opening theme while brass and percussion mark the rhythm within the bar, producing two strong, well-differentiated lines. In the continuation of the national hymn (at bar 213), he assigns the melody to the trumpets and trombones and the rest of the orchestra to the rhythm.

Composed in October and November 1876, *Francesca da Rimini,* op. 32, followed a synopsis that Tchaikovsky wrote at the head of the autograph score [91, 182–84; 372, 17–19], which is supplemented here with bar lines in parentheses (canto V of *The Inferno,* sometimes printed with the score, is far less faithful to the music):

Dante, accompanying Virgil's shade, enters the second circle of hell's abyss (1). The air is filled with groans, howls, and cries of despair (17). Amid the sepulchral darkness, a storm bursts forth and rages (67). The hellish whirlwind tears along inexhaustible, carrying in its wild swirl the souls of people whose reason was obscured in life by love's passion (139). Out of the countless multitude of whirling human specters, Dante's attention is especially drawn to the beautiful ghosts of Francesca and Paolo, tossed about in each other's embrace. Shaken by the vision of the young spirits, which torments his soul, Dante summons them and asks them for what sin they have been subjected to such a terrible punishment (295).

Francesca's shade, flowing with tears, tells her sad story (333, 368). She loved Paolo, but was married against her will to her beloved's hateful brother, the hunchbacked, one-eyed, vengeful Rimini. Her forced marriage could not banish Francesca's tender passion for Paolo. Once, they were reading the tale of Lancelot (414). "We were alone," Francesca relates, "and we read, fearing nothing. Often we grew pale and our embarrassed glances met. But one instant destroyed us both (463). When, at last, happy Lancelot takes his first lover's kiss, he, from whom nothing will separate me, lingering kissed my trembling mouth, and the book, having first revealed to us the secret of love, fell out of our hands!"

At this moment, Francesca's spouse had unexpectedly entered and stabbed her and Paolo (504). And, having told this, Francesca, in the embrace of her Paolo, is again carried off by the ceaseless and wildly disruptive whirlwind (520). Struck by eternal pity, Dante grows faint, loses consciousness, and falls, as if dead (654).

Laroche called *Francesca* "extraordinarily brilliant," noting that the "blinding play of the orchestral colors, inexhaustibly rich and incessantly changing, holds the listener from beginning to end as if held sway by some hallucination" [255 II 95]. Others have praised the orchestration for special effects—"timbral dramaturgy" [399, 440]—which place extraordinary combinations of instruments and unusual registrations in constant support of representation. These include, among many others, scoring the gates-of-hell imagery at the beginning with bassoon, tam-tam, and brass, *piano,* to create a darkly evil coloration.

Tchaikovsky admitted a "probable" indebtedness to Wagner in *Francesca* [vii 201], revealed in the undisguised Wagnerian sonorities in the work (at 511–19). The composer's visit to Bayreuth in 1876 notwithstanding, any Wagnerian connection might give way to Liszt, whose *Dante-Szimfónia* Tchaikovsky heard on 21 March 1875 and reviewed four days later. He wrote:

> In the first movement, which represents all the horrors of the underworld, there is much imagination, much sombre coloration which corresponds to the story, many loud and powerful external effects but little invention. . . . The middle episode of this part, which represents the love languor of Francesca and Paolo, is not without warmth and passion, but is too similar to many other such episodes in Liszt's works. [83, 268]

Everything about *Francesca* suggests invention, newness, organic connection, and concision—all, perhaps, in answer to Liszt.

By the recurrence of the opening theme, subdued thematic contrast, casting Francesca's narrative in variations, his dependence on adynamic strophic structures, and, not least, organizing the entire work around a single tonal center—E minor for the inferno and E major for Francesca's narrative—Tchaikovsky resisted dynamic change. "A certain passivity" that has been claimed for the love music [372, 45] enhances the impression of a profound consistency, nonmovement at the deepest level, regardless of the "infernal storm [that] roars and lashes about, like an ocean storm of Aivazovsky" [255 II 95]. In the hyperbolic love music, Tchaikovsky affirmed his sympathy for those who yield to their emotions despite the consequences. More than the dazzling inferno music, this was the centerpiece of *Francesca* in both location and pertinence.

The genesis of the *Variations on a Rococo Theme,* for cello and orchestra, op. 33, is obscure. Tchaikovsky drafted a finished version of the *Variations* in a cello-piano arrangement [CW 55-b], the full score corresponding to it elsewhere in the *Collected Works* [CW 30-b]. He showed it to the work's dedicatee, Wilhelm Fitzenhagen, who altered the cello part—in pitch, dynamic, agogic accent, phrasing, and fingering—directly on the manuscript and on strips of paper pasted onto it. Tchaikovsky apparently orchestrated the *Variations* from this modified cello-piano version. This score is wholly in Tchaikovsky's hand except the solo part, which, from the sixth bar of variation 1, was written in by Fitzenhagen, who also indicated critical changes to be made later in publication [CW 55-b, xi–xii]. A Soviet edition of the cello-piano version in Fitzenhagen's arrangement, edited by A. P. Stogorsky under the rubric "Author's Redaction," was published in Moscow in 1954, the full score in 1973. The standard version of the *Variations* is a second, more radical revision made by Fitzenhagen under circumstances now obscure. In it, he omitted one variation, relocated others, introduced repeats in another variation, and changed other details. All commercial editions except as noted, beginning with Jurgenson's in 1878, transmit this version of the music.

The word *rococo* applied to this work suggests that the *Variations* were Tchaikovsky's first nominal gesture toward eighteenth-century music. The Mozartian orchestra (though with clarinets and oboes) hints at this, as does the regular duple phrasing of the theme, for which (but not for the variations) he claimed a rococo quality. What was he attempting to do? In the orchestral introduction, even before the theme, he hints at some special expression:

Ex. 19

Abstract music does not behave like this; comic operatic music does. The gestural phrasing, seconded by the rising chromatic bass and its echo in the winds, mimics a lackey adjusting his master's hat. Its continuation in *pizzicati* strings and a horn solo, whose insipid tune languishes for seven unaccompanied bars as if unaware of playing beyond its cue, is a caricature of entrance music. And with this, we hear the arrival of the cellist/*bourgeois gentilhomme* and the beginning of the theme, whose stylistic propriety conveys the sense of someone striving for pristine elocution. The soloist has hardly finished before the winds blow his snobbish cover with bucolic sounds in eighteenth-century timbral code, with their drone and bassoon in octaves.

Tchaikovsky's introduction and theme support the imagery of actors looking ridiculous in powdered wigs. The stage set, he begins with variations audibly related to the theme, vignettes enlivened by our bumpkin whose theatrical airs project the music-structural aspects of the work. Tchaikovsky takes care not to let the *Variations* descend into slapstick. The solo cadenzas and pensive variations accomplish this with music distanced from the theme yet requiring some special interpretation, especially the cadenza at the end of variation II, which leads to the nonconformative variation III. Advancing both musical and theatrical lines of thought, he shows our fictional character's pensive side and offers a first, serious peroration on the theme as melody. When cadenza or peroration comes in midvariation, as in IV and V, a formal tension develops, of which variation V is the high point because its asymmetrical components juxtapose references to the theme with theatrical digressions. Variation VI begins to resolve the tension in its fidelity to the theme, then breaks in midstream for yet another cadenza, this one recalling Violetta's vocalizing before her cabaletta in *La Traviata*. After this *bizarrie,* Tchaikovsky shifts to the lovely variation VII in C major; its lyric outpouring is the dramatic pause, the upbeat to the finale, which in turn is based on a diminution of the opening motifs of the work.

Applied to music with two simultaneous layers of meaning, Fitzenhagen's later revision was a disaster. He rendered Tchaikovsky's concept incoherent, in part by placing historically proper repeats in either half of the theme. His relocation of variations produced a Liszt-reminiscent, all-movements-in-one imitation: variation VII became variation III, to serve as a kind of slow movement; the original variation IV, Tchaikovsky's vehicle of formal tension, was placed at the end, as if it were resolving, whereas Tchaikovsky's own ending, variation VIII, was simply dropped. The fanciful aspect of the *Variations* may explain why Tchaikovsky did nothing to rehabilitate the original. In light of his recent failure in comedy with *Vakula,* having to explain theatrical witticism was a humiliation even greater than subjecting his music to mutilation. Instead, he gave it up and made a present of his original manuscript to Anatoly Brandukov, from whom comes a story about Pablo Casals, who programmed the *Variations* and then withdrew them. To Brandukov's query as to why, Casals answered, "I cannot find the form in this piece, there is something lacking" [438, 36].

Of the numerous Jurgenson editions about which Tchaikovsky complained of errors, the *Valse-scherzo,* op. 34, from early 1877, elicited a strong protest for "completely impossible misprints" and "distortions for which I am not responsible" [vii 354]. A manuscript copy with the composer's corrections (which departs from published versions) reveals a dedication to *Eduard* Kotek, presumably Josef's real first name, and six additional measures in Tchaikovsky's hand at the end of the piece [97, 88]. Vasily Bezekirsky's edition is a mutilation in its own right.

The origins of the piece are obscure [348]. Judging from Kotek's letters to Tchaikovsky [96, 323], the composer promised to write him something as early as January 1877 (Tchaikovsky's letter describing his love for Kotek was dated 19 January). It is thought to have been composed about then. If the *Sérénade mélancolique* claimed its origins in song, the *Valse-scherzo* claims its origin in dance. One may speak of key and of pattern—the rounded reprise with rondo-like sections—but the point of the piece is bravura for the soloist, which echoes some virtuoso country fiddler. Like the *Sérénade mélancolique,* it is full of difficult ways to present simple ideas and demanding cadenzas which give them heft.

CHAPTER NINE

1877: The Year of Tchaikovsky's Marriage

THE YEAR 1877 DIVIDES TCHAIKOVSKY'S ADULT LIFE, FALLING 16 years after he achieved majority and 16 years before he died. That year his health, outlook, finances, artistic freedom, and composition were all affected. And yet his marriage, which happened during that year, remains obscure. Modest leapt deftly over it in *The Life,* leaving the impression of some woeful secret:

> I cannot set out in detail the whole sad history of the consequences of this marriage, first as I lack the requisite impartiality, second as I don't have in hand either the evidence *altera pars* or the possibility of ever ascertaining it, and third, wishing not to offend the rightful punctiliousness of many persons still alive. I shall say only that from the first days, even the first hours of Pyotr Ilyich's marriage he paid heavily for the flippancy and madness of his deed, and was profoundly unhappy. [1997 II 21]

Perhaps Modest's disclaimers should be allowed after his antimatrimonial arguments. Perhaps Pyotr gave offense by advising Modest to alter his inclinations and, among the family, informing him of the marriage last. In any event, one day (according to Modest), Pyotr received a letter from a woman who claimed to love him, which led him to propose within weeks. Modest cited nothing from May 1877, when they met and became engaged, nor did he explain why Anatoly, who was informed two weeks in advance, could not stop this "utterly mindless step." The nervous attack that Tchaikovsky suffered in St. Petersburg in September was bogus; to call the newlyweds' problems an "abyss of mutual misunderstanding" was obfuscatory. Modest's account, where not confected, vastly simplified the events, some ignoble, in which he himself was deeply implicated.

Reviewing *The Life* in 1902, Kashkin disputed Modest's account of the marriage, arguing that Tchaikovsky was "responding to some degree unconsciously to the external world around him" [MV020611]. Unable to take responsibility for it, he would attribute his marriage to *fatum*. Kashkin wrote a last memoir about the composer's marriage in 1918 [175], recalling a long discussion with him. Some modern opinions hold that he was lying in this memoir, that he knew Tchaikovsky and his future wife were acquainted in Pyotr's jurist years and that she may even have been a crush of his [407, 46–47]. From Tchaikovsky's wife, Antonina Milyukova herself, survive two memoirs and 16 letters to her husband between 1877 and 1889—reprinted or first published in a biography by Valery Sokolov, who presents the marriage, from her point of view in part, as a struggle against a brutish coalition of Tchaikovsky's henchmen [365]. Critiquing *The Life,* Nikolay Findeisen observed that Modest made no reference to Antonina's memoirs, the veracity of which stood unchallenged. Acknowledging the composer's nervous state in the autumn of 1877, Findeisen argued (in dispute of Modest) that marriage was not its cause, but rather the last dissonance that triggered it, the real reasons being Pyotr's teaching at the Moscow Conservatory and the circumstances of his life in general. Meanwhile, Findeisen cited Antonina's claim that others insisted that family life would kill Tchaikovsky's talent [RMG 1902/26–27, cols. 643–50; 365, 269]. Tchaikovsky's letters to her apparently do not survive; those to his brothers about the marriage have been heavily censored.

Tchaikovsky had been acquainted with Antonina for years before she wrote to him in 1877, as her brother had married the sister of one of Tchaikovsky's friends from the School of Jurisprudence [vi 144]. This couple lived near the Moscow Conservatory, where Antonina was once a student (she had also matriculated, in 1869–1870, at the Petersburg Conservatory [368, 243–44]). She wrote her first courtship letter to him sometime in late March 1877, after six weeks of daily prayer [365, 19]. He read it on 5 April, found it to be warm and sincere, and decided to respond [vi 144]. She claimed to have loved him for several years and to realize that he was too shy to propose [365, 265]. Unless she was the rankest opportunist, something made her think he might have feelings for her. At least two more letters followed before her first surviving one, dated 4 May. Her tone was sober; she was beginning to restrain her feelings in response to his admonition to do so. Tchaikovsky had apparently mentioned needing money, and she reported an expected inheritance of 10,000 rubles. Yet he dismissed her in a letter that day to Anatoly without mentioning her name. Might Anatoly have recognized it?

> The candidates for matrimony change every minute—but I cannot choose. One young woman even offered me hand and heart in a letter, explaining that she has loved me passionately for three years. In her letter she promised to be my "slave," adding that she has ten thousand [rubles] in capital. I once saw her and remember that she is pretty but unpleasant. Consequently I refused her peremptorily. [365, 23]

His financial need was manifest in five letters to his new correspondent, Nadezhda von Meck, in the first three days of May. He asked her for 3,000 rubles to deliver him from a "very, very wretched situation." It would take too long to explain (he wrote), but indebtedness was poisoning his life and paralyzing his inclination to work. What was this situation? And why was he borrowing again in three weeks' time? [vi 138, n. 2]. On 3 May, Meck sent him the 3,000 rubles. If money were the issue, why did he continue courting Antonina once he had it? Was he following the lead of Vladimir Shilovsky, whom he visited on 3 May, planning to marry to rehabilitate his reputation? If so, why did he keep it secret? And what of his passion for Josef Kotek (above, pp. 102–103)? On 4 May, Tchaikovsky was dismayed at Kotek for having taken up with a woman [365, 28]. By that date, a peculiar mélange found Antonina writing to him lovingly, Meck showing affection in the way she did best, and Tchaikovsky fretting over his love for another man.

Whatever her promise to behave, Antonina continued to be flirtatious. She claimed to have rejected a man who had loved her for the last five years and said that she was dying with anguish to see Tchaikovsky. In a famous passage, she wrote, "I cannot live without you and therefore soon, perhaps, I shall put an end to myself" [365, 221]. Posterity has construed this as a suicide threat, a conclusion encouraged by Tchaikovsky's later remarks to Meck:

> From the next letter I concluded that if, going so far, I suddenly turned my back on this young woman, I would make her truly unhappy, and lead her to

> a tragic end. Thus a difficult alternative was presented to me: to retain my freedom at the cost of this woman's destruction ("destruction" here being not an idle term: she in fact loves me without reservation), or to marry. I could not but choose the latter. [vi 145]

Yet in her next letter, Antonina retracted her extravagance: "Although I wrote many stupidities in my last letters, be assured that in fact I am not that bold, and could never permit myself to do that" [365, 223].

Tchaikovsky and Antonina met in person on 20 May 1877. He proposed three days later. She accepted, and the couple saw each other every day until 29 May, when he left for Konstantin Shilovsky's estate at Glebovo to work on *Evgeniy Onegin*. On 23 June, he informed Anatoly and his father of the engagement. Only after returning to Moscow at the end of the month, with barely a week before the ceremony, did he inform others: Meck on 3 July; Lev, Sasha, and Modest on 5 July; and Vladimir Shilovsky on his wedding day: "I am entering into marriage not without agitation and alarm, and yet with full confidence that it is necessary, and that it is better to do this now, when some remnants of youth remain, than later" [vi 150]. Only Ilya rejoiced:

> Praise God!! May the Lord bless you! I do not doubt that the person you have chosen deserves such an epithet as you have won from your father—an old man of 83, and from all my family, and indeed, from all of humankind who knows you.
>
> So I embrace you, then, kiss you and bless you. [1997 II 21]

The secrecy of Tchaikovsky's engagement may have been rooted in his resistance to submitting to the will of others and irritation at their intervention, although once he sensed his error he tried to deflect blame from himself. To Meck on 3 July, he claimed that, by so little as visiting Antonina, he had committed himself to marriage. Yet Tchaikovsky's regret and his brother Anatoly's pressure to seek a divorce are easily as responsible for Pyotr's subsequent anguish as anything Antonina ever said or did. On 6 July 1877, Tchaikovsky and Antonina were married in Moscow at the Church of St. George on Malaya Nikitskaya Street by Father Dmitry Vasilievich Razumovsky, the composer's colleague at the Moscow Conservatory. Anatoly and Kotek were Tchaikovsky's witnesses. Antonina remembered the day: a satin cloth on which she was supposed to stand had been forgotten, a bad omen; Pyotr and Anatoly left after the ceremony, sending a carriage for the others later to bring them to the wedding dinner at the Hotel Hermitage, described by one guest as "gloomy as a funeral"; after dinner, the parties returned to their quarters, to meet again at the train station at 7:00 p.m. for the newlyweds' departure for St. Petersburg, where Antonina met Ilya and members of the composer's circle.

At first there was little sign of tension over conjugal intimacy. To Anatoly Tchaikovsky recounted his anxieties when boarding the train in Moscow, but Prince Meshchersky got on at Klin and arranged a separate sleeping compartment for him. As a result:

> *In connection with deflowering her* absolutely nothing happened. I did not make the attempt, for I knew that until I finally get back to being myself, it makes no difference, nothing would come of it. But we had conversations which still further explained our mutual relations. *She agreed with everything absolutely and will never be dissatisfied.*

To this, he added, "I feel that it will not be long before I calm down permanently," and to Modest he went a step further: "I still cannot say that I love her, but I already feel that I shall love her as soon as we get used to each other" [369, 124].

By 9 July, Tchaikovsky had established a degree of intimacy with Antonina, making him feel "incomparably freer in relation to her" [369, 124]. But writing to Anatoly on the 11th, he had not renewed "the attack" because she had become "unconditionally offensive," though he still imagined a time when he would try and succeed [369, 131]. Other remarks suggest that he was reconciling himself with his situation: she is "very limited," but that is all right; she obeys him blindly, is well built, is satisfied with everything, and wants nothing except the happiness of being a support and consolation [vi 153; 369, 124]. Granting Tchaikovsky's anxiety in these difficult days, his letters betray neither sexual crisis—why, if he had secured Antonina's agreement to a platonic marriage, was he so committed to physical union?—nor any grating idiosyncrasy in her that would diminish his resolve to stay married.

That Tchaikovsky inclined to nervous upset and mood swings is clear from his letters. On 13 July, he claimed being "forever damaged" and suffering "unbearable spiritual agonies." And yet,

> the most horrible moment of the day began when I was alone with my wife in the evening. Having embraced, I began to walk around with her. Suddenly

I was feeling peaceful and satisfied. . . . I don't understand how this happened! Nevertheless, from this moment suddenly everything around brightened up and I felt that, whoever my wife was, *she is my wife* and in this there is something completely normal and as it should be. . . . For the first time I fell asleep today without a feeling of despair and hopelessness. My wife is not offensive to me in any way. I am already beginning to respond to her, like any husband who does not love his wife. But mostly, today I am already no longer shy with her, do not take her time with conversations and am completely tranquil. [365, 35]

After a week in St. Petersburg, the couple returned to Moscow, where, for domestic necessities, Tchaikovsky turned to Meck again for money. On 17 July, they visited Antonina's mother at Klin and learned of a delay and a reduction in Antonina's inheritance. On 26 July, he left Moscow for Kamenka, on the pretext of going south to take the waters. Antonina stayed in Moscow to set up house. What happened in the next six weeks was probably more complicated than the record shows. His brothers, especially Anatoly, developed a strategy to derail Pyotr's commitment to his marriage: reassert influence, vilify Antonina, and agitate the anxieties to which he was particularly vulnerable. The discernible facts are consistent with this hypothesis:

- After a few weeks of enforced cohabitation, Tchaikovsky was pining for his bachelor's life. In intimate letters, he made no reference to a sexual component in his unhappiness.
- In Kamenka, he began to compose and relished his freedom. The more he did, the more his resolve to make the marriage succeed diminished, a change surely encouraged by his brothers. By summer's end, a plan to separate Tchaikovsky from his wife had been conceived.
- Returning to Moscow, Tchaikovsky found it easy to be disenchanted with Antonina. Events themselves or his awareness of the plan produced anxiety, which led to a trip to St. Petersburg and escape to Western Europe at the end of September.
- In Switzerland with Anatoly, Tchaikovsky's attitude about Antonina changed from provisionally sympathetic to sharply negative by the middle of October. Henceforth, he rejected reconciliation. The tensions of this situation caused genuine emotional upset.
- Meanwhile, Meck regularized her financial support for him and stood ready to support a divorce. Tchaikovsky was able to withdraw from teaching.

He could have predicted a nostalgia for bachelorhood. He wrote to Sasha:

> I have become too used to bachelor life, and cannot recall my loss of freedom without regret. . . . Nevertheless, one cannot but give my wife her due; she does everything to please me, is always satisfied, makes no complaint and demonstrates in every way that I am the sole interest in her life. She is in any event a good and loving woman. [vi 158]

To Konstantin Shilovsky, he raised the possibility that he had erred:

> I need to be alone to assess my situation from a distance and decide whether in the end I acted well or stupidly. God knows, I don't know this now. Of my wife I shall tell you only this: she is doing everything to please me, and does not inhibit me in the least; she is very delicate and devoted. If I conclude that a bachelor's freedom is better than being married, then my wife will not have been the least guilty in this. [vi 159–60]

The change in Tchaikovsky's attitude may be observed in letters to Meck. On 26 July, he wrote, "A few more days, and *I swear to you,* I would have gone insane" [vi 160]. From Kiev two days later, Tchaikovsky claimed that right after the wedding Antonina was hateful to him, and being inseparable made it worse. Yet she was not to blame, which made it cruel of him to reveal that he did not love her and obligatory to pretend that he did. He contemplated suicide, but that was inconsistent with familial affection, and he loved life anyway and wanted to compose, as he had not yet said all that he could [vi 161–62]. But he faced a dilemma: breaking with Antonina would lose any gain in public image and increase the very suspicions he had hoped to allay, while the status quo was an agony of hypocrisy causing friction between him and his siblings.

In the six surviving letters from the summer of 1877, Tchaikovsky hardly referred to Antonina in the two to Anatoly [vi 172; 88, 293]. In the four to Meck, he referred to "my wife" or "new obligation" as he discussed music, lamented his illness, and objectified the mental state in which he married. On 30 August, he continued to write of salvaging his marriage [vi 170]. Earlier, on 11 August, he had been self-deprecating:

> I must confess I have displayed an unaccustomed faintheartedness and a total lack of courage in my ordeal. Now I am ashamed that I could so lose heart and

give way to such dark nervous agitation. Please forgive me for having caused you alarm and concern. I am *quite* sure that I shall emerge victorious from this rather difficult and ticklish situation. I shall have to overcome my feeling of alienation towards my wife and learn to appreciate the good qualities which she undoubtedly possesses. [vi 166]

We cannot know if his declaration was sincere or conditioned by a courtier's wish to please. Anatoly was there, and the two no doubt strategized how to regain Pyotr's freedom. Events after Tchaikovsky returned to Moscow were too staged to be spontaneous, which supports the contention that a rescue plan much like the following was conceived that summer:

- He would introduce Antonina to his circle there.
- Something would justify a trip to St. Petersburg, where a health crisis would require the composer's recuperation in Europe.
- Antonina would be persuaded to leave Moscow to meet her husband, but in fact would be abandoned in Odessa, three days' travel in the opposite direction, after Ippolit Tchaikovsky informed her of Pyotr's permanent separation from her, with assurances of her maintenance.
- Meanwhile, Tchaikovsky and Anatoly will have proceeded to Switzerland, Pyotr taking a year off from the Moscow Conservatory. He would protest the marriage, prepare the ground for a divorce, and be restored to a bachelor's existence.

The premeditated involvement in this plan of anyone besides Pyotr, Ippolit, Anatoly, and Modest cannot be established. Ilya was not told; Sasha did not know in advance; Pyotr surely counted on the generosity of Nadezhda von Meck, though not, apparently, as a party to the scheme. His letters to her continued for a time in the same newsy mode as those of August.

Tchaikovsky found it difficult to leave Kamenka, repeatedly delaying his departure until 7 September. That day Anatoly reported a curious incident: "In Tula, Tolstoy was sitting in the train. . . . He asked, incidentally, whether that person was your wife about whom you were speaking to him a year ago in terms of a young woman whom you liked and wanted to marry" [vi 172, n. 4]. "A year ago" would have been September 1876, the height of Tchaikovsky's resolve to marry and eight months before

Antonina's first letter. Tchaikovsky returned to Moscow on 11 September. To Meck, he wrote nothing of Antonina other than to praise the apartment she had prepared and alluded to escaping someplace [vi 175]. But to Anatoly: "I know that I must endure a little, whereupon, unnoticed, tranquility, satisfaction, and, who knows, perhaps even happiness will come. Now I dream of the trip to Petersburg, which must certainly happen soon, but I still cannot determine when!" [vi 177]. On 14 September, Kotek wrote of counting the days and hours before Tchaikovsky's arrival in the northern capital [365, 40]. People knew.

The only reported occasion on which Tchaikovsky and Antonina were seen together between 11 and 24 September 1877 was the name-day celebration for Jurgenson's wife, Sofia, on the 17th. Nikolay Kashkin described the evening in his dubious memoir of 1918:

> I saw Antonina Ivanovna for the first time, who produced a pleasant impression both in her exterior and in her modest conduct. I started to converse with her and could not but notice that Tchaikovsky stayed with us nearly the whole time. Antonina Ivanovna was either shy or had difficulty finding words, and Pyotr Ilyich would occasionally, during inadvertent pauses, speak for her or add to what she said. Our conversation, however, was so trifling that I would have paid Pyotr Ilyich's interference no heed had he not been so persistent when his wife started talking to somebody; such attention was not quite natural and seemed to indicate his fear that Antonina Ivanovna would find it hard to conduct a conversation in the hoped-for tone. In general our new acquaintance produced an impression which, although favorable, was quite bland. In the next few days . . . N. G. Rubinstein, recalling the evening at Jurgenson's and speaking of Antonina Ivanovna, said: "She is very nice and conducts herself well, but I didn't especially like her: indeed, she isn't genuine, there's something artificial." For all its vagueness this characterization was apropos, since Antonina Ivanovna did produce the impression of being somehow "not genuine." [175, 110–11]

This story must be considered in the totality of Kashkin's 1918 memoir. He is the only source for the tale that Tchaikovsky attempted suicide by wading into the Moscow River in the hope of catching some fatal illness, though the "icy bath passed without the least consequence" [175, 125]. If Antonina was informed of a permanent separation in Moscow, which Kashkin claimed, she would have had no cause to journey to Odessa, which she did. Yet one of Kashkin's speculations accords with other testimony: that Antonina was mad, if less obviously so in 1877 than when she was committed to an asylum in 1896, let alone before her death in 1917, long since deranged to the point of mistaking her doctor for the tsar. If, at first, Tchaikovsky did not perceive her mannerisms as symptoms of a mental disorder, growing awareness of the problem would explain his concern over how Antonina spoke at the Jurgenson soiree.

Antonina's mental state is an issue distinct from sympathy for the terrible life which befell her after her separation and from Tchaikovsky's state of mind during the courtship, which he was already beginning to disown. Anxiety over her sanity explains his retreat to St. Petersburg, but was it fact or contrivance? Antonina noted his drastic symptoms of illness as he departed for St. Petersburg on 24 September, the last day of their life together. His real reason may have been freedom—from her, from Nikolay Rubinstein, from the conservatory, from Moscow altogether.

Modest's claim in *The Life* that an attack of nerves struck down the composer in St. Petersburg, laid him low for some two weeks, and nearly killed him [1997 II 27] is a fiction. Twenty-five years after Tchaikovsky's death, Kashkin could still wonder how the best psychiatrist in Petersburg could discern from an unconscious man "his general condition and life circumstances," and "from the very beginning recognized the impossibility not only of Tchaikovsky living with his wife, but also expressed decisively the necessity of the couple's complete and permanent break, including the inadmissibility of any kind of future meeting" [175, 112]. But six days after arriving in St. Petersburg, Tchaikovsky wrote to Modest of "returning to life" [vi 179]. On 5 October, supposedly still unconscious in St. Petersburg, he was in Berlin, feeling much better, keeping his servant Alyosha informed of his status [356, 313]. The most plausible explanation for such obfuscation was the rescue plan. Had Pyotr been seriously ill, Anatoly would not have abandoned him. But Anatoly returned to Moscow, whence Modest was summoned from distant Grankino, Kolya Konradi's estate. Anatoly alerted the conservatory direction that Tchaikovsky was not returning soon and informed Antonina of Pyotr's alleged illness. Permanent separation was probably not mentioned; rather, Antonina was told that she would be meeting Pyotr on the road. Modest helped her to prepare for departure, which included acquiring copies of all of Tchaikovsky's music, and put her on the train to Odessa on 4 October. By then, Anatoly and Pyotr were in Berlin.

The strongest evidence of a strategy in progress was that it came unhinged. Instead of being informed of the break by Ippolit in Odessa, given some money, and left to cope, Antonina found refuge at Kamenka. Sasha exposed the willful cruelty of the plan, subjecting Pyotr to criticism, while Antonina's stay there foiled his return. The plan had failed: Antonina was still in their midst, and Pyotr had now to save face.

The reconstruction of events is speculative: before leaving Petersburg, Anatoly told Sasha of his intention to take Pyotr abroad; Sasha countered with an invitation to come to her in a telegram that arrived only after the brothers left. Having determined Antonina's route from Modest, Sasha contemplated intercepting her in Kiev, then found her in Odessa [365, 44–46]. Antonina arrived in Odessa on 7 October and on the 9th received a note from Anatoly, which, she claimed, said nothing about her husband's fate. It appears that Ippolit passed to Sasha the duty of informing Antonina of the break. Meanwhile, Tchaikovsky arrived in Geneva, writing in his first letter back to Russia, "I have still decided nothing. I await letters from *Odessa* from my poor spouse, in order to take some sort of decision. Today we went to the post office, but there were no letters. It is terribly sad!" [vi 182].

When Modest arrived in St. Petersburg, probably on 5 October, he found Sasha's letter and telegram and sent them to Switzerland together with an account of his time with Antonina, declaring her not without fault but not without virtue, even suggesting that, with appropriate transformation, she might become a life companion for Pyotr [365, 44]. This brought a furious response from Anatoly: "That she is immeasurably stupid and vacuous is the essential truth, but the goodness that you see in her seems to me more than doubtful. . . . No, not just Petya, but I as well would go insane living with her" [365, 47]. Modest moved quickly back into line. The distinction between Anatoly's corrosive tone and Pyotr's more synthetic anger in letters of this time suggests Pyotr's continuing acceptance of responsibility for the marriage.

Sasha, meanwhile, had accepted her sister-in-law without prejudice. On 20 October, she chided Modest for his "exaggeratedly cheerless view of Antonina the whole person":

> I have been home five days now, Nina is here with me, and I have already grown quite close to her and can say to you: she is not what you think. She has

> an honorable heart, she is endlessly loving, she has a mind, healthy and intelligent. . . . Do not think, Modichka, that I am carried away, or am dreaming up virtues in her out of pity. [365, 48–49]

Sasha shifted the debate to Pyotr's default of spousal responsibility. For a time she prevailed, leaving her brothers bereft of effective reply as they honed a rougher strategy: convince Sasha that the marriage is hopeless, get rid of Antonina, and press loyalty to Pyotr. Hence Tchaikovsky's new, more pointed negativism in a letter to Sasha, claiming that Antonina was wrong to let him take sole blame for the marriage:

> [P]ampered by you, it seems she imagines that *I* was striving to see us married, that I touched her heart with outpourings of love, in a word, that I am wholly guilty. But she was also guilty to some extent. I cannot hide from you that A[ntonina] I[vanovna]'s visit among you is the most sensitive wound in my heart. [vi 204]

Tchaikovsky wrote a long, almost mirthfully insulting description of Antonina to Meck on 25 October [vi 196–200]. In pages of uncharacteristic invective, he not only reversed his earlier stance of responsibility, but also supplied posterity with enough epithets to sully Antonina's image for a long time to come. She was fairly unhandsome, with expressionless eyes, lips too thin, and an unpleasant smile; her comportment was affected, her expression lacking any hint of inner spiritual beauty. Her head and heart were empty; she had never expressed a single thought or heartfelt gesture toward him. She showed no interest in his profession, which was odd considering she was a musician who had been in love with him for four years, but never in that time attended a concert of the Musical Society. She was loquacious about the men who have fallen in love with her, mostly generals, nephews of famous bankers, celebrated artists, even members of the imperial family; about the cruel and lowly deeds of her family; and about her life at the institute. She received the news of his illness with incomprehensible indifference, followed by several tales about men who were in love with her. "Some madness came over me," he claimed. From a letter Anatoly received the day before, she was no longer meek but angry and "very, very untruthful."

The tempers of these highly strung people, the distance between them, and their disjointed discourse produced an incorrigible babble, from which three critical developments emerged: Pyotr's "verdict" of permanent separation shattered Antonina; Sasha's frail health and the pressure to bend to her brothers' will brought her to change her mind about Antonina; and ambiguities in Pyotr's letters made Antonina continue to hope for some happy outcome precisely when his siblings were closing ranks against her. On 26 October, Tchaikovsky laid out his position [vi 202–3]. He would drop the matter of reconciliation forever; he would accept any punishment, but he could not live with Antonina. "This is quite possibly an *illness,* but it is incurable." He would see to her upkeep, but mostly, "I beg you *on my knees* to get her out of Kamenka; do this for the sake of all that is holy in this world: it is essential for my peace and yours."

On 31 October, Sasha reviewed the situation to Modest:

> My head is spinning. On the one hand Petya's letter, steeped with hate and revulsion for Antonina Ivanovna, which you both confirm; on the other A[ntonina] I[vanovna] herself, altogether undeserving such a sharp, decisive verdict. Am I really so blind, do I really misunderstand the appreciation of the human heart?
>
> . . . After lunch [the next day,] she began to talk: "Sasha, Sasha, what am I to do?"—and suddenly broke out in frightful weeping, almost crying herself out—no consolation would do. . . . Modya, do you really think this woman is capable of acting out such a comedy? I don't. If she were acting, the scene would have been much bigger. After this storm she fell quiet again, intending to write Petya and pondering her letter.
>
> . . . I am so worn out looking at her that I have ceased to understand things—compassion drowns any understanding in me. I will beg Anatoly to come and help me explain her situation to this poor woman. In the house she is quiet, modest, gives the children lessons, she is utmost kind to me, kisses my hands like a child and says: "God will not abandon me as long as you are near!"
>
> . . . Now here is my brief opinion of Petya: his behavior with A[ntonina] I[vanovna] is very, very ugly, he is no youth any more and can understand that he lacks even the shade of a tolerable husband's instincts. To take whatever woman he wants and try to make of her a shield for his debauchery, and then to shift onto her the hatred which should befall his own conduct—is not worthy of so highly developed a man. I am all but certain that her personal attributes play no role whatsoever in his hatred for his wife—he would come to hate any woman placed in obligatory relationships with him.

> . . . Petya's guilt before An[tonina] Iv[anovna] diminishes her faults in my view—all her blunders are explained, his behavior is unforgiveable—for the absence of endurance, self-possession, egotism and complete moral unsteadiness. [365, 53–55]

For all the misery in this situation, something brought Tchaikovsky to offer Antonina the slenderest hope. On 26 October, in a postscript of a letter to Sasha, he wrote, "If she is even to hope to live with me again at any time, then now, before I am fully recovered, one mustn't talk to me of this" [vi 203]. He expressed similar sentiments in another letter, confessing as much to Sasha and Lev as late as 2/14 December: "In fact I gave some remote hopes to A[ntonina] I[vanovna] in my last letter! And this was made all the worse because I *was lying,* telling her that I cannot vouch for the fact that there will be an 'afterwards'" [vi 270].

Tchaikovsky was trying to mediate his love for his siblings, his sympathy for the downtrodden, his embarrassment, his wish for a resolution, and his anger at Antonina's terrible persistence. Then, with more than a month left in her stay at Kamenka, he simply willed the problem out of his head. Declaring himself calm and happy, he wrote to Meck of his imminent trip to Italy to forget "the long nightmare" [vi 212]. Throughout November, his letters are about other topics except when forced to deal with news from Antonina. Often, his answer was unrelated to the question in the manner of a political debate: Sasha asked him why he didn't admit his guilt for the marriage; he answered that he had offered Antonina anything she wanted [vi 215, 227].

In Kamenka, Antonina asked Pyotr for an accounting of his actions. Reputedly 16 pages long, her letter is lost, though he described it to Sasha from Venice on 12/24 November. Antonina's sanity is questionable in her claim that Pyotr's servant Mikhail Sofronov, who lost his job when the composer married, paid a sorceress to bewitch him to hate his wife. Tchaikovsky restated his failed attempt to overcome his antipathy and insisted that he could not live with her. He avoided answering why he married in the first place and asked Sasha to restrain Antonina's whys and wherefores. He was a great artist with much to say and must look to that charge; he was busy with *Onegin* and set to finish the Fourth Symphony by year's end [vi 235–37].

By early November, Antonina was taking a serious toll on Sasha's health. On the 7th, she wrote Modest, acknowledging that Antonina must leave and awaiting Anatoly to end the situation. By 17 November, she had come around to her brothers' view. "You are correct—she . . . is *nothing,* she is full of negative traits," Sasha wrote to Modest, asking Pyotr's forgiveness and hinting that even Antonina was asking to be sent away. Antonina's last day in Kamenka was 4 December 1877. Two days earlier, Anatoly had recounted to Pyotr the last days of her stay. They were not taking her seriously, even her intention to drown herself. In Anatoly's telling, Sasha construed the matter such that it never crossed the minds of the inhabitants of Kamenka "even once, even for a second," that Pyotr "had done something bad" [365, 56].

With one additional speculation, the data concerning Tchaikovsky's marriage make sense: that in his resolve to marry in 1876, he revived his acquaintance with Antonina and contacted her. This would explain her weeks of prayer, her flirtatiousness, and other details of her account of their courtship [365, 265–67]; his continuing interest in Antonina even after receiving money from Meck; his faith in the marriage and his tendency to hold Antonina blameless; her being shattered at his insistence on a permanent break; Sasha's and Modest's equivocation; and Pyotr's genuine shock as he gradually became aware of her mental disorder.

Central to Tchaikovsky's 14-year correspondence with Nadezhda von Meck, the worldly heiress of a railroad magnate who became his patroness, was the stimulus it received from his marriage. Before the composer's request for money in May 1877, their surviving correspondence comprised eight letters. These would be insignificant were it not for the interest the two already had showed in each other. Antonina was a foil to their interest, and it is fair to ask how the Meck friendship would have developed had Tchaikovsky never married, or married happily. Antonina probably began her six weeks of prayer on 14 February 1877, and the very next day Meck wrote Tchaikovsky of her "profound affection" and that she would like to tell more of her "fantastic" relationship with him, which involved the "best, most elevated feelings possible in human nature" [86 I 4]. In time, she would tell him more than we want to know: she was long-winded, anti-Semitic, and politically reactionary.

The confessional aspect of their letters affirms the wisdom of their decision, notorious to posterity, to avoid personal contact. Kashkin wrote: "The bitter experience of life had already taught Tchaikovsky that only at a certain distance can people be endowed with all possible perfections, whereas closer one always sees defects, even if trivial, which rend the integrity of the imagination's vision" [MV020820]. The situation has encouraged amateur psychologists. A rich, socially reclusive widow is running a complex family business; her sole passions are her children and music; she supports students at the conservatory and other musical charities and has identified a composer whose music affects her deeply. A money-starved composer who lost his mother early in life is flattered by the attentions of a musically sensitive older woman who pays well for small tasks. Barriers to direct expression bring them to a vicarious passion that will blossom and fade in due course, but which at first seemed like a benevolent stroke of *fatum*.

Tchaikovsky's music was important to Meck; it was the point of supporting him. Perfectly aware of this, the composer came to link his ability to compose with his sense of well-being. The regularity with which he parlayed this linkage into a happy financial outcome was almost absolute. Over time, the "well-being to compose" became the "freedom to compose." From there, it was a short step simply to "freedom."

Whether Tchaikovsky was manipulating Meck, whether he coveted or resented her, whether he was ashamed to ask for money—we shall never know. Sophisticated in finance, why did she respond without hesitation to his requests? Was he unaware, bearing with valorous patience her digressions on sentiment and family lore, of her overstepping the most liberal bounds of patronage? On balance, their confidences, their shared ambitions, and their devotion to each other through many tragic circumstances bespeak sincerity. Their relationship may have been anchored in the decision to perceive each other as better than they really were. It was, in any event, replete with strong emotions. In her third letter to Tchaikovsky, Meck requested a funeral march (now lost) on motifs from *The Oprichnik*—all chosen from Natalia's passionate aria (no. 6), sung as she awaits her lover [220]. In her fifth letter, on 18 March 1877, she declared that "you do indeed personify my ideal and can compensate for all my disenchantment, mistakes, and sadness" [86 I 10]. To think that Meck was so naïve as to accept Tchaikovsky's marriage, discounting his sexuality, is about as silly as for Tchaikovsky to hint, in a letter to Anatoly on Christmas 1877, that Meck's recent silence was attributable to her discovery of it. His sexuality clearly made no difference to her. To idealize was her refuge after a hard marriage, and his after Antonina. He rejected Meck's invitation to use the familiar form of address but still managed to write:

> It was pleasurable not only to read your letter, but simply . . . to feel it in my hands, to see the dear, familiar handwriting, to feel at last completely satisfied because I was before now waiting for something to complete my happiness. And this something was your letter, my friend! You spoil me! From time to time, for my tranquility and well-being, I need to read your lines, to receive the affection you write. [viii 172]

The vicarious lover in him occasionally met an even headier response from her:

> I don't know whether you can understand that jealousy which I feel in relation to you in the absence of personal contacts between us. Whether you know that I am jealous of you in the most impermissible way: as a woman of a beloved man. Whether you know that when you married it was *terribly* hard for me, it was as if something had been torn from my heart. I became ill and bitter, the thought of your closeness to this woman was unbearable to me, and whether you know what a vile person I am. I rejoiced when things were bad between you and her; I reproached myself for this feeling; it seems I never let on to you about it, but nevertheless I could not expunge it—a person does not order one's feelings around. I hated this woman for the fact that things were going badly for you and her, but I would have hated her a hundred times more if things between you had been going *well.* It seemed that she had taken away from me what was perhaps only *mine,* to which I *alone* have a right because I *love you* as no one else, I value you higher than anything else in the world. [86 II 212–13]

Meck and Tchaikovsky indulged a symbiosis of dependency in a private world where their complementary traits were emphasized. Early on (7 March 1877), Meck was struck by the "coincidence" of their thoughts before his were expressed; Tchaikovsky affirmed this kinship. A recurrent motif of their letters, this "coincidence" initiated a riot of Antonina bashing. On 8 August 1877, Meck counseled him to stand firm and insist on happiness; on 12 August, Tchaikovsky agreed. On 11 October, Tchaikovsky explained how he tried to make his marriage work and failed; on 17 October, Meck agreed, praising Anatoly for saving him. To Tchaikovsky's insulting description of Antonina (above, p. 157), she responded with sympathy bolstered with meanness:

> It pains me that you accuse yourself and bother to sympathize with your wife. You are not to blame *for anything,* rest assured she will not suffer at all being separated from you. She is one of those happy characters . . . who cannot feel sorrow deeply or for long; they live on the surface, not knowing what really deep feelings are, because they can't feel *anything* deeply; they live an objective life, even a downright material one, which you have taken care of for her. [86 I 6]

They pursued the defamation of Antonina more earnestly in 1878, when a divorce seemed possible.

CHAPTER TEN

The Music of 1877

THAT TCHAIKOVSKY COMPOSED TWO OF HIS GREATEST WORKS THIS year speaks to the separation of his artistic and worldly spheres, a phenomenon he will describe to Meck in 1878 [vii 314–17].

The Fourth Symphony, the composing of which spanned the entire year, had no overt program until Tchaikovsky wrote one at Meck's insistence; she is the "best friend" of the symphony's dedication [vii 124–27]. His objection to doing so, to specifying undefined feelings in a "purely lyric process," seems contrived, given the arresting motto theme that begins the symphony, which not only implies specific content but also marks the non-Germanic pattern in the first movement and returns at the end of the finale. That Tchaikovsky's striking themes, unusual key patterns, and vivid sonorities could be justified as mere invention, as a "purely lyric process," would seem to stretch a point. The problem, instead, is one that we shall see again: the music is too strong to make credible Tchaikovsky's contention that the feelings are undefined, but rather, as Meck's request for an interpretation suggests, the impression is that he is not sharing them. The reasons for this are beyond retrieval, yet need not be confessional. The composer surely realized, and would learn again from later experience, that a program risked vulgarity and limited, unnecessarily, a listener's personal response to his musical ideas.

Had Tchaikovsky never written the program, some evidence of extra-musical meaning could be extrapolated from observing the Fourth Symphony in the context of his other music. The choice of A-flat minor and B major as important keys in the first movement recall the funereal passages of op. 21; the enharmonic reinterpretation of the pitch A-flat in pivoting between F minor and E major recalls a critical passage in *The Tempest,* as does the juxtaposition of these keys in later music, such as the beginning of the *Hamlet* Overture and that passage in *The Sleeping Beauty* where the Lilac Fairy commits Florestan's kingdom to a 100-year sleep. The association of E as a tonal center for *fatum* in *Francesca da Rimini* and the emergent association with death of the key of B, the arrival key of the movement I exposition—all suggest that the Fourth Symphony, in Tchaikovsky's private thinking, was more than a play of sounds.

A further barrier to understanding the Fourth is that much of Tchaikovsky's program [59, 163–66] was silly and unrelated to the music. He began to hedge before he closed the letter, finding the program's "insufficiency and lack of clarity" horrifying. To modern sensitivities, his reading smacks of kitsch, while its broad dissemination, coupled with a blithe disregard of his disclaimer, have done the work a disservice. What started out as a private act of diplomacy for a patroness has burdened the work with connotations—not least, the crude linkage of the entire work with Tchaikovsky's marriage—well beyond the composer's feeble attempt to explain it. An early interpretation in verse turns the first movement into a dialogue between Poet and Fate on a moonlit summer evening. It begins with the Poet:

Who are you? Answer, chance guest,
Why are you here in my little corner?
What are you whispering? What secrets
Are you idly tracing on the field?

To which Fate responds, after two more verses:

I am Fate, a world force,
Like a shadow I embrace the earthly sphere
Cooling outbursts of happiness
Or crowning them with sorrow. [131, 5–6]

For his part, Tchaikovsky labeled the fanfare at the beginning of the Fourth as *fatum:*

Ex. 20

He described this melody as the "kernel" of all that follows, which lends itself to interpretation as "cruel and unforgiving Destiny" [169, 9–10]. He later elaborated this point to Sergey Taneyev:

> In essence my symphony is an imitation of Beethoven's Fifth; that is, I imitated not its musical thoughts but its basic idea. What do you think? Is there a program in the Fifth Symphony? Not only is there, but also what it is striving to express is hardly arguable. Approximately the same idea lies at the basis of my symphony, and if you did not understand me, then it follows only that I am not Beethoven. [vii 201]

There is much Beethoven here, from parallels of general style [196] to complex motivic connections analogous to Beethoven's, to more specific allusions, particularly to the *Eroica.* One need but imagine the strings in the *Eroica* Scherzo played *pizzicato,* keeping the rubric, *sempre pianissimo e staccato,* to sense its proximity to Tchaikovsky's. The flourish that opens Tchaikovsky's finale is audibly similar to Beethoven's and signals deeper affinities: both movements contain variations on a popular tune within a formal pattern inimical to classical prototype. In their first movements, both composers initiate extraordinary chromatic exploration with a single dissonant pitch in the seventh bar.

S.V. Frolov has proposed an iconoclastic interpretation of the Fourth, especially of the finale [124]. Declaring the Meck program to be contrary to the music, he observed that the folk song in the finale, "In the Field Stood a Little Birch Tree," is unusual: its accompaniment is implicitly unstable tonally; Tchaikovsky introduces motifs that imply some alternate identity and treats them ever more violently. After statements at bars 10, 60, and 149, the tune disintegrates, its final appearance (at 268) being momentary and almost immediately destroyed. To suggest, as Tchaikovsky did to Meck, that this music expressed the spirit of folk festivity is nonsensical.

It is sooner an orgy, as in Berlioz's *Symphonie fantastique,* with its vulgar transformation and degeneration of an innocent theme. If one accepts that the beloved, represented by the folk tune, becomes monstrous and distorted, Tchaikovsky's need to confect a respectable explanation to satisfy his "best friend" becomes obvious.

The disintegration of themes and unusual key choices produce a pattern in movement I that negates sonata-allegro, not unlike Tchaikovsky's procedure in *The Storm*. Every theme is drastically modified, including the motto (introduced by trombones and tuba in bars 9–10). The limpid waltz at *moderato con anima* is the only time in the symphony we hear it thus. What poses as a transition (at 53–69) modulates but does not lead to a new theme; instead, Tchaikovsky returns to the first theme, shortened by half and overwhelmed by the noisy accompaniment of descending chromatic lines and blaring horns (70–77). Thereafter it is reduced to two bars (78–81) and then lost in passagework. Like someone drowning, it surfaces in the home key one last time (92–103), almost crazed, then vanishes.

At six bars, the *moderato assai, quasi andante* is too short for an interim key area. When the music moves to B major and the theme clarifies (134), the expression is striking: a disembodied waltz tune in thirds is accompanied by a funereal drumbeat below and an echo of the first theme above —all at the tritone from the home key. Tonally, we arrive at a plateau, but after a dozen bars Tchaikovsky begins dismantling this theme as he had the first; it leads to a return of the motto. The section proximate to a development does improvise and sequence, but provides no tonal reorientation at the end. Restating the first theme in D minor (at 284) leaves the recapitulation, sonata-allegro's most critical formal marker, without its crucial component, the return of the home key. Form as well as content are reconceived.

Frolov focuses on the "idea of duality, of transformation, of the rebirth of intonational imagic material," which occurs most conspicuously in the outer movements [124, 70]. To him, duality *is* the point of the piece, and this interpretation allows him to relate every manifestation of it to the motto, where it happens first. In the *Andantino,* free of thematic disintegration, Tchaikovsky reinterprets the principal melody rhythmically by shifting the bar line (at 199). In the Scherzo, the duality is timbral, as first the brass and then the winds mimic the opening theme (bars 170, 198). The finale forms symmetries with the first movement in the recycling of the motto, the process of thematic disintegration, and Tchaikovsky's rejection of classical pattern. He initiates intermovement unity as to motif in the first phrase of the waltz in the first movement, namely, the progressive clarification of a descending tetrachord, which recurs in every other movement:

Ex. 21 Movement I

Ex. 22a Movement II, opening

Ex. 22b Movement II, middle section

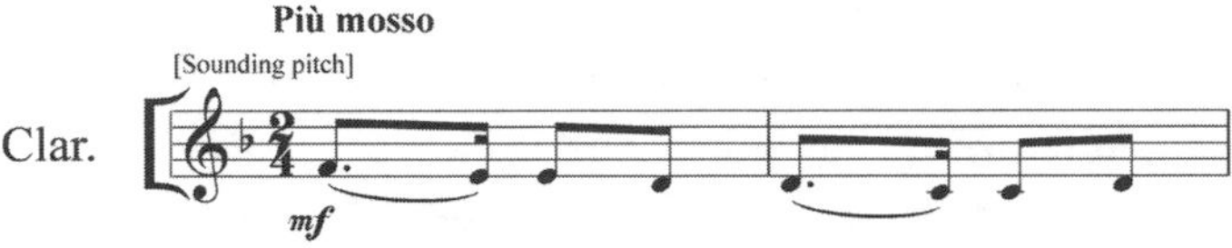

Ex. 23 Movement III

Ex. 24 Movement IV

Allegro con fuoco

The folk tune represents the lyric heroine of Tchaikovsky's symphony, invested (according to Frolov) with an "indelible impression of beauty and vulgarity" [124, 70]. Yet the tune might mean something more. It is among the last folk songs Tchaikovsky edited, in the month of his engagement [CW 61, 231]. Hearing it in the Fourth Symphony, Taneyev thought something was amiss: "Knowing how you worked out 'The Crane,' knowing what you can do with Russian melodies, the variations on 'In the Field a Little Birch Tree Stood' seemed not very relevant or interesting" [294, 32]. To this Tchaikovsky made no response, perhaps because Taneyev, like subsequent commentators, omitted consideration of an important aspect of the song: its text. Interspersed with the refrain "Ai, lyuli, lyuli," it tells of a little birch in a field; warm springtime days have arrived; we have gathered to make wreaths; for this, twigs are taken from the tree; then we dance beneath its branches. The birch is female in verbal gender and in description, "the curly-haired one" as defined by its branches; it is solitary; the refrain mimics the name Lel, the pagan god of springtime.

The ceremonial uses of flowers, fragrant grasses, and especially of birches as a symbol of springtime awakening from the death of winter are so numerous in Slavic folklore as to beggar recounting. But the weaving of wreaths from birch twigs relates to the prediction of marital happiness. For the most part women make the wreaths, then toss them in a river or stream to see what happens next:

> Since the earliest times the wreath served as an emblem of love and conjugal union. Just as in springtime Earth enters into a conjugal union with Heaven, and just as the goddess of spring (Life) was not only the representative of earthly harvests, but also more generally the patroness of marriage and the pleasures of love, so the celebration dedicated to her had to be considered the best time of year for the declaration of love and for divining future family happiness. Throwing wreaths into the water, youths and young women interrogate this prophetic element about their future destiny: if the wreath floats without touching the bank—it is a prediction of a desire fulfilled, a happy marriage and a long life; if the wreath circle[s] around in one place—it is a sign of failure (the wedding will fall through, love remains without a response), and if it sinks—it is a sign of death, widowhood or the lack of a family life (a person would remain unmarried). It is further noted: if a wreath remained whole and fresh, or if it faded from Semik to Trinity Sunday—in the first instance one

reckons on a happy marriage of many years, and in the second, one could expect an early death. [4 III 346]

Tchaikovsky's editing of "In the Field a Little Birch Tree Stood," his composing of the finale of the Fourth Symphony (the most errant movement in his explanation to Meck), and his courting of Antonina Milyukova—all in May 1877—prompt another speculation. Could his treatment of this tune be the musical enactment of a sinking wreath? The finale in this interpretation, with its progressive destruction of the folk melody, together with the "fate" motif of the beginning, may reflect his personal situation at the time.

The other great work of 1877 was *Evgeniy Onegin,* op. 24, based on Alexander Pushkin's novel in verse; the opera was begun in May and completed in January 1878. This synopsis is condensed from the standard performing version:

Act I. On Madame Larina's country estate, her daughters, Olga and Tatyana, are singing a duet inside the house as she and Filippievna, the children's elderly nurse, are making jam and reminiscing about the past in the garden. Peasants enter, celebrating the harvest, and perform a dance-song. Olga is ready to join the dancing, but Tatyana is immersed in her novel. Presently, visitors are announced: Lensky, Olga's fiancé and a poet, and Onegin, his new friend who has inherited a nearby estate. Like the sisters, the men are opposites. After an ensemble, they promenade in couples, Lensky declaring his love with increasing fervor, Onegin conversing with Tatyana, who comes to see him as the man of her dreams. In the next scene, Tatyana asks the nurse to tell stories from the past. Filippievna describes her arranged marriage at the age of 13 to a boy who was younger still. Tatyana, agitated, admits that she is in love. She asks the nurse to bring her pen and paper, then confesses her love to Onegin in a letter. When Filippievna returns to wake her, Tatyana sends her to deliver the letter. With girls picking berries to set the scene, Onegin informs Tatyana that he is not destined for family life. He is unworthy of her, but advises her to restrain her emotions. Tatyana is mortified.

Act II. At a reception on Tatyana's name-day, the guests sing and gossip. This irritates Onegin, who in turn annoys Lensky by dancing with Olga. Monsieur Triquet sings a name-day panegyric to Tatyana. The company is called to the cotillion, and Lensky has words with Onegin. Onegin tries to calm him, to no avail, and Lensky challenges Onegin to a duel. An ensemble begins with reflection and ends in an uproar. The scene changes to a field in winter at dawn. Lensky reflects on his life and fate. Onegin arrives, and they acknowledge the terrible irony of their enmity. Lensky dies in the duel.

Act III. At a ball in St. Petersburg four years later, Onegin, now 26, is unhappy with his life. After an éccosaise, Prince Gremin enters with Tatyana—his wife. Gremin introduces Onegin, then apostrophizes her. Tatyana makes her exit; Onegin regrets the past and realizes that he is in love with her. Alone in her drawing room, Tatyana reads Onegin's note. When he enters, she reproaches him. He remonstrates, but to no avail. She admits loving him, but cannot break her vows. She sends him away.

Several productions of *Onegin* make some claim to being the first: by students of the Moscow Conservatory on 17 March 1879, by professionals at the Bolshoy Theater in Moscow on 11 January 1881, by amateurs in the first performance in St. Petersburg on 25 April 1883, the first there by professionals on 19 October 1884, and the first complete performance (with the écossaise) on 19 September 1885.

The music has a complex publishing history [289]. Excerpts and a piano-vocal score had been published (and, by one account, sold over 1,000 copies [434, 77]) in 1878, months before any production, while a piano reduction, concert, and simplified editions of Pavel Pabst's paraphrase of the work, the full score, three editions of the libretto, an arrangement of the polonaise by Franz Liszt, and other excerpts had all been published before a note of the opera ever sounded on a professional stage. The Letter Scene was performed (against Tchaikovsky's wishes) by two divas in connection with the Pushkin celebrations of 1880. Tchaikovsky's indecision about the opera was reflected in differences between published librettos and scores (there being no assurance that a libretto matched a score), differing publication stemma of score and piano reduction, and continuing variance in editions after his death.

The early focuses of change were the last act, the transformation of Pushkin's "fat general" into the humane and protective Prince Gremin, and the final scene, after Tatyana admits to Onegin that she loves him [156]. Finding her rejection of Onegin in Pushkin too severe for opera, Tchaikovsky modified it, prompting Laroche to remark:

> Unyielding in the strict performance of her duty, but tormented within by the passion that consumes her, Tatyana in the last chapter of Pushkin's "Onegin"

> presents a genuinely tragic figure, the elevated purity of which is not without a tender and touching element. To the composer, however, it seemed that this latter impression would be greater if he nudged Tatyana somewhat off the pedestal on which we are accustomed to see her, and compelled her, in five minutes of kisses and embraces, to deny in practice her famous "I am given to another and will remain true to him forever." Perhaps operatic effect has profited from such a radical reform; but the figure created by the poet and (through the opera up to this scene) reverently preserved by the musician, is severely damaged by this. [255 II 107]

Sensitive about his instruction for Tatyana to fall into Onegin's arms, Tchaikovsky proposed, instead of an embrace, that Onegin would simply "come closer" to her; later in the passage, he substituted Tatyana's "I am dying" with "Farewell forever!" But the details of these changes do not survive, and the notorious rubric stayed in the 1881 libretto. The autograph score and the 1881 libretto have Prince Gremin order Onegin away, but this had been omitted by the second edition of the piano-vocal score later that year. In 1878, Tchaikovsky had misgivings about Onegin's final line and asked the noted actor Ivan Samarin to devise a substitute; hence Onegin's famous "Disgrace! Anguish! O my wretched fate!" to close the opera.

Before any public performance, familiar views of the work were emerging. Laroche attended the dress rehearsal of the student performance. He declared *Onegin* "among the joyful signs of our time" and placed Tchaikovsky in opposition to the "radicals":

> The cult of pure form, the roundedness of musical numbers, the predominance of melody, classical repetitions—all this so much strikes the eyes at even a superficial perusal of the score that the position of the composer is clearly outlined. Between him and the progressive party at the present moment there is absolutely nothing in common other than devices of orchestration.

The story (he continued) perfectly suited Tchaikovsky. "The deep, hopeless sorrow, which does not surface in Manfredesque imprecations but is half-obscured in a cloud of elegant calm—that is the tone which reigns in our composer's best pages." Tatyana and Lensky are the main characters, in whom "that elegiac side, which I consider predominant in Tchaikovsky's gift, has found such full realization as this element has very rarely achieved before now" [255 II 103–6].

The complete productions—except 1885 in St. Petersburg, the most emulated since—were given generous attention in both capitals. The conservatory staging produced a number of recollections [7, 105–7; 12; 434, 70–76]. Among the critics, Laroche declared *Onegin* to be one of Tchaikovsky's best scores, mentioning the Letter Scene and Gremin's aria: "It is difficult to imagine a more chaste gracefulness, a more attractive pensiveness; the fascination of the music does not for a moment break with the poetical truth, and the service of the truth does not for a moment restrain the free flight of the musical inspiration" [255 II 109]. Another complained, "The characters never *sing,* and recitative almost always acts on the public in a sleep-inducing way" [434, 79], and Tchaikovsky's "realism" involved setting vacant dialogues like "Hello. How are you?" and "Excellent, thank you very much."

"Ignotus" (Sergey Vasilievich Flerov) wrote extensively of the 1881 production [MV810115, MV810120], including details about the performance: Triquet sang the bowdlerized Russian text of his couplets, the last interval was filled with a performance of the *Capriccio Italien* and act II of Auber's *Fra Diavolo,* Gremin's appearance in the final scene was "now eliminated," and the Italian diva Augusta Verni's performance as Tatyana was not convincing. Flerov proposed an aria for Tatyana before the Letter Scene so the audience could get to know her (she was still a stranger in scene 1 and a completely different person in act III) and also a big, elegiac aria at the close to make the final scene "less agitated" and more in keeping with Pushkin's "marvelous calm."

When *Onegin* was first staged by amateurs in St. Petersburg two years later, the press was innocent of provocative insight and hardly lavish in good will. The imperial production in 1884 offered a grander pulpit just as the critical harangue was getting a little worn. Konstantin Galler claimed that Tchaikovsky's (Wagnerian) device of having the singer present the text while the orchestra elaborates it in characteristic motifs created a "duality of impression" [VI841110]. Nikolay Solovyov revived the old rag of Tchaikovsky the symphonist oppressing Tchaikovsky the opera composer. He ridiculed the row at Tatyana's name-day party, "seeing in the words and action only a pretext for his creative ardor as a symphonist." He also provided details of the performance: Triquet, a baritone, sang the French version of his couplets a third lower than notated; and the dancers of the polonaise had to improvise a closing, as the music ended before their steps [NO841023]. To Cui, *Onegin* was stillborn, insubstantial, and weak; the "melancholy monotony" of "little ideas repeated many times" was characteristic of music that weeps too much; after the "petty, monotonous, ungrateful, unstageworthy" first scene, the Letter Scene provided only momentary refreshment, "a beautiful decantation from the empty into the emptier," returning Tchaikovsky's insult to his songs (above, p. 84); Lensky's aria was "piteous diatonic whining," Gremin's was banal, Onegin's arioso was "common" [108, 88].

In *Onegin,* dubbed "lyric scenes," Tchaikovsky set a highly nuanced text with a gift for nuance. That is one reason it wears so well, especially among Russians, who have memorized the words. The characters were nearly contemporary with the audience. Human feelings pervade the opera without exotic spectacle, *coup de théâtre,* or plot tension. He conceded the absence of drama, but his characters are credible and his music on point. He kept the best of Pushkin's language, softening some of the poet's acerbic touches and casual treatment of tragic events. He omitted, for example, Olga's abandonment of Lensky's grave (7, vii), avoiding the issue of her shallowness, and deleted Tatyana's remark, when she and Onegin meet again, that it is her turn to give a lesson (8, xlii). Large issues inform the opera's narrative: an invocation to the muse; the flourishing and demise of inspiration; the clash of mores between old and new, country and city; the change of seasons; and the press of social imperative. These carry the work without hero or villain, love triangles, characters faced with odious alternatives, or simmering disaster.

We are aware of the muse from Lensky being a poet and Tatyana's romantic effusions, but it is first signaled in the girls' opening duet, where the curtain rises on absolute stasis. This *tableau* is so utterly unoperatic as to suggest that Tchaikovsky was attempting to be conventional and failed. In fact, he has reconceived the Pushkinian epigram. Madame Larina and Filippievna sing about fashions now distant, forecasting Tatyana's dialogue with Filippievna. The girls, in fragments of lines delivered unaware of deeper intent, are singing about the solitary singer of love and sorrow, the panpipe's simple sound (with Hellenic resonances in the Russian *svirel'*): Have you heard? Did you meet? Were you moved? It takes no effort to associate the solitary singer with Lensky, but Tchaikovsky was indulging other conceits. The girls sing a Pushkin text from 1816, of which at least 14 musical settings had been made before this opera. Tchaikovsky was allowing himself to be construed as the solitary singer as well, invoking the muse at the outset of composition. This scene prepares all later passages in the opera having to do with artistic inspiration, the disappointments of love, and the struggle of impulse against social convention. "The stylization . . . of the Larina sisters is not especially significant in itself, but for serving as 'a certain mask,' under which cover Tchaikovsky expresses his authorial idea—as would happen in an epigraph" [114, 18]. Signification proceeds as Tchaikovsky embeds the Introit from Mozart's *Requiem* in the music as Madame Larina and Filippievna sing, unwittingly, of Tatyana's effective death and the moral of the tale—"Habit is sent us from above as a substitute for happiness"—and introduces the churchly formula "Eternal memory" into the otherwise decorative chorus of peasants (no. 2 at 8, tenor) [126, 120].

By invoking the muse so artlessly, Tchaikovsky reminds us that we may not be aware of the inspiration present in those around us—as Olga did not realize of Lensky and Onegin did not realize of Tatyana. To emphasize this, two onlookers apostrophize Tatyana. Pushkin presents Triquet as a caricature, the dandified foreigner posing at sophistication who has brought a poem (with mis-accents) for Tatyana's name-day and sings it off-key. Tchaikovsky gave him alternative texts. One set of couplets (CW 4, 298–99), macaronic in French and broken Russian, affirms Pushkin. The other, all in French, exhorts "la belle Tatíaná," a perpetual star, to continue shining forever. Gremin's is the nobler apostrophe, whose text Tchaikovsky adapted from a verse later in Pushkin (8, xxix), partly because of his stature as a character and partly for Tchaikovsky's richly expressive melody (for Triquet, he borrowed the tune "Dormez, dormez, chères amours" from Dumersan and Colet's *Chants et chansons populaires de la France*). Tatyana inspires: she shines as a star and appears to him in the radiance of an angel.

These testimonials are all the more tragic as Tchaikovsky confirms, early in the opera, the blindness of Tatyana's intimates to her passions and sets in motion the death of inspiration as counterpoint to it; this runs throughout the work and forms its denouement. We learn this first from the chorus, the text of whose dance-song (within no. 2) describes a lad crossing a bridge with a cudgel; one of the girls on the other side must come out to see him. In a moment, Onegin will "cross the bridge" to the Larins' house and meet Tatyana. Then, in the opening lines of the Quartet (no. 5),

Onegin, an outsider himself, senses the inspiration in Tatyana and mentions his surprise that Lensky has not fallen in love with her, as he would have done had he been a poet. Tchaikovsky shows how tradition and simplicity compare with social pressure as forces in one's life. First, we realize (still in no. 5) that Lensky is too fervent in his love for Olga, which she accepts but does not reciprocate, and that Tatyana has no basis, other than instinct and impressions from her latest novel, to perceive Onegin as her ideal. At the outset, then, come two critical misreadings of inspiration. In addition to Lensky's, Tatyana's, fueled by love, is running high during the scene with the nurse (no. 8), telling of ancient marriage customs in which love had no place. Their viewpoints clash; Tatyana rejects the past and writes her letter to Onegin. For a moment the next morning there is hope as she hears the panpipe referred to in the opening duet (no. 10), but with Filippievna's return comes a certain dread—the affirmation of Tatyana's otherness pointed out by the nurse's inability to grasp the situation. Her distinctiveness deepens as the country girls pick berries (no. 11), a coquettish response to the threatening text of no. 2: when the young man appears, they will run away and pelt him with berries. These expressions of rural life intensify Tatyana's sense of isolation as her encounter with Onegin nears. His rejection tells her that she does not inhabit his world either.

To dismiss all of this as the problems of an adolescent 17-year-old would misconstrue Tatyana's character. Among Russian operatic heroines, she stands with Yaroslavna in *Prince Igor*—strong, autonomous, imaginative, self-aware, accountable. The resignation with which she builds another life after her encounter with Onegin is a concession to social dictates, which earlier found expression in her name-day party. At the duel, Onegin and Lensky realize that their feud is pointless but proceed with it anyway. It is as if the action of the opera were a net of social expectations in which its rebellious characters are caught. The Tatyana who would be true to herself is lost by the end of act I; Lensky loses his life at the end of act II. Onegin remains to be ensnared. Meanwhile, the seasons pass. The first two acts have taken us from late summer to the poet's death in winter. In another genre scene—the ball in St. Petersburg—the last act has hardly begun before Onegin laments the idle passage of his years. Tatyana inspires him, but it is too late. She accuses him of coveting her in the *monde* after rejecting her in the country. She is tempted but social dictates prevail: she is married to another. As rebels, she and Lensky have been defeated, and now Onegin, prey to rebellion, is rejected too. There is no peroration or catharsis; the end merely plays out the premises established earlier.

The crux of the opera, reflected in the connotations of its principal dances, waltz and polonaise [380, 49], comes in its two most celebrated soliloquies, Tatyana's Letter Scene and Lensky's farewell to life. Here, parallels of language and music affirm the death of inspiration and the true likeness of these characters [64, 160–64]. As Tatyana's passion is still in prospect, her speech is the more impulsive, divided into rhapsodic digressions and the sober moments when she actually writes. Lensky's passion is spent as he stands at the threshold of death, dividing his thoughts into what lies in the past and what lies ahead. As a matter of narrative, Onegin will be the agency of death—physical for Lensky, spiritual for Tatyana. As a matter of philosophy, both accept what the future will bring. Lensky expresses this in Pushkin's words:

> All is blessed: of vigil and of dream
> The appointed hour comes;
> Blessed is the day with its cares,
> Blessed also the coming of darkness! [6, xxi]

As does Tatyana:

> Perhaps all this is futile,
> The deception of an inexperienced soul!
> And a wholly different fate for me is judged . . .
> But so be it! [3, Tatyana's letter]

Both characters begin their speeches with reference to the beloved, Lensky even declaring his love for Olga and asking—ironically—if she will remember him. By the end, these references have been transformed. Immediately after "Ah, Olga I loved you!" Lensky shifts address and sings, "Ardent friend, desired friend, come, I am thy spouse, I await you." He never mentions Olga again. It is as if a loftier ideal had suddenly appeared to him. Tatyana asks, "Who are you? My guardian angel or an insidious tempter?" in another insight which supervenes her passions of the moment. Tchaikovsky elaborates his characters' intuition in these passages, Lensky's in the melodic climax of his aria and by setting off Tatyana's words with a separate introduction in the orchestra. Moreover, he links them verbally. Whereas Pushkin, near the end of Tatyana's letter, has her cry out "I await you!" Tchaikovsky interpolates these words into Lensky's aria. Should that detail be missed, he made the famous "Lensky sixth" in the refrain of his aria—a melody which begins on the third degree of the scale and proceeds downward to the fifth degree—a variant of Tatyana's question:

Ex. 25

Ex. 26

In *Onegin,* Tchaikovsky was seeking a richness of implication comparable to Pushkin, connecting Lensky and Tatyana by a depth of insight that amounts nearly to clairvoyance. Both characters sense their demise before the fact. In Pushkin, Tatyana foresaw Lensky's death in a nightmare. Tchaikovsky makes his point with a rhythm. Discounting the downbeat, which focuses the critical juncture in the manner of a call to attention, the verbal accents of the subsequent line correspond to words from the sixth song of the Orthodox funeral service, translated as "With the saints have rest":

Ex. 27

This phrase is associated not least with the *otpevanie,* or singing-off, of a departed soul. Tchaikovsky's appropriation of its verbal rhythm disguises the allusion by one note—the initial downbeat—in the same way that he had been curbing the obvious identity of allusions since his student days. This embedded meaning may explain why he will quote the phrase later in autograph albums to such un-Tatyana-like recipients as Platon Vakar, brother of Modest Vakar, whose son died of scarlet fever allegedly brought into his house by Tchaikovsky the child, and the chief procurator of the Holy Synod, Vladimir Karlovich Sabler [353, 146; 135, 75].

Around these central devices involving words, Tchaikovsky arrays purely musical ones. The vivid genre scenes—the folk choruses, the choral waltz at the beginning of act II, and the dances of act III—form a brilliant if uncomplicated foil to subtler manipulations of motif and key. A network of associative themes informs *Onegin,* primarily used in connection with Tatyana but not excluding Lensky and even Filippievna. Tchaikovsky marks Tatyana's critical act of writing by distinguishing her motifs on either side. Before the letter, she is represented by the melody at the beginning of the introduction:

Ex. 28

This is the demure Tatyana, who vanishes from the opera after she tears up her first attempt at writing Onegin (no. 9 at 34), to be heard again only in the closing scene (no. 22 at 88) at her words "As if I stood before him again as a young girl." In the interim, she is associated with two other themes: one is that of her question (example 25); the other is associated with her suffering, first stated in no. 8 at Tatyana's outburst to the nurse:

Ex. 29

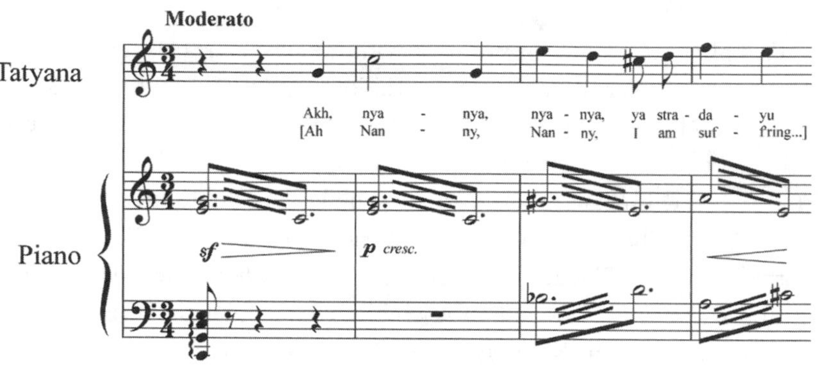

Other associative melodies are local to a scene, emphasizing a person or situation. Lensky's love song to Olga in no. 6 is illustrative, intensifying as Lensky expresses his feelings ever more fervently. Onegin's polite deference to Tatyana in the same scene reverts to the same musical line, which is unresponsive to the new text, producing not so much an associative motif as the expression of his state of mind:

Ex. 30

The opening phrase of his explanation to Tatyana in no. 12 creates a similar effect. To these readily audible devices, Tchaikovsky adds a network of subtleties, melodic and tonal, accessible through analysis [314, 116–51].

The key scheme of the opera is not unlike that of *Swan Lake:* characters and situations are assigned keys within the tonal system which are proximate or distant from one another in the same relationships as the characters or situations [432, 33–36]. Beneath its undramatic surface, *Evgeniy Onegin* lives by the verity of its characters' emotions, the portrayal of mores, its subtexts, and that multidimensional nuance of which the best operas are made. It is Tchaikovsky's strongest libretto in the connotative richness of its words.

CHAPTER ELEVEN

1878

TCHAIKOVSKY WAS IN WESTERN EUROPE UNTIL APRIL, THEN RE-turned to Russia. He started the academic year in Moscow in the autumn, resigned early in October, then went to Kamenka and to Vienna. From 15 November to the end of the year, he was in Western Europe again, spending almost a month in Florence with Meck; he then went to Paris in mid-December and to Clarens by year's end.

On the first of January 1878 (O.S.), he was in San Remo, his immediate source of anguish being a promise to serve on the Russian delegation to the Paris Universal Exhibition later that year [vi 186, 319, n. 2]. Reminded by an appointment letter just before Christmas, he would have to leave immediately, abandon the Fourth Symphony, and cancel the imminent visit of Modest and Kolya Konradi. Instead, he withdrew, declaring himself to the Russian consul in Paris to be too ill to leave San Remo despite his "ardent desire"; he was unable to answer the questionnaire sent to him in reference to the delegation and resolute that any substitute would require guidance and instruction [222, 19–20, 29–32]. Rubinstein's reaction to this would be unsettling, as Tchaikovsky was to return to the conservatory in the autumn and still depended on him.

Freedom had been a godsend, but had not proved easy. In the last two months of 1877, a disappointing tour of Italy forecast Tchaikovsky's powerful but aimless wanderlust of the coming years. Susceptible to impulse, moving from town to town, as soon as he was situated, he was miserable. En route to Italy again in 1878, he would write:

> In the traditions of youth, *abroad* still had some ill-defined prestige in my eyes—but every time, as the realization of *being abroad* is pleasant for the first moment, for me it loses its charm and starts to bring on melancholy. But such melancholy as now I have never yet experienced, since my life circumstances are fully excellent and I have no cause for complaint. . . . Consequently I am completely free and happy. All this I happily acknowledge, and yet I am sad to the point of tears. [vii 460–61]

Wanderlust had brought him to San Remo, but soon he was pining for the simple Russian landscape; on Russian Christmas, he declared that if Meck should offer him a little place near Moscow, he would accept and live out his days there [vi 336]. In time, freedom came to mean being nomadic and rootless, complicated in 1878 by Kolya Konradi's continuing illness and Tchaikovsky's servant Alyosha's contacting a venereal disease. Uncertainties of the mail threatened the Fourth Symphony, some Glinka text underlays Jurgenson had assigned him, and sketches for the First Suite. As a permanent home looked ever more attractive, he asked Lev Davïdov on 12/24 February for a room some distance from the main house at Kamenka, beyond reach of any musical sounds. By April, "a little cottage" off to one side had been arranged [vii 235]; by 16 August, he declared that he could find full satisfaction from life only in the solitude of the country [vii 372]; by 21 October, the Kamenka family had invited him to stay until Christmas [vii 433]. In the first years after his marriage, he considered Kamenka to be his permanent domicile, but by 1882 a home of his own was essential if life were not to be an endless series of visits. Finding one would be his first job upon returning to Russia in 1885.

Freedom spawned other problems. He had more money now but no talent for managing it [MV020820], making him a Maecenas to his devotees and a spendthrift to his providers. Any hope that he might effect any savings or put aside earnings from his music was never realized. In emergencies, he begged for more and pledged reform; but reform he never did, so when need arose, and that was often, his spending strained the ties of friendship. After giving Jurgenson the Fourth Symphony and *Evgeniy Onegin* in January [vii 42], following the *Rococo Variations* and the *Valse-scherzo*—probably contrite over the failure of Leuckardt to publish the last two—he proposed that Jurgenson pay for his work and advance large sums when needed, in return for projects simple and laborious [vii 72]. He would approve the last proofs and reissue his lighter pieces, "revised and corrected by the composer," preparing for the onset of the works' legal protection abroad. At times, Tchaikovsky pressed Jurgenson and Meck beyond their regular limits, once taking money from Meck's servants [vii 291]. No party to Tchaikovsky's finances ever explained how he spent it or cited a cause, leaving enigmatic his near-constant debt. We are left to wonder if Tchaikovsky suffered an extreme, perhaps pathological inability to forestall spending any money in his possession. At the same time, he was not simply profligate. In December, he returned 2,200 francs to Meck, but then regretted it. "I am sometimes quite horrified at my mercenariness and love of money," he wrote to Anatoly [vii 540].

That freedom enhanced Tchaikovsky's health and outlook is unclear because these were so dependent on overcoming his marital trauma. In one letter of 25 October/6 November 1877, "the wound was too fresh" for him to describe Antonina objectively, but in another his shattered nerves were "now in the best possible shape" [vi 197, 201]. At the end of November, his body was fine but his spirit might never recover from its wound [vi 258]. Bad days outnumbered good in the last months of 1877, as he completed the Fourth Symphony and *Onegin,* scoring them "as if they had been composed by someone else" [vi 259]. Throughout 1878 he regained creative fluency, from his claim in January that his depression was bad but he worked when he could [vii 23], to informing Anatoly that he had stopped twitching [vii 52], to attributing an attack of spleen to not composing on 12/24 February. In March, he declared himself free of mental illness [vii 183] and progressed on various pieces in April. Yet he was easily stalled. On 4/16 March, he complained of squeezing "frail and wretched little thoughts" out of himself and having to ponder every bar [vii 151]. The next day he explained to Meck, touching in effect on *prelest':*

> Only music which has poured out from the depth of the artistic soul by agitated inspiration can touch, stagger and move. There is no doubt that even the greatest musical geniuses sometimes worked unfired by inspiration. It is a guest that does not always appear at first call. Meanwhile one must always *work,* and the genuine, honorable artist cannot sit, arms crossed, on the pretext that he is not in the *mood.* If one waits for the mood and does not try to go out and meet it, it is easy to lapse into laziness and apathy. One must endure and believe, and inspiration will inevitably come to the person who can conquer *ill disposition.* [vii 154]

For the next three years, Tchaikovsky's productivity and occasional masterwork did not belie his uncertain inspiration. He wrote short pieces on sheer craft, but long works suffered when technique substituted for deep invention. He lacked "creative lust" [vi 238].

His well-being was linked to nonmedical palliatives, including company. At first Anatoly was his rod and his staff, but no sooner had Pyotr arrived in Switzerland than he lamented the "murderously burdensome" separation from his servant Alyosha [88, 299]. "He understands extremely well what I require of him nowadays, and satisfies all my requirements and more" [88, 327]. Tchaikovsky conceded "an unhealthy tenderness" for Kolya Konradi [86 I 139], which continued in 1878, and for Josef Kotek [369, 123], his fondness for whom cooled only after Kotek contracted syphilis, and Tchaikovsky focused on musicianly affinities when working on the Violin Concerto in March. In December in Paris, he was unhappy, among other complaints, with Kotek's pursuit of women, his reading of Tchaikovsky's letters, and his insistence that Tchaikovsky translate for him at the theater [vii 559].

Pyotr reserved a deeply emotional response for Anatoly, who departed in late November 1877 and to whom he wrote 23 times in December before Christmas. "I would express in words how I loved you, but there are no words for it," he wrote on 1/13 December, "It is a bottomless chasm of love" [88, 318]. The next day, "my soul is full of you," and at the end: "I kiss you a million times. What I wouldn't give to kiss you in fact" [88, 318, 320]. This intensity waned with the arrival of Modest and Kolya, but on 21 December Pyotr was covering Anatoly with kisses in his mind [88, 339]. Language so extraordinary revives issues about Tchaikovsky's correspondence: that so many of Anatoly's letters survive in copies, and that Anatoly led the charge after Pyotr's death to purge the letters. Similar remarks to Anatoly continued in 1878, mostly in effusive closings, which were censored in the academic edition with less obvious cause than those of 1877.

Tchaikovsky's principal companion in 1878 was Nadezhda von Meck, with whom he had a massive correspondence paralleled in letters to Anatoly and Modest. He was to her "like a child in its mother's caress" [vii 40] and was amazed by her clairvoyance [vii 34]. She continued to be infatuated at the "supernatural affinity of ideas and feelings that is apparent in almost every one of our letters," waxing effusive, possessive, and curious by turns. To Anatoly, he wrote on 1/13 February of difficulty expressing himself to her, unsure if the reason were shame or constantly having to thank her. For her part, Meck reaffirmed her justification for patronage. Only in voluntary relationships does her love give her the right to a person; reciprocated love places an unlimited obligation on her. Only one who loves and is loved by another has any right over another:

> [A]nd, as our relationship is of this kind, . . . my interest in all aspects of your life has no time limit. . . . It will be the same everywhere, in exactly the same forms as it has been up to now, more so because I have discovered during my long life that for a talent to be able to develop and receive inspiration, life must be materially secure. Otherwise it will stagnate, become sickly, tearful, and weak, and you know, my matchless friend, how precious your talent is to me, how I want to protect it: in your music I hear myself, my condition, I receive echoes of my thoughts, my anguish. [86 I 210–12]

Nothing in their correspondence better explains Meck's relationship to Tchaikovsky. A few weeks after writing it she came away from a performance of *Marche slave* in a swoon worthy of Johannes Kreisler, which led to a symbolic union: "the force of my feelings is enough to possess you wholly. In your music I merge into one with you, and no one can compete with me in that" [86 I 242].

Tchaikovsky adjusted to Meck's stance, if with a trace of embarrassment. He was discomfited by her closeness, inhibited by their near-meetings in Florence:

> But I cannot hide that N[adezhda] F[ilaretovna's] proximity somewhat embarrasses me. She walks and rides by very often. What happens if I meet her? How am I to act? She, evidently, is not the least afraid of this, as she even sent me a ticket to the theater for Saturday, where she will be. She proposes that I look at her villa, and although she says that when I do I shall not encounter a soul, it somehow frightens me. Sometimes it even seems to me that she might now be seeking personal acquaintance, though in her daily letters there is no hint of this. All this makes me not fully free, and to confess, in the depth of my soul I very much wish that she were soon to leave. [vii 479]

During the remainder of his Florence visit, Tchaikovsky was dispirited over her increasingly compulsive mothering [vii 519], though he felt guilty complaining of her and was sorrowful after she left. In addition, he noted to Modest, Florence was being spoiled by one "Napoleon," apparently a stalker, the avoidance of whom was keeping him from frequent visits to the town [vii 484, 496]. The early Meck correspondence is the richest repository of Tchaikovsky's unfeigned views on a number of topics, about most of which Meck inquired: the church [vi 251–52; 266, 80–81]; his family [vi 252–54; 266, 81–85]; the Mighty Handful and other musicians [vi 328–32; 266, 119–23]; the First Piano Concerto [vii 64–65; above, p. 89]; Schopenhauer, platonic and non-platonic love [vii 105–6, 122; 266, 82–83]; symphonic composition and the Fourth Symphony [vii 124–27; 266, 183–88]; Alexander Serov [vii 159–61; 266, 205–8]; Mozart [vii 179–81; 266, 219–22]; inspiration and composition [vii 314–21; 266, 293–98]; Edouard Lalo [vii 485–88; 266, 386–89]; and program music [vii 513–14; 266, 403–5].

After she left Kamenka, Antonina was next heard from in January 1878 in pestering letters about money to Anatoly and the aged Ilya. This enraged Pyotr: "Where can I escape from this intolerable plague with which I infected myself in the heat of quite inexplicable madness, of my own free will, without asking anyone's permission, and for no known reason? I cannot even blame anyone!" [vii 95]. In return for concessions, she promised never to bother him or his family again. The trip to San Remo helped him to recover:

> I was, to be sure, quite insane for several months running, and only now, having recovered fully, am I relating objectively to *everything* that went wrong during this short period of insanity. The person who in May intended to marry Antonina Ivanovna, in June, as if nothing had happened, wrote a complete opera, and in July married, in September fled from his wife, . . . was not I, but another Pyotr Ilyich, of whom now remains only the *misanthropy,* which, however, will probably never pass. [vii 98]

All of his divorce strategies failed. Tchaikovsky proposed that she take the initiative and he the blame; that he would pay all expenses and she would have the right to remarry; when it was over, she would receive 10,000 rubles from Meck [vii 243]. In response she accused him of egotism and perpetual self-interest; of deliberately causing her woe, subjecting her to mockery and profanation in Kamenka and now wanting her to divorce him without cause; of anticipating these designs early in their marriage; of acting in bad faith when taking 2,500 rubles of hers to set up house; and of making public their intimate letters. She distrusted Anatoly, whose behavior had been offensive, and preferred the Holy Synod to a court of law; she wanted the 2,500 rubles repaid before she defaulted on the loan which produced it. Only at the end was there a hopeful sign, when she invoked God to determine who was right and added, "I await notification as to how to proceed with the matter, so as to end it quietly and without scandals" [365, 226].

For the case to proceed, Pyotr had to perform an indiscreet act recorded by an eyewitness. Embarrassing as that would be, his greater concern was that Antonina would not change roles to be the aggressor [vii 294–95]. During 10 days at the beginning of June, the project derailed. Her discussion with Jurgenson went "round in small circles," producing no result [vii 304]. Never did she claim not to love him; she refused to lie in court; and if it came to proving his adultery, she would deny it. At some point, she learned of Meck's subsidy [365, 59], magnifying the complication of losing testamentary considerations if she divorced. Negotiations were revived on 24 July with new conditions: no divorce (as Antonina did not plan to remarry); a passport renewable without Tchaikovsky's permission; a guarantee of a one-time payment; and a pledge on her mother's "noble word of honor" that Antonina would never bother him again. Tchaikovsky paid his debt to her within a week, and her verbal attacks ceased [365, 59–60]. By the end of 1878, she had established a pattern of behavior: make contact, list misfortunes, claim to love him, and appeal for money. Her extremes, artless or willful, never lost their power to upset the composer. Yet, even at his angriest, Tchaikovsky never completely lost sympathy for Antonina, regardless of any threat of her suing him for his way of living "against nature" [369, 124–25].

Tchaikovsky's withdrawal from the delegation to the World Exhibition was one cause of his break with the Moscow Conservatory. Rubinstein called him idle and capricious and suggested that he withdrew from the exhibition because he was financially secure [vii 45]. He was joined in disapproval by Albrecht, Taneyev, Jurgenson, and even Anatoly [vii 53]. Yet Tchaikovsky was adamant. The thought of going to Paris made him ill [vii 57–58]. He felt alienated, and angry at Rubinstein:

> I have just reread your letter and was again amazed at your incomprehensible ignorance and lack of understanding of me generally and my present crisis in particular.

. . . I am quite aware of everything I owe you, but I very much dislike your seeing blessings where they do not truly exist. . . . I am obliged to [Meck] not just for life, but for being able to continue work, which is dearer than life to me. It is offensive to me on her behalf that you understand her as little as you do me. She is not an *eccentric.* For me she is the inexhaustible hand of providence. One must know her as I do now not to doubt that such infinitely good and trusting people still exist. [vii 45]

Meddling in the Tchaikovsky-Meck relationship may have been Rubinstein's critical mistake. It incensed Pyotr and induced Meck to follow suit in a hyperbole of invective. On 12 December 1877, she had attacked Rubinstein for keeping the conservatory at a low standard and using it to "gratify his despotism, vanity, petty spite, and other petty emotions" [86 I 120]. Tchaikovsky added that, when Rubinstein had not been drinking, he was distant, reminded Tchaikovsky that he owed him everything, and feared that Tchaikovsky wanted to become the director of the Moscow Conservatory [vi 332]. By 22 January, Meck had concluded that Rubinstein did not possess one decent quality:

He can understand only life's material side—he can feel only odious ambition, incessant envy, and vile love of power, and must have envied you because, although *you* never gave him reason to feel your superiority over him, *he himself* realizes it, and such natures never forgive this and it comes to the surface on every occasion. He envies me, too, but for my wealth, and, although he comes to me and assures me of his gratitude (why I don't know), he does vile things on every conceivable occasion. [86 I 176]

The next day, Tchaikovsky recounted the episode with the First Piano Concerto, but added: "Yesterday I began a letter to you in which I thought I'd give a complete account of my relations with Rubinstein. I had already completed three sheets when I felt revolted and ashamed to be writing all this empty, trivial, nasty rubbish" [vii 66]. Sensing that the September academic term was still too distant for such heated emotions, he calmed down just as Rubinstein took countermeasures. In March, Rubinstein appeared as the soloist in the First Piano Concerto to critical praise [vii 162, n. 6] and then revived the incidental music to *The Snow Maiden.*

From the outset of Tchaikovsky's crisis, Rubinstein understood that he might leave the conservatory, explaining that his classes were covered and no replacement would be invited if there were the smallest hope of his return [252, 162]. Tchaikovsky used this promise to negotiate reductions in his weekly teaching, assuring Rubinstein that the fewer hours he taught, the greater would be his zeal [vii 230]. As Rubinstein agreed to more reductions, Tchaikovsky's animosity revived. Outmaneuvered, Rubinstein agreed to ever more curtailed duties until none was left.

During Tchaikovsky's visit to Moscow at the beginning of June to learn the divorce procedure, he celebrated Rubinstein's birthday. "My numb feeling of *dislike* has blossomed into a quite excruciating *hostility,*" he wrote to Meck. Rubinstein still resented his withdrawal from the Paris Exhibition [vii 299], at which, it developed, Rubinstein was scheduled to conduct four concerts of Russian music, beginning with Tchaikovsky's First Piano Concerto at the first concert. Accordingly, criticism of Rubinstein fell silent through much of July. On the 25th, however, Tchaikovsky invoked the critical term *freedom* to Meck:

> I cannot hide from you that I enter upon the performance of my Conservatory duties with extreme aversion. Of course, it may well be that I shall quickly get used to it and manage, all the more that the awareness of my freedom will reassure me. Indeed, freedom is an ineffable blessing and happiness. With it one can always get on with life and reconcile oneself with all circumstances. [vii 346]

Not quite. To Modest on 29 August, he reported scabrous gossip about the Moscow Conservatory in a St. Petersburg newspaper. The piece mainly criticized Rubinstein [86 I 596–97] but mentioned Tchaikovsky on its way to matters more salacious:

> "There are in the Conservatory amours of another sort, but of them, for reasons eminently well understood, I shall not speak." It is clear to what this alluded. And so, that sword of Damocles, in the form of newspaper insinuation, which I fear most in the world, has grabbed me by the neck again. Let us suppose that the insinuation on this occasion does not touch me, but all the worse. My reputation is falling on the entire conservatory, and this makes me even [more] shameful and burdened. [88, 442]

For the next three weeks, his revulsion simmered. On a train ride earlier in August, he overheard two passengers gossiping about *him,* his marriage, and his insanity [vii 384]. Early in September, he received an offer from the St. Petersburg Conservatory at twice the salary and one-seventh the classroom time of his Moscow post [vii 396]. But he still needed Meck's express blessing to break with Moscow: "If you say I must stay then I shall of course, and fight this perhaps insane, but passionate, infinite thirst for freedom" [vii 393]. But after the exhibition concerts, Meck had gone to Italy, and she did not reply until 20 September. In the meantime, Tchaikovsky worked himself into a frenzy as the term began. Writing to Modest after his first class, everything was offensive—people, conversations, professors, students, rooms, walls, air—everything [vii 394]. To Meck he described his frustrations, with escape the only option [vii 397].

When Rubinstein returned to Moscow on 22 September, he described the enormous impression Tchaikovsky's music had made in Paris and how the conservatory was fortunate to possess such a celebrity. The next day, Tchaikovsky informed him that he would not stay past December. Rubinstein expressed no regret other than the loss of the prestige attached to the composer's name. On 24 September—Meck's approval still forthcoming—came the last straw. Adhering to the letter of her agreement if not the spirit, Antonina was back:

> [Her mother is] bombarding me with letters expressing the most tender love, invitations to visit her, and even a request to be a *proxy father* at the wedding of her youngest daughter, saying that *my blessing will bring her happiness* (!!!!). In one letter she tries to persuade me to live with a certain person and promises me *complete happiness.* Ah, my God, how good it would be to be a long way from all this. [vii 409]

He acted quickly. By 30 September, he told Rubinstein he would stay only for another month [vii 414]. Three days later, he could find no reason to wait that long. He hesitated, because Taneyev needed time to prepare to replace him, and Rubinstein was about to perform the First Concerto again, but he then decided: "these factors are outweighed by the fact that my life now is such a dreadful mess, is so insufferable, so insupportable, that I cannot bear even a month here" [vii 417]. He agreed to stay until the end of the week, citing, as he had when leaving the civil service, "domestic reasons." Thus, 6 October 1878 was Tchaikovsky's last day as a professor of the Moscow Conservatory.

On 3 October, Meck had written of her pleasure at his being liberated from the "Tartar yoke of our *eminent* and *undoubtedly worthy* friend." She was going to Florence for a couple of months [86 I 451]. He followed, after a sad farewell dinner, learning that Balakirev, claiming a lack of academic training, had declined to replace him [87 I 49]. Rubinstein's mood was dark. After a "friendly meeting" [vii 434], Tchaikovsky had doubts about his decision and would come to regret his treatment of Rubinstein. Congratulating him on his name-day (6 December), he also described to Anatoly a dream of his deep sorrow at Rubinstein's death. "Since then I cannot think of him without regret in my heart and without the most affirmative feeling of love" [vii 515].

At Kamenka in October, Tchaikovsky read proofs of the op. 40 piano pieces, corrected *Vakula,* and worked on the First Suite, three movements of which he had accidentally left behind in St. Petersburg. In Florence, Meck filled his days; he described his quarters to her and discussed music and composers (including himself), flirtation (passing by each other's homes, observing each other at events), and giving composition lessons to her house violinist, Vladislav Pachulsky [265]. There, he composed a substantial poem, "Lilies-of-the-Valley" [vii 542–43]. Early in December, Meck announced that she would soon be going to Paris, and he agreed to go there also. On the 28th, he and Alyosha left Paris for Clarens, arriving at noon on 30 December.

There were straws in the wind in 1878. In March, Alyosha took a romantic interest in Marie, a maid at the Villa Richelieu in Clarens; during this time his relations with Tchaikovsky suffered [vii 166, 176]; in October, the composer noted that Alyosha was nearing the age of military service [vii 424]. On 15 June, he observed to Modest that only morphine gave Sasha relief from the pain of her liver ailment, that Lev had grown thin and shadowy, and that their daughter Tanya was given to hysterics [vii 302]. In August, at Nizï, Pyotr reported to Anatoly that his friend Nikolay Kondratiev had been seriously ill for two months, had grown thin, and suffered from a strange body rash; Modest suspected syphilis [88, 436].

CHAPTER TWELVE

The Music of 1878

TCHAIKOVSKY'S RESUMPTION OF COMPOSING AFTER HIS MARriage dates from 11/23 February 1878; he composed a song between breakfast and lunch [vii 108]. Three days later, he informed Jurgenson that he wanted to compose some children's pieces, perhaps a liturgy [vii 120]. In March, after beginning a piano sonata, he was "succumbing to the lack of desire to work" [vii 152], but was in fact about to conceive the Violin Concerto, inspired in part by Josef Kotek, of whom the composer later remarked, "There is no denying that without him I could not have done anything" [vii 194]. Nor is there denying a return to his fluent invention of old, the concerto taking but 11 days to draft and nine to score, including the new slow movement. The manuscript was dated 30 March/11 April 1878. Tchaikovsky departed Clarens on 5/17 April and arrived at Kamenka on the 11th, where family matters and illness delayed any further composition until 23 April. On this date, he projected into May the *Children's Album*, songs, violin pieces, some sacred music, and some first thoughts about an opera. In general, the assessment of this music is inextricable from his convalescence.

On 20 March/1 April, Tchaikovsky finished recopying the first movement of the Violin Concerto [vii 191], the first work wholly conceived and composed after his marriage debacle, and two days later Kotek had recopied the solo part. On 27 March/8 April, he informed Jurgenson that the piano arrangement was very messy, and as he had not written the solo part into it, Kotek would take it all to a copyist in Berlin [vii 203]. For differences between the autograph and the academic edition, see the *Collected Works* [CW 30a, 171–72]; famous violinists (Auer, Oistrakh) have also edited it. This was the only work of 1878 about which Tchaikovsky had no doubts, reporting to Meck, "From the day that propitious mood struck it has not left me. In such a phase of spiritual life composition completely loses the character of labor: it is a veritable pleasure. When you write you don't know how time passes, and if no one interrupts you could work the whole day without getting up" [vii 164].

Early Viennese critics gave raucous voice to the concerto's atypicality, though what they heard is not disorder and incoherence. The first movement conforms in large part to the concerto variant of sonata-allegro: an orchestral introduction (if not a classic ritornello), then discernible exposition, then development. A solo cadenza, recalling Mendelssohn, precedes the recapitulation and coda. The second movement is a ritornello pattern, and the finale is a rondo.

The first movement is based on two winning themes, articulated by lengthy upbeats. The introduction approaches the first tonic cadence at bar 28 with the principal theme stated by the soloist. After this, the alternation is systematic: upbeat (34–40) to a restatement of the principal theme (41–46); elaboration incorporating the transition (47–68) acting as upbeat to the second theme (69–85); solo elaboration/upbeat (86–126), followed by orchestral close (127–40), which reprises the principal theme in a triumphal variant. As he had in the First Piano Concerto, Tchaikovsky reconceived the rhetoric of sonata-allegro.

This work lacks a big opening; the transition is unclassical, filled with soloist elaboration and moving to the second theme without a cadence (the second theme begins on the continuation of the dominant); the first sustained *tutti* is reserved to the very end of the exposition before trailing off to an uncertain 21 bars at the beginning of the development—themeless, non-improvisatory, wandering. From here, the music continues somewhat aimlessly, as if an exclamation point were expected and nothing happened. His powerful retransition spills over into the cadenza without a defining moment (at 211), and when (at 303) he withholds the *tutti* closing and begins the drive to the final cadence instead, the omission is almost palpable. In May, he wrote to Meck of the first movement: "Of course there is in it, as in every composition written for virtuoso display, much that is cold and calculated, but the themes were not forced, and generally speaking the plan of this movement came into my head at once, poured forth on its own, spontaneously" [vii 256]. If there is a flaw, it is that the unusual pattern risks leaving the customary architecture insufficiently marked.

Tchaikovsky wrote a magical slow movement. The introduction, which returns as a ritornello (bars 61, 96), so obscures the principal theme—another parallel with Mendelssohn's Violin Concerto—that its unexpected appearance is a ravishing deception. Throughout the movement he transforms themes, making those initially disparate closer to one another in melodic shape. This is first suggested in the likeness between the continuation of the principal melody at 28–30 with the introduction at 9–10, and again at 30–32 with 5–6. By the time the introduction returns at 96, the ear discerns this kinship. Meanwhile, the flute (at 34) stating the principal theme recalls the flute taking the principal theme in the movement I recapitulation.

Tchaikovsky elided the *Canzonetta* with the finale. The 52-bar introduction is another long upbeat to the classic pattern. The rondo itself is aclassical in that the second theme (at bar 149) proceeds to the middle section (at 197) without the return of the first. The abrupt changes of key and mood at this point affirm his exceptional behavior. The similarity of this middle theme to Lensky's farewell in *Evgeniy Onegin* cannot be accidental, any more than its assignment to the oboe, which presented the analogous melody in Tatyana's aria:

Ex. 31

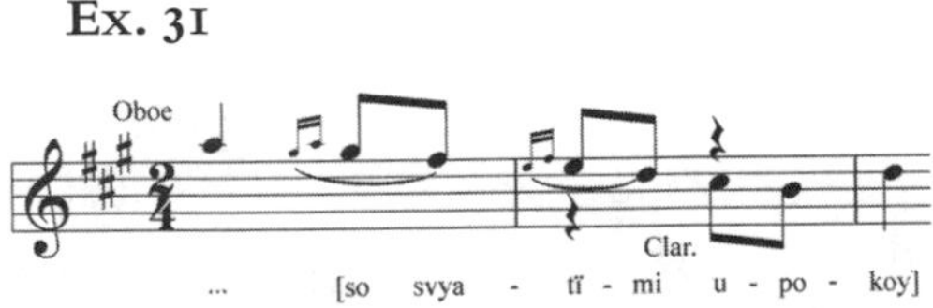

Alluding thus to the death of poetry, Tchaikovsky acknowledges the danger facing his own muse. At first, he softens the effect by spinning out the tune (217–30), but later yields to an aclassical peroration on it (400–445). Clearly, he could not expunge the memory.

Taking 38 minutes to perform, the Piano Sonata in G, op. 37a, yields to Beethoven's *Hammerklavier* at 43 minutes but overtakes Liszt's and Schumann's First. Unlike Beethoven's self-generating logic, Tchaikovsky's is based on contrast, reprise, and thematic transformation, virtuosity substituting for deep logic. Allusion in the Sonata is problematic. The brilliant octave writing and the surprise coloristic chord (e.g., mvt. II at 40) may have reminded Karl Klindworth, the dedicatee, of Liszt, his teacher. (To Klindworth, Tchaikovsky, the day after he left the conservatory, yielded full editorial control over the Sonata, which the pianist exercised on details unrelated to musical substance [213, 16; 227, 440, 446–47].) Elsewhere, it echoes Schumann's First Sonata, op. 11, which shares with Tchaikovsky's an impulsive, self-conscious, postclassical noisiness and hyperbole. Schumann's Gypsy-like melody in the introduction may have inspired the second theme of Tchaikovsky's opening movement; his fandango theme, a wrist étude of several pages, is echoed in the B section of Tchaikovsky's finale; the embedded reprise in Schumann's introduction is a device much used by Tchaikovsky; the dotted rhythm in Schumann's Scherzo anticipates a similar figure in Tchaikovsky's slow movement.

As in the Violin Concerto, Tchaikovsky adheres to classic pattern here, but produces formal tension in the unexpected omission and restoration of theme and key. Compared with Beethoven's subtleties, Tchaikovsky's form building is crude and unwieldy. Whether he drafted mvt. I, most affected by this problem, before setting aside the Sonata is not known. Its uninspired genesis raises questions about lesser, perhaps inadvertent allusions: to the Orgy Chorus in act I of *Les Huguenots* in Tchaikovsky's opening theme; to the *tempo di minuetto* to which the Catholic and Protestant nobles enter—in the same opera in act II—which lurks beneath the Schumannesque dotted flourishes of movement II (bars 24–26); and to the first phrase of the *Dies irae* in the second area (79) and close of movement I. Tchaikovsky frequently alluded to other music and admitted it, but allusion is ambiguous in a piece this pretentious. The effect of quoting the Mass for the dead, bellowed out with accents at the approach to the final cadence, forces a distinction between loftiness and kitsch, an ambiguity writ large across the Sonata which may speak to Tchaikovsky's state of mind at the time. *War es also gemeint?* Beethoven would not allow that question; Tchaikovsky stumbles on it.

Klindworth praised the Sonata; Tchaikovsky called Nikolay Rubinstein's performance "one of the most wonderful moments of my life" [viii 409], while describing it elsewhere as "somewhat dry and complex" [viii 403], "not without interest, but . . . one of the least lovable of my children" [viii 428].

The dedication to Anatoly of the *Six Romances,* op. 38, composed between February and May, acknowledges his help through Pyotr's marital crisis, which is recalled metaphorically in the songs. Op. 38 answers op. 28, the poetical motifs of which—obsession with and the denial of love—are reprised here with greater intensity: the singer's present is more drastic, the past more remote and ideal. Op. 38 sings of Tchaikovsky's preoccupations: mania, nostalgia, the affinities of mysterious love, coaxing the spirit back to joy from sadness, feeling passion after death, and escape to Italy.

In "Don Juan's Serenade," the wrathful Don, whose desire to see Nisetta can barely match his love of mortal combat on this night "reddened by the moonlight," personifies madness, which is conveyed in the accompaniment—the headlong, winding melody that frames the song and that returns the instant the voice falls silent. The key of B minor, echoing the combat music from *Romeo and Juliet,* is associated with death. The Don is less a predator than an irrational force; insanity and death are the measure of his song and of the composer's discontent that winter.

"It was in the early spring" (no. 2) enthuses over a distant love confession with imagery so vivid that the past fuses with the present in the singer's mind. The song is Schumannesque, the voice entering in midphrase and moving to cadence, the poem itself leading to an ecstatic moment. The strophic structure is illusory, changing at the ends of verses with the images: first, pure nature; then, nature and the beloved with a change of key (at 40) and echoes of the voice in the piano representing the beloved's "answer" to the singer's love. The ecstatic moment follows the last coherent line, "It was the morning of our years," with exclamations *ad libitum.*

No. 3, "Amid the din of the ball," echoes the imagery of "My Genius, My Angel, My Friend," as the beloved's presence visits the singer in the night, and refers, in "the call of a distant fife"—again, the *svirel'*—to the shepherd's pipe of song 2 and to the Hellenic panpipe at the opening of *Evgeniy Onegin.* Here, the singer actually meets the mysterious beloved, whose glance, voice, look, and laughter leave a mark, with the memory of which he merges as he falls asleep. The waltz rhythm persists throughout—the "din of the ball" providing a concrete image for the topical final line, "I do not know if I love you, but it seems I do!"

In "O, if only you could," the singer would recapture an earlier moment to dispel sorrow now. The mood is enthusiastic, the pace projecting a single burst of energy. Pitch and chord from the minor pass instantly but leave hints of sorrow, mostly in the minor sixth of the scale, first in the piano's opening gambit. It is the singer coaxing the beloved away from sadness. By setting aside the parallelisms of the poem in the music after the opening melody of each verse and by the sweeping upward gesture of the final cadence, Tchaikovsky creates parallels with song 2.

Lermontov's "The love of a dead man" expresses the eerie passion of a spirit beyond the grave who wrongly expected earthly feelings to abandon him at death. His soul is still fixed on his old love, and he suffers at the prospect of a rival. It is as if Don Juan, who offered up his life in no. 1, is looking back now as the *commendatore*'s heavy tread lurks the bass. Tchaikovsky sensed the tirade of the poem and used the first two lines as a frame—calmer, more majestic than the *più mosso,* where he limits range and cantilena. At the midpoint ("What to me is the radiance of God's power and holy paradise! / I have brought earthly passion with me there"), the words are set to Tatyana's and Lensky's funereal rhythm, already echoed in the Violin Concerto.

A memento of Florence, the borrowed tune in no. 6 was adjusted by Tchaikovsky to the trappings of the salon romance. His remarks about the ravishing voice of the young Vittorio, from whose singing he copied "Pimpinella," bespeak an exceptional fascination. Tchaikovsky had heard him in Florence in November 1877, but in February 1878, "I cried, languished, melted from delight," but also, to Anatoly, he reported being "permeated with one feeling" [88, 379]. The composer notated several of Vittorio's songs, but after that visit Vittorio dropped from view.

Drafted from 1 to 4 May 1878, little else is known about *The Children's Album: A Collection of Easy Pieces for Children in Imitation of Schumann,* op. 39, apart from a change in the order of the pieces. "The New Doll," "The Doll's Illness," and "The Doll's Funeral" were published in sequence, whereas in Tchaikovsky's original plan "The New Doll" came after the burial of the old one and just before the spirited dances which began in the publication with no. 9. The revision approximates the sequence of events in the first two chapters of Madame Segur's popular children's book, *Les malheurs de Sophie* (Paris, 1864), which was read to the children at Kamenka, where Tchaikovsky composed the piece and dedicated it to young Bob Davïdov. The reference to Schumann identifies the work's niche, but this music improves upon its namesake—briefer, more congenial, uncluttered in fingering and hand movement, less repetitive, densely textured, more diverse, and more engaged in external reference than Schumann. The *Children's*

Album is more lucid than the Piano Sonata—a quality less related to a young audience than to a perfect reckoning of length, balance between theme and elaboration, and the right contrast to follow.

In the preludial no. 1, "Morning Prayer," Tchaikovsky bows to Schumann, beginning with a theme reminiscent of the German master but also similar to no. 10 of the forthcoming *Liturgy,* "We hymn Thee, we bless Thee." A suite of borrowed pieces runs through the middle of the collection, like a divertissement. No. 12 in the published order is a Russian tune from his *Fifty Russian Folk Songs;* the "Kamarinskaya" in no. 14 is the wedding tune famous from Glinka; Vittorio from "Pimpinella" in op. 38 sings again in no. 15, the "Perche tradirme"; no. 16 is "Mes belles amourettes" from Weckerlin's *Echos du temps passé;* no. 18 is the "Neapolitan Dance" from *Swan Lake;* no. 24 quotes a Venetian street song. The *Children's Album* may draw on the composer's own memory. When he was a child, Fanny Dürbach saw to his prayers (nos. 1 and 23) and taught him the geography of Europe, echoed in the divertissement. She made Pyotr join in games, which might have included *petit cavalier* (no. 4) or wooden soldiers (no. 5); in quiet moments, he may have thought of *Maman* (no. 3) or listened to his own nurse's tale (no. 19).

Twelve Pieces of Medium Difficulty for piano, op. 40, is a miscellany composed between 4 July 1876, when Tchaikovsky offered a variant of no. 9 to Sergey Taneyev as a keepsake [CW 53, 235], through 11/23 February 1878, when he embarked on no. 12, to 30 April, when the set was finished. They were published in January 1879 and dedicated to Modest Tchaikovsky.

Unavoidable comparisons preclude flattering assessments. Tchaikovsky's opening, "Étude," evokes an uncomfortable Chopin in its elementary textures and blunt repetitions; in such company; the mazurkas of nos. 4 and 5 sound banal next to Chopin's rhythmic subtlety and expressive range (the engaging phrase extensions in no. 5 at 25–39 excepted). Similarly, no. 6, "Chant sans paroles," invokes Mendelssohn but disappoints with its nondescript cantilena. A fundamental problem is thus laid bare: excepting nos. 7 and 8, op. 40 is uninspired. Too often Tchaikovsky gives themes too ordinary elaboration too great. He is coaxing his muse, hoping to forestall embarrassing silences, even if in filling them he does not have much to say. The "Russian Dance" (no. 10), originally interpolated into act III of *Swan Lake,* shows what he is trying to regain; the Venetian song which forms the dream of no. 12, "Rêverie interrompue," breathes suavity just as

Tchaikovsky's original music around it is labored. It may be stretching a point to hear a likeness between no. 2, "Chanson triste," and Schubert's famous "Heidenröslein," but surely not the allusion to Schumann's op. 17, *Fantasia* (mvt. III at 44), in bar 5 of no. 3, the "Marche funebre"—at 10 minutes' playing time, easily the most overburdened of Tchaikovsky's simple thoughts. After the beginning of Beethoven's Sonata, op. 81a ("Les adieux"), no one could write the first two chords of no. 12 without risking accusations of theft. Op. 40 reveals the state of Tchaikovsky's muse soon after his marriage. The standard is low even if one considers piano miniatures to be a jaded repertoire.

Conceived in devotion [269, 200–202], Tchaikovsky's *Liturgy of St. John Chrysostom,* op. 41, became enmeshed in legal controversy. On 14/26 February 1878, Tchaikovsky wrote to Jurgenson, expressing interest in setting St. John's text. To Meck, he explained:

> In this regard a composer has an immense and still hardly touched field of activity. I acknowledge certain virtues in Bortnyansky, Berezovsky and the like, but their music is so little harmonious with the Byzantine style of architecture and icons, with the entire structure of the Orthodox service! Were you aware that church music composition comprises a monopoly of the Imperial Court Chapel, which prohibits the printing and singing in churches of everything not included among those works printed in the publications of the Chapel, which jealously protects this monopoly and decidedly does not want to allow new attempts to write on sacred texts? My publisher, Jurgenson, found a way to get around this strange law, and if I write something for the church, he will publish my music abroad. It is very likely that I shall decide to set the entire Liturgy of St. John Chrysostom to music. [vii 238]

Jurgenson cleared the verbal text with the Office of the Sacred Censor and published the *Liturgy* in January 1879. He did not consult the director of the Imperial Court Chapel, Nikolay Bakhmetev, who was empowered to censor all newly printed music for church worship. When Bakhmetev learned of the *Liturgy,* he halted further sales and confiscated all copies. Jurgenson sued. The outcome of complex litigation was that sacred pieces could be performed at home and in public. Approval of works rested with the Office of the Sacred Censor and could no longer be vetoed by the Imperial Chapel on the grounds of musical style [272, lxxxiv].

Such radical stylistic details as the *Liturgy* supposedly contained were thus rendered legally insignificant. That Bakhmetev acted in immediate response to the publication of the *Liturgy* veils a more deliberate provocation by Jurgenson and others who had considered the state of sacred choral music in Russia to be a problem for at least a decade. In 1869, Laroche had complained of chapel-authorized pieces in the Italianate operatic style of the eighteenth century:

> [They] stand, in content and form, in talent, in knowledge, at such a low level that it is impossible to acknowledge in them any advances on future development. It is time to confess that it is impossible to attribute serious meaning to the flat, routine imitations of Sarti and Galuppi, which unmask in their composers so much disrespect for the spirit and demands of the church, so much ignorance of the means and forms of the music. It is time for us to confess, in view of that amazing chain of musical geniuses from Dufay and Okeghem to Mozart and Cherubini, of which the Latin church is justly proud, that we do not have even one church composer, and that the dilettante compositions of our Bortnyanskys and Turchaninovs are at once not churchly and not musical. [256, 227–28]

Laroche renewed his attack the next year, praising a Palestrina motet:

> If there is a name by which one could designate all the insufficiency of our church music, it would be—Palestrina. There are ignorant judges who can rise up against the style of this world genius because he was a Catholic, who steer clear of the spread, in Orthodox music, of "Latinism," imagining that the music of the Catholics Sarti and Galuppi, which has received the right of citizenship in our Church, is somehow *more Orthodox* than Palestrina. [256, 291]

Laroche's critique could not have been lost on the guardians of the Imperial Chapel. Nor could Jurgenson, who would become the largest publisher of sacred choral music in Russia, look on with disinterest: 40,000 Orthodox churches, numerous teachers of choral singing, and new composers to encourage represented a significant opportunity. Over time, Tchaikovsky's efforts echoed those of Laroche and Jurgenson and the researches of Father Razumovsky, who had published an important book on Russian choral singing and who would counsel him when he was composing the *All-Night Vigil*. In 1875, Tchaikovsky had published *A Short*

Manual of Harmony, Adapted to the Study of Sacred-Music Works in Russia. Soon after the lawsuit he edited the sacred works of Dmitry Bortnyansky, a chore he came to hate but which Jurgenson commissioned to build his church music list. Laroche stated the problem prophetically: "The whole style of our church music is in need of reform and this reform can be conducted only through freedom of composition and the abolition of the murderous monopoly of the Court Chapel. At that point our choruses will see before them a new world of music" [256, 292].

The clerical response to the *Liturgy* was to prohibit it in church services for nearly two decades [272, lxxxiv]. After a performance in December 1880, Bishop Ambrosy of Moscow wrote, "We cannot begin to say how the combination of the words 'Liturgy' and 'Tchaikovsky' offend the ear of the Orthodox Christian, . . . since 'Liturgy' is supposed to be combined with 'St. John Chrysostom.'" Ambrosy defended singing in the service if the singers are not distracted by the play of sounds; he objected to the Divine Liturgy being sung outside of church, where recently it had been performed for money. He noted that applause, though disallowed, occurred anyway. And he disparaged Tchaikovsky's motivation:

> It is obvious that the songs of the Divine Liturgy were taken by Mr. Tchaikovsky only in the guise of material for his musical inspiration (since he did not designate them for church use), as historical events and folk songs and legends are taken; the elevated worth of the songs and our people's esteem for them were for him only reason to attach his talent to them; they were the libretto for his sacred opera. [1997 II 374]

By the time Tchaikovsky declared himself "powerless to fight against these wild and senseless persecutions" in 1881 [x 265], he had long since accepted the challenge of reforming church music. One can hardly believe that he did not write the *Liturgy* for church use. He was the first to treat the Divine Liturgy as a "single, continuous musical entity" [272, lxxxvi–lxxxviii]. Of the 50 notated bars in the first number, most comprise statements of "Lord, have mercy," each a choral response to the deacon's prayer. Performing 13 run-on statements of this phrase without the prayers produces aesthetic nonsense in concert and misrepresents the music. This could not have been Tchaikovsky's purpose. Discounting other similar liturgical requirements, 10 numbers in the *Liturgy* assign the choir more lengthy texts calling for musical elaboration. Here, Tchaikovsky develops his own counter-Italian aesthetic for Orthodox polyphony: mostly syllabic, simple-textured, mostly in four parts, with little or no repetition, and observing proper verbal accent. This word-favoring approach, which predominates in the *Liturgy,* affirms Tchaikovsky's opinion that St. John's text is one of the greatest artistic creations of all time [vi 251].

In the *Liturgy,* Tchaikovsky explained, he "completely gave himself over to his own artistic instinct" [x 130]. Most listeners would dispute its similarity to Tchaikovsky's other music. Orthodox polyphony had no guidelines comparable to the rules of dissonance and voice leading that developed in the Renaissance West, leaving Tchaikovsky to decide these matters for himself. He made dissonance rare but free in its astringency, as in the Creed near the beginning:

Ex. 32

[Crea-]tor of heaven and earth, all things visible and invisible.

Or later:

Ex. 33

[Was crucified under Pontius Pilate, and suffered, and was buried,]

To vary texture and sonority while preserving clarity of text, he indulged in the simplest artifice. In no. 6, the Cherubic Hymn, imitation is either split between voices and repeated by each pair, or obscures only the first word of a phrase, moving promptly to homophony. The most elaborate counterpoint comes in no. 14, the Communion Hymn, where 53 of 86 bars set the word "Alleluia," while the most systematic points of imitation—all brief—come in no. 11, one to almost every phrase. Tchaikovsky was nevertheless criticized in the *Liturgy* for unsatisfactory prosody, in part because he set the text in regular meter (a restraint on natural declamation) or distorted intelligibility with hemiola. Sometime in the next decade—possibly in the late 1880s—Tchaikovsky made an undated setting of the Lord's Prayer that is virtually identical to no. 13 of the *Liturgy* [CW 63, 270–72].

The first indication that Tchaikovsky was planning the *Souvenir d'un lieu cher,* op. 42, came in a letter to Meck of 24 March/5 April 1878: "Today I wrote another andante, more suitable to the adjacent movements of the concerto. The first will become an independent violin piece, which I shall join with another two violin pieces I have conceived. They will comprise a separate opus, which I shall also supply you with before publication" [vii 196]. Neither movement title nor expression refers to Meck's estate at Brailovo, which is the *lieu cher.*

Like the Piano Sonata and op. 40, the *Souvenir* suggests the composer's trying too hard to recapture inspiration. "Meditation" opens with a long introduction leading to an unexpected cantabile theme. But the theme does not bear repetition well, and the second idea (at 40) descends into note spinning, as does the pair of themes comprising the middle section (at 74), the eightfold cadence of which (82–90) risks monotony. This is also true of the Scherzo, which overworks conventional ideas and makes its case on sheer energy. The third piece, "Melody," hints at Fritz Kreisler; it is effective when it stays on point, but when it lapses, as at bar 18, the train of thought is lost until the peroration (from 59).

The *Souvenir* was suitable for domestic performance and was a *donné* to Meck, to whom he owed much that he could only repay in art. She especially liked violin pieces [vii 229], and he had still not composed an answer to Kohne's "Le Reproche," which she had requested of him on 30 April 1877. This may be his belated substitute.

Two other short projects took Tchaikovsky's attention this year. Before 27 November 1877, he had refused to produce a composition in support of the Russo-Turkish War. In April 1878, the Committee for the Organization of a Volunteer Fleet opened a subscription for donations, and on the 24th Tchaikovsky wrote the March for the Volunteer Fleet, also known as the Skobelev March, in response. It was published for piano in May 1878 under the pseudonym P. Sinopov, which Tchaikovsky wrote on the autograph [96, 408–9]. He declined to orchestrate it. A standard March and Trio, it alludes to the national anthem at the end. It is published in the *Collected Works* [CW 52, 65–70].

In a letter of 5 September 1877 (N.S.), Laoro Rossi, director of the Naples Conservatory, invited Tchaikovsky's contribution to the *Album per pianoforte alla memoria di Vincenzo Bellini*. On 11 May 1878, Rossi prompted him, and Tchaikovsky again simplified the Russian Dance from *Swan Lake,* already included in op. 40 as no. 10. This version is not in the *Collected Works* [Rossi's edition is reproduced in 398, Tchaikovsky's manuscript in 230, 192–93].

CHAPTER THIRTEEN

1879–1881

CIRCUMSTANCES IN THESE YEARS PRODUCED A MALAISE THAT brought Tchaikovsky in 1881 to the nadir of his life. That year, *The Maid of Orleans* kept him in St. Petersburg, but the others he began and ended in Western Europe, while every summer (in 1880, from April to November), he stayed at Kamenka.

Tchaikovsky spent January 1879 in Clarens working on *The Maid of Orleans.* Two points of biography are important to the composition of this opera: the obscurity of why he chose it and his manner of composition once he did. Early in 1878 he had indicated to Taneyev that what he needed in opera was an intimate, powerful drama, specifically ruling out grand opera with its "tsars, tsaritsas, people's rebellions, battles, [and] marches" [vii 21–22]. Eleven months later, in choosing *The Maid,* he had reversed himself without explanation:

> The thought of writing on this topic came to me at Kamenka when I was paging through Zhukovsky, in whose work there is a translation of Schiller's "Maid of Orleans." There are wonderful things for music in it, and the story is still not worn out. . . . I had thought about the subject sometimes before, and even last trip to Petersburg once dreamed of it—but now I am beginning to be drawn to it seriously. [vii 467–68]

The clichés of French grand opera in *The Maid*—a large cast, panoramic dimensions, the portrayal of the highborn as irrelevant or degraded—are mediated by the strong title character, the earnest treatment of religious themes, and the lyrical elements in Joan's part. These traits, placed in the context of national struggle, align *The Maid* with Russian historical opera of the 1870s, though it lacks the harsh tone and bluntness of that genre.

One cannot identify a specific stimulus for this composition. Like *Mazepa* and any number of operatic projects that Tchaikovsky abandoned, *The Maid* fulfilled a need he had to be writing opera. In this case, he proceeded without a libretto or even a complete scenario [viii 36–38, 59–62]. Using historical accounts and other librettos [171], he began on 5/17 December 1878, reporting three days later, "Tomorrow I shall have fully ready an entire large scene, capital among its neighbors" [vii 520]. His problem was that he got carried away; he was overflowing with ideas [vii 523–24]. Early in 1879 he settled on a procedure: prepare text one day to be composed the next. Such inchworming almost guaranteed sprawling growth to the detriment of dramatic focus.

The marriage debacle was so recent that he could appreciate progress, even of this kind. He admitted to Meck on 3 January that his labor over the number of syllables, poetic feet, and rhythm was exacting a price, though he finished composing on 21 February/5 March in Paris. In Russia, meanwhile, Nikolay Rubinstein was still under attack in the press. On 18/30 January, Tchaikovsky appealed to Vladimir Stasov, the chief attacker, to desist. Stasov refused [401, 129–34]. Tchaikovsky hesitated to defend Rubinstein because he still feared publicity about himself [87 I 76–77]. Meanwhile, Rubinstein was threatening to leave the conservatory [viii 107].

For the most part, Tchaikovsky's life was aimless. He spent most of February in Paris at the theater but not enjoying it; after the middling success of *The Tempest* at a Concert Colonne, he publicly apologized to the conductor [viii 136]. In March, social duties in St. Petersburg were odious, Ilya was failing, and Antonina seemed to be stalking him. On 26 April, he began to orchestrate *The Maid* [viii 187] and decided to alternate the completion of the full score with completion of the piano-vocal reduction [viii 256]. But once act II was scored, he suggested that Yury Messer, the "blockhead" who would defile the *Capriccio Italien,* do the job. By the end of August, he acknowledged that he must finish the piano reduction himself [viii 344]. It took almost a year. On 18 July 1880, he finally returned the third proofs of the piano-vocal score with corrections. The presses ran, and still the dedication to Nápravnik was omitted.

In May 1879, he spent 10 days at Brailovo before returning to Kamenka, where the family was ill. In June Alyosha was declared the illegitimate father of a child born of a chamber maid in Clarens, to whom Tchaikovsky sent money and on whose behalf he lobbied her employers to let her return to work. Later June was spent with Kondratiev at Nizï, attending their pal Nikolay Bochechkarov, who would die in August, his last treatment prescribed by a local medicine woman. July was relieved by an amateur theatrical, Octave Feuillet's *La fée,* for which he composed a song [143, 258].

September was spent in travel, first to St. Petersburg to help Anatoly deal with what turned out to be a noncrisis in his job, then to Modest in Grankino, 65 miles on horseback beyond the last train station. At Kamenka in October, he found two more children in Sasha's home, the youngest of their late half sister, Zinaida. Out of sorts, he was working on the Second Piano Concerto, Meck was negotiating for a performance of the Fourth Symphony in Paris, and Nikolay Bakhmetev erupted a second time over the publication of the *Liturgy.* During this time, Tchaikovsky received his first letter from Leonty Tkachenko, an emotionally troubled youth who approached him wishing to become an artist. In the coming years, he supported Tkachenko at the expense of much time and anguish. He spent November in St. Petersburg and Paris, where he finished drafting the concerto. In December, he revised the Second Symphony in Rome.

Through all of this, his major preoccupation in 1880 was to prepare *The Maid of Orleans* for production. On 1 February, he requested that the direction of the Imperial Theaters consider the opera [ix 353], and six weeks later he was in St. Petersburg politicking for it. Every day, he breakfasted in three places, lunched in five, and dined in ten; he was tired as a dog [ix 92]. An important consequence of this activity was that he met Grand Duke Konstantin Konstantinovich Romanov, known as K.R., whom he would later engage in lively correspondence. Tchaikovsky described his lobbying to Meck:

> One must plunge up to one's neck into a sea of theatrical and bureaucratic rubbish, must breathe in to the point of stifling this rotten atmosphere of petty intrigues, microscopic but poisonous ambitions, all manner of chicanery and manifestations of coarse petty tyranny. What to do! Either don't write operas or be ready for this. [ix 234]

On 6 September, it was the complaints of artists who lacked a printed piano-vocal score [ix 260]; on 12 September, the theater censor was demanding

> *that the Archbishop is to be called a Hermit (?) and that all conversation about a cross be removed, and that these crosses not appear on stage.* How stupid this is! The fact is that at the end of the opera, when Joan is being led to the pyre, she asks for a *cross,* and one of the soldiers makes a cross of two fragments of a cane bound together, and gives it to her. This entire scene is prohibited. [ix 279]

Tchaikovsky successfully argued for changing the archbishop to a cardinal because the censors had permitted one in Halévy's *La Juive* [87 I 178].

After official notification on 18 September that *The Maid of Orleans* was to be staged, Nápravnik called for large cuts and alternatives. Tchaikovsky admitted that he must "take the advice of such an honorable, truthful, experienced man, very well disposed towards me and my music" [ix 326], however burdensome the changes [ix 327–29]. Orchestral rehearsals began on 27 January 1881. On 1 February, Tchaikovsky took stock: Nápravnik knew his music, but the production was derived from old works. Maria Kamenskaya, but lately assigned the role of Joan, was superior to Maria Makarova in the second cast. He also liked Ippolit Pryanishnikov as Lionel, and Fyodor Stravinsky, who was making an early appearance on the Petersburg stage as Dunois.

The Maid of Orleans was first performed at the Maryinsky Theater on 13 February 1881, a month after the first professional staging of *Onegin* in Moscow (11 January). On 2 March—hardly two weeks later—the assassination of Alexander II closed the theaters for the rest of the winter and spring seasons. The opera was revived in the fall of 1881, went unperformed in 1882 (much of which was taken up in a revision of Joan's part to make it more suitable to Kamenskaya's voice), and was revived again in 1883, reaching its 17th performance by 11 December 1884 [D&Y 333]. Meanwhile, through Nápravnik's advocacy, it was staged in Prague in the summer of 1882, the first opera by Tchaikovsky to be produced outside of Russia.

At the first performance Tchaikovsky took 24 curtain calls, which little reassured him. Critics served up platitudes about whether he had created something new and his gift for opera compared with his gift for symphony

[GO810215, GO810223]. Cui found his talent to be "alien to power, dramatic properties, humor, merriment—it is soft, feminine, lyrical, with continual shades of sorrow and melancholy." His orchestration was peerless, but generally his music was "good-soundingness without content—as tiresome as some people's persistent civility." Insignificant numbers had disproportionately magnificent conclusions; the lyrical being enormously favored over the dramatic. Kamenskaya's performance was exemplary, certain passages even striking, such as the end of Joan's hymn in act I. Cui was hardly the first to make sport of Tchaikovsky's near-quotation—he compared the beginning of Joan's hymn with Mathilde's "Sombre forêt" in *Guillaume Tell;* Joan's final song in act I with "Su! Del Nilo al sacro lido" in *Aïda;* and the Agnes-King duet with the duet of Valentine and Raoul in *Les Huguenots*—which he attributed to Tchaikovsky's wish to oblige his public. Of Schiller's dramatic clashes but one remained, between Joan and Thibaut in act III, while the last act arrived before Joan gave voice to the struggle between love and duty. There is "little stage movement; there are no upheavals which take possession of all the spectators' attention" [GO810219].

The continuing issues in Tchaikovsky's life in the years 1879–1881 may be summarized for the entire period. Among his personal contacts, Meck was most important. Ill much of this time, she proposed in May 1879 that they again enjoy a "close living relationship." Tchaikovsky balked, then traveled to Brailovo in August. He was troubled, as in Florence, by the very factors that consoled her: proximity and her obsession with his nearness [viii 308]. Her greeting on 12 August was so tactile as to undermine formal address:

> What happiness, getting up every morning, to feel that you are so close to me, my dear, priceless friend, to imagine you in a dwelling so familiar and precious to me, . . . to feel that you are *with me,* that *je Vous possède,* as the French say—all this a pleasure I am enjoying at this moment and for which I am infinitely grateful to you, my incomparable, excellent friend. [86 II 170]

On 15 August 1879 the inevitable happened—a face-to-face encounter. It passed in a moment, and while it distressed Tchaikovsky, Meck described her pleasure at experiencing him "not as a myth but as a real person" [86 II 176]. Ten days later she proposed to match one of her sons to one of his nieces, and Tchaikovsky agreed to another "vicarious meeting" at Brailovo to survey improvements and sense her presence. His claim that outliving her would be unbearable (in response to her question) brought a torrential response:

> My God, how grateful I am for that remark, how kind, how inexpressibly precious this sentence is to me. If you only knew how I love you. It is not only love, but adoration, idolization, worship. However burdensome, bitter, painful something is, a few of your good words makes me forget everything, forgive everything. . . . O my God, how grateful I am to you, and how precious you are to me! [86 II 195]

Taken aback, Tchaikovsky expressed joy at her assurances but concern that her friendship was loftier than he deserved [viii 343]. From Grankino a month later, after Meck had vented her feelings about Antonina (above, p. 163) and described an almost physical response to hearing his Fourth Symphony, he wrote:

> I was expressing an outpouring not only from myself, but also from you; this is not my, but *our* symphony. Only you can understand and feel everything I was understanding and feeling while writing it. . . . I shudder to think what would have happened to me if fate had not led you to me. I am obliged to you for everything: for life . . . freedom and such fullness of happiness as I thought unattainable before. [viii 370–71]

Meck underwrote a performance of the Fourth in Paris conducted by Edouard Colonne on 13/25 January 1880. Tchaikovsky encouraged her at first, but after the concert wrote that he would find it offensive and unpleasant had she paid Colonne, concerned about bad publicity if word of it were to reach the Russian press. Eight months later, he relented, inviting her to send to Colonne any of his music that she wished [ix 315]. According to the *Gazette musicale de Paris* for 1 February (p. 37), the piece was "sometimes disorderly and a little savage, sometimes rich and powerfully colored," mixing tenderness and brilliance, refinement and vulgarity.

The close living relationship Meck advocated again at the end of 1879 was marred by illness and distress over an attempt on the tsar's life. From Brailovo, she asked, "Will we ever again be close to one another," and if so "when and where?" [86 II 279]. There was no such occasion in 1880, though Meck, who spent three months in Florence, invited him to join her in the hope of recreating the visit of 1878. Their relationship continued askew;

their correspondence dwindled. On 18 June, Tchaikovsky proposed to write less often; in November 1880, Meck declared herself content with one letter a month from him [86 II 446]. From Simaki, his residence at Brailovo, he described familiar sights and experiences, and Meck could still respond in an ecstatic tone:

> Dear incomparable friend! Yesterday I received your precious letter. . . . Words cannot transmit that deep gratitude, that infinite love for you that I feel upon reading such expressions. Yes, my priceless friend, it is true that with all my heart, all my mind, all my organism I feel your music and worship its creator. . . . I hear the spirit of a kind unique upon this earth. [86 II 434]

In February 1881, business affairs prevented Meck's writing. On 6 March, she reviewed her husband's legacy: railroad debts of some 4.5 million rubles secured with personal assets and a 500,000-ruble mortgage against Brailovo, with a yearly loss of 200,000 more. Add to this conspiracies against her business and family, and she was frightened. She had not lost hope of uniting the Mecks and the Davïdovs, but knowing that Lev would expect guarantees of security for any of his daughters, she wondered if her children would be able to keep the 700-mile railway from one of the best ports in Russia, her 24,000-acre estate, the most luxurious home in Moscow, and a collection of diamonds and art worth millions, which were all at risk [86 II 508].

Antonina had last been heard from through her lawyer late in 1878. In 1879–1881, she continued to waver between the financial benefits of a divorce and those of staying married. On 24 March 1879, she called on Tchaikovsky, declaring her love and that she could not live without him. After two hours, he gave her 100 rubles to leave [viii 159–60]. She followed the meeting with an incoherent ramble four days later.

> My dear Petichka!
>
> What is happening with you, that you don't give the slightest bit of news? Are you ill? This minute I am moving into a separate room. . . . Come, excellent man, visit me. I would be very sad, however, if you came only to get rid of me, having made but a ceremonial visit. I know that you don't love me, which tortures me, agonizes me and never leaves me in peace. At least you could satisfy yourself that you are everything in the world to me. No powers will force me to stop loving you; react to me albeit with pity. I belong to you,

> body and soul, make of me what you will. After meeting you I cannot put my nerves in order, and I start crying several times a day. [365, 227]

On 9 April she called again, and her tone was utterly businesslike. She claimed that Meck had guaranteed her 15,000 rubles, which she needed to go abroad and devote herself to music; a fortnight later, she asked for a divorce in order to marry someone else. Consenting, Tchaikovsky gave Anatoly his power-of-attorney on 4 May [viii 195]. Wrangling continued until mid-June, when Tchaikovsky refused to pay any more until a divorce was final. The episode looked to be a ploy to get money. In May 1880, he demanded that she cease all contact and set a deadline:

> I gave her a year, during which I asked her to consider and be advised about her situation, try to determine what she would gain or lose from a divorce, and to write me, without cursing or reproaches, etc., clearly and precisely, what she wants. If from her letters I see that she has at last lost hope of taking up with me and understands that divorce is the best resolution of the matter, then I for my part will consider, will see if I can get the necessary money, and use a specialist in these matters. [ix 135; see also viii 446–47]

On 25 June 1880, Antonina responded. She agreed to a divorce but would not lie to get it. Addressing him in the formal second person and as "Kind Sir," she reproached him for spreading rumors about her, for judging her without telling "the terrible truth" about himself. Her faith in reconciliation was gone: "Between us all is finished" [365, 229]. It was a major change, and the reason would soon be known: Antonina was pregnant. Through the summer Tchaikovsky received letters, including one from her mother which assured him of her daughter's crystal purity [ix 192]. To uphold Antonina's virginity at this point may speak to the extremity of her situation, including the onset of her mother's final illness and discord between Antonina and the child's father, her lawyer, Alexander Alexandrovich Shlïkov. That she did not divorce when Tchaikovsky agreed to accept the blame and give her a small fortune beggars explanation, as does his not obtaining one in light of her condition. In January 1881, Tchaikovsky ceased paying her pension. She gave birth to a daughter on 13 February (the same day as the premiere of *The Maid of Orleans*) and baptized her the next day with Shlïkov's patronymic. There was no further talk of divorce.

If Meck was his patroness and Antonina his wife, money was Tchaikovsky's mistress in 1879–1881, and she treated him badly. His spending was incorrigible. On 30 January/11 February 1879, he wrote to Meck that he had wrongly informed her that he had the funds to travel [viii 82], and at the end of February he left Paris so short of money that he ran out in Berlin. An appeal to Jurgenson met no response, whereupon he wrote to Meck with another embarrassing admission: the shortfall was due to a "mania for dandyism" in Paris, where he had indulged himself in new clothes and underwear [viii 146]. When Jurgenson (who was away) remained silent, he asked Meck for money; meanwhile, Kotek had pawned his watch to buy food [viii 151]. Hardly another month had passed before he was complaining to Anatoly of miscalculated finances and having too little to buy summer clothes [viii 177]. In Paris at the end of the year, he went shopping again [viii 424].

On 10 May 1879, Tchaikovsky responded to Vladimir Shilovsky's accusation of ingratitude after accepting 28,000 rubles. His real debt, he reckoned, was 7,550 rubles:

> It is little if you consider the innumerable spiritual torments this money cost me; it is little if you recall that you are a rich Maecenas and I am a poor artist; it is very little if you recall your countless declarations of love for me and readiness to make any sacrifice, and finally it is absolutely nothing compared with what you so often promised! [viii 213]

To save money was the main reason that Tchaikovsky stayed at Kamenka in the summers of 1879–1881. In June 1879, Meck suggested he be more moderate, just as he was awaiting her August payment. Of this 2,000 rubles, he owed Lev Davïdov 1,300 and Alyosha 300. The remaining 400, he rued, was not much to live on [viii 246, 340]. He asked Meck for his February 1880 payment early, on 22 January, having admitted squandering to Anatoly and declaring that he must live until October without another kopeck. In July 1880 he was 4,000 rubles in debt, 1,000 more than Meck's subsidy for the rest of the year, on which he had already taken an advance. The cause of his shortfall, as ever, was unclear. To Jurgenson on 3 July, he admitted running up debts the previous winter, that Meck would give him what he needed but he simply could not ask, nor could he live in prolonged isolation deep in the country. He asked Jurgenson to arrange a special loan of 4,000 rubles from Pavel Tretyakov, who was a business magnate, art collector, and member of the Russian Musical Society. The composer agreed to pay Lev, Alyosha, his creditors General Dmitry Semyonovich Shenshin and "a Kamenka Jew," and several smaller debts—and then settle his life [ix 171–72]. In 17 days, Jurgenson had made it so [ix 204]. Yet by September, Tchaikovsky was urging Meck to send his stipend because he needed it [ix 267–68], and in December he put the touch on his Moscow friends again.

Tchaikovsky's most extraordinary request for money came during the summer of 1881. Meck's fortune had been threatened, Modest had helped himself in May to 850 rubles from Jurgenson [x 95], with whom Pyotr had abused his own credit, and had borrowed from Kolya Konradi [x 118]. On 19 May, he wrote to Konstantin Petrovich Pobedonostsev, a jurist and advisor to the tsar, asking him to intercede with the emperor for a repayable loan of 3,000 rubles. On 2 June 1881, Alexander III responded: "I am sending you 3000 rubles for transfer to Tchaikovsky. Tell him that he need not return this money" [243, 235–36]. Tchaikovsky was deeply touched and duly grateful, but within three weeks could write to Jurgenson, "It is shameful that, receiving so much, I am forever sitting without money and my freedom is forever paralyzed" [x 150]. In October, he apologized to Meck, claiming that he was going to cease his childish and wasteful squandering [x 251]. Yet in December, he was borrowing again from the Russian Musical Society [x 305].

Tchaikovsky was expensive to maintain: clothes, travel, gifts, and support to others. But he also coveted money. His attitude toward a valuable, heartfelt gift from Meck—a watch depicting Joan of Arc on one side and Apollo and the Muses on the other, the fellow travelers of his inspiration—was that he would have preferred the cash she spent on it. Like Wagner, he wanted others to forgive him when he overspent; at all times, he was sensitive to criticism about his excesses.

Apart from providing money, Jurgenson worked to consolidate control of Tchaikovsky's music in 1879–1881. He wanted to acquire exclusive rights to all of it, including the music Bessel had published and Tchaikovsky had resold to him on 20 March 1880 [D&Y 230]. On 9 April 1880, the composer authorized Jurgenson to take over his financial affairs, negotiate agreements, and conduct judicial proceedings [D&Y 232]. After a summer of haggling, he could no longer cope with Bessel and relinquished his contract [ix 295–96]. On 12 February 1881, he agreed to sell

Jurgenson 37 compositions for 7,000 rubles [D&Y 250]. This brought his income for 1881 to at least 16,000 rubles, discounting royalties—a phenomenal sum for someone so deeply in debt who lived nearly eight months of that year in the country.

Subordinate to Meck, Antonina, and money during 1879–1881 were family matters. Tchaikovsky was in Rome when his father died on 9 January 1880, and the composer eulogized him as "a marvelous old man, angelic in his soul" [ix 24]. A year earlier, he had been alarmed over Sasha's health [viii 179–80]. In 1881, she had a nervous breakdown over Tanya's volatile behavior and over Lev's finances, taking refuge in morphine [ix 290–91]. The Kamenka family deteriorated as Sasha and Tanya, both addicted, played upon each other's woes. Tchaikovsky's patience with Tanya grew thin. In the summer, as Tanya's addiction became acute, he claimed that his worst punishment was spending two hours with her [x 133]. Sasha's condition kept Lev from managing Brailovo for Meck and stayed Tchaikovsky from composition. Pyotr's own complaints of illness during 1881 were less frequent than in 1877 and 1878. In 1880, they had been more numerous, as from Rome in January, when he wrote Meck of a night that he thought he was going to die [ix 32].

His affections continued to be evasive. Early in 1879, he was still expressing strong feelings for Kolya Konradi, if not so intense or often as before [viii 74; ix 75]. His passionate language to Anatoly fell off (though expurgations continued in the letters of 1879). His letters to Modest from Paris in March 1880 were printed with ellipses in the sections in which he described how he was idling away his time [ix 66–67]. To these sundry observations may be added two unusual ones. On 9/21 January 1879, he described to Anatoly a passionate erotic dream about his cousin Anna Merkling: he abstained because of incest and woke up when her demands became urgent [369, 122]; on 25 May 1879, he remarked: "I find myself in a period of complete indifference to the fair sex" [x 233].

Alyosha's conscription was shortened after he passed an examination in June 1880, but for a technicality had to take it again [ix 144]. On 16 October he reported for duty, to Pyotr's dismay: "you will always be *mine,* and never for a minute will I forget you" [ix 308]. In two months, he had interceded to have Alyosha posted to Moscow and pressed for relief from his terrible living conditions from his cousin Mitrofan Petrovich, an army general [ix 336–37]. Leonty Tkachenko formed a counterpoint to Alyosha's conscription. In December 1880, he returned Pyotr's letters with a suicide threat after Pyotr had rebuffed his ambitions to become a musician. In January 1881, Tchaikovsky enrolled him in the conservatory for a term [x 17], during which he behaved irrationally; the composer discouraged further study of music [x 273–74].

Early in 1881, Nikolay Rubinstein fell ill [x 17]. "Rubinstein worries me very much," Pyotr informed Anatoly, "it seems this is *le commencement de la fin,* and I am simply horrified at the thought that he will be no more" [x 48]. On 11/23 March, three hours after oysters for lunch at noon, Nikolay Grigorievich Rubinstein died in Paris. Griefstruck, Tchaikovsky could not finish a description of the funeral to Meck [x 68]. The next day, after the *panikhida* (an Orthodox funeral service), he accompanied the coffin for dispatch to Moscow, and wrote an account of Rubinstein's last days for the *Moscow News* [x 65–67]. Rubinstein's death was the focal point of Tchaikovsky's hyperbole of woe in 1881, his personal dismay yielding to a sober awareness of the loss to Russian music and the changes in his own life. One wonders what role guilt played in a discourse on Christian forgiveness to Meck on 16/28 March, which reflected his response to Rubinstein since 1878: hatred, reluctance to stand with him against his enemies, and now sorrow [x 69–70]. Other disasters were arrayed on either side of Rubinstein's death. Ten days before, Alexander II had been assassinated by a terrorist bomb. Eleven days after, Meck wrote that her son was rumored to be a nihilist conspirator who had put up a million rubles for the emperor's assassination. She also reviewed her personal and financial woes. Brailovo would have to be sold [86 II 518].

On 6 May 1881, Tchaikovsky wrote to Karl Yulevich Davïdov of the Petersburg Conservatory, requesting the libretto on Pushkin's *Poltava* that Davïdov had abandoned; it was the story of an old warrior in love with a young woman, who betrays her and his tsar in the pursuit of political ambitions. By August, he had composed only four numbers, citing a lack of enthusiasm [x 204].

Tchaikovsky faced the summer of 1881 having lost a mentor, a refuge, and possibly a benefactor. He wrote to Eduard Nápravnik, "Now, with Rubinstein's death, you are my sole support and fulcrum!" [x 143]—wishful thinking, given that Nápravnik would resign from the Russian Musical Society before the year was out [x 287]. The terrible situation with Sasha and Tanya at Kamenka was ongoing. His spending was out of control pre-

1 Tchaikovsky as a young man in 1862,
when he entered the St. Petersburg Conservatory.

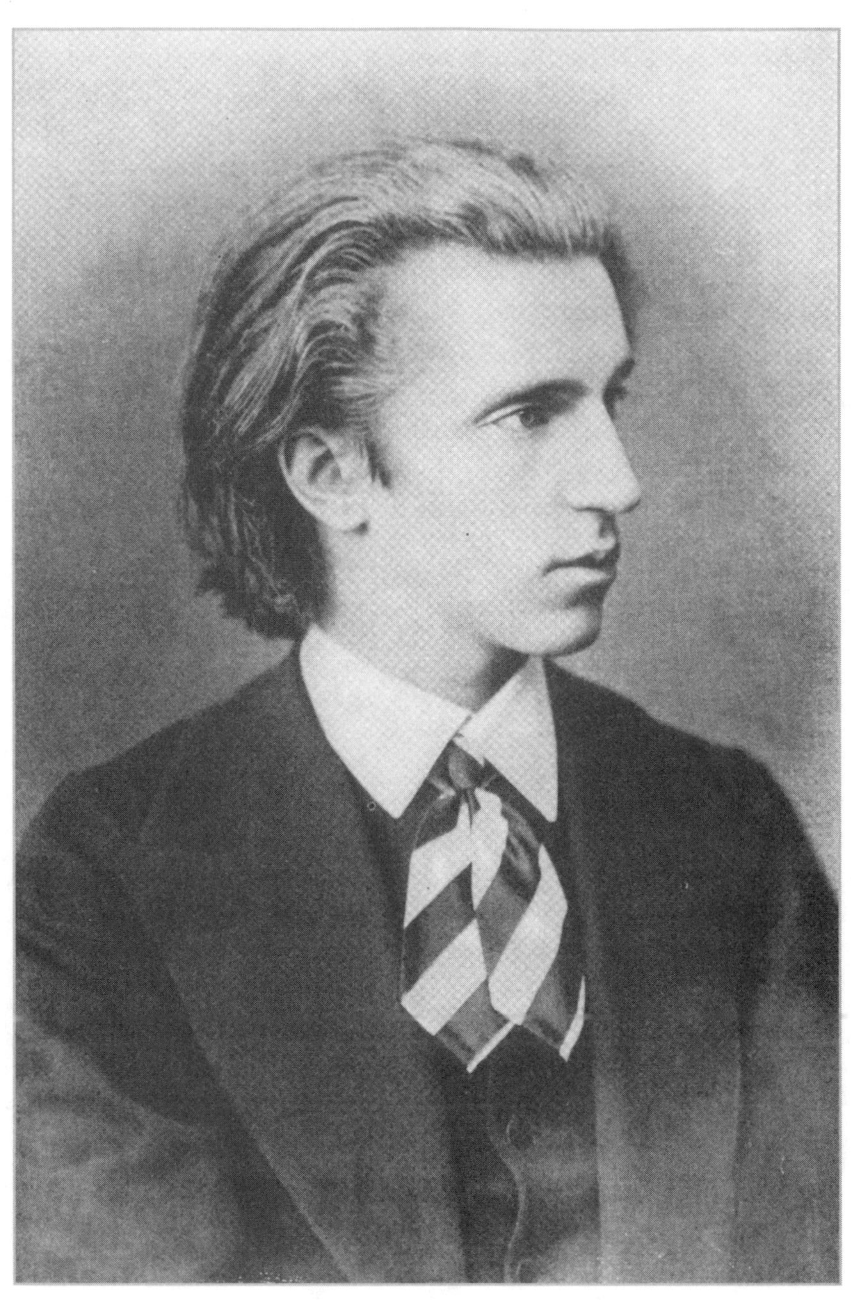

2 Hermann Laroche as a young man.

3 Anton Rubinstein.

4 Nikolay Rubinstein.

5 Pyotr Jurgenson.

6 Nikolay Kashkin.

7 Modest Tchaikovsky.

8 Vlatimire ("Bob") Davidov as a student at the School of Jurisprudence.

9 Tchaikovsky and his wife, Antonina Milyukova.

10 Nadezda Von Meck.

11 Pavel Khokhlov as Evgeny Onegin.

12 Maria Kamenskaya as Joan in *The Maid of Orleans.*

13 Nikolay Figner as Hermann in *The Queen of Spades.*

14 Tchaikovski in the 1890s.

cisely when his resolve to return to work was soft. He wanted another year of freedom and had declined to shoulder any of the burden caused by Rubinstein's death, on 28 April energetically rejecting the Russian Musical Society's attempts to make him its director [x 86–87]. His remorse for Rubinstein, genuine in its way, did not run to self-sacrifice. Meanwhile, former colleagues Kashkin and Nikolay Zverev, a professor of piano, were ill, Albrecht without Rubinstein was half his former self, and Klindworth had left, leaving the young Taneyev as the focal point of the institution's future. Tchaikovsky was terrified, on the eve of the new term, that the Moscow Conservatory should be opening without Rubinstein [x 194].

As 1881 ended, Tchaikovsky's situation was dismal. His relations with Tanya Davïdova were plumbing new depths. He was editing the sacred works of Bortnyansky, a project without end. Rubinstein's replacement had yet to be found; in St. Petersburg, *The Maid of Orleans* was about to be dropped. Adolf Brodsky had performed the Violin Concerto with the Vienna Philharmonic under Hans Richter to a hostile reception. Klindworth had published an edition of Tchaikovsky's works in Berlin, which vexed Jurgenson. In November, Vera Davïdova married, the last family event before Tchaikovsky left for Rome. There, he lamented his loss of creative fervor.

CHAPTER FOURTEEN

The Music of 1879–1881

SOME COMPOSITIONS OF THIS PERIOD EMERGED FROM AN INSCRUTABLE, sheltered corner of Tchaikovsky's mind, while most were affected by what he called "servitude," or work obligations. On the day he began *The Maid of Orleans*—5 December 1878—the lost movements of the First Suite were found in St. Petersburg. He proceeded with the opera, and then the suite went missing again [vii 564]. He was overjoyed when it turned up in Clarens. Similar progress and delay marked the Second Piano Concerto, which was sketched in two weeks, composed in less than two months but delayed for another five, in part by a hurried commission early in 1880 for a piece called "Montenegro at the Moment of Receiving Russia's Declaration of War against Turkey" to accompany a program of *tableaux vivants* comprising a "Dialogue of the Genius of Russia and History." It celebrated the 25th anniversary of Alexander II's reign [324, 163–64], to which others contributed (including Borodin, with *In Central Asia*). Tchaikovsky wrote "Montenegro" in six days, just to have the performance canceled and the score lost. He composed nothing else before June 1880 (a duet for op. 46) and no new orchestral work until September. He was still uncertain about *1812* in late September [ix 286–87].

Servitude marked the last half of 1880. *Capriccio Italien* and the Second Piano Concerto required a second set of proofs because Jurgenson's arranger had been tampering with the goods: "The obligation of that blockhead Messer is to follow the manuscript, making everything as I have it;

instead, this idiot and son-of-a-bitch allows himself to correct and edit my harmonies after his own fashion, and in place of an intelligent modulation has got up some rubbish" [ix 237]. In 1881—the least productive year of Tchaikovsky's life—a revulsion for work came in the wake of Rubinstein's death, a lethargy in stark conflict with his financial need. On 4 May 1881, Jurgenson prevailed against Bakhmetev in the senate. The next day, he asked Tchaikovsky to edit the complete works of Dmitry Bortnyansky "for an excellent reward" [87 I 189]. With *Schadenfreude,* Jurgenson described the fines and costs levied against Bakhmetev and the chief of police for wrongful confiscation, then added:

> Publishing Bortnyansky, I shall deal a powerful blow to the [imperial] chapel and its privilege. This is an idea of the longest standing, on which I shall absolutely carry through, and I would be *very* pleased if you would not be averse to being editor of this edition: it would eliminate competition. [87 I 190]

Editing would allow Tchaikovsky to ponder Orthodox music in his "present religious mood." From the beginning, however, he was antithetical to the plan: he wanted to write the *All-Night Vigil* and might follow this with an opera if he found a subject. By 21 June, he realized that most of the Bortnyansky pieces were trivial, and some 60 percent called for instruments, which were proscribed in the Orthodox service. Jurgenson brushed this aside, Tchaikovsky yielded, and months of editing began, proceeding to November. On 1 September, Tchaikovsky reported the *All-Night Vigil* as "completely ready" but not recopied; that awaited January and February 1882.

Tchaikovsky's only completed opera in this period, *The Maid of Orleans,* begun in the late days of 1878 and first staged in February 1881, was made to his own scenario.

Act I. Country girls decorating a venerable oak are interrupted by Thibaut, Joan's father, and Raymond, an aspirant to her hand. Thibaut finds their amusements frivolous during war, when a woman's best defense is a spouse; he would have Joan marry Raymond. Joan declares that fate has decided otherwise. Enraged, Thibaut claims she is in league with impious powers. Peasants enter, fleeing the English. Among them, Bertrand reports that Orleans is under siege, but Joan insists that the English warrior Salisbury has been killed, and prophesies victory for France. A straggler confirms

Salisbury's death, and the people, marveling at Joan, sing a prayer. Alone and melancholy, she is accosted by a chorus of angels reporting that her hour has come; she begs them to pass her by. The angels inspirit her.

Act II. In the castle of Chinon, the pensive King Charles, his knight Dunois, and his beloved Agnes are listening to minstrels. The king orders them paid, but the treasury is empty. Agnes offers her jewels. As the king languishes in love, Dunois urges him to lead the army in defense of France. He hesitates, and when a wounded knight announces defeat, he decides to flee. Dunois renounces him and exits to lay down his own life. Agnes consoles the king. Fanfares; the stage fills with people. Dunois reports a miracle: the French are victorious. The archbishop tells how a young woman wrested victory from the enemy; Joan enters to cheers. The king and Dunois exchange places, but she is not deceived, and by divine insight reveals the king's prayers. She tells her story; the king entrusts his army to her.

Act III, scene 1. In a clearing near Rheims, Joan battles Lionel. As she raises her sword against him, she sees his face in a ray of moonlight and cannot kill him. They are interrupted by Dunois and others; Lionel, a Burgundian, returns to the French side as Joan, bleeding, falls into a swoon. Scene 2. At Charles's coronation, the king calls Joan the savior of France. Thibaut declares her victory a deed not of heaven but of hell. He calls upon her to account, and her silence as the archbishop thrice questions her purity is taken as an admission of guilt. After an ensemble, she remains alone; Lionel reassures her; she calls him her most dangerous enemy and rushes away.

Act IV, scene 1. In a forest, Lionel is pursuing Joan. First she curses him, then yields to her passion. A duet. The English are approaching; she curses herself and him again. The angelic choir reappears, informing Joan that because she has not rejected earthly love she cannot complete her task, but heaven does not curse her. If she meets her fate without complaint, eternal bliss will be hers. The English capture her and kill Lionel. Scene 2. Rouen. A funeral pyre and march. Joan is led in. The people would prevent her execution. Joan loses heart at the sight of the fire, but the angelic choir supports her to the end. She proceeds. A priest makes a cross from sticks and holds it before her. The fire flares up.

The publication history of *The Maid of Orleans* is complex. In the first edition, a piano-vocal arrangement (461 pages) that passed the censor on 16 August 1880 and was issued in April 1881, the archbishop is called that;

there is an optional, 50-bar cut in the act III finale (no. 20). The second edition (censor's approval on 26 August 1884; issued later that year; 421 pages) transmits changes of detail and the composer's cuts in nos. 12, 15, and 20 (the last exceeding his optional cut in the first edition). These reflect the first production, as does a rubric omitting the episode with the cross in act IV "when performed in the Imperial Theaters." A German translation has been added. To Jurgenson on 25 May 1881, Tchaikovsky specified that the archbishop be a cardinal in the Russian text of a new edition [x 123], but an archbishop in translation; in this edition he is a cardinal in both. The first edition of the orchestral score (633 pages), passed by the Moscow censor on 16 January 1899, was issued by Jurgenson in separate volumes, with supplements at the end of acts I, III, and IV containing transpositions, presumably made for Maria Kamenskaya. The *Collected Works* [CW 5 and 37] conflates Jurgenson's versions, from which (through notes and supplements) they can be reconstructed. The editors changed punctuation and the transliteration of "Salisburi" to the Frenchified "Salisbyuri." The *Collected Works* also transmits changes that Tchaikovsky made in his full score—cuts, transpositions, and rewriting. The third edition of the libretto (censor's approval on 26 July 1886) was possibly made for a staging at Tiflis in December of that year. The text and numbering of scenes differ from the piano-vocal scores. The duet of Agnes and the king is retexted; the cardinal appears throughout; other changes tend to follow the second piano-vocal score. The *Collected Works* editors refer to a third edition of the music, with "two minor changes in the Introduction and one in no. 15" [CW 37, xviii]. These are too slight to match the musical changes implied by this libretto.

The Maid of Orleans is overblown, a quality affirmed by the tendency, beginning with the first production, to make lavish cuts. The big choral scenes of acts II and III cannot bear the weight of Tchaikovsky's ungainly elaboration—a trait recalled from *The Oprichnik*—while the lovers' intimate scenes, of hopeless ambivalence as drama, do not begin to achieve the expression that intense personal feeling inspires in the finest opera. The customary explanation for this is the influence of French grand opera, that event-ridden, least personal of genres, abetted by extraordinary projections of the composer's psyche onto the work, which is presumptuous and unflattering to any assessment of Tchaikovsky as a man of the theater. Mediating these assessments is the fact that *The Maid* is glorious to listen to, a quality made plain to anyone who listens with closed eyes during a performance and allows the demands of theater to lapse. By any feasible measure, it is more beautiful than any French grand opera save *Don Carlos.*

A more reasonable explanation for these infelicities is the composer's deficiencies as a librettist, especially concerning two important turns in the drama, namely, Joan's condemnation, based on her father's accusation that she conspired with the devil, and her loss of divine agency, effected by her love for Lionel. These events are not undramatic, but simply unconvincing as Tchaikovsky presents them. In the libretto, Thibaut, angered by Joan's disobedience in refusing to marry Raymond, accuses her of conspiring with evil. This accusation stands in act III, when he repeats it, shifting the crowd's praise for Joan into condemnation. As regards credibility it is too petty, and Thibaut too much the curmudgeon to sway the crowd. The archbishop, seeking proof of the accusation, does not ask Joan if she conspired with the devil, a matter easily denied. He asks her if she is pure, and the crowd, amid thunderclaps—heaven, hell, or simply bad weather—reads her silence as guilt. Thus, one old man's suspicions demean the agency whereby Joan restored the crown of France and defeated its enemies, accomplishments so virtuous that no right-thinking person, least of all the king, present onstage and inexplicably muddled, could possibly construe as diabolical. Schiller did not allow this; his Raymond disputes Thibaut's accusation and claims that the supposedly diabolical site is a holy shrine, whereupon Thibaut himself describes a dream in which he saw Joan astride a throne in Rheims, and warns her against an excess of pride, which is clearly not her problem in act III of the opera.

Joan's silence before the archbishop is rooted in her loss of divine protection—the purity about which he inquires—and thus the two flaws in Tchaikovsky's libretto intersect. In act I, the angels inform her that she will "know not earthly love," that wedding candles will not burn for her, and that God will glorify her in battle. These are given; Joan has no free will in choosing them. Her response—asking to let pass the bitter cup—laments not love (as in Schiller), but leaving home and flock. In a later-omitted passage (between bars 180 and 181 of no. 15 in CW 5 and 37), the Virgin Mary urges Joan to take up the sword but exacts no vow. Thus Joan is rebuked in act IV for breaking a vow she never made. Meanwhile, her sparing Lionel is not explained. He converts instantly from belligerency to love; Joan is flummoxed and gives no hint that love is the reason. Her ambiguous posturing, initiated by a moonbeam that illuminates Lionel's face, seems too little to seal her fate and diminishes the credibility of their belated love duet in act IV. She thrives without love and suffers with it. Moreover, Tchaikovsky avoids the androgynous nuances in Schiller by changing the name of Joan's nemesis from the masculine Isabeau to Isabella, and by having Joan protest when an angel tells her that she, like a man, must don armor and take up the sword. This initiates a tension between Joan the warrior and Joan the shepherdess.

Among the composer's contemporaries, Laroche identified the fundamental problem with *The Maid of Orleans:* Schiller struck no deep chord in Tchaikovsky, moving him to substitute Schiller's confection of Joan's death with her real death at the stake. For this he used Jules Barbier, from whom, according to Laroche, he might also have taken the rest. By making his scenario four-fifths Schiller and one-fifth Barbier, Tchaikovsky sought to reconcile romantic poetry with historical fact [255 II 207–8]. The preponderance of Schiller precluded this, and trying to de-Schiller the libretto, including significant borrowings from Auguste Mermet's opera *Jeanne d'Arc* [171, 133–36], only worsened the problems of continuity.

While Tchaikovsky would have been the first to admit that he was no genius at confecting librettos, it strains belief that he would let such transparent blunders stand, and one aim of modern criticism has been to explain them. Part of this effort comprises apologetics from Soviet commentators, overriding the faults of the libretto in washes of praise and marking the composer's fascination with Joan since he was a child. "Using the high drama of the history of the life and ruin of the French maiden, who battles for her homeland's freedom, who is handed over and sold out to her enemies, provided scope for the creative imagination" [149, 214], or "Joan of Arc's patriotism was for Tchaikovsky the main ideological core of his remarkable opera about the maid of Orleans" [314, 187]. Western readings are psychologically more invasive, the work crying out for "interpretation as a psychological autopsy" [190, 239]. These include Freudian free-associations of Tchaikovsky's dreams [443, 310–12] and more plausible interpretations of how the character of Joan accorded with Tchaikovsky's feelings at the time he chose the topic [394, 181–84], including the possibility that he saw Joan as a liberating artistic vehicle through which he might reassess his own place in society and his relationships with others [190, 241]. This would explain his fundamental allegiance to Schiller's portrayal of Joan as "other" and as full of contradictions, at the same time that he wished to avoid

Schiller's rhetorical extremes. The conclusion of all such interpretations is still to recognize flaws in Tchaikovsky's libretto, either by disregarding them or by embracing the late twentieth century's rejection of primary meaning. In the process, he is made to be either so brazen as to put the vagaries of his own psyche onstage, or the helpless prey of his own draconian subconscious.

As drama, the opera collapses around these problems, leaving Joan perplexed and confused, urged to die without credible cause by the heavenly choir. Granting that any adaptation of Schiller would require drastic reduction, Tchaikovsky was not up to the task. The instantaneous shifts of Joan from shepherdess to warrior, Lionel and Joan from combatants to lovers, and the people from adulation to hostility are simply not persuasive, whatever his reasons for allowing them.

A libretto thus constituted will inevitably have consequences for the music. *The Maid* echoes French grand opera in that the score entertains or accompanies the action of historical forces, and thus rarely indulges an individual's passionate or intimate expression. The popularity of Joan's farewell to the forests is attributable to the convergence of sincerity, emotion, and powerful musical expression, a rare combination in the work at large. By contrast, the love duets of Charles and Agnes, then Joan and Lionel, do not move listeners because they lack emotional credibility. Yet Tchaikovsky's command of idiom in *The Maid of Orleans* is flawless. Whatever the moment—overture, opening chorus, recitative, ensemble, finale, dance, or march, even the processional in act III—the music attests to a quick sensitivity and profound assimilation of French repertoire, including its exteriority and disregard of Italianate passion, what César Cui harshly declared of the first production "good-soundingness without content." This combination—of continuous acuity of imagination and a scarcity of wonderful moments—produces overall an impression of no more than "a basically functional level of inspiration" (a remark made in reference to *Mazepa* [442, 52]).

More susceptible to critique are Tchaikovsky's musical allusions. Are they a sport of his muse, evidence of imperfect recuperation from his marriage, or a conscious strategy? The duet of Charles and Agnes, 29 bars at the end of no. 13, so clearly refers to Raoul and Valentine in *Les Huguenots* that Tchaikovsky surely realized his audience would notice. Both situations typify the genre in that personal calamity yields to historical forces. Tchaikovsky's restrictive brevity and imperfect rendition of the model make a point—that Charles and Agnes are facing mere embarrassment whereas Raoul and Valentine were facing death. His unheroic, even pitiable portrayal of them by means of this degraded counterfeit recalls the experimental readings of *The Oprichnik*. Later, when Thibaut, about to menace Joan, lingers within earshot of the organ inside the cathedral (act III, no. 19), the allusion to Mephistopheles menacing Marguerite in Gounod's *Faust* is unmistakable. It imparts a satanic coloration to Thibaut's belief in his daughter's guilt.

The opera's piecemeal genesis may explain why effectiveness in the music and unifying devices in the score tend to be local. Soviet analysts labored to show how Tchaikovsky's treatment of Joan extended over larger spans, citing a much-varied rising melodic sixth as an *Ur-melodie* representing Joan's heroic aspect [245, 105–7]. The first prominent manifestation of "Joan's sixth" comes in her farewell to the forest at the point when she acknowledges her higher calling:

Ex. 34

A variant comes a scant 10 bars later, in D minor, bridging the reprise of the opening theme in the orchestra:

Ex. 35

(*continued*)

Ex. 35 *(continued)*

These occurrences of Joan's sixth are countered by the understated chromatic line embedded within the opening phrase of the aria, suggestive of her sorrow:

Ex. 36

An important motif makes Joan's farewell a site of melodic unity. But is its dramatic importance made clear? Joan's claim that her hour has come is resolute, accompanied by the triumphal variant of the motif, and yet when the angels appear to her in the next number, she asks to be exempted. Dramatic pertinence aside, Joan's sixth lacks panache as a musical thought. It is insufficiently marked on its first appearance to make later ones recall the circumstances of that moment, reducing what should be aurally significant to discovery by analysis. It lacks the arresting properties of the "kiss" music in *Otello* or the "fate" motif in *Carmen* and supports the cliché that Tchaikovsky's truest gift was for the orchestra.

Tchaikovsky began sketching the First Suite, op. 43, on 15 August 1878 at Verbovka; 24 April 1879 is the date on the autograph; four months after that, he wrote a new movement for it, the Divertimento. Composition was protracted and confusing, involving repeated changes of movement name, the inclusion and exclusion of movements, and uncertainty about their number and order. In November 1879, Jurgenson, contrary to Tchaikovsky's express wish, published the score (plate no. 3905), parts, and a piano, four-hands arrangement [D&Y 221] before the first performance, in the order of introduction and Fugue, Divertimento, Andante (marked in the score as Intermezzo), Scherzo, Gavotte; the Marche miniature was deleted. On 8 December 1879, Nikolay Rubinstein, after complaining about its difficulty, conducted the First Suite with the Marche miniature, which was repeated. Jurgenson then wrote: "And so we were naughty having left out the March. Better late than never, for which reason I am making a present to the public of the March, that is, I am adding it to the edition in the form of an appendix" [87 I 126]. A "new edition" perpetuated many of the errors of its predecessor, including the order of the movements [CW 19a, 5]. The editors of the *Collected Works* do not indicate when the music was first published in its present order, apparently as performed by Rubinstein.

Tchaikovsky recalled that, upon sketching an orchestral scherzo, "there came into my head a whole series of pieces for orchestra, out of which a *suite* in Lachner's manner must be formed" [vii 375]. An organist and acquaintance of Beethoven, Franz Lachner was a Mendelssohnian stylist whose suites recycled baroque genres with a modern chord vocabulary, thick scoring, and cumbersome replicas of archaic counterpoint. His Suite no. VI contains an introduction and Fugue, an Andantino, and a Gavotte, as does Tchaikovsky's, but also a *Trauermusik und Festmarsch* with a very un-Tchaikovskian quotation of "Ein feste Burg." How much his music was a model for the First Suite is open to question.

To Tchaikovsky, a suite was a group of movements based primarily on attractive sound, or *prelest'*. Free of confession, philosophy, or program, it emphasized the present moment over long-term coherence; its rule was freedom from established rules [xii 352]. Allusions to eighteenth-century music may be present; formal schemes may proliferate subsections and thus increase thematic and timbral diversity. The opening sound of the First Suite—a high bassoon solo—anticipates *Le sacre du printemps* and signals a propensity of the suites to *bizarrie*. The fanfares (at 50), echoing the Fourth Symphony, hint at personal relevance. The Fugue, which the young Debussy admired [86 II 394], connects to the introduction by these fanfares at 159.

Tchaikovsky referred to the Divertimento as a "quiet waltz" [ix 54–55]. The editors of the *Collected Works* translated his whimsical title of "Divertimento" as "Divertissement," which points at the movement's theatrical properties. The Intermezzo is also misnamed. This rondo is the weightiest movement yet, a "cruel romance" tune [195, 30] with Neapolitan cadence (26ff.) and impassioned elaboration of the second theme (from 38), which echoes the Third Symphony in motif and key (mvt. III at bar 35). The intense C theme (154) suggests a significance beyond the play of sounds, as do the fanfares of the opening movement, echoed here in the denouement (188).

After the Marche miniature relieves the Intermezzo in expression and sonority, the Scherzo wearies in its proportion of length to content. Tchaikovsky gives the wind choir much to do, but the recurrence of the Scherzo theme in the principal section is inane, like some reflexive action of the body, and the attempt to parlay the Trio theme (bar 52) into significance ends in a vacuous swirl (135). The un-gavottish Gavotte is the remnant of a movement once called Dance of the Giants, which title better fits the disjunct opening phrase, the grotesque connotations of the accompanying winds, and the garrulous recurrence of its principal theme. Tchaikovsky confected a new final section, with an increase of energy and a variant of the Fugue subject from movement I (bar 145).

Composed between 7 October and 3/15 December 1879, the Second Piano Concerto, op. 44, was scored in the first months of 1880 (dated 28 April) amid politicking for *The Maid of Orleans*. Like Tchaikovsky's other concertos, it lacks the solo part in the autograph [CW 28, xvi]. It is dedicated to Nikolay Rubinstein, to whom Tchaikovsky, with understandable trepidation, showed the work for criticism. After reporting to Jurgenson that no changes were needed [ix 236], he wrote to Meck that Rubinstein had found the piano part too episodic and set off from the orchestra [ix 287]. It is likely that Rubinstein would have played the first performance had his death not intervened; Tchaikovsky's memorial to Rubinstein was a trio for the same instruments as the concertino in the second movement.

He endured much advice about the concerto. Sergey Taneyev thought the first two movements long, and the violin and cello solos in the slow movement preemptive of the piano [294, 80]. In 1887, Tchaikovsky reputedly made cuts [xvi-a 82, n. 7; xiv 613–14]; the changes he made for pianist Vasily Sapelnikov in 1888 are noted in the *Collected Works* [CW 28]. On 17 December 1888, Alexander Siloti proposed radical changes [251, 89–92, 149–56], including passing from the big interior cadenza of the first movement directly to the coda and deleting much of the music for solo violin and cello in the Andante. Tchaikovsky rejected the first, claiming it would spoil the form, and yielded little on the second [xvii 147]. His last pronouncement on the matter came on 20 August 1893 to Jurgenson: "I have agreed to some of Siloti's changes, but absolutely cannot to others. He goes too far in his wish to make this concerto easy, and wants me literally to mutilate it for the sake of simplicity. The concessions that I have made, and the abbreviations that we both have thought up, will perfectly suffice" [xvii 173]. The edition entrusted to Siloti in 1893 was ready only in 1897. He made a small cut in movement I, reduced movement II from 332 bars to 141, and left the finale intact, claiming that all were "according to the composer's intentions."

In Anton Rubinstein's manner, the movement I exposition has two areas, with two keys apiece (G and e, then E-flat and C major, tinged with minor); the development has solo cadenzas at beginning and end, the latter running more than 100 bars and serving as a retransition; and the recapitulation is radically curtailed. Tchaikovsky states his themes sparingly and elaborates them generously. The soloists in movement II, a tripartite reprise pattern, emulate friends in intimate conversation. The finale, a Sonata with elements of the first movement's key scheme, returns to the public arena. It is quixotic and overblown—the Don is attacking windmills.

The slow movement refers to the concerto grosso at the same stylistic remove as the introduction and Fugue in the First Suite refers to Bach, or the Third Symphony to a classical divertimento. More openly, the Second

Concerto (as the First) recalls Beethoven's Fourth: in its home key, a second theme in E-flat that returns in B-flat, a new theme in the development. A trace of Beethoven's Andante echoes in it literally (cf. mvt. II at bars 286ff. with Beethoven's second movement at 64ff.), homage to the work Tchaikovsky once called the "miraculous pearl of Beethoven's inspiration" and "one of the most capital works of musical creation" [83, 171].

The *Capriccio Italien* may have occurred to Tchaikovsky in 1877, when Jurgenson asked him to arrange Glinka's Spanish overtures on the eve of a trip to Italy. He wrote of emulating Glinka [xi 29], and the conceptual likeness of the *Capriccio* to Glinka's *A Night in Madrid* is his closest to any Russian predecessor. Its components are diverse. Tchaikovsky claimed to have notated some of the tunes and taken others from a collection he did not identify [ix 29]. The opening fanfare was taken from a cavalry signal audible from his hotel in Rome [1997 II 353]. The *Capriccio* is a rondo-like elaboration of themes which provides for clarity of pattern, key variety, peroration, and climax. Within it, he formulates an engaging beginning and powerful drives to cadence, in contrast with the limp starts and rhetorically abrupt, often weightless endings of earlier Russian composers in this genre.

The *Capriccio* comprises an exposition of song and an exposition of dance—introduction (180), first dance (198), and tarantella (291)—interspersed with song and ending with a coda. The opening fanfare frames the exposition of song, a brooding, Gypsy-like melody inflecting major and minor that yields to a swaggering cantabile in thirds (96). These themes return later, the first (at 259) after the first dance, and the second (at 455) after the second dance and just before the coda. The exposition of song comprises a large cadence in A major, the swaggering cantabile moving to the tritone at the end, signaling a variety of keys to come in the dances (E-flat, D-flat, B-flat, A minor, and B-flat). The new keys produce a structural tension, affirmed when the cantabile returns in a distant key and resolved in the extensive coda. The tunes are vivified through orchestration. All the strings take the opening melody, accompanied by the rest of the orchestra in guitar-like rhythms. The primary scoring of melodies, everywhere evident (not least in the second theme at 96 and 117), and the rich percussion have antecedents in Glinka, echoing Tchaikovsky's initial goal. Tchaikovsky claimed no ambition for the *Capriccio* other than to please. In Moscow, it did; in St. Petersburg, it was found to be vulgar and a sign of declining invention [86 II 630–31].

Tchaikovsky first mentioned the *Six Duets* of op. 46 to Meck on 5 June 1880; by 10 July, he was making a clean copy. Except for no. 2, for soprano and baritone, all are for soprano and mezzo. The stance of the dueting voices, their similarity of *facture* and phrase recall the opening of *Onegin,* as does the precedence of clear delivery over musical illustration. The poems' time sequence, from nightfall to dawn, and most of the topics seem relevant to the dedicatee, Tanya Davïdova, who at the time was mired in an unsuccessful engagement: (1) night relieves day without lifting the heart's sorrow; (3) the endless, inconsolable flow of tears; (4) the maiden crushed in sorrow by the arrogant young man; (5) passion is dead, yet one cannot blend in with vulgar life; (6) nature's beauty, a prayer, and let us be on our way. Only no. 2—the blood of the father is on the son's hands—does not fit this interpretation.

In "Evening" (no. 1), conflated from two poems, the lethargic play of two-note phrases in the introduction conveys the lassitude at day's end, followed by a coquettish little arabesque which sounds when the voices are silent; in the second stanza, about silencing the day's alarms and nocturnal quiet, Tchaikovsky shortens the interval between vocal phrases as if to exclude the arabesque, but this will not be; it pervades the accompaniment as the mezzo drops out and the text shifts to a confession marked by a new key, successive dueting, and rich accompaniment. After asking God to grant rest, Tchaikovsky repeats the confession and the opening two verses, bringing with them a riot of the disquieting arabesque.

The "Scottish Ballad" (set by Brahms in Herder's translation) in Tchaikovsky's redaction nearly suppresses the fact that the soprano is Edward's mother and gives no hint of her culpability in persuading Edward to kill his father. Her shift from pressing inquiry to lyrical outpouring as she asks about her fate is bereft of treachery if her identity is not clear. For dramatic effect, Tchaikovsky intensifies the near-strophic setting by raising the key of verses 3 and 4 a step higher and by more forceful vocal lines as the dialogue intensifies. He indicated that the "Scottish Ballad" should not be sung, but almost declaimed [x 163].

"Tears," Tchaikovsky's favorite from op. 46 [x 163], deploys the voices in a litany of repeated phrases to represent the flow of tears—early and late, endless, unseen, innumerable, inexhaustible. It thus complements Tyutchev's poem—short, mellifluous, folk-like, doting upon repeated syllables, and relaxing strict syntax. The litany is enhanced by the freedom of formal pattern and structural key change. Only the piano catches the hyperbole, beginning with plain chords and gradually becoming more animated; after the voices cadence, Tchaikovsky wrote an 18-bar epilogue, a peroration on the tears' ceaseless flow.

"In the garden" (no. 4) hymns the people's travails in "sorrowful songs, like autumn days." Here, the abandoned girl mimics nature—withered as the poppy, parched as the hops, bent low as the willow. The poem is set as a narrative song. The dueting voices sing as one, with much repetition against a near-constant, strumming accompaniment, offsetting vivid contrasts of verbal image. The principal motif is relaxed only in the final verse, with the girl's weeping and sobbing.

Tchaikovsky set Tolstoy's "The passion has waned" (no. 5) using relative keys in the first verse to point out the dilemma: passion is gone, but the speaker is still in love. He marks love's "disquieting ardor" with a Neapolitan chord and feints toward a new key at "to fall out of love." "But to stop loving you is impossible" (22–29) is a melody that will permeate the love duet in act I of *The Queen of Spades.* The voices begin to overlap, merging to show how everything that is not the beloved is empty and false, and they sing in rhythmic unison in the central verse, lamenting the inability to blend back into "vulgar life" now that the blood has calmed.

Surikov's "Dawn" (no. 6) contrasts personal elation with a hallowed appreciation of nature. Each of the three sections begins with elated motifs from the introduction and proceeds to octaves in the voices in reference to nature, concluding with declamation on a single pitch. In the third, as the poem refers to a prayer before leaving on a journey, the voices sing alternating phrases before the last reference to nature, a striking if momentary shift to a theatrical mode of thought. Tchaikovsky orchestrated "Dawn" in 1889 [CW 27, 473–85].

Reprising the poetical motifs of op. 46 with greater force, the *Seven Romances,* op. 47, reflects the more ravishing setting at Brailovo during Tchaikovsky's holiday in July 1880: the thrall of nature, which brought him to kneel and thank God for the blessedness he felt [ix 184]; a sense of refuge; and, in contrast, a euphoria-dashing letter from Antonina [ix 186–87, 191–92]. The first and last songs are about a young woman disappointed in love, no. 1 because the lover on his shining steed never showed up, no. 7 because of "marriage to a hateful, grey old man." The other poems share a hallowed tone, nos. 2 and 5 blending nature imagery with personal sentiment, nos. 3 and 4 placing the singer's personal sorrow and the lure of oblivion in the context of natural beauty. No. 6 is an ecstatic love lyric.

The introduction and postlude of no. 1, "If only I had known," emulate folk music, as does the strumming accompaniment. Calm at first, the singer grows animated describing her efforts to be attractive (*meno mosso* at 66–74). In the surge of excitement, Tchaikovsky replicates the introduction, setting and then abandoning a folkish drone, reaching low into the piano's range. The middle verse also begins with drones, which are abandoned as the peak of emotion is approached. An inner-outer dichotomy emerges between the agitation in the voice and the implication of disappointment in the piano. It is parallel to Tchaikovsky's externally vented anger at Antonina, concurrent with a wordless yet sympathetic inner meditation.

In "Calmly the spirit flew up to heaven," a soul asks to return to earth "whomever to pity and console." Transport is expressed by vocal phrases of litany-like regularity passing through the words without repetition or emphasis, before a linear motif in the piano (at 19) refers to "a long line of tears." This motif, abetted by modulation, fills the interludes as the spirit ponders earthly suffering. Its prominence increases as lines of the poem are repeated—about distress and woe and the wish to be returned to earth.

In no. 3, "Dusk fell upon the earth," the poet sorrows in darkness and the resplendent morning to music indirect and enigmatic. The shifts of perspective, passionate expression growing quiet and halting (fermatas at bars 21, 66, 117); the dotted figure that focuses the ends of lines (4, 39, and the postlude at 139 and 142); a variant of the Lensky sixth (108–11) on the words "I am sorrowful, as before"; and the ongoing tension between G minor and F major—all suggest an evasive beauty in relation to perpetual sorrow.

"Sleep, poor friend" (no. 4) is a lullaby marked by the nearly hypnotic return of its opening phrase of solace and reassurance. The key and the lyric recall Gremin in *Evgeniy Onegin,* the vocal part conveying maturity and experience, the song again illustrating the reciprocity between Tchaikovsky's operas and his songs. An enharmonic modulation (at *più mosso*) refers to oblivion, as does a gentle dialogue in the tenor range of the piano (at 20) between descending tetrachords urging the onset of sleep and sighing motifs which echo the sleeper's travails. At the end, the sighs vanish, as if sleep has prevailed.

"I bless you, forests" expresses Tchaikovsky's exalted feelings at Brailovo. Introduced with two-note figures that herald repetitions later ("valleys . . .

meadows . . . mountains . . . waters" at 16–18), the ear is prepared for a burst of melody to follow. The voice is set above a rich, seamless chordal texture, intensified to ecstatic effect in the fourth verse, when the singer merges the soul with all of life, to embrace enemy and friend alike. The new accompaniment, in repeated triplet chords, persists to the final cadence in the voice, whereupon, in the piano postlude, Tchaikovsky returns with emphasis to the initial two-note figure, now transformed.

In Apukhtin's "Does the day reign?" a substantial improvisation precedes the voice before rushing headlong into the poem, which, like no. 5, is a hyperbole: in every thought, the beloved initiates all that is good and sacred. The continuous accompaniment urges on the voice, leading to the most energetic postlude in op. 47. In mood, the song anticipates the Strauss of "Zueignung" and "Heimliche Aufforderung"—heady and exalted. Tchaikovsky orchestrated "Does the day reign?" in 1888, but the score is lost.

Surikov's folk-like "Was I not a little blade of grass?" (no. 7) likens the singer to natural phenomena: as one cuts the grass to dry and a rose to make a bouquet, so the maiden is cut off from her family when she marries. The main theme (like that of no. 1) descends in arabesques to the low range of the piano. The introduction and postlude trade more in the chord progressions of Western art music than much of the modally harmonized vocal setting, to haunting effect doubling the vocal line and the bass of the accompaniment at the nearly untranslatable refrain, "Oh, you my woe, my little woe!" The third verse (bars 45–54) is unabashedly operatic. Tchaikovsky orchestrated "Was I not a little blade of grass?" in 1884 [CW 27, 489–500].

First mention of the celebrated *Serenade for Strings,* op. 48, was to Meck on 9 September 1880; by 10 October, it was composed; he dated the finished score on 23 October. It was performed privately in Moscow on 21 November, before Nápravnik conducted the public first performance in St. Petersburg on 18 October 1881. Imperial period editions and the *Collected Works* [CW 20] advise: "The more numerous the complement of the string orchestra, the more it will conform to the composer's wishes." Because the *Serenade* arose from an inner compulsion, Tchaikovsky claimed genuine merit for it. "In the first movement I paid tribute to my worship of Mozart; this is an intentional imitation of his manner" [x 206]. Although not his language: the *Serenade* nowhere sounds like Mozart, though it emulates his motif and witticism, as in the introduction of movement I with the migration of the opening theme from treble to bass and back again, reharmonized and inverted, hinting at the importance of counterpoint later. The *Allegro moderato* starts with a jest: two chords of indeterminate syntax turn upon each other, as if uncertain how to proceed. This palindromic moment forecasts larger arch-like gestures, including the reprise of the introduction at the end of this movement, modified as the principal theme of the finale, and again in its original form in the closing pages.

The *Pezzo in forma di Sonatina* signals, as do the other movement titles (all in Italian), Tchaikovsky's inspiration in southern climes, borne out by the extraordinary buoyancy and melodic richness of this music. Movement I, like the Overture to *The Marriage of Figaro,* forms an exposition through the first and second key areas, then recapitulates without a development. Thus, Tchaikovsky initiates a formal tension across the entire work, resolved by the inclusion of a development in the finale. Within its thematic contrasts, the first movement coheres by embedded falling tetrachords from the opening theme:

Ex. 37

Ex. 38

Ex. 39

The principal theme of movement II is anticipated in a brief but noticeably waltz-like passage in movement I:

Ex. 40

Ex. 41

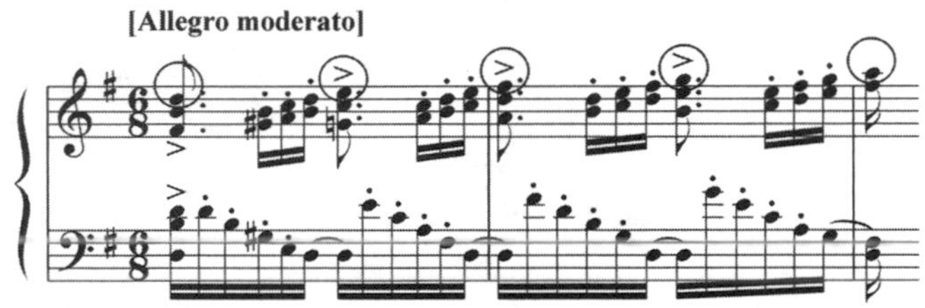

Then, in the *ritenuto* and fermata (30–33), which suggest the chic hesitation of dancers, Tchaikovsky hints at that mere thread of sound that links movement III with movement IV. The *valse* does not emulate Mozart, though the simple reprise pattern is closer to the Minuet and Trio than to the waltz ritornelli of Tchaikovsky's symphonies and ballets.

He frames the *Elegia* with its opening melody, then sets out the main part in strophes, as he did at the beginning of movement I, composing it, as he did the waltz, on a rising scale. We do not know for whom Tchaikovsky here was expressing lament and praise. The introduction admits otherworldly connotation, the parallel sixth chords rising as the bass line, with its beguiling initial dissonance, descends. The main part is a song rich in counterpoint and ecstatic phrase extensions—the praise implicit in *Elegia*. Lament comes later, after the reprise of the opening, with the unexpected return of the central melody, hushed in *pianissimo,* over a pulsating tonic pedal, with distinctive coloration of the minor. The movement ends with an extraordinary gesture—a three-octave climb in scales and leaps, as if ascending to a higher sphere.

The finale begins atop that three-octave climb. One senses an allusion not to Mozart but to the same location in Beethoven's String Quartet no. 6. While the subtitle, *Tema Russo,* refers to the Allegro theme, the ethereal melody after the end of the *Elegia* is a Russian tune as well, "As through the meadow," no. 6 in Balakirev's collection [24]. Another folk song, "Beneath the green apple tree" (Balakirev, no. 29), launches the sonata-allegro pattern. It begins in changing background, then moves to the second key area, individualizing a Western transition with balalaika imitations (bars 72–83). Chromatic digression forestalls cadential affirmation before the development (at 168) improvises on the main themes. A dominant pedal (256) leads to a recapitulation with an abbreviated first area. As the recapitulation is about to end, the opening of movement I returns and is juxtaposed with "Beneath the green apple tree" to affirm the likeness between these movements.

"As through the meadow" is about a young lad pining for his beloved, "Beneath the green apple tree" about an unmarried man who takes up his *gusli* to sing about his marriage: the bride vanished, the victim of foul play. The latter relates the *Serenade* topically with the texts of opp. 46 and 47 and suggests sympathy for Tanya Davïdova or even Antonina. The theme that opens movement I may not have been invention so much as conscious borrowing: the folk song, chosen first, projecting back from the fourth movement to animate the first. In that event, as Machaut once wrote, "Ma commençement est ma fin."

A festive Jurgenson title page refers to Tchaikovsky's op. 49 as *1812: Solemn Overture for Large Orchestra, Composed on the Occasion of the Dedication of the Cathedral of the Savior;* in plainer Jurgenson editions, *1812: Overture solenelle pour grand orchestre.* Rahter called it *1812 Overture für grosses Orchester;* the *Collected Works* calls it *The Year 1812, Solemn Overture,* where it is edited by Vissarion Shebalin; the imperial hymn has again been deleted and banished to an appendix (CW 25, 177–81, bars 398–403), replaced by the concluding *slava* of Glinka's *A Life for the Tsar.*

In May 1880, Nikolay Rubinstein asked Tchaikovsky to choose a topic to compose for the All-Russian Exhibition of Arts and Manufacture the following summer: an Overture for the opening, something to mark the 25th anniversary of Alexander II's reign, or a cantata with religious shadings for the consecration of the Cathedral of the Savior in Moscow. Tchaikovsky procrastinated. On 18 September, Rubinstein exhorted him: the exhibition should have "exceptional new things"; his piece would be dearer than the others; it will be a favor, not a commission. It was to be 15–25 minutes long, without soloists but possibly with chorus, and it was due in December. Rubinstein thanked him, then quoted the song Tchaikovsky had dedicated to him, no. 5 from op. 16, "Kill me, but love me" [252, 181–82]. Tchaikovsky composed *1812* in a week, between 30 September and 6 October 1880, admitting that his inspiration was more commissioned than spontaneous. This may explain the many borrowings: the prayer "Save, Lord, thy people," at the beginning; a duet of Maria and Olyona from *Voevoda* (CW 1 suppl., 252–53; *1812* at 164; this suggests that he had not yet burned the opera in 1880); the folk song "At the gates" (Balakirev no. 38 [24]) at 207; the imperial hymn "God Save the Tsar!" and "La Marseillaise."

The Overture *1812* has endured vitriolic criticism, from an early reviewer who found it banal [108, 397] to a commentator 60 years later who dubbed it "one of the most dreary and repulsive works in the whole of music," preposterous in its array of performers and obnoxious, noisy, vulgar, and empty [1, 95]. These remarks animate a meager literature. Modest did not comment on it in *The Life;* Soviet authorities hardly sniffed at a work so redolent of tsar and Orthodoxy; even the Eulenburg miniature score (no. 624) has no preface. An eyewitness wrote:

> The national anthem, the inevitable finale of this kind of piece (his Serbo-Russian March, A. Rubinstein's "Russia," etc.) is introduced at the very end, in a powerful fanfare-like transcription. . . . The weakest part of the overture is the battle, strongly, so to speak, "seasoned" with the pealing of bells, the ears rent by three hundred drums, etc.—in a word, by all those Wagnerian effects, which press for overwhelming grandeur but in fact only bring listeners to a tiny smile which condescends to overindulgence in the loud. The string instru-

ments are completely overwhelmed; the roar of the "winds," the rattling of the tympani and cymbals, the wall-shaking screech of the tam-tam, and the uninterrupted, breathtaking trilling of the snare drums—all this calls forth but one desire—"If only it would end soon!" And then more bells. [GO820817]

According to Kashkin, *1812* was to be played in front of the cathedral with a colossal orchestra, military ensembles, and cannon [187, 128; MV020820]. Recalling the Cantata for Peter the Great, Tchaikovsky may have decided that blunt externals and familiar borrowings promoted intelligibility—including "La Marseillaise," a song born not of Napoleon but the revolution, highlighted in Litolff's *Robespierre* Overture, a favorite of Tchaikovsky the student.

There is no written program. The work opens with "Save, Lord, thy people" in the strings [166, 154–55]. The oboe solo, *piangendo e molto espressivo,* hints at alarm and escalates into a stormy *tutti* which leads to the military Andante (77) with its fanfares. The *Allegro giusto* initiates a sonata-allegro, followed in the coda by a grand mélange of themes culminating in the triumphant Russian anthem. In the first theme group, an *agitato* theme spins out the alarm of the introduction; next we hear, amid the tumult, fragments of "La Marseillaise." The second group joins a lyrical interlude—the music from *Voevoda*—with Russian folk song. As Russian and French music vie with each other, Russian is favored. With so many themes and so much counterpoint in the outer sections, Tchaikovsky abbreviates the development and places the Russian part of the recapitulation over a dominant pedal (bar 279) extended through the coda, including a moment (328ff.) when "La Marseillaise," in long notes to the accompaniment of cannon, suggests that the French have gained the advantage. But rescue is at hand with the return of the *largo,* reinforced by military music, prayer, and the national hymn.

No mention of the Trio "To the Memory of a Great Artist," op. 50, survives before 15 December 1881 [x 292], though Kashkin wrote that Tchaikovsky took almost all of that year to compose it [187, 131], finishing in January 1882. By omitting Rubinstein's name in the dedication, he distinguished personal from artistic memory [178, 50]: that a two-movement scheme, sonata and variations (the last variation set off from the rest and cast as a sonata movement of its own), should memorialize an important interpreter of Beethoven links the Trio to Beethoven's last piano sonata.

The ensemble of strings and piano, to which Tchaikovsky once objected [ix 306], replicates the slow movement of the Second Piano Concerto, to the same dedicatee. The ever-darker coloration of the Trio, from the ruminating *moderato* to the funeral march in the closing bars, memorializes Tchaikovsky's own foreboding about Rubinstein's death and the death itself. Pausing in the movement I development at the tritone seems to be a structural pivot, followed by an enharmonic shift to B major, preparing the key of movement II. It brings Tchaikovsky to E-flat minor, the tonic of the Third String Quartet, another memorial work, which emulated the intonations of a funeral service.

Disputing responses to the work, Tchaikovsky claimed he was writing "without the feeblest intention to represent something, suddenly to learn that it represents this or that" [xi 266]. Taking him at his word, one may liken the freedom of expression in the Trio to that of the *Rococo Variations,* or consider the second movement, in a more rarified comparison, proximate to Bach's *Goldberg Variations* as a review of the current state of music: Tchaikovsky's variation 3, the scherzo; variation 4, the folk song; variation 5, the pastoral (recalling the shepherd's *svirel'* at the end of scene 2 of *Evgeniy Onegin*); variation 6, the waltz; and after the return to theme in variation 7, the fugue, the dirge, and the mazurka in variations 8–10. Self-reference persists in the melody and rhythm of the theme to movement I and the allusion to the opening of the Second Piano Concerto in the *Allegro risoluto e con fuoco* of the last variation [20, 28–41].

A more tempting rationale is to hear the Trio, regardless of the composer's claim, as an unabashed memorial full of references to the great artist of the dedication. Soon after *The Snow Maiden* in 1873, at a picnic in the Sparrow Hills, "N. G. Rubinstein loved genuine folk songs very much and for that reason made the peasants sing," Kashkin wrote. "This scene lingered in Pyotr Ilyich's memory, and the recollection of it was awakened almost nine years later in the variation theme of the piano trio dedicated to the memory 'of a great artist.'" In movement II, "recollections of Rubinstein and his musical characteristics are manifest, in various situations in his life" [187, 87, 131]. Twenty-five years after Rubinstein's death, Kashkin reiterated: "For those close to the deceased his image is sketched in each variation of the Trio" [MV060310].

The headmotif is never abandoned; Rubinstein is present in every variation. Other connections are easily imagined. The scherzo of variation 3 recalls Anton Rubinstein, variation 4 a raucous drinking song, variation 5 a music box which leads directly to a *valse* which recalls the Christmastide *svyatki* from *The Seasons.* In this circumstance—masquerading guests dropping in for cheer—Rubinstein's theme is delayed for 50 bars, a fresh key, and pompous augmentation—appropriate mimetic choices. The fugue of variation 8 brings to mind Anton Rubinstein's remark that theoretical wisdom came much easier to Nikolay than to him. Variation 9 may recall the Bayan in Glinka's *Ruslan and Lyudmila* or some Gypsy music in a café as easily as the death-like, pre-Mahler *Kondukt* in its resonance of bells and nasal, listless melody in the muted strings. Variation 10 conjures up visions of Rubinstein and Wieniawski improvising dances at the Artistic Circle of the 1860s [MV990212]. The last variation is infused with Schumann, on whom, according to Laroche, Nikolay Rubinstein bestowed the treasures of his genius. "Rubinstein was able without coercing Schumann, and remaining true to his spirit, to give the [*Fantasia in C*] a plastic clarity and captivating brilliance; the literally bogatyr-like hand of the inspired pianist lifted the motley crowd of listeners to the pure heights of Schumannesque poetry" [255 V 89–90].

To a first listener, the Trio can seem overstated; Tchaikovsky realized this and authorized cuts. He described it as an orchestral work set upon three instruments [xi 24], a mannerism of the habitually orchestral composer. There had to be a piano in a memorial work for a pianist; at the same time, a concerto or fantasia seemed too gala [187, 131]. To Kashkin, the Trio had no parallel in musical literature, being equally huge in dimensions and content [178, 50].

CHAPTER FIFTEEN

1882–1884

NO ARTIST IS GUARANTEED A FAITHFUL MUSE, AND TCHAIKOVSKY'S, in these years, continued along the fretful course begun in 1878. He was ever less in control of his finances; Kamenka had long since ceased to be a refuge; more and more, he wished for a little piece of earth with a house on it. This wish became insistent in 1884, in painful conflict with his chronic lack of money. Most of his compositions from this time, including music for the coronation of Alexander III, remain obscure. *Mazepa,* after a desultory gestation, moved into production, Tchaikovsky indiscreetly declaring the 8 percent performance royalty to be an affront at a time he could not boast of a single work in the continuing repertoire.

1882

After the Piano Trio was finished in January, there was little composition in the first third of the year. Nikolay Bernard, the publisher of *Nouvelliste,* had asked Tchaikovsky for six piano pieces at 100 rubles apiece, but Jurgenson intervened, preferring to pay the price and keep the pieces, which would become op. 51. Having little to do magnified the distractions: the death of Jurgenson's son, talk of a trip to Algeria, and Anatoly's engagement. In Rome during Tchaikovsky's stay, Sergey Flerov, a music critic from Moscow, presented him with his translation of E. T. A. Hoffmann's "The Nutcracker and the Mouse-King." Returning to Russia in March, Pyotr attended Anatoly's wedding on 4 April and discussed (without consequence) the possibilities for a new opera with Mikhail Lentovsky, an impresario of garden theaters in Moscow [xi 97].

Meck's woes continued. She was writing less than before, her zest for complex discourse diminished. She still waxed passionate from time to time, and Tchaikovsky was still the courtier. There is no sign that he was any less grateful to her, nor that she did not cherish her relationship with him [e.g., 86 III 160], but they wrote mostly in the summer about domesticity and bringing together Anna Davïdova with Nikolay Meck. At the end of April 1882, Meck bought a new estate, Pleshcheyevo, in the environs of Moscow.

As spring passed into summer, Tchaikovsky was again at Kamenka. In April, he had noted with displeasure the presence of the music tutor Stanislav Blumenfeld, whom he had recommended six years before [vi 79, n. 2]. Blumenfeld's proximity intimidated Tchaikovsky as he composed, and he had a negative reaction to Blumenfeld's advances to Tanya Davïdova. On 6 May, Kolya Konradi's father died; his will brought Modest 10,000 rubles. Midsummer was spent at Grankino, which now belonged to Kolya. In May, Tchaikovsky learned of a successful Brodsky-Richter performance of the Violin Concerto in London. Tchaikovsky completed the second third of *Mazepa,* but despite a warm feeling toward the opera, he worked without enthusiasm. On 16/28 July, *The Maid of Orleans* was produced at a summer theater in Prague. In August, he traveled to Moscow to hear the first performance of *1812;* he finished op. 51 in September. Meanwhile, Jurgenson, smarting from the piracy of foreign publishers, agreed to revise Tchaikovsky's prints.

Through all this comes a sense of the sands shifting beneath Tchaikovsky's feet. On 20 August, he urged Jurgenson not to forget to locate "the tiniest little cagelet" for him in his house, perhaps to reduce expenses, perhaps to disengage from Kamenka. He was vexed to find Blumenfeld at Kamenka when he returned, and within a month declared that Tanya was unblushing at behavior in which "only public women engage" [xi 212]. His irritation, and Sasha's continuing illness, did not stay his composing progress: in mid-September, he finished *Mazepa* and began to score it, and he revised *The Maid of Orleans* before year's end. In October, he said that he hoped to live out his days in Moscow after Alyosha's military service [xi 246–47]. Several days later, the Davïdovs moved him out of his quarters to make room for a teacher [xi 252].

The end of 1882 was suddenly busy. He delivered the *All-Night Vigil* to Jurgenson, discussed coronation pieces, attended concerts and operas, rebuffed Balakirev's program for a *Manfred* Symphony, met Max Erdmannsdörfer (Nikolay Rubinstein's replacement as conductor) [37], reconciled with Vladimir Shilovsky, accepted an invitation from the new director of the Imperial Theaters, Ivan Alexandrovich Vsevolozhsky, to join the theatrical operatic committee, awaited the revised *Maid of Orleans* (though Maria Kamenskaya, for whom he revised it, had fallen ill), left for abroad on 28 December, and heard *Tristan und Isolde* for the first time two days later in Berlin. It was a taste of crowded schedules to come.

1883

In Berlin, Tchaikovsky did not visit Josef Kotek, apparently unaware of his failing health; he was en route to Paris to orchestrate *Mazepa*. Arriving on 2/14 January 1883, he was thus engaged when he wrote to Anatoly 12 days later asking him to confirm that Tanya was on her way [xii 32]. Two days after that—16/28 January—Modest arrived with her. The official purpose was to treat her morphine addiction, but there was another reason, which is suppressed in most correspondence and *The Life:* Tanya was more than halfway to term with Blumenfeld's child. It is hardly credible that her parents were not aware of this. Three months before, after conferring with Blumenfeld, Tanya had been "flushed and anxious" [xi 262]. Even still, Tchaikovsky recommended him again—for an institute in Kiev for young women of the nobility [xiii 24].

Tatyana Davïdova kept Tchaikovsky in Paris until mid-May, while he orchestrated *Mazepa,* composed for the coronation, and arranged a foster home for the infant Georges-Léon. He was assisted in Tanya's care by Parisian specialists, a companion sent from Russia, and the finances of Meck and Jurgenson, who had already provided 5,000 rubles 30 days before the birth. In September 1882, he had written of Tanya, "How this will turn out simply makes my hair stand on end" [xi 213], whereas now he spoke of *fatum,* predicting that she would never be free of drugs and might come to an early, unhappy end. Whatever his reputation for softness of character, Tchaikovsky dealt calmly and efficiently at this time with Tanya, his professional responsibilities, the future of the Moscow Conservatory, the health of Meck and Sasha, and other serious issues.

Before leaving Moscow, he had agreed to arrange the final chorus of Glinka's *A Life for the Tsar* to accompany Alexander III's entry into the Kremlin during the coronation. On 15 January, Jurgenson reminded him and on the 27th sent the music and reiterated the charge: repattern the chorus into unison couplets, omitting mention of the opera's hero, then write a short transition into the national anthem, all accompanied by strings. The music arrived on 1 February, and Tchaikovsky sent off the arrangement three days later. Modest listed it as "in manuscript" [1997 II 514]; the latest thematic catalog said that it was presumably published by Jurgenson [423, 760]; and a German catalog indicated that Jurgenson published only the choral part [378, 96–97]. On 6/18 February, Tchaikovsky received a telegram querying his coronation cantata. He hadn't written one, as he had never received a text. He proposed something from the Peter the Great Cantata of 1872 [xii 58]. On 1 March, Jurgenson exhorted him to fulfill a commission for a coronation march, which he started on the 5th [96, 298] and hoped to dispatch by the 17th [xii 78]. Three days later, he received a formal commission for the cantata. Tempted to ransack *Mazepa* to discharge these "unexpected and very oppressing labors" [xii 80], he composed them afresh, and on 26 March he posted both scores to St. Petersburg [96, 348]. He refused any fee for these works, citing his indebtedness to the emperor and his wish not to reject an imperial commission.

Adding to his burden late in February were thoughts of Antonina, and he asked Jurgenson to investigate her situation. If she had been spurned by a lover, Tchaikovsky must extend a helping hand [xii 72–73]. This sentiment may have been prompted by Tanya or by Anatoly and his wife, who shortly before this letter were awaiting the birth of their daughter: "I would give dearly if your fears could be mine. It seems to me that the crown of human happiness is to have children. How many joys lie ahead for you" [xii 32].

On 25 April, his 43rd birthday and the eve of Georges-Léon's birth, Tchaikovsky mused that he had never spent it thus, totally uncelebrated, awaiting an increase in his nieces and nephews. Much remained to do. The child was baptized and taken to foster parents on the third day. Bills had to be paid, against which, on 7/19 May, the composer calculated a shortfall of 2,000 francs. The solution, he rued, was Meck—again [xii 159]. He left France on 10/22 May 1883, the day his Glinka arrangement was being sung in Red Square by 10,640 strong. He arrived in Petersburg on the

15th, the day his new cantata was being performed in Moscow, lingering in St. Petersburg to avoid the crowds in Moscow, relieved to be free of family burdens and claiming no appetite for work. By the end of May, he was living in Anatoly's new home at Podushkino; by 1 June, he and Meck had matched her son Nikolay with his niece Anna.

One senses a quickening of the pace of his life. On 10 June, he presented *Mazepa* to the Petersburg theater direction. On the 15th he entered the fray at the Moscow Conservatory, urging Nikolay Hubert to rejoin the faculty after stepping down as director. He began to compose the Second Suite. On the 20th, he informed Modest of Nikolay Kondratiev's illness, a presentiment of his terrible end. On the 21st, an imperial favor acknowledged the *Coronation March* and Cantata. During the rest of the year, he finished proofreading *Mazepa* on 10 August; he disputed with Nápravnik over casting, threatening to withdraw the opera until better singers were available. Near year's end, the Ministry of Court increased his royalties for it. The Second Suite was completed on 13 October. A few days before, notice had gone out from the International Union of Composers in Paris, requesting a new piece from Tchaikovsky and his agreement to conduct it there. By 24 October, he was selecting texts for the *Children's Songs,* op. 54, finished and dispatched 10 days later. On 19 November he was in Moscow to hear Erdmannsdörfer conduct his First Symphony, unperformed since 1868. In the autumn, he lobbied on behalf of the pathologically idle Laroche for a job. Fearing his friend's perdition, he began in December write down articles as Laroche dictated them.

Relations with Meck continued to draw the best from Tchaikovsky the courtier. He hosted her sons at Podushkino in July; he calmed her worry that they might fail their examinations at the School of Jurisprudence, though Nikolay, Anna Davïdova's fiancé, actually did. He attended their engagement celebration in September and looked forward to their wedding. He needed money only once, though in typically awkward circumstances. Learning of the imperial recognition of his coronation music, valued at 1,500 rubles, he started spending against it; he was disappointed that, instead of money, he received a ring and that it pawned for only 375 rubles; then, he lost his wallet containing both the money and the pawn ticket.

From the south, meanwhile, came hints that Lev and Sasha did not know about Tanya. After a family baptism in October, Sasha questioned Pyotr about Blumenfeld, who had never aroused her curiosity before [xii 260].

Some days later, Alyosha reported a rumor that Blumenfeld had spent several nights with Tanya last summer, that she had become pregnant and had gone to Paris to give birth. He was little consoled that all Kiev knew it from Blumenfeld's intemperate boasting.

The year 1883 ended on a curiosity and an imperial favor. On 30 December, Meck sent New Year's greetings and asked Tchaikovsky why Modest had never married. On 31 December, Nápravnik received imperial permission to produce *Evgeniy Onegin* during the next season [D&Y 304].

1884

Once the premieres of *Mazepa* had passed, this was one of the most unusual years in Tchaikovsky's life. He focused on small deeds as his fortitude of 1883 fell away. This year's diaries survive, revealing mystifying alphabet codes and a surge of affection for his nephew Bob Davïdov. The Third Suite, the Concert Fantasia, the op. 57 songs, and cherubic hymns form the bulk of his composition, augmented by small pieces and thoughts of a revision of *Vakula the Smith,* realized early in 1885.

On 9 January in St. Petersburg, Tchaikovsky met with Nápravnik and Lev Ivanov, the balletmaster of *Mazepa,* on the 11th he attended the wedding of Anna Davïdova and Nikolay Meck, and then it was back to Moscow on the 14th for rehearsals of *Mazepa* there. His weariness was such that he doubted he could endure it all twice [xii 299], and when summoned to St. Petersburg on 20 January, he assigned Nápravnik his authorial rights in matters of learning and performing the opera and declined any future claim of imperfect execution [xii 302]. According to Kashkin, Tchaikovsky's anxiety was extreme at rehearsals of *Mazepa:*

> At the dress rehearsal of *Mazepa* I was sitting in a box in the *bel-étage,* and in an adjacent box the composer was hiding behind a door curtain. The rehearsal was going very smoothly, everyone was satisfied, only the composer had the look of someone sentenced to death.
>
> At the end of rehearsal I wanted to say something to him, but looking him in the face I stopped; he was visibly making every effort to fend off a nervous attack, and if I had said a word to him at that moment, hysterics would have ensued. . . . Pyotr Ilyich regained his self-possession, and though he had an extremely disordered look he could, it seems, go onstage and thank the performers. [187, 132]

The premieres of *Mazepa*—3 February in Moscow, 6 February in St. Petersburg—revealed characteristic differences. In Moscow, acting was stressed; in Petersburg, historical accuracy. Muscovite errors in staging *Mazepa* did not hinder the noble impression, whereas in Petersburg there were no blunders of locale or history, but the precision of it all left the spectator cold [NV840208]:

> All the decorations are executed by Mr. Bocharov after drawings made by him personally from life during a trip last autumn, undertaken especially for this purpose to Dikanka, Baturin, Whitechurch and other places where the action occurs. . . . The costumes . . . are most faithful copies of the costumes of that time; . . . among the models were original and personal costumes of some of the principal characters, preserved as family treasures and mementos . . . put at the direction's disposal by the descendants of the Kochubey family, famous in Little Russia, by the Princes Kochubey, Volkonsky and others. [NO840131]

If in Moscow there was "not the slightest confusion in the movement of groups" [MV840207], in Petersburg the action was sometimes muddled:

> [In Moscow] Korsov admires Maria, the latter offers wine from the winebowl, whereas here [the Mazepa] Mr. Pryanishnikov only twirls his moustache, and is so absorbed in the dance that he doesn't pay a bit of attention to Maria, who ought to be filling his heart at this very moment as he contemplates telling Kochubey his secret. [NV840208]

The dungeon scene was graphic, probably more so in Moscow where the executioners rushed at Kochubey, tore off his clothes, and dragged him to the torture wheel. A critic complained of anti-artistic realism, including live horses onstage: "The tramping of their hooves on the wooden boards rends every scenic illusion, and the constant fear that their getting frightened and throwing the singers would produce a commotion—did not enhance artistic impression in the least" [MV840207]. Critics thought the narrative was extreme: abduction, torture, treason, execution, insanity, suicide, retrieving a corpse. The display of the torture apparatus was crude and sensational, as was the "completely unnecessary" drunken Cossack [PG840207].

Sergey Flerov in Moscow objected to Tchaikovsky's interpolations of Pushkin's verse, and said that his "ideal center"—the Battle of Poltava—had been reduced to an entr'acte. Mazepa was superfluous in acts I and III;

his love for Maria was too complex for the crude brushstrokes of opera. Writing in 1889, Laroche reiterated that Tchaikovsky's operas were subject to the odd disparities of his genius: a "wide, bloody river flows through his operas," and yet "the weakest places . . . are those in which he must represent dramatic clash." Cantilena lies at the heart of his muse; therefore when Mazepa ceases to be a bloody tyrant and turns into a simple, loving baritone, magnificent music pours out of his mouth. *Mazepa* is full of truth and beauty in its lyric moments, even as the dramatic side shows a great talent on an alien path [255 II 130–31, 134]. Konstantin Galler found evidence of a declining muse in Tchaikovsky's borrowings [NO840211]. Perhaps alluding to Musorgsky, Tchaikovsky used the folk song Musorgsky had used in the Coronation Scene of *Boris Godunov* and referred to Varlaam in the drunken Cossack and to the chorus of monks as Pimen takes his crutch and finds his way to matins in the prayer offered up by Kochubey and Iskra. There is no holy foolishness in Maria's deranged lullaby, but otherwise she resembles Musorgsky's *yurodivïy*—meek and vulnerable. The similarity of the Lyubov-Maria duet to the *Sterblied* in act II of *Tristan und Isolde* (at 1564), which Tchaikovsky first heard late in 1882, was probably accidental.

Impressions of *Mazepa* come down to us from the young Vasily Kalinnikov in a letter of 26 September 1884, a day after seeing the opera:

> The music is so likeable and so amazing in its grandeur that in the emotional [*pateticheskikh*] passages I simply lost track of my surroundings. Before the last act the music in an entr'acte represents "The Battle of Poltava." Tchaikovsky carried out his musical idea so well, that in spite of oneself you imagine with the sounds all the horrors of this glorious battle and its course. The public especially loved this "Battle of Poltava," proof of which was that it was played twice. . . . The orchestra, consisting of 120 players (22 first violins), performed so beautifully and nicely that it was simply a miracle. Yesterday Tchaikovsky himself conducted the third and fourth acts. He was given a laurel wreath, and there was no end to the public's delight and calls. . . . You know from Pushkin's "Poltava" that Maria goes insane at the end and then encounters Mazepa as a fugitive. This scene is remarkably well expressed by Tchaikovsky. The prayer prior to death of Kochubey and Iskra also stands out. [314, 221]

It's difficult to decide which is more striking: Kalinnikov identifying two of the bloody scenes as the most impressive or the performance details—

including the size of the orchestra and that Tchaikovsky was conducting two years before the widely assumed date of his return to this activity.

The day after the premiere in Moscow, Tchaikovsky went abroad, missing the first performance in St. Petersburg, which was attended by the emperor—a serious lapse of protocol. He also missed, the next day, hearing Max Erdmannsdörfer conduct the first performance of the Second Suite. Erdmannsdörfer did not appreciate the slight, though his excellent performance was repeated four days later [1997 II 536–37].

Tchaikovsky arrived in Berlin on the morning of the *Mazepa* performance in Petersburg. When he reached Paris, Tanya Davïdova was there again for treatment. He resolved to stay until she was ready to travel, and he visited Georges-Léon, a "colossal, beautiful, merry child" who looked "frightfully like his father" [xii 318]. But as much as his family, *Mazepa* was in his thoughts. By the end of February, Tchaikovsky had grown skeptical of Tanya's medical treatment, and when Nápravnik reported the emperor's surprise and sorrow that Tchaikovsky had missed *Mazepa,* advising him to return immediately [xii 332], the composer departed straightaway. He was granted an imperial audience at Gatchina on 7 March, officially to receive the Order of St. Vladimir, Fourth Class. He described the occasion to Anatoly [xii 334–35], then wrote to Meck that his despair over *Mazepa* was unjustified: the opera had pleased in St. Petersburg, the press had misrepresented the general opinion, and the emperor was first among his sympathizers [xii 335–36]. In Moscow he revised the opera [xii 340] and began pursuing "very diligently" the quest for a home of his own [xii 344–45]. Beyond this, there are signs of extraordinary changes in Tchaikovsky during the spring and summer of 1884.

The evidence suggests that he was engaging eternal questions, and the cause was illness. Tchaikovsky had often suffered physical distress, from nerves or emotional turmoil, but for the first time in 1884 his complaints, mostly of gastric upset, persisted. On 1 April, he reported to Taneyev that he had been ill for two weeks, forced to refuse dinner invitations; on 7 April, he was still unwell and informed Meck that "catarrh of the stomach" had delayed his departure from Moscow for several days; on 26 April, he noted that the obnoxious condition of his stomach was beginning to poison his life. Nor was composition going well. In Paris, he had planned to write a symphony at Kamenka [xii 328], but he lacked ambition now that he was there. Music came to him but the genre was not clear, and he was dissatisfied with the commonness of his ideas [Dnev 13]. At month's end, he began the Third Suite after realizing that it was a suite, but it and the Concert Fantasia, op. 56, remained conflated in his mind for a time.

He was pondering religion and philosophy. On 7 April he wrote of attending many church services. Five days later he was thinking about church music and its reform. On 22 April he read the First Book of Kings (which begins with the death of David, the biblical psalmist). Five days later he wrote to Anna Merkling:

> I do not wish to die and would like to reach a hearty old age, but would not agree if asked to become young again and to relive my life. Once is enough. . . . Every age has its charms and excellent sides, and the point is not to be young forever but to suffer physically and morally [*nravstvenno*] as little as possible.
>
> . . . And something else is needed—that there be no fear of death. That I cannot boast. I am not so infused with religion as to see with certainty a new life beginning in death, and I am not so much a philosopher as to be reconciled with that abyss of nonbeing into which one must sink. I envy no one as I do completely religious people. [xii 362–63]

Tchaikovsky resolved to do his best with what remained to him. Health and sluggish composition darkened his assessment on 24 April, the eve of his birthday: "How long I have lived and—truthfully, without false modesty—how little I have accomplished! Even in my own present *occupation:* you see, hand on heart, there is nothing *perfect* and *exemplary.* I am still searching, doubting, wavering. And in other things? I read nothing, know nothing" [Dnev 14–15].

As April passed into May, he was thinking about Mozart—preparing recitatives for *The Marriage of Figaro* and playing over the gigue that would go into *Mozartiana* [213, 32]—but ill humor set the stage for some notorious coded references in his diaries, the first on 23 April: "The Butakov persecution during whist. There was much Z. Ah, what a monster I am!" Z, invariably mentioned in connection with playing cards, has companions in X and "the feeling"—all such references can be found in 13 diary entries between 23 April and 4 June 1884. The only completely inscrutable code is X, which occurs once on 12 May: "While playing vint I was terribly angry, not on account of the cards, but in general, so-so, at something undefined that could be called Z. Yes, this Z is less tormenting and better founded than X—but even still it is unpleasant" [Dnev 21]. Without further clues, X will remain obscure. On 2 June, he wrote: "There was a little *feeling,* but now I am not afraid of the enemy for I know him; it is still the same thing—my stomach" [Dnev 28]. The English translator of the diaries has speculated that Z was "the secret symbol that, it appears, Tchaikovsky employed to refer to his homosexuality" [253, 27]. That Tchaikovsky should let this diary survive, encoding his homosexuality in pages that openly express his love for Bob Davïdov, is nonsensical; the linkage is untenable if he wrote truthfully on 12 May that Z was something undefined—his homosexuality undefined at the age of 44?—or if Z, as he wrote on 4 June, had a thousand other causes besides playing cards [Dnev 28]. Affirmative evidence suggests another meaning for Z, which explains his twinges of guilt and why Z is burdensome, irritating, melancholic, and associated with cards. He was dissatisfied living at Kamenka, his fondness for Bob was impossible, and corrosive family gossip transpired at cards. To be openly ungrateful toward his family made him feel guilty, and Z was its symbol.

Tchaikovsky left Kamenka on 8 June, writing his last diary entry for 19 months in Kharkov the next day. He proceeded with Modest to Grankino, relieved after the "smelly, noisy, many-peopled Kamenka" [xii 388]. There, he proofread his translation of da Ponte's *The Marriage of Figaro* made in 1875 but published in 1884, revised *The Oprichnik,* which would have to be two-thirds changed in order to qualify as a new work, finished drafting the Concert Fantasia (30 June), and dated the Third Suite on 19 July. Three days later, he was at Anatoly's summer home near Moscow. He continued work on the Concert Fantasia, took up dictation again with Laroche, and felt well enough on 8 August to cancel a trip to Vichy [xii 417]. After this, however, he had nowhere to go. He asked Meck if he could stay at her new estate, and spent from 3 September to 4 October at Pleshcheyevo, where on 24 September he finished and dated the Concert Fantasia.

By 6 October, he was in St. Petersburg for the first imperial performance of *Evgeniy Onegin* on the 19th. It was not an instant success despite Vsevolozhsky's fussing over its dances and costumes, the duel "with the wintry view of mills," and the last scene, where the Neva and the Peter and Paul Fortress were visible from Tatyana's window. The first scene was coldly received, the second succeeded as a result of Emilia Pavlovskaya's impassioned rendition of Tatyana, the ball at Madame Larina's enjoyed a huge success, and the duel was praised [316, 178, 181].

On 25 October came news of Josef Kotek being near death from consumption at Davos. Tchaikovsky rescheduled his January trip to visit him sooner [xii 468–69] and composed two cherubic hymns en route in response to a promise made to the tsar. He explained to Modest on 3/15 November that he had written a high official "whom I am asking to explain to the emperor why I have not yet fulfilled my promise to write something for the church" [xii 476]. Other details are not known. In Berlin on 6 November, he wrote a short piece for string orchestra, to be performed 16 December, celebrating the 50th anniversary jubilee of the actor Ivan Samarin, who had first produced *Evgeniy Onegin* at the Moscow Conservatory. When Tchaikovsky arrived in Davos on 11 November, he found Kotek better than expected. By the 17th, he had composed a third cherubic hymn; Kotek's situation, he concluded, was grave but not hopeless. That day, he received a new request from Vladimir Stasov for the originals of five scores: "your best things ought to be preserved in the original in our national collection, together with the best works of Glinka and Dargomïzhsky," he wrote [401, 137]. Tchaikovsky referred him to Jurgenson. In several days, Stasov contacted him again, reporting a 500-ruble award from an "unknown patron" (Mitrofan Petrovich Belaïeff) to Tchaikovsky for *Romeo and Juliet.*

A few days later in Paris, he looked in on Georges-Léon and began preparations for the child's adoption and return to Russia. Elliptical remarks to Jurgenson suggest that Tchaikovsky wanted to adopt Georges-Léon himself:

> Remind me when we see each other that I have mentioned to you a matter very important to me, in which I cannot get by (however I tried) without someone's advice and moral support. You can render me an immense service. I have wanted to talk to you about it for a long time, and resolved not to: it is unpleasant for the unmasking of a secret that touches on someone close to me. [xii 490]

To Modest he was more forthcoming: "I decided to go to Paris, for . . . I now must look in on Georges, pay the money . . . and generally try to decide something" [xii 493].

He lingered 10 days in St. Petersburg to attend the first performance of Modest's play *Lizaveta Nikolaevna* on 11 December. On the 14th, Rimsky-Korsakov sent a warmly inscribed copy of his harmony textbook. On the

29th, the Slavonic Philanthropic Society requested "some musical piece" to mark the thousandth anniversary of St. Methodius. But the news was not all bright: on 23 December 1884/5 January 1885, Josef Kotek died in Davos.

Among domestic issues in 1884, a permanent home was the most pressing. Lacking one revealed the bankruptcy of Tchaikovsky's nomadic life and made him reevaluate that freedom he so had prized upon leaving the conservatory in 1878. By now, he had taken three years to absorb the tragedies of 1881: Meck's financial catastrophe, the imperial succession, Nikolay Rubinstein's death. From all this, some of it unmentioned (Tanya, the alphabet codes), Modest nevertheless concluded that Pyotr's "rest" from official public responsibilities and the complete, uninhibited reign of the "real" Tchaikovsky "make the period 1878–1884 the brightest and most joyful of his life. Never before or after was he happier, and without suspecting it, never, creating freely and tirelessly, did he more piously perform his duty before humanity" [1997 III 7]. Bizarre.

 CHAPTER SIXTEEN 

The Music of 1882–1884

THE WORKS OF 1882–1884 ECHO THOSE OF 1878–1881: OP. 51, like op. 40, is a set of notated improvisations; the *All-Night Vigil* came in the wake of Nikolay Rubinstein's death, just as the *Liturgy* came after the events of 1877; the Second Suite, op. 53, is an experimental orchestral work like the First; the *Children's Songs* of op. 54 echo the *Children's Album,* op. 39, as the Third Suite, op. 55, with its elegy, waltz, and variations, echoes the *Serenade for Strings;* the Concert Fantasia for Piano and Orchestra, op. 56, returns to the dashing pianism of the Piano Sonata. *Mazepa,* a historical opera, recalls *The Maid of Orleans* in that respect.

On 3 January 1882, Nikolay Bernard requested more pieces for *Nouvelliste* after *The Seasons.* He asked that they be easy and suggested titles: Nocturne, Daydreams, Salon Waltz, and Russian Dance [96, 411]. They became the *Six morceaux pour piano,* op. 51, composed between August and September 1882. Five pieces are dances, the sixth a song. The "Valse de salon" mimics a real dance at home, changing with the age of the couple dancing. The "Polka peu dansante" is less about a polka than about a young woman brooding over romance. The "Menuetto scherzoso," which slides from the first phrase into the second—the only passage in the piece that might occur in a real minuet—is for Anna Merkling, with whom jest was the order of the day. Did it echo her recollections of him playing at home in his youth? The lovely "Nata Waltz," named for Sasha Davïdova's friend Nata Plesskaya, had been composed in 1878 and breathes the air of the composer's Italian trip that year. The "Romance" is closer to its

Chopinesque namesake in Op. 5 than to a song; Tchaikovsky spins out its sentimental opening motif before giving way, after the fermata, to a contrasting section more distinctively pianistic. The "Valse sentimentale" is dedicated to Emma Genton, the governess of Nikolay Kondratiev's children, who had a crush on Tchaikovsky for several years. Quiet and meditative, it could be his apology.

The *All-Night Vigil,* op. 52 [tr. 391, 101–11], comprises unaccompanied, four-part choral settings of monophonic, unmetered melodies from publications sanctioned by the church. Tchaikovsky selected and arranged them, adapted them to musical meter, and set them mostly in chords, occasionally relieved by florid counterpoint and imitation. The work is variable according to liturgical need; performed exactly as printed, it makes no sense. Drafted by 1 September 1881, the *Vigil* was published in March 1883 [CW 63, 14]. It was Tchaikovsky's first project after Nikolay Rubinstein's death. Mention of it came 11 days before his appeal to the emperor for money, suggesting a connection between the project and nationhood.

An integrated polyphonic setting of the *All-Night Vigil* had never been composed before, the reasons for which Tchaikovsky was about to learn. After studying official books, it became clear that the *Vigil,* unlike the *Liturgy,* was extremely flexible in its music and text; one modern scholar computed its variants at about 10,000 [CW 63, 13]. The books were little help [x 120]:

> Imagine, having in hand all this assistance, I cannot come up with either text or melody. I went to Father Alex[ander] for clarifications, but he confessed to me that he knows nothing and conducts the service according to some routine, not dealing with the *tipikon* and regulations. . . . I asked Father Alex[ander] what his junior deacon does, performing the canon with verses, and how he is able to know what and how to read and sing (for the church designates with improbable precision on what days in what voice, how many times, what and how to sing and read). He answered: "I don't know! Before each service he seeks out something for himself!" If those conducting sacred services don't know, then how am I, a sinner, supposed to proceed! [x 148]

In fact, Father Alexander Tarnavich, priest at Kamenka, and Father Dmitry Razumovsky of the Moscow Conservatory supplied Tchaikovsky with the orders of service from which he arranged the *Vigil.* But the task of setting the melodies was no less imposing, as they were modal and resisted elegant harmonization [x 110]. Wondering if the original sound was irretrievable [x 120], Tchaikovsky avoided Italianisms and wrote as he thought appropriate to the Orthodox service, favoring monastic singing as a model over that of churches. He never denied that his approach was personal, "more obeying instinct than reflection and any preconceived theories":

> I have not been shy about forcible placement of the melodies in some particular rhythm, sometimes having deviated, changed and in places quite abandoned [them] and given free rein to my own invention. There is almost no contrapuntal element. *The melody is always in the upper voice.* As for the harmony, it is always severe, that is, without chromaticism, without six-four and seventh chords. The dominant chord appears not otherwise than in passing. [x 186]

The essentials of his style are clear by the end of the first phrase of the first number:

Ex. 42

[Bless, my soul, the Lord]

The sense of acclamation is subdued compared with the *Liturgy,* but not the joyousness conveyed by the limpid melody, which leads the chorus and thereby focuses the ancient chant. Polyphonic elaboration in the *Vigil*—the *jubilus* on "Alleluia" in bars 68–81 of no. 8—is brief and rare, some passages being utterly un-Western. The first line of no. 5, "Gladsome light of the holy glory," uses a point of imitation of four repeated notes, too short and uncontoured for Palestrina; set up as call-and-response, it has yielded to familiar style by the 10th bar. A sense of brightness flows from the text and music in all its aspects.

On 8/20 March 1882, Tchaikovsky drafted a foreword to the publication of the *Vigil,* explaining his view of Russian sacred music and how he set liturgical melodies. The second part (unpublished during the composer's lifetime) defended those who would change Orthodox music:

> It seems that the Russian musician's feeble intention to take pains for his country and all his church cannot be regarded as a crime, and might sooner warrant, if not praise, at least some encouragement. In fact, however, that turns out not to be true. Some people look at this matter differently, who observed in my first work of church music the violation of sacred rights, the impertinent infringement on certain exclusive privileges. A series of actions took place, the sense of which was: the most cruel persecution of my work as something criminal, worthy of destruction, removal from the face of the earth. Fortunately the matter proceeded to judicial scrutiny, which shed the light of truth on the right of Russian musicians to set down churchly song, and of Russian publishers to print these songs. These rights were triumphantly upheld. [CW 63, 273]

Jurgenson suggested that Tchaikovsky's *Festival Coronation March,* composed 5–24 March 1883, be short, patriotic, and intelligible. It comprises a brassy, festive main section and a subdued Trio. Overlooked is its topical and musical relationship with Tchaikovsky's *Festive Overture on the Danish National Anthem* of 1866. That piece celebrated Alexander's marriage by quoting the national anthems of the tsarevich and his bride. Here, in a piece that marks the tsar's ascent to the throne, Tchaikovsky quoted both again. The Russian hymn occurs near the end of the Trio, the Danish hymn in the March (at bars 27–29, then 31–33, in the horns and bassoon). It returns in counterpoint with the Russian hymn at 90–94. In the *Collected Works* [CW 25], which contains the academic edition of the March, the Russian national hymn (at 91–93, trombones and tuba) has been emasculated, its rhythms smoothed over to make it lame and unrecognizable. The proper tune is cited in a footnote:

Ex. 43

Maykov's poem for *Moscow* [tr. 387, 5–8], the text for Tchaikovsky's coronation cantata composed in March–April 1883, like Polonsky's for the Peter the Great Cantata, traces the history of Rus' with epic intonations. The version of *Moscow* in the *Collected Works* presents the most extensive retexting of any composition in that edition, without acknowledging the new words by Mashistov, which replace references to the deity, people who once were enemies, and the autocracy—with drivel. The reference to Russia as the third Rome was allowed to stand, but the prayer in no. 5 and the *slava* (greeting) near the end of no. 6 were replaced by self-conscious alternatives:

No. 5, Maykov	*No. 5, Mashistov*
Is it to me, Lord, according to my strengths That you give the heavy cross? Unworthy am I of Your love! Art Thou truly giving me the powerful strength, Make me wise, with Thy wisdom!	Am I commanded to raise the banner of battle, To engage in mortal struggle? Who will help me on my path? Art thou to me alone, bright truth Giving me the powers, strengthening me, in this threatening hour!
I as a faithful slave give myself to Thee I am ready for the fire and for every grief, For dear to me is not earthly honor, But the crown of Christ!	If I am fated to perish in battle, I am ready to meet death face-to-face, For dear to me is not life, not human honor, Dearer to me than them is the work of truth!

No. 6, near the end, Maykov

Praise God in the heavens, glory!
To our Lord on this earth glory!
To the Empress, his spouse, glory!
To the Lord Successor, glory!
To His entire imperial household,
glory!
And to all His people, glory!
To His true servants, glory,
To his distinguished guests, glory,
That there be truth in Rus
More beautiful than the spring sun,
glory!

No. 6, near the end, Mashistov

Praise the sun in the heavens, glory!
To all our mighty land, our homeland,
glory!
To the wise helmsmen of our power,
glory!
To our valiant warriors, glory!
To all who labor for our good, glory!
Forever to our people, glory!
To the brethren of all peoples, glory,
To all our desired guests, glory
That there be truth in Rus
More beautiful than the bright sun,
glory!

Tchaikovsky did not emulate Maykov's vivid images; rather, he expressed heroic events with religious accents and hints of Russian style. In no. 1, *Andante religioso,* depicting the plight of ancient Rus, there is a distinctive echo of folk song in the 13-syllable phrase on which the vocal part is built, its gentle but persistent recurrence, and within it the first five syllables on a rising scale with an accent on the fifth. These devices continue in no. 2, the rise of Muscovy, where Tchaikovsky responds to epic references again with a repeated line, here of 15 syllables. The text begins with a folkish negation:

That was not a little star which twinkled in the impenetrable darkness;
That bright wax candle caught fire in stone-built Moscow.

The victory of the prince of Moscow, portrayed in no. 3, shifts to military clichés—everything is duple, march-like, fanfares, and bells. The movement is brief, the chorus rhetorical and unmodulated except for the key inflection (at 80) to convey the dispersal of storm clouds. The text at the reprise (52) alludes to the actual circumstances of performance:

And in the bepatterned palace
Sits, brightest and most joyous of all
The Prince of Moscow on his throne,
Autocrat of all Rus'.

A learned introduction prepares the baritone's lengthy narrative in no. 4, which begins with the prince of Moscow rallying the world's Slavs and then elaborates his religious aspect, unto Slavs as the star of Bethlehem, chosen by God, defender of orphans, and deliverer of the imprisoned. Tympani play a tattoo through the account of Slavdom's woes, shifting to harp and tremolo strings to describe the prince's aspect. Sacred and secular merge in the closing: chorus joins soloist as the victorious sounds of no. 3 return to express Muscovy as the third Rome. No. 5 of *Moscow* is modeled on the romance though the text is a prayer in which the emperor accepts the burden and asks for wisdom and strength; the melody and key, E-flat minor, anticipate Paulina's song in *The Queen of Spades.*

In the first of three sections of the finale, the baritone solo, to forging motifs, describes the arming of Rus'. As the text addresses the present emperor (at 24), the orchestra calms and then is silent for the recitative, "Today anointed to reign for us, / Adorned with virtues, / Given to us by God's mercy!" The chorus proclaims the tsar's greatness in the final *slava,* a melodic call-and-response for each individual who is praised. It is at once churchly and folkish:

Ex. 44

Allegro con spirito ♩ = 144
Mezzo-soprano soloist
Baritone soloist
Chorus
Сла - ва солн - цу на не-бе сла - ва! Всей зем-
[Glory to the sun in the heavens, glory! in all the
Glo - ry, glo-ry, glo - ry!
Allegro con spirito ♩ = 144

ле мо-гу-чей, на-шей Ро-ди-не, сла-ва!
Муд-ым корм-чим дер-
earth mighty, to our Homeland, glory!
To the wise helmsmen]
ff
ff
ff
ff
Glo-ry, glo-ry, glo - ry!
f

The concluding apostrophe to bread (as a symbol of hospitality) is a free fantasia on the melody bearing this text, presented in nonsystematic imitation.

Moscow was performed at a ceremonial meal in the Kremlin Palace of Facets, which symbolized how the emperor and empress, dressed in the same robes and seated on the same thrones as earlier at the Uspensky Cathedral, represented the unity and indivisibility of emperor and state [128]. After a performance in St. Petersburg on 8 January 1884, *Moscow* was next heard at concerts memorializing Tchaikovsky on 17 and 22 February 1894.

Mazepa was composed from May 1881 to April 1883. Here is a synopsis:

Act I. Maria's girlfriends want her to join them in divination with wreaths (referenced in the finale of the Fourth Symphony), but she declines, as the Cossack hetman Mazepa is a guest in the house. Alone, she is expressing her love for Mazepa when Andrey, a young Cossack, confesses his love for her. During celebrations, Mazepa discloses his love for Maria to her father, Kochubey, who is scandalized, as the elderly Mazepa is Maria's godfather. Mazepa presses, Kochubey banishes him, and Maria, faced with a dilemma, leaves with Mazepa. In scene 2, Kochubey's wife, Lyubov, laments the loss of Maria, Kochubey denounces Mazepa to Peter the Great, and Andrey volunteers to deliver the denunciation.

Act II. Peter has rejected Kochubey's denunciation and turned him over to Mazepa, who will execute him and his friend Iskra the next day. In prison, Kochubey ponders his end, yet refuses to give up his wealth to Orlik, Mazepa's henchman. In scene 2, Mazepa, troubled, apostrophizes the night. In an interpolated aria, he declares his love for Maria just as she arrives and protests when she doubts his love. He counters her doubts with his dream of being the leader of an independent Ukraine. Enraptured, Maria pledges sacrifice and reaffirms her love. Alone, Maria gazes out at the night and senses misfortune. Lyubov enters, begging her to intercede with Mazepa to save Kochubey. When apprised of the situation, Maria faints. Revived, she and Lyubov rush off to the execution. Scene 3 is the execution. Crowds are waiting; a drunken Cossack, much reviled, sings and dances. Mazepa and Orlik pass by. Kochubey and Iskra are led in and pray, joined by the people. The axes fall as Maria and Lyubov arrive.

Act III. An orchestral entr'acte depicts the Battle of Poltava. When the curtain rises, we see the ruins of Kochubey's house. Andrey enters, recalls better times, and wishes death upon Mazepa, who presently arrives, fleeing the Russians. Andrey challenges Mazepa, who urges restraint but shoots Andrey when provoked. Maria enters, witless after her father's execution. She refuses to go with Mazepa, and he leaves. She takes the dying Andrey for a child and sings a lullaby. He dies. People rush in. Maria recalls singing of the divination with wreaths and drowns herself in the river. The people retrieve her body, place it next to Andrey's, and grieve.

Into librettist Victor Burenin's text Tchaikovsky incorporated passages from Pushkin, verbatim or nearly so: in the dungeon; Mazepa's scenes with Maria in acts II and III; and the scene with Maria and Lyubov in act II. This enrichment increased likenesses to *Onegin:* the heroine is in love with an older man; a more appropriate lover dies by the older man's hand; the tragedy is set in motion by quarreling at a party. Even still, the characters are ambiguous. Is Kochubey righteous or just insulted? Maria acknowledges the peril of loving Mazepa but lacking any Tatyana-like insight. Affirming her love after he proposes to become king of the Ukraine, is she ambitious or naïve? Pushkin had stressed Mazepa's villainy; Tchaikovsky underplays it. He is loving enough to win the girl and treacherous enough to wreak havoc.

Twice before rehearsals, Tchaikovsky wrote a new aria for the Moscow Mazepa, Bogomir Korsov, "something lyrical, loving, where Mazepa's feeling of love for Maria would pour forth" [316, 171]. Korsov was unhappy with the first substitution, now lost, whereupon Tchaikovsky wrote "O Maria," no. 10a in modern prints. In March 1884, he made three more changes, which went into production in Petersburg and stayed with the work: a shorter ending for act I, scene 1; a large cut in act II, scene 2, mostly affecting Mazepa in his duet with Maria; and the creation of the standard ending by extending Maria's lullaby and cutting the final scene by the lake shore [xii 340].

In *Mazepa* Tchaikovsky's scoring is exemplary, especially the continuously fresh writing for winds. Local color in the opening folk scene, the gopak, and the execution is appropriately evocative. His use of reminiscence themes, including that of Mazepa (the opening bars of the opera) and the fateful fanfares (first in no. 11) reminding us of Kochubey's execution, are effective and restrained. Much of his dramatic recitative and arioso project character well, especially Kochubey in the dungeon, with its hints of Beethoven's Florestan, and providing Maria with Onegin-like repetitions of emotionally nondescript melody (at 20 of no. 2). The central difficulty with *Mazepa,* a relapse after *Onegin,* is Tchaikovsky's inability to catch the right music for the right moment. Part of the problem rested with the libretto in the central characters, in whom love and political ambition were not effectively distinguished, and with the avoidance of a direct personal clash which would sharpen motivation: Mazepa reveals his love for Maria to Kochubey offstage and, instead of going himself to confront Kochubey in prison, he sends Orlik, who fatally trivializes Kochubey's righteous tirade with vulgar demands for money.

Tchaikovsky wrote musical extensions that diminished the powerful situations implicit in the drama. Andrey threatens to kill Mazepa, and then they duet for 38 bars before the shot is fired. He announces to Maria that he is dying, and they duet for 67 bars before he breathes his last. On the other hand, Kochubey's shock at Mazepa's love for Maria; Mazepa's leisurely recitative at the beginning of no. 11, which lacks any sign of passion after his interpolated love aria; and his almost nonchalant decision to abandon Maria at Orlik's merest reminder (no. 18, 129–47)—ostensibly fleeing pursuit when none is in evidence—are all embarrassing understatements, though they are potentially effective moments had they been given music of appropriate intensity.

The perception of flaws, however, should not preclude the acknowledgment of daring. To have the ruthless Mazepa ride off into the night so unmotivated reduces him in comparison with Tchaikovsky's other operatic heroes. Letting him do this permits the extraordinary closing of the opera, in which the dying Andrey seeks one last communication with the deranged Maria, an unprecedented scene of powerful effect, echoed in Stravinsky's Anne Truelove and Tom Rakewell in Bedlam.

Mazepa played in the imperial repertoire every year from 1884 to 1891, was taken up by private theaters in the 1890s, and revived every few years after that until World War I. In 1900 Kashkin warmly recalled the first performance but still remarked on the "heavy impression from the dark subject, which had an oppressive effect despite the excellent music" [MV000208].

Practical factors have marred the reception of the Second Suite, op. 53 (composed between June and 13 October 1883), the least beloved of Tchaikovsky's orchestral works: technical difficulty, much obbligato writing, rhythmic intricacy, and extravagant scoring, including the need for four 10-valve accordions that play but 36 of 1,607 bars. Apart from a broad distinction between singing themes and colorful, pantomimic musical ideas, folkish intonations help to overcome an impression of heterogeneity rooted in passing allusions to Tchaikovsky's earlier works (mvt. I at bar 10–13 to Symphony no. 1/I, bars 180–89; 174–90 to *Onegin,* no. 2 at 51–52; mvt. II at 138–45 to Symphony no. 3/V, 118–28). While the emphasis on sonority and contrast links the Second Suite with the First, the highly colored themes at times are overextended, even in their final form which was, in the case of movements III–V, much shorter than originally written. Tchaikovsky reduced the *Scherzo burlesque* to 333 bars from 590 in the autograph and the remaining two movements by 32 and 90 bars [CW 19-b, 3, 213–91].

In movement I, transient emphasis on the tonic triad in the opening phrases moves to a dialogue between strings and winds, no sooner established than a new key and theme introduce a striking contrast (the dotted melody at 24), no less puzzling (at 48) with the realization that all this was just an introduction. From here, Tchaikovsky continues to avoid familiar structural references. He continues to downplay the tonic at the beginning of the Allegro with a theme that disorients the meter, and delays a sense of key until the pedal point at 122. He breaks this off (at 146) and moves directly to a new theme in B minor, suggestive of some balletic coquette coming onstage. After this comes a fugue on the Allegro theme, which works its way to a reprise (310). To close, he revisits the introduction. Such is the "play of sounds."

The *valse* offers pleasant if discursive relief, doting on the main theme and providing two episodes in the Trio. In the *Scherzo burlesque,* the insubstantial theme does not promote a sense of pattern but rather a kaleidoscope of volatile ideas passing rapidly through cadences before coming together at huge climaxes. The Scherzo unfolds in two spans (1–88, 89–205) which drive to an emphatic cadence with the accordions. The Trio, announced by a folkish melody in the horns, is soon accosted by the Scherzo theme (at 280), abbreviated, which again drives to a cadence with accordions.

The winning *Rêves d'enfant,* like the *valse,* is a lyric outpouring after a boisterous, unusual movement. It begins with a dialogue between choirs of the orchestra; its key—A minor (colored by the opposite mode)—was the first key change in movement I. The formal pattern, obscured by the slow tempo and the complexity of ideas, consists of three melodic groups (bars 1, 28, 74), each with an introduction, the reprise of the first interrupted by the third. They make a convincing metaphor of dreaming, of falling ever deeper into slumber before reapproaching consciousness. Tchaikovsky underscores this effect with increasingly elaborate presentations of his themes proceeding to an ever more distant key, E-flat minor in group 3, where the music takes on the ethereal, free-associative aspect of real dreaming, muted and anxious. He thus continues a tendency to imbue his music addressed to children with somber expression. At 74–101, he anticipates the so-called Dream Entr'acte of *The Sleeping Beauty.*

Invoking Dargomïzhsky justifies *grotesquerie,* but nothing in the finale approaches the eccentricities of the preceding movements. Tchaikovsky's charming counterfeit emulates the Scherzo in texture, the popular treatment of the tune, and the buildup of sound. The key is clear, the train of thought is easily followed, all in a breathless rush of sound.

On 15 February 1881, Alexander Pleshcheyev, whom Tchaikovsky had known since his early days in Moscow, inscribed a volume of his poetry called *Snowdrop* "To Pyotr Ilyich Tchaikovsky as a sign of esteem and gratitude for his beautiful music to my poor words" [D&Y 251]. The composer made notes in the margins of most of these poems, and by May was pondering a substantial project, asking Jurgenson for collections of children's songs [287, 18]. He completed one song in 1881, later included as no. 16 in op. 54. After finishing the Second Suite in October 1883, he returned to the project, abbreviating and reshaping all but four of the poems into the *Sixteen Songs for Children,* op. 54. They raise a question of genre. They are not written for children to perform, nor are they, like Musorgsky's *Nursery,* theatrical portrayals of a child. The poetry raises adult issues, Tchaikovsky's musical alchemy tempering the adult implications of the poems into something proper to a child's world view.

In no. 1, the grandmother, knitting socks, keeps an eye on her pensive grandson. She thinks he wants a toy; he really wants to go to school. The sad expression of the beginning gives way to declamation in the grandmother's urgings, pressed energetically in the piano's repeated notes and accented fragments of melody. The sad introduction returns to answer the child's wish.

As it flies, a little bird in no. 2 reports to God the human suffering it sees, which nudges its song out of tune. It asks God to support the poor, that they meet their end without complaint. Tchaikovsky's conversational arioso is perfect for storytelling, gently inflected from the major tonic to express human suffering.

Springtime in no. 3 brings the return of the lark with a song from afar. As the poem enthuses over spring, Tchaikovsky centers the voice around an energetic, recurring 8-bar phrase which begins with a drone-like effect and accounts for much of the song. The result resembles something that might be sung by schoolchildren.

An overgrown village garden in no. 4 is better than a well-ordered but cheerless urban one. The singer would tarry in it, listening to the bees. Tchaikovsky strikes a march-like stance and indulges in wordplay. The parallel introduction and close sound the bees' hum in the left hand; the sturdy 4/4 in the voice becomes the sunflower standing sentry.

In no. 5, the Christ child had a garden of roses, which the children picked, leaving him only thorns to make a wreath. Distress is but suggested in the insistent, accented phrases of the introduction and postlude. Winning is the stately, hymn-like tune, austerely accompanied at the outset and simply elaborated, like an organist accompanying a congregation. At the high point, Christ is asked how he will weave a wreath without the roses. Tchaikovsky orchestrated this song in 1884 [CW 27, 501–5] and arranged it for chorus in 1889 [CW 63, 267–69].

A fisherman's family in no. 6 is alarmed when he does not come home on time, and rejoices when he arrives. Tchaikovsky sets this long text in four strophes with simple accompaniment and folkish, even sing-song turns of melody, producing the effect of a unison song for children. The joyful expression of the postlude contrasts with the sad beginning.

Most of "Winter Evening" (no. 7) is about children in domestic happiness, while the last verse is about orphans who are not so lucky. Using strophic form and minor key, Tchaikovsky darkens the verses describing happiness. Then follows an intrusive, syncopated piano interlude, admonishing the embrace of the unfortunate. Taneyev complained that the mood of the second part of the song too much colored the whole [294, 106–7]. Tchaikovsky concurred [xii 397].

In no. 8, the cuckoo asks the starling about the other birds, and the starling tells of the nightingale, lark, and thrush. When the cuckoo asks about himself, the starling has no answer, whereupon the cuckoo vows to repeat the word "cuckoo" forever as his vengeance upon man. Of this, Tchaikovsky makes a substantial song filled with proto-Mahleresque onomatopoeia, running to a hyperbole of "cuckoos" at the approach to the final cadence.

The coming of spring delights children most of all. The poem of no. 9 unfolds in two parallel spans with different endings, the first essaying the descriptive potential of "storms," hearts "beating," and "troubles," the second building on the emotional warmth of the "laugh of playful children" and the "singing of the carefree birds," who most love nature's renewal.

A mother in no. 10 commands the storm to subside, that her child not be disturbed, then bids the child sleep, promising that when the child awakens in the morning, there will be sunlight and love. The lullaby is cast above the range of the right hand of the piano, suggesting the wind, and ominous if nondescript growls of the left. This implies the mother's strength and steadfastness, which falter when her grammatically complete text is left wanting a cadence in the music.

Merry flowers in the field espy a pale, solitary flower behind a trellis in no. 11. They urge it to join them but it will not; it blooms for one inside who suffers, to remind him of the green hills. The music is controlled by the six-verse text, which Tchaikovsky deployed in 6/8 time to accommodate the words and sustain a sense of movement. The breezy opening melody suggests that flowers communicate with one another through the wind. In verse 4, recitative-like, the solitary flower refuses to heed the others' call.

In no. 12, Granddad wakes the children to announce the arrival of winter; they are first incredulous, then overjoyed. Tchaikovsky makes a genre scene of it, with repeated, strongly gestural phrases which are annunciatory, chattering, or joyous as befits the moment, and which are molded to imply the wintry activities of sledding, ice skating, and decorating the Christmas tree.

No. 13 is a sentimental address to spring, the dew, the aroma of the flowers—everything which delights the eye and affirms the presence of God. A waltz, Tchaikovsky subsumed its diverse images within a single mood, *dolce, molto expressivo,* and cast the entire poem in the manner of a modern popular song—two choruses, disparate verse, and chorus.

In no. 14, an address to the dreariness of autumn, three verses are set to the same melody, slow-moving harmony, and syncopated effects in the piano. The nicely contoured voice part sustains the repetitions, which parse the dreariness: lethargic, cloudy, joyless, pale, desolate.

A swallow hovers over a young girl in no. 15, and she asks it why. It brings greetings from her brother, languishing in prison. Does she remember and shed tears? Music preempts a topic seemingly inappropriate for children in a network of repeated phrases which neutralize the implication and emulate a child's song. The principal theme is agreeable, devoid of wordplay, and nuanced to the text, especially at the end in the parallel minor. The repetition of small units and lack of musical artifice impart a folkish sense.

In the last song, a little girl is so small that she can use bibs made from gnats' wings, a chair from a walnut, slippers from a crabshell, an umbrella from a lilac leaf—and more. Set to highlight the words, the music is deployed in small units which preclude distinguishing the contrasting images.

Several devices suggest that op. 54 is a cycle. The division into two groups of eight, marked by the jesting songs 8 and 16, is bolstered by the likeness of the poetic motif linking the seven other songs of each half (1 with 10, 2 with 15, etc.). Each division has a prevailing key (G and its satellites in songs 2–8, F major/minor in songs 9–13), the entire collection tonally rounded by songs in A minor. The anomaly within this scheme is song 14 in F-sharp minor, the unchild-like "spiritual center" of the collection, which combines the most somber images of nature with the unhappiest situation of humankind [155, 150–52]. The dark coloration may convey the composer's guarded view of domesticity at the time—Kamenka in the autumn of 1883—after seeing Tatyana Davïdova through childbirth and rehabilitation.

In footnotes to the score of the Third Suite, op. 55 (April–May 1884), the *Collected Works* [CW 20] reports discrepancies in performance indications between the autograph and early prints—mostly in metronome markings, which the composer insisted be observed exactly. The most striking differences come in the finale, where the printed version is slower than that indicated in the autograph. Tchaikovsky also made changes in the second movement: 16 bars after 214 (as counted in CW 20) were omitted in early editions, and a cut is observed—the reprise of bars 2–137 as they originally recurred later in the movement (the CW editors note that a comparable cut in printed editions was smaller, corresponding to bars 93–137). Tchaikovsky did not explain these changes.

The Scherzo, composed first, resembles that of the Second Suite in its sonorous theme. The tempo, at *presto,* does little to mitigate the difficulty of distinguishing 6/8 from 2/4, any more than does the assignment of music to constantly shifting instruments. An important motif for the entire work comes in the opening bar in G major with stress on the submediant:

Ex. 45

Tchaikovsky plays with this emphasis throughout, sometimes enriching the tonic triad with the addition of the sixth, creating a chord with the pitches of both triads simultaneously, and so creates a merging of G major and E minor throughout the Scherzo. No less important is the unobtrusive accompaniment on offbeats (at 34), revisited in the middle section of the waltz. The Trio is a march, punctuated by snare drum and triangle, which continues the melodically insubstantial Scherzo proper. The juxtaposition of Scherzo and march echoes the Third Symphony and anticipates the Sixth.

Tchaikovsky referred to the *Valse mélancolique,* composed next, as the "obligatory waltz number" [xii 365]. Typical it is not. The key, E minor, anticipates the Scherzo. The somber expression of the principal melody was exceptional, and the second subject (at 51) drew close to the Scherzo with syncopation, the tension between notated triple and effective duple time, and the loss of discrete melody. The unusual periodicity in long, uneven spans is acharacteristic, as is the formal pattern, a tripartite reprise that also mimics the Scherzo. Lilting movement is put aside in the Trio when Tchaikovsky attaches the melody, with absolute persistence and eccentric dynamics, to the unusual sonority of alternating octaves:

Ex. 46

C. ingl.
Fag.
V-le.
V-c.
C-b.
mp
sf
mf

Oboe
C. ingl.
Fag.
V-le.
V-c.
C-b.
I
crescendo
mp
sf
mf

The unwaltz-like result, sustained for 100 bars, is enigmatic. Abbreviating the reprise makes the Trio even more striking.

Tchaikovsky conceived the Third Suite in five movements but soon discarded the first, leaving the *Elégie* to begin. The premises of the Scherzo affect it as well, elaborating the G-major triad with the added sixth—in melody, at cadences, and in adornments like the harp coloration of bars 15–19. But the nearly continuous lyric melody produces an entirely different effect. A pivot from B to B-flat (at 70) produces tension in the misalignment of theme and key. The first theme group returns in the key of the second (143), then to a bridge (154), timorous in expression and faltering in melodic strength, as Tchaikovsky returns to the home key (179–89), reprising the second theme group in the key of the first. Only then does he align the first theme and key before the lengthy epilogue (225–98).

The celebrated Theme and Variations was composed last, starting with the polonaise. Having an eye on the ending may have clarified the strategy leading up to it: an attractive if benign theme followed strictly for a time, then ever-freer characteristic elaborations, then recalling the *thema* near the end before a grand finale. Tchaikovsky links the *thema* with the other movements: its opening chord is presented as a triad with added sixth, and, like the *Elégie,* the movement is resolutely melodic; he changes orchestral color without shifting focus from line to sonority. Variation 4 liberates the *thema* to new musical realms, here in midvariation with a brassy statement of the *Dies irae.* The mold broken, he keeps only the head-motif of the *thema* in the next several variations: faux Bach-like points of imitation, a gigue-hornpipe, slow meditations (variations 7 and 8, the second a lament joining English horn, tremolo strings, and folk-like turns of phrase), and a 4-bar vamp, producing a folkish aura with changing background. If these devices point to Russia after the nonnational music earlier, the vamping makes bizarre entrance music to a specific image in variation 10, elided with its predecessor and beginning with a cadenza for solo violin. It is a ballerina's music in the sparse texture, nuances of tempo, and unobtrusive arabesques in the winds, which appear briefly before the ornamented reprise. Tchaikovsky has introduced an imperial, even Petersburgian image into his finale. After variation 11, a meditation which revisits the *thema,* he affirms the Petersburg imagery in variation 12 with a massive polonaise. In its spacious dimensions and long approach to the main theme, it presses the boundary between theatrical conceit and the direct musical representation of imperial grandeur.

Prelest' in the Third Suite is too prominent for a symphony, while at the same time the suite's coherence advances well beyond the casual miscellany of the Second. "I wanted to make a symphony," Tchaikovsky quipped, "but it didn't come out" [xii 397]. The continuity here casts doubt on the freedom he so cherished when writing the First Suite six years earlier, freedom that, in his life and recently in his music, had proved wanting. The Third Suite also reflects Tchaikovsky's dark outlook in mid-1884: *Elégie, Valse mélancolique,* the quotation from the Mass for the dead, and the persistence of E minor, the key of *fatum*. The juxtaposition of worldly and eternal is hinted in the contrast between the *Elégie* and the polonaise and its stylistic subsidiary throughout the Suite, the contrast between coherent melody and music based purely on sound.

On 13 April 1884, Tchaikovsky "[s]tumbled on the idea of a piano concerto, but it was wretched and not new" [Dnev 12]. A month later, he was rewriting the discarded first movement of the Third Suite, called "Contrasts," which would become the second movement of the Concert Fantasia for Piano and Orchestra, op. 56. By 30 June, he knew the work for what it was to be [xii 397]. He dated the manuscript on 24 September.

The Fantasia draws on folkish/popular themes (except for the operatic first-movement cadenza, melodically related to "O Paradies!" from Meyerbeer's *L'Africaine*). Untroubled by subtleties of structure (the misleading first-movement title, "Quasi Rondo," covering for a sonata-allegro with a cadenza replacing a development), it is not fantasia-like, the outer sections of the pattern being symmetrical and bereft of the least surprise. Movement II is based on themes that Tchaikovsky noted in his diary on 11 May 1884, the first impassioned and sorrowful, the second upbeat and boisterous (first at bar 57). He presents each in turn, twice, and adds a coda. One critic wrote, "[T]he absorbing quality of its second movement redeems the common passages of the first" [108, 458]. But the redemption is heavy with virtuosity, and recalls the Piano Sonata in G. To Meck on 14 July 1884, Tchaikovsky may have been saying something about the music when he pointed out that Taneyev (who played the initial performances) lacked that particular virtuoso artistry which magically transports the public [xii 402].

Was the composer again writing, to paraphrase Laroche, with less concern about what was played than how?

Both the Jurgenson score and the *Collected Works* [CW 29] provide confusing instructions about how to play the first movement separately (in Jurgenson, follow the § from the end of p. 51 to the first page of the appendix; in CW 29, proceed from the end of p. 53 to the beginning of p. 55). The piece is dedicated to different pianists: the Jurgenson two-piano arrangement (plate 6539, December 1884) to Annette Essipoff, and the orchestral score (plate 6537, March 1893) to Sophie Menter. The announcement of a performance in November 1892 indicated, without elaboration, that Tchaikovsky had made changes [MV921105].

With one exception, the pieces in *Six Romances,* op. 57, finished by December 1884, are dedicated to opera singers, and the music shows this: no. 1 to Fyodor Komissarzhevsky, the first Vakula; and others to those who created *Mazepa* in Moscow: Bogomir Korsov (Mazepa), Emilia Pavlovskaya (Maria), Dmitry Usatov (Andrey), and Alexandra Krutikova (Lyubov). The exception is Vera Butakova, born Vera Davïdova, who was the object of Pyotr's dubious courtship at Hapsal in 1867.

The answer to the poem's questions in no. 1—what does the nightingale sing? what makes the maiden tremble in her dreams? what brings happiness in the midst of torment?—is the same, love; the point of the song is to present various interpretations of this word. Tchaikovsky wrote impassioned ariosos which end in repetitions of the word with appropriate inflection—declamatory, high note beneath a fermata, hushed and in a distant key, and again declamatory.

As silence settles on the golden cornfields in no. 2, the wail of the singer's soul erupts. A bitter parting from the beloved is conveyed by the stark texture of the voice and dissonant, strummed accompaniment. Repeated accented notes convey the singer's agony, the interjection of D-flat major into D minor the soul's parting with the beloved. Especially effective is the reprise of an interior line at the close: "My soul is full of parting with you." The first time, these words lead to self-reproach; the second time, reproach is stifled as the music simply dies away.

Mignon's "Heiß mich nicht reden" from Goethe's *Wilhelm Meister* is transformed in Alexander Strugovshchikov's translation, as illustrated by the middle verse:

Goethe	*Strugovshchikov*
At the right time the sun's course drives out	There eternal ice covers the mountaintop,
The dark night, and it must brighten,	Here o'er the fields the nighttime shadow lies,
The hard rock opens its bosom,	With spring the source will rush along anew,
Begrudges not the earth its deeply hidden sources.	With the dawn God's day will be seen again,
	And to all consolation given in the hour of sorrow.

Mignon's enigmatic utterance is lost in translation. A vow has sealed her lips. Her appeal not to speak is recitative-like, *con disperazione, ma quieto;* the shift to aria (at 10) speaks to the tension between her urge to speak and her vow of silence, recalling Tatyana's Letter Scene, a gesture to the dedicatee, Pavlovskaya, who would be the first Tatyana at the Maryinsky within a month of the composition of this song:

Ex. 47

(*continued*)

Ex. 47 *(continued)*

[There eternal ice covers the mountaintop, . . .]

This arching lyricism continues to the end, transforming the reprise of the opening (at 20), and is relieved only by the suddenly hushed closing line, "And only God can release my vow."

In no. 4, Merezhkovsky's "Sleep!" the singer would yield forever to the poem's sweet invitation: the cradle of grasses, the lark's song, the buzzing of the bees, and the rustling of the fields. Much of the text unfolds in rapid, conversational melody, which is found in the other songs as a foil to aria-like passages, but here is without the aria. Wordplay complements the informal setting: rapid figuration in reference to the singing lark is reprised in reference to buzzing flies and rustling fields. The melodic sigh in the singer's line intimates drowsiness, the absence of motion at the final downbeat drifting off into slumber.

Merezhkovsky's "Death" in no. 5 marks its approach in the falling rose petals, the dimming stars, and rays of sunrise—but describes its effect as free of struggle, captivating, promising rest, "nature's best gift" to be greeted smiling, without resistance. The gait is waltz-like, the line utterly coherent in the accepting of death. The Tristanesque figure in the left hand at the beginning and close may be intended, though the chromatic producing this allusion is omitted at the end of the phrase—free of yearning.

No. 6, "Only you alone," from the German of Ada Christen (Christine Friderik), apostrophizes the kindness of someone who believed, supported, reached out, and cared—but never loved the singer. The dark mood, conveyed by strumming, speaks to unrequited love, which overwhelms gratitude. The voice, in litany-like repetitions linked to the phrase "You alone," proceeds to a burst of anguish on the final words, "And you never loved me," with stentorian dynamics, shifting tempos, and a theatrical contrast as the singer repeats the line, full voice, in the low register.

The songs of op. 57 are musically unified. The strumming accompaniment that opens the first and closes the last produces a bard-like effect; the operatic repetition of a critical word or phrase connects the apostrophes of nos. 1 and 6; D minor across the songs is associated with anguish. The close of all the songs, often in the accompaniment, resonates or summarizes the sense of the text. The poems reflect Tchaikovsky's thoughts in 1884: the virtues of love and compassion, a reconciliation with death, and the agonized expression of earthly torments. Earthly trials can be acute, as Mignon tells us, and compassion proffered without love.

Two short pieces are adjuncts to Tchaikovsky's complex compositions of 1884. The *Impromptu-caprice,* written in September, is his contribution to an *Album du Gaulois* in Paris to raise funds for impoverished musicians. It expresses the qualities referenced in its title: the framing sections of impromptu are brief improvisations on a salon-like melody given in the first four bars; Tchaikovsky's characteristic broken style fills in the texture. In between, the caprice riffs on a Slavic motif, two bars quickly expanded in range and texture and quickened in tempo. The *Elegy in Honor of I. V. Samarin* was composed in November to celebrate Samarin's 50th year of artistic activity; the work was renamed *Elegy* at the time of its publication in 1890, five years after Samarin's death. The music is a tripartite reprise form with an epilogue; the principal theme is elegiac in being sweetly melodious but almost continuously (if mildly) dissonant. The beginning of the epilogue (at 89) recalls in its part writing the *Elégie* from the Third Suite (at 39) and the opening bars of the Second. A bow to the dedicatee may be intended in the long upbeats to sections, as if to mark some character's entrance, and the frankly melodramatic middle section (at 40), which mimics an actor's gestures. Tchaikovsky reused this piece in his incidental music to *Hamlet* as an entr'acte before act IV.

CHAPTER SEVENTEEN

1885–1888

TWO MONTHS INTO 1885, TCHAIKOVSKY WAS LEADING A NEW LIFE. The most potent change was putting down roots. This was important for the benefits of domesticity and relief from wandering, but even more for clarifying who he was, bringing him to assume some responsibility for Russian music after his nomadic life. It marked the onset of his civic duty, supporting enterprises still threatened by Nikolay Rubinstein's death. As the leading Russian composer of his time, he decided now to promote his music by conducting [214, 65], while Jurgenson formalized licensing agreements for Tchaikovsky's works in Paris and Hamburg, after sporadic arrangements with foreign publishers since the late 1870s [224, 47–52]. He also took advantage of imperial favor, requesting that the emperor build a new opera house in Tiflis (which happened) and engaging Grand Duke Konstantin Konstantinovich in correspondence. No less important was the mentorship of Ivan Alexandrovich Vsevolozhsky, the Director of the Imperial Theaters, who had shown interest in his work since coming to the post in 1881 and whose advocacy would rival that of Nikolay Rubinstein.

His life became dense with letters. Complaints of exhaustion cannot be feigned, nor was their negative effect on his creativity, which he claimed, some sport of artistic temperament. The Meck correspondence continued to diminish despite reassurances of affection. His personal affairs showed the same *clair-obscur* as before, the problem being, as ever, to avoid overreaching the *clair* to arrive at glib conclusions about the *obscur*. The sustained relationship still eluded him; his affection for Bob Davïdov met with an increasingly cool response. Illness returned in 1886 with special virulence, which he attributed to everything from excessive drinking to a tapeworm to living near swamps. These complaints frightened him; they seemed to herald his death. His inability to manage money continued; his resolve to settle down prompted Jurgenson and Meck to lavish assistance. They preferred to pay a great deal for a permanent home than even more for temporary ones. Among family matters, murkiest was the arrangement whereby Georges-Léon was adopted by Nikolay Tchaikovsky and his wife. After a silence, Antonina stepped back into the picture, wretched and irrational, arousing his temper and compassion. Anatoly's posting as procurator in Tiflis literally expanded Pyotr's horizons, bringing him south to a warm reception as an artist and acquainting him along the way, and thence to Marseilles, with Constantinople and other marvelous sights.

Mortality and remembrance dominated his thinking. There was much to do and think about "while death is already beginning to lie in wait around the corner." He recalled the deaths of others and chided himself for keeping diaries. In letters he revealed the existence of diaries for 1882 and 1883 (no longer extant) and found the experience unrewarding. "Disgusting," he grumped on 19 September 1886. Why should he persist, if death is really nigh? He recorded extended meditations on music and philosophy in a journal of these years known as Diary no. 8.

These preoccupations were reflected in his music. Mortality is the subtext of *Manfred, Hamlet,* and the Fifth Symphony. Remembrance lies behind *Cherevichki* and the songs for Désirée Artôt. The attentions of the imperial family gave rise to the *Romances,* opp. 60 and 63, and his sacred music. Thrice within this time, *Swan Lake,* last seen in Moscow in January 1883, rose again in revivals proposed or realized.

1885

The first of January was a busy day. Tchaikovsky placed a notice in the *Police News* of Moscow: "Single person seeking a dacha-estate for rent." He was also proofreading the Third Suite, to be conducted in 11 days in St. Petersburg by Hans von Bülow and later in the year by Karl Klindworth in Berlin [213, 19]. A sadder duty was to contemplate Josef Kotek's death, which made him feel "solitary under the pressure of this sorrowful event" [xiii 16]. Bogomir Korsov, who sang Mazepa in Moscow, was now to sing it in St. Petersburg and wanted changes in his part. Emilia Pavlovskaya was pressing him to be there on the 8th, when *Onegin* was to be performed before the tsar. Judging from their correspondence, Tchaikovsky held Pavlovskaya in high regard. She sang the first performances of Maria in *Mazepa* and Kuma in *The Enchantress,* was a prominent Tatyana and Oxana, and shared her knowledge on topics from librettos to backstage gossip. In response, Tchaikovsky was too kind, offering her roles she could no longer sing.

The Third Suite enjoyed an unqualified success. "I saw that this mass of the public was struck and grateful to me. These moments are the best adornment of an artist's life." On 15 January at a performance of *Onegin,* the tsar conversed with Tchaikovsky "at length and in a friendly manner" [xiii 25]. On the 19th, Bülow, who had played the premiere in Boston, performed the First Piano Concerto, for which his enthusiasm subsequently waned [119, 40], in Moscow on the same program with the Third Suite. That day, the composer read Ippolit Shpazhinsky's play *The Enchantress,* which immediately decided the topic of his next opera. Within a week, composer and librettist had met.

On 5 February, he took a year's rental on a house at Maydanovo:

> [It is two versts (1.3 miles)] from the town of Klin, on the banks of the river Sestra. . . . The house . . . stands picturesquely on a high bank of the riverlet; around it is a fine park with wide pathways lined in linden trees, with the remains of "corbeille de roses" in front of the façade, with summer houses, with ponds and their inevitable little bridges, with rare species of trees, with a marble vase in a shady corner. . . . The environs of Maydanovo are drab, . . . but Pyotr Ilyich so loved nature in Great Russia that the birch grove, the little pine forest, the swampy meadow, the distant view with the watchtower of the village church and the horizon with the dark stripe of the great forest—fully satisfied him. . . . [I]t was far enough away . . . to scare off the accidental visitor "dropping in." [1997 III 21]

To Meck he admitted that he hadn't seen the house before renting it, nor anticipated the noisy neighbors that summer would bring. On 6 July, he declared that Maydanovo was not going to work, but he didn't leave; in September, he traded homes with his landlady [xiii 147].

Tchaikovsky's professional stature at this time was higher than that of any other Russian composer. Accordingly, the Moscow branch of the Russian

Musical Society, on 10 February 1885, elected him its director. He was also involved with the Russian Choral Society, and the head of the synodal press invited him onto a commission that overlooked the affairs of its school [1997 III 9]. Thus began several years of good works, for which he would pay with time, productivity, and his health: on the day of his election, he described to Meck a headache so severe that he feared losing his mind [xiii 32].

In February, he turned to composition, revising *Vakula the Smith* "with fiery enthusiasm" on the 16th [xiii 35]. *Manfred* and *The Enchantress* followed. On 22 April, the Moscow theater direction approved *Cherevichki,* as the revised *Vakula* was called; two days later, stage designer Karl Valts, creator of the flood in *Swan Lake,* left for Tsarskoe Selo to study the amber room to be depicted in act III. On 2 May Tchaikovsky sent the revised libretto for printing, and he finished proofing the piano-vocal score by the end of July. The first performance was scheduled for January 1886, though by 19 November there had been "not a whisper" about it. The indisposition of Bolshoy conductor Ippolit Altani brought Tchaikovsky to offer his services instead.

Begun in April, *Manfred* did not go well. The sketches for it (as later for *Hamlet*) are hectic and nonsequential [116, 155–57; 18, 33–39]. On 13 June and again on 3 August, he informed Meck that *Manfred* was demanding "immense exertion and labor" [xiii 99, 122]. On 3 July, he admitted to Laroche:

> Balakirev so pestered me with *Manfred* that in a weak moment I gave him my word; after that I tried, I began—and then like a snowball turning into a huge avalanche, from these attempts a huge symphony crawled out into the light, à la *Berlioz*. I swear that I am writing a program symphony for the last time in my life: what falsehood, how much conventionality in the spirit of the Mighty Handful, how cold and false all this is, in effect!! [304, 95]

On 13 September, he reported its completion to Balakirev. A week later, Tchaikovsky promised to send the four-hands arrangement, but asked him not to propose changes [xiii 145–46, 149].

To Pavlovskaya Tchaikovsky boasted that within an hour of finishing *Manfred,* he had begun *The Enchantress.* He noted the completion of act I to Meck on 27 September; reckoned from the completion of *Manfred,* he composed that act in five days. On 9 October, he praised Shpazhinsky as the ideal collaborator, the first act being magnificently written, with life and movement everywhere. On 6 December, the poet promised to deliver act II.

Tchaikovsky did not leave the Russian Empire in 1885, though circumstances were shaping his travel plans for 1886: Anatoly's transfer to Tiflis, Felix Mackar's purchase of the rights to Tchaikovsky's music for France and Belgium, and the retrieval of Georges-Léon. Mackar's deal with Jurgenson produced 10,000 francs for Tchaikovsky [224, 47] and an energetic correspondence [120]. Mackar reported on performances in Paris and converted important musicians to Tchaikovsky's cause. Through him, Auguste Dupont in Brussels approached Tchaikovsky in November for a score of *Swan Lake* with plans (unrealized) for a staging. Mackar also negotiated to publish Tchaikovsky's music under Bessel's imprint. Writing piano pieces, he contended, would make the composer's way in Paris easier.

The circumstances of Georges-Léon's adoption remain mysterious. In February, Tchaikovsky asked Jurgenson to send 500 francs to the Bélards in Paris, who coordinated his finances with the child's foster parents. In June, he wrote of a plan disrupted:

> Up to now I never said anything to *the mother* about the proposed change in her son's fortunes. Now, with only the deed left to do, I thought it my duty to write to her about it. Unexpectedly I received a letter in which she entreats me to do nothing right now. She asks that the child be left for another year where he has been; she says that in a year she hopes for an important change in her life (what it is she doesn't write), hopes that it will be possible to manage something close to her, etc. In a word, she begs me to wait. . . . I cannot but yield to her request. [xiii 103]

Events proceeded unrecorded until 19 August, when Tchaikovsky wrote to Nikolay, "I rejoice greatly in everything you write about Georges; thank you, my pet, for visiting him" [xiii 128]. That is the last surviving mention of Georges-Léon in 1885.

In May, Tchaikovsky attended the unveiling of a monument to Glinka in Smolensk, but returned to Moscow before the ceremony, fearing that the rush of acquaintances would deny him a moment's freedom and peace [xiii 89]. On 11 June, he and Modest helped to extinguish a fire that destroyed two-thirds of the town of Klin [xiii 115]. On 13 October, Gustav

Kross died; he was the composer's classmate at the St. Petersburg Conservatory who had played the premiere of the First Piano Concerto there [xiii 179, n. 2]. Six days later in Moscow, Tchaikovsky met Georgy Lvovich Catoire, an aspiring composer whom he would mentor. On 6 November, he celebrated Sasha and Lev's 25th wedding anniversary in Kamenka [xiii 189]. Later that month, he received 500 rubles from "an unknown benefactor" (Mitrofan Belaïeff again) for *The Tempest.*

Ongoing issues proceeded as before. Tchaikovsky and Meck affirmed their friendship, offered each other sympathy, and helped where it counted. She continued to love his music and support him. He found a post at the Moscow Conservatory for one of her protégés, Genrikh Pachulsky, brother of Vladislav [xiii 144–45], who held it until 1921. Finances were causing friction in the autumn when Jurgenson's outlays were high. By 9 October, money was a delicate topic [xiii 167–68], though not enough to keep him from borrowing 1,000 rubles from Jurgenson in September and donating to musicians' benevolent funds, nor from pressing Jurgenson, for a party over Christmastide, to bring three pounds of the best Swiss cheese, three pounds of pressed caviar (also the very best), cans of salmon, and crevettes in addition to 10 bottles of red wine, two bottles of excellent port, and two bottles of fine champagne or the best cognac [xiii 230]. Clearly, frayed moments were smoothed over by some greater understanding. If letters and diaries are any indication, Tchaikovsky's libido was subdued in 1885. On 6 October, he encouraged Modest to write candidly about Bob Davïdov and was dismayed when Modest seemed to be right [xiii 168]. The major issue coming into focus in 1885 was illness; Tchaikovsky's letters were dotted with complaints, mostly of stomach pain.

1886

Early this year, he strove to honor agreements made to increase Moscow's exposure to Petersburg musicians, including Alexander Glazunov, who began giving Tchaikovsky warmly inscribed prints of his music. Tchaikovsky offered to yield his own place on programs, but Erdmannsdörfer objected. Having stabilized the administration of the conservatory, Tchaikovsky turned to sacred music, assessing Vasily Orlov, the successful candidate for regent of the Synodal Choir, at a concert of Tchaikovsky's works on 17 February [MV020219]. In July, he wrote:

> Generally in recent times our sacred music is beginning to move forward along an excellent road. The person responsible for this movement is the emperor himself, who is very interested in its perfection and who has indicated the path it should follow. He has twice discussed this matter with me, and my latest pieces were written at his invitation and in the spirit which he desires. [xiii 285–86]

Letters and diaries suggest Tchaikovsky's heightened religious feeling at this time. On 19 January 1886, he began rereading the Bible, the New Testament in parallel with the Old. On 22 February, he essayed the Old and New Testaments in Diary no. 8. In 1886, he marked his Bible 49 times [445, 22]. Christian charity brought him to sponsor a school in Maydanovo.

In composition, he proceeded with *The Enchantress,* finishing two acts by 6 February, making changes as he went, and recasting five acts into four. On 4 February, he initiated another habit of his later years: he would begin a piece and put it aside, perhaps to finish later. That day he was looking over pieces by Mozart to orchestrate. On 28 February he informed Modest that Grand Duke Konstantin Nikolaevich, patron of the Russian Musical Society, would be in Moscow on 4 March. This was probably when K.R., who accompanied his father, relayed to Tchaikovsky the empress's wish to have something dedicated to her. It would be the songs of op. 60.

The trip south and on to Paris was an utter contrast to these occupations. On 6 February, Tchaikovsky informed Anatoly's wife that he was coming for relaxation. After visiting with Ippolit and his wife in Taganrog, he set out:

> On Sunday morning the 30th we got into the carriage, harnessed to four horses, and having settled in we left. . . . The whole night preceding I did not sleep from the horrible, unimaginable bed and the fleas . . . and for that reason I was thinking that the beauties of the Georgian Military Road would have little effect on someone tired and annoyed by lack of sleep. But it was so astonishing, magnificent, strikingly beautiful, that I didn't give a thought to sleeping the whole day. The variety of impression[s] was such that my interest never flagged for a minute. First, for a rather long time you approach the mountains, which seem to be right in front of you, but you keep going and going. Then the valley of the Terek gets narrower. Then you come to the Daral Gorge, frightening, somber, wild. Then little-by-little you enter the snowy heights. Before I passed through there had been a huge avalanche, which veritably hundreds of somber-gazing natives had only just managed to clear and were still clear-

ing. We climbed, finally, ever higher between two steep walls of snow. We had to put on our furs. At six in the evening we descended into the Aragva Valley and spent the night in Mlety. We took the *imperial rooms.* After the filth of the Vladikavkaz hotel it was amazingly pleasant to find ourselves in marvelous, clean rooms, with glorious beds, with a nicely set out table, etc. I dined, walked through the gallery by moonlight and went to bed at 9 o'clock. We left early the next morning. Already the scent of the south wafted towards us. The mountainsides were cultivated; we came upon picturesque Caucasian villages and all manner of dwellings without end. The descent is speedy, sometimes even frightening, especially at turns in the road. Not far before the Dushet Station there opened before us a view of the distance so astonishingly marvelous that I wanted to weep from delight. The further we went the more one sensed the south. Finally we passed through Mtskhet (where there are castle ruins and a famous cathedral) and about 4:30 in the afternoon we were already in Tiflis. [xiii 306–7]

On 4 April, Tchaikovsky responded to Jurgenson about *Swan Lake,* one act of which had been requested for staging at the summer theater at Krasnoe Selo [xiii 314]. He insisted on act II; Lev Ivanov, who had set the dances in *Mazepa,* probably was the choreographer, as he was when this act was first staged in St. Petersburg after Tchaikovsky's death. On 6 April, Tchaikovsky asked Shpazhinsky for the remainder of act III of *The Enchantress* by the 26th.

In Tiflis, Tchaikovsky could not avoid the adoring local musicians, headed by Mikhail Ippolitov-Ivanov, who performed his music (including a staged *Mazepa* and a concert). Yet his stay centered on two others. First was Anatoly's wife, Praskovia, a vivacious woman with whom the composer usually got along well. On 4 April, he noted in his diary her mania to arouse passion in everyone. Second was a military officer, Ivan Verinovsky, whose name Tchaikovsky first noted in his diary on 6 April and who, judging by his frequent mention during this time and the composer's agony later, had aroused *his* passion. A competition arose between Tchaikovsky and Praskovia for Verinovsky's attentions, the composer noting her unbecoming behavior (as if jealous), which peaked on 26 and 27 April: "Infinitely sorry for Verinovsky and am angry at that hussy" [Dnev 54]. The passion of this love triangle, if such it was, was expressed only by Tchaikovsky. Praskovia, interviewed much later by Nina Berberova, recalled: "'I did him out of an admirer in Tiflis when he was staying with us,' she said to me, smiling merrily. 'It was Verginsky,' I answered. 'Yes, it was Verginsky, and Petya could never forgive me for this'" [35, 10].

Verginsky? Praskovia responded with bubbly inaccuracy to this question calling on her authority as a family member. A few days after the composer's departure, Verinovsky shot himself. Praskovia, when queried about it only weeks later, was nonresponsive. On 7 July, two months after Verinovsky's death, Tchaikovsky appealed to Ippolitov-Ivanov for information, complaining the next day that "I cannot get out of anybody what happened with *Verinovsky,* and it has been since Paris that I asked you to give me precise details." Ten days later, he knew: Verinovsky had killed himself because he had failed an admissions examination to the Academy of the General Staff [Dnev 100, n. 1]. There is no evidence, except for Berberova's inconclusive comment, that Verinovsky reciprocated Tchaikovsky's feelings:

> Verinovsky put an end to himself out of love for Anatoly Ilyich's wife Praskovia Vladimirovna, and in part because of Tchaikovsky himself—he was a young officer in love with the composer's sister-in-law who had flirted with him cruelly. When Tchaikovsky came to Tiflis, Verinovsky felt an attraction towards him. He fired a bullet into his forehead the day after Tchaikovsky's departure. [35, 218]

Tchaikovsky left Tiflis innocent, the family coming to Batum to see him off. He continued to remark on the places he saw: Trapesund, Kerasund, the Bosporus and Constantinople, an eruption of Mount Aetna ("it is impossible to convey the beauty of this combination of moonlight with the fire of Aetna and the raging sea" [xiii 339]), sunrise over Messina, Stromboli. He instructed Modest on 28 April: "I am not going to get to Vichy. But tell everyone that is in fact where I am going." This would give him several weeks in Paris instead of a few days. He got acquainted with Felix Mackar, through whom he met Gabriel Fauré and the librettist Léonce Détroyat. His greater purpose was to arrange Georges-Léon's return to Russia (apparently despite Tanya's veto), as was clear from the arrival of Nikolay's wife, Olga, on 4 June to accompany them on the trip. They arrived in St. Petersburg on the 15th. Two days later, Tchaikovsky stood as godfather at Georges-Léon's baptism, writing to Praskovia of Nikolay and Olga without mentioning the ceremony: "Imagine: they want to take on the upbringing of some orphan boy. It will utterly change the flow of their life" [xiii 369]. Georges-Léon's identity was an open secret; when Ippolit visited Nikolay, he repeatedly observed the child's resemblance to Tanya [xiii 430]. Tanya's trip to Petersburg on 30 October was surely inspired by her child's presence there; on 8 November, Tchaikovsky noted in his diary, "Tanya and the boy were late." The day after the baptism, he was sad at losing "a father's rights" over Georges-Léon.

Tchaikovsky's assurance to Meck that he would not tire when he returned to composition, together with Shpazhinsky's telegram (19 June) reporting the completion of *The Enchantress,* held promise for a productive summer. Three days later, he received a letter from Antonina; in two days, she had written again. "Intense moral suffering," he agonized. "And hatred and pity" [Dnev 75]. Antonina reverted to allure and promises of love; she wanted to live together, she was ready to be all his [xiii 388]. Tchaikovsky thought her utterly mad and offered 600 rubles a year to avoid contact [xiii 387]. She took the money and in a letter thanking him, described her recent life [365, 230–34]. A year ago, she was burned out by a fire in her quarters, evacuated before she could retrieve even small personal items. She was grateful for the resumption of his payments and made three requests: to adopt one of her three children—Maria who was five, Pyotr who was four, and Antonina who was just under two; to sign off on a new passport; and finally, for a dedication, preferably of a song. She recalled that he once wanted her to leave Moscow, and now, six days hence, she will do so—to Kursk.

Tchaikovsky judged her letter to be strange and wild [Dnev 81], though a month after he yielded up his rights as a father over Georges-Léon, her proposal did not evince the least curiosity. Through 1886, she stayed in Moscow and continued to ask for help, making this appeal seem more an attempt to manipulate than to bid farewell. In August, Tchaikovsky declared he would not answer Antonina's letters; in September, he approved her new passport; on 16 October, she wrote again about adoption, then vanished again, surfacing in Italy in July 1887.

Being free of civic responsibilities in 1886 after opening the conservatory and celebrating the 25th anniversary of Jurgenson's business, both on 1 September, encouraged Tchaikovsky's creative projects. He wrote op. 60 between 19 August and 8 September, after beginning act IV of *The Enchantress* on 7 July and finishing it by 18 August. When he played through the opera, he found it too long [xiii 455]. He began to orchestrate it on

19 September, making cuts as he went, determined to complete both the score and piano-vocal reduction by Lent. He was immersed in these tasks when the call to conduct *Cherevichki* came on 19 November. His first orchestral rehearsal, on 4 December, went better than expected. The entire project, including lessons with Altani, filled his schedule from 20 November to the first performance on 19 January 1887.

In St. Petersburg from 18 October to 9 November 1886, Tchaikovsky basked in celebrity. He had written to K.R. in September asking help to secure permission to dedicate op. 60 to the empress and *The Enchantress* to the emperor [xiii 447]. On 27 October, the two men met; by 5 November, Jurgenson had been contacted by Fyodor Adolfovich Oom, the empress's secretary, to begin the complex process of imperial dedication. On 10 November, the composer summed up:

> In the highest spheres, besides the emperor and empress who are favorably disposed towards me, I have a particular, special patron, namely the Grand Duke Konstantin Konstantinovich. In this visit to Petersburg I often spoke and visited with him. His person is unusually charming. He is a talented poet and not long ago, under the initials K.R., a collection of his verses was issued, which is enjoying a great success. . . . Despite my shyness, especially with people of the highest spheres, I feel completely free in the company of these most likeable, most august personages, and derive sincere pleasure from conversation with them. [xiii 493]

Tchaikovsky was poised to leave on 8 November when he was invited by Vsevolozhsky to discuss a ballet with balletmaster Marius Petipa and Alexander Frolov, supervisor of the Petersburg Theater School. They agreed on *Undine,* which Tchaikovsky would begin after he finished *The Enchantress.* By Christmas, confronted with the enormity of his responsibilities, he requested an extension, and *Undine* was banked, to be revived as *The Sleeping Beauty.* Similarly, a concert by the St. Petersburg Society of Chamber Music on 5 November had celebrated Tchaikovsky's honorary membership. Out of this would come, after similar delays, the *Souvenir de Florence.*

Tchaikovsky's private life continued private, the exception in 1886 being Verinovsky's death. Home from Paris, he wrote to Praskovia, "I have wept much apropos this situation . . . all the while it seeming to me that had I stayed another week in Tiflis, this would not have happened" [xiii 369]. In

October, he was still "weep[ing] without ceasing" over Verinovsky [Dnev 100]. Tchaikovsky's feelings for Verinovsky were much stronger than for others noted in his diaries before he learned of Verinovsky's death, including a Turk, an American, a kind-hearted German, a good-looking flat-chested young man, and two unusually dark young men. He also indulged in a lusty relationship in Moscow with a man named Vanya, a driver with whom the composer did not shrink from being seen and over whom, he reported to Modest in September, he had "fallen deeply into Cupid's nets" [xiii 455]. The composer's affection for Bob Davïdov continued this year, but he could no longer deny Bob's lack of reciprocity. On 8 November, he wrote in his diary, "I have a strange feeling when I am with Bob. I feel that he not only dislikes me, but really feels something like antipathy towards me."

Among old friends, Meck was remembered with 32 letters in 1886. Laroche, suffering, claimed in February that he could not tolerate Tchaikovsky's music [Dnev 41]; in September, he took a leave from the Moscow Conservatory; in October, Tchaikovsky again volunteered to take his dictation (of an article about Liszt). Among new friends, Julia Shpazhinskaya, the estranged wife of the librettist of *The Enchantress,* engaged the composer to help build a writing career for her. On 28 October, he referred to "charming Volodya," Nápravnik's son and an official of the Russian Musical Society, who would leave memoirs about the composer [316, 254–62].

The most significant development in Tchaikovsky's life in 1886 was a dramatic increase in complaints about his health. At first, it was upset stomach, but then other maladies piled on: 17 July, terrible chest pain, could not lie, sit, or stand; 29 July, his "disgusting condition" continued. The hyperbole ran into autumn: on 12 October, "An absolute invalid. At the least exertion it seems to me as though I have a nail in my brain. My stomach refuses to function. And to die, how I dread it!" On 13 November, his intestinal pain was "unbearable." On 29 June, his name-day, Tchaikovsky had thought he was dying and wrote his will [Dnev 75].

Half of Diary no. 8 was written in 1886. On 22 February, Tchaikovsky compared psalms with gospels and found David's words nothing compared with Christ's "Come unto me all ye that labor and are heavy laden." On 29 June, he wrote of Tolstoy, "alone in his inscrutable greatness." On 20 September, he compared Beethoven, his Jehovah, with Mozart, his Christ, the intermediary of love and human compassion. He preferred middle Beethoven and detested the late music, but loved all Mozart, especially *Don Giovanni.* [On Tchaikovsky and Mozart, see 223; on Tchaikovsky and Beethoven, see 202, 170–75; 225.] He also left opinions in his regular diaries: on 4 August, Massenet's *Manon* was nauseating, but he felt some kinship with the nausea; of Brahms on 9 October: "It angers me that this presumptuous mediocrity is declared a *genius.* Compared to him Raff is a giant, not to mention Rubinstein" [Dnev 85, 101].

The year 1886 had its musical high points. Early in the year, Anton Rubinstein was performing his "historical concerts" in Moscow, at the last of which he played four of Tchaikovsky's pieces. The first performance of the *Manfred* Symphony was given on 11 March, the fifth anniversary of Nikolay Rubinstein's death. On 31 May, at Pauline Viardot-Garcia's home in Paris, Tchaikovsky studied the autograph of *Don Giovanni.* On 6 July, at the Uspensky Cathedral in Moscow, he heard one of his sacred pieces in a service for the first time. On 27 November, he received another 500 rubles from the "unknown benefactor" for *Francesca da Rimini.* On 31 December, K.R. informed him that he had asked the emperor personally about the dedication of *The Enchantress* and was told everything would be settled if no obstacles were encountered.

1887

This year was marked by Tchaikovsky's rise to prominence as a conductor, visits south (May–July) and to Aachen (July–August), standing watch over the decline of Nikolay Kondratiev, staging *The Enchantress,* and a tour of Western Europe.

On 16 January—3 days before the premiere of *Cherevichki*—Alexandra Krutikova, scheduled to sing the part of the witch Solokha, withdrew, obliging Tchaikovsky to coach her substitute, Alexandra Svyatlovskaya. Here is his description of the first performance:

> Altani led me to the orchestra; just then the curtain swished up and the presentation of wreaths began from the orchestra and the chorus, etc., amidst a storm of applause. During this procedure I put myself in order somewhat, began the overture well and towards the end was already conducting with utter confidence. The overture was loudly applauded. The first act went well, although far worse than at the dress rehearsal. After the first act more wreaths were presented. . . . By then I was utterly tranquil and conducted the rest of the opera

quite calmly. In the first scene of act II the public laughed a great deal. Between the scenes of this act I rose and bowed several times. The third act, it struck me, pleased less than the second, but was applauded even still, something was encored and the artists and I were called several times. At the end they were calling warmly and often. It is difficult to say whether the opera really pleased. The theater was half-filled, if not more, with my friends, and it is hardly surprising that I received many ovations; but time and the *true* public of subsequent performances will tell whether it was for the opera or for me personally for prior services. It was a great misfortune that, due to Krutikova's illness, Svyatlovskaya sang Solokha. This role does not suit her at all, whereas Krutikova is excellent in it. Klimentova would be perfectly fine if she did not overact just a little; even still she greatly pleased. Usatov was quite excellent. Korsov took the role of the devil extremely subtly and intelligently, and I was delighted in places with his acting. . . . In general I am completely satisfied with the artists and the public. Now, you ask, how did I do? I am embarrassed to speak of this. . . . The production as regards decorations is *magnificent,* and for this I am obliged to I. A. Vsevolozhsky. If he continues as head of the theaters the costumes will also be *magnificent,* which cannot be said of them now. In general, *economy* reigns in the local direction. After the performance there was a big dinner with the customary speeches, etc. I was improbably tired, but the fatigue would have been pleasant were it not for the sorrowful news which came this morning. [xiv 20–21]

In St. Petersburg, while her uncle was conducting *Cherevichki* in Moscow, Tanya Davïdova had died at a costume ball. Tchaikovsky was shattered. He wrote to Meck, still without mention of Tanya's having given birth and her rehabilitation from her addiction: "Though it often occurred to me that the best and desired outcome for this unfortunate person was death, I was still deeply struck by the news. She . . . was a shadow of the former Tanya; morphine destroyed her, and one way or another a tragic end was unavoidable" [xiv 23].

Word of Tchaikovsky's conducting was quick to spread. Five days after the first performance of *Cherevichki,* the St. Petersburg Philharmonic Society invited him to conduct its annual Lenten concert on 5 March [xiv 43, n. 5]. After social duties—the weddings of Alyosha (whose intended bride failed to show up) and of Alexander Siloti—and tying up strands of compositions, on 28 February he was rehearsing his Lenten concert. The

Second Suite, parts of *The Enchantress* and of the *Serenade for Strings,* piano music and songs, and *1812* came off well. "Tchaikovsky conducts beautifully, with assurance and complete technique. Calls for the composer of 'Onegin' yesterday were endless, just as there was no end to the praise of his likeable talent" [PG870307].

As winter turned to spring, Tchaikovsky continued to be ill. On 15 February, he was "feeling terrible, as in November"; on the 20th, his headaches returned. In March, he put Vichy on his schedule. In St. Petersburg between 22 February and 11 March, he attended his friend Nikolay Kondratiev. To Meck, he described the sadness of bidding farewell to his friend, both men thinking it was their last meeting [xiv 61–62]. It was in fact the first of three farewells. On 28 March, Anton Rubinstein wrote, announcing a new opera company and asking for *The Enchantress*—or if it were committed, a new work by 1 September. Tchaikovsky declined [xiv 77–78] and settled into a nondescript April. On 22 April, he learned that Kondratiev's illness was incurable and made excuses not to see him. By 5 May, he had decided "to perform the duties of friendship of many years" and visit Kondratiev again, then go south to Tiflis [xiv 106–7]. His friend was almost unrecognizable; Tchaikovsky departed on the 16th after "painful goodbyes," returned to Moscow for conservatory examinations, and went south on 20 May.

This time, he steamed down the Volga to Astrakhan, then onto a stormy Caspian Sea to Baku, thence by train to Tiflis. As before, he left descriptions of the journey [Dnev 145–47; xiv 116–17; 386, 531–32]. After a fortnight of complaining of medical problems, he hoped to find relief in the mineral waters at Borzhom, where he arrived on 12 June. The doctor there claimed that his liver had "moved somewhere it shouldn't have" [Dnev 153], and the composer's reaction to treatment was weakness, lethargy, and aching. But he liked the city, and in a few days he began work on *Mozartiana* and the *Souvenir de Florence.* On 18 June, he wrote to the emperor, asking for assistance in building a new opera house for Tiflis [xiv 124–25]; two days later, he informed Ippolitov-Ivanov that he had agreed to conduct the first performance of *The Enchantress* there soon after the premiere in St. Petersburg [xiv 127].

His plan to substitute Borzhom for Vichy changed when on 30 June he received a telegram from Kondratiev, now at Aachen: "Supplie venir, votre arrivé peut me ressusciter" [xiv 141]. He took the waters for another week and composed "The golden cloud has slept," a chorus dated 4 July, then departed on the 7th. From 15 July to 25 August, with a break in Paris, Tchaikovsky for the third time attended Kondratiev, whose decline he reported graphically in letters. Yet he finished *Mozartiana,* composed the *Pezzo capriccioso* for Cello and Orchestra, and wrote 16 bars of an "Aachen Waltz" of which we know nothing further [426, 87]. He feared he would have to accompany Kondratiev back to Russia, but his friend "stretche[d] on, like a candle" [xiv 175], abhorring death [Dnev 165]. When the last farewell came, there were no excessive tears [Dnev 173]. Home by 30 August, Tchaikovsky redrafted his will before the day was out [Dnev 175].

In September, his thoughts turned to Eduard Zak after a 13-year silence in the official record. He wrote on 5 September:

> Again was thinking and recalling *Zak.* How amazingly vividly I recall him: the sound of his voice, his movements, but especially the unusually marvelous expression of his face at times. I could not imagine that he was not *really* here now. Death, that is *his* utter nonbeing, is beyond my understanding. It seems I have not loved anyone so much as him. My God! What they did not say to me *then* and however much I reassure myself, my guilt before him is terrible! And meanwhile I loved him, that is, not *did* love him, but continue to love him now and his memory is sacred to me! [Dnev 176–77].

Tchaikovsky's susceptibility to intense existential moments (e.g., kneeling and thanking God for the blessedness of nature at Brailovo in 1880) cautions against necessarily taking these remarks as proof of long-smoldering passion. He rued the loss of Verinovsky and had suffered alongside Kondratiev; his language here could be expressing the guilt of the survivor.

He noted on 11 September the "feeling in my left side which I have long considered the onset of a fatal disease" [Dnev 178]. On the 21st, he wrote his only entry for 1886 in Diary no. 8:

> How short life is! How much one wants to do, and ponder, and say! You put things off, imagining that so much still lies ahead, while death is already beginning to lie in wait around the corner. For exactly a year I have not touched this book, and how much has changed! How strange it was for me to read that 365 days ago I was still afraid to acknowledge that despite all the fervor of sympathetic feelings awakened by Christ I was able to doubt his divinity. Since then my *religion* has become infinitely clearer; I thought much about God, about

> life and death all this time, and especially in *Aachen* the fateful questions: why? how? for what reason? often occupied me and hovered disturbingly before me. I would like sometime to set out my *religion* in detail, if only for myself, once and for all, to clarify my belief and that border beyond which, after speculation, it begins. [Dnev 213]

On 26 September, Tchaikovsky asked, "And what is happening in Aachen? It is frightening to think about it." He learned the next day that Nikolay Kondratiev had died.

Life rushed on. On 28 September, he left to rehearse *The Enchantress,* which took up much of October. His account of the preparations and the first performance was guarded:

> There were very few orchestral rehearsals; nevertheless . . . I proceeded with them quite meticulously. I was quite satisfied the whole time by the artists' and the direction's relationship to me. And their performance, with one exception. *Pavlovskaya,* given the title role as compensation for past services, has completely lost her voice. . . .
>
> On the day of the performance . . . I was greeted with friendly clapping. The first act went not especially well. *Pavlovskaya* . . . delayed her exit in one scene to the point that commotion and bewilderment ensued, and finally I had to stop the orchestra. Fortunately *Koryakin* prompted her, . . . and everything returned to order. . . . The second act went very well; in the third Pavlovskaya overacted and sang very unbeautifully, and it left a cold impression. In the fourth many numbers pleased, and the storm with Melnikov's magnificent acting had a deep effect.
>
> . . . "The Enchantress" is not much liked, and the blame for this lies with me, and chiefly with Ip[polit] Vas[ilievich Shpazhinsky]. He knows the stage very well, but is still too little attuned to operatic demands. There are too many words in him, conversation too much predominates over lyricism. And however I shortened his text, . . . the scenes came out too long. But in much I too am guilty. [xiv 249–50]

First performed on 20 October, *The Enchantress* met with familiar complaints. Superior in everything orchestral, Tchaikovsky could not write for the voice. He lacked a strong dramatic instinct [NO871023]. Dramatic high points were musically uninspired; Nastasya's declaration of love to Yury was too long and no more than pretty, in a lyric-sentimental style which lacked power [PL871023]. *The Enchantress* could sooner be called a music drama than an opera, given the Wagnerian relationship of voice to orchestra, even though the dramatic content was distant from Wagner's "foggy images." The music tried to flow together with the text into a seamless whole [PL871022]. More pertinent was the scarcity of lyrical numbers in *The Enchantress* due to Shpazhinsky's wordiness. After conducting four performances, Tchaikovsky left town, apologizing to Vsevolozhsky on 25 November: "I am ashamed before you, before the artists, before the whole world. All the same, deep in my heart I believe that the fiasco was undeserved, that the opera . . . is not so bad as the Petersburg newspapers report with unanimous hostility." He was fired by revenge and hinted about a revival of *The Maid of Orleans* [xiv 271–72].

But other projects were at hand. In October he asked Ippolitov-Ivanov to postpone *The Enchantress* at Tiflis [xiv 233], agreed to conduct in Prague early in December [xiv 237], set dates in Moscow for the next month, informed the Berlin Philharmonic Society of his availability between 15 January and the end of February, and accepted an invitation from Siloti to conduct in Leipzig. In fact, he conducted *Mozartiana* in Moscow on 14 and 15 November and in Petersburg on 12 December. On 15 December he departed for Western Europe, postponing Prague until February. By 19 December, in Leipzig, he had met Brahms, Grieg, and Dame Ethel Smyth. On the 28th, he was in Hamburg. At the end of 1887, he was in Lübeck and learned on 1 January 1888 that the emperor had awarded him an annual lifetime pension of 3,000 rubles, apparently at Vsevolozhsky's suggestion [1997 III 185].

Such a frenzied schedule was inconsistent with Tchaikovsky's illness. On 27 November he did not want to consult a doctor [xiv 277], yet on the 30th he wrote to Meck:

> I often have unprecedented attacks, as if asphyxia or asthma, with pounding heart and powerful nervous upset. It seems that there is nothing serious about that and it is but again the same nerves added to a stomach that is capricious and not always obedient to me. . . . [I]t is impossible to be more strict and abstemious in hygiene than me, and meanwhile I am incessantly ill. At the moment as I am writing you I am not well: my heart is pounding and my breathing is strained. [xiv 279]

Was Tchaikovsky a good conductor? He was cautious at first; his close friends disapproved; audiences loved him perhaps more for his celebrity than his skill; and critics were of varying opinion [214; 436, 411–16]. Of

The Enchantress, one complained: "As a composer conducting his own work, Mr. Tchaikovsky was too agitated, too carried away to the detriment of the obligations he assumed, which for him, as for any other unaccustomed person, were quite difficult, taking away that feeling of self-possession so necessary for a conductor" [PL871024]. Writing in 1890, Tchaikovsky agreed: "I find that when the composer conducts he causes an unwilled nervousness, uncertainty, unsteadiness in the performers. How much more calmly and assuredly singers and chorus and orchestra perform if the accustomed, assured hand of a real conductor is leading them!" [xv-b 290].

Kashkin, who praised Tchaikovsky's conducting of Beethoven's Ninth Symphony [202, 171], was more damning when Tchaikovsky conducted his own pieces:

> Conducting his own music was . . . attended by loss of time and money and by extreme violence to his nature. It was a very sad and mistaken urge, partly responsible for the premature death of this voluntary martyr. . . . Standing before an orchestra he completely lost himself and utterly forgot the piece—even one of his own—and its performance instructions. His perplexity and ill assurance showed in the movements of his baton, which he waved with his entire arm, from the shoulder, as if engaging in heavy physical labor. . . . Tchaikovsky was not the least successful at conducting, and to the end remained just as feeble before an orchestra as at the outset. [MV030627]

Conducting burdened his composition. The year 1887 rivaled 1881 as the least productive year of Tchaikovsky's life. He composed no large work, completing only *Mozartiana*—four orchestrations—a handful of short pieces, and the *Pezzo capriccioso.* On 3 November, he signed the autograph book of Baron Boris Fitinhof-Schell [MV990105], whose ballet *The Tulip of Haarlem* was first performed during rehearsals of *The Enchantress.* According to Schell, they discussed working with a balletmaster and the dimensions of music in relation to dance—to help avoid making unceremonious changes in rehearsal. This may also be the reason that Marius Petipa, when the time came, gave Tchaikovsky written instructions for the music of *The Sleeping Beauty.*

1888

Tchaikovsky described the beginning of his concert tour in the "Autobiographical Account of the Journey Abroad in 1888" [83, 355–91; 84,

331–64; 278]. It covered only the first three towns in which he conducted —Leipzig, Hamburg, Berlin (then Prague, Paris, London). His repertoire included the First Piano Concerto and the Violin Concerto, the First and Third Suites, *Romeo and Juliet, Francesca da Rimini, 1812,* and shorter works. In Leipzig, local Russians welcomed him (Siloti, Brodsky, the pianist Arthur Friedheim); he met other important musicians and heard new music: Brahms's Double Concerto (with Joachim and Hausmann, conducted by Brahms), which left no impression; *Das Rheingold* under Nikisch; and at his own request, *Die Meistersinger.* Tchaikovsky's wariness of Brahms persisted after meeting him and was apparently mutual. He now considered Brahms to be an immense talent with no melodic gift, who drowned his ideas in complex harmonies which drove them off-point. In the tour diary, he cited Brahms's "very attractive personality" but made no effort at personal conversation; to Anatoly and Praskovia he wrote that he and Brahms got drunk together [xiv 295].

Tchaikovsky conducted the First Suite in Leipzig at the New Gewandhaus on 24 December/5 January in a program shared with Beethoven, Spohr, Reinecke, Mendelssohn, Rubinstein, Schubert, Franz, and Schumann. An incoherent speech in German at rehearsal won the artists' good will, and the concert went well. The next day, he was touted at a concert of the Liszt Verein, which included his First Quartet and the Trio. Here he heard Karl Halíř, who would play the Violin Concerto in Prague: "He is a genius" [Dnev 187]. Tchaikovsky observed of his own debut, "Conducted well." Edward Bernsdorf in the *Signale für die musikalische Welt,* fearing "the monstrous, distorted and perverse," was pleased at the composer's discretion and refinement. He liked the introduction and Fugue best, and the Marche miniature—an imitation of a music box—least [#4/1888, p. 54]. To Bernhard Vogel, the Suite, lacking philosophical engagement, won an easy victory [NZ880111, p. 21]. Critics praised his chamber music for its compelling ideas, "the deeply thought Trio dedicated to Nikolay Rubinstein and the Quartet, wholly magnificent in every movement and simply wonderful in its Andante" [MW880112, p. 33].

From Lübeck on 2/14 January 1888, Tchaikovsky warmly thanked the emperor, the minister of the Imperial Court, Vsevolozhsky, and his assistant Vladimir Pogozhev for his annuity. Otherwise, as throughout his tour, he complained of illness, homesickness, and boredom and admitted to heavy drinking. In Hamburg, which visit has been extensively documented

[119], he conducted the *Serenade for Strings,* the First Piano Concerto with Vasily Sapelnikov, and the Theme and Variations from the Third Suite. The audience liked the *Serenade,* was indifferent to the other pieces, but loved Sapelnikov (*Famos, unglaublich, kolossal!* [83, 385]). To the critic of the *Musikalisches Wochenblatt,* "The first movement of the piano concerto is a horrible piece, scatterbrained and uncouth in shape, intellectually empty and often downright unbeautiful in sonority. . . . the orchestral variations are a piece of Asiatic music, . . . an instrumental witches' sabbath one must have endured to have believed" [MW880216]. In a footnote, the editors disowned these remarks. In Hamburg, Tchaikovsky made important acquaintances: Daniel Rahter, a former Petersburger who would become his German publisher and soon busied himself with concerts and stagings of Tchaikovsky's works; Julius Laube, who would conduct at the Pavlovsk Railway Station; the historian-theorist Hugo Riemann; Joanna and Willy Burmester, aspiring pianist and violinist, who would maintain contact with Tchaikovsky in letters [230, 266–67, 270–94]; and Theodor Ave-Lallemant, director of the Hamburg Philharmonic Society and member of its governing committee since 1832 [119, 59], who told Tchaikovsky that he had the makings of a good German composer and should consider emigrating to Germany, where his faults could be corrected [83, 387].

Tchaikovsky's next engagement was 17 days later in Berlin. Officials of the Berlin Philharmonic, with Bülow's concurrence, persuaded him to exchange *Francesca da Rimini* for something that the public would favor; Tchaikovsky chose *1812.* He spent the week of 14–21 January in Leipzig, visiting old friends and making new, including Ferruccio Busoni ("very talented") and "the conductor *Mahler*" [Dnev 193]. On private matters, he wrote to Modest, in reference to Sapelnikov, "Not since Kotek's time have I loved anyone as fervently as him" [xiv 354], which explains the increasingly warm references to the pianist. Another echo, of a time even further removed, was the composer's reunion with Désirée Artôt. Of a dinner given by the impresario Hermann Wolff, he wrote:

> Artôt was there. I was inexpressibly happy to see her. We quickly became friends again, without a single word about the past. Her husband *Padilla* suffocated me in his embrace. Day after tomorrow there will be a grand dinner at her place. The old lady is just as captivating as she was 20 years ago. [xiv 354]

Tchaikovsky's visit to Prague was exceptional. He was welcomed by crowds of citizens and a host of officials important in politics and music. Instead of solitude in hotels, it was one lavish reception after another. Instead of hostility in the press, he read analyses of his pieces prepared by leading musicians. The reason for this was partly Slavic solidarity. While cautious about this openly anti-Teutonic celebration of Slavdom on the heels of leaving Germany, Tchaikovsky delighted in his welcome and wanted to emphasize Slavic unity with the Czechs at his next audience with the tsar. The German musical press, which reported events from all over Europe and America, omitted mention of Tchaikovsky's concerts in Prague. The undercurrent of Russophobia referred to in the "Autobiographical Account," stemming from an inflammatory speech by Bismarck the year before, may have been responsible.

Amid visits, deputations, formal dinners, rehearsals, new acquaintances, even purchasing a clock and a small mechanical organ [Dnev 196], Tchaikovsky wrote to Modest:

> In the station before Prague, *Kralupy,* a large crowd and a deputation awaited us, which accompanied us to Prague. At the station a mass of people, deputations, children with bouquets, two speeches: one in Russian, the other—long—in Czech: I responded. I walked to my carriage between two walls of people amid shouts of "Slava!" At the hotel, magnificent lodging. That evening a performance of [Verdi's] *Otello* at the opera. A mass of acquaintances and greetings. . . . Yesterday morning a visit from *Dvořák,* who stayed two hours; a trip around the city and a look at the sights with the director of the museum and the Russian priest (who sends warm greetings to Sasha and Nata), dinner at *Valechka's* (a famous bookseller and Russophile), a ball in the best local hall, during which I sat on view in a box and everyone looked at me. Today at 10:30 liturgy in the Russian church, the visit of a circle of students, lunch with Dvořák, a trip around the city with the same museum director (he speaks excellent Russian) and a grand soiree honoring me at the *Music Society.* [xiv 359–60]

Tchaikovsky conducted twice. After the first concert, on 7/19 February, came a banquet and speeches, including his own, much rehearsed. Two days later at the National Theater, he conducted the first half of the performance; the second was a staging of act II of *Swan Lake.* Tchaikovsky noted, "*Swan Lake. A moment of absolute happiness.* But only a moment"

[Dnev 198]. The production, by August Berger, was given seven more performances [346, xliv–xlv]. The next day, he wrote to Meck: "I am received here as if I represented not Russian music but all of Russia. . . . I never suspected how much the *Czechs* are devoted to Russia and how deeply they hate the Germans" [xiv 363]. He bade farewell to Siloti and to Jurgenson, who had made the trip to Prague, paid calls, received visitors, signed photographs, and amid well-wishers and flowers, left for Paris.

Prompted by Mackar, Tchaikovsky courted the influential in Paris from 12/24 February to 6/18 March. The cellist Anatoly Brandukov, a recent graduate from the Moscow Conservatory, was his frequent companion. Pyotr wrote to Modest midway through the visit:

> Ambassador Morgenheim gave a celebratory dinner and reception; at the Russian Circle there was also a celebration; at Colonne's there was a grand soiree in my honor; yesterday there was an enormous society at Diémer's (who is very rich and receives luxuriously); today I was at M-me *Adam*'s at her reception. . . . At the concert Gounod was demonstratively expressing delight; the young musicians are also very kind to me. I am getting acquainted with them. *Delibes* is most likeable of all. The newspapers are very involved with me; I have had a host of interviews with various journalists. . . . At "Figaro" next *Wednesday* there will be a big celebration. . . . In a word, I cannot complain of a lack of *glory*. It is impossible to retell everything that has happened, and to recount all my new acquaintances. [xiv 375]

His first concert was a soiree at Maria Benardaki's on 16/28 February attended by 300 of the city's cultural elite. Tchaikovsky conducted the Colonne Orchestra in the elegy and waltz from the *Serenade for Strings;* songs and other short works followed, performed by the hostess, her sister, Jean Louis Lassalle (of the Opéra), Edouard and Jean de Reszke, Brandukov, flautist Claude-Paul Taffanel, and pianist Louis Diémer. "Remarkable evening," Tchaikovsky noted with breathtaking understatement. He conducted the second half of public concerts on 21 February/4 March and again a week later; the Benardaki program, augmented, was repeated in the meantime [1997 III 209]. Amédée Boutarel in *Le Ménestrel* wrote, "Mr. Tchaikovsky has preferred to give us works of a less lofty genre," noting that his style "shows neither great daring nor powerful originality" [ME880311]. In *Le Temps,* the absence of capital works was also noted, and Tchaikovsky was described in the words of César Cui: productivity as inexhaustible as it is premature, themes for the most part charming but lacking in power, grandeur and profundity, but in their elegiac quality providing some cachet of individuality [LT880312]. Three more concerts honored him. The first, sponsored by *Le Figaro* on 2/14 March, was marked by the publication that day in *Le Figaro* of "Don Juan's Serenade" from op. 38. The second was on 4/16 March at the chamber society La Trompette, where Tchaikovsky played second piano to Diémer in the Concert Fantasia. The next day at the Salle Erard, Diémer and his students played some 40 of Tchaikovsky's piano pieces [D&Y 444]. Exhausted, Tchaikovsky left for London on 7/19 March. Leaving Paris in a storm, two hours late into Calais, on the channel crossing, he observed:

> There wasn't a single soul besides myself who didn't puke. I finally convinced myself that I was not prone to seasickness. Arrived in London at midnight instead of 7:00 p.m., with masses of snow everywhere, as by us in January. I have yet to see anyone. Rehearsal tomorrow, day after tomorrow, and concert in the evening. [xiv 384]

On 10/22 March in the St. James Hall, he conducted the *Serenade for Strings* and the Theme and Variations from the Third Suite in a diverse program of the London Philharmonic Society. The critic of the *Times* found the *Serenade* not very Russian and said that it precluded the display of orchestral color; he also thought that Tchaikovsky might have chosen something grander. The *Musical Times* reported, "Amateurs would have preferred music of greater pretence, . . . to allow a comparison between the Russian master and his contemporaries on the ground of the highest art" [MT880401, p. 216]. When he departed London on 12/24 March, Tchaikovsky proceeded to Vienna, passing Aachen with its memories of the preceding summer. It took six nights on the train to reach Ippolit in Taganrog, and then he went to Anatoly and Praskovia in Tiflis for three weeks. At resting points, he caught up on correspondence, writing to Meck of the impulse, when exhausted by travel, to want to travel again. "I dream of some distant sea journey, and I shall try, next year or in two years, to get invited to conduct concerts in America" [xiv 395].

He never summed up this concert tour, though the main points are clear. Social obligations were a strain: "The fact is that if my journey had consisted only of rehearsals and concerts, I would sooner have experienced pleasure than weariness, despite the intensity of my nerves" [xiv 385]. As the tour proceeded, he grew more sensitive to taking great trouble for little pay: "Of course I regretted the huge sums spent on the trip, but this had to be or there was no going" [xiv 401]. Yet his concerts had made an impression and his name was well known. Before he reached home, Mackar sent him the sketch of a libretto by Détroyat and Gallet ("The Georgian Woman"), stressing that it was time to compose an opera for Paris. Mindful of Ave-Lallemant's suggestion to correct his faults, he returned to Russia and wrote the capital work of his next tour, which would show the Germans a thing or two about symphonies and would be dedicated, after some consideration of the London Philharmonic Society [119, 88–89], to Ave-Lallemant.

Tchaikovsky had hardly reached home before the anthill of his local affairs burst into activity. In April, Shpazhinsky had been full of ideas for an opera on Pushkin's "The Captain's Daughter," a project first discussed in 1885 to follow *Mazepa,* but delayed by the composition of *The Enchantress.* In April, the composer wrote to Meck that any thought of setting "The Captain's Daughter" was provisional, and in May to Vsevolozhsky that he had cooled toward the topic [xiv 416, 429], despite the director's attachment to eighteenth-century topics and the emperor's esteem for Catherine the Great, during whose reign the events depicted in the story took place [56, 171–73]. On 23 April, he arrived at his new home in Frolovskoe, still in the Klin area but further removed than Maydanovo. "The house stands on a hill," he wrote to Meck, "the view is marvelous, the garden moves directly into the forest, there are no summer residents, the ceilings are high, [the rooms are] outfitted in old furniture, and, in a word, I am completely satisfied with my new situation" [xiv 415]. The first letter he had received in it, he noted with pleasure, was from her.

There was no calm. He thanked the emperor for his pension in an audience on 2 May, though he was barely given time to mention his welcome in Prague. The Petersburg visit was mostly taken up with family: Sasha was going abroad (she had aged, become grey, and was constantly sick), and Bob was abnormally corpulent. On 22 May, Léonce Détroyat wrote from Paris, inviting him to choose any topic, whereupon he and Gallet would write a scenario and, upon the composer's approval, send him the libretto act by act [6, 115]. At the end of May, he spent 10 days in Moscow on business of the Russian Musical Society and attending conservatory examinations.

His productivity disputed complaints of declining powers. Between June and December 1888, he composed the Fifth Symphony and the *Hamlet* Overture (both in some three weeks in June), refurbished his house, arranged future concerts, prepared a production of *Evgeniy Onegin* in Prague, maintained good relations with the imperials, tended the Russian Musical Society in Moscow, worked with Marius Petipa on *The Sleeping Beauty,* and, not least, dealt once again with Antonina. He rejected all opera proposals before Détroyat's *The Enamored Courtesan* (or *Sadia*) in August. He was taken by Vsevolozhsky's proposal for a ballet on Charles Perrault's "La belle au bois dormant," praising it as "enchanting beyond all description" [xiv 509].

The drain on Tchaikovsky's finances from the conducting tour was crippling when added to his customary mishandling of money and the expense of a new house. On 4 June he admitted to Meck that she might wonder how he could be short of money with her stipend, the emperor's pension, and receipts from his labors and "other sources." But it was true, exacerbated by the absence of revenues from *The Enchantress.* If his October allowance from her were sent now, he could, as he put it in his next letter, "get down to work for himself, not others" [xiv 448, 452] and install a hearth in his house to warm and dry it out, relieving the illness that had returned during the summer. She sent the money, but on 22 August, he wrote again: "You cannot imagine, my dear, kind friend, the agonizing shame and displeasure with myself taking up this letter. For I am again turning to you for financial help! It strikes me you must be rather angry with my endless extravagance, my childish inability to keep my affairs in order." He asked for another 4,000 rubles and gave his word of honor that it would be the last time [xiv 510–11]. At year's end he wrote again, thanking her effusively and asking her "to forgive me for writing rarely and to believe that until the last minute of my life I shall love and esteem you without limit" [xiv 609–10]. On the day of this letter—26 December 1888—Meck was writing to him, lamenting her inability to correspond due to ill health. Sometimes, she visited Vera's grave, a reference to Tchaikovsky's niece, the second of his nieces to die in as many years. In September, he had also lost one of his oldest friends, Nikolay Hubert.

The sea of life left little time for grief. In June, Yuly Ivanovich Zet from St. Petersburg, a "highly recommended concert agent," inquired of his response to an American offer of $25,000 for a series of concerts. There was talk of other countries and the Paris Exhibition of 1889 [xiv 472–73], but nothing materialized. The first performance of the Fifth Symphony was scheduled for St. Petersburg on 5 November [xiv 506], and *Evgeniy Onegin* was to be staged in Prague. In September, he contributed to the preface of a Czech translation of the opera and indicated his wish to conduct the first performance. On 1 October, he thanked his Petersburg colleagues for assisting with the Czech production [xiv 547–48]. On 27 October, he wrote to Meck:

> The membership [of the Russian Musical Society] has again declined, and this is a very sad phenomenon; every year it is smaller, and the finances of the Conservatory, whose primary support is revenue from concerts, is becoming more critical. . . . After Nikolay Grigorievich [Rubinstein's] death one could have expected our Musical Society to lose all its prestige; but this did not happen, and to the contrary, the number attending concerts even increased—but about 4 years ago it started to go down, and one must think the decline will be progressive. It is frightening for the Conservatory, which might have to close if we cannot think of how to attract the public to our concerts. [xiv 580]

He discoursed with K.R. on aesthetics. On 10 September, the latter wrote of brevity in art, citing Tchaikovsky's *Manfred* as an example of prolixity. The composer answered him in a remarkable letter of 21 September, addressing *remplissage* with a stirring defense of Beethoven:

> But can one say that one encounters *remplissage* in Beethoven? In my opinion, absolutely not. On the contrary, studying him one is astonished to what extent in this giant among all musicians *everything* is equally important, everything is full of significance and power, and additionally at the fact that he was able to contain the improbable pressure of his colossal inspiration and never lose track of equilibrium and finish of form. Even in his late quartets, long considered the work of a man who has lost his wits and was, moreover, deaf, the *Himmlische Längen* seem such [i.e., long] until you study them completely. But ask people especially well acquainted with these quartets, members of a quartet society who perform frequently, if they find anything superfluous in the C-sharp minor quartet. Probably if it isn't some old man brought up on Haydn, he will be horrified if you propose to shorten or omit something. . . . Let someone be found who in the "Eroica" Symphony, unusually long, will find even one superfluous bar, even one little place which could be thrown out as

> *remplissage.* And so, not everything long is long-winded; verbosity is not quite verbiage, and *brevity* is not at all, as Fet says, a condition of absolute beauty of form. The same Beethoven who in the first movement of the "Eroica" Symphony builds a grandiose structure with an endless series of varied, ever newer, astonishing architectonic beauties on the most simple and seemingly meager motif, can sometimes amaze the listener with beauty and concision of form. Don't you recall, Your Highness, the andante of the G major piano concerto[?] I know no greater work of genius than this brief movement and I always pale and chill when I hear it.

If there is prolixity in music (Tchaikovsky continued), it occurs frequently in music after Beethoven, and Brahms is Beethoven's caricature because his music lacks content. Wagner may be a genius, but when he carries forward Beethoven's spirit, he is simply overreaching:

> As for your most humble servant, all his life he has suffered from the awareness of his inability *in form* in general. I have struggled much with this limiting defect and can with a certain pride say that I have achieved significant results, but I shall die without having written anything *perfect* as regards form. *Remplissage* by me is endless; *la ficelle* is always noticeable in a bad way for the experienced eye, and one can do nothing about it. As for "Manfred," without the least wish to appear modest I shall say that it is a repulsive work that I hate profoundly, *with the exception only of the first movement* . . . , and out of a large symphony, utterly impossible in length, I shall make a *Symphonische Dichtung*. . . . I do not presume to be angry at Your Highness's observation about "Manfred." You are completely correct and even too kind. [xiv 541–43]

After many years of aphoristic remarks about Beethoven, some damning, some admiring, this apostrophe puts Tchaikovsky's appreciation of the German master in perspective.

The composer's schedule made this the worst time for Antonina to reenter his life. Yet she did, in October, with a hyperbole of woe: ill for three years, she had recently endured a serious operation, been swindled out of her modest inheritance, and would seek employment but for the lack of connections and patronage. Her common-law husband was about to die, and she asked Pyotr to increase her subsidy: "God has given you exceptional genius, which makes it possible for you to do much—but God has given me no talent. Besides your subsidy I have nothing. I have come to the point that I do not have a decent dress to be seen anywhere" [365, 238–39]. He increased her subsidy as of 1 November; her husband died four days later.

On that day, Tchaikovsky conducted the first performance of the Fifth Symphony in St. Petersburg. When he was made an "honored member" of the St. Petersburg Philharmonic Society afterward, "applause was transformed into cries of delight, and even shouts of 'Hurrah!'" [SV881108]. Reviewers favored the first two movements. "Especially fine was the first," Solovyov declared, "constructed with a great understanding of form. . . . As regards originality, the first movement . . . leaves the finale far behind" [NO881107]. The next week, Tchaikovsky conducted it again, together with the Overture to *Hamlet.* Of the latter, a critic insightfully explained:

> *Hamlet* is a difficult assignment for a musician, for the philosophical basis of Shakespeare's tragedy does not lend itself to music. How in fact does one illustrate in sounds the doubts consuming Hamlet, his lack of character? Willy-nilly one must either set secondary episodes of the tragedy or give something quite ill-defined, elusive of the central concept. [NV881115]

Six days later, Tchaikovsky conducted the Fifth Symphony in Prague: "I concluded that this symphony is unsuccessful. There is something repulsive about it; some excess of motleyness and insincerity, artificiality" [xiv 600]. Of *Onegin,* which he conducted on 24 November/6 December at the National Theater: "The performance was very fine, and especially the singer of the role of Tatyana [Berta Foerster-Lautererova] I liked very much" [xiv 594]. He brought the Fifth to Moscow on 10 and 11 December, and complained about it again [xiv 610]. On 18 December, he attended a meeting about *The Sleeping Beauty* and received Petipa's instructions for acts I and II. By 26 December, he was back in Frolovskoe, where, in his absence, Jurgenson had arranged with Alyosha to present him with a Christmas gift—the complete Mozart in the Breitkopf and Härtel edition. He was delighted.

As 1888 ended, Tchaikovsky looked forward to another winter of conducting, followed in the summer by composition and a busy autumn. Henceforth, he would compose while traveling, navigating the sea of life with confidence and tranquility. He grudgingly assented to *Sadia,* embarking upon a long and contentious correspondence with its librettists [230, 239–58; 6, 104–7, 114–24], at the same time that he enthusiastically accepted

The Sleeping Beauty. Responding to Vsevolozhsky's scenario, he wrote: "For some time I have been feeling a striving for topics *not of this world,* ones where they don't cook jam, hang people, dance mazurkas, get drunk, forward petitions, etc. etc." [xiv 505]. This distinction must have occurred to him at Frolovskoe in the early winter, when he began work on the ballet, the piece he would be composing on the road.

CHAPTER EIGHTEEN

The Music of 1885–1888

Tchaikovsky revised *Vakula the Smith into Cherevichki* (the Fancy Slippers) [tr. 383, 72–120] between 3/15 December 1884 and 22 March 1885. Like his earlier operas, *Vakula* had upset him as soon as he saw it. In October 1878, he wrote to Meck, wishing he would "better restrain my purely musical inspiration and forget less the conditions of *theatricality and decorativeness* inherent in the opera style. . . . I very acutely recognize all the opera's defects, which, alas, are uncorrectable" [vii 440]. By the time he changed his mind, *Mazepa* had failed, and a new *Vakula* may have been Tchaikovsky's rebound from that failure.

The story was unchanged from *Vakula* to *Cherevichki*. The principal revisions were lightening the orchestration and simplifying the harmony, improving the vocal melodies [cf. CW 35, 333–420], and writing new numbers—the duet of Oxana and Vakula in the final scene of act I, the Schoolteacher's Song and quintet of act II, an interpolated arioso for Vakula at the end of the Rusalka Scene (to words by Nikolay Chaev, this was composed only at the end of 1886), and couplets for His Excellency in act III (cf. CW 35, 412–13). Of the 3,945 bars of *Vakula,* Tchaikovsky cut more than 500 and composed 934 anew (CW 7a, xii). He sent the revised libretto to Jurgenson, instructing that his own words be printed in cursive, which was made so in the print of *Cherevichki* that passed the censor on 14 June 1885. That libretto was the basis for additional changes in the autograph score (which retained 411 pages of *Vakula* [CW 35, xvii]) and reduction, Tchaikovsky's conducting score (see CW 7 supplements),

Jurgenson's piano-vocal prints of 1885 and 1901, and the full score, with a Moscow censor's date of 28 March 1898. Changes of detail comprised an overhaul of the rubrics, elaborations of the devil and Solokha's dance-song and Oxana's confession in act I, the quintet, the caroling chorus and Vakula's aria near the end of act II, and new wording in the final ensemble.

In seven performances between 19 January 1887 and 6 March 1888, *Cherevichki* brought the same response as *Vakula:*

> Tchaikovsky responds intelligently and sensibly to the story of *Cherevichki,* putting much talent, knowledge and mastery into it . . . but . . . neither Polonsky nor Tchaikovsky is adept at comedy; they do not yield to it; more often one hears violence and artificiality in their humor; it often passes unnoticed in their work for the unwilled, at times prominent notes of grief and meditation; neither can laugh for very long. . . . In a word, *Cherevichki* is . . . a *comic opera in the minor.* [quoted in D&Y 402]

To Laroche, Tchaikovsky excelled in the ethnic and fantastic, and *Cherevichki* stood "at a very lofty height," but luxurious orchestration blunted the sharp Gogolesque wit and made it counter-comedic. The more pointed Tchaikovsky's witticism, the stronger the sense that it was exceptional: "in this mass of complex, ingenious, 'learned,' not rarely sad and somber music, sewn onto a capricious, merry Gogolesque canvas, perhaps lies the work's principal defect, developed with obvious zeal and love and which charms us at every step as witness to the brightest and most noble talent" [252 II 128–29; see also 383, 244–47].

Tchaikovsky's promise to the tsar to compose for the church (above, p. 288) raises the possibility that the style in the *9 Sacred Music Compositions* (1884–1885 [tr. 391, 315–82]) results from exalted advocacy. In them, he proceeds, often after some annunciatory gesture, to distinctive, thick textures in which the outer voices move faster than the inner ones and roughly in contrary motion (e.g., no. 7, 12–15, 27–37). This "Russian counterpoint" virtually excludes the possibility of elaborate imitation—the word "Alleluia" being a possible exception—just as strophic organization precludes any pointed response to particular meanings of words. Some of the pieces are marked by irregular periodicity (the structural strophe of the second cherubic hymn, for example, comprising 4 + 7 + 13 bars with hints of imitation) and voice pairing to vary the texture and to highlight words (such as "mystically," also in the second cherubic hymn). As regards scale, they are mostly diatonic and triadic, but not to the exclusion of dominant seventh chords.

A setting of the Lord's Prayer in no. 6 is exceptional for its frequent tonicization and imitation. As the phrase "Who art in heaven" unfolds, the upper voice climbs to a high point while the two lower voices engage in imitation—a graphic analogy. The imitation on "Give us this day our daily bread" suggests that each entry is a supplicant. Striking is the descending sequence with which Tchaikovsky progresses toward tranquility from "Forgive us our debts" to "Deliver us from the evil one."

On 7 March 1885, Tchaikovsky wrote the *Gimn v chest' Sv. Kirilla i Mefodiya* (Hymn in Honor of Saints Cyril and Methodius [tr. 391, 412]). His own translation of a Czech text, the hymn is "in four voices, suitable also for one voice" [xiii 37, n. 2], namely the uppermost, which carries the melody. Set in Western hymn style to phrases of ancient Slavic songs [xiii 37, n. 4; CW 63, 278], each of the two verses divides melodically as AABA′ and is inflected with shadings of dynamic and key appropriate to meaning.

When composing *Manfred,* a symphony in four *tableaux* after the dramatic poem by Byron, op. 58 (April–September 1885), Tchaikovsky revised Balakirev's program except for mvt. 2, "The Alpine fairy, appearing to Manfred in the rainbow from the spray of a waterfall." The other movements are as follows [22, 75–76; Eulenburg Miniature Scores, no. 500]:

Movement I

Balakirev/Stasov

Manfred is wandering in the Alps. His life is shattered, importunate questions remain without answers; nothing remains of his life except reminiscences. The image of the ideal Astarte rushes through his thoughts, and he calls out to her in vain. Only the echo of the crags repeats her name. Memories and thoughts consume and gnaw at him. He seeks and begs for oblivion, which no one can give him.

Tchaikovsky

Manfred is wandering in the Alps. Wearied by fateful questions of existence, tormented by the burning melancholy of hopelessness and the memory of his criminal past, he is experiencing spiritual torments. Manfred is deeply imbued with the secrets of magic and imperiously in communication with the mighty powers of the netherworld, but neither these nor anything on earth can bring *oblivion,* which is the only thing he seeks and

Balakirev / Stasov	*Tchaikovsky*
	begs for in vain. Memories of Astarte, who has perished and whom he once loved passionately, consume and gnaw at his heart, and there is no limit or end to Manfred's despair.

Movement III

The way of life of Alpine huntsmen, full of simplicity, geniality, and patriarchal mores. Manfred clashes with this way of life, forming a stark contrast.	Scene of the simple, meager, free life of the inhabitants of the mountains.

Movement IV

A wild, unbridled Allegro, representing the halls of Ariman (hell), where Manfred has made his way, seeking a meeting with Astarte. The *calling* and *appearance* of Astarte will represent a contrast to this hellish orgy. . . . The music must be light, transparent as air, ideal, and real. Further on, the pandemonium again, and then Manfred's sunset and death.	The subterranean halls of Ariman. A hellish orgy. Manfred's appearance in the middle of the bacchanal. Calls and the appearance of Astarte's shade. He is forgiven. [From the French at this point: She predicts the end of his earthly trials.] Manfred's death.

In the first movement, the music fits the program perfectly: Manfred wandering in the Alps, etc. (bars 1–79), deeply imbued with the secrets of magic, etc. (80–110); . . . he seeks and begs for oblivion in vain (111–70); memories of Astarte (171–288); . . . Manfred's despair (289–338). After vignette appearances of the motto in the middle movements, the finale conforms to the program: the bacchanal (1–160); Manfred's appearance (161–205) and the resumption of pandemonium (206–65); the invocation and appearance of Astarte (mvt. I recall, 266–393); and Manfred's death (394–491).

The motto theme, with its climbing melodic phrases against the downward movement of the bass, nicely conveys the tension between Manfred's aspirations and his despair. The tonic-evasive Astarte music conveys her inaccessibility through death, a detail new to Tchaikovsky's program which justifies the violent reprise of the Manfred theme in response (mvt. I at 289). In the second movement, the realm of the Alpine Fairy is presented in athematic, ephemeral ideas, recalling Balakirev's exhortation to Tchaikovsky to write an instrumental scherzo in the manner of *Queen Mab* [22, 69]. (A nod to Balakirev's own style comes at 220 in the elaboration of the Alpine Fairy's song.) After creating a fine lyric movement, Tchaikovsky wrote the finale outward from the fugue, a paradoxical approach in a program focused on pandemonium. He objected that the program suited "a symphonist disposed to imitate Berlioz" [xi 280], surely aware of the Berliozian referents in his finale: the bacchanal to the witches' sabbath (or to the "Orgie de Brigands" in *Harold*), the fugue to the witches' round dance, and the *Dies irae* (the bass of *Manfred* at 472).

Avoiding formal paradigms in *Manfred,* Tchaikovsky used strophic structures and literal repetition to shape the music. In movement I, the discursive introduction effects a bridge to the *più mosso* (at 80), an upbeat to a first key area in B minor. But the Allegro no sooner begins than stops 30 bars later, having moved to E minor. A tentative re-beginning at *moderato con moto* (111) prepares for the Astarte theme (171), which leads to a return of the Manfred theme, strongly in B minor, and the movement ends. There is no paradigm. The middle movements are tripartite reprise patterns with unpredictable interiors. The Trio of the Alpine Fairy's song is in two strains, the first giving the tune six times, the second but once; the motto returns (at 250) as this asymmetry is playing out. In the Pastorale, Tchaikovsky quotes selectively from the first section in the second, and from the second in the third. At the end of the second, he states the motto and extends it with a tolling bell (163–81). The furtive horn melody that follows (from 37) echoes the horn melody in movement I (at 120). The finale moves to A minor before rushing into a second theme (81–140), cadencing in E minor, followed by a reprise of the motto (161–205). After this, the fugue (206–65) ends with two statements of the motto (266–302), reminiscences of movement I, and a restatement of the motto (394–447) parallel to movement I at 289. These produce a form-giving symmetry with movement I to end the symphony, but Tchaikovsky moves instead to the transfiguration music, *tutti* with organ (448–77), and a quiet final cadence.

Through-composed in effect, *Manfred* relies on contrast and repetition for coherence. Tchaikovsky asks much of a listener to hear such a complex piece solely in the aggregate of local devices, though he embraces the whole in a rational key scheme. It is based on the familiar association of E minor with *fatum,* prominent in *Evgeniy Onegin* and *Francesca da Rimini* (the sketch for Astarte's theme in one of his notebooks is headed, after Dante, "Nessun maggior dolor[e] . . . "), and the linkage of B minor with death. In movement I, these associations vie for precedence in establishing the home key. The prominence of C major (the Neapolitan of B minor) at the climax of the Astarte theme, the transformation of the motto at the end of movement I (302–4), the return of the motto in the Trio of movement II and at the climax of movement IV with organ—all seem consistent with Astarte's transformative power in relation to Manfred's death. Importance attaches to the scheme of the whole:

I			II	III	IV
e b	e–D . . .	b . . .	b–D–b	G	b
Intro	Allegro	Reprise			

The interaction of the keys, especially E minor and B minor, and between them and D major, will inform the structure of later music:

Pezzo capriccioso

e D	b–D . . . b . . .
Intro	Allegro

Fifth Symphony

I		II	III	IV	
e	e – D e	(b) – D – – D	A	E	e D e E
Intro	Allegro			Intro	Allegro

Sixth Symphony

I	II	III	IV
e b – D b	D b D	G	b
Intro Allegro Recap			

Tchaikovsky spoke harshly of *Manfred,* which is gratuitously extended and artificially energized, as if a formidable technique were vying with an indifferent muse. All the same, he seems to have identified deeply with its music, marking in its keys associations that will inform the capital works of his late period.

In the autumn of 1885, Tchaikovsky wrote two pieces for the 50th anniversary of the founding of the School of Jurisprudence, the Jurists' Song and the Jurists' March. The song is a 46-bar chorus (soprano, alto, tenor, bass) in familiar style, "which the students should sing at the celebration" [xiii 160]. The text is Tchaikovsky's and is set without artifice in two parallel strophes:

The pure flame of bright truth
That man kept in his soul
Until the very end who laid
The first stone of our school.
Like a father, with affectionate care
He did not spare his labors and his
  strength.
Out of us trustworthy sons
He formed for the homeland.

Jurist! How he, high aloft
Holds the banner of truth.
For his native land,
Vigilant foe of every falsehood . . .
And, striving for good with the times,
Remember the testament of school days:
Citizen and man
The jurist was and ever shall be.

Tchaikovsky had agreed in May 1885 to write a celebratory cantata on a text by Apukhtin, which was received in July. He soon opted for the chorus to his own text [96, 354–55]. Choral parts and score for the Jurists' Song were published by Markova in St. Petersburg in 1885.

He began the Jurists' March, also called the Jurisprudence March, on 27 October 1885 and dated the manuscript on 5 November [CW 26, xii–xiii]. Its premiere was a month later at the St. Petersburg Noble Assembly. With doubled winds, expanded brass, and percussion, including triangle, military and large drum, two harps, and strings—it has a certain swagger. It opens theatrically, with fanfares over a dominant, leading to a main theme that catches the ear by avoiding tonic emphasis in the chord progression. An unmarked Trio begins at 59, with contrasts in every respect, before the reprise of the theatrical introduction (at 90), an abbreviated statement of the main theme (101–14), and an expansive coda (115–39).

Early in 1886, as he had 19 years before, Tchaikovsky responded to a request for incidental music from Ostrovsky, now a new monologue for the second edition of *A Dream on the Volga*. The result was Domovoy's monologue from Ostrovsky's *Voevoda,* composed 13–17 January. This wordless music comprises 45 bars with an optional 14-bar repeat. Ostrovsky requested the sounds of night and Tchaikovsky complied. With muted strings throughout, the music begins and ends with tremolos, between which a four-bar melody is gently expounded with occasional harp flourishes. The music was apparently used only once, on 19 January 1886.

His first extended work of the new year was the *Dumka,* or "Little Reverie," op. 59 (15–21 February 1886), which was issued by Jurgenson although written in response to Felix Mackar's request for something to be published in France. A bravura salon piece in the manner of Tchaikovsky's opp. 7 and 8 with a descriptive subtitle, *Scène rustique russe,* it is a collage of five folkish themes, often in changing background variation but deployed asymmetrically with improvisatory flourishes. The stately opening promises a work of considerable extent and is followed after one variation with a second theme of only four bars, given four times, and a third theme of but two bars, given eight times. One suspects a game with proportions when a fourth theme of two bars passes to a near-Lisztian cadenza. The third theme receives four more variations interspersed with yet another new theme before the Adagio returns for the restatement of the opening cantabile.

In the spring of 1886, Konstantin Romanov told Tchaikovsky that the empress would like the dedication of a piece of his, even a single song [xiii 438]. In response, Tchaikovsky wrote the *Twelve Romances,* op. 60, between 19 August and 8 September, although the dedication to the empress was suppressed in Soviet editions. He and K.R. soon began a lively dialogue about poetry and music centered on Afanasy Fet, whose words were chosen for no. 2.

In no. 1, Khomyakov's "Last Night" apostrophizes nature, love, and friendship, tempered by a thought from the singer's childhood at the end: "Life would be better there, at that starlit height!" The piano announces the melody, a rising line dropping quietly to a cadence with the merest hint of sadness (in the F-flat in bar 1). The voice mimics it, then inflects the description of the nightscape with tessitura or hushed phrases of wonderment, though a minor coloration (17–20) stays the lavish imagery from transport. The last line, almost recitative, slows the momentum and elides with the postlude, which repeats the opening hint of sadness.

In "I'll tell you nothing," the singer is withholding something, perhaps something alarming. Still, nothing will be said. The ambiguity of the spoken versus the unspoken lies at the heart of both poem and music in the number of bars without words (30 of 67); the casual, almost detached vocal lines in relation to meaning (such as "I tremble"—nondirectional chords leading to a fermata); lines which do not close with the harmony; and the wordless cadence figure for "what I silently repeat." Perfection in the piano seconds distraction in the voice.

No. 3, "O, if only you knew," is a hyperbole: to ease the singer's misery, the beloved might pass by, look in the window, rest in the doorway, even come inside. Each verse runs from ebullient to sad, operatically: the grand melodic arch at the beginning and its more anguished continuation, ending with a fermata, is close enough to strophic to accumulate impact through the verses but different enough to convey the change from the singer's solitude to an expression of love by volume, tessitura, and the impatient crowding of phrases.

As Karadži's "Nightingale" has three songs, the singer in no. 4 has three worries: whether young men marry early, a tired horse, and that evil people keep him from his beloved. He wants a grave near the flowers and brook, where girls will weave garlands and old folks will draw water. Tchaikovsky merges clichés of folk song with conceits of art song. The first is responsible for the chirping and the *barform* of the opening verses; the second for the volume and tessitura of the extended line about evil people, the dense chromatic reharmonization of the opening line at the Andante, and the new melody at the close, near the top of the singer's range.

"Simple Words" joins a salon waltz to Tchaikovsky's own hyperbole. "God has not given me the gift of song," he asserts, "so I speak in simple words." Apostrophes to the beloved alternate with labored, distantly Hellenic praise, all to waltz music no less trite than the words. The second strain, beginning with the third verse of text, is a quotation and marked *a piena voce,* as if to signify something familiar.

In "Frenzied Nights" (no. 6), Apukhtin's singer is fixated on the beloved, whose whisper drives out the sounds of day and kills his sleep. Tchaikovsky's version of the frenzy is deadening—hypnotic, slow music with animated texture on incoherent talk; short phrases for the flickering fire; rising arpeggios for the grasp of time's merciless hand; quiet figuration in sixteenth notes for the stealthy whisper. He frames the image of the last verse—the drowning whisper—in a steady crescendo, culminating in dissonance and the voice's highest, loudest notes.

Polonsky's "A Gypsy Song" in no. 7 tells of how a girl will bid her lover farewell by the bridge tomorrow. Will someone else soon love her, or him? The campfire is dying down. Tchaikovsky centers the song around the opening strain, anticipated in the piano sounding as a guitar. He responds to Gypsy clichés with seductive repetitions of cadence and vocal strains based on the opening, alternating with more earnest emotions in less characteristic music. Her swagger lapses at the thought of a rival (at 48)—her voice falters, her tessitura drops as she regains composure—before the Gypsy patina returns. Does the swagger shield a broken heart?

Nekrasov's "Forgive" urges that ill feelings yield to remembrance of the love felt when "we were completing our journey." Tchaikovsky marks this by distinguishing a near-diatonic vocal part (five chromatic pitches in the song) from a discordant accompaniment (four occurrences of the tonic triad before the vocal cadence). The first verse sweeps along with a *Tristan*-like rising chromatic figure in the voice; after a pause, the appeal to brighter memory subdues the accompaniment, while the voice, invoking a blessing, gradually falls, leaving a long peroration for the piano.

In "Night" (no. 9), Polonsky disowns the ravishing night, to which Tchaikovsky responds in a somber reverie. In the first verse, the piano periodically echoes the voice, but in the second, as the singer questions the night, he becomes more rhetorical and insistent, and the sense of flow and reverie is lost. Tchaikovsky persists thus in the second half with strumming chords, as if to suggest the singer's heightened awareness of his disquiet, and his ever-intensifying declamation is relaxed only in the dreamy postlude, "Because, perhaps, my peace is far away."

Polonsky's "Behind the window in the shadows" is, like no. 5, a jolly song. A tryst results when the beloved is found awake; the lovers will escape by disguise and cleverness. Ranging between impish delivery—for stealth and impudence—and gentler lyricism with hints of feeling, Tchaikovsky makes his point with timing, deftness, playful mimicry, and a folkish tinge.

Khomyakov's "The heroic deed" (no. 11) declares at the outset that patience, love, and prayer are more valuable than heroic deeds in battle, which Tchaikovsky expresses at the beginning and end by spinning out the piano's strained opening motif. The homily-like middle verses, about human sorrow and the power of heroic deeds to rise above malice and the hue and cry, are fashioned into parallel strophes that achieve a Wolf-like intensity, with muscular bass movement and sequential, thickly textured, and dissonant chords, before tapering off to the framing verse.

Pleshcheyev's "The mild stars shone for us" recalls a beautiful night and queries where it has gone and when the singer will forget it. The first two verses indulge in sweet remembrance, the piano inflecting and highlighting the voice, before the singer asks in anger where the ravishing images have fled. But the *agitato* yields again to the calm of the opening as the singer again surrenders to memory, half sad, ever seductive, his reality overcome.

Tchaikovsky's only original opera of this period, *The Enchantress,* occupied him from September 1885 to May 1887. The following scenario is summarized from the 1887 libretto:

Act I. Pastimes at the wayside inn of the young widow Nastasya, or "Kuma" (Godmother). Balakin, a guest, warns that officials see what happens here as immoral. Kuma enters, clever and worldly but kind and welcoming; then Lukash, a flirt, and Kichiga, a scrapper, take their turns in song. Prince Yury stops with his hunting party; he accepts the crowd's greetings while Kuma, standing apart, reveals her love for him. After his departure, Yury's father, the governor-general Prince Nikita, arrives with his clerk Mamïrov; the crowd fears punishment, but Kuma nullifies Mamïrov's effort to rouse Nikita's indignation, defends the reputation of her inn, and denies practicing magic. Nikita accepts wine and converses; the crowd is incredulous as he thanks Kuma with a present of his gold ring. He consents, finally, to watch the dancing of the *skomorokhi* (vagrant entertainers). Kuma suggests that the righteous Mamïrov might join them, which Nikita commands, to the clerk's humiliation. Nikita falls in love.

Act II. Mamïrov informs the Princess that her husband has taken up with Kuma and proposes that Kuma die. Yury enters and queries his mother's distress; the Princess admits nothing. Mamïrov orders the vagabond priest Paisy to spy on Kuma, then ponders revenge for being made to dance. Nikita enters and dismisses him. He is distraught over his wife's gloominess, but also that his heart is drawn to Kuma. The Princess confronts him; he dissembles. She threatens to denounce Kuma to the Father Superior; he counterthreatens a cloister for her. In a commotion outside, the townspeople pursue one of Nikita's huntsmen. Trying to calm them, Mamïrov is rebuffed, and Yury intervenes. Prince Nikita is not at hand, and when they learn that he is visiting Kuma, Yury understands his mother's distress. Yury vows to kill Kuma.

Act III. In Kuma's chambers the moody Nikita admits to loving her, but she hints at a rival. He presses his suit; she threatens to kill herself; and Nikita, furious, leaves. Kuma learns that Yury has sworn to kill her for enchanting his father. She feigns sleep as he enters with Juran, his chief huntsman; she protests her innocence, explains the situation with Nikita, and begs Yury to believe her. He claims to; Kuma confesses her love; he resists and tries to leave. She urges him to stay; he reconsiders and admits that she has conquered his heart. A love duet.

Act IV. In a gloomy forest near the river, the sorcerer Kudmá watches the approach of Yury's hunt. The Princess knows from Paisy that Yury and Kuma are in love and plan to flee. And Nikita is pursuing them. The huntsmen exit. Yury thanks Juran for preparing their escape; Kuma is nearby. Juran counsels him not to go, but Yury affirms his love and notes the danger of staying. Kudmá sells the Princess poison. After Kuma bids farewell to her friends, the Princess, disguised as a pilgrim, persuades Kuma to drink some poisoned water, then withdraws. Yury arrives; he asks about strangers; Kuma is describing the pilgrim as the Princess returns. Yury accuses his mother of murder as Kuma dies. The Princess orders Kuma buried in the river. Yury rushes to the river bank, where he learns of Nikita's pursuit. Yury tells him of Kuma's death, and Nikita kills him in a rage. The Princess reproaches him. A storm rises. She is led away. For a moment, Nikita knows that he faces eternal torment, but as the storm increases he sees visions, hears voices, and senses blood everywhere. Kudmá curses him for murdering his son. Nikita takes him for a demon, sees a vision of hell, and falls in a faint.

On 23 February 1887, eight months before the first performance, censors in Moscow approved a piano-vocal score and a libretto of *The Enchantress.* The words of these sources do not match. To all appearances, the libretto represents Shpazhinsky's text before production changes. Otherwise, its publication is inexplicable, though it remained the only separate edition of the libretto before 1901 [375, 439]. In the piano-vocal score, issued by Jurgenson in April 1887, the biggest change was the introduction of a *décimet,* a 10-part ensemble in response to the Prince's gift to Kuma of his ring. In the libretto, Mamïrov declares that Kuma has "wound her diabolical net" around the Prince, a thought echoed by Kuma's friends; in the *décimet,* he rails, but less intensely; Kuma's friends say nothing of her wiles; and the others call the Prince's ring "an exquisite gift of kindness." Kuma is thus less boldly an enchantress, and passion has faded as the centerpiece of the drama [151, 148–50]. Various cuts include nine lines from the Princess's arioso in act II where she compares the blessedness of morning with the darkness in her heart and sings of her justification for killing

Kuma, who "lived for evil, and by evil." The love duet was shortened. Tchaikovsky then made additional changes in response to singers' complaints. By September, the February version had been superseded; a new edition, incorporating these changes and those made in rehearsal, was published in 1901 in score (passed by the Moscow censor on 2 February) and piano-vocal arrangement. The Yury-Princess duet in act II was recast, the love duet trimmed, and short scenes in act IV omitted.

The Enchantress is Tchaikovsky's wordiest libretto, the sheer volume of text precluding concision and inhibiting dramatic effect. It is his only opera of which the editors of the *Collected Works* printed the libretto separately from the music, assuring readers that it was what Tchaikovsky set. It lacks operatic simplicity, a virtue which ran against the grain with Shpazhinsky, whose surfeit of folk, archaic, and colloquial expressions, unconventional grammar, missing parts of speech, and contorted word order made the text difficult to project on the lyric stage. Its genre, moreover, was ambiguous. Was *The Enchantress* a folkish opera, in which "the people" were a protagonist, or was it a drama of passion? Shpazhinsky's words enhanced the folkish moments but obscured the plain language of a lover's confession. Genre ambiguity, in turn, confused the perception of the characters as literal or metaphorical. Much about *The Enchantress* is unexplained or illogical, including the moral outrage over Kuma's tavern, Mamïrov's idiosyncratic rectitude, and what brought Nikita and his wife to an unhappy state. At the same time, the characters lack the symbolic attributes typical of a parable. Nikita in particular lacks character: hating vice in act I, then joining in the fun; wondering why his wife is unhappy in act II, then making failed advances to Kuma in act III; wreaking havoc in act IV as he goes mad. The lovers are not much better off. The Kuma-Yury scene calls for an instant shift from murderous to passionate in Yury, who theretofore (recalling Joan) had not shown any interest in romance at all. The audience must negotiate a thicket of words and unusual behavior in the characters just to learn that love cannot surmount hatred and does not conquer in the end.

Tchaikovsky did what he could. By 1887 his handling of the Russian folk manner was peerless—in the choruses of act I and, more subtly, among the principals when Kuma tenderly admits that she loves Yury (no. 17, at bar 282) or Yury responds to Kuma's death in the moments before Prince Nikita arrives (no. 23, 106). Kuma's apostrophe to the rivers and the countryside (no. 4, 49) begins with the folkish melody stated at the outset of the opera, then alternates with a winning, anthem-like melody. This list could be extended [400, 201–14]. Occasionally, his inspiration flagged, as in the lyric-sentimental, overly long love duet, which lacks expressive power [PL871023], or in Kudmá's comic song in act IV, which slows the pace and blunts nothing of the horror to follow. Sometimes he miscalculated, as in the Prince's confession to Kuma in act III (no. 15, 120). Here Nikita protests his love for a younger woman in the manner of a romance [NO871023]:

Ex. 48

The parallel with Prince Gremin in *Evgeniy Onegin* is clear enough, but falters in light of Nikita's situation and emotional instability: the song is too glib for a tyrant.

Tchaikovsky's muse lapsed with faults in the libretto. The first sustained lyric outpouring, in the Yury-Princess duet in act II, is musically rich if overheated for an exchange between the hero and his mother. Yet in the next act, with Kuma and Yury's coming together, Tchaikovsky's abbreviations curtail the very breadth of expression needed to overcome the emotional contrivance of the situation; on the other hand, the labyrinthine preparatory conversation before the lovers pour out their feelings, which is set in recitative with diminished emotional warmth, is prolix.

For Tchaikovsky in 1887 to engage such liabilities revisits the question: was he pressing opera in a new direction, combining "the people's element" with Wagnerian declamation, reconciling a Russian story with the mainstream? The story echoes *Tristan* in Mamïrov's likeness to Melot, the effect of illicit love on succession, the impressionistic use of the hunt, even the lovers coming together in death, but not in the halfhearted lovers themselves. It also contains motifs of Tchaikovsky's beloved *Carmen,* in that Kuma, like Bizet's Gypsy, lives in a vivid ethnic setting and dies in an attempt to free herself from the exploitation of her shadowed life. Or was *The Enchantress* an outright experiment, moving beyond the mainstream? This possibility resides in the tension between realism and stylization. The libretto uses archaic language, contorts everyday logic, suppresses background, and includes the Princess's Snow White–like poisoning episode—all of which point toward stylization beneath the realism which first meets the senses. *The Enchantress* may be more evidence of a new Tchaikovsky.

On 18 February 1887, Tchaikovsky composed *Angel vopiyashe* (The angel cried out) [tr. 391, 393], on a text from the Divine Liturgy in Paschaltide. Commissioned by the Russian Choral Society in Moscow, it is filled with enthusiastic text repetition in support of rejoicing, praise, and exultation. After three variants of the same phrase, Tchaikovsky marks the fourth with a dissonance, G against F-sharp, on "*Your* Son has arisen [in] *three days*" and bursts into counterpoint at reference to the dead rising up. He set "Shine, new Jerusalem" with a point of imitation, moving again to familiar style at the exhortation for Zion to exult and dropping to *pianississimo* for "Be Thee radiant." The dynamic swells to *fortissimo* on "resurrection of Your Son!"

Although he pondered a suite from Mozart in May 1884, anticipating the centenary of *Don Giovanni* in 1887 [xiii 221], Tchaikovsky selected the pieces for *Mozartiana,* or Suite no. 4, op. 61, only in February 1886 and fashioned the work in June–August 1887. He wrote to Jurgenson: "My position as regards *Mozartiana* is very delicate, for how can I receive much money for the fact that Mozart was a genius, and yet on the other hand my labor is worth something" [xiv 243]. On 5 October, he wrote to Jurgenson with a foreword to be printed with the score [xiv 619].

Tchaikovsky set Mozart's Gigue (K. 574)—short, fast, and linear, with its slightly tipsy rhythm and theme—for strings except where bulk was needed before a cadence. In the Minuet (K. 355; K. 576b), with its modern dissonance and lacking a trio, strings predominated again, with discrete doublings in the winds. The immediate origin of the "Preghiera," based on Mozart's ravishing *Ave verum corpus* (K. 618), is ambiguous. According to the score, it is "D'après une transcription de F. Liszt," whose *Collected Works* contain no such source. Tchaikovsky probably used "À la Chapelle Sixtine: Miserere d'Allegri et Ave verum Corpus de Mozart," as he paraphrased Liszt's introduction and took most of his closing, adding eight bars at the end. Otherwise, his "added details of harmony and lightly changed things" [xiv 172] were un-Mozartian. He replaced Mozart's introduction with a somewhat rouged one with winds, horns, and harp, reserving strings for the principal melody. The ensemble took the next phrase *cantabile,* led by the cellos, then reduced to strings and harp for the hushed "Esto nobis." The *divisi* violins at the end, dying away to *pppp,* recall the act I prelude to *Lohengrin.* In the finale, arranging Mozart's variations on a tune known in German as "Unser dummer Pobel meint" from Gluck's *La recontre imprévue* (K. 455), Tchaikovsky emphasized the concertante: obbligato flute in variation 3; exchange of bassoons and *tutti* in variation 4; variation 6 for winds alone; and the violin solo in variation 9, which echoes the Third Suite, mimicking a ballerina's solo. After a clarinet cadenza in variation 10 and an elaborate coda, the duple pulse of the theme returns at the *tempo del comincio.*

Nochevala tuchka zolotaya (The golden cloud has slept; 2–5 July 1887) is the piece Tchaikovsky finished in Borzhom before departing for Aachen to attend Kondratiev:

> A golden cloudlet passed the night
> On the breast of a giant cliff;
> In the morning it set out early on its way,
> Playing merrily about the azure sky.
>
> But a damp trace remained in a crease
> Of the old cliff.

It stands solitary; it has been deep in reverie,
And it weeps silently in the wilderness.

Homophony complements the external objectivity of Lermontov's poem, while understated choral effects add poetic coloration: the crescendo on "cliff" suggests imposing might; the inflection of E-flat on *velikana* ("giant") imparts a sense of awe; setting off the final line with a fermata, a slower tempo and shift to duple meter implies the inexorable, monumental aspect of a cliff in the wild. In the first two lines, flowing, almost conversational movement results from phrases of different lengths. Then, after extensions and elisions, this manner returns in the last two lines to heighten the mystery of "weeps silently in the wilderness."

The *Pezzo capriccioso* for Cello and Orchestra, op. 62 (12–19 August 1887) was, in Tchaikovsky's words, "the sole fruit of my *creative spirit* the whole summer" of 1887 [xiv 202]; it was composed in Aachen. It begins with an introduction in the "wrong" key and an unreprised theme; the A of the ABAB structure comprises song-like themes for the cello arranged asymmetrically in different keys, the first B a nondescript framework for a frenetic solo theme, organized into two asymmetrical strophes. The A reprise introduces a surprise modulation at the end; the abbreviated B reprise—a coda—changes key for the drive to the final cadence. In short, the *Pezzo is* capricious. Tonally, it metaphorizes Nikolay Kondratiev's fatal illness. The principal keys (E minor and B minor) and the secondary ones (D major and C major) are those of *Manfred,* with implications of fate, death, love, and transfiguration. The imperious, tonic-assertive opening melody in the key of *fatum,* the sweet, tonic-evasive principal melody, gently but insistently reprising in B minor, the prominent seventh—E to D in the opening melody, D major to C major in the A reprise, clearly echoing *Manfred* and anticipating the Fifth Symphony, and the sudden, unsettling ending—all speak of death.

After Tchaikovsky asked him to secure the dedication of op. 60, K.R. sent him a book of his own poems, from which the composer selected the *Six Romances,* op. 63, composed in November and December 1887. The songs reflect issues that the two will take up in correspondence: the niceties of expression where music and word merge. Piano introductions are curtailed, and fewer melodic ideas serve more poetic ends. Attention is paid to prosody, poetic foot, enjambment, and the rise and fall of the voice in accordance with spoken intonation. Arguments have been advanced to the effect that opp. 63, 65, and 73—Tchaikovsky's last groups of songs—may be perceived as cycles [262].

"At first I did not love you" is brief and finely nuanced. Not in love, the singer fears the lover's declaration but yields to it; this disperses her fears and revives her heart with sacred fire. Tchaikovsky's symmetrical opening of each couplet expresses the singer's new emotional state. A tonicization in the first verse conveys fright; a longer key change in the second indicates the singer's yielding to love; and a rise in volume and tessitura emphasizes the words "new life."

In no. 2, "I opened the window," the singer whiffs the scent of lilacs, hears a nightingale's song, and recalls the distant homeland. Tchaikovsky catches the moment in the prelude—the singer's breath in the rising line, his kneeling in the descending bass, traversing the great distance in the chord progression that arrives in the tonic just before the voice enters. He begins every couplet except the last with the piano's rising melody, where the thought of the homeland pushes the music to a new key, a faster bass, and "breathless" syncopations before the voice comes to an incomplete cadence, and the piano reprises the introduction to close.

When the beloved finally realizes the singer's unreciprocated adoration in no. 3, "I do not please you," it is too late. Already, dreams resuffered have ceased to caress the heart. The introduction suggests the despair of unanswered love, as does the lament-like repetition of this phrase in the voice, extended with sudden outbursts and unresolved chords until "It will be too late," whereupon it vanishes until the postlude. Those words initiate a chord progression suddenly aimless, while the voice reverts to one pitch (on "springtime flowers") before Tchaikovsky frees it from rhythmic constraints entirely with the *ad libitum*. The singer closes indefinitely, away from the home key, as if searching for it.

"First Meeting" (no. 4) is about the moment, after separation and hardship, when love is inflamed with the prospect of delight. Tchaikovsky summarizes the poem in the introduction, which carries on to inspirit the vocal part. In the third verse, where the emotion is personalized ("our hearts will beat in unison"), the insistent momentum relaxes, with modulations and the merest hint of word painting—*espress*[*ivo*] (at bars 33–34) to suggest the heartbeat. The fourth varies the first with an operatic high note and fermata at the end ("our love will take heart!").

"The fires in the rooms were already out" is a hyperbole of sentimental reminiscence: what has become of the lovers now? Tchaikovsky alternates the opening melody with chromatic forays ("the aroma of the roses," "the radiance of the moon") and hushed parentheses. In the second verse, the lovers engage in "mute conversations more eloquent than words," and he begins to focus on the moment, chord and rhetoric producing tension in reference to thoughts that the singer dares not believe, to be released at the end, "All this the nightingale's song said on our behalf."

The "Serenade" in no. 6 is not to a lover but to a child. Word and philosophy yield to an irresistible gait and a swaggering tune in the manner of a Neapolitan song. The intense third verse departs from the strophe with a new melody and key, invoking a guardian angel to pamper the beloved's virginal sleep and sing a song of paradise whose echo will inspirit.

In *Blazhen, kto ulïbaetsya* (Blessed is he who smiles [tr. 389, 16]), composed on 7 December 1887, Tchaikovsky set K.R.'s words with voice pairing and simple imitation—good-sounding devices in a men's chorus. Eliding phrases produced bursts of energy which override harsh passing references (crown of thorns, harsh destiny, alarm and grief, etc.). Elision gave special power to the unexpected repetition of the second verse: the slowing and quieting on "Who, recalling a cherished goal / With an assured stride" are not an illogical reversal of mood, but an upbeat to the concluding outburst.

For his Parisian concerts in February 1888, Tchaikovsky arranged two earlier works as vehicles for the cellist Anatoly Brandukov. In the *Andante cantabile,* movement II of the First String Quartet, he added double bass to the ensemble, raised the key from B-flat to B major, reducing the notes playable on open strings, and added mutes to all parts. Deferring to the soloist, certain motifs were moved to other parts, and dynamics were changed. Bars 106–13 of the original were omitted. The new version of the "Nocturne," op. 19, no. 4, for cello and orchestra, is also transposed up a semitone, but scored for small orchestra—paired winds and horns and five-part strings. This richer sound resource enabled Tchaikovsky to idealize the original textures for piano by contrasts of *pizzicati* with *arco,* winds with strings, and an elegant reprise (at bar 45) varied by the addition of an obbligato flute.

The preliminary stages of the Symphony no. 5 in E Minor, op. 64 (May–August 1888), are obscure. Sketches for it were sent to Ippolitov-Ivanov but never returned and are considered lost [424, 19]; inchoate jottings could place first thoughts of the work as far back as Tchaikovsky's visit to Aachen in 1887 [426, 86]. His uncertainty over the Fifth, in letters during composition, was reflected in changes marked in the autograph [CW 17a, 223–27]. In Geneva on 24 February/6 March 1889, he referred to a cut in the finale, and three days later in Hamburg to correcting parts [Dnev 227]. Nadezhda Tumanina called the alterations for Hamburg a "final variant" [400, 240], which came five months after Jurgenson published the score. The editors of the *Collected Works* make no reference to this change, and all editions accessible to the present writer follow Jurgenson.

The four movements are linked by a motto theme, which is presented in the introduction to the first; all conform in the large to classical pattern. In movement I, Tchaikovsky approximates a three-key exposition:

Exposition	e	(V/b)	D
Recapitulation	e	(V/C-sharp)	E

The striking, folk-rooted progression from E to D is replicated in the finale and in the keys between movements I and II. Movement II, with its celebrated horn solo, is a tripartite reprise pattern, the first section hinting strongly at the F-sharp minor of the second in its first cadence (bar 16) and at the second strain of the principal melody (24). It also drifts toward the seventh degree, from D major to arrivals in C-sharp minor in the middle section. With dramatic surprise and strident accents, the motto intrudes before the reprise (99) and again, even more emphatically, near the end (158). In the third movement, a gracious waltz also in tripartite reprise, it appears in the closing bars. The finale is a sonata-allegro with introduction and concluding march.

Tchaikovsky placed unifying devices into the motto theme, thought to be a reintonation of a *bïlina,* or Russian folk epic [446, 330]:

Ex. 49

(*continued*)

Ex. 49 *(continued)*

The initial plagal chords return at the opening of the Allegro (thematically, a similar reintonation [446, 331]), are telescoped later in the exposition (84–94), and used in the coda (487–94); they forecast the key relationship of movements III and IV, and return in the finale at the beginning and to move from the development into the recapitulation. The march-like gait implicit in the motto is clarified at the beginning of the Allegro and anticipates the grand march at the end of the symphony. The prominent Phrygian cadence at bars 9–10 is restated emphatically at the end of the introduction, then returns in the waltz (at 20) and at the beginning of the finale.

Other unities of key and chord are scattered throughout the work. First inversion triads occur dramatically in movement I (at 84, 255, 285) and again in the finale, where the Allegro begins over the third of the scale:

Ex. 50

In the interim area of movement I, Tchaikovsky establishes B minor by emphasizing its dominant, especially in pitch (bars 116–27), and avoids a strong tonic cadence. He does this again in the middle of movement II and in the second key area of the finale. He visits distant E-flat minor in the development of movement I (267), the middle of movement II (83), and the development of movement IV (250). In the outer movements, he makes an unusual if inaudible juxtaposition of F-flat major and E major in moments of repose (mvt. I at 244–46, mvt. IV at 266–70). C major is a cadence point in the introduction, accented melodically at the pickup to the Allegro—C when the ear calls instinctively for B, the fifth of the scale.

The Fifth Symphony echoes the Fourth and *Manfred,* in that the outer movements open with a motto, or use the three-key exposition, or highlight plagality, the march, and C major. Indeed, the Fifth may be a reconceived *Manfred* free of an explicit program: the outer movements are less eccentric in pattern, the themes and keys of all movements more diverse and deployed in better balance. Intermovement unities are more deeply seated in the Fifth, offsetting the obviousness of the motto, itself simpler. Tchaikovsky's point-to-point logic is flawless, the succession of ideas perfectly timed to enhance rhetorical effect, ensuring brilliance even in less than pristine execution. The piece speaks to first-time listeners, who can sense a narrative based on expression alone. As if to link the two symphonies, Tchaikovsky left a gentle reminder of *Manfred* (at 151–56) in the finale of the Fifth (at 122–25).

The presence of a motto theme in the Fifth has prompted debate over its meaning [194; 277, 122–34; 342], despite Tchaikovsky's remark to K.R. that he was writing a symphony without a program [xiv 454]. In a sketch dated 15 April 1888, Tchaikovsky in fact jotted down the themes used in the Fifth proximate to sketches for a program for the first movement:

> Introduction: Complete and utter bow before fate, or also before the inscrutable design of Providence
> Allegro: I) Grumbling, doubt, complaint, reproaches to . . . XXX
> II) Can one not throw oneself into the embrace of *faith??*
> A marvelous program, if only it can be executed. [96, 239]

While this is no program and is not much related to the finished work, references to fate and faith resonate with Tchaikovsky's preoccupation with mortality at the time of composition, especially to "thinking about

God, life and death while at Aachen" [Dnev 213]. Given evidence of his appropriating verbal rhythms in earlier music, the similarity of the motto's rhythm with the words of the Paschal troparion, "Christ is risen," may not be idle:

Ex. 51

This reference to the resurrection, the "not of this world" of his praise for *The Sleeping Beauty* (above, p. 311), suggests a meaning for the work. The motto's somber presentation in movement I and triumphant reprise in the finale affirm the darkness-to-victory sense of the outer movements. In between, its extraordinary transformations, which rend the mood in the Western symphonic Andante and *valse,* may assert that aspect of the melody rooted in Russian epic song. Its ebullient appearance in C major in the finale recalls this key in the finale of *Manfred.* Yet one can understand, if the motto's reference were intentional, Tchaikovsky's reluctance to broadcast it. This would have trivialized a lofty thought and risked the same result as his explanation of the Fourth Symphony to Meck. Lest such speculation beguile, it should be recalled that the composer declared the Fifth to be motley, massive, and insincere. Was he acknowledging, as did his friend Ivan Klimenko later, that the mellifluous Andante was partly based on the street cry of a sausage monger? [199, 76–77; the theme appears first at bar 56]. Among works exhibiting the *Manfred* key complex, the Fifth may be the turning point, the "after" to which *Manfred,* the *Pezzo capriccioso,* and even *Hamlet,* with its cursed question, represent the "before."

Tchaikovsky made unambiguous reference to the Fifth in *The Sleeping Beauty* when Aurora rises in a vision from her hundred years' sleep. The possibility that he was also beginning to think about *The Queen of Spades* when he composed the Fifth may explain the links between the symphony and that opera. It is the gateway to his late period. Resuscitated in the concert hall by German conductors after Tchaikovsky's death, the Fifth has since been scorned by German thinkers, including Adorno, for whom the Andante is kitsch, the return of its principal melody "the depraved reflection of that epiphany which is vouchsafed only to the greatest works of art" [3, 43]. Carl Dahlhaus used the same movement to show that the trivial originates through the emphatic representation of the simple, and kitsch through the transfiguration of the trivial [197, 176]. These claims stand apart from the rich implications of the music.

Tchaikovsky had intended to write an Overture on *Hamlet* at least since 1876, the cure at Vichy, his first acquaintance with Kolya Konradi, the Bayreuth Festival, his resolve to marry—and Modest's letter containing a program for it [96, 301]. At that time, he composed *Francesca da Rimini* instead. In 1885, he wrote a melody with the words "To be or not to be" (in English) on a blotter [96, 302]. In his diary for 9 September 1887, he wrote, "Unsuccessful second theme of Hamlet." He did all this before actor Lucien Guitry's request in January 1888 to write an overture if possible, and perhaps some entr'actes, for a gala performance [6, 108–9, 209–10]. When the gala was canceled [96, 302], the composer returned to the *Hamlet* Overture/Fantasia, op. 67, the first performance of which he conducted in St. Petersburg on 12 November 1888.

It is in eight sections followed by a coda:

I (1–82). Elaboration of the opening theme in E, with inflections to F minor and elsewhere

II (83–143). Elaboration of a new dotted theme, in F minor. Agitated, distantly march-like

III (144–95). Comprising an introduction in b (144–62), with solo oboe, and a lyric theme (*moderato con moto,* 163) in D

IV (196–215). Fanfares over a G pedal, returning to the dotted theme from II (208–15)

V (216–59). An abbreviated reprise of II

VI (260–330). An expanded reprise of III, again in two parts, but here a semitone lower

VII (331–58). Reprise of part of II (104–43) that was omitted in V, mixed with theme I

VIII (359–85). Fanfares from IV, now over a firm C pedal (preparing for an F minor tonic)

Coda (386–434). Comprising (1) a dotted theme to dissonant cadence (386–401), and (2) preparation (402–22), based on bars 20–21, and funeral march (423–34), in F minor

The music is ambiguous in relation to the play [but see 211, 147], the composer providing the merest hint with the word "Fortinbras" on a sketch of the fanfares [96, 303]. Apart from this, the themes of *Hamlet* resist association.

The day after scoring *Hamlet,* Tchaikovsky wrote to Jurgenson of his intention to write incidental music for the play, deferring separate publication of the Overture/Fantasia [xiv 563]. For Guitry's farewell benefit in February 1891, he revised the Overture and produced 16 additional numbers. The *Hamlet* for which Tchaikovsky composed was a French adaptation in rhyme by Alexandre Dumas *père* and Paul Meurice, who made cuts, joined scenes, and added dialogue:

> [Act I, scene 2,] is an insipid love scene between Hamlet and Ophelia. Dumas has Hamlet give her a love letter, which much rejoices Ophelia. . . . The passage in II.2 between Hamlet and Ophelia, after the monologue "To be or not to be," is the most misrepresented. . . . In the scene with Ophelia Hamlet does seem mad; at the entrance of the king he does not exit, but rather rushes at him and shakes him by the collar. This is not and could not be in Shakespeare. Probably wishing to introduce a comic element, the French authors have turned Polonius into a complete idiot. [NV910211]

The Entr'actes were borrowed: the "Alla tedesca" of the Third Symphony before act II (no. 5); Kupava's Complaint, no. 10 of *The Snow Maiden,* before act III (no. 7); and the *Elegy in Honor of I. V. Samarin* before act IV (no. 9). To these, Tchaikovsky added fanfares (nos. 2, 5a, 6, and 15), songs—two for Ophelia (nos. 10 and 11), one in act V for Shakespeare's First Clown, redubbed "Gravedigger" (no. 13)—marches (nos. 12, 14, and 16), and melodramas (nos. 1, 3–4, 8). Locating these numbers in the play is problematical (a notated score with cues apparently survives but remains undescribed in print [143, 321]). Guitry wrote to Tchaikovsky with additional instructions on 4 October 1890 and requested changes late in rehearsal [6, 111–12, 212].

The revised Overture uses the same themes as the Overture/Fantasia but with abbreviations and the deletion of various passages. Ophelia's derangement in act IV was reconceived as she wavers between love's sorrow and grief at being orphaned. Tchaikovsky begins no. 10 with a Grétry-like *ariette* in which Ophelia betrays her true state with a declaimed outburst, "A bas! à bas! qu'on le jette à bas"—not in Shakespeare—accompanied by a sudden crescendo. After the dull accompaniment at the beginning of no. 11, she lapses into speech again as another *ariette* sounds in the orchestra. She tries to sing but only half succeeds, drifting back and forth from speech ("I am the bride! Ah! But I no longer truly know what I am seeing") to song ("His coffin, draped in snow, passed by all spread in flowers"). The most curious numbers are the four *mélodrames.* The published score includes neither text nor cues (perhaps because cues based on Dumas and Meurice might have precluded using the music in other versions). Alexander Glumov believes that the melodramas were played during appearances of the ghost of Hamlet's father [143, 319], a claim more reasonable with respect to the first and third, which are short enough to accompany the ghost during a pause in the spoken text, than to the second and fourth, which may have accompanied the ghost's speeches.

Guitry performed *Hamlet* with Tchaikovsky's music three times, the first on 9 February 1891. The music was missed, one reviewer observing that "the audience is little inclined to forgo its custom of talking during entr'actes and treating orchestral numbers played in this theater as a pleasant noise which made it all the more suitable to converse" [MV910219]. In October 1891, parts of Tchaikovsky's music were used in Moscow, to a similar result [MV911021].

Like the Fifth Symphony, the *Hamlet* Overture/Fantasia may have involved some reconception of *Manfred,* both heroes coping with the slings and arrows of outrageous fate, both pieces based on unconventional formal patterns. Among musical similarities are the opening theme (of which he explicitly wanted to avoid a likeness with *Manfred*), an idiosyncratic formal pattern, and an intertextual reference in *Hamlet* (at 363) to the Pastorale in *Manfred* (at 267).

In three weeks before 9 September 1888, Tchaikovsky orchestrated an Overture by Hermann Laroche because Laroche's lack of concentration prevented him from doing so, then conducted the first performance on 5 November at the St. Petersburg Philharmonic Society. Much editorial commentary notwithstanding, this work in D major [CW 59, 60–178] is not the Overture to *Carmosine,* which is in E minor, composed and orchestrated by Laroche and conducted in Moscow in 1868 by Nikolay Rubinstein, in Petersburg by Nápravnik in 1873, and again by Tchaikovsky at his last concert on 16 October 1893 [255 I 7; 352, 120].

After perusing the poetry of Paul Collin in the spring of 1888, Tchaikovsky wrote the *Six mélodies,* op. 65 (summer to 10 October 1888), after his reunion in Berlin that autumn with Désirée Artôt [337, 53] and dedicated them to her. Light and for the most part flirtatious, the poems suggest a residual affection.

Edouard Turquety's "Sérénade" queries whither the newborn breeze of dawn, then directs it to the beloved. The coquettish opening motif—the breeze's sigh—carries the song until the admonition to approach the beloved focuses the voice on single pitches, with the breeze's sigh beneath. By the time the voice regains the motif, the breeze has borne to the beloved the scent of the woods and mosses and words "soft as the roses of May."

The introduction to Collin's "Déception" (no. 2) conveys the poem's sense: the singer, deceived into thinking he will meet the beloved as of yore, will be disappointed. The funeral march, extended at cadences, passes between voice and piano, yielding to stark outcry in recitative-like acknowledgments of reality. The closing lines—of faded sun, silent birds, and love lost—return to the dirge, but with frozen chords beneath.

In no. 3, Collin's "Sérénade," the singer, seeing the beloved in the beauties of nature, is inspired to passionate hyperbole. Four metaphors are set to the opening theme, then the hyperbole, while more *volupté* ("And I love the sighs of your breast which throb in the long moans of the wind") brings more complex accompaniment. Tchaikovsky tries at "I love the proud ardor / Of which your heart senses the flame" to restore the initial motif, which cannot accommodate an image so ardent. The final verse, with the singer's highest and loudest point, comes on "Et j'aime la douceur de ta *mélancholie* dans le vague déclin des soirs!" a line approaching Verlaine.

"What does it matter" (no. 4, again by Collin) dismisses winter's blight by taking refuge in the beloved's beauty. Well-wrought but emotionally indifferent lines convey a disregard for winter's ravages; their destination is the last line, slowed from allegro to andante, placed in a different key, and marked *dolce.* Here, fervor is invested in the beloved: "You whom I love," "Oh my dearest," and, at the end, "My dear love."

In "Les larmes," to a verse by Madame A.-M. Blanchecotte, consoling tears are welcome, but "murderous" ones are banished. Tchaikovsky expresses the singer's hesitation at the prospect of weeping by avoiding the tonic chord throughout the first verse, even through the outpouring on "hidden griefs," adorned by the motif of "fall, o my tears!" The second verse begins as if strophic, but the symmetry is abandoned as the singer begs the tears to forbear.

Tchaikovsky ends op. 65 with a light touch in no. 6. The rounded element in Collin's "Rondel" is the opening couplet, "Hidden in your grace is a sweet sorcery." The beloved carries hearts away, and her glance is the net which gathers up our souls. The *ariette*-like setting is built around the opening motif. A mock-serious moment refers to the beloved's glance, set to a descending bass. But the *parlando,* the unaccompanied "God knows how!" sets up the answer: *un doux ensorcellement . . . a sweet sorcery.*

Perhaps because he was setting French, Tchaikovsky curbed word repetition and emulated recitative in op. 65 (e.g., song 5 at *più vivo,* bar 27), hinting at the austere treatment of poetry he will invoke in Russian in the songs of op. 73 [424, 106–8].

CHAPTER NINETEEN

1889–1893

In the last five years of Tchaikovsky's life, celebrity obscured his real preoccupations, the most important of which was his muse, the ability to compose. In addition to revisions, arrangements, short pieces, rejected or destroyed works, and unrealized projects, his accomplishment in those years comprised *The Sleeping Beauty, The Queen of Spades,* the *Souvenir de Florence, Iolanta, The Nutcracker,* and the Sixth Symphony. If the composer's difficulties with *Iolanta* and *The Nutcracker* bespeak faltering inspiration, there remain four big works composed or completed in the fluent manner of old. *The Sleeping Beauty, The Queen of Spades,* and the *Souvenir* were completed in 1889–1890 and the Sixth Symphony in the winter of 1893. They encourage a distinction between feast and famine, the latter in 1891 and 1892. Being written out is no childish complaint. Nor is it accidental that Jurgenson published during this time some old pieces, such as the Overture to *The Voevoda* and the *Overture on the Danish National Anthem,* as if surrogates for new composition. Tchaikovsky's efforts to write a grand symphony between 29 October 1889, when he declared this intention, and 16 October 1893, the first performance of the Sixth, spanned the high and low points of his inspiration and included his last completed work, the Third Piano Concerto.

Mortality continued to be his principal philosophical concern. Nikolay Kondratiev's death, which brought him to metaphysical rumination, was one of many losses. The death of Sasha Davïdova, preceded by two of her children, left the deepest mark, followed by lifelong friends whose passings came in the months before Tchaikovsky's own. In this period he wrote his will a third time, notarizing it and specifying bequests. Metaphorical deaths were no less important; the demise of Tchaikovsky's relationship with Meck in September 1890 matched anything on the mortal ledger. It contributed to the composer's lapse of creativity, which he came to describe in mortal terms—as his muse dying within him, gradually, as the body lived on. A second figural death occurred some weeks after the premiere of *The Queen of Spades* in Tchaikovsky's concern that imperial favor for his music had died. Vsevolozhsky's rebuttal did little to discourage his concern, and the fact remains that Tchaikovsky, after a spate of imperial commissions, went to his grave without one. Productivity affected his late style, in that the focal points "of this world" and "not of this world," which define it, apply to capital works and presuppose inspiration commensurate with the task. A composer's late style implies a particular awareness of the imminence of death, its philosophical outcomes being the themes just cited with their religious overtones; in Tchaikovsky, it lacked perfect form, which he would admit to K.R., with an attendant relaxation of obvious unifying devices, such as the motto theme of the Fifth Symphony, and the granting of a noticeable stylistic heterogeneity, sensed in *The Sleeping Beauty* and particularly in *The Queen of Spades.* But it did not imply, as Edward Said argued (via Adorno) of Beethoven's late works, any concurrent negativity or rejection of the acceptable, let alone the abandonment of communication with the established social order of which he was a part [339, 8–18].

1889

Tchaikovsky gave much of 1889 to conducting—in Moscow, in Europe, and for Anton Rubinstein's 50th anniversary jubilee, which was in the autumn between a revival of *Evgeniy Onegin* in September and a charity concert in November which included Beethoven's Ninth. Tchaikovsky's concern for the Moscow concerts was driven by the Russian Musical Society, whose revenues continued to decline even as the Moscow Conservatory faced paying higher salaries to attract good faculty and the concerts themselves required star-quality guests. In composition, 1889 is most important for *The Sleeping Beauty,* besides which he wrote only four short compositions and arranged two others. Of *Sadia* and another opera, *Béla,* from a text by Lermontov, there was only talk.

Throughout the year, Meck was in decline. On 2 January she indicated that several letters each year from him would be fine, and on 27 February complained of bad health. By 14/26 October she reported suffering headaches all the time, intending for weeks to write a few words and ending up dictating them instead. She feared losing her shares in her husband's enterprise—her only source of income and the only means of helping her children through life. Tchaikovsky might thus have been alerted to the coming break.

Documents from 1889 show Tchaikovsky less swayed by personal passion than before. He noted the pleasant company of the student Vladimir Sklifasovsky while traveling between Marseilles and Constantinople in the first week of April. His affection for Bob continued. The last significant reference to him before autumn was to Modest on 31 August: "Seeing how Bob's significance in my life is ever increasing, I have finally decided from next year to live in Petersburg. To see him, to hear and sense his closeness, it seems, is quickly becoming for me the very first condition of well-being" [xv-a 174]. He never moved there.

Early in 1889, Tchaikovsky's enthusiasm for *The Sleeping Beauty* was sparked by the beauty of the Russian winter. On 6 January he asked Vsevolozhsky for a meeting; he wanted more instructions from Petipa and estimated finishing the *répétiteur,* a rehearsal score arranged for two violins, by August and the full score by November. He finished *The Sleeping Beauty* in fact on 26 May, in "about 40 days," and scored it by 20 August. Meanwhile, he arranged concerts and put out fires in Moscow. He proposed that the conservatory invite star conductors, whom he volunteered to contact: Artur Nikisch, Antonín Dvořák, Johannes Brahms, Jules Massenet, Edouard Colonne, Karl Klindworth, Alexander Siloti, Anton Rubinstein, and Nikolay Rimsky-Korsakov.

On his Western tour Tchaikovsky made debuts in Cologne, Frankfurt [137], Dresden, and Geneva and revisited Berlin, where he conducted *Francesca da Rimini* after its deferral the year before, and where Désirée Artôt was again his "consolation in a life dominated by social engagements" [xv-a 51]. He reserved his principal novelty, the Fifth Symphony, for Hamburg. There, he again met Brahms, whom he asked to conduct in Moscow. Brahms declined but stayed to hear the new symphony. While he found Brahms kind and congenial ("I liked his directness and simplicity"), and they breakfasted together after rehearsal, he noted that Brahms did not like the finale of the Fifth, nor did the musicians, nor did he himself [xv-a 68]. As Kashkin later explained:

> [Tchaikovsky] quite destroyed his Fifth Symphony by his performance in Russia and abroad, such that its revival awaited Mr. Nikisch after Tchaikovsky's death, with whom it had a great success everywhere. . . . Tchaikovsky was ready to attribute the failure of the Fifth Symphony more to its actual composition than to his performance of it. [MV030627]

Tchaikovsky passed three milestones early in 1889: the death of Father Dmitry Razumovsky, who had presided at his marriage and who later helped him to navigate the complexities of Orthodox song; his reunion after 17 years with Ivan Klimenko, his chum in the early Moscow days; and the death in February of Karl Yulevich Davïdov, a professor of cello who had also served as the director of the St. Petersburg Conservatory and who had supplied him with the libretto of *Mazepa*. In February, Antonina asked for a larger stipend, and Tchaikovsky gave it to her [xv-a 78].

Among the constant distractions, two in midsummer were extraordinary. The first was a dispute at the conservatory: since April, Taneyev had wanted to withdraw as director and Vasily Safonov wanted to replace him. But Safonov, whom Tchaikovsky thought ambitious and proud, refused until the forced retirement of the inspector of the conservatory, Konstantin Albrecht—one of Tchaikovsky's oldest comrades. Within days of completing *The Sleeping Beauty,* Tchaikovsky was negotiating Albrecht's retirement. Soon, he wished to appoint Anatoly Brandukov to replace Wilhelm Fitzenhagen as professor of cello. He would fail, and leave the society as a result. The second was to lobby the imperial family for Anatoly's appointment as governor of Tiflis. K.R.'s delayed response was not encouraging. The composer insisted that, if it were the least awkward or inappropriate to intervene, K.R. should let the matter drop. And that is apparently what happened. Anatoly spent the remaining years of Pyotr's life in dispirited moves to Revel (now Tallinn), Estonia, and then to Nizhny-Novgorod.

Two days after conducting *Onegin* in Moscow on 18 September, Tchaikovsky was in St. Petersburg for rehearsals of *The Sleeping Beauty* (where he would appear with a 10-pound box of chocolates, drawing children like bees to their hive [113, 114]) and meetings with the Rubinstein jubilee committee. The concert season he had organized in Moscow began on

21 October, conducted by Rimsky-Korsakov, surely the occasion recalled by student Nikolay Averino, who was sent to play tam-tam in Balakirev's *Tamara.* Averino missed his entrance, for which Tchaikovsky rebuked him before Tchaikovsky took his place in the orchestra as the castanet player in Rimsky-Korsakov's *Capriccio espagnol,* just to miss *his* entrance when the moment came. He leaned over to Averino and whispered, "It's frightful, and . . . how shameful!" Afterward, the conductor thanked his percussionist *manqué,* who broke out laughing [21, 98; for season review, 176].

After encountering Tchaikovsky at his concert of 28 October, Antonina wrote to the empress of their marriage (apparently making good on a threat), then exploded on 15 December in some 4,000 words of abuse against Jurgenson, including anti-Semitic slurs, and detailed his and Tchaikovsky's vilification of her back to 1877 at Kamenka. She made no reference to her own behavior, yet her description rings true and suggests, as before, another side to the story of Tchaikovsky's marriage [365, 242–48]. It was her last extant letter to Tchaikovsky. He answered it three days later, but we don't know what he wrote.

Early in November he was in St. Petersburg rehearsing Anton Rubinstein's oratorio *Babel,* which he conducted on the third of three jubilee days, 18–20 November. On the first, his "Greeting to A. G. Rubinstein" was performed and a gift album to Rubinstein from his former students was presented, to which Tchaikovsky contributed an Impromptu for piano. The next day, he conducted Rubinstein's Fifth Symphony, the musical picture "Russia," and a *Konzertstück* for piano with Rubinstein at the keyboard.

In the last months of 1889, public service lost its charm. "The fact is that I consider it my duty, while my powers last, to struggle with my fate—not to distance myself from people—and to act in the public view while this is desired," he assured Meck on 12 October [xv-a 197]. Yet he wondered if he could ever distance himself from it. By the time he wrote again on 17 December, he claimed that composition was his true business and the rest accidental, pointless, and a curb on his lifespan [xv-a 219]. In this spirit, on 29 October, he made a heady declaration to K.R.: he would write a grand symphony to end his compositional career and dedicate it to the emperor. "The ill-defined plan of such a symphony I have carried around in my head for a long time—but I need the confluence of many beneficial circumstances before this plan can be completed. I hope not to die without having realized this intention" [xv-a 205]. He memorialized his ill-defined plan in verbal and musical sketches on two undated leaves, thought to be written in the early 1890s, which point to a symphony yet to be composed:

> Furthest essence of sketches for the symphony *Life!* First movement—all upsurge, confidence, thirst for action. Must be short. (The finale is *death*—the result of destruction) 2nd movement is love; 3rd disappointment; 4th ends with a dying-out (also short). [CW 62, vii]

A focus on program in the literature tends to obscure the less specific, more poetical element that lay at the heart of Tchaikovsky's symphonies. Program and graphic representation, as Boris Asafiev reminds us, were not on point, compared with the stimulus to compositional imagination that lies in a basic thought or a psychological factor with implications for musical architecture. A symphonic work need not eschew descriptive ideas, but when present they do not necessarily assume a defining role in meaning or structure [193, 29].

The first obstacle to "the confluence of many beneficial circumstances" was to compose *The Queen of Spades,* which was decided by 17 December 1889. To Meck, he summarized: Modest had written the libretto three years earlier for the composer Nikolay Klenovsky, who began but never finished; Vsevolozhsky wanted something new, and Tchaikovsky wanted to get away from Russia for a time; the committee convened, the libretto was accepted, decorations were projected, and roles were even discussed [xv-a 219]. He omitted mention of his prior rejection of the project, in the face of Modest's prompting, in 1887 and 1888 [e.g., xiv 400].

There were other remarkable events in 1889: in June Rimsky-Korsakov opened the Russian concerts at the Paris International Exhibition with Tchaikovsky's First Piano Concerto; Tchaikovsky wrote his autobiography for Otto Neitzel, a German music critic [418, 302–11; 309 I 521–28]; in October, Julius Block, Thomas Edison's representative, offered Tchaikovsky a private demonstration of the Edison phonograph; on one occasion, Tchaikovsky's voice was recorded [45; 413; 392]. About then—12–14 October—Tchaikovsky met Anton Chekhov, who dedicated his collection of short stories *Gloomy People* to him and inscribed a copy to him as his future librettist.

1890

The high and low points of this year were the composing of *The Queen of Spades* and the break with Nadezhda von Meck. *The Queen of Spades* made it easy for him to defer *Sadia,* which irritated his librettists and required personal diplomacy to keep the project alive. He was in midcomposition of a tone poem called *The Voevoda* when the break with Meck came.

On 1 January Tchaikovsky dined with Modest, Lucien Guitry, and his wife, then stayed for the first performance of *The Sleeping Beauty* on the 3rd, which was preceded the day before by an officially closed dress rehearsal attended by the emperor. "Very nice!!!" was the tsar's response. Despite this apparent condescension, *The Sleeping Beauty,* some balletomanic carping aside, was a triumph. Young Alexander Benois wrote of the mastery of the performers and the charm of each one combining in the beauty of the ensemble. "Thus the good fortune befell me in fact to see a genuine *Gesamtkunstwerk*" [34 I 606]. Balletomanes complained of vast expenditures for a ballet-*féerie,* a genre of extravagant display and superficial content. "Luxury has its limits," wrote Konstantin Skalkovsky, "stipulated by the nature of the art" [351, 198]. Tchaikovsky expressed his profound gratitude to ballerina Carlotta Brianza for her sharp, precise dances [297, 145]. "All her dances—*entrée, adagio,* and variations on *pointe,* are extremely elegant, masterfully and accurately executed" [NV900105]. Laroche approved:

> The Russian way in music, besides being strong in Tchaikovsky in recent years, is at issue here. The music completely suits the costume, the characters; it has a French nuance, but all the same it savors of Rus. . . . It may be said, without lapsing into contradiction, that the local color is French, but the style is Russian. [255 II 143]

A Moscow critic put the staging into perspective when observing the unprecedented elegance and luxury of *The Queen of Spades:*

> This aspect of the work is . . . such that no other stage in Europe can compete with the Maryinsky Theater. Our press appreciates the Maryinsky altogether too little; we must needs be convinced of this, having seen and listened to the ballet *The Sleeping Beauty,* also by P. I. Tchaikovsky. If something like it were produced on one of the big European stages, its praise would resound throughout the world, while in Petersburg the press took this work and its production to be quite ordinary. [MV910101]

The Sleeping Beauty dominated the ballet schedule for the remainder of the winter. Tchaikovsky went abroad on 14 January, arrived in Florence four days later, bought a new notebook, and began work on *The Queen of Spades* the next day.

The new opera filled Tchaikovsky's life from January to May. Unhappy with Florence at first [xv-b 22], by 7/19 February he was inspired to the point of madness and facing difficulties as well. "At times it seemed I was living in the eighteenth century, and that beyond Mozart there was nothing" [Dnev 255]. The distance separating him and Modest brought Pyotr to peremptory changes in the libretto. At first praising Modest's work, he then complained of wordiness and tough and rigid verses [xv-b 23–24]. He disapproved of the opening chorus and modified the ballroom scene. He wrote sections himself, including the Russian dance tune in scene 2, Yeletsky's aria in scene 3, much of scene 6, and the final chorus. A second tier of problems arose from Nikolay Figner's complaint that the role of Hermann was too demanding. Never free of distraction, Tchaikovsky took on this trip Modest's valet, Nazar Litrov, who kept a diary of the composer's moods and actions but who also fell ill and carried on with the local women. On 23 January, Jurgenson reported a maverick production of *The Oprichnik* and threatened to sue Bessel; he also forwarded a letter from Antonina, who "kills work." In mid-February, Siloti reported the failure of the only performance in Moscow of *The Enchantress,* attributed to the intrigues of people whom he would name in person [xv-b 143, nn. 1–2]. But Tchaikovsky's greatest distraction was his decision to resign from the Moscow Russian Musical Society when Safonov again refused the Brandukov appointment. Tchaikovsky took back his promise to conduct six concerts in the coming year and complained that his advice was not being taken when his desires, instructions, and recommendations must be the law. Among the odder circumstances of the period was that he completed *The Queen of Spades*—a dark tale of St. Petersburg—as Buffalo Bill's Wild West Show was playing in Florence; he attended a performance on the day he finished, 3/15 March 1890. On 7/19 March, he fell ill and was incapacitated for a week.

On 27 March/8 April, he arrived in Rome, and on 15/27 April, he finished orchestrating scene 3. He arrived in Frolovskoe by 3 May, embarking upon a quiet summer. His mood improved, and by 30 June he had finished drafting the sextet begun two years before [xv-b 194]. In the meantime, the ownership of the holograph score of *The Queen of Spades* had been disputed. As the commissioning entity, the theater direction considered it theirs, whereas Jurgenson, by agreement with the composer, considered it his. Tchaikovsky sided with Jurgenson, who had paid him 5,000 rubles for the opera [56, 31–32], but did not object to giving the manuscript to the theater direction. In mid-June, he suggested that Modest write a preface to the libretto [xv-b 183], explaining the changes in Pushkin's story. By 30 June he and Nikolay Kashkin had corrected the preface, and on 15 July, Pyotr took responsibility for any remaining corrections of detail.

A disturbing moment that summer came from Détroyat, who wrote on 23 June/5 July asking for news of *Sadia*. After Tchaikovsky agreed to write *Sadia* (Détroyat claimed) only if it were accepted by a Paris theater, Détroyat secured this acceptance, but now Tchaikovsky wanted a Russian piece staged first, which, if successful, he would follow with *Sadia*. Détroyat had upheld his part of the bargain, and his agreements were breaking down [6, 122–23]. Tchaikovsky advanced the deadline for reasons of ill health and a new imperial commission.

Tchaikovsky and Meck had not corresponded during the composition of *The Queen of Spades,* and when he wrote on 27 March/8 April, it was to Vladislav Pachulsky (now Meck's son-in-law). He naïvely wished they might start again as of old; Meck responded that she was still recovering; he wrote again, pleased to see her handwriting and reminding her of her strength; she answered that she was not as strong as he thought. Even as her letters continued to report ill health, she sent Tchaikovsky a year's subsidy on 1 July, honoring her obligation to him until June 1891. On 22 July, she thanked him for the vocal score of *The Queen of Spades* and wrote that her health was bad, her house in a turmoil, the weather cold, and her brother Vladimir had died [86 III 600]. On 13 September, she reported disastrous financial problems. It was her last surviving letter to Tchaikovsky. The next one canceled his subsidy.

Angry and shaken, he replied that such a radical reduction of his budget would have less impact than she thought. He disputed that he would remember her only for her money; he would remember her great kindness and generosity and bless her until his last breath [xv-b 263–64]. One measure of his shock was the delay in telling others; six days passed before he informed Jurgenson and three weeks before he told Modest. Now he must live a different life and might have to find a job. During their correspondence, her generosity had never burdened him, but now it did. His pride was hurt, his faith betrayed: "But you see, I well know that from our point of view she is nevertheless fantastically rich; in a word, it has been some banal, stupid joke." As a result, he needed money and asked Jurgenson for 500 rubles [xv-b 267–69].

Responses to the break have brought posterity to find Meck blameworthy, not least in *The Life,* as Modest described Pyotr's last illness: "he became somewhat delirious and constantly repeated the name Nadezhda Filaretovna von Meck, angrily reproaching her" [1997 III 579]. Reviewing *The Life,* Kashkin defended Meck:

> [H]er chronic consumption was complicated by acute pneumonia, and while her organism bore these illnesses her strength was greatly diminished, and she had almost lost the use of her hands. . . . [S]he spent her remaining time not really living but expiring, gradually losing her sight and hearing. A profoundly mystical tendency possessed her, and only in it did she seek consolation and support. Nevertheless, as I had occasion to hear from persons very close to her . . . she continually recalled Pyotr Ilyich, . . . and would say that their friendship remained the best recollection of her life. [MV030316]

The editors of the Tchaikovsky-Meck correspondence cite a letter of Alexey Sofronov suggesting that Pachulsky might be up to mischief, so envious was he of Tchaikovsky's lavish manner of living [86 III 610]. The correspondence had cooled in recent years and might soon have ended of its own accord. More provocatively, the editors propose that Meck's children—shocked by her relationship with Tchaikovsky, with its amorous overtones and "patina of scandal," and by his partaking freely of family wealth long past the point he was well provided for—may have spread word of his homosexuality, which would explain Meck's early, secretive payment of Tchaikovsky's stipend in 1890 and Tchaikovsky's anguish, as much at the fear of disclosure as the loss of revenue [86 III 613–14]. He nevertheless deserves some credit: his press to return to the old ways, extreme to the onlooker, may not have been disingenuous to either party.

Had he not been preparing for a trip to the United States before Meck's final letter, one might interpret that journey as a flight from bad news. Weeks earlier, Eugene Weiner, president of the New York Philharmonic Club, had requested a new piece; Tchaikovsky agreed and received official thanks on 16/28 November. In September, Hermann Wolff had written that Walter Damrosch hoped to propose several concerts to Tchaikovsky in the spring of 1891. The matter seemed decided by 15 September [xv-b 259], but as late as 21 December he was still awaiting word, while on 23 December/4 January 1891, Frederick Grant Gleason wrote to him, soliciting his view of the organization of the music division of the World's Columbian Exposition of 1894 [6, 88–89].

There is little in the public record about Tchaikovsky's personal life in 1890: on 4 October, he wrote to Bob Davïdov, concerned that Bob was getting too friendly with Apukhtin.

The last two months of 1890 were taken up mostly with *The Queen of Spades*—appeasing Nikolay Figner by retransposing his last aria and reassigning the part of Lise to his wife, Medea; nearly continuous editing; coping with the piano-vocal score; and pondering special effects, such as toy instruments for the children to play in the opening scene, a church choir in scene 5, and a harpsichord for visual effect in scene 2. As ever, this principal occupation proceeded amid a medley of counterpoints. After declining any celebration of his 25th anniversary of musical activity [xv-b 286], it was celebrated anyway, on 3 December at the St. Petersburg Conservatory by the Russian Musical Society, Anton Rubinstein, professors and students, a concert, and his own speech [NV901205]. A proposal from Bernhard Pollini, his agent in Hamburg, to acquire *The Sleeping Beauty, The Queen of Spades,* and *Evgeniy Onegin* for all German and Austro-German stages (and, subsequently, *The Maid of Orleans, Mazepa,* and *Iolanta* [119, 109]) was much debated before Tchaikovsky agreed, whereupon manuscript copies of *The Sleeping Beauty* and *The Queen of Spades* were sent to Hamburg and lithographed there. The 20 copies of *The Sleeping Beauty,* rendered unusable by the incorrect sequence of numbers, comprised the only publication of the full score before the *Collected Works* was published in 1952 [CW 12; 112, 245–46].

On 5 December, *The Queen of Spades* went into dress rehearsal, but not without mishap. Nikolay Figner, the tenor lead, had received permission to put on his costume at home, some distance from the theater. When it was torn, finding a replacement delayed the rehearsal. Attending the tsar, Vsevolozhsky was obliged to explain: "Figner split his trousers, Your Majesty." The emperor's laughter echoed through the entire hall [316, 214–15]. The first performance followed on the 7th amid rumors that

Figner had broken his collar bone and might not sing. On that night, private carriages stretched a kilometer beyond the theater; the auditorium gleamed with uniforms and diamonds [MV901211]. Tomsky's ballad and the love duet were repeated, despite Medea Figner's "defects of execution." The *intermède* was performed amid groups of guests, "as was done in the seventeenth century in Italian courts and at Versailles" [177, 793]. Tchaikovsky was called to the stage after every scene and given a silver wreath and a lyre fashioned of laurel leaves. Many luminaries, including Anton Rubinstein, attended the dinner after the performance. Laroche recalled:

> I spoke several times and in the last speech made a parallel between Hermann and Tchaikovsky. There are moments when life offers a game of blind chance, when a person looks at success and failure as a peasant farmer looks at a future harvest. Some idea like this took hold of me that evening, and accordingly I said that Hermann placed a large sum of money on the Queen of Spades and met with failure, while Pyotr Ilyich placed a large sum of money on the same lady and won. [255 II 254]

The reception of the new opera was led by Nikolay Kashkin in support, arrayed against Nikolay Solovyov, who had declined an offer to compose *The Queen of Spades* himself [PL901220]; Mikhail Ivanov, Tchaikovsky's former student but no ally; and the blustery Vladimir Baskin, who took aim at Kashkin and raged over being deprived of a piano-vocal score on which to write his review [VI910112]. The initial critique faulted Modest's adaptation for being a pale remake of *Evgeniy Onegin* and the production for emphasizing magnificence over content. Its most impressive accomplishment, Petipa's *intermède,* "The Shepherd's Sincerity," at which the audience "literally gasped," caused widespread delight [MV901211] after a similar pantomime on the tale of Daphnis he had made for Anton Rubinstein's *Goryushka* the year before [56, 247–53]. Tchaikovsky's orchestration was peerless; in addition to his expected lyricism, he showed a powerful dramatic gift, especially in the scenes with Hermann and the Countess; elsewhere, his music was "accessible on first hearing to any listener" [MV910101]. Nikolay Figner stole the show; his "high notes sounded extremely full" [NO901209].

Modest, "the insignificant brother of the significant brother" (Baskin), was an easy target. The large cast atomized singers' opportunities, restricting everyone but Hermann and Lise to one or two moments and little else. "It is interesting in excerpts," snipped Solovyov, "while *Evgeniy Onegin* is charming in general" [NO901209]. Kashkin commended Modest for avoiding *longeurs* and providing strong situations for music [RV901214]. Pyotr's music pleased in the widely admired scenes of the Countess's bedchamber and the barracks, where the fantastic was treated as if it were "undoubted actuality" [MV901211], and was disparaged in the confected scene by the Winter Canal and the much reconceived ending. Mikhail Ivanov complained that the chorus of tipsy gamblers praying for the repose of Hermann's soul was like the bystanders in *Carmen,* kneeling and praying for the heroine in the wake of her murder [NV901210].

Insight in the critique of *The Queen of Spades* resided in the tension between complaints of nonconformity with operatic norms and praise for the composer's ingenuity. Baskin pointed out the issue: "[I]f the old woman is excluded, who is sketched more clearly than the others, one is left with secondary characters who could almost not exist" [D&Y 509]. Such Philistinism is beside the point. Tchaikovsky himself rejected a chiming bell in the scene by the Winter Canal as "too real and inartistic" [xv-b 110]; Ivanov praised the bedchamber and barracks scenes, with their supernatural occurrences, as "artistically true without being coarsely naturalistic" [NV901210]. Critics were beginning to sense Tchaikovsky's theatrical gift. To Kashkin, it resided in his supraconventional autonomy. Modest's lack of definition in portraying Lise gave Tchaikovsky greater scope for expression [177, 785]. He praised Modest for writing prose in the libretto, increasing dramatic effect and discouraging a lapse into conventional numbers [183, 174]. The Lise-Hermann duet in scene 2 illustrated the new approach: Lise's aria prepares for Hermann's arrival, compensates for the absence of any prior explanation of their love, and makes comprehensible why she is astonished but not frightened at Hermann's entrance. In act I, he concluded, "we encounter all Tchaikovsky's best attributes—melodic richness, immense mastery of technique, and that healthy realism which constitutes one of the most characteristic traits of his talent, much more clearly testifying to his blood relationship with Russian artists, poets, novelists, than any use of folk song" [177, 787–88].

Faulty declamation, noted by first-night reviewers, was another literal fault that had already been taken up by K.R., who also complained of word repetition, as in the governess's text in the second scene [244, 77]. The composer's response was polite but candid:

> Truth to tell, however, I do not respond too scrupulously to details of this kind. Our music critics, who forget that the main thing in vocal music is truth in reproducing feelings and moods, seek out mis-accents in melodic devices and all manner of petty faults of declamation at odds with spoken discourse—collect them with malicious delight and use them to reproach the composer with a zeal worthy of better aspirations. . . . But, Your Highness, please agree that the absolute absence of error in musical declamation is a negative quality and that one ought not exaggerate its significance. . . .
>
> As for the repetition of words and even entire phrases, . . . I find nothing untruthful when an old, dull-witted governess . . . repeats an eternal refrain about proprieties. But even if this never happened in real life it would not trouble me to abandon real truth in favor of artistic truth. . . . I am, of course, a child of my era and do not wish to return to outlived operatic conventions and nonsense—nor do I intend to submit to the despotic demands of a theory of realism. [xv-b 237–38]

It took Laroche to synthesize the opera's early reception, reviewing the 37th performance of *The Queen of Spades* some 18 months after the composer's death. Only lately and gropingly did Tchaikovsky, after many a succès d'estime, find an operatic project that fit his powerful, sincere, but sharply outlined, inflexible, and disobedient talent. On the strength of a misunderstanding, he had expended energy on dramatic stories for many years, but in his last four stage works he found himself, a new Tchaikovsky unfolded before us, in which instinct and impulse won out over conformity to fashion:

> *The Queen of Spades,* its libretto motley, its music bereft of style, is rich in charming detail, in which we recognize the elegiac, pensive Tchaikovsky with his elegant disappointment, and the brilliant, worldly Tchaikovsky, incomparable master of transmitting the baronial magnificence and carefree merriment of Catherine's time. Because of his cool, artisan-like way of writing, striving for effect was not and could not be part of Pyotr Ilyich; he went for effect because the story called for it and the externals of the theatrical task inflamed his imagination. [255 II 191]

As usual, Tchaikovsky did not linger: he was in Kiev by 11 December for the first performance there. By then, a new proposal from the direction must have been firm, as he wrote to Modest on 21 December of a commission to write a new opera and a new ballet—*Iolanta* and *The Nutcracker*—for the coming season. Tchaikovsky was pleased with *The Queen of Spades* in Kiev [xv-b 304, 309–12], and after the first performance on 19 December, he left on the 22nd for Kamenka. Was nostalgia or commemoration responsible? Sasha's health? In any event, he greeted the new year in the bosom of his family. "It was very merry," he reported to Modest.

1891

The year 1891 was marked by desultory concentration and no grand event after his trip to the United States. Neuralgia in his right arm impeded his conducting, and his composing was unenthusiastic, while diaries and furtive notes suggest attempts to write the symphony announced to K.R. in 1889. *Iolanta* and *The Nutcracker* were not finished in time for the 1891–1892 season. Throughout the year (likely a response to Pollini's project for his works in Germany), he labored over a new edition of *Evgeniy Onegin* that would reflect the Petersburg performance version, be free of errors, and reconcile the Russian and German texts [289, 165–68].

Tchaikovsky set his affairs in motion in January with correspondence, breaking his promise to Rimsky-Korsakov to conduct *The Voevoda* on 26 January, claiming not a note had been written. Citing his neuralgia, he began to cancel engagements, declaring to Friedrich Sieger, a concert organizer in Frankfurt, that he was "completely vexed" at missing a second visit there [137, 218]. By 22 January, he knew that the American trip was on for April. The next day he agreed to conduct for charity in St. Petersburg. The concert took place on 3 February with a roster of stars unmatched since his Paris concerts of 1888, including Marcella Sembrich, Felia Litvin, Nellie Melba, and Édouard de Reszke, who again sang the "Serenade of Don Juan." On 9 February, he attended Lucien Guitry's farewell benefit, having been assured an orchestra of at least 50 to play his *Hamlet* music with the house lights down. He reported its success to Anatoly [xvi-a 55].

To Vsevolozhsky on 12 February, Tchaikovsky first indicated his discomfort with *Iolanta* and *The Nutcracker*. The letter started with complaints about the withdrawal of *The Queen of Spades* after several weeks of full houses:

> [From no one] have I heard an explanation of why myself and my opera have been so pitilessly offended. Meanwhile it is *essential* for me to have some ex-

planation, for otherwise I cannot, with the necessary calm, undertake a new work for that same theater, on the boards of which my best and most beloved composition suffered so wretched and undeserved a fate.

He acknowledged the official reason for the opera's withdrawal—Medea Figner's pregnancy and Nikolay's "antagonism to all prima donnas not his wife" [xvi-a 46]—but argued that even the caprices of such important artists should not determine the director's marching orders:

> I shall not list all the times when the emperor's coolness towards me was more or less obvious. But what happened at the rehearsal of "The Queen of Spades" is probably still fresh in mind. I cannot hide that I was saddened, chagrined, and wounded by imperial disapproval so manifest yet so negatively expressed. Then I learned that the emperor was not present at one performance of "The Queen of Spades," another negative but very clear sign of ill favor. It explains everything that has happened to my opera.

As director, Vsevolozhsky must do his monarch's bidding but may not see the truth, and so he had commissioned something else to regain imperial favor:

> Beginning "The Daughter of King René" and "Casse-noisette" I feel like someone re-invited to a house whose host showed a clear inclination not to have him as a guest the time before. If the emperor does not encourage my works for the benefit of the theater, how can I work with love, with the necessary tranquility and warmth, for an institution of which he is proprietor?

He asked if the emperor approved the new commission. If the composer were wrong, he would proceed with pleasure; otherwise, he would be freed of his commission [xvi-a 49–51].

Vsevolozhsky was quick to refute him: court officials emphasized favor at the highest levels. Then, he noted that the emperor had called for Tchaikovsky at the dress rehearsal just when the composer was trying to hide in a corridor, and at the end of the opera Tchaikovsky was hiding behind the backs of others. "You are indeed a Russian talent," he wrote, "genuine, not inflated, for which reason in you there is no arrogance, and too great a modesty" [1997 III 383]. The issue calmed until Tchaikovsky departed on 6 March, though he wrote to Praskovia on 25 February that he had "nearly quarreled" with Vsevolozhsky in St. Petersburg [xvi-a 62].

Tchaikovsky left Russia a month before departing for the United States. He wrote to Anatoly that he could finish *Iolanta* in two uninterrupted weeks. In Paris on 24 March/5 April, he conducted a Colonne concert, a hefty program of the Third Suite, the Second Piano Concerto, the *Sérénade mélancolique,* songs and a duet, the *Andante cantabile* from the First Quartet, *The Tempest,* and the *Marche slave.* The next day, he left for Rouen to work on *The Nutcracker* until 3/15 April, when he wrote Vsevolozhsky again. After a week in Rouen, he had sketched the first two scenes of *The Nutcracker.* And yet:

> I had to resort to unlikely exertions of will, to agonizing outlays of strength in order to work. It produced as a result something colorless and dry, hasty and wretched. Knowing that *things are not going well* torments and agonizes me to tears, to the point of illness; burning anguish constantly gnaws at my heart, and for some time I have not felt so unhappy as now. . . . "Confiturembourg," "Casse-noisette," "King René's Daughter"—I do not rejoice in these images, they do not inspire but rather frighten, horrify and pursue me, waking and sleeping, mocking me that I cannot cope with them.

He appealed to Vsevolozhsky to substitute these topics with others or to postpone the production [xvi-a 84–85]. Vsevolozhsky postponed, and the issue calmed again. In some degree, Tchaikovsky was justified: the scenario of *The Nutcracker* was flawed, in that young Clara, after a Christmas party, is accosted by mice and saved by a toy nutcracker who comes to life as a prince. After he battles the mice, the two withdraw to the Land of Sweets, leaving the story open-ended. But the scenario was not his complaint. Nor is it clear why the Land of Sweets should challenge someone who had already composed for witches and devils, ghosts, water spirits, wicked fairies with retinues of rats, and evil genies who change into owls.

Rouen was not all. The next day, 4/16 April 1891, passing through Paris, Tchaikovsky read in a Petersburg newspaper of the death of his sister Sasha a week before. In *The Life,* Modest, gratuitously injecting himself into the circumstances, claimed to have heard about Sasha's death as early as 29 March, resolved to tell his brother in person, went to Rouen from Paris for this purpose on 4/16 April, and then held back, wishing not to break the mood of their joyous meeting, let alone threaten Pyotr's American trip [1997 III 387–88]. But if Modest and Pyotr were together, why would Pyotr write to him on that very date, asking for details [xvi-a 88]?

On 6/18 April, Tchaikovsky boarded the *Grand Bretagne* for New York, a stormy Atlantic crossing that took nine days. He began a diary, which he would keep throughout the U.S. visit and circulate among family when he returned. Two days later, on 8/20 April, he wrote the only significant entry about his recent tribulations: "Sasha's death and everything of torment linked with thoughts of her, seem as if recollections from a very distant past which I, without special effort, endeavor to drive away, again to think of the momentary interests of that non-I who within me is going to America" [xvi-a 93].

The U.S. visit, from 14/26 April to 9/21 May, has been generously documented [Dnev 263–94; 347; 439]. Tchaikovsky enjoyed the lavish reception, though he grew weary of being touted. He was gratified that his music was so much performed so far from Russia. He suffered culture shock—the "ridiculously colossal" 13-story buildings [Dnev 268]; the private baths, hot and cold running water in his hotel room; "electric and gas lighting; absolutely no candles" [xvi-a 100]; the niceties of wealth, including ices served mid-dinner in little boxes, to which slates were attached on which excerpts from his works were finely etched in pencil, which he had to autograph; callers free of ulterior motive who asked if he needed anything. Only in Russia, he wrote, would you encounter anything like American hospitality [Dnev 271].

He conducted at four concerts celebrating the opening of the (Carnegie) Music Hall, still unfinished when he arrived. He shared the podium with Walter Damrosch and found the orchestra splendid. His repertoire: the *Coronation March* on 23 April/5 May; the Third Suite on 25 April/7 May (his 51st birthday); unaccompanied choruses "Our Father" and "Legend," op. 54/5, on 26 April/8 May; and the First Piano Concerto with Adèle Aus der Ohe on 27 April/9 May. The last concert also included one of his songs, "So schmerzlich," probably op. 6, no. 3. With the exception of "Our Father," all his music was received enthusiastically, as was his person:

> The Music Festival of 1891 will be chiefly remembered as the occasion of the opening of the finest music-hall in America, if not in the world, and for the first appearance in America of Mr. Tchaikovsky. . . .
>
> The engagement of Mr. Tchaikovsky is in itself a significant fact, as it is perhaps the first time that an invitation has been sent from this country to a musician who is a composer only, and not a virtuoso (except at the conductor's

> desk). If this should signalize [*sic*] the opening of a new era, when the general public will begin to realize that a creative artist is of infinitely more importance than a mere interpreter—singer or player—something will have been gained apart from the pleasure afforded by the performance of five of Mr. Tchaikovsky's compositions under his direction, which insured correctness in all things. [439, 112]

He made two excursions. Of Niagara Falls, he wrote, "The beauty and majesty of the sight are truly breathtaking, . . . the verdure is quite fresh and the *dandelions,* my darlings, are showing." He descended by elevator to see the falls from below, "very interesting, but a little frightening" [Dnev 281–82]. He also went south to Baltimore, Philadelphia, and Washington. In the first two, he conducted the Victor Herbert Orchestra, whose namesake took the remainder of the program. It had but four first violins, which forced the substitution of the *Serenade for Strings* for the Third Suite; Aus der Ohe played the First Concerto. In Washington, his Piano Trio was performed at a musical soiree. In New York on 7/19 May, there was just enough time for farewells amid preparations for departure. After the return crossing, from 9/21 to 17/29 May, he stopped in Hamburg; St. Petersburg, 20–28 May; and was home in Maydanovo on the 29th. One detail of his shipboard diaries was important for composition. On 10/22 May, he referred to "sketches for a future symphony" with fragments of music in a sketchbook of the same date [CW 62, vii–viii]. A finished musical idea in E-flat minor is separate from more fragmentary sketches in E minor, labeled "Beginning and basic idea of the entire symphony," over which he has written "Why? Why? For what?" On later pages, he has written above another musical sketch, "Motif for the finale, after *why?* At first there is no answer, but then suddenly celebration." The sketchbook contains themes for the Symphony in E-flat and *The Nutcracker.*

Well before the journey was over there was talk of returning, with a choir that would perform sacred music, which had so pleased Andrew Carnegie in Moscow. Announcements of a second American tour appeared in Russia as early as 3 June [MV910603]; another round of negotiations ensued. Only in July was a fundamental misunderstanding laid bare. Tchaikovsky thought that Carnegie would sponsor a second journey, but instead Morris Reno, manager of the Music Hall, offered $4,000 for 20 concerts, with no Russian choir. Insulted, Tchaikovsky replied in French with one word: *Non.* Then came a second proposal for 20 concerts, asking his fee. He specified $12,000. In November came the response: his prior fee was for an extraordinary occasion funded by a millionaire, and his present demand exceeded appropriate risk. There was talk, but no further action taken about a return trip [439, 173–87].

Meanwhile, new productions were stirring. An inquiry in January about *The Queen of Spades* from Prague caused materials to be sent there from St. Petersburg. On 30 September, Tchaikovsky agreed to go; on 23 December, it was postponed. A similar fate befell a staging in Hamburg. The opera did enjoy a successful premiere at the Bolshoy Theater in Moscow on 4 November. On 15/27 December, Mackar proposed that Petipa come to Paris to stage *The Sleeping Beauty* in the spring of 1892. It never happened. An opera-ballet called "Watanabe," on a Japanese story, had been sent to him by the stage machinist Karl Valts on 17 June [362, 331–34; 77, 474–76]. It took the composer but a day to reject it [xvi-a 151].

Tchaikovsky composed fitfully in 1891. His main job was to complete *The Nutcracker* and *Iolanta,* both of which he had done by February 1892. He declared *The Nutcracker* "infinitely worse" than *The Sleeping Beauty* and complained of lack of inspiration [xvi-a 156, 161]: "I wrote the ballet with effort, sensing a decline in my ability to invent. . . . I am experiencing a kind of crisis. I shall either emerge from it victorious and still, for a few more years, fill up sheets of music paper, or I shall lay down my arms" [xvi-a 165].

He composed *Iolanta* from early July to early September, with scoring to follow. On 11 July, it was proving difficult and would take at least two months. The composition sketches were completed only on 4 September. He agreed on 2 September to conduct the first performance of *The Voevoda* [xvi-a 199] and finished orchestrating it on the 22nd. He would revise the *Souvenir de Florence* [xvi-a 126], but proceeded only in December and tarried until January—all for one new movement.

Composing proceeded in tandem with the afterpiece of the drama of Nadezhda von Meck. Tchaikovsky continued to correspond with her indirectly after their formal break, receiving at least 11 letters from Vladislav Pachulsky between 28 October 1890 and 13/25 June 1891 [xvi-a 133, nn. 1–2] and responding to two of them. Pachulsky wrote about family, discussed Meck's health, and conveyed greetings. At the end of October, her illness returned. In a week, Pachulsky wrote: "Nadezhda Filaretovna ordered me to convey to you her most heartfelt greetings and profound gratitude for your attention." Two months after this, Pachulsky insisted that Meck's relationship with Tchaikovsky was unchanged [86 III 611–12].

On 6 June 1891, Tchaikovsky wrote to Pachulsky for the last time, outlining his grievances with Meck, the recent correspondence notwithstanding:

> I *wished,* I *needed* my relations with N. F. not to change whatever after ceasing to receive money from her. Unfortunately this proved impossible because of N. F.'s patently obvious cooling towards me. Thus it happened that I stopped writing her, ending almost all contact, *after I was deprived of her money.* This situation demeans me in my own eyes, makes it unbearable to recall receiving her financial transfers, constantly tortures and hangs over me beyond measure. Last autumn in the country I reread N. F.'s earlier letters. Neither illness, nor grief, nor material difficulties, it seemed, could change the feelings expressed in these letters. . . . I could not imagine inconstancy in such a demigoddess; it seemed the earthly sphere might sooner break up into little pieces than N. F. change in her relationship to me. But that has happened, and it has turned upside down my view of people, my belief in the best of them; it disturbs my peace, and poisons that measure of happiness fate has allotted to me. [xvi-a 132]

Pachulsky insisted that Tchaikovsky was mistaken. If he would write as of old and ask about her, she would respond wholeheartedly. "[Y]ou need not at all ask why she has changed," he declared, "*because there is no change*" [86 III 612]. Yet all communication between the parties ceased, and 14 years of kinship ended, apparently within reach of conciliation. The demise of the Meck relationship overlapped with complaints of diminished inspiration in June, his vexation in Rouen, and his insistence on a large fee for the second American trip. In August, when his payment would have arrived in former years, Tchaikovsky complained to Anatoly that he must deal with a radical reduction in his budget, "depriving him of material benefits" [xvi-a 193].

The plan had been to conduct *The Voevoda* at a concert of the St. Petersburg Russian Musical Society on 14 December. The first performance in fact was at a Siloti concert in Moscow on 6 November. It was applauded. The music, "which most successfully illustrates the content of the program, gleams with the mastery of instrumentation and melodic beauty"

[MV911109]. There was no justification for Tchaikovsky to find it "so foul that the next day I tore it up into little pieces" [xvi-a 283]. Siloti, after assuring the composer that he had destroyed the orchestral parts, admitted that he hadn't, and the score was ultimately published from them.

Destroying *The Voevoda* forced Tchaikovsky to postpone the Petersburg concert of 14 December, which was rescheduled for 7 March, by which time he needed something else to offer. Meanwhile, on 1 December, Tchaikovsky conducted, Siloti played, the Figners and the chorus of the Russian opera sang at a benefit concert in St. Petersburg: the Overture to *Cherevichki, Marche slave,* "O sommo Carlo" from Verdi's *Ernani*—the only occasion on which Tchaikovsky ever conducted Verdi's music—excerpts from *Carmen, Lohengrin,* and *The Maid of Orleans,* and even songs by Cui. A huge sum was collected [NV911203].

Over Tchaikovsky's unsettled life in 1891 one issue hovers—his health. Siloti sent name-day greetings, adding that his great desire was for Tchaikovsky to stay healthy. In the summer, the composer returned to abstinence, writing to Modest on 17 June: "I have stopped drinking *vodka* and I am immensely pleased that I resolved to get along without this poison. If only I could discipline myself to smoke less!" In September he notarized the final version of his will. Any property at the time of his death would go to Georges-Léon, except for a seventh part, to Alexey Sofronov. Royalties to his compositions would go to Bob, who was instructed to make distributions every year to Modest (1,800 rubles), Antonina (1,200 rubles), George-Léon (1,200 rubles), and Alexey (600 rubles). His personal estate would go to Alexey [D&Y 608]. Before this, Tchaikovsky had written his will after confronting death. Was he doing that again now?

On Christmas Day from Kamenka he wrote to Bob of Sestritsa, already an adult when Pyotr was a child and now 84, who invited him to tea, oblivious to anything else:

> After tea she uttered such oddities and nonsense that three times Boris [son of the estate manager] broke out in laughter. It appeared to me that *she* . . . has seriously declined and is much more muddled than before. . . . At about 6 o'clock I was awakened by the squeaking door, and from behind the cupboard I heard Sestritsa's sepulchral voice: "My pet, wouldn't you like some tea?" I answered nothing: she left, muttering some absurdity. [xvi-a 298–99]

On 27 December he left for Warsaw, where he arrived on the 29th and attended a performance of *Cavalleria rusticana,* which moved him. On the 30th, he rehearsed for his concert.

1892

This year Tchaikovsky was never long in one place, a schedule consistent with his flawed concentration. The year started on a sour note with Jurgenson—their relationship was more vulnerable after Meck's subsidy ended—Tchaikovsky apologizing sheepishly for his spendthrift ways. At Vichy, which speaks to his health concerns, he mostly fretted. Once home, he resolved to finish the new symphony. *Iolanta* and *The Nutcracker* were given their first performances on 6 December.

In Warsaw, where he conducted on 2 January (O.S.), a performance by a Russian music luminary was a rare event. Reports of his conducting there, as in the United States, ran contrary to the Russian view:

> He has all the gifts needed for conducting an orchestra. Remarkable self-possession, complete clarity and definition of baton movements, and outstanding musicality. . . . Inspiring the orchestra, this extraordinary conductor acts irresistibly on his listeners as well. He produces an indelible impression with artistry of genius not only on persons initiated into the secrets of the musical art, but also on the entire mass of listeners. [D&Y 543]

In Hamburg, he rehearsed *Onegin* but left the German premiere on 7/19 January "not [to] some mediocrity, but simply a *genius* who is burning with the desire to lead the first performance" [xvi-b 16]. This was Gustav Mahler, whose conducting "was positively magnificent" [xvi-b 17]. According to outside accounts, Tchaikovsky was put off by the German translation of his opera, and his conducting was such that Mahler stood behind him in rehearsal and gave cues for entrances [119, 112]. On 10/22 January in Paris, where he had gone to rest and to revise the *Souvenir de Florence,* a trip to Holland was postponed [1997 III 465], as was the production of *The Queen of Spades* in Prague until the following season [xvi-b 21]. Returning early would placate Jurgenson, who had complained on 2 January that Tchaikovsky's constant demands for money were endangering his own finances [87 II 309, n. 2 to no. 347]. That remark made the composer "horribly uncomfortable" [xvi-b 21].

He began orchestrating *The Nutcracker* on 28 January in Maydanovo, while debating another change of residence. By 9 February, he had rented a house in Klin [xvi-b 37], not far from the birthplace of Alexey Sofronov and the hereditary estate of Antonina's family [32, 57]. It was his last home and would be purchased by Sofronov after Tchaikovsky's death and sold in 1897 to Modest and Bob, who would make it into the Home-Museum that continues to the present day. The *Nutcracker Suite* was also ready that day [xvi-b 37], after which Tchaikovsky agreed to conduct Gounod's *Faust,* Rubinstein's *The Demon,* and his own *Onegin* for Ippolit Pryanishnikov, who had staged *The Queen of Spades* in Kiev [xvi-b 46]. In Petersburg on 3 March, he conducted a charity concert of the School of Jurisprudence [MV920307], and that day he asked Alexander Khimichenko in Kiev about a flute technique, *frulato,* anticipating its use in act II of *The Nutcracker* [xvi-b 49–50]. On 7 March, he conducted the first performance of the *Nutcracker Suite* for the Russian Musical Society, vexed with tuning the new celesta mustel to Petersburg concert pitch. For a piece that would be so identified with Tchaikovsky later, it received middling notices, though Mikhail Rimsky-Korsakov (the composer's eldest son) recalled that it caused a furor [323, 359]. Five of the six dances were repeated. "The celebrated composer's success was immense" [NV920309].

In March, Tchaikovsky learned that Fanny Dürbach was still alive and renewed his correspondence with her, receiving 13 letters before the last on 1/13 October 1893 and visiting her before 1892 was over [232; 228]. Her letters fuss over Pyotr and congratulate him, and one, from July 1893, records a warm reminiscence of Votkinsk. Modest claimed that Pyotr was agitated upon learning that she was still alive—the fright of witnessing miracles—but that he quickly warmed to seeing her [1997 III 467]. His last letter to her had been 36 years before, belatedly reporting his mother's death. Tchaikovsky returned to St. Petersburg to commemorate the anniversary of Sasha's passing [xvi-b 65], then, in Moscow, wrote to Siloti, "I am already pondering a new large composition, that is, a symphony with a *secret* program" [xvi-b 70].

Tchaikovsky devoted most of April to the Pryanishnikov Opera, which performed in Moscow from 7 April to 1 May. Its repertoire was extraordinary for a volunteer collective, including big works like *Prince Igor, Carmen,* and *Aïda,* and everything—singers, orchestra, chorus, production apparatus—was brought in from Kiev. According to newspaper announcements, Tchaikovsky conducted on 20 April (*Faust*), 22 April (*The Demon*), and 26 April (*Onegin*); Pryanishnikov later claimed he conducted three performances of each work [317]. Executed with good ensemble, *Faust* was marred by a cat running between the performers and the audience and the smell of smoke, which alarmed the hall, forcing Tchaikovsky to stop the performance [MV920422; 316, 304]. Years later, Pryanishnikov recalled: "several passages, especially in act III (in Marguerite's garden) received in his conducting new and very beautiful shadings, or, better put, Pyotr Ilyich added something fresh and unusual" [D&Y 549–50]. *The Demon* passed without incident, while interest focused on Tchaikovsky's own interpretation of *Evgeniy Onegin*. In his own opera, "he was not just the president of the republic, nor even a constitutional king; he was a sovereign monarch, which, it seems, somewhat inhibited the other participants but provided as a result a *true* coloration to the whole" [MV920429].

His life continued busy. The day he conducted *Faust,* Tchaikovsky finished the proofs of *Iolanta*. Then he visited St. Petersburg to proof his early *Festive Overture on the Danish National Anthem,* which kept him out from underfoot as Alyosha readied the new house, where the composer spent May negotiating a return to the United States. For $10,000, he wrote to the American consul in St. Petersburg, he would go to the World's Columbian Exhibition in Chicago for four weeks and conduct Russian concerts [xvi-b 89]. On 20 May he began his new symphony [xvi-b 96], and on 24 May he wrote to Eugen Zabel, a German biographer of Anton Rubinstein, with reminiscences and praise for his teacher [xvi-b 100–103]. By 28 May, Tchaikovsky was on his way to Vichy with Bob Davïdov. The pleasure of making the trip with Bob was dampened by the presence of Anatoly's wife, Praskovia, who, Tchaikovsky suspected, insisted on going because she was in love with Bob [xvi-b 108], though she was "unbearable to Bob as a result of special circumstances about which it is awkward to write" [xvi-b 111]. If her rambling, half-incoherent letter from the following October is any indication, these had to do with pressing Bob to declare himself sexually:

> I like your essential being: external form, your heart, (not always) your mind, (always) your *general* Manière d'être—all this like a magnet draws my organs, my eyes, my heart, my thoughts, etc., etc. . . .

> I was frightfully happy when I noticed that you liked me; but when in the carriage, to my question, was it true what they said about you, you answered that "you can go one way or the other" (that is, for a man or for a woman) . . . I thought . . . that . . . I . . . am the first woman who had an effect on your sensitivities. . . .
>
> After your departure I learned that . . . you said that you definitely cannot understand amorous relations of a man with a man or a woman with a woman. . . .
>
> I learned also that Uncle Petya feared and endeavored to make you not thus. . . . And it is not difficult to divine whose company and what entourage had this baneful influence on you. . . . I would give much to cure you, but alas! What can I do—only pray for you. If I were free—I swear, I would cure you. [365, 200–201, n. 181]

The stay at Vichy lasted until 4 July. Bob was declared seriously ill, but not Tchaikovsky.

The rest of the summer was nondescript. On 13 July, Tchaikovsky urged that Laroche be invited to the St. Petersburg Conservatory as a teacher of counterpoint or the history of music and that Adèle Aus der Ohe be invited to play; the first was declined, the second awaited Tchaikovsky's last concert in October 1893 [359, 119, 122–23]. By 27 July, the proofs of *The Nutcracker* were finished, and Tchaikovsky turned back to *Iolanta,* which proved vexatious as Modest complained about errors in the libretto and Taneyev about errors in the score. On 3 August, the new symphony was not progressing, and only on 23 October did he begin to orchestrate. Meanwhile, announcements of the 1892–1893 concert season in St. Petersburg listed Tchaikovsky's "Sixth Symphony" among the novelties [MV921013; NV921014]. One senses the same lack of fire that had marked the composition of the opera and ballet. Modest recalled a change coming over his brother at about this time:

> This mysterious "something" was an inexplicably alarming, somber, hopeless feeling. . . . [I]n general I decline the excessive task of solving this last psychological evolution in the depths of Pyotr Ilyich's soul—but in pointing it out I cannot but mark the parallel with what had occurred prior to every sharp turn in his life. As before choosing a career in music at the beginning of the 1860s, as in Moscow before his marriage, as in 1885 before emerging from solitude

to "show off to people"—so now one sensed that "*things cannot continue thus,*" that a new turning point was at hand. . . .

Death, which was the turning point, had the look of chance, but I have no doubt that it occurred when *things could no longer continue thus.* [1997 III 502]

Tchaikovsky finished proofing all of the music for *Iolanta* and *The Nutcracker* on 29 August 1892; the next day from Moscow he wrote to a young poet, Daniil Rathaus, agreeing to compose songs to some of his verses. Then he went to St. Petersburg and to Vienna, arriving on 6/18 September for the International Musico-Theatrical Exhibition, where his works were on display [215, 9–10, 15–17, 25–27]. His concert was scheduled for 10/22 September in what had been described in the invitation as a *Grosse Musikhalle,* but which Tchaikovsky learned was a colossal "restaurant, full of stuffiness and the stench of foul butter and other consumables. I immediately decided either to demand the tables be removed and the tavern's transformation into an auditorium, or to withdraw" [xvi-b 164–65]:

[At rehearsal] Tchaikovsky began the second number on the program. After a few bars he tapped his baton and asked where the first trumpet was. He was told that the performer was very tired from rehearsal but was such an excellent musician that he [would] play the concert even without rehearsal. At that point the astonished Tchaikovsky exclaimed, "But my God, this is impossible, I have a trumpet solo here, and the part includes such difficult passages that the most experienced artists cannot perform it at sight!" [1997 III 504]

He abandoned the concert because conditions augured ill [xvi-b 167–68]. A Russian newspaper added that he called for a second and a third rehearsal, but the orchestra would not hear of it, at which point he gave up [NV920918]. He spent a fortnight at Sophie Menter's castle in Itter before *The Queen of Spades* in Prague and began to negotiate a visit to Odessa in the new year. On 25 September/7 October, Ilya Ilyich Slatin invited Tchaikovsky to conduct in Kharkov, after which the composer went to Prague, and he was back at Klin by 7 October. He arrived in St. Petersburg on 27 October to attend rehearsals of *Iolanta* and *The Nutcracker* and to be honored at the hundredth performance of *Evgeniy Onegin* at the Maryinsky that night.

During this visit to the northern capital, he was nominated as a corresponding member of the Institut de France, invited to accept an honorary doctorate at Cambridge University [1997 III 510], attended the first performance of the revised *Souvenir de Florence,* and rehearsed the double bill. The novelty of children onstage playing toy instruments—considered for the opening of *The Queen of Spades*—was proposed again in *The Nutcracker,* but after trying for several days, "our achievements were declared unsatisfactory, and after a rather long discussion in French between M. I. Petipa, the gentleman in the white suit [Tchaikovsky], and R. Drigo, the latter told us that whoever could play was permitted to" [316, 463–64]. On 12 November, an exceptional interview with Tchaikovsky, full of opinions, was published in *Peterburgskaya zhizn'* (Petersburg Life). Wagner was superior to Brahms; Mascagni heralded a rebirth by his talent and the proximity of his opera to real life. Tchaikovsky challenged Russia's naysayers and took pride in the country's successes. The Mighty Handful was a misleading nickname because no musical philosophy or principle ever marked the group's collective identity. Its much-touted innovations were atypical of the members' practice, as they never severed all connection with the past nor disdained traditional forms. Meanwhile, their hostility toward the rest of Russian music prompted the idea of a struggle between the Handful and everyone outside it. Tchaikovsky found this absurd. Presently, he would propose gymnasiums in all the principal Russian cities, which would prepare gifted students for whom music was a true calling. This should be done at government expense [84, 367–73].

The dress rehearsal of *Iolanta* and *The Nutcracker* was on 5 December 1892. The chief *régisseur* perpetuated the sense that these works were born of travail: "That it was the ballet orchestra, not the opera orchestra, much hampered the performance. That the costumes and decorations are not ready—is the chronic suffering of first performances" [316, 229].

If his nonconformity to operatic practice in *The Queen of* Spades was beginning to dawn on its critics, *Iolanta* and *The Nutcracker* risked appearing flawed or extremely experimental. *Iolanta* was resolutely atheatrical, resembling a cantata or an oratorio. The heroine is a blind princess sheltered from even the concept of sight until a knight discovers her and explains her condition. A Moorish physician, bolstered by Iolanta's faith and newfound love, restores her sight. It is what Laroche called elsewhere "unsuitable for the stage but full of poetry and profound thought, eminently suitable for musical illustration" [255 IV 93], and Kashkin called it a step forward in Tchaikovsky's command of the forms of dramatic music:

"Numbers fully suitable to regular operatic forms are not especially plentiful; the main parts are written in a mixed, free style, where recitative and arioso are blended, alternating and forming one harmonious whole" [RV921212]. *The Nutcracker* was also unconventional: a mimed first act with child principals to the near-exclusion of virtuoso dancing preceded a final act with no plot resolution and almost nothing but dancing. The ballerina made no appearance in the first act and refrained from dancing at all until her *pas de deux* just before the closing number.

By external measures, the premieres went well. A new aria for Vaudémont and his duet with Iolanta were encored, despite breaks in Figner's voice. *The Nutcracker* was less successful because the story little suited Tchaikovsky, and the shift to Lev Ivanov after Marius Petipa's illness disadvantaged the choreography [316, 229–30]. Even still, the Winter Scene and the Chinese Dance were approved, the latter encored for the dancing of Maria Anderson, whom Tchaikovsky had chosen to perform Puss 'n' Boots in *The Sleeping Beauty.* Writing to Anatoly the next day, he recalled the dress rehearsal with the emperor present: "He was delighted, called [me] to his box and spoke a mass of sympathetic words. The production of both is magnificent, the ballet even too magnificent—the eyes weary from such luxury" [xvi-b 201].

The unconventional aspects of these works nevertheless drew fire. *Iolanta* might be touching, but the libretto was "written in an unbeautiful, coarse style, in places so affected, suffering from *longeurs,* needless chatter, that it could hardly inspire a composer" [NO921210]. Mikhail Ivanov declared it too lavishly anointed in rose water and objected to the heroine's blindness as an atheatrical, pathological circumstance similar to Rigoletto's hump [VI930206]. He ridiculed Modest's philosophizing, especially from the Moorish doctor, and wickedly hinted that Tchaikovsky set Modest's inept verses in recitative and arioso because his melodic inspiration had lapsed. Worst of all, he was repeating songs and earlier operas, most obviously between the duet and Anton Rubinstein's song, "Desire." *Iolanta* was more a *pièce àpropos* than an opera; its musical interest diminished as it went along; the best numbers were at the beginning [NV921214].

Kashkin called *Iolanta* purely lyrical, "the coloration of tender sensitivity lies upon all, passively yielding to the course of events" [RV921212]. Another critic observed that heartfelt gesture was not common in Tchaikovsky: "Until now one has found bigness of expression and grand outbursts of heart only in the first act of *The Maid of Orleans,* in certain romances and two symphonic poems, *Romeo and Juliet* and *Francesca da Rimini,* whereas fine, delicate things, at times sickly in character, are innumerable in all his works." The grand pieces in *Iolanta* "are of an inspiration less noble and personal than in the works we have listed" [JS921209].

Kashkin later construed the absence of theatrical tension as the centrality of feeling:

> No external drama takes place onstage; the whole drama is reduced to what happens in Iolanta's soul and the gradual if rapid development of her awareness and feelings. Thus the main task for the musician becomes the depiction of the internal process of a young soul enveloped by new impressions and nearly exhausted under their burden. Not many opera composers would find such a story suitable, unsupported by powerful theatrical effects and situations. . . . P. I. Tchaikovsky in this sense never was a genuine opera composer; in him . . . stood a refined, sincere musician to whom external effect said little and the process of internal, intimate feelings—infinitely more. . . . Our late friend . . . knew that customary operatic devices would not do; one had to be content with the means provided by music alone, without depending on stage action. [174, 112–13]

The reception of *The Nutcracker* was polarized between ballet and music specialists. Balletomanes found little to love: "The production of ballets like *The Nutcracker* can quickly and easily lead the ballet troupe to its downfall" [BV921208]. Konstantin Skalkovsky concurred: "In general, the new ballet is produced primarily with children for children and for everything that can have value in their eyes as regards external brilliance; for the ballerina there is very little in it, for *art* precisely nothing, and for the artistic fate of our ballet, it is one more step downward" [NO921208]. Lack of substance was the principal complaint of "Old Balletomane" in a pompous letter to the editor of the *Peterburgskaya gazeta:* "What poverty of imagination! Such absurdity in the characters!" In the old days, he claimed, aesthetic enjoyment in ballet derived from a story that allowed the entire company to show its strengths in mime and dance, and a ballerina who took the leading part. *The Nutcracker* had only decorations and costumes

[PG921210]. The ballerina, Antonietta Dell' Era, had enjoyed a middling reception in her earlier appearances in St. Petersburg. At the second performance of *The Nutcracker,* the audience began to leave before the end [NV921210]. She was gone by the third.

Lev Ivanov was neither denied his virtues nor forgiven his faults. Most critics dubbed the battle of the mice and toy soldiers a failure, confused and chaotic on a dark stage, but the mime of Clara with the toy nutcracker won praise. Whereas the dances of Drosselmeyer's gifts in act I (dancing mechanical dolls) and the divertissement in act II were found to be excellent, the Waltz of the Flowers was "not bad as regards groupings, but the dances of the excellent soloists are completely lost in the general mass" [NO921208]. Dell' Era's *pas de deux* with the celesta made no particular impression, but the Waltz of the Snowflakes and the interlude preceding it struck a sympathetic chord among critics in a Petersburg winter: "The ballerinas were in white dresses, adorned as if in fluffs of snow, with snowy boughs they brandished and snowy rays around their heads; when they sat down and lay down, beckoning to each other, the effect was a pleasant, even warming pile of snow" [NV921207]. "Downy pompoms on white tunics, and on the headwear as rays of stars, and in fluttering little bundles on the accessories, represent the movement of snowflakes fully and picturesquely, the original grouping producing an elegant impression of the artistic allegory of a snowdrift" [NO921208]. "Mr. Bocharov's decor was much applauded, and yet more the sparkling waltz, so original in rhythm and orchestration. . . . The final grouping, on which electric light is suddenly shone, produces a magical effect" [JS921209].

Balletomanes objected to Tchaikovsky's music for not being *dansante,* but their musician colleagues disputed this, claiming that *The Nutcracker* marked a new era of ballet music: "Of Mr. Tchaikovsky's three ballets, . . . *The Nutcracker* is best, its music indeed not for the customary visitors to the ballet" [PG921209]. Conceding that it lacked the magnificence and orchestral panache of *The Sleeping Beauty,* another declared, "Clearly, ballet music is a domain where Mr. Tchaikovsky's genius is not beating its wings just once [but] is taking flight, and has profusely sown flowers as rich in color as they are beautiful and original in form" [JS921209]. Even Mikhail Ivanov, who had written a score for Petipa four years earlier, was humbled by *The Nutcracker:*

> The composer's technical mastery is expressed here brilliantly at every step, and to list those pages where Mr. Tchaikovsky showed himself a beautiful symphonist and savant of the orchestra would take too long, for such pages are too numerous. . . . As for the complexity of its music, ballet has now started out along a completely different path from before, and the most inveterate balletomanes . . . would doubtless find that a series of waltzes . . . no longer satisfies. Mr. Tchaikovsky was completely right to compose *The Nutcracker* . . . as he understands ballet music now. [NV921214]

Implicit in these remarks is that sense of breaking away, of perfecting a new individuality that Laroche sensed throughout Tchaikovsky's late theater works.

Were *Iolanta* and *The Nutcracker* successes? Claims of lapsed creativity echo the composer's own assessment, seconded by critics who named allusions too transparent or who found Tchaikovsky too inclined toward the miniature. And yet, the works show refinement in technique, orchestration, and motivic relationships [379, 133–38], and they clarify Tchaikovsky's place in the theater. They explain why, despite his talk of writing a piece like *Cavalleria rusticana,* he never tried to do so, and why he never wrote *Sadia*. These may have been the *dernier cri,* but he could not write them without reembracing clichés, clashes which in the past had led to grief. His art was evolving in another direction.

Tchaikovsky never took criticism well, but his mood for the rest of 1892 merged authorial irritation with the possibility that his critics were absolutely right. Scheduled to conduct in Brussels and to see Fanny Dürbach, he left St. Petersburg on 12 December, stayed in Berlin from 14/26 to 17/29, went to Basel overnight and on to Montbéliard. From Berlin, he wrote to Bob:

> These days I have devoted myself to important thoughts fraught with consequences. I have carefully perused and, so to speak, objectively responded to the new symphony, which fortunately I have not yet managed to orchestrate and launch. The impression is unflattering, for it—the symphony—is written simply to have something to write—there is nothing of the least interest or likeable in it. I decided to cast it out and forget about it. This decision is irreversible, and it is well to have taken it. But does it not generally follow from this that I am extinguished and dried up? That is what I've been thinking these

> three days. Perhaps a *scenario* could still inspire me, but pure music, symphonic and chamber, I ought not write. Meanwhile to live with nothing to do, without work swallowing up time, thoughts and powers—is very boring. What remains for me to do? Wave my baton and forget about composing? That is very difficult to decide. And so I think, think and do not know on which to settle. In any case, I have lived through these three joyless days. Yet I am completely well. [xvi-b 208]

Thus, he lived on as his muse died within him.

The prospect of visiting Fanny filled him with dread: "Tomorrow I go to Montbéliard, and, I confess, with a kind of sickly fright, almost horror, as if into the realm of people long vanished from the world's stage" [xvi-b 212]. He saw her on 20–21 December 1892 (O.S.), New Year's Day and 2 January in France. She was living in the house where she was born. He recognized her immediately, little changed for her 70 years. For a moment, he feared there would be tears and a scene, but there were not. He wrote to Nikolay:

> Forthwith began endless recollections and a veritable stream of the most interesting details of our childhood, Mama and all of us. Then she showed me our *notebooks* (*mine, yours and Venichka's*), my compositions, your and my letters, but most interesting of all several amazingly nice letters of Mamasha's. I cannot express the enchanting, magical sensation I was feeling, listening to these stories and reading all these letters and notebooks. The past in all its detail was so vividly recalled to mind that it seemed I was breathing the air of the house at Votkinsk. [xvi-b 213]

From Montbéliard, Tchaikovsky went to Paris and Brussels. The last letters of 1892 complain of melancholy; he resolved never to come abroad again except for pleasure or with someone to keep him company [xvi-b 219–20].

1893

After Brussels, Tchaikovsky went to Paris, then left for Odessa, arriving on the 12th. Meanwhile, on 10 January, the *Moskovskie vedomosti* reported that he, Sophie Menter, and Vasily Sapelnikov were to give concerts in London before their trip to Chicago [MV930110]. Tchaikovsky would later write to Menter in July 1893 confirming a concert in London for the following

May [234, 50], which implies that negotiations with Frederick Grant Gleason for appearances in Chicago had been successful. For now, Odessa from 12 to 24 January was, along with Prague in 1888, the greatest triumph Tchaikovsky ever enjoyed. He attended performances of *The Queen of Spades* and conducted five times, beginning with the Russian Musical Society on 16 January and two charity concerts. At a second Russian Musical Society concert on 23 January, he offered the most unusual program of his career: Borodin's First Symphony; Ernst's Violin Concerto in F-sharp Minor (K. A. Gavrilov the soloist); a Scherzo for Orchestra by Porfiry Iustinovich Molchanov, a professor at the Odessa Music School; the first performance of Sophie Menter's *Hungarian Fantasia* for piano (Menter, conducted by Sapelnikov), which he had orchestrated; and *1812,* which was encored. Nikolay Dmitrievich Kuznetsov sketched and painted his likeness, the composer's only portrait made from life [xvii 278]. "They honor me here in every possible way," he wrote to Vladimir Nápravnik. "[T]hey tear me to pieces until I am weary to the point of derangement" [xvii 20]. "All this very much fatigues me," he reported to Merkling, "but to complain about it would be laughable" [xvii 24–25]. In Kamenka he welcomed the return of merriment after Sasha's death, though Sestritsa was failing. He responded to an insistent Charles Villiers Stanford, who was pressing to know what he would conduct in Cambridge, and then, to Anatoly, pondered canceling that trip altogether [xvii 28]. He planned a nonstop return to Klin, so great was his need for solitude, but had to disembark at Kharkov because of a stomach ailment [xvii 29, n. 1 to no. 4854]. He was home by 3 February.

The next day, he began writing down the Sixth Symphony. He completed the first movement in five days and began the Scherzo. We do not know what had revived his muse—an act of God, a change in brain chemistry, recent events, including "the most powerful impression" from visiting Fanny [xvii 17] and being honored in Odessa as "all but the savior of society" [xvii 24], or the breath of mortality that forced him off the train at Kharkov. As recently as 28 January, he had written to Modest, "I need to believe in myself again, for my faith has been severely undermined, it seems that I have come to the end of my role." On 11 February, he wrote to Bob:

> During the journey another symphony came to me, programmatic this time, but with a program that shall remain a riddle to all—let them guess, but the

> symphony is thus and will be named: Program Symphony (no. 6); *Symphonie à Programme* (no. 6); *Programm-Symphonie* (no. 6). This program is nothing if not suffused with subjectivity, and often during my wandering, composing it in my head, I wept a lot. Now, back at home, I started writing sketches, and work was so impassioned and fluent that the first movement was completely ready in less than four days, and the others are clearly outlined in my head. Half of the third movement is already prepared. In its form much will be new in this symphony, and incidentally, the finale will not be a loud allegro but rather the most unhurried *adagio*. You cannot imagine what bliss I am experiencing, that my time is not yet past and that I can still work. [xvii 42–43]

With the symphony in his head he left for Moscow, where he conducted a benefit concert that marked his reconciliation with Safonov [1997 III 534]. After visiting Anatoly, he accepted Robert Kajanus's invitation to conduct in Helsinki (postponed until 1894) and his cousin Andrey Petrovich's request for a march for his regiment. He learned that Lev Davïdov was to remarry. On 8 March, he reported to Modest a headache of two weeks' duration that ended mysteriously in time for his departure to Kharkov to conduct on the 14th. There he met Ivan Klimenko for the last time. Home again, he finished composing the Sixth on 24 March, after some 23 days of work; the draft included sketches for a concertante piece for cello [425, 283–91]. The next day, he wrote the "March for the Yurievsky 98th Infantry Regiment" for his cousin. By 28 March, he had completed his new vocal quartet, "Night," based on Mozart [xvii 72]. Part of his time was devoted to the advocacy of young musicians. The orchestral suite "From a Child's Life" by Georgy Konyus had won his admiration [xvii 48–49]; he urged Bessel to publish the work and scheduled to conduct it. In Odessa, he had assessed candidates to direct its music school and the concerts of its musical society. Of two worthy prospects, Felix Blumenfeld and Andrey Schulz-Evler, he thought Blumenfeld especially suitable [xvii 74]. On 7 April, he commenced an income-producing project—to compose a new piano piece or song every day for a month. By the 15th, cooking his 10th such pancake, he wrote, "At the beginning it wasn't easy, and the first two–three pieces required an exertion of will, but now I can hardly deal with the thoughts that occur to me, one after another, every passing day" [xvii 81–82]. He stopped on 22 April with 18 pieces, adding the op. 73 romances on 5 May. He left for St. Petersburg on the 6th, and a week later for England.

Tchaikovsky's English adventure comprised two public events. First was a concert in London, as his agent, Francesco Berger, wanted to take advantage of the important musicians converging on the town—Max Bruch, Arrigo Boito, and Camille St.-Saëns all being there to accept honorary doctorates (Grieg fell ill and stayed home). Second was to celebrate the 50th anniversary of the founding of the Cambridge University Musical Society at a concert given the day before the conferral of degrees. There, he would conduct *Francesca*. The concerts were two weeks apart, leaving him time to spare in a city he did not especially like, where he didn't know anyone and did not speak the language. Even before arriving, he described his pining, suffering, and weeping and diagnosed himself as having "some psychological illness [*psikhopatiya*]." He then invited himself to Grankino, to Bob and Kolya, on his return trip [xvii 93–94].

The composer described little of what happened in England, though later a scholar noted important activity for almost every day [283]. On the day he arrived, 17/29 May, Tchaikovsky described his current state:

> I suffer from melancholy . . . and hatred of foreigners, from some undefined fright and who knows what else. Physically this condition is marked by pain in the lower abdomen, and by aching and weakness in the legs. . . . And I still have two weeks to stick around here! It seems an eternity!!! I arrived this morning. . . . Only with difficulty did I find a room in my hotel; it is high season, and all the hotels are overflowing. London is a most disagreeable city; I cannot find anything here; there are no *pissoirs,* no *money-changing shops,* it's hard to find the hat on your head!!! [xvii 97]

He stayed at the Hotel Dieudonné in Ryder Street off lower Regent Street—an exclusive lodging, with a French staff and a French proprietress. During Tchaikovsky's visit, Louis Diémer, Pablo Sarasate, and Camille St.-Saëns were also staying there. It had but one bathroom.

At Tchaikovsky's first rehearsal on 19/31 May, Sir Alexander Mackenzie was touched by his modesty and kindness [283, 350]. The next day, Sir Henry Wood memorialized the anecdote in which Tchaikovsky exhorted the players in the finale of the Fourth Symphony by shouting "Vodka—more vodka!!" [283, 351]. Later that day, he could not find the stage door and hoped to gain entry by the box office. The clerks thought he was trying to buy a ticket; he was finally discovered by an assistant. "The concert went brilliantly," he wrote to Modest, "that is, by the unanimous opinion of all I had a genuine triumph, such that *St.-Saëns,* who appeared after me, suffered somewhat as a result of my extraordinary success" [xvii 102; notices in 283, 352–58].

London, he decided, was pleasant but punishing. He went to receptions, soirees, and performances by others. He called on Friedrich Cowan and George Henschel, was photographed at Herbert Barraud's in Oxford Street, visited Mackenzie at the Royal Academy, and rehearsed at the Royal College of Music for the Cambridge concert. He met with Polish composer Zygmunt Stojowski, giving him the score of the Fourth Symphony he had used in the Philharmonic concert (it would be auctioned at Sotheby's in December 2000).

On 31 May/12 June, Tchaikovsky left for Cambridge, sharing a compartment on the train with the music critic Hermann Klein [283, 388–90]. In addition to the composers, receiving doctorates on this occasion were two physicians, a general, and a rajah—this after Anton Rubinstein, Johannes Brahms, Giuseppe Verdi, Charles Gounod, Antonín Dvořák, and Joseph Joachim had declined. Tchaikovsky had accepted Frederick William Maitland's invitation to stay in his home and was delighted with his welcome and obviously fascinated with the ritual of it all:

> The celebration itself ran for two whole days, and consisted the first day of the concert, gala dinner and gala reception, and the second of the ceremony of elevation to doctoral rank, gala breakfast and reception by the chancellor's wife. The ceremony was as follows. At 11:30 we gathered in a special location and donned our doctoral robes, which were made up of a white cloak (silk), covered in crimson velvet, and a black velvet beret. Together with us there were raised to the level of the doctorate four persons, of whom one, an Indian vassal princeling (a rajah), wore a turban adorned with precious stones worth upwards of millions, and one field marshal. In the same hall all the professors and doctors of the university gathered in costumes similar to ours, but of a different color. At 12 o'clock a procession took place according to the printed ceremonial. I processed next to Boito and behind *St.-Saëns.* We passed through a huge courtyard before numerous crowds into the University Senate, which was overflowing with the people. Each of us sat at a prepared place on a high eminence, the *public orator* came in (so named is a gentleman who specializes in making speeches at these ceremonies), and by turns addressed each of us in Latin, extolling our services to science and art. . . . During that discourse, the

person in whose honor it was being spoken came forward and stood motionless. Moreover, according to medieval tradition the students, comprising choruses, whistle, whine, sing, cry out, to which one ought not pay the slightest heed. After the discourses the orator takes the doctors by the hand and forms them into a semicircle facing the chancellor, who occupies a special place. The latter takes the doctors by the hand and says to each in Latin, "In the name of the Father and the Son and the Holy Spirit I declare you a doctor." After enthusiastic handshakes, you are led back to your place. When everything is over the procession, in the same manner, returns to the first hall, and in an hour and a half, all, in their costumes, depart for the gala breakfast, at the end of which the ancient, rounded chalice passes to all the guests, and thus everything is finished. I immediately left for London, and the next morning for Paris. I am still not completely myself. [xvii 109–10]

Between 7/19 June, the first day of a week at Schloss Itter with Sophie Menter, and 19 June at Grankino, no letter of Tchaikovsky survives. When he wrote to Anatoly on 19 June, he lamented the deaths of Konstantin Albrecht, a friend from his earliest days in Moscow, and Konstantin Shilovsky, who helped him with the libretto of *Evgeniy Onegin,* and he was concerned about Alexey Apukhtin, a friend since his school days, who was alive but mortally ill. At Grankino he began to adapt the Symphony in E-flat into the Third Piano Concerto and asked Modest to think about a libretto, claiming to prefer something like *Carmen* or *Cavalleria rusticana* [xvii 85]. He then traveled to Ukolovo to visit Nikolay, bypassing Kamenka. He stayed 10 days and was back at Klin by 18 July.

The next day, he agreed to conduct the first performance of the Sixth Symphony in St. Petersburg on 16 October; Adèle Aus der Ohe would perform the First Piano Concerto; he also agreed to three more concerts in the 1893–1894 season. On the 21st, he answered the call from Bernhard Pollini of Hamburg for the revival of *Iolanta* on 8 September, and they discussed a production of *The Queen of Spades.* His main business at Klin was to complete the Sixth:

I am up to my neck in the symphony. The further I go, the more difficult the instrumentation. Twenty years ago I forged ahead as fast as I could and it came out well. Now I have become fainthearted, unsure of myself. Today I sat the whole time over two pages, and nothing came of it, however much I tried. [xvii 142]

At this time, Siloti was again pressing him to shorten the Second Piano Concerto, but still he resisted [xvii 147, 160]. His assessment of the Third Concerto (to Siloti) was perfectly sane—the piece is not bad, but not very worthwhile [xvii 151]. Early in August, personal irritations found their way to the surface. He wrote to Bob, "Why are you angry with me? It is otherwise difficult to explain why you utterly despise my effort, however modest, to exchange news. . . . Truly, I never presumed to deserve special attention, but I am simply sad that you are so little interested in me." He threatened for a breath to reconsider the dedication of the new symphony to Bob, then affirmed his faith in the work: "I positively consider it the best, and especially the *most sincere* of all my things. I love it as I have never loved any of my musical offspring before" [xvii 155]. On 12 August, he completed the Sixth Symphony—score and four-hands arrangement—and worried about the cholera epidemic facing Anatoly in Nizhny-Novgorod [xvii 164–65].

As Tchaikovsky made ready to leave for St. Petersburg and Hamburg, Apukhtin died. "At the very moment I am writing this letter, they are 'singing off' my comrade Apukhtin in Petersburg. So many deaths among my old pals: Karlusha [Albrecht], both Shilovskys, Apukhtin!!" [xvii 174]. The Hamburg visit passed without incident. Tchaikovsky met the Czech composer Josef Foerster, with whom he had been in friendly correspondence, and recommended him to a publisher. On the way home, he stopped in Mikhailovskoe to visit Anatoly [xvii 180]. He informed Stojowski that he would conduct his Suite, op. 9, on 15/27 January 1894 [xvii 181].

On 20 September, Grand Duke Konstantin wrote to him. Since Apukhtin's death, he had been thinking about Tchaikovsky and proposed the composition of an oratorio based on Apukhtin's poem "Requiem." At Klin, Tchaikovsky reread Apukhtin's poem. Much in "Requiem" did not require music and even contradicted it, he observed:

> There is yet another reason why I am little inclined to compose a requiem of any kind, but I fear touching indelicately on your religious sensitivity [K.R.'s wife being originally a Roman Catholic]. In the [Latin] Requiem much is made of God the Judge, God the Punisher, God the Avenger (!!!). Forgive me, Your Highness, but I make bold to suggest that I do not believe in such a God, or at least such a God cannot cause those tears, that delight, that worship for the creator and source of all good which would inspire me. . . . [H]ow many

> times I have dreamed of illustrating Christ's words: "Come to me all ye who labor and are burdened," and then: "for my yoke is sweet and my burden is light." What endless love and compassion for humankind reside in these marvelous words! What endless poetry in this, one could say, *passionate* striving to dry the tears of grief and ease the torments of suffering humankind! [xvii 194]

From September to October we can observe Tchaikovsky's world in microcosm. Eduard Strauss wrote from Vienna, proposing conducting dates in February 1894 [6, 19–20]. Death claimed another friend, Nikolay Zverev, Tchaikovsky's colleague at the Moscow Conservatory and a teacher of Rachmaninov. On 1 October, Fanny Dürbach wrote. On 3 October, he finished scoring the Third Piano Concerto; on 6 October, he entertained the cellists Brandukov and Poplavsky; on 7 October, he departed Klin for the last time. In Moscow he attended Zverev's funeral service, visited Nikolay Rubinstein's grave [367, 157], showed Taneyev the Third Piano Concerto, and at the conservatory attended a performance of "Night" and a read-through of the Sixth Symphony. Konstantin Saradzhev, who was 15 at the time, left an account of the latter:

> There were many stops, clearly they were correcting mistakes in the parts and in the playing of the performers. . . . Then I saw Tchaikovsky, Safonov and Grzhimali come out of the hall, and behind them the other teachers at some distance. Tchaikovsky was carrying the huge score. His face was especially flushed, powerfully agitated. Safonov and Grzhimali walked a step or two behind him and all were silent. It is difficult to explain what these people were experiencing, but it was clear to me that something exceptional and outstanding had happened. [316, 372]

In town from Hamburg, Pollini proposed that Safonov and Tchaikovsky, conducting a German orchestra sent to Moscow for rehearsal, would tour provincial Russia the next summer. Kashkin wrote of his last meeting with Tchaikovsky later that evening:

> Imperceptibly our conversation shifted to our most recent losses: the deaths of Albrecht and Zverev. . . . Unwilled the thought entered our heads: who would be next along the path of no return? Utterly assured, I told Pyotr Ilyich that he would probably outlive us all; he disputed this, but in the end said that he had never felt so healthy or happy as now. On that very evening Pyotr Ilyich had to take the express train to Petersburg, and it was already time to leave for

> the station. He was to conduct his new symphony there, the Sixth, completely unknown to me; he told me that he had not the slightest doubt about the first three movements, but the last still posed questions for him, and perhaps after the Petersburg performance it will be destroyed and replaced. The Musical Society concert in Moscow was set for 23 October; Tchaikovsky proposed to return to Klin several days earlier, and come to Moscow the day of the concert; in case we did not meet at the concert, he arranged a meeting afterwards at the Hotel Moscow, where he wanted several people to come to dinner. . . . Our conversation ended on that, we took each other's leave and Tchaikovsky left for the train station. . . . [T]he possibility of eternal separation never crossed our minds. [187, 159–60]

The last 15 days of Tchaikovsky's life were extraordinary because of his unexpected death and its ambiguities. Accounts disagree in major points and in details. Whether testimony was given in the confusion and dread of the composer's final illness or later, no witness to Tchaikovsky's last days was exempt from exaggeration. Accounts of his passing abound [307; 44; 363; 286]. Let us first summarize the data and describe Tchaikovsky's funeral.

That Tchaikovsky's death was unanticipated is implicit in the scheduling of so many future commitments and is confirmed in sources from the days before he fell ill. His late correspondence was all business as usual; the last letter, dated 21 October to Ivan Nikolaevich Grekov, was about arranging a concert in Odessa. In *The Life,* Modest mentions meeting his brother on 10 October, that he looked well and then proceeded to rehearsals and performance (on 16 October) of the Sixth Symphony. The symphony was applauded and his brother recalled, but the enthusiasm was no greater than in the past. In this, Mikhail Rimsky-Korsakov concurred: it was a succès d'estime, though the applause after each movement was not markedly warm [323, 360]. Yuly Konyus, who had heard Tchaikovsky play the Sixth at the piano at Klin, thought that "he took it all too fast, as if fearing to descend into vulgar sentimentality" [241, 370]. Modest found the critical response middling. Never long on compliments, Nikolay Solovyov thought the first movement had a beautiful second theme and a development "marked by great energy and thrilling external power"—but it risked disintegration from the contrast of the first and second themes. He liked the Scherzo; the ensuing Adagio, he wrote, was the natural consequence of exceptionally fast tempos earlier in the work [NO931018]. Laroche wrote:

> As for melody, recent years have revealed in Mr. Tchaikovsky an extraordinary richness and an impassioned beauty of themes. . . . I cannot recall one Tchaikovsky composition of my very favorites which in greater degree would combine originality of design and artistry of execution, the agility of a master and the inspiration of a creator. [255 II 159–61]

These reports contained nothing about art imitating life, or about the finale signifying death.

Modest cut to the following morning when Pyotr, unsure of what to call the new work, adopted Modest's suggestion, "Pathétique," and wrote it on the title page. Modest elaborated:

> Hugo Riemann, one of the most brilliant and esteemed music theorists, in a thematic elucidation of the content of the Symphony no. 6, sees the solution of the riddle of its title "Pathétique" in the "kinship, which immediately strikes the eye, of the basic thought of the composition and the principal theme of Beethoven's *Sonate pathétique,*" which Pyotr Ilyich was not contemplating. [1997 III 572]

He next reviewed the days before 21 October. Pyotr looked forward to conducting Konyus's "From a Child's Life"; he spoke of revising *The Maid of Orleans* [316, 230–31]. On Wednesday, 20 October, he dined with Vera Vasilievna Butakova, his flame from Hapsal in the summer of 1867, and after the theater at the Restaurant Leiner—macaroni washed down with white wine and mineral water. He came home healthy and calm [1997 III 572–75].

From the morning of 21 October to his brother's death early on the 25th, Modest recounted his brother's final illness in great detail. On the 21st, Tchaikovsky took a salty laxative water instead of castor oil for his chronic stomach upset; he left to visit Eduard Nápravnik but returned without doing so because of indisposition; he felt well and wrote letters at midday; he also drank a glass of unboiled water and dismissed Modest's fright over this; and at 5:00 p.m. Modest ceased to heed his brother's protests and called a doctor. Vasily Bertenson arrived at a little past 8:00 p.m. and suspected something serious. He called his brother Lev as Tchaikovsky's symptoms worsened. Lev Bertenson arrived at 11:00 p.m. and diagnosed cholera. The battle with the increasingly terrible symptoms was aggressively pursued until 5:00 a.m. on 22 October, when they began to ease. At 9:00 a.m. a new doctor, Nikolay Mamonov, arrived, and by midday all symptoms had subsided except for thirst. This improvement lasted for the rest of the day, though the doctors feared it might be the calm before a new, more drastic complication. On 23 October, Tchaikovsky's symptoms were stable but his mood had deteriorated, as he no longer hoped for recovery. His doctors tried to reverse the cessation of kidney function, and when nothing availed they planned to give the composer a hot bath to stimulate the passage of fluids. Pyotr, Modest, and Nikolay were hesitant about this because their mother had died soon after this treatment. Scheduled for that evening, it was not carried out because of the patient's diarrhea. On the 24th Tchaikovsky was weak, felt terrible, slept more fitfully, and suffered occasional delirium, repeating the name of Nadezhda von Meck in reproach. When he awakened, he found it more difficult to return to full awareness than before. He was completely bereft of strength, and when Lev Bertenson arrived at about 1:00 p.m., he immediately ordered the bath. Tchaikovsky was hardly immersed in it before he complained of weakness and asked to be taken out. For all this, he seemed stable through the afternoon and into the evening; he was injected with musk to stimulate his heart when his pulse weakened. At a little past 8:00 p.m. it weakened significantly, and Lev Bertensen was summoned. It was the beginning of the end. At about 10:00 p.m. emphysema set in, and a priest was summoned. By the time he delivered the last rites, Tchaikovsky was beyond comprehending them. The doctors applied stimulants, but to no avail. His breathing slowed, and when asked questions, he nodded:

> Suddenly his eyes, up to then half-closed and having begun to roll, opened wide. There occurred an indescribable expression of clear awareness. He rested his gaze, in turn, on the three persons closest to him, then gave himself up to heaven. In a few moments something lit up in his eyes, and with his last breath it went out. It was a little past 3 o'clock in the morning. [1997 III 575–81]

The only other relative to recount Tchaikovsky's last days in print was his nephew Yury Lvovich Davïdov, Bob's younger brother, a 17-year-old student at the time whose recollections were published "with abbreviations" only in 1943 [316, 382–95]; they fill in some of the events about which Modest wrote little. Davïdov could not comment on Pyotr's illness because (he wrote) he was not admitted into his uncle's apartment out of fear of infection. He was allowed, as a student, to attend rehearsals of the 16 October concert, where he recalled seeing K.R., Glazunov, Nápravnik, Lyadov, Laroche, and Modest at the dress rehearsal. Tchaikovsky was relatively calm in contrast to his usual agitation, expressed in continuous smoking, silence, and pacing about, agitation which had nearly disappeared since the mid-1880s. This was a surprisingly authoritative remark from someone born in 1876 who had spent most of his life away from his uncle's conducting. Davïdov recalled audience reaction "with almost photographic precision": the first movement was warmly received but without ovations; the second produced a storm of applause that was not sustained; the third was received again more warmly; the end of the finale brought prolonged silence until Tchaikovsky signaled his appreciation to the orchestra. After the concert, Tchaikovsky asked Anna Merkling if she had grasped the program of the new symphony. She construed it as biographical, to which Pyotr generally concurred, referring to the last movement merrily as "that by which everything is ended, but, I am still a long way from that." Later in the evening, Tchaikovsky indicated his plan to depart for Klin the next day, and Modest asked him to stay for the first performance of his new play on the 25th. Tchaikovsky hesitated, then agreed [316, 384–87].

On 20 October, Davïdov joined his uncle at supper *chez* Butakova, where the composer described his recent trip to Hamburg and joked about the suitability of voices accustomed to Wotan and Hunding singing the lyric parts of *Iolanta*. He then went to the Alexandrinsky Theater and after that to the Restaurant Leiner. There, Davïdov claimed, the composer, when informed there was no more bottled water, ordered a glass of unboiled water, "the colder the better." It was brought to him just as Modest, who arrived late, came into the restaurant:

> Modest Ilyich got seriously angry with his brother and exclaimed: "I categorically forbid you to drink unboiled water!" Laughing, Pyotr Ilyich leapt up and went to meet the waiter, and Modest Ilyich rushed after him. But Pyotr Ilyich left him behind and, holding him at bay with his elbow, managed to drink the fateful glass at one draught. [316, 390]

Neither Modest's nor Davïdov's account withstands scrutiny. Why did Modest downplay the critical response to the new symphony and magnify his own importance in choosing the work's title, which his brother had already chosen in August or September [307, 27–28]? Given the family's sensitivity to cholera, why did he make prominent the incident with unboiled water in the apartment and then omit mention of the incident with unboiled water at an important restaurant? Publicized in newspapers the day after Tchaikovsky's death [307, 146], this report caused a downturn in the Restaurant Leiner's business [307, 178]. The vivid detail and sole authority of several particulars in Yury Davïdov's account must be weighed against the distortions of 50 years of memory and his motive at the time of publication to dispel rumors that Tchaikovsky had committed suicide. He wrote like someone having nothing to hide, while later evidence indicated that his account was partly fiction, and he did not witness the events in the Restaurant Leiner that he so vividly described [307, 76–78]. How are we to interpret the assurances of Tchaikovsky's good mood, or his alleged agreement to stay in St. Petersburg until 25 October when he was to conduct the first performance of the Sixth in Moscow on the 23rd?

Sorting out what was true or false, what was doctored or misremembered (let alone impossible to verify) in accounts of Tchaikovsky's passing leads to ambiguities which place all evidence at the mercy of the reader's interpretation. Invoking the legal principle whereby a person known once to bear false witness thereby taints all other evidence he gives, we must dismiss both Modest and Davïdov. If doubt is this evident in the composer's devoted relatives, what is to be made of the newspaper rumors, conflicting accounts, and conspiracy theories?

Of the honor bestowed upon Tchaikovsky after his death, however, there can be no doubt. The grandeur of his funeral was extraordinary for a head of church or state, let alone a private citizen and a musician. There were at least 12 religious services in Modest's apartment before the funeral and others at the School of Jurisprudence, the Moscow Conservatory, the St. Petersburg Conservatory (where classes were suspended for three days), Tchaikovsky's church in Klin, and many other venues. The night before the funeral, commemorative wreaths lined the walls of Modest's apartment and nearly covered the coffin [NO931028]. Two days after his death, there was already talk of making his home in Klin a national property [367, 153].

Some grief was couched in oratory. "Tchaikovsky is dead! . . . I cannot convey to you the deep impression this death has caused. . . . After Lev Tolstoy—Pyotr Tchaikovsky: two names in which lived the expression of Russian genius, and half of this is no more!" [quoted in 367, 152]. The aloof

Rubinstein was taken aback. "Could this be God's will?" he wrote to his sister. "What a loss for music in Russia! And it happened in the prime of life—he was only 50!—and all this from a glass of water! Everything indeed is nonsense—life, creativity, and all the rest" [25 III 140].

The extremity of the grief was clear from the composer's funeral, which was paid for by the emperor, lasted eight hours, and brought together some 100,000 souls. The theater direction, charged with planning it, hoped to limit deputation to 8,000 people by issuing passes to the funeral procession, and 6,000 more would be given places inside the Kazan Cathedral, where the memorial liturgy and funeral service would take place. Tens of thousands of requests were received [NV931028].

Tchaikovsky was buried on 28 October 1893. Early in the day, the emperor sent a magnificent wreath of white roses. At about 9 o'clock, officials and deputations began to assemble in front of Modest's apartment, unofficial mourners having gathered earlier. Carriage traffic was suspended, and the pavement was lined with police. Wreaths delivered after this were placed onto carriages. At 10:00 a.m., as a short service was conducted in the apartment, the master of ceremonies began to arrange the deputations. Here is a sample, the first of eight sections, each with its own manager:

State comptroller and inspectors of the Ministry of the Imperial Court
Imperial Academy of Arts
Court Chapel
Imperial St. Petersburg Philharmonic Society
Imperial St. Petersburg Theater School
Imperial Theaters of Moscow
Imperial St. Petersburg French Drama Troupe
Imperial Russian Drama Troupe
Imperial St. Petersburg Ballet
Orchestra of the Imperial St. Petersburg Theaters
Imperial Russian Opera [NO931028]

When representatives of concert-giving societies, educational institutions, and press organizations; literary figures; members of the School of Jurisprudence; clerics, civic and court officials, and the nobility are counted, some idea of the task becomes clear. Deputations stretched from Modest's apartment, just off Nevsky Prospect, to St. Isaac's Square. Along the funeral route, thousands of people observed from windows.

The coffin was placed on a hearse, a carved white carriage in the Russian style, gilded and draped in white damask. Preceded by singers, clergy, and the deputations, it was led by a porter in funeral livery and students from the School of Jurisprudence carrying a velvet pillow with the cross of St. Vladimir, Tchaikovsky's imperial award [VI931106]. Behind it came three carriages of wreaths, Prince Alexander Oldenburg (patron of the School of Jurisprudence), other persons of rank, family members, and intimate friends. The procession began shortly after 10:00 a.m. and moved to the Maryinsky Theater. Theater Square was a sea of people; the Maryinsky entrance was draped in black, its lights shrouded, the piers between its windows adorned with palm wreaths intertwined with black crepe; near the entrance was a huge funeral lyre with Tchaikovsky's initials. Across the square, the scaffolding of the new conservatory, its fences, windows, and balconies, and the roofs of coaches were all covered with onlookers; 14 new deputations from music institutions both local and as distant as Kharkov and Prague met the procession here. Passing around the conservatory, the procession moved back to Nevsky Prospect and the Kazan Cathedral, the vast semicircle in front of which had been cleared. As a result, people crowded in from the sides. The hearse approached from a side street, the deputations from the front. It was almost noon.

The cathedral was overflowing, complicating the entry of the deputations when the public crowded in on the heels of Tchaikovsky's family, adding to worshippers who had stayed on after an earlier service. Entry was suspended, and order restored only after an exhortation to respect Tchaikovsky's memory. These words had a magical effect; the doors were reopened, and those with passes were let in [NO931029]. A wreath of white roses from the city of St. Petersburg was placed on Tchaikovsky's coffin. In company with fellow clergy, the Most Reverend Nikander, bishop of Narva, who possessed a beautiful bass voice, offered the memorial liturgy, a celebration of the resurrection. The cathedral's own choir sang during the hieratic service, but during the liturgy as a whole the chorus of the Russian Opera sang music by Glinka and Vinogradov, and three choruses by Tchaikovsky. Bishop Nikander celebrated the singing-off, while the numerous clergy in white vestments were joined by the chorus of the Imperial Opera [NO931029]. Afterward, the deputations reassembled for the procession down Nevsky Prospect to the Alexander Nevsky Lavra:

> In expectation of the bearing of P. I. Tchaikovsky's coffin out of the cathedral, thousands of Petersburgers waited several hours on Nevsky Prospect, [in] Kazan Square and on Kazan Street; the public formed two veritable walls. Mounted policemen cleared a path for the deputations. On the balconies of houses opposite the cathedral cameras were in near-constant use. On Kazan Street opposite the cathedral a trumpet ensemble from the Life Guards Finnish Regiment was deployed. It [was] 1:30 p.m. [NO931029]

The procession moved with difficulty through the people massed on Nevsky Prospect. It seemed that all of Petersburg had poured out onto the boulevard. The journey of some two miles took about two and a half hours. By the time the procession arrived, about 1,000 people were already at the open grave, located near those of Musorgsky and Borodin. It was so crowded that each deputation had to limit entrance to one member. Bishop Nikander conducted the burial service, the coffin was lowered into the earth, and addresses followed. Safonov spoke of the woe which had befallen the art of music. Senator Vladimir Gerard, the composer's classmate, spoke on behalf of the School of Jurisprudence: "Farewell, dear, beloved colleague. The earth will rest lightly upon you, there is no doubt of this. It always rests lightly on him who leaves behind good memories of himself; and for Tchaikovsky 'eternal memory' lies in his work, and in the love of them who knew him. Farewell!" [NO931029].

One observer described the scene:

> The twilight fell darker over Petersburg, as did the twilight of the heart. . . . In the dusk of a Petersburg day it was so mournful—a cemetery covered in light snow and overgrown with leafless trees! People everywhere looked black in the darkness—on the monuments, crosses, the gravestones. . . . I did not see much, and was hearing badly, and mainly saw and heard an immense grief. . . . But the crowd kept pressing and pressing, when suddenly, in a moment of the most intense silence, playful, merry voices rang out. I glanced around and saw not far away on a roof a small group of children, rummaging about happily in the snow, who with lusty cries were expressing the fullness of their joyful feelings. Such is the renewal of life, infinite and immutable. [367, 154]

By five o'clock, it was done.

 CHAPTER TWENTY 

The Music of 1889–1893

TCHAIKOVSKY BEGAN COMPOSING IN THE YEAR 1889 WITH TWO choruses commissioned by Fyodor Bekker, chorus master of the Imperial Opera in St. Petersburg. One was an arrangement of "Legend" [tr. 391, 420], the fifth of his *Children's Songs,* op. 54, from which he deleted the 8 bars of introduction and postlude and assigned choral parts to the original accompaniment, adjusting the texture when the accompaniment turned more florid. He enlivened the rhythm with rests on the downbeats and occasionally altered the song melody, as at the beginning of Christ's words. The new voicing, including low octave displacements for the bass, enhanced an effect of gravity. *Solovushko* (The Little Nightingale) [tr. 389, 18], to his own words, was composed 9–12 January. As "Legend" was religious in tone, so "The Little Nightingale" was folkish. The call of the opening call-and-response, with mixed meter and cadence on the seventh, returns near the end in reference to the coming of spring. The melodies, their litany-like repetition, the nonprimary scale degrees at cadences, the cadence chords themselves, and not least the reserved, almost sorrowful expression sustain the folk-like ethos.

The major work of 1889 was *The Sleeping Beauty,* op. 66, which originated in the proposal three years before for a ballet on the story of Undine. The orchestral score was first typeset in the *Collected Works* [CW 12]; honoring Tchaikovsky's arrangement with the impresario Pollini in Hamburg (above, p. 350), a performance score from St. Petersburg was lithographed for rental only and fitted with Jurgenson title pages in Russian and German. The music, however, not only conveyed the Petersburg redaction, omitting the Entr'acte (no. 18), the Sapphire Variation, and the *entrée* of the act III *pas de deux,* but also contained crippling errors, such as placing the Gold Variation from act III before the act I waltz instead of its intended relocation after no. 15a in act II. These errors were apparently never corrected and precluded the practical use of this score. The following scenario is condensed from the 1890 libretto [tr. 431, 327–33; analyzed 110, 136–50]:

Prologue. In King Florestan's banquet hall, courtiers prepare to congratulate the King and Queen and Princess Aurora's fairy godmothers at the child's baptismal feast. The master of ceremonies, Catalabutte, verifies the guest list; the royals and fairy godmothers enter; pages and girls present gifts from the King to the fairies, who then bestow their gifts upon the child. As the Lilac Fairy makes her gift, there is a commotion in the entranceway: it is the uninvited fairy, Carabosse, who punishes Catalabutte for excluding her by feeding tufts of his hair to the rats in her retinue. Her gift is a prediction: as a young woman, Aurora will prick her finger and fall asleep forever. The Lilac Fairy intervenes: instead of eternal sleep, Aurora will be awakened by a prince's kiss, to be followed by a happy and contented life. Enraged, Carabosse departs.

Act I. Aurora is 20. Catalabutte dispatches some villagers to prison for working with needles in front of the royal palace. The King and Queen enter with four princes seeking Aurora's hand, who beg mercy for the offenders. Amid rejoicing, the peasants dance. Aurora makes her entrance and dances with each of the princes. Her parents urge her to choose one, but she declines out of love of freedom. At the princes' urging, she dances. She espies an old woman with a spindle, takes it, continues dancing, pricks her finger, and falls. The old woman is Carabosse, who vanishes in smoke and fire. The Lilac Fairy, revealed in a fountain, consoles the despairing parents and sends everyone to the castle, where they fall asleep at her command; verdure overgrows the scene; she posts her minions to protect the sleeping realm.

Act II. A century has passed. Prince Désiré's hunting party is taking its rest. Hunters and ladies divert him with dance, archery, and games. Galifron, his tutor, urges sociability, as he must choose a wife, but the Prince's heart has not spoken. When he is alone, the Lilac Fairy appears. She summons a vision of Aurora and her friends, who enchant Désiré until they disappear among the rocks. Mad with love, Désiré chooses Aurora, then sails with the Lilac Fairy to Florestan's castle. They enter, and when Désiré kisses Aurora, the castle awakens.

Act III. A divertissement of fairytale characters invited to the wedding of Aurora and Désiré, whose dances are followed by *entrées* of Romans, Persians, Indians, Americans, and Turks; a dance for the entire ensemble; and, to close, an apotheosis, the "Gloire des Fées."

Unlike the Moscow Ballet, for which Tchaikovsky composed *Swan Lake*—a work of undocumented collaboration made upon a neglected company—the Imperial Ballet in St. Petersburg in 1889–1890 was arguably the greatest in the world. He composed *The Sleeping Beauty* in collaboration with the director of the Imperial Theaters and balletmaster Marius Petipa, who guided Tchaikovsky and resolved rehearsal issues, setting his highest art to music that well exceeded his norms of intricacy. Vsevolozhsky made costume designs and funded the production.

The score may be judged by its adherence to the stage action and its conformity with genre. Tchaikovsky's knack for the characteristic produced such *dansante* yet right-sounding variations in the prologue as those for the Breadcrumb Fairy (pizzicati) and "Canari qui chante" (the warbling piccolo). His music grew more vivid when the narrative recommenced, at Carabosse's entrance (no. 4 at 37), conveying the evil fairy's grotesque yet threatening aspect:

Ex. 52

Other examples of *prelest'* in *The Sleeping Beauty*—a long list—include the action scenes that begin acts I and II; Aurora's dance with the spindle, the stages of her demise meticulously described; the so-called dream chords, at the moment when "Tout le monde est petrifié" at the Lilac Fairy's command (no. 9, 151); and not least no. 19, "Le Sommeil," where Tchaikovsky turns music that his collaborators intended merely for a scene change into philosophy.

The balletomanic evaluation of *The Sleeping Beauty,* which risked misconstruing vivid sound as disregard for the basic necessities of dance, was indirectly a compliment. It spoke to how Tchaikovsky recognized these necessities and also repaired the breach that specialist composers had opened between the music of narrative and the obligatory *dansante.* Petipa did not prescribe nor did Tchaikovsky yield to the primitive standard of a bass drum marking out a hackneyed melody. In his variations, *dansante* simplicity, animated with sounds appropriate to the situation, grow richer throughout the work, culminating in the precious stones variations for the fairies in act III, where the composer's gift for metaphor reaches heights of acuity and synesthesia, especially in the dazzling Sapphire Variation, where horns, bassoons, and piano establish the dark-hued background for the glints of pizzicato strings, and the sparkling Diamond Variation, whose flashes become audible in wisps of flute, clarinet, and violin. Variation music had never sounded like this before, which was true of much of the rest of the ballet. The extended upbeat and winning melody of the *Valse villageoise, mouvementé* and perfect for the situation, is followed by the ballerina's entrance—enriched, as is every facet of the work—and the Rose Adage, a *pas d'action* unprecedented in majesty and fullness. After *The Sleeping Beauty,* Laroche rightly expressed pleasure that "such a powerful talent as Tchaikovsky, following the general trend of the time, has turned to ballet and promotes thereby the ennobling of musical taste in this sphere as well" [255 II 41].

The continuous discourse that emerges from Tchaikovsky's attention to detail reconciles the competing demands of *dansante* and narrative. *The Sleeping Beauty* is unified motivically by the introduction themes, which announce Carabosse and the Lilac Fairy. While the Lilac Fairy's theme maintains its gait and contour, Tchaikovsky transforms Carabosse's—a metaphor of the shiftiness of evil—even down to its initial double semitone, most prominently at the end of act I as the kingdom falls asleep. The keys of the ballet are diverse and open-ended in keeping with its far-flung story. The principal key in the first half of the ballet (where *fatum* plays into Aurora's future) is E major/E minor, associated with both the Lilac Fairy and Carabosse. The earthly concern for dynasty, expressed in the Rose Adage and the awakening, is set by Tchaikovsky a semitone lower, in E-flat. These and other important keys, abetted by enharmonic respellings and presented in rapid succession, inform the first 16 bars of the introduction.

One could mock Tchaikovsky's choice of a children's story to compose something "not of this world," but its parables—of birth, death, and rebirth—immediately disarm the mockery while the sophistication of the music affirms that he was perfectly serious. E major and E minor reinforce the association with *fatum* and link the ballet with other pieces drawing on the *Manfred* key complex. Intertextual reference to movement II of the Fifth Symphony is made in no. 15 of the ballet, when the Lilac Fairy has just brought Aurora back to life in a vision:

Ex. 53 Symphony No. 5, mvt II

Ex. 54 The Sleeping Beauty

(*continued*)

Ex. 54 *(continued)*

If the motto of the Fifth and, by extension, the symphony's sense centered on the Easter greeting "Christ is risen!" then citing that work as Aurora rises up from death is surely not accidental. Greater subtlety informs no. 19, the Dream Entr'acte which accompanies a *tableau* of the kingdom after 100 years asleep. Tchaikovsky forms much of it out of earlier music, opening with the Lilac Fairy's dream chords from the end of act I. At bars 66–73, he restates, transformed, the chord progression from Carabosse's appearance in the prologue (at 196–203). There, the passage was rubricked: Carabosse was waving her wand over Aurora's cradle. It is rubricked here as well: *Les nuages se dissipent* (at 70). After a last statement of the dream chords, Carabosse's motif is never heard again. Evil has been banished.

If one senses formality and even sadness as Aurora and Désiré appear in act III, it may portend some further moral to the tale. The piano, introduced in the Silver Variation, here accompanies the ballerina with arpeggios more typically played on the harp. The connotations of nostalgia in the *adage* are powerful. The melody, the earthiness of the piano's timbre, together with King Florestan's persistent inability to make the right decision or to exert a positive impact on events, would have been quite enough to demote Alexander III's enthusiasm to the "Very nice!" which Tchaikovsky noted with a certain hurt. His achievement nevertheless raised the bar of ballet music forever, while the merging of fairytale and philosophical rumination suggests that his late style, essaying the distinction between this world and the next, had begun.

Tchaikovsky composed a *Valse-scherzo* in August 1889 for a new journal, *Artist,* which went into publication in Moscow the next month, a time when he was involved with staging *The Sleeping Beauty* [xv-a 158]. The piece comprises simple clichés, from the coy, rhythmically curtailed principal phrase, to the figuration in waltz style with hints of Chopin. The middle section echoes the grand upbeats in the act I waltz of *The Sleeping Beauty.* Even so, the music editor of *Artist,* thanking the composer, wrote, "It will be a true adornment to the issue, doubly so: it is signed by your name, and in addition the piece itself is all charm, grace and elegance" [96, 415].

In September 1889, anticipating Anton Rubinstein's jubilee celebrations, Tchaikovsky composed "Greeting to Anton Grigorievich Rubinstein" [tr. 389, 18], a ceremonial welcome, or *slava,* which was probably sung the moment Rubinstein was introduced on 18 November. The fanfare-like framing sections acknowledge Rubinstein's universal recognition and the delight which he has created, while the two middle verses, to fresh music, contain chromatic touches that may refer to Rubinstein's own style. The Impromptu for piano, for the same occasion, was included in the album *From Former Students of the St. Petersburg Conservatory to A. G. Rubinstein,* which was presented to him the same day. The music may be referential: the ever so slightly sentimental cantabile at the beginning recalls the student Tchaikovsky presenting his work to his teacher, the middle section reminds one of the improvisations for which Rubinstein (his teacher) was remembered, and the reprise, adorned with the flat sixth chord so typical of Tchaikovsky, was emblematic of the composer's own maturity.

The Queen of Spades was the great work of 1890, the action of which is summarized here from the 1890 libretto:

Act I, scene 1. In the Summer Garden of St. Petersburg, children play while adults admire the fine weather. Two gamblers, Chekalinsky and Surin, speak of Hermann, who always watches but never wagers, when Hermann enters and declares he is in love. His beloved is of noble birth but if he cannot win her, his only choice is death. Prince Yeletsky announces his engagement, whereupon Lise, his bride, enters with the Countess; Yeletsky's bride is also Hermann's passion. After the principals react to one other, Count Tomsky sings the ballad of the Queen of Spades. In her youth in Paris, the Countess was a gambler. One night, she lost her fortune, but for the price of a single tryst she learned the secret of three cards and won it back. She revealed the secret to her husband and to a handsome youth, but an apparition warned that she would die by the hand of a third man, who "ardently and passionately loving" would try to learn the secret by force. A storm.

Scene 2. In Lise's room, she and Pauline sing a duet, then Pauline sings Lise's favorite song. Lise's girlfriends take up a merry Russian tune, are scolded by Lise's governess, and leave. As Lise confides her secret love to the night, Hermann appears on the balcony. He would die but wanted to meet her first, now that she is promised to another. Lise weeps and Hermann, ecstatic, declares her his beauty, goddess, and angel. The Countess knocks, objecting to the noise. When they are alone again, Hermann would now reject death, but Lise must decide his fate. She orders him to leave, then bids him live. They embrace and declare their love.

Act II, scene 1. A ball. Hermann's friends ponder his fixation on the Countess's secret; Yeletsky affirms his love. Hermann enters with a note from Lise asking for a meeting. Chekalinsky and Surin tease him, unobserved; he wonders if he is delirious. An entertainment is announced: "The Shepherd's Sincerity." When it is over, Catherine the Great arrives.

Scene 2. On his way to Lise, Hermann, in the Countess's bedchamber, ponders her portrait and realizes that their fates are linked and that one of them must perish. He tarries; the Countess returns; she reminisces as she is readied for bed, almost whispering a song she once sang for the King of France. Alone with her, Hermann begs for the secret. The Countess says nothing; Hermann draws his pistol; and she slumps over, dead. Lise enters; Hermann protests that the Countess died without telling her secret. Shocked, Lise rejects him.

Act III, scene 1. Hermann is in his barracks, reading a letter from Lise, who asks to meet him at midnight. He feels remorse; he recalls the Countess's funeral and thinks he hears a choir singing her off to the next world. After a knock at the window, the door opens, and the Countess's ghost enters. Against her will, she has been commanded to fulfill his wish. She exhorts him to marry Lise and names the cards: a three, a seven, and an ace.

Scene 2. Lise awaits Hermann by the Winter Canal. Weary from the darkness in her life, she acknowledges that her soul is linked with his in damnation. Shortly after midnight, he arrives, and a hectic love duet ensues. Hermann would leave for the casino. She thinks him mad; crazed, he then mistakes her for the Countess and claims not to know her. Despairing, Lise drowns herself in the canal.

Scene 3. In a gambling house full of merry guests, Yeletsky, unfortunate in love, expects good luck at cards. Hermann enters, places a huge bet, and wins. He bets again, wins again, and sings of life being a game. He invites someone to bet against him a third time, and Yeletsky volunteers. Hermann bets on an ace and loses: he is holding the Queen of Spades. The Countess's ghost appears, and Hermann, in shock and despair, stabs himself. He begs Yeletsky's forgiveness and sees a vision of Lise, who forgives him. The gamblers pray for his soul.

The Queen of Spades was printed in three piano-vocal arrangements, all bearing a censor's approval date of 2 June 1890. The first was a limited tirage published that month for the artists to learn their parts; the second was in November, with metronome marks, changes in Hermann's and Lise's parts, and Hermann's final *brindisi* transposed from B major to A major. The third was issued early in 1891, after Nápravnik complained that the earlier editions were too difficult; the *brindisi* in that one is in B-flat [96, 97–98]. The *régisseur*'s score from the summer of 1891, made by Osip Palechek, calls for (among other changes) the opening chorus to be sung not by little girls but by four governesses and omits the chorus of gamblers in the last scene, which was also cut in the piano-vocal score Tchaikovsky prepared for Nikolay Figner [411, 231, 239–40].

The opera was part of a web of collaborations linking many composers and librettists in Vsevolozhsky's effort to develop Russian opera after the Imperial Italian Opera was abolished in 1885 [56, 152–87]. Pushkin was his preferred libretto source, including "The Gypsies," "The Captain's Daughter," and "The Queen of Spades." A libretto on the latter written by Kandaurov in 1885 and another by Ippolit Shpazhinsky passed to composer Nikolay Klenovsky to no result [96, 87]; Klenovsky wrote to Modest on 12 September 1887 asking him to collaborate. Meanwhile, Vsevolozhsky had approached Nikolay Solovyov to write the music. Modest delayed responding until Pyotr came to St. Petersburg for *The Enchantress,* and supposedly urged him to write *The Queen of Spades* to avenge that work's failure. Pyotr refused, but kept abreast of Modest's work with Klenovsky, who by 20 March 1889 had composed four scenes [96, 90–91], and subsequently even used part of it [420, 155–59]. Modest continued to lobby Pyotr, who subsequently changed his mind and agreed to compose [xv-b 26]. Vsevolozhsky, who apparently contemplated a work with comic features [56, 175], was in for a surprise.

Tchaikovsky had more control over the words of *The Queen of Spades* than he had over *The Enchantress* [420, 166–77] and pressed for an explanatory foreword in the separately issued libretto [73]; a separate synopsis was also published [74]. Modest apologized for the "necessary condition" of altering Pushkin if an opera were to be made of his story, shifting the action to the time of Catherine (already advocated by Vsevolozhsky in the Kandaurov version [96, 87] and concordant with Tchaikovsky's own fascination with eighteenth-century literature, including the historian Karamzin [205, 167]). He also intensified the love interest, Pushkin's Hermann having "strong passions and a fiery imagination." In the opera, Hermann loves Lise and would take her to a new life; his guilt over the Countess's death is genuine.

The adaptation involved two other major changes, one sacred, one demonic, neither acknowledged. In Pushkin, Hermann attends the Countess's funeral, where the eulogist claims that the "angel of death found her awake, in the midst of holy meditations, awaiting the midnight bridegroom." In the story, Hermann had waited for her past 2:00 a.m., and she never engaged in holy meditations. The Tchaikovskys moved the encounter of Hermann and the Countess back to midnight, and had Lise specify in her letter that Hermann meet her before midnight if she is to absolve him of the Countess's death. Hermann is late to this meeting and, fixated on playing the cards, declares to Lise, "I don't know you!" All this echoes the parable of the wise and foolish virgins from Matthew 25, identifying Hermann darkly with the midnight bridegroom. An additional aspect of the parable coheres with the story. It derives from the oil—*eleon* in Greek—the source of light by which the virgins replenish their lamps. Pushkin refers to light and darkness randomly; the librettists encouraged the perception of the entire opera as a metaphor of light yielding to darkness. Lise and the Countess die at night; there are many references to candles lit and extinguished (the one by which Hermann reads Lise's letter goes out when the Countess's ghost appears); day is overcome by darkness in the first scene; even the opening lines of the libretto, sung by little girls at play, urge that the light not be extinguished. And yet it is. Is this *fatum,* or do the characters will what happens to them? Hermann twice alludes to his freedom of choice—after Tomsky's ballad, in reference to the cards: "What's there for me in them? Even if I had them?" Again, in the Countess's boudoir, he realizes that his quest may be folly. He willingly capitulates to impulse at these moments, but appears to have lost his free will after the Countess's ghost accosts him.

After a landmark study by Viktor Vinogradov in 1936 [429], the scrutiny of Pushkin's "The Queen of Spades" for hidden meanings has become an industry. From simple relationships—the importance of the cards to the structure of the story (seven parts, each with three events in the plot [260, 419–20])—to ones of intermediate complexity (how the numbers in the tale relate to the game of faro as played in Pushkin's time [328, 256])—to arcane computations of *gematria* ("a numerical system whereby the letters of a word are connected to their numerical equivalents, added up, and then replaced by another word whose numerical equivalents add up to the same total" [260, 434]), these devices reveal Pushkin's fascination with cards, his sympathy with the Decembrist uprising in 1825 (marked by his visits to Kamenka, the estate of Decembrist Vasily Lvovich Davïdov, in the early 1820s [98, 23–36]), and his awareness of the Cabala and other occult traditions, including Freemasonry [430]. Whatever Tchaikovsky's love of Pushkin's words, this tale provided many points of contact with his own life—his residency in Kamenka, his brother-in-law Lev (Vasily Lvovich's son, born when his parents were in Siberian exile), his love of cards, and recent claims of his own association with Freemasonry [298].

What response to Pushkinian detail do we find in the libretto and score? Again, simple devices of organization yield to more complex ones—forecasting doom by means of the storm in scene 1 and Tomsky's ballad preparing for Hermann's encounter with the Countess in her boudoir; revealing dichotomies in musical language [51]—to "a net of composerly correspondences, resonances and echoes," including the "mysterious play" of love and death, imaginary and real, obsession and *fatum,* reflected partly in the *Doppelgänger* relationship between the narrative and the *intermède* [263]. Pushkin jests about the cabalistics of the cards: in the three, Hermann sees an enormous flower; in the seven, Gothic portals; in the ace, a paunchy man or a huge spider. This humor did not engage the librettists, but the numbers apparently did: phrases of libretto and music are formed into groups of three and seven syllables or notes. Such groupings could be random, but their frequent occurrence in reference to mysterious events is striking. Simplest is the three-syllable "Tri kartï!" (Three cards!) and its orchestral counterpart, which run throughout the opera. More subtle is the beginning of the quintet in act I, where the first two phrases of Lise, the Countess, and Hermann, "I'm frightened! He is again before me!" juxtapose 3 + 7 syllables while the parallel phrases of the unaffected Tomsky and Yeletsky do not. It is hardly surprising that Hermann's lines to the Countess's portrait, "The Venus of Muscovy! / By some mysterious force / I am linked to you by fate," and his remark as the scene draws to a close, "I did not learn her secrets," should each contain seven syllables. Five-syllable groupings, referring to sorcery or to the Countess as a witch, may have pentagrammatic connotations, as Hermann's outburst, "Staraya ved'ma!" (You hateful old witch!) just before he threatens her or, reciprocally, the Countess's response to Hermann when he is first identified to her in no. 4, "How frightful he is!" Some evidence is problematic, perhaps intentionally so to avoid making the relationships obvious, as when an innocent reference is spread upon the fateful numbers. The rubric at the head of no. 16 describes the Countess's bedchamber as "illuminated by lamps," which Tchaikovsky belies with 40 bars of seven-note melodic phrases. These persist after Hermann enters, falling silent for a moment at his lucid "And what if there is no secret?" which is followed (in seven-syllable phrases) by "All this is only empty / The raving of my sick soul?" Later, the Countess mutters, "This world is hateful to me!" seven syllables not directly related to the cards.

Light and darkness, biblical allusion, and the manipulation of numbers deepen the work's meaning. But what, in all this, is the point? Juxtaposed with mystifying effects are depictions of reality—the Summer Gardens, the Winter Canal, the officers' barracks, the casino—to be found in a Baedeker and even visited today. The point of the opera *is* discontinuity and puzzlement. The score reflects this, showing right appearances at a given moment and elsewhere indicating that things are not as appearances suggest. The shifting perspective produces a tension in the drama, making it unstable and chaotic, and is abetted by Tchaikovsky's unabashed heterogeneity of style, alluding to musical genres and nuances of earlier periods, and Modest's interpolation of other poets, which were already part of his libretto for Klenovsky [420, 158]. One proceeds through the opera realizing that, whatever else it may be, the story is only provisionally coherent and is bursting with hidden meanings.

The introduction states four apparently unrelated motifs. The first, a rhythmic echo of the Allegro of the Fifth Symphony, raises the possibility of Paschal associations, though this is hardly obvious. After a fermata, the second anticipates Tomsky's "O Bozhe!" (O God!) from before his first mention of the three cards, followed by the tempestuous card motif in E minor, which leads to a statement of the love theme (at *molto espress*[*ivo*]) in D. E minor moving to D major echoes the *Manfred* key complex, permitting the analogy between Hermann and Manfred. Before this, the interplay of B minor and E minor in the first three motifs, being limited by the pitches B and F-sharp (implying B minor, pitch emphases which return at the first mention of Hermann), not only impose an element of unity onto the introduction and sustain familiar key associations, but also distinguish the first three motifs from the last, which is associated with love.

No. 1 is a conventional operatic beginning—regular folks enjoying a day in the park, set out cinematically, with instantaneous shifts of key and melody. Adding to right appearances is an unambiguous reference to *Carmen* as the little boys play soldier. When their march turns to B-flat (at 91), as the one in *Carmen* does (no. 3, at 94), Tchaikovsky's well-heeled aristocrats become Bizet's street urchins' musical cousins. By then, the indirect elements of the drama have started up, in the little girls' urging that the light not be extinguished, and in the opening rubric, *Vesna* (springtime). In contrast to Pushkin's November, the composer specified that the trees in the opening scene should not have leafed out yet, which tilts the time setting toward April [xv-b 109]. The action thus falls within reach of Easter, linking the first notes of music with the first rubric and with the parable of the wise and foolish virgins in the liturgical calendar. In no. 2, Tchaikovsky moves to the dominant of E minor at the first mention of Hermann, whose recitative contains a melody that becomes the refrain of his brief aria at the words "I do not know her name, nor do I want to!" This device recurs in no. 3 (*con amarezza* at 87), setting up the storm. Upon their arrival, Lise and the Countess recognize Hermann, the music moving into F-sharp minor for the quintet, which brings the first sounds of the storm at its cadence. Tomsky's ballad returns to E minor. In no. 6, Tchaikovsky reprises E minor, F-sharp minor, and B minor. The key of F-sharp minor, in reference to dread or fright, is added to the associations of E minor with *fatum* and of B minor with death.

In scene 2, Tchaikovsky presents Lise using similar devices. After a beginning of right appearances (the duet of Lise and Paulina), mystifying issues follow in Paulina's song. That she should sing is a right appearance, but she drastically rends the mood. In the morning of her days, love thrived, but what has befallen her is . . . the grave. This forecasting of Lise's fate is transparent; its Arcadian setting anticipates the *intermède* of the next scene, which will also be about her; and the key, E-flat minor, harks back to the funereal Adagio of the Third String Quartet. The song introduces an inexplicable disjunction of mood for an engagement party.

Much is deferred to the long finale. Tchaikovsky presents a theme in the English horn (no. 10 at 31), the subject of Lise's first embedded aria (53–102). It comprises phrases of 7 + 3 notes at the beginning and is played as her maid is extinguishing the lights in her room:

Ex. 55

Lise takes it up: "Whence these tears? My girlish daydreams, you have betrayed me." She extols Yeletsky but does not love him. She is fearful, as if she were losing her free will. And she has a secret, which is told in her second embedded aria (no. 10, 109–38): she loves Hermann, who is handsome like a fallen angel. Tchaikovsky gives her ravishing music, including anticipations (at 116–19) of the coming duet. The shift to E minor at the end of her confession signals Hermann's presence. As Hermann protests her betrothal and makes to bid farewell (180–231), Tchaikovsky states the love theme and, with it, a profound ambiguity which reaches to the end of the opera. What does it express? Lise's love, still subject to rational constraint? But she tells him to leave. Hermann's vow to love or die? It is tamed in a moment, despite his ecstatic "Beauty! Goddess! Angel!" and his morose aria (232–86), which mimics Paulina's deathly melody, here in the key of dread. The Countess interrupts. The card motif pervades the music as if to depict Hermann's perception of her, but her words do not sustain this image: she is just a cranky old lady. She leaves; Hermann insists that Lise command him to die. "No, live!" she cries. Her resistance breaks with only six bars left to sing in the act, having shifted to the familiar second person only

10 bars earlier. Tchaikovsky thus conveys the height of the love interest in the opera in some 50 bars, most of it with the lovers in dispute. By the end of act I, we question whether love is true, or a right appearance.

Act II time-travels to the age of Catherine. The centerpiece is a play with songs and dances watched by the stage audience. Artifice and history mingle in the quoted or paraphrased period music and in genre: the *intermède* or aristocratic entertainment. In the French manner, it paraphrases the opera: innocent Prilepa prefers Milozvor ("Good Looking"), who is sad and weary, having hidden his passion too long, to Zlatogor ("Mountain of Gold"), expressed in lines rich with seven-syllable phrases relatable to Yeletsky's recent aria. The near-quotation in the Prilepa-Milozvor duet of Papageno's "Ein Mädchen oder Weibchen," where the birdcatcher sings that a "soft little dove" would mean blessedness for him, is Tchaikovsky's most direct reference to Mozart. Afterward, Catherine's imminent arrival (in the 1890 libretto, the curtain fell just before her appearance) rouses the guests to a *slava,* for which Tchaikovsky borrowed a choral polonaise from Iosif Kozlovsky, one actually sung in praise of the empress [354, 202–7; 53]. A reference so direct suggests his acknowledgment of Vsevolozhsky's fascination with the eighteenth century and the emperor's with the age of Catherine. Yeletsky's aria before the *intermède,* of such nobility as is rarely bestowed on spurned lovers, is nearly celibate in effect, like Gremin's in *Evgeniy Onegin:* "In no way do I wish to inhibit the freedom of your heart." Stressing Lise's liberty to choose, he is unaware that she has already chosen Hermann.

In scene 4, no. 16 progresses to where Hermann confronts the Countess in her boudoir. We again see her as she really is, in counterpoint with Hermann's aurally intense image of her, in the pervasive seven-note accompaniment and demonic groupings of syllables. The real Countess lives in a past unrelated to the cards that essentialize her. She recalls socially exalted names and barely sings an *ariette* from Grétry's *Richard Coeur de Lion,* preceded by "Vive Henri IV!" (the theme of the apotheosis of *The Sleeping Beauty*) in the background. No. 17 presents confrontations of Hermann with the Countess and of Hermann with Lise. He appeals on bended knee not to the old woman's sorcery but to her virtuous instincts. And she dies. What might she have done? Scold, repudiate, curse? Hermann is shattered; ambiguity deepens. Lise enters "with a candle," after which the recital of what took place cadences in F-sharp minor, the key of dread.

In act III, scene 5 is the height of enigma in the opera, scene 6 resolves Hermann's earthly relationship with Lise, and scene 7 his fixation on the cards. In her boudoir, the Countess was old and dotty. In scene 5 she is aware, her demonic ghost commanded to grant Hermann's wish; he must marry Lise, "and the three cards will win in succession." That she urges him to virtue and provides the means to achieve it would seem to put her on the side of the angels. But the cards she names will fail for reasons we are left to guess. Has Hermann somehow willed his own destruction [328, 259–70], or is there some inexplicable, ungodly cause?

Tchaikovsky evokes both sacred and secular in scene 5. The first theme emulates a church choir, with military signals at the cadence. The opening is made problematic by the initial phrase in seven notes, while the key, E-flat minor, links this music with Paulina's song in scene 2 and so to Lise, whose letter Hermann is reading as the curtain rises and whose future will be clouded by what is about to happen. As Hermann ponders the letter he recalls the Countess's funeral, a recurrent "frightful dream and dark pictures," set to a sacred choir of eerie sentience singing the troparion "I Pour Out My Prayer unto the Lord":

> I pray to the Lord that He heed my sorrow,
> For my soul has been filled with evil and I fear the captivity of hell,
> Look down, O God, on the sufferings of Thy slave!

He hears something and thinks it is the wind. The 1890 libretto leaves open the possibility that an actual service might be within earshot. It omits the choir's text, but as Hermann sings "I can't make it out," "a distant funeral song is heard," and as he describes the service, "the candles and the censors, and the sobbing," "the singing becomes more distinct." The troparion, however, refers to someone still alive and is sung to the opening melody of the introduction, which points to Lise. The Countess's ghost arrives in no. 19 to the card motif and rapid phrases of accompaniment grouped in sevens, the chord progression arriving at the dominant of E minor as she appears in the doorway. She sings in a monotone, accompanied by a descending whole-tone scale (no. 17, 41–48). While this signal for the supernatural moves the action beyond any precinct of everyday rationality, it is nevertheless, in one critic's words, "undoubted actuality," and with the specter's words, the scene ends.

In scene 6, Lise waits by the Winter Canal. The mood is turbulent, the key is E minor. She sings of Hermann metaphorically, in the manner of a folk lament (*Andante molto cantabile*): when life promised joy, he was the dark cloud, the storm in the opening scene. She ends this with five-syllable phrases, "I am exhausted, / spent with suffering!" As midnight tolls Hermann is not there, and her despairing melody ("His criminal hand has taken my life and honor") recalls Yeletsky's love song for a moment. She fears damnation; the troparion was being sung for her, subtly affirmed by the connotations of *eleon,* referring at once to the oil that the foolish virgins left behind and the *eleison* of the Roman Mass: at this moment, Lise has neither light nor mercy. Her joy at Hermann's arrival is illusory, the lovers' duet a gratefully brief but strange right appearance. Hermann would march off to the casino. Lise can hardly give voice to the wrongness of this; Prilepa chose Milozvor, who suddenly is raving about "mountains of gold." And now Hermann's "Who are you? I do not know you!" echoes St. Matthew. Bereft of light, Lise chooses death as the music drives to F-sharp minor again.

The merriment that opens scene 7 is symmetrical with scene 1: the chorus embedded with a serious matter of the heart (Yeletsky's broken engagement), a set number by Tomsky to words of Derzhavin, an ensemble (about gambling, to words of Pushkin), and a final scene, sparked by the shock that Hermann has actually come to gamble. After his first bet, a septet ensues, parallel to the quintet in scene 1. Breaking the tension after the second bet with a conventional aria gives Hermann a last bravura display and reminds us how far he has come since refusing to sacrifice the necessary in the hope of gaining the superfluous. Not least, it predicts the outcome of his last hand. The card motif returns for the last wager against Yeletsky and the whole-tone scale for the last appearance of the Countess's ghost. The opera closes with the love motif.

The historical place of this most studied of Tchaikovsky's operas [e.g., 11; 293; 373] is partly rooted in the composer's shattering of the realist premises on which Russian opera in his day was based, effected here through contradictory time references (the Countess, for example, at the age of 87 in the 1790s, could not possibly have sung an aria from Grétry's *Richard Coeur de Lion* in her youth) and extraordinary shifts in perception from everyday to phantasmagorical, as if to mock the very concept of normal consciousness. This disjunction, which confounded early reception of the opera, was precisely what made it a precursor to developments in Russian culture, inspiring both conservatives, such as Alexander Benois and the World of Art group, and the Russian symbolists, for whom "it played out all of their creative obsessions: the relationship between fortune and fate, dream and reality, societal death and societal rebirth" [273, 48, 51–114; 204, 14–29]. In a context personal to the composer, *The Queen of Spades* was another complex, multilevel piece that invited autobiographical readings without letting speculation partake of certainty. Yet the analogy of Lise, the Countess, and Hermann with Antonina, Meck, and Tchaikovsky is not a good fit. Ambiguity remains its point and message.

The Queen of Spades coheres by the density of its relationships. No catharsis presents the moral of what has taken place: at the end, the piece makes little of insanity, or obsession, or the blandishments of passion, or death. It ends with a chorus of gamblers in a key, D-flat major, basically unrehearsed, in four-part churchly style (echoing the beginning of act III), stepping out of character after a night of carousing to ask forgiveness for Hermann's "rebellious and tormented soul." Only the love motif is familiar, which suggests that Lise grants forgiveness as well. But what has love meant? Passion? Hardly. The lovers were too contentious. Hermann's right appearance was of passion, but it was never independent of his fascination with the Countess's secret. Like Boris Godunov, suspended between virtue and suspicion, Hermann is a tainted hero, mired in circumstances too complex for us to judge.

Tchaikovsky deferred serious attention to the Sextet for Strings, *Souvenir de Florence,* op. 70, until the last half of June 1890, after completing *The Queen of Spades.* "I am writing with unlikely effort," he wrote to Modest. "[W]hat is making it difficult for me is not the lack of thoughts, but the novelty of form. One must have six independent, generically similar voices. This is improbably difficult" [xv-b 184]. He urged the players of an 1890 performance to report any deficiency in the part writing or articulation or performance instruction [xv-b 227–29]. He rejected his original Trio of movement III, apparently making a gift of its manuscript during his trip to America. It is preserved in the Isabella Stewart Gardner Museum in Boston [230, 172–83].

The sextet is clear in structure and broadly laid out, its movements cast in sonata-allegro, tripartite reprise, scherzo/trio, and sonata-allegro. An exception to normative pattern comes in the finale, where the development ends early, the recapitulation begins (at 201), and a fugue ensues (247–324) which reengages developmental improvisation. This learnedness demonstrates Tchaikovsky's mastery of six voices (and may explain his rejection of the original Trio, which would have placed a fughetta in the middle of the third movement).

He never explained the title. Modest offered the slenderest connection: "The first theme of the Andante was sketched in Florence in the winter of 1890. Hence the title of the sextet" [1997 III 496]. The Italian journey held no small fascination for Tchaikovsky, and the *Souvenir* may be its timbral embodiment, in the saucy rhythm of the third movement, in the folkish drone of the finale, and not least in song, that fundament of Italy, found in every movement. The richest of these, the *Adagio cantabile,* makes uncanny (and surely coincidental) reference to Hugo Wolf's "Kennst du das Land" in the opening chromatic motif (first at bar 10), recalling Wolf's piano introduction and veering close in movement I (first at 198–202) to Wolf's refrain, "möcht' ich mit dir, o mein Geliebter, ziehn," where Mignon sings of being drawn to the land of blossoming lemon trees. The invocation of Goethe calls to mind Tchaikovsky's own setting of "Kennst du das Land," in which the poet's last two stanzas were reversed so that the song ended not with crags and dragons but with the utopian vision. Goethe, Wolf, Tchaikovsky—all were *oltramontani* wistfully picturing the south. The possibility that Tchaikovsky, in this cache of souvenirs, is recalling further back than the most recent summer is signaled by the introduction of the slow movement, which clearly alludes to its counterpart in the *Serenade for Strings,* another Italianate excursion exceeding four string parts. When that work was composed, he had quoted Goethe's "Italian Journey" to Meck [viii 486–87]. In his late style, the *Souvenir,* which is very much of this world, contrasts with *The Queen of Spades* in its brightness and cheer. If the mixed metaphor will be forgiven, it is a luminous piece, the ideal of chamber music that seeks only to delight.

The Voevoda, a symphonic ballad on a poem by Adam Mickewicz as translated by Alexander Pushkin, was the work Tchaikovsky was composing at the time of the final break with Nadezhda von Meck. A provincial governor returns at night from a battle to discover his wife is missing from her bed. He calls for his weapons and sets out with a retainer to wreak vengeance. In the garden, they overhear the wife's tryst with a young man. It is a farewell, emotionally wrenching if physically benign: she has yielded to the Voevoda's wealth and power despite her affection for the young man and his years of devotion. Observing this, the retainer loses heart and cannot bring himself to fire. As the Voevoda takes aim, a shot rings out. The retainer has killed the Voevoda.

The first sign that Tchaikovsky was composing *The Voevoda* came after the first break with Meck, in a letter to Modest on 10 October 1890 reporting that he had finished composing, but not scoring the work. Lacking the autograph, we do not know if he included a program or rubricked the music. The relationship of poem to music is nevertheless clear. Two lengthy crescendos open the work (bars 1–152), based on a hoofbeat rhythm and a motif above it associated with the Voevoda. A sense of urgency and even wrath gives way to a quiet interlude where the Voevoda's motif mixes with nondescript phrases for the bass clarinet (153–236); master and retainer are finding their way by stealth. Two lyrical themes in soprano and tenor registers alternate through most of the work (237–425). The first—the Voevoda's wife—languishes in the manner of Rimsky-Korsakov; her lover's is forthright. The interlude returns (426–69), interrupted by a loud chord in the full orchestra—the shot (470)—then wails in the brass and winds and rhythmic outbursts as the Voevoda cries out, then dies.

Tchaikovsky's reasons for destroying "such filth" are not based on any failure of technique, as the ideas sound beautifully and are effectively elaborated. The restrained praise of Siloti and Taneyev may have disappointed him ("weaker than *Romeo and Juliet* and *Francesca*" [96, 306]), as this earthbound text, unlike Shakespeare or Dante, lacked expressive height or philosophical rumination. Writing to Modest in 1901, Taneyev observed that at least one theme (bassoon at bar 275) fit the verbal rhythm of a fragment of Pushkin's text, and he suggested that this passage may have been composed not as an orchestral work but as a song. "Performed without words by orchestral instruments, this romance produces a somewhat indefinite impression and loses much set in this way" [96, 307]. Based on *The Voevoda* (bars 1–54 of 63 bars corresponding to bars 276–330 of the orchestral score) and unpublished before the *Collected Works,* the manuscript of *Aveu passionné* resides in the Library of Congress. Could Tchaikovsky have written it for an American admirer? A sketch appears among the autograph fragments of *The Voevoda.*

Tchaikovsky wrote three unaccompanied choruses in a few days before 14 February 1891. They are his last secular choruses and were requested by teachers for students: the first mixed, the second for men, the third for women. In *Ne kukushechka vo sïrom boru* ('Tis not the cuckoo in the damp pinewood) [tr. 389, 18], the musically identical first two verses describe a sorrowful girl and a flirtatious lad in folkish terms ("it is not this, but *this*"). Tchaikovsky breaks the strophic structure in verse 3, a theatrical report of a young lad's death on the battlefield, reprised in a hushed 5/4. The last verse is parallel to the first except for an extension that dotes on the maiden's sigh. Expression throughout is constrained by the pervasive rhythm of the first six notes, which serve an ostinato-like function that enhances the overall effect of folkishness.

In *Chto smolknul veseliya glas* (What silenced the merry voice?) [tr. 389, 16], a *brindisi*-like mood at the beginning finds its way to the praise of light at the end, with juxtapositions of thought and image in between of a kind to be expected from the tipsy. Hence the first basses' persistent anticipation of the coming text in the opening verse—the group cannot begin a phrase together—rolling into new meter and polyphony in the second (though strict imitation, appropriate to "Pour the glass fuller!" is beyond their reach), then on to loud declamation in the third. The toast to reason and the muses clears our singers' minds for a moment before they engage the apostrophe to light with a downward-sliding bass, mixed meter, and a cadence avoiding the home key on "immortal sun of intellect." All is reoriented in the final line, or nearly so, as the tenors, *con tutta forza,* sing the word "darkness" on a high B-flat.

Bez porï, da bez vremeni (Without time, without season) [tr. 389, 16] is the subtlest of the three, Tsïganov's complex, folkish text comprising nature images gradually personalized to depict the plight of a young girl with a grumpy old husband. Tchaikovsky returns to the strophic approach of the first chorus, generalizing despair in two identical strophes rather than painting details of the dead grass, the stream, the nightingale, the berries, the flowers. The last half of the setting, which complains directly of the old husband, is freer in treatment and more dramatic, leading to the final *fortissimo* lament of the loss of freedom.

Composing *Iolanta* and *The Nutcracker* was Tchaikovsky's principal achievement of 1891, the finishing of details of the latter spilling over into 1892. This scenario of *Iolanta* is based on the second edition of the piano-vocal score:

In her garden, Iolanta is attended by her nursemaid, Martha, and others. When Martha notices, without touching Iolanta's eyes, that she has been weeping, Iolanta senses wanting something she cannot describe. She is referring to sight and, perhaps unwittingly, to passion. Thought to be darkening her mood, the musicians are dismissed. Iolanta urges Martha to explain her longing. Girls run in with baskets of flowers, singing in praise of their scent and texture. Tired, Iolanta asks Martha to sing for her. A lullaby. Iolanta falls asleep and is borne offstage.

Alméric, King René's messenger, announces the King's arrival with Ebn-Hakia, a Moorish physician. Alméric learns that Iolanta is betrothed to Robert, Duke of Burgundy, and is here because René wants her blindness kept secret until she can see again. No one in Iolanta's presence may refer to light or what is seen, nor tell her that she is the daughter of a king. René and the doctor arrive. Ebn-Hakia examines Iolanta as René, in an aria, asks God's mercy on his sins for her blindness. Ebn-Hakia believes that Iolanta can be cured, but first she must know her condition, and she must fervently desire a cure. René protests.

Robert, seeking release from his engagement, and his friend Vaudémont approach, despite a sign threatening death to trespassers. Robert sings of his beloved Matilda, Vaudémont of his desire for someone angelic and pure. Discovering Iolanta asleep on a terrace he is captivated, but Robert fears bewitchment and urges escape. This awakens Iolanta, who asks who they are. Vaudémont responds, but Robert leaves to find help. Vaudémont's ardent words confuse her, and when she thrice gives him a white rose after he asked for red, he realizes that she cannot see. In a triumphant aria, Vaudémont describes the beauty of nature and of light, which the perplexed Iolanta joins with guileless inquiry. Angry that she has discovered her disability, René interrupts them, but Iolanta is exultant; René's threat to execute Vaudémont intensifies her desire for sight. She touches Vaudémont's face and withdraws with Ebn-Hakia. Fanfares signal Robert's return. René disowns his threat to Vaudémont, who asks for Iolanta's hand. As she is already betrothed, the King refuses and is about to identify her fiancé when Robert enters. He recognizes the King; he will honor his promise to Iolanta, but explains his love for Matilda of Lorraine. The King frees him from his vow and grants Vaudémont Iolanta's hand. She enters, in wonderment and fright at the experience of vision. Vaudémont vows to protect her. The principals offer up a prayer of thanks and praise for the miracle that has occurred.

From the opera's contention that, with hope and belief, the soul grows stronger emerges a parallel with *Die Zauberflöte:* "in both the finding of light is achieved on a course of serious trials, . . . the heroes of Mozart and Tchaikovsky are subject to initiation which transforms their spirits" [379, 131]. The gaining of light locates *Iolanta* in Tchaikovsky's late style as a companion piece to *The Queen of Spades,* in which light is overcome by darkness. One commentary links *Iolanta* and *The Nutcracker* with Tchaikovsky's reading of Benedict Spinoza [444, 165].

The first edition of *Iolanta* in piano-vocal score passed the censor on 25 April 1892 and was issued later that month. A corrected second edition, with Russian and German text, passed the censor on 22 May, together with the full score [96, 107–8]. It is the standard Jurgenson issue; it did not include Vaudémont's interpolated aria, marked in later editions as no. 6a. A libretto of *Iolanta* issued by Jurgenson had already passed the censor on 22 May 1891, a month before Tchaikovsky took up the music. It may represent Modest's version, as it differs from the words of the second piano-vocal score. Besides variants in punctuation, rubrics, and word order, Robert, Duke of Burgundy, who is "Robert" in the second edition, is in this one simply "the Duke." Ensembles are the most drastically revised, either by the deletion of lines printed in the separate libretto, or by the expansion of ensembles and choruses that the separate libretto does not include.

The obscurity of Henrik Herz's play *King René's Daughter* hides the extremity of Modest's adaptation. In Herz, Iolanta was sighted as an infant; at the age of one, in a palace fire, she was dropped from her window in order to save her life, and in the fall she lost her sight. The accident prompted the guilt that René laments in his aria, and a memory of it could be driving Iolanta's sense at the beginning of the opera that something is the matter with her. Ebn-Hakia (Ebn Jahia) has studied Iolanta's horoscope and raised hope that she would regain her sight in her 16th year, which time has come. He frightens the palace household and René with his amulets and other charms, but otherwise his ethnicity is not stressed; the libretto's repeated "Allah is great!" is Modest's. René must comply with Ebn-Hakia's requirements before sundown or forfeit his skills. The knights —Tristan of Vaudémont (Robert) and Geoffrey of Orange (Vaudémont)—

are considerably recast. Tristan/Robert has come to seek release from his marriage, and it is he who falls in love with Iolanta; his companion goes for help. The returning knights attack René's palace; Tristan/Robert accuses René of being a sorcerer. It is Geoffrey/Vaudémont who recognizes the King.

After Modest reduced the narrative clutter, background, and action, a tale of rigorous simplicity emerged: no real crisis threatens, and a different outcome would bring little change in Iolanta's world. Modest intensified two elements mentioned in the play: a sensual, almost pre-Raphaelite beauty, represented by the Eden-like garden and its aromatic flowers, and a religious element, stressing the deity's role in the otherwise miraculous restoration of Iolanta's sight. The religious language ran afoul of Soviet authorities, who retexted the opera until 1997 [360, 200], degrading the spiritual intensity of the words, as in the lullaby:

Modest	*Soviet Retexting*
Sleep, let the angels with their wings	Sleep, let the sounds of the lullaby
Waft sleep upon you,	Waft sleep upon you,
Soaring calmly among us	Blowing in a limitless caress
Full of blessings.	Full of tenderness.
Sleep, child, let blessed sleep	Sleep, child, let blessed sleep
Shield you.	Shield you.
From heaven the Lord universal	Loving, we hold your rest
Gazes down on you,	Sacred for us,
God hearkens to the child's prayer,	Wearied by tears, woe and
Generously,	Melancholy,
Sending down from on high	In dreams you will know
Happiness and joy!	Happiness and joy!

Modest imposed a structure on the text, the first half of the opera being taken up with exposing Iolanta's condition and the second with her love for Vaudémont. He divided the work between Vaudémont's interpolated aria (no. 6a) and the three following ensembles (nos. 7–9), which resolve the story. To Pyotr, the opera before no. 7 was expository, its format conventional: around arias in which the principals express their feelings, recitative provides background and choruses provide color. This music betrays no shortage of invention: the soft lyricism of the opening number, the vivacious "flower" chorus—a cross between Tatyana's friends picking berries and Senta's friends at their spinning wheels—the reverent prayer, the King's anguish, Ebn-Hakia's faux exoticism, Robert's impassioned apostrophe to Matilda of Lorraine. Motif and key take on associations in these numbers (Martha, René, Ebn-Hakia).

In the last three numbers, Tchaikovsky's musical approach turns Wagnerian. Recurrent motifs as part of an orchestral web, keys which organize the score, cadentially marked musico-dramatic divisions, even the occasional allusion to Wagner's music or scenarios—are all present. A single tonally rounded dramatic unit spans encounter to love to revelation, with symmetries of text. The introduction as the generator of theme (the motif from the opening bars of the opera) and sonority (the English horn, reminiscent of the shepherd's song in *Tristan*) are Wagnerian, as are key associations that are formgiving without being rigid, including:

C—light
D—the King; the gloomy past, the old order
G—ravishment, including the beauty of the garden
A-flat—resolution; restoration of Iolanta's sight

Numbers 8 and 9 complete the dramatic resolution, the first by determining Iolanta's cure (conveyed by a reprise of Vaudémont's extolling of light from no. 7), the second in Wagnerian fashion by revealing the characters' identities at the end and by tying up the remaining strands of the story. Much of this unfolds with diverse allusions in passing—to *Lohengrin* in the closing bars of no. 8 and to Beethoven's "Seid umschlungen, Millionen!" in Iolanta's final hymn (no. 9 at bar 194).

Laroche understood *Iolanta* as a departure, the destination of which death kept Tchaikovsky from reaching:

> Together with *The Queen of Spades* and *The Sleeping Beauty, Iolanta* gives us the latest Tchaikovsky, . . . who found himself and, it seems, was poised for the most marvelous and distant voyage when fate suddenly cut short this new strength. From this point of view *Iolanta,* although Henrik Herz counts among its authors, represents for me the spiritual property of Pyotr Ilyich much more than do his other operas, in the libretti of which he took a direct hand, or which he even planned himself. [255 II 203]

It continued his experiment with new theater. Tchaikovsky was drawn to Wagner's aesthetic (if not the details of his style) for its indirect, non-literal approaches to meaning, which so influenced the avant-garde of Russian letters at the time of Tchaikovsky's death and which remained important for the next three decades [273, 2–14, 46–51]. The perception of Tchaikovsky as proto-avant-garde by Alexander Benois and others, Tchaikovsky's reconception of the eighteenth century (an era which held no small fascination for Russian modernists), the phantasmagorical visions of *The Queen of Spades* and *The Nutcracker,* the subtle, forward-looking changes in his use of the orchestra—all showed him evolving toward or with important currents of thought. In this context, *Iolanta* is a forebear of *La damoiselle élue,* or even *Pelléas.*

The double bill which offered *Iolanta* in the first half was completed by *The Nutcracker,* op. 71, the scenario of which is here summarized from the 1892 libretto [tr. 431, 333–37]:

Act I, scene 1. In Silberhaus's home, a Christmas tree is being decorated; when it is ready, the children are called; Silberhaus distributes gifts to them; they dance. New guests arrive. The wall clock sounds, and at its last stroke Counselor Drosselmeyer appears. After greeting the Silberhauses, he summons his godchildren, Clara and Fritz, to receive his gifts: life-sized, keyed dolls that dance. The children are entranced, but Silberhaus orders the dolls put away. Drosselmeyer then offers them a Nutcracker and demonstrates it. Fritz breaks the Nutcracker, and Clara comforts it as Fritz and his friends make noise with musical instruments; she wraps the Nutcracker in a blanket and puts it in her favorite doll's bed. Silberhaus proposes a last dance, after which the guests leave and the children go to bed.

The moonlit room is empty when Clara comes downstairs to see the Nutcracker. But scratching sounds and the chiming clock with Drosselmeyer's image on its face frighten her. The room fills with mice; the Christmas tree grows to an enormous size; the dolls and toy soldiers come to life. A detachment of mice devours the gingerbread soldiers arrayed against them. The Nutcracker rises up and takes command, making a formation of tin soldiers as the Mouse King appears. A battle ensues; the mice are thrown back; the Mouse King engages the Nutcracker in single combat and is about to prevail when Clara throws her slipper at him, shifting advantage to the Nutcracker. The mice disperse, and the Nutcracker turns into a handsome prince. He and Clara pass through the branches of the Christmas tree. In scene 2, a winter forest, snowflakes begin to fall; as the blizzard quiets, the scene is illuminated by moonlight.

Act II. In Confiturembourg, the Land of Sweets, the Sugar Plum Fairy and her consort greet the Nutcracker and Clara, who is praised for saving him. The Sugar Plum Fairy orders confections and the guests to be entertained with dances, in which she and her consort take part. Clara, dazzled, thinks that what is happening is a dream from which it would be terrible to wake up, while the Nutcracker tells her of the wonders and unusual customs of Confiturembourg. An apotheosis presents a beehive with flying bees guarding their riches.

Knowing who was responsible for the scenario of *The Nutcracker* might explain some striking details in the libretto and a troubled collaboration. Vladimir Pogozhev, supervisor of the Petersburg Imperial Theaters from 1882 to 1897, recalled categorically that the story was selected by Vsevolozhsky [316, 227–28], whose quip that Marius Petipa was *vieux genre* [362, 241] suggests that he was preempting the balletmaster's prerogative to decide new repertoire. That Petipa was *assigned* the piece might explain its flaws: the unexplained attack by the mice and the irresolution of the visit to Confiturembourg. Nor would an experienced balletmaster permit the imbalance between mime and dancing in acts I and II, nor give leading parts to child dancers, reserving the ballerina's only solo for the penultimate number of the last act. Evidence pointing to Modest as the librettist [332, 100; 340, 76–79] is unpersuasive.

The question may be asked of *The Nutcracker* as of *Iolanta:* do flaws so obvious point to a new type of drama? The motifs of the growing Christmas tree and the winter forest, missing in Hoffmann, echo ancient representations of the underworld, regular world, and heavenly realm being joined by a tree, as does the meaning of winter not just as a demise before rebirth but also, joined with the forest (as in no. 8), as a path to another world, possibly the realm of the dead. Supporting this are blatant contrasts between the acts: action/stasis, day/night, house/forest, earthly/heavenly, actual/magical, life/death, passing time/eternity [361, 41–44]. All of this suggests a sophisticated subtext. Complexity is implicit in Tchaikovsky's promise from Rouen to create a "very bold conjuration" [xvi-a 84], and as Laroche would point out, Hoffmann's essential irony makes the reader constantly aware of not believing the beguiling magic being described—

which is to say, it *is* a conjuration. After Tchaikovsky learned of his sister's death, he never complained of the imagery of Confiturembourg again. The passage in his ocean diary, that thoughts of Sasha seem as recollections from a very distant past, may have solved the problem of composing it, reconceiving it at a stroke into a fresco of Kamenka, the "torment linked with thoughts of Sasha." The entire first scene is a family gathering, fresh in memory from Christmas 1890, a few months before Sasha's death. But Confiturembourg is what Tchaikovsky found so vexing, and the Sugar Plum Fairy and the divertissement look to be conjured: the *Danse arabe,* based on a melody provided to Tchaikovsky by Ippolitov-Ivanov, stirred memories of Tiflis and its Asian district; the Chinese dance, with its shuffling rhythm and the whistling piccolo, depicted Sestritsa and her steaming teapot (Laroche observed that it lacked any hint of Chinese music [255 II 274]); *La mère Gigogne* encoded myriad occasions playing with the children in Kamenka, the stormy interludes in the Waltz of the Flowers its buffeting winds. If there is one dance that permits these speculations a higher order of credibility, it is within the *pas de deux,* the only number in the ballet which the Sugar Plum Fairy performs. The luminous celesta of the matriarch's solo speaks for itself. Before that, in the *entrée,* the rhythm of the *panikhida* is heard again, as before in the music of Tatyana and Lensky. Here, it occupies the insistent principal melody, the blunt, even violent repetition of a falling octave scale—Sasha's *otpevanie,* or singing-off, linking Confiturembourg with her death. In this light, *The Nutcracker* becomes a document of commemoration not free of sorrow in its external merriment, a quality which one critic detected but could not explain [275].

The gravest flaws in *The Nutcracker* were the absence of a cohering metaphor (such as the Lilac Fairy and Carabosse, to which melodies could be assigned) and of a significant love interest. Lacking a point, a moral, romance, and simple closure, the ballet may have been declaring itself experimental. On a mundane level, Tchaikovsky followed Petipa's instructions, which called for borrowed tunes—the *Grossvatertanz,* "Bon voyage, Mr. Dumolet," for the galop in no. 3 and the *carmagnole,* a revolutionary ditty, for a divertissement ultimately deleted from act I. To these, Tchaikovsky added, besides the *Danse arabe* and the *panikhida* rhythm, songs from Colet and Dumersan's *Chants et chansons populaires de la France,* which had already supplied him with the melody of Triquet's couplets and "Vive

Henri IV!" used in *The Sleeping Beauty* and *The Queen of Spades.* Nos. 63 and 58 from Colet and Dumersan, "Giroflé, Girofla" and "Cadet Rousselle," were used in *La mère Gigogne.* The heterogeneity which comes of their juxtaposition with his own style approximates the same result in *The Queen of Spades* and may again be signaling that meaning is not what it seems on the surface.

Tchaikovsky appears to have reconciled with the open-ended scenario by building the score around an arch-like arrangement of keys, proceeding from the opening B-flat to E major at the midpoint and back again. A concern for symmetry explains other analogies. In act I, the battle is followed by the forest scene in C major (no. 8), leading to the waltz in e/E major; in act II, the arrival in Confiturembourg, in E, makes a prominent recall of C at the musical high point (falling octaves in no. 11, bars 19–29) just before a reprise of the battle music as Clara describes how she saved the Nutcracker. The trepak in no. 12 echoes the rhythm of the *Pas diabolique des poupées à ressort* in no. 4; the *Danse des mirlitons* in act II, a polka in D major, echoes Clara's polka in D major in no. 5; the Waltz of the Flowers balances the Waltz of the Snowflakes.

Tchaikovsky observed E.T.A. Hoffmann's distinction between the everyday and a special reality perceived by select characters, with extraordinary sonorities attached to things magical. He marked each instance of special reality with sound: in the first number, the clarinet-bassoon duet when the clock strikes nine (bar 40), when the Christmas tree lights up "as if by enchantment" (arabesques in the winds, from 73), and even when the children, upon beholding it, are struck with astonishment (oboe, harp cadenzas, tremolo strings, from 117). Magic is the point; at the entrance of the adults, whose magic is external, being costumed *en incroyables* in no. 3 (at 45), there is a change of melody and meter, but no special sound. Magical sonorities prepare Drosselmeyer's arrival at the beginning of no. 4, where conventional orchestration ceases as if by shock. Only as he interacts with the other guests does his spare, distinctive introduction, in violas, trombones, and tuba, punctuated with stopped horns, give way to less eccentric sounds (as at 19, where he and Silberhaus probably exchange pinches of snuff), but it returns as his gifts for the children are brought in (at 44) and when he winds the mechanical dolls (67ff.). Drosselmeyer's timbral world accompanies the magical events of the night scene (no. 6), the battle of the mice (no. 7), the Waltz of the Snowflakes (especially at the beginning), and Confiturembourg—all perceived only by Clara among the regular human characters. Tchaikovsky uses the celesta at the first appearance of the Sugar Plum Fairy, having discovered the instrument in Paris in the summer of 1891 and having asked Jurgenson to buy one covertly, so that Rimsky-Korsakov and Glazunov would not preempt his first use of its bell-like sonority [xvi-a 129–30].

The composer's personal experience may have vivified *The Nutcracker*. Not long after he received a translation of Hoffmann's story in 1882, he reported to Meck from Naples about his lodgings:

> I suffer a shameful weakness: I am afraid to the point of insanity (literally) of mice. Imagine, dear friend, that at this moment, as I write to you, above my head in the attic, perhaps a whole army of mice should be conducting manoeuvres. If even one of them falls into my room, I am condemned to an agonizing, sleepless night! [xi 64]

The importance in the scenario of the clock—in the face of which Drosselmeyer's image appears—may have reminded him of Prague in 1888, when he repeatedly visited a clockmaker and bought a clock and a small mechanical organ [Dnev 196–97]. For someone who loved Dickens (responsible for his study of English), it would not have been exceptional for Tchaikovsky to have read "A Christmas Tree," in one passage of which a narrator, "alone, the only person in the house awake," is describing the intricately decorated Christmas tree of his childhood, whose myriad toys included "a demoniacal Counsellor in a black gown," various dolls, drummers, a regiment of soldiers in a box, a little tumbler. For a moment, "the very tree itself changes, and becomes a bean-stalk—the marvelous beanstalk up which Jack climbed to the Giant's house!" and presently "all common things become uncommon and enchanted" [104, 13–16].

The so-called *Nutcracker Suite*, op. 71a, was mentioned in the press as early as 15 November 1891 [NO911115]. Tchaikovsky began scoring the entire ballet with the movements of the suite (for which copies have been substituted in what is otherwise the holograph score of the ballet) and finished these on 8 February 1892. He pondered alternative titles: "Suite from the Ballet 'Christmas Tree,'" "From the Kingdom of Delicacies and Toys" for the second number, and, among the dances, "Final Waltz" for the Waltz of the Flowers, "Russian Gingerbread" for the trepak, "Little Reed Pipes" for the Dance of the Shepherds, and "Fairy of the Sweets" for the Sugar

Plum Fairy. At one point, he considered including the Spanish Dance. The autograph, long lost, was rediscovered in 1946 [96, 182–84].

In June 1892, Tchaikovsky agreed "as soon as possible" to provide a short piece for Velebin Urbanek to publish in Prague in a collection called *Pianoforte.* This was the *Impromptu (Momento lirico),* and "as soon as possible" was 26 October. Sergey Taneyev completed a draft of a different version at Klin, published by Jurgenson in 1894 [xvi-b 118, n. 3]. Tchaikovsky extemporized on the rhythm of the opening bar, then quickly built a dissonant climax (38–39) from a repeated beginning, followed by a coda, epilogue-like, stating the motif in ever simpler transformations.

The *Ungarische Zigeunerweisen,* or "Gypsy Songs" (also known as "Hungarian Rhapsody"), which Tchaikovsky orchestrated, is identified in performance reviews as being the work of Sophie Menter, but after scrutiny has been shown to be music of Franz Liszt, elaborated by Tchaikovsky in the process of scoring, with occasional passages by Menter, who drew the title and certain formal features from the work of the same name by her teacher Karl Tausig [428]. The piece is a bravura potpourri, mostly of two-part themes in a conventional Gypsy style, interspersed with thematically nondescript cadenzas very elaborate at the beginning (some emulating the repeated notes of the cimbalom, and so labeled) and abbreviated as the piece unfolds. One theme (first at rehearsal 6 in CW 59) unifies the piece by its recurrence. The work was published in score by G. Schirmer in 1909, apparently unbeknown to Jurgenson in Moscow. This version differs slightly from the autograph, housed in the Pierpont Morgan Library in New York City. Tchaikovsky orchestrated the piece from a four-hands arrangement in September–October 1892.

The symphonic project of Tchaikovsky's last years comprises the music he wrote in connection with his plan to write a grand symphony upon which to end his career. It includes two big works: the Sixth Symphony, composed early in 1893, and the Symphony in E-flat before it. Diverse sketches (above, pp. 345, 358; 46), to which both these symphonies show some connection, suggest that his disparate verbal jottings about a symphony were to some degree of a piece [CW 62, vii–viii]. The fresh inspiration described in Tchaikovsky's explanation to Bob (above, p. 374), however, relegates them to a nondescript preliminary stage.

We know the E-flat Symphony—also called the *Life* Symphony after a reference in the sketches—only in reconstruction, for much of which the editor, Semyon Bogatïrev, looked to the Third Piano Concerto (excepting the first 248 bars of movement I, which Tchaikovsky had written out); the concerto was itself an adaptation of the symphony, the scoring of which was what Tchaikovsky probably changed the most. He never composed the Scherzo past sketches.

It is easy to understand why he suppressed the work. Little about it suggests the culmination of a compositional career; the quality of the ideas and the fulsome *remplissage* were precisely the faults that Tchaikovsky confessed to K.R. The formal pattern, especially in the outer movements, is straightforward in contrast with Tchaikovsky's customary individuality. The first movement is bland where he is typically striking; the transition between the first and second areas is crude, the closing area labored, the development and retransition mechanical. The hackneyed themes anticipate the worst of optimistic socialist realism (though the second area's theme begins to reclaim Tchaikovsky's lyric) and point to an uncertainty of genre confirmed by Tchaikovsky's transformation of it into a concerto. The jazzy opening bassoon solo, climbing into its high register, and the rambunctious closing theme (first at the *Allegro molto vivace*) point out the concertante element and suggest a more suitable home in some other kind of music:

Ex. 56

Ex. 57

The slow movement is thoughtful and spacious, its motifs elegantly spun out. The scoring, presumably Tchaikovsky's, with its rich emphasis on winds, recalls the allusions to concerto grosso in the Third Symphony and the Second Piano Concerto. The theme at the closing (bar 33, sixth chords above a tonic pedal) is especially eloquent. The Scherzo is problematic because it was editorially mandated, based on the merest of sketches, and is concordant with a piano piece ostensibly composed later. Even if Tchaikovsky had written the "Scherzo-fantaisie," op. 72, no. 10, early enough to serve him in the symphony, we cannot assume that he would have borrowed it whole in the form that we have it. One curiosity is the principal theme of the middle section, which resembles "The Crane," which Tchaikovsky used in the finale of his Second Symphony, presented here in the manner of a *cantus firmus:*

Ex. 58 E-flat Symphony

Ex. 59 Symphony No. 2

The finale echoes the first movement with proletarian musical ideas inconsistent with Tchaikovsky's aspirations. Added to much swirl and passage work, they rush to the closing cadence without a sense of weight. The lack of coherence overall in the Symphony in E-flat—the sense that it is assembled—forestalls the urge to seek allusion in its themes, though the march diverts the listener away from abstraction to something played in front of a fairground theater:

Ex. 60

In the middle section of the rondo, Tchaikovsky introduces another theme, picturesque but also awkwardly contoured for a dashing finale, then keeps it through a sizable development:

Ex. 61

The symphony lacks the ability to engage. Middling inspiration places it alongside the Piano Sonata and the op. 40 piano pieces as regards allusion. The Trio melody is insufficiently bold to determine whether its similarity to "The Crane" is intended. But was Tchaikovsky in fact referring to the slow movement of Borodin's Second Symphony at page 65 in the slow movement, or to movement II of his own Third Symphony on page 119? He did not destroy the symphony when he reported doing so to Bob, but changed movement I into the Third Piano Concerto later.

To impose some interpretation on the Symphony no. 6 in B Minor, op. 74, has proved irresistible and may result from the progressive refinement of Tchaikovsky's approach to program after *Manfred*. There, the program was explicit, the symphony's hectic music linked by a cyclic theme. In the Fifth, he used a cyclic theme again, with no external hint of its meaning. The result, so removed in the implication of referentiality from any notion of "abstract" music, may have been an attempt to strike a balance between guiding his audiences and letting them hear as they pleased. In this context, the Sixth represents a further step, in which the cyclic theme was eliminated, a title was added, and the music continued to invite the listener to interpret. And that is exactly what has been going on for more than a century. We can only wonder what the reception of the Sixth would have been had Tchaikovsky lived for decades after the premiere. Interpretations linking the piece with his death were soon to emerge:

> [I]t ended with the Adagio lamentoso, which leaves the listeners in the most sorrowful mood. In this Adagio the composer is as if bidding farewell to the living; . . . one could hardly find anywhere such a shattering picture of human grief at the sight of irresistible death, to which one must submit however burdensome it is to part with life. . . . This Adagio served as if for a "Requiem" for Tchaikovsky himself. [31, 144]

In the early Soviet era, no less than Boris Asafiev, founder of the new regime's music scholarship, wrote:

> He commissions a Requiem for himself, for he composes the terribly intense sixth symphony, in which the tragic battle of the spirit with death unfolds. . . . Oh, what a cruel, what a sharp sorrow Tchaikovsky likely suffered, composing it, foretelling in music what he was soon experiencing in reality, at the hour of his death! [140, 34]

With time, hypotheses of its meaning have become more elaborate [322; 231; 292; 212]. It is a testament to Tchaikovsky's gift in the Sixth (and a measure of its superiority over the E-flat Symphony) that it submits to extraordinary interpretation. Timothy L. Jackson proposes:

> [A]ccording to the "plot" of the Sixth Symphony, Tchaikovsky believed that the relationship with Bob was an "illness" which would prove deadly. I shall suggest that this "fatal" aspect derives from two considerations: (1) by obstinately pursuing their "forbidden" love, the lovers "gamble" with Fate, i.e., they call its bluff and Destiny responds by destroying them, and (2) their love proves to be fatal because *Eros,* as a form of divine madness, cannot survive in the phenomenal world. . . . In the first movement, the "scherzando" first group portrays Bob as a pubescent boy, while the second group constitutes an idyll depicting idealized love between the composer and Bob as young man and angelic Muse. [170, 40–41]

In Jackson's reading, the scherzo/march invokes the tradition of "amorous combat," and the finale represents, in musical symbols, the self-crucifixion of the composer [170, 45, 50ff.]. He marshals a host of arguments to support his thesis, both internal to the Sixth and from surrounding works, reaching into the cultural spheres of Western European music and philosophy.

In the massive report of a symposium in memory of Archpriest Dmitry Razumovsky [162], Father Mikhail Fortunato argues that the program of the Sixth Symphony is a statement of Tchaikovsky's faith in the resurrection of Jesus Christ:

> The key to solving the secret of the Sixth Symphony lies in the device which Tchaikovsky used in composing several melodies of the work, basing them on the *rhythm of key words of the Orthodox service. . . .*
>
> The realization of human death is set out in the first movement of the symphony. In the opening sounds of the bassoon we hear the rhythm—not the melody but in fact the rhythm—of the celebrated funeral song "Holy God, Holy Almighty, Holy Immortal." This theme then receives symphonic development.
>
> In the third movement of the symphony, the theme of the victorious march is based on the rhythm of the words of another churchly song, which in truth can be considered central to the life of the Orthodox Church and which Tchaikovsky knew well from childhood. This is the Easter *troparion,* "Christ has risen from the dead, having driven death to death, and having given life to those in the grave." Counting insignificant dislocations on one accent, the words of the *troparion* are entered [into] the theme of the march. [162 II 595]

Such interpretations obscure the typical elements of Tchaikovsky's thinking in the Sixth. Its pattern is similar to that of his other symphonies: a complex, unusually articulated first movement yields to Schumannesque interior movements of striking sound and a finale that balances the intensity of the first. Its principal keys are concordant with the *Manfred* key complex (above, p. 317), particularly in the mix of E minor/major, B minor, and D major. No prominent device in the Sixth is new. The somber introduction recalls the finale of *Winter Reveries,* and the funeral march recalls the finale to *Romeo and Juliet;* the lyrical themes have many precedents; 5/4 time had been used in *The Sleeping Beauty;* the Scherzo idiom in the third movement runs from the First Symphony to the Third and Fourth, thence to the Third Suite and the *Souvenir de Florence;* the triumphal march had been rehearsed in the finale of the Fifth; even the religious accents in the Sixth echo the Third String Quartet, while the quotation or emulation of Orthodox song was anticipated in *1812* and *The Queen of Spades.* At the same time, one cannot speak of *remplissage* in the

Sixth, as one can of the Symphony in E-flat—surely a source of satisfaction for the composer.

Beethoven is a presence both obvious and subtle in the Sixth, as he was in the Fourth by Tchaikovsky's own admission. Modest thus risked appearing ignorant when he rejected Hugo Riemann's observation that the opening of the Sixth alludes to Beethoven's "Pathétique" piano sonata. But there are deeper affinities in Tchaikovsky's Sixth with Beethoven's Sixth, in the shift of the center of gravity and intensity from the outer movements into the interior. In both, after an energetic opening Allegro, all factors which normally contribute to tension—dynamic, rhythmic, and chordal intensification; dissonance—are deferred not to the finale but just before, releasing the finale proper from these very elements. Thus, Tchaikovsky's Scherzo finds its dynamic and gestural counterpart in Beethoven's Scherzo and in storm movements.

That Tchaikovsky gave no more idea of his meaning than can be connoted from the adjective *pathétique* suggests the possibility of hidden complexity. Indeed, diminishing the temptation to divine meaning may explain why he omitted a motto theme and why, compared to *Manfred,* he simplified the formal pattern and key in the Sixth:

Mvt. I			Mvt. II			Mvt. III, strophic				Mvt. IV, strophic			
			Tripartite			Strophe		Strophe		Strophe		Strophe	
Int	Sonata	Allegro	reprise			1		2		1		2	
Exp		Rec	A	B	A	Scherzo	March	Scherzo	March	1st	2nd	1st	2nd
e	b–D	b–B	D	b	D	G	E	G	G	(b)	D	(b)	b

Echoing this simplicity, Arkady Klimovitsky's thought, the Sixth is paradoxical in the lapidary separation of movements and the misalignment within them of both content and clichés of genre [208, 110]. It is here, as in Tchaikovsky's reconception of genre in opera and ballet, that the point and message of the work may lie.

Does the Sixth speak to Tchaikovsky's belief? Possibly. Father Mikhail's interpretation aligns it with the religious implications of other late-period works, abetted here by Tchaikovsky's atypical thanks to the deity in the sketches and the unambiguous melodic quotation of "With the saints give rest" in the development section of movement I (at bars 201–5), a citation long noted in commentaries. Fortunato's observation that the opening motif embeds the prayer rule of Orthodox services (the same passage that alludes to Beethoven's piano sonata) signals the possibility of several layers of meaning in the Sixth, framed, as it were, by the invocation of "Holy God" in its first notes and closing with the intimation of death at the end of the finale.

Tchaikovsky's unambiguous quotation of "With the saints have rest" justifies this line of inquiry and focuses on the sixth ode (of eight) of the *Kanon* of the Orthodox memorial service, perhaps its most recognizable line, being found in the brief *litiya* (most of the services in Tchaikovsky's apartment after his death); the more extensive *panikhida,* containing all eight odes; and the *otpevanie,* or singing-off, a more elaborate service to be celebrated in church. This text is the basis of speculations earlier about verbal rhythms in *Evgeniy Onegin,* the Violin Concerto, and *The Nutcracker.* Tchaikovsky also considered these famous words for the barracks scene of *The Queen of Spades* before choosing "I pour out my prayer unto the Lord." Traceable to his student days, the incorporation of verbal rhythms into his melodies, like the pattern of movements, key schemes, and the allusions to Beethoven, is a well-tried device.

The three funeral services have features in common: the *Trisvyatoe* at the beginning and end, the sixth song of the *Kanon,* just referred to, and the *Vechnaya pamyat'* (Eternal memory) before the return of the *Trisvyatoe.* The rhythmic imprint of these important words informs the beginning and end of movement I of the Sixth, with the direct quotation in between:

Ex. 62a Tchaikovsky, Symphony No. 6

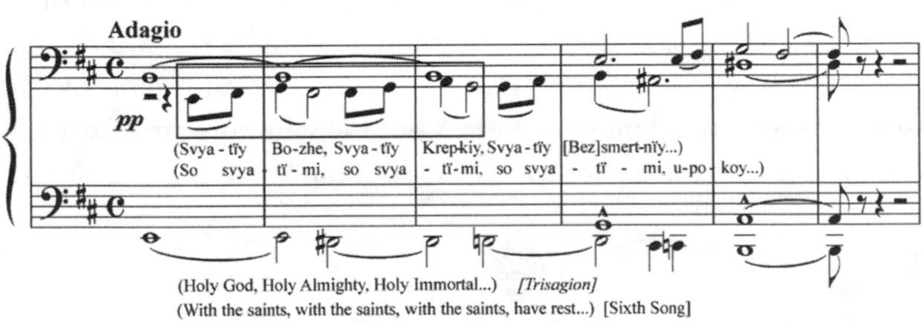

Ex. 62b Beethoven, Sonata for Piano No. 8

Ex. 63 Tchaikovsky, Symphony No. 6, mvt. I, postlude

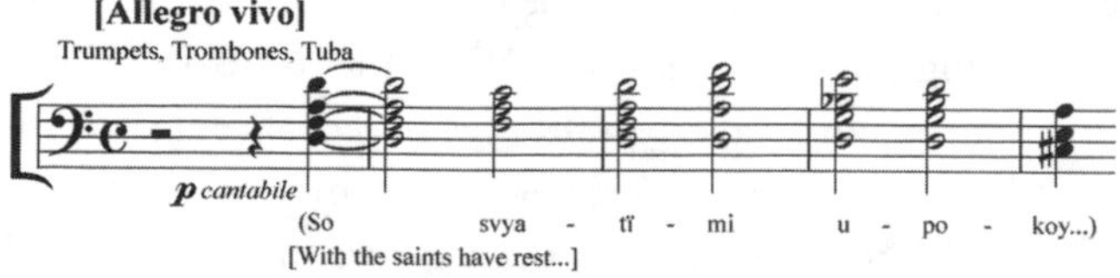

Ex. 64 Tchaikovsky, Symphony No. 6, mvt. I, second area theme

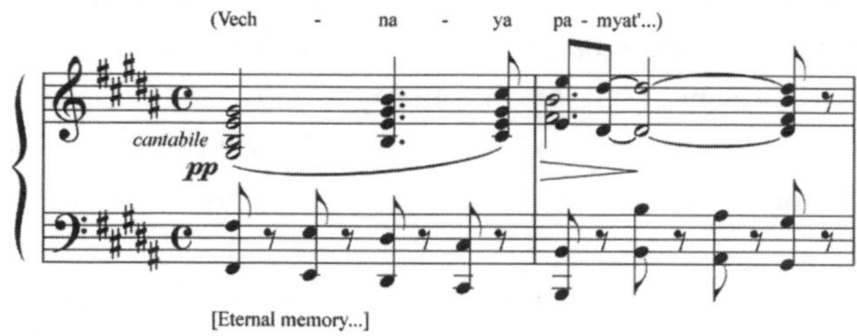

If such references impart a somber element to the first movement, it waxes less intense as the references become freer and the prosody less precisely applied, flowing into symphonic discourse (recalling the "drowning" effect of the folk melody in the Fourth Symphony, Tchaikovsky's disputation with K.R., granting himself exceptions to correct declamation, and his lifelong tendency to make allusions with one or two changes on the model). With these provisos, the famous lyrical theme fits the prosody of the respondent phrase of "With the saints give rest," namely, where there is no sickness nor sorrow nor sighing but everlasting life:

Ex. 65

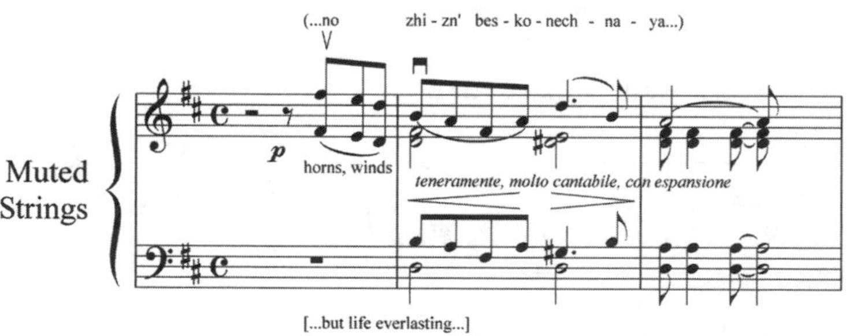

The text underlay taken from the italicized phrase is repeated, suggesting a less ironclad appropriation of the thought. Its implications are both universal and personal, the latter echoing the composer's illness at the time of composition and the death of his close friends; that this section is set apart from the rest of the movement by fermatas speaks to a special meaning.

The development, which shatters the calm, is taken up at first with the opening motif of the Allegro. Soon, however, frenetic activity leads to more ominous accents which correspond to yet another passage from the sixth ode. In the funeral service, the priest gives out the words, "For earth thou art and into earth thou shalt return, whither all dust will make its way," which is then continued by the choir, *our lamentation at the tomb creating the song: Alleluia, alleluia, alleluia.* At this point (bars 189–97), just before Tchaikovsky quotes "With the saints have rest," the italicized words are represented rhythmically in the outburst of the trumpets. Only in the recapitulation, when he returns to these accents in a newly composed section (277–96), does the music align with the textual underlay for a moment, just before the return of the second area's theme:

Ex. 66

(Nad - - - grob - no - e rï - - - da - ni - e

ff *sempre*

Nad - - - grob - no - e rï - - - da - ni - e tvor

fff

(*continued*)

Ex. 66 (*continued*)

(...nadgrobnaya rïdanie tvoryashche pesen, Alleluya, alleluya, alleluya)
[...our lamentation at the tomb, creating the song: Alleluia, alleluia, alleluia)

—Choral response from the Sixth Song of the funeral service

The middle movements seem, as did the middle movements of the Fifth, detached from the philosophy and expression of their neighbors. The second was composed last and makes no clear prosodic allusion. Does the 5/4 time perhaps refer to Vsevolozhsky, the composer's important mentor, whom Alexander Benois once described as walking with a "measured, just dance-like gait"? The Scherzo, especially its march, expresses the sense of the opening of the sixth ode: "The sea of life, surging with the tempest of temptations, I behold." The rhythmic allusion to Beethoven's "fate" motif (e.g., at 93–96) may thus be connoted for what it is. But therein Tchaikovsky makes a subtle point: Beethoven's motif is here adorning a movement that is about to leave the key of *fatum* behind forever. In the Sixth, the introduction to movement I, in E minor, does seem to echo the Fifth Symphony, but if the sequence of Tchaikovsky's sketches is any indication, the introduction occurred to him after the rest of the movement had been drafted and before he began movement III, the only other movement where E is prominent. The sequence of composition thus supports the proposition that he decided to link the Sixth with the Fifth tonally, then expunge its key after glorious exposure in the Scherzo.

Given the importance of the last movement in readings of the Sixth Symphony's meaning, it is well to recall that the lamenting of the *Adagio lamentoso* also links it with the connotations of the sixth ode. The opening period, allowing a modicum of flexibility in the prosodic underlay, would seem to incorporate yet another text from the sixth ode:

> Where are the passions of this earth?
> Where are the dreamings of the moment?
> Where is the gold and silver? Where is the host of servants? And fame?
> All is dust, all is ashes, all is a shadow.

Ex. 67

(Gde mirskoe pristrastie?
Gde privremennïkh mechtanie?
Gde zlato i srebro? Gde rabov
mnozhey?

Vsya perst',
Vsya pepel,
Vsya sen'...

—from the *stichera* of the memorial service

Where are the passions of this earth?
Where are the dreams of the moment?
Where the gold and silver? Where the
host of servants?

All is dust,
All is ashes,
All is shadow...)

Indisputably somber, the finale nevertheless offers some mitigation of "negation," "annihilation," "suicide," and similar descriptors. The second theme in D major is repeated in ever more prominent and secure presentations, as if offsetting despair. At its return (bar 90), the opening theme has lost the tortured voice crossing of its initial statements, suggesting relief and clarification. At the consequent of this theme (108), Tchaikovsky makes a breathtaking octave displacement of transformative effect, reversing the dark connotations of this phrase in its earlier occurrences and launching the upward-spiraling sequence which will lead to the chorale before the return of the second theme. Here (at 147), one may speak of desolation, but at that, as the melodic phrases descend into the lowest registers, the graphic metaphor of the music parallels the verbal metaphor that runs throughout the memorial service, which refers not to death but to falling asleep, which is precisely the image at the close of the symphony.

The Sixth Symphony can be considered many things, but shows evidence of being a salute to Beethoven and the grand tradition and a reconciliation of Tchaikovsky's personal approaches with Western symphonic thought. That he infused his themes with verbal rhythms is a hypothesis like any other, but the philosophical theme implicit in the rhythms is signaled by the outright quotation from the sixth ode. It is not a vocal setting, and so, in keeping with his customary habits of disguise, Tchaikovsky avoids a literal, *cantus firmus*–like treatment of his melodies in favor of the transformation and motivic play expected of a symphony. It is a contemplation informed by particular rhythms. The result, if the hypothesis has some basis, conforms to Bishop Amvrosy's characterization of the *Liturgy of St. John Chrysostom* as songs of the Divine Liturgy taken by Tchaikovsky only in the guise of material for his musical inspiration. That claim had no merit in 1880, but does in 1893 in light of the circumstances of Tchaikovsky's life. To this may be added an observation from Yury Davïdov's dubious memoirs to the effect that K.R. (who had urged Tchaikovsky to set Apukhtin's "Requiem") exclaimed after a rehearsal of the Sixth Symphony, "What you have done, you see, it's a requiem, a requiem!" [316, 384].

As ever with Tchaikovsky, one may be imagining the legitimacy of interpretation, stylistic evidence notwithstanding. Whatever else it may be, expression in the Sixth is consistent with the sense of resolution and farewell that informs Tchaikovsky's late work. No wonder he was pleased. The shade of Pushkin, upon hearing it, would surely have approved.

The Third Piano Concerto, op. 75, is the only remnant of the Symphony in E-flat that passed through Tchaikovsky's hands from start to finish. Structural changes, apart from adding a cadenza for the soloist, were minimal. He expanded two bars in the symphony (132–33) to four in the concerto (132–35); introducing the cadenza involved the deletion of 19 bars of the symphony, which had continued after the point where the cadenza began. Modeled thus so closely on the symphonic movement (always assuming that the reconstruction is accurate), of what did this revision consist? Probably the reconception of sound, which is important precisely because he did not alter the structure to make it more concerto-like.

After 10 bars from the symphony, Tchaikovsky rescored the concerto to produce more of a dichotomy of orchestral sonority and soloist. Applying the *concertato* principle to music lacking a concerto structure supports the hypothesis that one problem with the Symphony in E-flat was a misalignment of music and genre. The concertante element in the first movement was pulling away from the symphony into a concerto for orchestra. Moreover, the popular themes may have been more acceptable in a concerto than in a symphony. In this light, the piece was not so bad as to exclude it from his list of works.

As music, much the same can be said of the Andante and Finale for Piano and Orchestra, op. 79, as for its counterparts in the slow and last movements of the Symphony in E-flat, on which they were based. Again, adaptation brought changes. The Andante adds 8 bars and a cadenza between bars 138–39 of the symphony and 3 bars after the final cadence. In the finale, bars 33–35 in the symphony are omitted in op. 79, and bars 245–60 in op. 79 are not included in the symphony. But Tchaikovsky left op. 79 incomplete, having prepared the movements only in piano score by the time he died. The orchestration is Taneyev's. In the Andante, one senses Tchaikovsky's hand in the eloquent scoring of the reprise, deploying solo violin, viola, and cello with the piano in the manner of a concertino ensemble and recalling the slow movement of the Second Piano Concerto. In contrast, the *cantus firmus*–style presentation, in the trumpet, of the trite march theme near the end of the finale does little to redeem its ineptitude as an idea. This contrast speaks to the fundamental problem of op. 79, which is the disjunct impression of the whole. It cannot help sounding like the last two movements of a piece that began with something else.

It is too involved for an introduction, it deploys too much beauty for the bumpkin-like finale. The piece is a monument to practicality; he realized that these movements made too long a concerto when linked to op. 75, but not that they made imperfect sense when standing alone.

By 3 March 1893 (the date on the autograph), Tchaikovsky had composed the chorus *Noch'* (Night):

> O, what a night! How bright it is! What an expanse!
> In the heavens the stars are sparkling.
> Already everything is silent,
> Only in the distance a stream babbles mysteriously.
>
> Everything sleeps, peace, welcome guest, descends into the heart.
> The tired spirit has savored rest anew!
> O, nocturnal hour, give me oblivion and send blessed sleep down upon me!
>
> O, what a night and what an expanse!
> Such a night, bright and quiet!

He arranged it from the Andantino of Mozart's Fantasia in C Minor for Piano, K. 475. Judging from his treatment, Tchaikovsky was drawn to it as pure music. What in Mozart is a quiet, dramatically tentative improvisation in Tchaikovsky tilts toward *volupté*. He follows Mozart for 32 of 39 bars, then substitutes for the original disquieting bridge a leisurely 154-bar extension, freely rhapsodizing on Mozart's two principal melodic ideas, onto which, earlier, he had grafted the two stanzas of his verse. It becomes a radical transformation.

A few weeks later, on 24 March 1893, he composed the March for the Yurievsky Regiment at the request of his cousin for "three strains in all, [and] some melody in a noisy setting," and later a Trio [96, 417]. It was to be scored by the regimental bandmaster.

The dismissal of the *Eighteen Pieces for Piano,* op. 72, as a diversion to make money is offset by the importance of the music and its dedicatees. It may lie on "the periphery of Tchaikovsky's world, but [this is] a periphery which possesses a completely unique coloration—indeed, here Tchaikovsky makes direct contact with the atmosphere of his times, with the images surrounding his life" [448, 95]. Op. 72 restates important aspects of his musical thinking, including ballet and dance (three pieces from op. 72

were orchestrated by Riccardo Drigo for inclusion in *Swan Lake* in the celebrated staging of 1895), memory, his place in the musical world, the characteristic, and even the idea of variety itself [448].

In no. 1, "Impromptu," the elaboration of the two short ideas in the outer sections of the piece encloses a middle section in the manner of a music box. Tchaikovsky's treatment of the framing sections, especially the end, is mimetic, as if the music represented the gestures of an actor or dancer.

The lovely cradle song in no. 2 suggests the regular movements of the cradle and the mother's singing in the irregularly placed, sweet consonances of the melody. Tchaikovsky's style brings to mind the exquisite "Sterb' ich, so hüllt in Blumen meine Glieder" from Wolf's *Italianisches Liederbuch,* published a year before this music, with its tonic pedal on A-flat, offbeat rhythm in the left hand, mellifluous melody, and profound sense of calm.

"Tender Reproaches" is a contentious dialogue. This is clarified when the second statement of the opening melody, in the tenor, proceeds independently, at which the soprano cannot forbear interruption (at 29). The frequent nuancing after this—*poco meno, animato, crescendo, riten*[*uto*]—all within nine bars—depicts increased animation, while the middle section (at 49) imposes an artificial calm, and the brief coda (at 113) permits an exit from the stage.

No. 4, "Danse caractéristique," is of Russian cast with a quirky bass pattern at the beginning. It is easy to imagine orchestrated—not just drumbeats of the left hand at the outset, but some other percussion, perhaps a tambourine, in the syncopated figures in sixteenth notes, a harp in the *glissandi,* possibly a voice in the distantly Schumannesque *pochissimo meno allegro.*

The trite opening of the "Meditation," no. 5, echoes Schumann. The dedication to Safonov encourages a topical reading of the striking rising line in duple (9ff.), which cuts painfully through a repetition of the opening melody. This idea is omitted in the reprise, implying the overcoming of differences.

The unmazurka-like music at the opening of no. 6 jests at the title "Mazurka for Dancing": the downbeat stress, the clipped phrases, nothing that draws attention to the weak beats of the bar. The jest is made clear (at 33) by adhering to paradigm and by the resemblance to the mazurka at the end of *The Sleeping Beauty* (no. 30 at 42).

The "Polacca de Concert" was dedicated to Pavel Avgustovich Pabst, a virtuoso who had written a paraphrase of *Evgeniy Onegin* in 1880 and a four-hands arrangement of themes from *Mazepa.* Clear in structure, ambitious in technique, it is reminiscent of Beethoven's *Emperor* Concerto in its key movement from E-flat to B major (which happens again in nos. 8 and 11).

In no. 8, the "Dialogue" between the soprano and baritone registers may refer to the spousal disputes of the dedicatee, Hermann Laroche's wife, Ekaterina. At first, the soprano holds sway with brief responses from the baritone. As early as bar 14, however, the absence of time intervals between the voices and the phrase repetition suggest a more impassioned discourse. Emphasis shifts to the baritone with the change of key at *un poco sostenuto.* By *un poco animando* (43), the duet is unrestrained, and by bar 49 it has become operatic.

Tchaikovsky mimicked other composer's styles typically as an evocation, not a counterfeit. In "Un Poco di Schumann," the beginning melody is perfectly Schumannesque, especially in its transformation at bar 19. The middle section (31ff.) is *un poco di Tchaikovsky.*

In its exacting technique and wan personality, the "Scherzo-fantaisie" (no. 10) recalls Tchaikovsky's early virtuoso pieces and challenges the player to sustain an artistic point through extensive repetition. The dedicatee, Alexander Siloti, was a student of Liszt, which may explain additional referents from Mephisto waltzes to wild hunts to the flight of a will-o'-the-wisp.

The "Valse-bluette" (no. 11) is a *dansante* waltz, the regularity of which is interrupted only by the retransition to an internal reprise (95–105) and the chromatic wandering which just precedes it (at 81–94), perhaps an act of memory: the dedicatee, Melle Dina Kondratieff, was Nikolay Kondratiev's daughter, and the peregrinations echo the composer's travels in her father's last days.

"L'espiègle" (no. 12) may be a portrait of its dedicatee, Alexandra Svetoslavskaya, Pyotr Jurgenson's daughter. Tchaikovsky was vexed in 1890 not to attend her wedding. "Please kiss her chubby pink cheeks and tell her that I love her frightfully," he wrote at the time [xv-b 258]. This impishness is borne out in the music—*con grazia, in modo di scherzo*—as if putting childish pranks to music. Its *dansante* qualities prompted Marius Petipa to use the piece in *Swan Lake,* as orchestrated by Riccardo Drigo. In this capacity, the middle section (18ff.) was omitted.

No. 13, "Echo rustique," is dedicated to Alina Bryullova, mother of Kolya Konradi, who had lived deep in the countryside at Grankino. Tchaikovsky begins this beguiling evocation with a folkish tune, out of which a rounded pattern emerges, based on varied melodies of irregular periodicity all related to the first. A music box *quasi campanelli* echoes through the piece.

"Chant élégiaque" (no. 14) is dedicated to Vladimir Nikolaevich Sklifasovsky, the 14-year-old who traveled on the steamer taking Tchaikovsky back to Russia in April 1889. He died in 1890, which explains the memorial dedication and the heartfelt expression. The principal theme mimics Liszt's famous "Liebesträume," as too the treatment of the melody in the reprise, which is placed in the middle voice with elaborate figuration on either side. The *più mosso, moderato assai,* confirmed in the peroration at 86–90, alludes to the end of the Entr'acte of *The Sleeping Beauty* (no. 18, 72–76); it is doubly topical for the connotation of elegy and because Tchaikovsky was composing the ballet at the time of his acquaintance with the dedicatee.

No. 15, "Un Poco di Chopin," is more referential for charm than mimicry. Tchaikovsky builds his piece from a pristine mazurka to begin, with a hint of Chopin in the Neapolitan chord over a tonic in the bass, then a more neutral, even waltz-like second theme (at 17), and a third theme poised between an *obertas* and Chopin's "Minute" Waltz.

In no. 16, "Valse à cinq temps," the sparkling effect of the piano textures recalls the Sapphire Variation from *The Sleeping Beauty,* the difference being that Sapphire is concise and the *valse* is a garrulous *moto perpetuo.* This may be the connection to the dedicatee, Nikolay Lenz, a jurist/graduate of the School of Jurisprudence and an accomplished pianist who co-arranged two-piano, eight-hands arrangements of *Manfred* and *Francesca da Rimini.*

A stately melody in the upper voice and the title "Passé lointain" reference the dedicatee, Nikolay Zverev, a teacher of piano at the Moscow Conservatory and Tchaikovsky's long-time friend. He died on 30 September 1893; had Tchaikovsky known of his illness when he composed this piece, the "Passé lointain" could be seen as an elegy in advance of death.

The last of op. 72, "Scène dansante (invitation au trépak)," is self-explanatory, a rousing encore for the dedicatee, Vasily Sapelnikov. It is a simulated folk scene, in which three large upbeats to the dance proper (1–67), including a tantalizing slowdown (at the *moderato assai*), after which the tempo comes up to speed and the texture focuses. The permutations in the bass, with instant shifts of texture and melody in the upper voices, emulate the variegated gestures of the real dance, which increase in tempo, volume, and frenetic movement.

Tchaikovsky dedicated the *Six Romances,* op. 73, to the tenor Nikolay Figner after composing them, between 22 April and 5 May 1893, without preliminary sketches (except for no. 4) [424, 94, 108] or changes in the texts. The sentiment of the poems suggests his sorrow over the deaths of friends—in references to the extinguishing of light and to what has been left unsaid, which the ardor of the passionate poems never quite overcomes.

In no. 1, "We were sitting together," the singer regrets not having said anything to the beloved. The song begins in E major, recalling the beloved by a river, its waters depicted by a falling chromatic figure which cadences on a tremolo deep in the bass, anticipating the next verse, "Far off it began to thunder." Tears and silence mark the lovers' distress: the key begins to drift, the vocal line is volatile and unsettled. Shifting to *poco più* [*mosso*], an insistent, agitated syncopation and a recurrent bass pattern bring us into the present: the beloved is gone but the anguish persists. The final cadence in C-sharp minor—a rare instance of progressive tonality in Tchaikovsky—underlines the distinction between past and present.

The text and music of "Night" recall no. 3 of Musorgsky's *Without Sun:* darkness creeps in as the candle fades, and anguish grips the heart; as sleep descends, the grief-struck soul invokes the beloved, if only in a dream. The music is Musorgskian in its drooping melodies and eccentric chromaticism. Tchaikovsky based the vocal part on the introduction: a rising diminished fifth, which falls to the root of the scale, and a phrase beginning on the root and descending to the fifth. While the accompaniment may reverse the downward flow of the music, darkness resides in the tonic pedal, which runs unbroken throughout the song. These devices anticipate no. 6.

In no. 3, "On this moonlit night," the singer cannot restrain confession, but words are futile and the heart is exhausted. The rushing sixteenth notes suggest a nervous awareness of the waning night, the prevailing motion ceasing at the final couplet, "Dearest, farewell! Again the wave of life brings us a day of anguish and sadness!" The voice cadences enigmatically—on a dominant ninth chord.

No. 4, "The sun has set," is an apostrophe to night, the entire vocal part, as it had been in no. 2, based on the motif from the introduction. Thematic uniformity focuses the poem's emotion, yet a subtle tension runs throughout the song, finally relieved at the outset of the last verse. Only here, with the return of the music of the first verse, do the words point to the sense of the poem directly: "All is enveloped by the languor of this impassioned night, / You have inclined your head upon my shoulder and I am insanely happy."

In "Amid somber days" (no. 5), the singer all but denies the present with remembrance, carried away by the wish to relive passion. This intensity is caught in Tchaikovsky's expansive introduction. The power of his melody downplays other devices: the sighing figure which subtly underpins the voice in the left hand; the home key, A-flat major drifting to F minor, gently undermining the rush of emotion; and the operatic final cadence in the voice, underlaid by chords borrowed from the minor. If the beloved's memory is bright, the days are nevertheless somber.

"Again, as before, alone" (no. 6), popularized in an orchestral arrangement by Leopold Stokowski called "Solitude," is an intimation of death. The singer, parted from the beloved in a beautiful nocturnal setting, is indifferent to the whispering leaves and the sky aflame with stars. He asks for her prayer, as he is praying for her. The motif of the piano introduction is part sigh, part lament. The vocal melody through the first half of the song is limited to a third, suggesting the constriction or relaxation of consciousness, which intensifies one last time as the singer's emotions quicken at the thought of the beloved. When this outburst has quieted, the tempo has slowed and nothing remains but the lament, which drifts into silence on the indeterminate second inversion of the tonic triad.

In fact if not in name, op. 73 is a song cycle, progressing from an ardently remembered "then" to a despairing "now." Four songs refer to light being extinguished, four are set at night. They are balanced among elation (nos. 4 and 5), happiness mixed with melancholy (nos. 1 and 3), and despair (nos. 2 and 6). Among the links of detail: the text of no. 1 embeds the title of no. 6; the introduction of no. 5 embeds the concluding vocal phrase of no. 3; songs 3–5 begin with a rising scale in the principal melody; similar devices convey the heaviness of nos. 2 and 6.

The key scheme of the songs at first seems random, but a coherent rationale arises out of the tension between A minor as the home key for the group, representing despair, and A-flat major, representing hope. The E major songs anticipate the A minor of no. 6 as dominant to tonic. More subtly, E major, masking F-flat, also acts as a flat submediant of A-flat and thus, metaphorically, as an intermediary between happiness and despair. The significance of A-flat in nos. 3 and 5 is rooted in its poetic content: no. 3 is filled with delight until the end, and no. 5, after opening with a reference to the weight of misfortune, turns to delight in the beloved. In song 5, in the last phrase of the vocal part, the cadence in A-flat is approached with chords borrowed from the minor—triads on F-flat and B double flat (at 32)—embedding an enharmonic cadence in A, the key of no. 6, and thus anticipating despair. The songs of op. 73 thus never lose sight of the A minor of no. 6, despite the key of the moment:

	No. 1	No. 2	No. 3	No. 4	No. 5	No. 6
	E to c-sharp	f	A-flat	E	A-flat	a
			(signals F-flat = E)		(embeds V–I in A)	
a:	V	vi	(V)	V	(V–I)	i

 CHAPTER TWENTY-ONE 

The Circumstances of Tchaikovsky's Death

SOON AFTER TCHAIKOVSKY'S DEATH, THE QUESTION AROSE: HOW did he die? Probably from natural causes, but foul play or suicide cannot be excluded [e.g., 161, 386–88]. Controversy arose, as it will when famous people die; speculation flourished in the confusion of data; the unanswerable questions spawned hypotheses well beyond rational boundaries. Inexplicable disparities in statements by Modest and by Tchaikovsky's doctors inspired hardy suspicions about what really happened without proof of any dread circumstance or motive in these people to deceive.

Explanations of Tchaikovsky's death have hardened into orthodoxies. One, following *The Life,* is that he died of cholera. It is the cause of death listed on Tchaikovsky's death certificate [367, 147; 307, 162]. The late Nikolay Blinov summarized the argument for cholera [44], reconciling oddities in the accounts of Modest and the doctors, reviewing the doctors' competence, establishing the actuarial plausibility of death from cholera, explaining sources of infection, and in his own opinion, dismissing any other possibility. Blinov worked with great care but relied on assumption and interpretation. A second explanation is that other people killed Tchaikovsky or forced him to commit suicide. Its adherents dismiss the lack of evidence because conspirators are secretive. A third explanation is that death resulted from a totality of influences conspiring over a long period. Tchaikovsky sensed death was near, but it occurred in its own good time.

Claims that Tchaikovsky's death was intentional are not the work of recent generations casting suspicion in hindsight, but rather are early allegations of pernicious vitality [307, 192–221]. By a week after his death, enough doubt had been sown to reap suspicion forever. The day after he died, the *Petersburg Gazette* queried, "How could Tchaikovsky, having just arrived in Petersburg a few days earlier and living in excellent hygienic conditions, have contracted cholera?" [307, 91]. In Moscow, the *News of the Day* editorialized: "In the city yesterday the sole topic of all talk and conversations was P[yotr] I[lyich's] tragic end. His Moscow friends, who know his concern for hygiene, his strict routine, were perplexed—how could he get infected with cholera?" [367, 150].

The graphic if conflicting accounts of Tchaikovsky's condition within days of his death, and medical bulletins placed on the door of Modest's apartment while Pyotr was still alive, suggest an open disclosure of his illness. In light of subsequent controversy, however, they can look like planted evidence. Lev Bertenson, Tchaikovsky's senior physician, published a clarification of the composer's illness two days after the death [NV931027; 161, 440–42], before which the editors of the newspaper explained: "Contradictions which have appeared in the press about the illness of the late P. I. Tchaikovsky compelled us to turn to Dr. L. B. Bertenson." Modest's account on 1 November was similar [NV931101; 160]. "To supplement the short but completely accurate account by L. B. Bertenson of the last days of my brother's life," he began, "I find it necessary to clear up all manner of conflicting rumors, to provide for you, for publication, as complete as possible an account of everything to which I was witness." Clearly, rumors were circulating.

One need not be a conspiracy advocate to wonder why Tchaikovsky died in the absence of his senior physicians. Vasily Bertenson left St. Petersburg and sent condolences to Modest from Moscow. Lev Bertenson, distraught and exhausted, left his patient's side in the last hours and went home. Given Tchaikovsky's importance and his imminent demise, one might have expected his doctor to stay. Yet at the point of death, only family members and the junior physician, Mamonov, were attending. Soon questions about Tchaikovsky's medical care were being raised. Two days after he died, commentators queried why the latest treatment (a type of enema) had not been used when doing so was indicated [367, 159]. On

3 November, Alexey Suvorin, editor of the widely circulated *Novoe vremya,* attacked Lev Bertenson:

> Mr. Bertenson did not do everything needed, and it seems to me there is basis to ask, why did he not convene a consultation? Could he have believed his own authority, or that his patient would recover? Either way he was wrong, and the dying man's words at the outset of some improvement, "You have wrest me from death's clutches," sound like a cruel and just irony for Mr. Bertenson now. Mr. M[odest] Tchaikovsky's letter does not diminish this irony, who registers the forenames and patronymics of the Bertenson brothers and affirms their indefatigable solicitude about the patient. Everything, he says, was done but death was inexorable. No, everything was not done. [367, 160]

Two days later, a call for a public investigation of Bertenson's treatment regimen [307, 175–76] alleged that he was not familiar with treating cholera (his practice being to high society) and should have consulted with doctors who were. (The Bertensons admitted never having treated cholera before Tchaikovsky [44, 96].) Such reproaches brought Modest, on 7 November, into print again, dismissing criticism of the Bertensons [367, 164–65; 307, 179]. Did camaraderie alone bring him to this appearance of stifling debate? In response, Modest himself was declared responsible for his brother's death in part by delaying the initial call for medical help and for not insisting on a consultation [307, 180]. He was manifestly suspect. It matters little that disparities among medical accounts seem less heinous now or that Suvorin later apologized to Lev Bertenson. Doubt about Tchaikovsky's death was raised *at the time,* as if accounts of unboiled water, delays in seeking medical help, methods of treatment—even openness of disclosure—were misfired attempts to conceal his intimates' letting Tchaikovsky die with malice aforethought. This inference may be totally unjust and lacks credible motive. But that is the point: never was a crisis outside his illness signaled, while the sense lingers that something mysterious occurred.

More than a century after the fact, the cholera theory accords with medical plausibility and allows for disparities in the reports of a gossipy press. Cholera was a threat in St. Petersburg at the time, and Tchaikovsky was neither assured of contagion by drinking unboiled water nor excluded from it on the basis of his social status or living conditions. Seven others died of it the same day as he did; two more cases were reported on his street within five days of his death. Reports of the outbreak at the time suggest that the strain he contracted was particularly virulent [44, 38]. Such data place a tremendous burden on claims that his illness was falsified and that famous doctors risked their reputations so that Tchaikovsky might die by suicide for unknown reasons. Yet the singular failing of the cholera theory is that it cannot disprove that Tchaikovsky poisoned himself with something similar in its effect [161, 386–89]. This flaw leaves open the possibility that the descriptions of Tchaikovsky's illness came out of a medical book while his intimates watched him die of poison. Modest's periodic recital of witnesses takes on an eerie subtext in this light, as does the absence when death came of Tchaikovsky's senior physicians, who would not have chosen to witness such a fundamental breach of the Hippocratic oath.

Conspiracy theories are categorically different. The focus shifts from others to the composer, and from generous documentation to virtually none. The debate moves from biographers and scholars mostly detached from the events to persons directly conversant with Tchaikovsky's life. Valery Sokolov has observed that, for all the fuss about Modest and the doctors, no source immediately after his death ever suggested that Tchaikovsky took his own life [367, 144]. That idea came later, after incubating. Many envious people might have wished Tchaikovsky dead, but the idea that envy was responsible for his death yields to another, which finds him more susceptible because of his sexuality.

The hardiest conspiracy theory subjects Tchaikovsky to possible exposure and punishment for pursuing a young man who found his attentions unwelcome. To escape the consequences, the composer took his own life. One variant traces to Olga Tchaikovskaya, Nikolay's wife. She could have easily been the source of information passed along to her sister, whose son's diaries indicate that Tchaikovsky committed suicide by a means he chose and administered; that his family knew about it; and that the cause was the composer's exaggerated attention to a young man of high status [307, 204–5]. In another variant, the emperor offered an ultimatum of suicide or prosecution; Tchaikovsky chose suicide, and Lev Bertenson administered the poison (which he supposedly admitted in old age [307, 198; 286, 131]). In another version, the judgment for such a transgression was passed by a "court of honor" of Tchaikovsky's former classmates at the School of Jurisprudence, who voted for his suicide to protect the school's reputation. In this case, Alexandra Orlova, who first published the theory, gave names: Tchaikovsky was making advances to the nephew of Duke Alexey Alexandrovich Steinbok-Fermor; the duke's accusation to the emperor was entrusted to Nikolay Jacobi, a graduate of the School of Jurisprudence, who convened the court of honor before delivering it. The account comes from Jacobi's widow, to whom Jacobi told all and who was doing her needlework in the next room as the proceeding was conducted. Jacobi's widow told Alexander Voitov, another jurist, when the 20th anniversary of Tchaikovsky's death was being celebrated, and Voitov told Orlova [286, 132–34]. In more recent times, Voitov's widow claimed no knowledge of a court of honor [307, 220, n. 20].

The conspiracy theories have been scrutinized in detail [e.g., 161, 396–400; 36; 308]. Here are the principal elements of their refutation:

Tchaikovsky's pressing for sexual favors in 1893, at the age of 53, would have come seven years after the latest (surviving) reference to homosexuality in letters to Modest [369, 122]. The hypothesis assumes Tchaikovsky's promiscuity, but does not indicate where or when the offense took place. It cannot have occurred during the final visit to St. Petersburg, as a fortnight is too little time for the composer to get in trouble, wait for the bureaucracy to act, and take five days to die. In St. Petersburg, it would have to have fit into three days in August and a week in September, or else happened earlier or someplace else. The earlier it happened, the more fraudulent would appear Tchaikovsky's many professional activities scheduled for after his death, including a second trip to the United States and various conducting appearances; if it took place in St. Petersburg closer to the time of his death, it must be explained in relation to Tchaikovsky's affection for Bob Davïdov, who was living there. That he would press for sexual favors after being rebuffed contradicts what little we know about his retiring personality, in addition to the disparity between a lamb-like submission to suicide and the aggressiveness of a sexual predator.

That Tchaikovsky could not have died of cholera (and must have died of poison) because sanitary precautions were not observed in Modest's apartment is refuted by his doctors' knowledge that cholera is transmitted only by ingestion. This leaves open the possibility that he died of cholera, but refutes conspiracy.

That the emperor threatened Tchaikovsky with death is rebutted by his leniency in other cases and his favor toward the composer and by tolerant attitudes toward homosexuality in the Russian upper classes despite anti-sodomy laws and the strictures of the church [308]; Tchaikovsky's worst outcome would have been exile.

The court of honor, as it involves the School of Jurisprudence, raises issues of allegiance that defy credibility. The school did promote an image of rectitude and tried to live up to it, but extending this requirement to the behavior of its graduates later in life is stretching a point. Alexey Apukhtin, Tchaikovsky's chum, was an unabashedly public homosexual whose poetry K.R. wanted Tchaikovsky to set just weeks before the composer's death. It is easy to imagine Apukhtin's response to indictment by a court of honor. Moreover, if the court of honor comprised Tchaikovsky's available classmates, it would have included Vladimir Gerard, who delivered the school's funeral oration at Tchaikovsky's grave, and Avgust Gerke, who visited him on the morning of 20 October (and could have delivered poison at that time) and who sent highly commiserating messages to Modest. Hypocrisy on such a grand scale diminishes rectitude.

Because some variants attribute Tchaikovsky's suicide to an ultimatum from the emperor, conspiracy theories have prompted a review of the imperial family's response to Tchaikovsky [44, 73–81; 367, 176–81], who had feared a loss of favor in 1891. While Vsevolozhsky assured him of his monarch's approval then, an awkward liaison cannot be excluded. If so, we know nothing of it, and nothing suggests imperial disfavor at the time of Tchaikovsky's death. In his diary, K.R. noted his own sorrow and the emperor's and empress's; in subsequent weeks, he twice referred to playing through parts of the Sixth Symphony, once "with Kündinger," presumably Tchaikovsky's teacher from 1857 [44, 81]. On 2 December, Modest requested that K.R. consider an imperial pension for Georgy Konyus on the basis of Pyotr's approval. It was made so. The emperor's paying for the funeral, the dispatching of eight telegrams of condolence from the imperial family to Tchaikovsky's relatives, K.R.'s attempt, stayed by grief, to write a memorial poem, and his acceptance of cholera as the cause of death—all speak to an unfeigned sense of loss.

The conspiracy theories are worthless in an evidentiary sense. They rationalize why Modest and Tchaikovsky's doctors protested so much that he died of cholera. They survive by hints of plausibility and the blandishments of sensationalism. A more reasonable explanation accounts for other forces in his life and is fairer to his memory, which suffers from having no alternative to mystery and wrongdoing to explain his death. A different explanation also would cease to essentialize his sexuality. If, in addition, one reconnected with the broader dimensions of Tchaikovsky's art, details about how he died, should any of the theories prove true, would still seem myopic and off point. His death and his music are linked only in that the richer the appreciation of his music, the less important the details of his death. The critic who finds that the Sixth Symphony is about suicide never insists that Brahms's late chamber music is about liver cancer. Evidence of the imminence of death cascades through Tchaikovsky's last years: illness as near-constant companion, thrice drafting his will, ruminating over the deaths of others, trips to Vichy. Vasily Bertenson described the composer's principal ailment as catarrh of the stomach, then added:

> Pyotr Ilyich drank a lot of vodka and wine. Evenings, especially in periods of "little seizures," he abused cognac, and there was a time when, according to his brothers, he was close to genuine alcoholism. . . . He smoked without restraint from the age of fourteen, especially when he was working. He inhaled not only cigarette smoke, but also cigar smoke. [316, 399]

In a letter to Modest from July 1898, Bob Davïdov took this line of thought to its logical conclusion: "You see, Uncle Petya had terrible catarrh of the stomach, which in my time was, obviously, less intense, but which carried forward to an extreme and finally served as the basis of his mortal illness" [367, 192].

The year 1893 had been full of portent. From his refusal to attend rehearsals of *Iolanta* at Schwerin for health reasons, to the unscheduled stop at Kharkov because of medical distress, to the letter of 8 March reporting the end of a two-week headache, to the report from London of pain in the lower abdomen with aching and weakness in the knees, to complaints of stomach problems at Ukolovo and Moscow in July, to the ominous debt obligation written to Ekaterina Laroche on 1 August which indicated how she should be repaid if he died within the next seven months—there is reason to suppose that death would not have come as a surprise. Nikolay, in a letter to Modest of 28 July, reported Pyotr's illness at Ukolovo as "cholerina" [367, 186]—a less virulent form of the parent illness which might have been dormant in his system.

A death premonition is implicit in reports of Tchaikovsky's last house guests at Klin. Anatoly Brandukov recalled Tchaikovsky's wish to be buried at Frolovskoe as they left Klin on his final journey. Ever meddlesome, Modest pointed out that many beautiful locales delighted his brother to the point of wishing to be buried there, but Petersburg was where his parents and sister were buried and where he spent his best years [367, 156–58]. Whatever the case, Tchaikovsky was thinking about death. Illness, with *fatum* as its metaphor, underlay the last years of his life. Above it, he deployed philosophy, muse, commemoration, and his professional activities. His preoccupation with things "not of this world" in the late works does not preclude sexual mischief, but certainly burdens the arguments that assume it. This tension underscores the most serious flaw in the suicide theories, namely, a lack of credible motive. It might have been reasonable for Tchaikovsky to take his life after the break with Meck shattered his finances and his muse, but it was unreasonable after his muse revived. His authorial pride in the Sixth Symphony is inconsistent with the final episode of a soap opera. Moreover, for the Sixth to be a premeditated announcement of Tchaikovsky's death calls for an even more mystifying sequence of events than the one mandated by the suicide theorists. Tchaikovsky must have committed the deed and sensed the certainty of prosecution before February 1893, by which time he had already conceived the *Adagio lamentoso.*

Nothing argues better that Tchaikovsky had come to see death as life's natural end than his acts of commemoration. One is the referentiality of his late music: the images in *The Nutcracker,* self-quotation in *Souvenir de Florence,* allusion in the Sixth Symphony. Another is his homage to first things and to Mozart (in the chorus "Night"), whose music was an object of abiding affection. A third resides in the events of his life: seeing Fanny Dürbach; accepting the doctorate; systematic reunions with siblings; returning to the Moscow Musical Society after a period of estrangement; contemplating the revision of *The Oprichnik* and *The Maid of Orleans;* visiting Nikolay Rubinstein's grave during his last visit to Moscow; even dining with Vera Butakova a few nights before he died, which surely revived memories of Hapsal in the summer of their flirtation. These were spread out over his final year, not the manic activities of a person with a death sentence, but moments of resolution to be savored as one ties up the strands of memory.

As 1893 passed from summer into autumn, his life was neither at a peak nor in a trough, but one can imagine him perceiving a crossroads at which many aspects of it converged. His pledge to write a symphony that represented the culmination of his compositional career had been fulfilled. In the theater, he had moved away from the mainstream in *The Queen of Spades* and *Iolanta*. With Lev Davïdov's remarriage, the door symbolically closed at Kamenka. He had been isolated by the death of family members and close friends. Bob had graduated from the School of Jurisprudence, and Modest had broken with Nikolay Konradi after 17 years. Of the 12 works Tchaikovsky offered to conduct for the St. Petersburg Musical Society in August 1893, only one was by him and half were by younger composers: Konyus, Stojowski, Glazunov, Taneyev, Rachmaninov, and Arensky [xvii 156]. That so many of his conducting responsibilities in 1893 were charitable betrays a self-awareness impossible in the absence of historical perspective. And all of this with the court of honor presumably yet to come. From this perspective, Tchaikovsky's death is more reasonable than contrived, and the extraordinary focus on his last two weeks is extreme. Yet still the nagging question: why did Modest and the doctors act as they did? The events of those last days are now obscured beyond hope of clarity by time and human intervention. We do not and probably never will know beyond doubt the cause of Tchaikovsky's death.

Afterword

TO SOME DEGREE, TCHAIKOVSKY WILL REMAIN A PARADOX. WE may learn more when his letters that are in private hands become public, but even then, barring some extraordinary rediscovery (such as his letters to his wife), a sense of not-knowing will remain. This is due to circumstances already noted—the gaps in his correspondence, together with letters known to have been mutilated or destroyed. But it is also due to facts we know: he was an avid reader and yet said so little about the issues of his day. He lived in momentous times; what was he thinking beyond his immediate preoccupations? An answer to this question applies to more than his amorous pursuits; Tchaikovsky, an important figure in the culture of his day, is difficult to place within that culture. The one exception is politics—his allegiance to the emperor, from whom he accepted money, in whose theaters he strove to have his works produced, and with whose ministers and relatives he maintained friendly relations. His one reference to communism, to Meck in April 1883, was an embarrassment to the Bolshevik regime: "What you say about communism is completely true. A more mindless utopia, something more discordant with the natural attributes of human nature is impossible to conceive" [xii 123–24].

But what of the rest? Not every composer is Wagner or Stravinsky, drawn to excessive pronouncement. Apart from outpourings in the early correspondence with Meck (above, p. 187), Tchaikovsky was not inclined to record his opinions. Did his reading extend with any regularity to the celebrated "thick journals" of his day, organs of social thought, reminiscences, and literary criticism? Did he have an opinion on serfdom, or revolutionary foment, or political reform? We have a few of his thoughts on Lev Tolstoy, but what did he think of Dostoevsky? What does his receptiveness to Western art mean when so many factions on the political spectrum in his day were anti-Western? Was his dislike of Musorgsky's music simply a matter of personal taste, or was it rooted in some philosophical rejection of populist art? Is this why Ilya Repin, who painted Musorgsky, Vladimir Stasov, and even Anton Rubinstein, never painted Tchaikovsky? What was Tchaikovsky's response to the "mad summer" of 1874, a few months after the first performance of Musorgsky's *Boris Godunov,* in which, unbidden, young intellectuals from the cities dressed as peasants and went to the country to live among them, landowners gave away their possessions, and Jews were baptized Orthodox to be closer to "the people" whom Musorgsky so esteemed? Did Tchaikovsky even notice, at a time when his discontent with his life in Moscow was intensifying? Or did he notice profoundly, ultimately rejecting graphic realism and pristine speech intonations in *The Queen of Spades* and elsewhere, channeling the advances and reconceptions of his art toward what realists would consider artifice?

For the most part, Tchaikovsky avoided public rhetoric, in part (one presumes) to protect the quality of concentration he needed for artistic creation. But it defies credibility to suggest that protecting his inner world caused him to stand aloof from circumstances around him which were by no means benign and to which he left hints of being aware. He certainly did not stand aloof from contentious issues as a music critic. Was he, in defending the listener against that narrowly construed truth by which a real apple is better than a drawn one, or in comparing César Cui's judgments to those of an earlier age that found Beethoven, Mozart, and Raphael no better than chefs or gardeners, acknowledging an awareness of, let alone opposition to, Nikolay Chernïshevsky (e.g., *The Aesthetic Relation of Art to Reality*), who belittled art and artists, including Raphael, beloved of traditionalists? Or was this an accidental allusion?

Emphasizing the absence of direct interactions between Tchaikovsky and the ideas of his time are those occasions in which he made nothing of being in touch with important people or events. When Prince Vladimir Odoevsky presented him, in congratulation, a pair of cymbals at the time of *The Voevoda,* did they discuss anything outside the immediate occasion? Had Tchaikovsky read any of Odoevsky's philosophical papers, his predictions of the decline of the West, or his futuristic *The Year 4338,* in which Great Britain is sold at public auction to Russia and the world is divided between Russia and China? The composer left no opinion of the politics of the Franco-Prussian War, the mobilization for which he observed first-hand during a trip in 1870, and when he conducted the first performance of *Marche slave* in 1876, a riot of patriotic fervor ensued, about the pan-Slav implications of which he did not elaborate. Was this an oversight, or was Tchaikovsky indicating that he was not an anti–Romano-German xenophobe?

These enigmas surrounding the man extend to his music, but with different effects. However justified the conclusion that Tchaikovsky was a social and political conservative, his music was not. Snobbishness and personal taste excepted, all but the most prejudiced observer now recognizes the boldness of his thinking in symphonic writing, concertante, and theater. Of greater import is not what he meant in his music, but its ability to prompt a variety of responses. While this is true of any great artist, in Tchaikovsky's case more sophisticated interpretation has enabled a shift in reception away from the easy dismissal of his music as personal and overly indulgent.

Referentiality external to the musical notes, as unexplained as Tchaikovsky's views on important issues of the day in relation to his life, began with his student works and became more noticeable in and after 1877, the year of his marriage. This intensification was thus related to his life and may be measured—approximately—by the enthusiasm with which posterity has sought to explain the Fourth, Fifth, and Sixth symphonies compared with its lack of curiosity about the Third, Second, and First. The fallacy in such a lapidary distinction is to assume that his music was persistently and abjectly autobiographical. That assumption, already untenable in reference to *Evgeniy Onegin* in 1877, was certainly so by the time of the *Serenade for Strings* in 1880, and was positively silly a decade later in reference to *The Sleeping Beauty* and *The Queen of Spades.* In these later works, as always in the theater, the fable rationalizes compositional choices without raising additional meanings. Or nearly so. Tchaikovsky's method, it would appear, was to use little external flaws as gateways to the internal world of his thought. Hence, the little flaw of *ennui* with which *Evgeniy Onegin* begins, which opens the door to awareness of the epigraph, or the little flaw with which *The Nutcracker* ends (by not returning to reality), which suggests his belief in the reconciliation of opposites and the immanence of God in all things, a passage he underlined in Letter 21 of Spinoza's *Correspondence* [444, 164–65], a focus of his reading in the years 1892–92. This passage also relates to an arid period of composition and the last throes of the Meck friendship in 1891, but yields in the artwork to considerations larger than Tchaikovsky's life. After 1887—Nikolay Kondratiev's last summer—such idiosyncrasy as we notice in his works aligns with a late style based on fundamental dichotomies: darkness and light, death and life, this world and the next.

The sense that Tchaikovsky's music generates meanings beyond its immediate impression mitigates the harsh criticisms leveled at his music and locates his thinking as pan-European. If there is a Russian-German distinction to be made between Tchaikovsky and Beethoven or Brahms, it is not because Tchaikovsky was untrained or "Asiatic," to cite an early term of abuse. He was Russian in the same sense that Musorgsky and Glinka and any number of other compatriots were—in borrowing and individualizing European models. It is not absurdly reductive to suggest that the difference between Tchaikovsky and Brahms, the negative response to each other's art being exaggerated in the popular imagination, is that Tchaikovsky the Russian favored melody not totally at the expense of able construction, while Brahms the German favored an excellent bass line not totally at the expense of attractiveness in the other dimensions of a piece. Brahms's concern for the developmental potential of his musical ideas limits their distinctiveness as themes, while Tchaikovsky's focus on striking melody limits contrapuntal potential and the propensity for motivic coherence. From this distinction, the two composers progressed to quite different results. Even still, the motto theme of Tchaikovsky's Fourth Symphony and the Alphorn theme in the finale of Brahms's First share common ground: they stand out within their symphonic settings, they are most effective of a piece, and they do not function well when fragmented. The striking moment in Tchaikovsky has been emphasized in these pages in reference to musical thoughts too attractive to let pass, thoughts that reveal the composer's gift for the charming or the bold or the striking, thoughts more pertinent in the moment than in the long term. In loving such ideas, Tchaikovsky was no more pointedly non-Teutonic, let alone anti-Teutonic, than Verdi or Delibes. But unlike those two masters, he was willing to engage the German symphony using his own language, the brightness of which contrasts with the more subdued symphonic themes from Mozart through Brahms. The critical flaw is to assume that the delight implicit in Tchaikovsky's invention of attractive sound precludes the achievement of artistry associated with the German tradition, and so warrants declaring any attempt to do so a failure. The logical end point of Tchaikovsky's symphonic writing is thus denied him, in simplistic historiography, on the assumption that everybody should write like Beethoven.

In sum, Tchaikovsky—person and music—warrants evaluation in a much wider context than occurred in the twentieth century and should be given the benefit of the doubt in comparisons or when subjected to fearsome clichés of criticism. Apart from the continuing scrutiny of documentary sources [239], this calls for seeing him as he really was, a well-networked musician interacting constantly with other professionals in and outside Russia. To demonstrate this would offset the journalistic preoccupation with his personal problems, which are introspective by definition and secretive by choice. Lucinde Braun's study of late imperial operatic institutions contributes to this context-broadening effort [56]. Proceeding from Tchaikovsky to Rimsky-Korsakov and Sergey Taneyev, she places their operas within the reforms of the Imperial Theaters, the abolition of the Italian opera, and the rise of private opera companies. Projecting opera onto the totality of Tchaikovsky's accomplishment, the evidence is mounting for a long-apparent if insufficiently acknowledged conclusion: he was a wholly functional artist and human being even in light of his woes. Wounded people cannot do what he did. Second, Tchaikovsky deserves to be raised up from the status of historical oddity—a lamentable mix of talent and vulgarity—to interact with today's cultural issues. To do this would accord him a place in scholarly discourse comparable to the generation-transcending appeal of his music. In this regard, two other studies, by Susanne Dammann on genre and its implications [93] and by Kadja Grönke on the fate of women in the Pushkin operas [153], show the way. Given the unlikely prospect of additional biographical revelations, thoughtful reflection on Tchaikovsky's art shows the greatest promise for understanding him better. One suspects that he would have preferred it this way.

APPENDIX A

Calendar

Year	Age	Life	Contemporary Events
1840		Pyotr Ilyich Tchaikovsky born at Votkinsk, in the Urals, son of Ilya Petrovich Tchaikovsky, a mining engineer, and his wife, Alexandra Andreyevna Tchaikovskaya	Death of Paganini; Schumann (30) marries Clara Wieck (20); Lermontov writes *A Hero of Our Time;* Great Britain is ascendant in the industrial revolution; Napoleon's ashes are returned to Paris; China is in the midst of the Opium War; Cherubini is aged 80, Auber 58, Meyerbeer 49, Rossini 48, Donizetti 43, Berlioz 37, Glinka 36, Mendelssohn 31, Chopin 30, Liszt 29, Wagner, Verdi and Dargomïzhsky 27, Gounod 22, Dostoevsky 19, Lalo 17, Smetana and Bruckner 16, Johann Strauss, Jr. 15, Lev Tolstoy 12, Anton Rubinstein 11, Hans von Bülow 10, Brahms and Borodin 7, St.-Saëns, César Cui, and Nikolay Rubinstein 5, Mussorgsky 1

Year	Age	Life	Contemporary Events
1841	1	Pyotr's sister Alexandra "Sasha" is born on 29 December	Schumann's "song year"; birth of Dvořák; Wagner composes *The Flying Dutchman*
1842	2		Death of Cherubini; birth of Massenet; Gogol publishes *Dead Souls;* building of railway service between St. Petersburg and Moscow begins
1843	3	Pyotr's brother Ippolit born on 10 April	Birth of Grieg; Britain annexes the Sind
1844	4	Fanny Dürbach joins the Tchaikovsky family as governess to the children	Births of Rimsky-Korsakov, Ilya Repin, and Nietzsche; electric telegraph opens between Washington and Baltimore; Marx meets Engels
1845	5		Birth of Fauré; premieres of Wagner's *Tannhäuser,* Mendelssohn's Violin Concerto
1846	6		Premieres of Berlioz's *La damnation de Faust,* Schumann's Second Symphony
1847	7		Deaths of Felix Mendelssohn and Fanny Mendelssohn Hensel
1848	8	The family leaves Votkinsk, visits Moscow and St. Petersburg	Death of Donizetti; antimonarchical revolutionary uprisings throughout Europe; Marx publishes *The Communist Manifesto;* Cavour effects the political reorganization of the Piedmont
1849	9	Family moves to Alapaevsk; Anastasia Petrova, to whom Pyotr dedicated his first surviving music, joins the family as the children's governess.	Death of Chopin; Britain conquers the Punjab, the last important Indian territory outside British control; the California gold rush begins
1850	10	Modest and Anatoly Tchaikovsky are born; Pyotr is enrolled in the preparatory division of the School of Jurisprudence in St. Petersburg; Nikolay Vakar dies	Death of Wordsworth; the Bach Gesellschaft is founded
1851	11		Birth of d'Indy; premiere of Verdi's *Rigoletto;* Great Exhibition in London
1852	12	Pyotr's parents move back to St. Petersburg; he enters the School of Jurisprudence	The Bach Gesellschaft begins the systematic publication of Bach's works

Year	Age	Life	Contemporary Events
1853	13		Russia's war with Turkey initiates the Crimean War; the first railway line is opened in India
1854	14	Pyotr's mother dies; he writes down his first surviving composition, the "Anastasia Waltz"; contemplates an opera, *Hyperbole*	Birth of Janáček; Liszt composes *A Faust Symphony;* Wagner finishes *Das Rheingold*
1855	15	Pyotr begins the study of piano with Rudolf Kündinger	Emperor Nikolay I dies; Sevastopol falls; Alexander II ascends the Russian throne; aluminum is introduced to the public at the Paris Exhibition; the Panama Railway opens
1856	16	Takes up the study of Italian and singing with Luigi Piccioli	Births of Sergey Taneyev, Sigmund Freud; the Treaty of Paris ends the Crimean War
1857	17		Death of Glinka; birth of Elgar
1858	18		Birth of Puccini; the East India Company transfers the administration of India to the British Parliament
1859	19	Pyotr graduates from the School of Jurisprudence, joins the civil service in the Ministry of Justice	Premiere of Gounod's *Faust;* Darwin publishes *The Origin of Species*
1860	20	Pyotr's sister Alexandra marries Lev Davïdov, moves to his estate at Kamenka in the Ukraine	Births of Mahler, Hugo Wolf, Chekhov
1861	21	Travels to Western Europe as a translator during the summer; takes his first course in music theory in the autumn	Russian serfdom is abolished; the American Civil War begins; proclamation of the kingdom of Italy; Britain annexes Lagos as a Crown colony
1862	22	Enters the St. Petersburg Conservatory	Births of Debussy, Walter Damrosch; premiere of Verdi's *La Forza del destino* (in St. Petersburg); Tolstoy begins writing *War and Peace;* Turgenev writes *Fathers and Sons;* Otto von Bismarck becomes chief minister of Prussia, makes his "blood and iron" speech; the "Wanderers" revolt against the St. Petersburg Academy of Art
1863	23	Resigns from active service in the Ministry of Justice; begins study	Wagner conducts in Russia; Abraham Lincoln issues the U.S.

Year	Age	Life	Contemporary Events
		with Anton Rubinstein	Emancipation Proclamation; birth of Mascagni
1864	24	Composes *The Storm,* an overture to Ostrovsky's play	Death of Meyerbeer; birth of Richard Strauss; Dostoevsky publishes *Notes from the Underground*
1865	25	First public performance of Tchaikovsky's Characteristic Dances, conducted by Johann Strauss, Jr.; graduates from St. Petersburg Conservatory	Lincoln is assassinated; births of Sibelius and Glazunov; premiere of Wagner's *Tristan und Isolde;* American Civil War ends
1866	26	Moves to Moscow; begins teaching music theory; debuts as professional composer with the revised Overture in F; Moscow Conservatory opens in September; composes the First Symphony	Births of Busoni and Satie; Dostoevsky publishes *Crime and Punishment;* first transatlantic cable is laid; British foreign investment reaches £500 million
1867	27	Begins *The Voevoda;* flirtation with Vera Davïdova in Hapsal; composes the *Souvenir de Hapsal,* op. 2; greets Berlioz during his visit to Moscow	Marx publishes first volume of *Das Kapital;* United States purchases Alaska from Russia; the British North America Act creates the dominion of Canada; Alfred Nobel granted a patent in Great Britain for dynamite
1868	28	First serious engagement with Balakirev and the Mighty Handful; finishes *The Voevoda;* composes *Fatum;* flirtation with Désirée Artôt leads to some thought of marriage; writes his first music review; his op. 1 is published	Death of Rossini; premiere of Wagner's *Die Meistersinger;* Disraeli becomes prime minister of Great Britain
1869	29	Premiere of *The Voevoda;* composes *Romeo and Juliet* and op. 6 songs; composes the opera *Undine*	Death of Dargomïzhsky; birth of Gandhi; opening of the Suez Canal; the transcontinental railway across United States opens
1870	30	Visits Vladimir Shilovsky in Germany; is caught up in the turmoil of the Franco-Prussian War; revises *Romeo and Juliet; Undine* is rejected in St. Petersburg; begins *The Oprichnik*	Franco-Prussian War begins; birth of Lenin; First Vatican Council affirms the principle of papal infallibility as Rome is being occupied; refrigeration is introduced on trains and ships
1871	31	Tchaikovsky's benefit concert in March features the First String Quartet; he obtains separate living quarters for the first time	Death of Auber; premiere of Verdi's *Aïda;* Paris capitulates in the Franco-Prussian War; proclamation of the German Empire under Kaiser Wilhelm I; Rome

Year	Age	Life	Contemporary Events
			becomes the capital of a united Italy
1872	32	Takes up music criticism in earnest, finishes *The Oprichnik;* composes the Second Symphony; first signs of serious discontent with Moscow; his nephew Vladimir "Bob" Davïdov is born	Births of Scriabin and Vaughan Williams; internal self-government in South Africa begins
1873	33	Composes *The Tempest,* the piano pieces opp. 19 and 21, incidental music to Ostrovsky's *The Snow Maiden;* as critic, engages César Cui in polemic; tours Europe in the summer; suicide of Eduard Zak	Birth of Rachmaninov; Tolstoy begins *Anna Karenina*
1874	34	Composes *Vakula the Smith,* the Second String Quartet, the First Piano Concerto; *The Oprichnik* is staged; his newspaper criticism shows discontent for Moscow; Nikolay Rubinstein critiques First Piano Concerto; reviews Hans von Bülow, who begins to praise him in print	Births of Schönberg and Ives; premiere of Musorgsky's *Boris Godunov;* birth of Guglielmo Marconi, inventor of the radio
1875	35	Discontent with Moscow increases; sends the First Piano Concerto to Bülow for its first performance (Boston, October); composes the Third Symphony, songs opp. 27–28; wins a competition for setting *Vakula the Smith;* begins to compose *Swan Lake*	Birth of Ravel; premiere of *Carmen;* death of Bizet
1876	36	Composes the Third String Quartet, *Marche slave, Francesca da Rimini, Variations on a Rococo Theme;* hears *Carmen* and *The Nibelung's Ring* for the first time; abandons music criticism; fiery infatuation with Nikolay Konradi, Modest's deaf mute student, brings on a resolve to marry; *Vakula the Smith* is staged; meets Lev Tolstoy; receives his first letter from Nadezhda von Meck	Telephone is invented; premiere of Brahms's First Symphony; the first Bayreuth Festival; Custer is defeated at the Battle of the Little Big Horn
1877	37	Composes the Fourth Symphony and *Evgeniy Onegin* over the	Russia declares war against Turkey over Slav nationalism in the

Year	Age	Life	Contemporary Events
		course of the year; *Swan Lake* staged in February; acknowledges a passion for (student) violinist Josef Kotek as he looks for a suitable marriage partner; he chooses Antonina Milyukova in May and marries her in July; retires to Kamenka (without his wife) for the summer, probably conceives a divorce strategy; feigns illness to cover an escape to Western Europe, abandoning his teaching post in Moscow; Sasha Davïdova initiates a bitter dispute with Pyotr and Anatoly, who press for Antonina's banishment; they finally prevail in November; Pyotr travels to Italy at the end of the year	Balkans; the Turkish fortress at Plevna falls; Thomas Edison invents the phonograph; Henry Morton Stanley returns from his journey down the Congo River
1878	38	(Unsuccessfully) attempts legal avenues of divorce; Pyotr returns to Moscow Conservatory in September, but resigns in October; develops his affinities with Meck; visits Florence in November to be near her; finishes *Evgeniy Onegin;* composes the Violin Concerto, Piano Sonata (op. 37a), *Children's Album,* op. 40 piano pieces, songs of op. 38, and the *Liturgy of St. John Chrysostom;* decides on *The Maid of Orleans* as his next opera	Nikolay Rubinstein conducts the first performance of the Fourth Symphony in Moscow (February) and other works at the World Exhibition in Paris
1879	39	Composes *The Maid of Orleans,* First Suite, Second Piano Concerto; *Evgeniy Onegin* is staged by students; a lawsuit regarding the *Liturgy* is initiated; a period of nomadic travel begins, interrupted by summers at Kamenka; the Meck relationship achieves a vicarious intimacy; the two matchmake a marriage of one of his nieces with one of her sons; revises the Second Symphony	First edition of *Grove's Dictionary of Music and Musicians;* Dostoevsky begins *The Brothers Karamazov;* birth of Stalin; Thomas Edison demonstrates the carbon filament lamp; Bismarck initiates a series of alliances aimed at determining European political alignments

Year	Age	Life	Contemporary Events
1880	40	Tchaikovsky's father dies; the Meck correspondence begins to dwindle; he lets pass his best prospect for a divorce, based on Antonina's pregnancy; his sister's health begins to fail; he prepares *The Maid of Orleans* for production; composes *Capriccio Italien,* op. 46 duets, op. 47 songs, Serenade for Strings, and *1812*	Meck finances a performance of the Fourth Symphony in Paris; birth of Ernest Bloch; death of Offenbach
1881	41	Livelihood is affected by threats to Meck's business and the death of Nikolay Rubinstein; his sister and his niece Tatyana ("Tanya") descend into morphine addiction; appeals to the tsar for a loan; Jurgenson prevails in the lawsuit over the *Liturgy;* Pyotr agrees to edit the sacred works of Dmitry Bortnyansky; *Onegin* and *The Maid of Orleans* are staged professionally; Antonina gives birth to a daughter; in Vienna, Adolf Brodsky gives the first performance of the Violin Concerto	Alexander III assassinated; birth of Bartók; Repin paints Musorgsky's portrait; deaths of Musorgsky and Dostoevsky
1882	42	Finishes Piano Trio; begins to disengage with Kamenka as a residence; finishes composing and begins scoring *Mazepa;* composes the *All-Night Vigil*	Birth of Stravinsky; death of Darwin; premiere of Wagner's *Parsifal*
1883	43	In Paris, attends to the detoxification of Tatyana Davïdova and the birth of her son until mid-May; completes *Mazepa;* composes a March and a Cantata for Alexander III's coronation, then the Second Suite and op. 54 songs later in the year; niece Anna Davïdova marries Meck's son Nikolay	Coronation of Alexander III; deaths of Wagner and Marx; Fabian Society founded in London
1884	44	Premieres of *Mazepa* in Moscow and St. Petersburg; composes the Third Suite, the Concert Fantasia, op. 57 songs, three cherubic	Birth of Boris Asafiev; premiere of Massenet's *Manon;* death of Smetana

Year	Age	Life	Contemporary Events
		hymns; receives the Order of St. Vladimir, Fourth Class, at an audience with the emperor; complaints of illness increase; letters take on a philosophical tone; writes unusual alphabet codes in diaries; premiere of *Evgeniy Onegin* in the St. Petersburg Imperial Theaters; visits the dying Josef Kotek in Davos; makes preparations in Paris for the return of grandnephew Georges-Léon to Russia; desire for a permanent home increases	
1885	45	Rents a house at Maydanovo; revises *Vakula* as *Cherevichki;* composes *Manfred;* begins *The Enchantress;* elected director of the Russian Musical Society in Moscow; Hans von Bülow conducts first performance of the Third Suite	Birth of Alban Berg; Repin paints *Ivan the Terrible with his Murdered Son;* Gottlieb Daimler patents a high-speed internal combustion engine; Berlin Act formalizes decisions of colonial powers about claims to territory in Africa; organization of the Indian National Congress; Mark Twain publishes *Huckleberry Finn*
1886	46	Experiences a period of heightened religious feeling; increased complaints about his health; drafts his will; continues work on *The Enchantress;* visits Tiflis; meets Verinovsky; in Paris, meets several luminaries in the musical world; agrees to write a new ballet; prepares for his conducting debut	Death of Liszt; the first Home Rule Bill (for Ireland) is introduced in the British Parliament
1887	47	Premiere of *Cherevichki* initiates his conducting career; death of Tatyana Davïdova; his own illness continues; attends the dying Nikolay Kondratiev at Aachen; conducts the premiere of *The Enchantress;* arranges *Mozartiana* and composes the *Pezzo capriccioso;* begins a conducting tour of Western Europe	Death of Borodin; birth of Nadia Boulanger; premiere of Verdi's *Otello;* the United States acquires Pearl Harbor
1888	48	Continues his first conducting tour; learns of his annuity from the emperor, with whom is he	Wilhelm II becomes emperor of Germany

Year	Age	Life	Contemporary Events
		granted an audience; takes a new home in Frolovskoe; composes Fifth Symphony, *Hamlet* Overture; agrees to compose *Sadia,* on a libretto by Détroyat and Gallet, for Paris, and *The Sleeping Beauty* for St. Petersburg	
1889	49	Makes second foreign conducting tour; engagements in Moscow, and in St. Petersburg for the 50th anniversary jubilee of Anton Rubinstein; composes *The Sleeping Beauty*	Births of Adolf Hitler, Jean Cocteau; Rimsky-Korsakov conducts at the World Exhibition in Paris; premiere of Mahler's First Symphony
1890	50	Premiere of *The Sleeping Beauty;* goes to Florence to compose *The Queen of Spades;* the break with Nadezhda von Meck; premiere of *The Queen of Spades*	Daimler-Motoren-Gesellschaft founded; premiere of Borodin's *Prince Igor,* completed by Rimsky-Korsakov and Glazunov; Bismarck dismissed; premiere of *Cavalleria Rusticana*
1891	51	Suffers difficulties of concentration, caused by doubts of imperial favor; death of Sasha Davïdova; travels to United States for the opening of the Music Hall in New York; the final stage of the Meck relationship; begins work on the Symphony in E-flat	Birth of Prokofiev; construction on the Trans-Siberian Railway is begun; British foreign investment reaches £2,000 million
1892	52	Conducts in Warsaw, Hamburg, Moscow (for the Pryanishnikov Opera); renews acquaintance with his childhood governess, Fanny Dürbach; completes *Iolanta* and *The Nutcracker,* both first performed in December; moves into his last home, at Klin; continues work on the Symphony in E-flat	Death of Lalo; births of Honegger and Milhaud; premiere of *I Pagliacci;* dancer Vladimir Stepanov publishes a treatise on movement notation, which is taken up by the Imperial Russian Ballet
1893	53	Conducts in Odessa, Moscow; composes the Sixth Symphony, op. 72 piano pieces, op. 73 songs; visits England; receives honorary doctorate at Cambridge; conducts there and in London; conducts premiere of Sixth Symphony; falls ill on 21 October, dies on 25 October/6 November	Deaths of Alexander III, Gounod, Apukhtin; premiere of Verdi's *Falstaff;* Labor Party founded in England; Franco-Russian alliance takes effect; Gandhi moves to South Africa

APPENDIX B

List of Works

Adapted from 96; 217; 309; 423; for a bibliography of the musical works, see 309 II 569–785.

I-A. Completed Music for the Stage

Music for the Fountain Scene from Pushkin's *Boris Godunov* (1863–1864?), lost [96, 190; 309 I 123; 423, 754].

Introduction and mazurka for Ostrovsky's play *The False Dmitry and Vasily Shuisky* (Jan. 1867). First performance, Moscow, Maly Theater, 30 Jan. 1867.
Piano arrangement of the mazurka. First performance, Klin, May 1986 [412].

Recitative and couplet for P. Fedorov's vaudeville *The Tangle* (Dec. 1867), lost [96, 191; 309 I 124; 423, 754]. First performance, Moscow, Dec. 1867.

Opus 3: *The Voevoda* [Provincial Governor], opera, libretto by Ostrovsky and Tchaikovsky (1867–1868). First performance, Moscow Bolshoy Theater, 30 Jan. 1869.

Undine, opera, libretto by V. A. Sollogub after Zhukovsky and de la Motte Fouqué (1869), lost [96, 18–22; 309 I 15–17; 423, 23–28]. Performance of excerpts, Moscow Bolshoy Theater, 16 Mar. 1870.

Chorus of Flowers and Insects from Rachinsky's projected opera *Mandragora* (1869–1870). First performance, Moscow, 18 Dec. 1870 [96, 115].

The Oprichnik, opera, libretto by Tchaikovsky after I. I. Lazhechnikov's play (1870–1872). First performance, St. Petersburg Maryinsky Theater, 12 Apr. 1874.

Almaviva's couplet, "Vous l'ordonnez," tr. M. P. Sadovsky, from Beaumarchais's *Le barbier de Séville* (Feb. 1872) [96, 192; 309 I 124–25; 423, 282–83]. First performance, Moscow Conservatory, 12 Feb. 1872.

Opus 12: Incidental music for Ostrovsky's *The Snow Maiden* (1873). First performance, Moscow Bolshoy Theater, 11 May 1873.

Opus 14: *Kuznets Vakula* [Vakula the Smith], opera, libretto by Yakov Polonsky after Gogol′ (1874). First performance, St. Petersburg Maryinsky Theater, 24 Nov. 1876.

Recitatives for Mozart's *Le nozze di Figaro,* tr. Tchaikovsky (1875) [96, 486; 309 I 381; 423, 740–41]. First performance, Moscow Conservatory, 5 May 1876.

Opus 20: *Lebedinoe ozero* [Swan Lake], ballet, libretto attributed to V. P. Begichev and V. F. Gel′tser (1875–1876). First performance, Moscow Bolshoy Theater, 20 Feb. 1877.

Opus 24: *Evgeniy Onegin* [Eugene Onegin], lyric scenes, libretto by Tchaikovsky and K. Shilovsky after Pushkin (1877–1878). First performance, Moscow Conservatory, 17 Mar. 1879.

New aria for Prince Vyazemsky in act II of *The Oprichnik,* text by G. H. Lishin (Oct. 1878) [349]. Not performed in Tchaikovsky's lifetime.

Orleanskaya deva [The Maid of Orleans], opera, libretto by Tchaikovsky after Zhukovsky/Schiller, Barbier, and Mermet (1878–1879, rev. 1882). First performance, St. Petersburg Maryinsky Theater, 13 Feb. 1881.

Chernogoriya [Montenegro, or "Montenegro at the Moment of Receiving the News That Russia Had Declared War on Turkey"], music for a *tableau vivant* (Jan.–Feb. 1880), lost [96, 199–200; 309 I 132; 423, 755].

Mazepa [Mazeppa], opera, libretto by V. Burenin and Tchaikovsky after Pushkin, plus text by Kandaurov for interpolated aria in act II (1881–1883). First performance, Moscow Bolshoy Theater, 3 Feb. 1884.

Cherevichki [The Fancy Slippers; revision of *Vakula the Smith*], opera, libretto by Yakov Polonsky and Tchaikovsky after Gogol′ (1885). First performance, Moscow Bolshoy Theater, 19 Jan. 1887.

Charodeyka [The Enchantress], opera, libretto by I.V. Shpazhinsky (1885–1887). First performance, St. Petersburg Maryinsky Theater, 20 Oct. 1887.

Domovoy's monologue from Ostrovsky's *The Voevoda* (Jan. 1886) [96, 200; 309 I 132; 423, 283–84]. First performance, Moscow Maly Theater, 19 Jan. 1886.

Opus 66: *Spyashchaya krasavitsa* [The Sleeping Beauty], ballet, libretto by I. A. Vsevolozhsky after Perrault (1888–1889). First performance, St. Petersburg Maryinsky Theater, 3 Jan. 1890.

Opus 68: *Pikovaya dama* [The Queen of Spades], opera, libretto by Modest Tchaikovsky and the composer after Pushkin (1890). First performance, St. Petersburg Maryinsky Theater, 7 Dec. 1890.

Opus 67a: Incidental music for Shakespeare's *Hamlet,* tr. Dumas and Meurice (Jan. 1891). First performance, St. Petersburg Mikhaylovsky Theater, 9 Feb. 1891.

Opus 69: *Iolanta* [Iolanthe], opera, libretto by Modest Tchaikovsky after Hertz (1891). First performance, St. Petersburg Maryinsky Theater, 6 Dec. 1892.

Opus 71: *Shchelkunchik* [The Nutcracker], ballet, libretto by I. A. Vsevolozhsky(?) after E. T. A. Hoffmann, tr. Dumas *père* (1891–1892). First performance, St. Petersburg Maryinsky Theater, 6 Dec. 1892.

I-B. Incomplete, Projected, or Rumored Works for the Stage (see also 96, 154–55; 423, 779)

Hyperbole, projected opera, to a libretto by Viktor Ol'khovsky (1854) [135, 76; 96, 112–13; 309 I 395; 423, 770].

Grozá [The Storm], opera after Ostrovsky (c. 1864); claimed by Modest Tchaikovsky [1997 I 176; 96, 113–14; 309 I 396; 423, 771].

Pal'ma [The Palm Tree] (1867–1868?) [309 I 396–97].

Alexander the Great, opera proposed to a libretto by Ostrovsky (1868) [v 144; 96, 114; 309 I 397; 423, 771].

Virgilia (before 1869), referred to in a letter of 18 Oct. 1869 from Modest Tchaikovsky to the composer [96, 115].

Mandragora, opera to a projected libretto by Sergey Rachinsky (1869–1870) [96, 115–16; 309 I 397; 423, 761–62].

Raymond Lully, opera after a scenario by Sergey Rachinsky (1870) [v 202; 96, 116; 309 I 398; 423, 771–72].

The Lake of Swans, a rumored house ballet performed at Kamenka (1867 or 1870) [95, 26; 362, 89].

Volshebnïy bashmachok, ili Sandril'ona [The Magic Slipper; or, Cinderella], ballet in four acts to a libretto by Karl Val'ts (autumn 1870) [v 234–35; 362, 80–81; and libretto, 297–303; 96, 185; 309 I 398; 423, 780; 402, 104–6].

Snegurochka [The Snow Maiden], opera after Ostrovsky's play; claimed by Modest Tchaikovsky (1873?) [1997 I 381–82; 96, 117–18].

Efraim, opera to a libretto by Konstantin Shilovsky (1875–1876) [96, 120–21; 309 I 399–400; 423, 772].

Tsaritsa ponevole [The Princess against Her Will], opera to a libretto by Konstantin Shilovsky (1875) [96, 118].

Francesca da Rimini, opera to a libretto by Konstantin Zvantsev (1876) [96, 119–20; 187, 106–7; 309 I 400; 423, 773].

Dobrïnya Nikitich [The Good Bogatïr Nikitich], opera based on ancient Russian epic to a libretto by V. P. Avenarius (Dec. 1876) [96, 121–22; 423, 773].

Othello, opera to a libretto by V. V. Stasov after Shakespeare (Nov. 1876–Apr. 1877) [96, 122–25; 309 I 400; 423, 773–74].

The Cardinal, opera considered to a scenario by V. V. Stasov after de Vigny (1877) [96, 125–26].

Ines de Las Sierras, opera to a scenario proposed by Modest Tchaikovsky (1877) [96, 126–27].

Undine, opera to a libretto by Modest Tchaikovsky after Zhukovsky and de la Motte Fouqué (1878) [96, 128–29; 309 I 401; 423, 775]. Modest in 1893 offered a libretto of this title to Rachmaninov, who did not set it.

Romeo and Juliet, opera after Shakespeare's play in A. L. Sokolovsky's translation (1878–1881) [96, 129–32; 309 I 401–2; 423, 762–63]. Sketches for a duet, based on themes familiar from Tchaikovsky's overture/fantasia of the same name, were completed by Taneyev [CW 62, 211–63].

Prikhoti Mariannï [Les caprices de Marianne], considered for an opera after Musset (Aug. 1878) [96, 132–34; 309 I 403; 423, 775]. The possibility of an opera on this topic may have been revisited in 1888 with Léonce Détroyat.

Taras Bulba, opera to a libretto by V. Al'feriev after Gogol (Oct. 1878) [96, 134; 423, 775].

Cradle song and waltz for Feuillet's *La fée* (July 1879) [96, 198–99; 309 I 131–32; 423, 754–55], lost.

Cradle song reconstructed by V. L. Davïdov [143, 258]. First performance, Kamenka, summer 1879.

Sakuntala, opera after Kalidasa, briefly considered (1880) [96, 134–35].

Sasha and Vanya, opera to a story and libretto by I. E. Simakov (1880) [96, 135].

Van'ka klyuchnik [Vanka the Steward], opera to a libretto by L. N. Antropov after Averkiev (Oct. 1881–Jan. 1882) [96, 135–37; 309 I 404; 423, 776].

Dolya-gore [Woe Is One's Portion], opera after A. N. Potekhin; *Koromïslova bashnya* [The Tower of Havoc], opera after a legend from Nizhnïy-Novgorod; *Sadkó,* opera after the old Russian epic (all 1882) [96, 137–38]. Topics discussed in negotiations with the impresario Mikhail Lentovsky.

Alësha i prachka [Alyosha and the Laundress], sketches for a possible opera (1883) [309 I 405].

Tsïgane [The Gypsies], opera to a scenario by V. A. Kandaurov after Pushkin (Dec. 1884–Jan. 1885) [96, 138–39; 423, 776].

Nakanune [On the Eve], opera to a libretto by P. A. Pereletsky after Turgenev (1885) [96, 139].

Kapitanskaya dochka [The Captain's Daughter], opera to a libretto by I.V. Shpazhinsky after Pushkin (Jan. 1885–May 1888) [96, 140–43; 309 I 407; 423, 776].

Undine, ballet to a libretto by Modest Tchaikovsky after de la Motte Fouqué (Nov.–Dec. 1886) [96, 186–87; 309 I 408–9].

Vlyublennaya bayaderka [The Enamored Bayadère], opera to a libretto by I.V. Shpazhinsky after Goethe's "Der Gott und die Bajadere" (May–Aug. 1888) [96, 143–44; 309 I 411; 423, 777].

La courtisane; ou, Sadia, opera to a scenario by Léonce Détroyat, libretto by Louis Gallet, after Goethe's "Der Gott und die Bajadere" (Oct. 1888–Jan. 1891) [96, 144–46; 309 I 412; 423, 777].

Béla, opera to a scenario by A. P. Chekhov after Lermontov's *A Hero of Our Time* (Jan. 1890–1893) [96, 147–48; 309 I 413; 423, 778].

Chernïy prints [The Black Prince], opera subject proposed by Désirée Artôt, briefly considered by Tchaikovsky (1890) [96, 148].

Venetsianskiy kupets [The Merchant of Venice], an opera after Shakespeare suggested by Kolya Konradi (1891–1893) [96, 152].

Burya [The Tempest], tentatively considered ballet scenario by N. Nikolaev after Shakespeare (1891) [96, 187–88].

Vatanabe [Watanabe], ballet to a scenario by Karl Val'ts after a Japanese fairy tale (1891) [362, 331–34; 77, 474–76; xvi-a 151; 96, 188–89; 423, 780].

Legenda o prekrasnom Pekonene i prekrasnoy Bol'dur [The Legend of the Handsome Pekonen and the Beautiful Boldour], briefly considered opera to a scenario by B. B. Korsov after Victor Hugo (1891) [96, 149–50].

Shil'onskiy zamok [The Castle of Chillon], briefly considered opera to a scenario by A. F. Fedotov after Byron (1892) [96, 151–52].

Pechal'naya sud'ba prepodobnogo Bartona [The Sad Fortunes of the Reverend Amos Barton], opera after George Eliot referred to by Modest Tchaikovsky (1893) [309 I 420–21].

Lyubov' Mistera Gil'filya [Mister Gilfil's Love Story], opera after George Eliot to Tchaikovsky's own libretto (1893) [96, 153–54; 309 I 421; 423, 778].

Adam Bede, brief consideration of an opera after George Eliot (1893) [309 I 421–22].

Vechnost' v mgnoven'i [Eternity in a Moment], opera after T. L. Shchepkina-Kupernik's drama. Sketches in a copy of the text. Date is uncertain [309 I 424].

II-A. Completed Orchestral Music

Early Student Works, 1863–1864 (CW 58)

Allegro ma non tanto in G, for strings.

Largo and *Allegro* in D for 2 flutes and strings.

Andante ma non troppo in A for small orchestra.

Agitato and *allegro* in E, for small orchestra.

Allegro vivo in C for winds and strings.

Rimlyane v Kolizee [The Romans in the Coliseum] for orchestra(?) [309 I 348; 423, 755], lost.

Later Student Works

Opus 76: *Grozá* [The Storm], overture to Ostrovsky's play (summer 1864). Not performed in Tchaikovsky's lifetime.

Characteristic Dances [rev. as Dances of the Serving Maidens in *The Voevoda*] (winter 1864–1865), lost [96, 273–74; 309 I 176; 423, 756]. First performance, Pavlovsk Railway Station, 30 Aug. 1865, cond. Johann Strauss, Jr.

Overture in F, first version for small orchestra (autumn 1865) [309 I 177; 423, 345]. First performance, St. Petersburg, 14 Nov. 1865.

Overture in C Minor (1865–1866) [96, 274–75; 309 I 176; 423, 348–49]. Not performed in Tchaikovsky's lifetime.

The Official List

Overture in F, second version for large orchestra (Feb. 1866) [309 I 177–78; 423, 346]. First performance, Moscow, 4 Mar. 1866.

Opus 13: Symphony no. 1 in G Minor, *Winter Reveries* (Mar.–Nov. 1866; rev. 1874). First performance of the complete work, Moscow, 3 Feb. 1868.

Opus 15: *Ouverture triomphale sur l'hyme national Danois* [Festive Overture on the Danish National Anthem] (1866). First performance, Moscow, 29 Jan. 1867.

Opus 77: *Fatum* [Fate], symphonic poem (1868). First performance, Moscow, 15 Feb. 1869.

Romeo and Juliet, fantasia/overture.
- First version (1869). First performance, Moscow, 4 Mar. 1870.
- Second version (1870). First performance, St. Petersburg, 5 Feb. 1872.
- Third (standard) version (1880). First performance, Tbilisi, 19 Apr. 1886.

Serenade for the Name-Day of N. G. Rubinstein (Dec. 1872). First performance, Moscow, 6 Dec. 1872.

Opus 17: Symphony no. 2 in C Minor, *Little Russian.*
- First version (1872). First performance, Moscow, 26 Jan. 1873.
- Second version (1879). First performance, St. Petersburg, 31 Jan. 1881.

Opus 18: *Burya* [The Tempest], symphonic fantasia after Shakespeare (1873). First performance, Moscow, 7 Dec. 1873.

Opus 29: Symphony no. 3 in D, "Polish" (1875). First performance, Moscow, 7 Nov. 1875.

Opus 31: *Serbo-Russkiy marsh* [Serbo-Russian March, *Marche slave*] (1876). First performance, Moscow, 5 Nov. 1876.

Opus 32: *Francesca da Rimini,* symphonic fantasia after Dante (1876). First performance, Moscow, 25 Feb. 1877.

Opus 36: Symphony no. 4 in F (1877). First performance, Moscow, 10 Feb. 1878.

Opus 43: Suite no. 1 in D (1878–1879). First performance, Moscow, 8 Dec. 1879.

Opus 45: *Capriccio Italien* (1880). First performance, Moscow, 6 Dec. 1880.

Opus 48: Serenade for String Orchestra in C (1880). First performance, St. Petersburg, 18 Oct. 1881.

Opus 49: *1812,* festival overture (1880). First performance, Moscow, 8 Aug. 1882.

Festival Coronation March (Mar. 1883). First performance, Moscow, 23 May 1883.

Opus 53: Suite no. 2 in C (1883). First performance, Moscow, 4 Feb. 1884.

Opus 55: Suite no. 3 in G (1884). First performance, St. Petersburg, 12 Jan. 1885.

Elegy in Honor of Ivan Samarin (Nov. 1884). First performance, Moscow, 16 Dec. 1884.

Opus 58: *Manfred,* symphony after Byron (1885). First performance, Moscow, 11 Mar. 1886.

Pravovedskiy marsh [Jurists' March] (Nov. 1885). First performance, St. Petersburg, 5 Dec. 1885 [96, 300–1; 309 I 192; 423, 382].

Opus 64: Symphony no. 5 in E Minor (1888). First performance, St. Petersburg, 5 Nov. 1888.

Opus 67: *Hamlet,* fantasy/overture after Shakespeare (1888). First performance, 12 Nov. 1888.

Opus 78: *The Voevoda,* symphonic ballad after Mickiewicz (1891). First performance, Moscow, 4 Nov. 1891.

Opus 71a: Suite from the ballet *The Nutcracker* (1892). First performance, St. Petersburg, 7 Mar. 1892.

Opus 74: Symphony no. 6 in B Minor, *Pathétique* (1893). First performance, St. Petersburg, 16 Oct. 1893.

II-B. Incomplete, Projected, or Considered Orchestral Works (see also 96, 313)

Taras Bulba, projected symphonic poem after Gogol´, suggested by V.V. Stasov (1872) [96, 308–9].

Symphony in B-flat. Sketches from June–July 1873 [96, 256; 309 I 398–99; 423, 781].

Hamlet, a symphonic poem, proposed by Modest Tchaikovsky (1876) [vi 59].

Tamara, a symphonic poem, proposed by Modest Tchaikovsky (1876) [vi 59].

Ivanushka-durachok [The Foolish Ivanushka], topic for a symphonic poem suggested by V. V. Stasov (1876) [96, 309–10].

Suite compiled from the music of *Swan Lake,* contemplated (1882) [309 I 404–5]. Such a suite was published by Jurgenson in 1901; Tchaikovsky may or may not have selected the numbers before his death.

Shil'onskiy uznik [The Prisoner of Chillon], topic for a 3-movement symphony, suggested by E. M. Pavlovskaya (1886) [96, 310–11].

Symphony in E Minor/E Major. Sketches (autumn 1887–Apr. 1888) [423, 781–82].

Suite. Sketches noted for an "And[ante] (for the suite)" (Jan.–May 1889) [309 I 412–13; 423, 782].

Suite compiled from the music of *The Sleeping Beauty,* contemplated (1890) [309 I 414]. Such a suite was published by Jurgenson in 1899; Tchaikovsky may or may not have selected the numbers before his death.

Symphony in E-flat, sometimes projected as the *Life* Symphony, and completed by S. S. Bogatïrev under the title "Symphony no. 7." Conceived by Tchaikovsky, who composed mvts. I, II, and IV and who scored only part of mvt. I between May 1891 and Dec. 1892 [96, 244–49; 309 I 415–17; 423, 764–66].

March (projected for orchestra?) based on White Russian and Ukrainian folk tunes (Sept. 1893) [96, 311–13; 309 I 420; 423, 782–83].

III-A. Completed Music for Solo Instrument and Orchestra

Opus 23: Concerto no. 1 for Piano and Orchestra in B-flat Minor (1874). First performance, Boston, 13/25 Oct. 1875.

Opus 26: *Sérénade mélancolique* for violin and orchestra (1875). First performance, Moscow, 16 Jan. 1876.

Opus 33: *Variations on a Rococo Theme,* for cello and orchestra (1876). First performance, Moscow, 18 Nov. 1877.

Opus 34: Valse-scherzo for Violin and Orchestra (1877). First performance, Paris, 8/20 Sept. 1878.

Opus 35: Concerto for Violin and Orchestra in D (Mar. 1878). First performance, Vienna, 22 Nov./4 Dec. 1881.

Opus 44: Concerto no. 2 for Piano and Orchestra in G (1879–1880). First performance, Moscow, 18 May 1882.

Opus 56: Concert Fantasia for Piano and Orchestra (1884). First performance, Moscow, 22 Feb. 1885.

Opus 62: Pezzo capriccioso for Cello and Orchestra (Aug. 1887). First performance, Paris, 16/28 Feb. 1888.

Opus 75: Concerto no. 3 for Piano and Orchestra in E-flat (1893). First performance, St. Petersburg, 7 Jan. 1895.

III-B. Incomplete or Projected Works for Solo Instrument and Orchestra

Concerto for Two Pianos and Orchestra, reported by Laroche after Tchaikovsky's death as a piece the composer was planning to write (1891–1892) [309 I 414; 423, 783].

Concerto for Cello and Orchestra; sketches included with sketches for the Sixth Symphony (end of 1892–Feb. 1893) [425, 285–90; 96, 340; 309 I 423; 423, 784].

Opus 79: Andante in B-flat and Allegro [Finale] in E-flat for Piano and Orchestra (= mvts. II and IV of the Symphony in E-flat). Conceived by Tchaikovsky in 1893, completed by S. Taneyev. First performance, St. Petersburg, 8 Feb. 1896 [96, 338–39; 309 I 418–19; 423, 767–68].

Concert work for Flute and Orchestra. Brief sketches (Oct. 1893) [309 I 422; 423, 783].

Waltz for cello and piano, 18-bar sketch (1893?) [309 I 424].

Pieces for violin, reputedly planned at the time of Tchaikovsky's death [309 I 422–23].

IV-A. Completed Chamber Music

Early Student Works, 1863–1864 (all in CW 58)

Adagio in C for 4 horns.

Adagio in F for wind octet.

Adagio molto in E-flat for string quartet and harp.

Allegretto in E for string quartet.

Allegretto moderato in D for string trio.

Allegro in C for piano and string quintet.

Allegro vivace in B-flat for string quartet.

Andante ma non troppo in E for string quintet.

Andante molto in G for string quartet.

Later Student Work

Quartet for Strings in B-flat [1 mvt.] (1865) [96, 367; 309 I 293; 423, 480–81]. First performance, St. Petersburg, 30 Oct. 1865.

The Official List

Opus 11: Quartet for Strings no. 1 in D (Feb. 1871). First performance, Moscow, 16 Mar. 1871.

Opus 22: Quartet for Strings no. 2 in F (1874). First performance, Moscow, 10 Mar. 1874.

Opus 30: Quartet for Strings no. 3 in E-flat Minor (1876). First performance, Moscow, 18 Mar. 1876.

Opus 42: *Souvenir d'un lieu cher* [Remembrance of a Beloved Place] for violin and piano (1878).

Opus 50: Trio for Piano, Violin, and Cello "To the Memory of a Great Artist" [Nikolay Rubinstein] (1881–1882). First performance, Moscow, 11 Mar. 1882.

Opus 70: Sextet for Strings, *Souvenir de Florence* (1887–1892). First performance of rev. version, St. Petersburg, 24 Nov. 1892.

IV-B. Unfinished or Projected Chamber Music

Uprek [Le reproche] for violin and piano. Requested by Nadezhda von Meck (1877) [423, 786–87].

Sonata for Cello and Piano in G Major. 8 bars in Sketchbook no. 13 (1891) [96, 425; 423, 787].

Waltzes for violin and piano. Sketches (before 1893) [423, 787].

Pieces for violin and piano (1893).

Waltz for cello and piano [possibly orchestra]. Fragment, possibly related to the projected Concerto for Cello and Orchestra (see above, under III-B) [96, 426].

V-A. Completed Music for Piano

Valse dedicated to Anastasia Petrova ["Anastasia Waltz"] (1854) [96, 385; 309 I 305; 423, 502; transcription in 440].

Student Works

Jest on the tune "Vozle rechki, vozle mostu" ["By the river, by the bridge"] (1862) [96, 386; 309 I 305; 423, 757], lost.

Opus 80: Sonata for Piano in C-sharp Minor (1865).

The Official List

Opus 1: Two Pieces (1867).

Scherzo à la russe [based on themes from the String Quartet in B-flat]. First performance, Moscow, 31 Mar. 1867.

Impromptu

Opus 2: *Souvenir de Hapsal* (1867).

Ruines d'un château

Scherzo

Chant sans paroles

Potpourri on themes from the opera *Voevoda* (1868) [96, 393]. Published under the pseudonym H. Kramer.

Opus 4: Valse-caprice (1868).

Opus 5: Romance in F (1868).

Opus 7: Valse-scherzo in A (1870).

Opus 8: Capriccio in G-flat (1870).

Opus 9: Trois morceaux (1870).

Rêverie, D

Polka de salon, B-flat

Mazurka de salon, D [based on the mazurka from the incidental music to Ostrovsky's *The False Dmitry and Vasily Shuisky*]
Opus 10: Deux morceaux (1871–1872).
Nocturne
Humoresque [arr. vn, pf by Tchaikovsky (1877)]
Opus 19: Six morceaux (1873).
Rêverie du soir
Scherzo humoristique
Feuillet d'album
Nocturne [arr. vc, small orch. by Tchaikovsky, Feb. 1888]
Capriccioso
Thème original et variations
Opus 21: Six morceaux, composés sur un seul thème (1873).
Prélude
Fugue à 4 voix
Impromptu
Marche funèbre
Mazurque
Scherzo
Opus 37b: Les saisons (1875–1876).
Janvier: Au coin de feu
Février: Carnaval
Mars: Chant de l'alouette
Avril: Perce-neige
Mai: Les nuits de mai
Juin: Barcarolle
Juillet: Chant de faucheur
Août: La moisson
Septembre: La chasse
Octobre: Chant d'automne
Novembre: Troika
Décembre: Noël
Waltz in F-sharp Minor (4 June 1876) [309 I 321]. Written in an album of Sergey Taneyev; rev. as op. 40, no. 9. One source indicates a date of 4 June 1878 and dates Taneyev's album as 1880 [423, 541].
Funeral march on themes from *The Oprichnik,* for piano, 4 hands, written at the request of Nadezhda von Meck (Mar. 1877), lost [96, 403–4; 309 I 321; 423, 757].
March for the Volunteer Fleet [Skobelev March] (1878) [96, 408–9; 309 I 325–26; 423, 545–46]. Published under the pseudonym P. Sinopov.
Nathalie-valse (5 Aug. 1878) [309 I 330]; rev. as op. 51, no. 4.
Opus 39: Album pour enfants: 24 pièces faciles à la Schumann (1878). Listed and titled in sequence of publication; parenthetical numbers show Tchaikovsky's original order:
1 Prière de matin (1)
2 Le matin en hiver (2)
3 Maman (4)
4 Le petit cavalier (3)
5 Marches des soldats de bois (5)

6 La nouvelle poupée (9)
7 La poupée malade (6)
8 Enterrement de la poupée (7)
9 Valse (8)
10 Polka (14)
11 Mazurka (10)
12 Chanson russe (11)
13 Le paysan prélude (12)
14 Chanson populaire (Kamarinskaya) (13)
15 Chanson italienne (15)
16 Mélodie antique française (16)
17 Chanson allemande (17)
18 Chanson napolitaine (18)
19 Conte de la vieille bonne (19)
20 La sorcière (Baba Yaga) (20)
21 Douce rêverie (21)
22 Chant de l'alouette (22)
23 A l'église (24)
24 L'orgue de barberie (23)

Opus 40: Douze morceaux (difficulté moyenne) (1878).
Étude
Chanson triste
Marche funèbre
Mazurka in C
Mazurka in D
Chant sans paroles
Au village
Valse [in A-flat]
Valse, F-sharp [first version, 4/16 July 1876; rev. 1878]
Danse russe
Scherzo
Rêverie interrompue

Opus 37: Sonata for Piano in G (1878).

Opus 51: Six morceaux (1882).
Valse de salon
Polka peu dansante
Menuetto scherzoso
Natha-valse [revision of *Nathalie-valse*]
Romance
Valse sentimentale

Impromptu-caprice (1884) [96, 413; 309 I 332; 423, 558–59].

Opus 59: *Dumka: Russian Rustic Scene* (1886).

Valse-scherzo in A (1889) [96, 414–15; 309 I 333; 423, 560–61].

Eksprompt [Impromptu] in A-flat (Sept. 1889) [96, 415–16; 309 I 334; 423, 561–62]. Composed for Anton Rubinstein's 50th anniversary jubilee.

Aveu passionné, largely a transcription of part of the symphonic ballad *The Voevoda* (1892?) [96, 416; 309 I 335; 423, 562–63].

Impromptu (Momento lirico), written at the request of the Czech publisher Urbanek (26 Oct. 1892) [96, 416–17; 309 I 335; 423, 563–65]. This version, apparently unknown to Tchaikovsky's intimates, was superseded by a variant completed by Taneyev from one of Tchaikovsky's manuscripts at Klin.

Military march [for the Yurievsky Regiment] (1893) [96, 417–18; 309 I 335; counted as an orchestral work in 423, 390–92, though there is no evidence that the published orchestration is Tchaikovsky's].

Opus 72: *Dix-huit morceaux* (Apr. 1893).
- Impromptu
- Berceuse
- Tendres reproches
- Danse caractéristique
- Méditation
- Mazurque pour danser
- Polacca de concert
- Dialogue
- Un poco di Schumann
- Scherzo-fantaisie
- Valse bluette
- L'espiègle
- Echo rustique
- Chant élégiaque
- Un poco di Chopin
- Valse à cinq temps
- Passé lointain
- Scène dansante (invitation au trépak)

V-B. Incomplete or Projected Works for Piano (see also 96, 421–22)

Allegro in F (1864) [96, 386; 309 I 395–96; 423, 682]. Incomplete; restored by Kalinenko as a Sonata (pub. 1978).

Theme and Variations in A Minor (1863–1864) [96, 386–87; 309 I 306; 423, 503–5]. Completed by Taneyev (pub. 1909).

Étude in A Minor, a fragment (1885) [309 I 407–8; 423, 785].

Waltz in E Major ("Aachen Waltz"), 16-bar sketch (12 Aug. 1887) [426; 309 I 409–10; 423, 785].

Nocturne in B Major, 7-bar sketch related to sketches for the Piano Pieces, op. 72 (winter 1891–1892) [309 I 418; 423, 785].

Étude in E-flat, included with the sketches for the Sixth Symphony (Feb.–Mar. 1893) [309 I 418; 423, 786].

Momento lirico, sketches (July 1893) [423, 786]. Two jottings on the original version of mvt. II of the Third Piano Concerto, arr. 2pf.

Fragmentary sketches, possibly for piano [309 I 424].

Fragment of a piano piece in A Minor (the ending of an apparently finished work), of unknown date [309 I 425; 423, 758].

VI-A. Completed Songs and Duets for Voice and Piano

Moy geniy, moy angel, moy drug [My genius, my angel, my friend] (Fet, 1855–1860).

Mezza notte (text supposedly by Tchaikovsky, c. 1855–1860).

Nochnoy smotr [The nocturnal review] (Zhukovsky, before 1866) [96, 429–30; 309 I 252–53; 423, 758], lost.

Opus 6: *Shest' romansov* [Six Romances] (Nov. 1869).

Ne ver', moy drug [Do not believe, my friend] (A. K. Tolstoy)

Ni slova, o drug moy [Not a word, o my friend] (M. Hartmann, tr. A. Pleshcheyev)

I bol'no, i sladko [It is both painful and sweet] (E. P. Rostopshina)

Sleza drozhit [A tear quivers (in your jealous gaze)] (A. K. Tolstoy)

Otchevo? [Why?] (Heine, tr. L. Mey)

Net, tol'ko tot, kto znal [No, only one who has known] (Goethe, tr. L. Mey)

Pesn' Zemfirï [Zemfira's Song] (Pushkin, 1870s?).

Zabït' tak skoro [To forget so soon] (A. Apukhtin, 1870).

Opus 16: *Shest' romansov* [Six Romances] (1872).

Kolïbel'naya pesnya [Cradle Song] (A. Maykov), arr. pf, 1873

Pogodi! [Wait!] (N. Grekov)

Poimi khot raz [Accept this once] (A. Fet)

O, spoy zhe tu pesnyu [O, Sing That Song] (Felicity Hemans, tr. A. Pleshcheyev), arr. pf (1873), and pf and vn (1873)

Tak chto zhe? [So what then?] (N.N. [= Tchaikovsky]), arr. pf (1873)

Novogrecheskaya pesnya [New Greek Song] (A. Maykov)

Unosi moyo serdtse [Take my heart away] (Fet, 1873).

Glazki vesnï golubïe [The blue eyes of spring] (Heine, tr. M. Mikhailov, 1873).

Opus 25: *Shest' romansov* [Six Romances] (1875).

Primiren'ye [Reconciliation] (N. Shcherbina)

Kak nad goryacheyu zoloy [As over burning embers] (F. Tyutchev)

Pesn' Min'onï [Mignon's Song] (Goethe, tr. F. Tyutchev)

Kanareyka [The Canary] (L. Mey)

Ya s neyu nikogda ne govoril [I never spoke to her] (L. Mey)

Kak naladili: Durak [As they kept saying: "Fool"] (L. Mey)

Opus 27: *Shest' romansov* [Six Romances] (1875).

Na son gryadushchiy [At Bedtime] (N. Ogaryov)

Smotri, von oblako! [Look, the cloud there!] (N. Grekov)

Ne otkhodi ot menya! [Do not leave me!] (Fet)

Vecher [Evening] (Mey, after Shevchenko)

Ali mat' menya rozhala [Did my mother bear me (for such great sorrow)] (A. Mickiewicz, tr. L. Mey)

Moya balovnitsa [My little favorite] (A. Mickiewicz, tr. L. Mey); rev. later

Opus 28: *Shest' romansov* [Six Romances] (1875).

Net, nikogda ne nazovu [No, never shall I tell] (Musset, tr. N. Grekov)

Korol'ki [The Little Corals] (V. Sïrokomli [= L. Kondratowicz], tr. L. Mey)

Zachem? [Why?] (Mey)

On tak menya lyubil [He loved me so] (Apukhtin)

Ni otzïva, ni slova, ni priveta [Neither response, nor word, nor greeting] (Apukhtin)

Strashnaya minuta [The Fearful Moment] (N.N. [= Tchaikovsky])

Khotel bï v edinoye slovo [I should like in a single word] (Heine, tr. L. Mey, 1875).

Ne dolgo nam gulyat' [We have not far to walk] (N. Grekov, 1875).

Opus 38: *Shest' romansov* [Six Romances] (1878).

Serenada Don-Zhuana [Don Juan's Serenade] (A. Tolstoy)

To bïlo ranneyu vesnoy [It was in the early spring] (A. Tolstoy)

Sred' shumnovo bala [Amid the din of the ball] (A. Tolstoy)
O, esli b tï mogla [O, if only you could] (A. Tolstoy)
Lyubov' mertvetsa [The love of a dead man] (Lermontov)
Pimpinella (Florentine song, tr. N.N. [= Tchaikovsky])

Opus 46: *Shest' duetov* [Six Duets] (1880).
Vecher [Evening] (Surikov)
Shotlandskaya ballada [Scottish ballad] (from the poem "Edward," tr. A. Tolstoy)
Slyozï [Tears] (Tyutchev)
V ogorode, vozle brodu [In the garden, near the ford] (Shevchenko, tr. Surikov)
Minula strast' [The passion has waned] (A. Tolstoy)
Rassvet [Dawn] (Surikov), arr. orch., 1889

Opus 47: *Sem' romansov* [Seven Romances] (1880).
Kabï znala ya [If only I had known] (A. Tolstoy)
Gornimi tikho letala dusha nebesami [Calmly the spirit flew up to heaven] (A. Tolstoy)
Na zemlyu sumrak pal [Dusk fell upon the earth] (Mickiewicz, tr. N. Berg)
Usni, pechalnïy drug [Sleep, poor friend] (A. Tolstoy)
Blagoslavlyayu vas, lesa [I bless you, forests] (A. Tolstoy)
Den' li tsarit? [Does the day reign?] (Apukhtin), arr. orch., by 12/24 Feb. 1888, lost
Ya li v pole da ne travushka bïla? [Was I not a little blade of grass?] (Surikov), arr. orch., by 25 Sept./7 Oct. 1884

Opus 54: *Shestnadtsat' pesen dlya detey* [Sixteen Songs for Children] (1881–83).
Babushka i vnuchek [Grandma and grandson] (V. Sïrokomli [= L. Kondratowicz], tr. Pleshcheyev)
Ptichka [The little bird] (V. Sïrokomli [= L. Kondratowicz], tr. Pleshcheyev)
Vesna (Travka zeleneyet) [Spring (The grass is turning green)] (from Polish, tr. Pleshcheyev)
Moy sadik [My Garden] (Pleshcheyev)
Legenda [Legend] (from English, tr. Pleshcheyev); arr. orch., Apr. 1884; arr. unacc. mixed chorus, 1889
Na beregu [On the bank] (Pleshcheyev)
Zimniy vecher [Winter evening] (Pleshcheyev)
Kukushka [The cuckoo] (Gellert, tr. Pleshcheyev)
Vesnya (Uzh tayet sneg) [Spring (The snow is already melting)] (Pleshcheyev)
Kolïbel'naya pesn' v buryu [Lullaby in a storm] (Pleshcheyev)
Tsvetok [The little flower] (L. Ratisbonne, tr. Pleshcheyev)
Zima [Winter] (Pleshcheyev)
Vesennyaya pesnya [Spring song] (Pleshcheyev)
Osen' [Autumn] (Pleshcheyev)
Lastochka [The swallow] (T. Lenartowicz, tr. I. Surikov)
Detskaya pesenka [Children's song] (K. Aksakov)

Opus 57: *Shest' romansov* [Six Romances] (1884).
Skazhi, o chyom v teni vetvey [Tell me, of what, in the shade of the branches] (V. Sollogub)
Na nivï zhyoltïe [On the golden cornfields] (A. Tolstoy)
Ne sprashivay [Do not ask] (Goethe, tr. Strugovshchikov)

Usni! [Sleep!] (Merezhkovsky)
Smert' [Death] (Merezhkovsky)
Lish' tï odin [Only you alone] (A. Christen, tr. Pleshcheyev)

Opus 60: *Dvenadtsat' romansov* [Twelve Romances] (1886).
Vcherashnyaya noch' [Last Night] (Khomyakov)
Ya tebe nichevo ne skazhu [I'll tell you nothing] (Fet)
O, esli b znali vï [O, if only you knew] (S. Prudhomme, tr. Pleshcheyev)
Solovey [The nightingale] (Vuk Karadžić, tr. Pushkin)
Prostïye slova [Simple Words] (N.N. [= Tchaikovsky])
Nochi bezumnïye [Frenzied Nights] (Apukhtin)
Pesn' tsïganki [A Gypsy Song] (Polonsky)
Prosti [Forgive] (Nekrasov)
Noch' [Night] (Polonsky)
Za oknom v teni melkayet [Behind the window in the shadows] (Polonsky)
Podvig [The heroic deed] (Khomyakov)
Nam zvezdï krotkie siyali [The mild stars shone for us] (Pleshcheyev)

Opus 63: *Shest' romansov* [Six Romances] (all by Konstantin Romanov) (1887).
Ya snachala tebya ne lyubila [At first I did not love you]
Rastvoril ya okno [I opened the window]
Ya vam ne nravlyus [I do not please you]
Pervoe svidaniye [First Meeting]
Uzh gasli v komnatakh ogni [The fires in the rooms were already out]
Serenada (O ditya, pod okoshkom tvoim) [Serenade (O child, beneath thy window)]

Opus 65: Six mélodies (all tr. A. Gorchakova) (1888).
Sérénade (O, vas-tu, souffle d'aurore) (E. Turquety)
Déception (P. Collin)
Sérénade (J'aime dans le rayon de la limpide aurore) (Collin)
Qu'importe que l'hiver (Collin)
Les larmes (A.-M. Blanchecotte)
Rondel (Collin)

Opus 73: *Shest' romansov* [Six Romances] (all by D. Ratgaus [Rathaus]) (1893).
Mï sideli s toboy [We were sitting together]
Noch' [Night]
V etu lunnuyu noch' [On this moonlit night]
Zakatilos solntse [The sun has set]
Sred' mrachnïkh dney [Amid somber days]
Snova, kak prezhde, odin [Again, as before, alone]

On idyot [He goes] (Apukhtin) (before 1866) [423, 758], lost.

VI-B. Incomplete or Projected Works for Solo Voice and Piano

Adagio in G Major, sketch for voice and piano (early 1860s?) [309 I 395].

Nas ne presledovala zloba [Spite has not pursued us]. Sketches, apparently for a duet (1880).

Mudrenïy sluchay [A strange instance]. 26-bar sketch of a song, medium voice, to words of P.V. Schumacher (after 1880) [96, 472; 309 I 423; 423, 792–93].

Strelochek [The Little Rifleman], humorous canon on a folk melody (1882) [96, 471; 309 I 390; 423, 759], lost.

Songs for Children, possibly sketched in connection with the composition of the op. 54 songs, some on the pages of a copy of Pleshcheyev's collection of poems *Podsnezhnik* [Snowdrop], from which the texts of op. 54 were taken.

Kaplya dozhdevaya govorit drugim [A raindrop speaks to others], after M. Hartman [423, 788].

Na dache [At the summer house] (Pleshcheyev) [423, 788].

Iz "Pesen o prirode" A. Shul'tsa [from A. Schultz's "Song about Nature"] [423, 788].

Noch' [Night], 10-bar sketch to words of Pleshcheyev (1883) [96, 473; 309 I 405].

Nishchie [The Beggars] (Pleshcheyev) [309 I 405]

Rodina [The Homeland] (Pleshcheyev) [423, 788]

Lyublyu ya pod vecher tropinkoyu lesnoyu [I love, eventides, by the forest path] (Pleshcheyev) [423, 788]

Blengeymskiy boy [The Battle of Blenheim] (Pleshcheyev) [423, 788]

Koroleva maya [The Queen of May] (after Tennyson) [423, 788]

Zimniy vecher [Winter Evening] (Eichendorff) [423, 788]

V sude on slushal prigovor [In court he heard the verdict] (V. Hugo) [423, 788]

Nochnïe golosa [Nocturnal Voices] (after Eichendorff) [423, 789]

Ottsovskiy ochag [The Paternal Hearth] (after Eichendorff) [423, 789]

Stariki [Old Men] (from Scottish poets) [423, 789]

Vse lyudi brat'ya [All men are brothers] (Pleshcheyev) [423, 789]

Ozhidaniya [Expectations] (Pleshcheyev) [423, 789]

Ya tikho shel po ulitse bezlyudnoy [I walked quietly along the empty street] (Pleshcheyev) [423, 789]

Bol'noe ditya [The Sick Child] (Tumansky) [309 I 405]

Zhaloba [Complaint] (Tumansky) [309 I 405]

Vurdalak [The Vampire] (after Pushkin, 8-bar sketch; Oct. 1883) [96, 472; 309 I 406; 423 790]

Pesn' torzhestvuyushchey lyubvi [Song of Triumphant Love], 5-bar sketch for a vocal work after Turgenev to words by K. A. von Tavastern (1883) [96, 473; 309 I 409].

O net! Za krasotu tï ne lyubi menya [O no! You do not love me for my beauty], sketch to words of K.R. made by Tchaikovsky in a volume of K.R.'s poetry (1886) and completed by Boris Asaf'ev [96, 473–74; 309 I 408; 423, 790–91].

Tebe ya videla vo sne . . . [I saw you in a dream . . .], sketch to words of K.R. made by Tchaikovsky in a volume of K.R.'s poetry (1886) and completed by Boris Asaf'ev [96, 474; 309 I 408; 423, 790–91].

French songs, possibly sketched in connection with the composition of op. 65, some on the pages of poetry books (1888).

Prière, to Paul Collin [423, 791]

Rondel à Madame I. Triery, to Paul Collin [423, 791]

Rondel d'automne, to Paul Collin [423, 791]

À la mémoire de Madame Marie [423, 791]

Lamento, two sketches (5 and 7.5 bars) for medium voice to words of Paul Collin, written in the margins of a book of Collin's poetry (1888) [96, 474; 309 I 410; 423, 792]

Mai, four sketches to words of Paul Collin, comprising some 25 bars [96, 474–75; 309 I 410; 423, 792]

Elle est malade, to words by J. Reboul, from Eugène Borel's *Album lyrique* (after Feb. and before 10 Oct. 1888) [96, 475; 309 I 410; 423, 792]

Ne prosïpaysya, moy drug [Do not awake, my friend], sketches for a quartet of voices (1891–1892) [309 I 415; 423, 793].

VII-A. Completed Choral Music

Early Student Work

Oratorio (1863–1864?), lost.

Later Student Works

Na son gryadushchiy [At bedtime] (Ogaryov), a capella version (1863–1864).

Na son gryadushchiy [At bedtime] (Ogaryov), version for chorus and orchestra (1863–1864).

K radosti [To Joy], cantata (Aksakov et al. after Schiller, 1865). First performance, St. Petersburg, 29 Dec. 1865.

The Official List

Priroda i lyubov' [Nature and Love] (Tchaikovsky, Dec. 1870). First performance, Moscow, 16 Mar. 1871.

Cantata in Commemoration of the Bicentenary of the Birth of Peter the Great (Polonsky, 1872) [309 I 218–21]. First performance, Moscow, 31 May 1872.

Chorus for the Jubilee of Osip Petrov (Nekrasov, 1875). First performance, St. Petersburg, 24 Apr. 1876.

Opus 41: *Liturgy of St. John Chrysostom* (1878). First performance, Kiev, June 1879; arr. pf, 1878.

Cantata for the Patriotic Institute, for [unaccompanied 4-pt.?] women's chorus (Aug.–Sept. 1880) [96, 346–47; 309 I 234; 423, 756], lost.

Vecher [Evening] (N.N. [= Tchaikovsky], 1871), for women's chorus, rev. 1881 for men's chorus; first published in Moscow in 1876 for 3-pt. children's chorus in Chevé notation [309 I 230; 423, 440–41].

Vesna [Springtime] (N.N. [= Tchaikovsky]), for 3 same-voiced parts, first published in Moscow in 1876 in Chevé notation; long considered lost [419, 136–41; 425, 291–95; 309 I 229; 423, 440–41].

Opus 52: *Vsenoshchnoe bdenie* [All-Night Vigil] (texts and melodies of liturgical songs, 1881–1882). First performance, Moscow, 27 June 1882.

Moskva [Moscow], coronation cantata (A. Maykov, Mar. 1883). First performance, Moscow, 15 May 1883.

9 Dukhovno-muzïkal'nïkh sochineniy [9 Sacred Music Compositions] (1884–1885).

- *Kheruvimskaya pesnya* [cherubic hymn]. First performance, Moscow, 17 Feb. 1886
- *Kheruvimskaya pesnya* [cherubic hymn]. First performance, Moscow, 2 Nov. 1903
- *Kheruvimskaya pesnya* [cherubic hymn]. First performance, Moscow, 22 Oct. 1891
- *Tebe poyom* [We hymn Thee]. First performance, Moscow, 17 Feb. 1886
- *Dostoyno est'* [It is truly fitting]. First performance, Moscow, 2 Nov. 1903
- *Otche nash* [Our Father]. First performance, Moscow, 12 Dec. 1893
- *Blazheni yazhe izbral* [Blessed are they, whom Thou hast chosen]. First performance, Moscow, 17 Feb. 1886
- *Da ispravitsya* [Let my prayer ascend]. First performance, Moscow, 17 Feb. 1886
- *Nïne silï nebesnïye* [Now the powers of heaven]. First performance, Moscow, 28 Mar. 1891

Gimn v chest' Svyatïkh Kirilla i Mefodiya [Hymn in Honor of Saints Cyril and Methodius] (Tchaikovsky, 1885). First performance, Moscow, 6 Apr. 1885.

Pravovedcheskaya pesn' [Jurists' Song] (Tchaikovsky, Sept. 1885) [309 I 242–43; 423, 756–57], to celebrate the 50th anniversary of the School of Jurisprudence. First performance, St. Petersburg, 5 Dec. 1885.

Otche nash [Our Father] (late 1880s?).

Blazhen, kto ulïbaetsya [Blessed is he who smiles] (Konstantin Romanov, Dec. 1887). First performance, Moscow, 8 Mar. 1892.

Angel vopiyashe [The angel cried out] (scripture, 1887). First performance, Moscow, 8 Mar. 1887.

Nochevala tuchka zolotaya [The golden cloud has slept] (Lermontov, July 1887).

Privet Antonu Grigor'evichu Rubinshteynu v den' prazdnovaniya 50-ti letnyago yubileya ego artisticheskoy deyatel'nosti, 18-go Noyabrya 1889 g. [Greeting to Anton Grigorievich Rubinstein on the Day of Celebration of the 50th Year Jubilee of his Artistic Activity, 18 Nov. 1889] (Polonsky, Sept. 1889). First performance, St. Petersburg, 18 Nov. 1889.

Solovushko [The Little Nightingale] (Tchaikovsky, 1889). First performance, Moscow, 13 Dec. 1892.

Ne kukushechka vo sïrom boru ['Tis not the cuckoo in the damp pinewood] (Tsïganov, 1891).

Bez porï, da bez vremeni [Without time, without season] (Tsïganov, 1891).

Chto smolknul veseliya glas [What silenced the merry voice?] (Pushkin, 1891).

Noch' [Night], based on Mozart's Fantasia for Piano in C Minor, K. 475 (Tchaikovsky, 1893). First performance, Moscow, 9 Oct. 1893.

VII-B. Projected or Uncompleted Choral Music

Noch' [Night], a cantata suggested by Balakirev, to include the "Chorus of Flowers and Insects" Tchaikovsky had composed for the projected opera *Mandragora* (1871) [423, 784–85].

VIII. Album Leaves and Musical Letters (see also 96, 470–71)

Sobaka nizkaya [Lowly Dog], 21 bars, words by Tchaikovsky, set for bass voice and piano in an album for M. A. Golovina (22 Sept. 1876) [96, 470; 309 I 389; 423, 673].

Chizhik [The Siskin], 9 bars to words by Tchaikovsky, set for high voice and piano in an album for M. A. Golovina (22 Sept. 1876) [309 I 389; 423, 674].

Ne znayu! [I don't know!], words by Tchaikovsky, set for high voice. Included in a letter to A. N. Littke dated 22 July 1891 [96, 471; 309 I 390; 423, 674–75].

Ot milogo netu vesti [No news from the beloved], 22 bars, "Allegretto, ma doloroso," words by Tchaikovsky, set for medium voice and piano in a letter to Vladimir "Bob" Davïdov (1893) [96, 471; 309 I 391; 423, 675–76].

Nessun maggior dolo che ricordarsi del tempo felice nella misera, citation from Dante in various forms, including as a short score with voice above. In a letter to Meck of 6 June 1881 [96, 468–70; 309 I 403–4].

Polka de Salon, for Tchaikovsky's great-nephew Georges-Léon, included in a letter to "Bob" Davïdov (15 Apr. 1993) [96, 422; 309 I 390–91].

IX. Transcriptions of his own music (excluding his piano arrangements for two and four hands of various theater, vocal, and orchestral works)

Voevoda, Entr'acte and Dances of the Serving Maidens. Arr. pf, 2 hands (June 1867): [unpublished], and 4 hands (1868).

Incidental music to *The False Dmitry and Vasily Shuisky,* no. 2, Mazurka. Arr. pf, 2 hands (June 1867).

Potpourri of themes from the opera *Voevoda,* for pf, 2 hands (1868), published under the pseudonym H. Kramer.

Song, op. 16, no. 4 ("O Sing That Song"), arr. vn, pf (1873). Attribution of this arrangement to Tchaikovsky is uncertain.

Songs, op. 16, no. 1 ("Cradle Song" [versions in A-flat Minor and in A Minor]), no. 4 ("O Sing That Song"), and no. 5 ("So what, then?"), arr. pf, 2 hands (1876).

Humoresque, op. 10, no. 2, for piano, arr. vn, pf, before Apr. 1877(?) [309 I 298].

String Quartet no. 3, mvt. III, *Andante funebre,* arr. vn, pf, before Apr. 1877(?) [309 I 297–98].

Nathalie-valse, revised for inclusion in op. 51 as no. 4, "Natha-valse."

Waltz in F-sharp Minor [309 I 321], revised in op. 40 as no. 9.

Russian Dance, interpolated into act III of *Swan Lake* (1877), arr. pf as op. 40, no. 10, and again as Tchaikovsky's contribution to an album in memory of Vincenzo Bellini [398; 230, 192–93].

Liturgy of St. John Chrysostom, op. 41, for piano (May 1878) [309 I 234].

Song, op. 54, no. 5 ("Legend"), scored for voice and orch. (1884).

Song, op. 47, no. 7 ("Was I not a little blade of grass?"), scored for voice and orch. (1884).

String Quartet no. 1, mvt. II, *Andante cantabile,* arr. solo vc and string orch., Feb. 1888(?) [309 I 212; 423, 699–700].

Song, op. 47, no. 6 ("Does the day reign?"), scored for voice and orch. (1888), lost.

Piano Pieces, op. 19, no. 4, Nocturne, arr. solo vc and string orch., Feb. 1888(?) [309 I 212–13; 423, 701–2].

Song, op. 54, no. 5 ("Legend"), arr. for mixed chorus before Mar. 1889 [309 I 245–46; 423, 702–3].

Duet, op. 46, no. 6 ("Dawn"), scored for vocal duet and orch. (Dec. 1889).

X. Orchestrations and Arrangements of Music by Other Composers

Weber, Menuetto capriccioso (mvt. III) of Piano Sonata, op. 39 (J 199), orchestrated 1863.

Beethoven, Piano Sonata, op. 31, no. 2, mvt. I, 4 versions orchestrated 1863(?), lost.

Beethoven, Sonata for Violin and Piano, op. 47 (*Kreutzer*), mvt. I exposition, orchestrated 1863–1864.

Schumann, Adagio and Allegro brilliante [Variations 11 and 12] from *Études symphoniques,* op. 13, orchestrated 1864.

Johann Gungl, valse, "Le retour," for piano, orchestrated before 1866.

A. Dubuque, polka, "Maria Dagmar" for piano, orchestrated autumn 1866.

A. Dubuque, "Lyubi, poka lyubit' tï mozhesh" [Love while you can], sketch of an arrangement for pf, 2 hands. Published in a completed version by B. I. Rabinovich.

K. Kral, Triumphal March for piano, orchestrated May 1867. First performance, Moscow University, May 1867 [423, 759], lost.

E. P. Tarnovskaya, song, "Ya pomnyu vso" [I remember everything], op. 281, arr. pf by Dubuque. Arr. pf, 4 hands, by Tchaikovsky before 1868 [96, 490].

Dargomïzhsky, *Malorossiyskiy kazachok* [Little Russian kazachok], fantasia for orchestra, arr. pf, 2 hands, before 1868.

Glinka, song, "Zhavoronk" [The Lark], orchestrated for Désirée Artôt's benefit performance of Rossini's *The Barber of Seville* (Apr. 1868): [423, 759].

Dargomïzhsky, a song, orchestrated for Désirée Artôt's benefit performance of Rossini's *The Barber of Seville* (Apr. 1868): [423, 759].

Auber, *Le domino noir,* Introduction to a Chorus and Recitatives (1868). First performance, Moscow Bolshoy Theater, 10 Jan. 1870.

A. Rubinstein, *Ivan Groznïy* [Ivan the Terrible], characteristic musical picture for orchestra, after Mey, op. 79, arr. pf, 4 hands, Oct. 1869.

Stradella, aria, "O del mio dolce ardor," arr. for voice and orch. (29 Oct. 1870) [309 I 362–63]. The music is sometimes attributed to Gluck.

Cimarosa, *Il matrimonio segreto,* trio, "Le faccio un inchino," from act I, scene 4, orchestrated before Jan. 1871.

Weber, Piano Sonata, op. 24 (J 138), Perpetuum mobile (Rondo-finale). Right-hand part shifted to the left, with a newly composed right-hand part, before Mar. 1871.

A. Rubinstein, *Don Quixote,* humorous musical picture for orchestra, op. 87, arr. pf, 4 hands, after Jan. 1871.

Gaudeamus igitur, student song, arr. under the pseudonym "B.L." for 4-pt. men's chorus and pf, not later than 1874 [96, 488].

Gott erhalte Franz den Kaiser, Austrian national hymn, arr. orch., 1874.

Schumann, "Ballade vom Haideknaben," melodrama, op. 122, no. 1, for voice and piano, arr. for voice and orch., 1874. The Russian title is translated as "The Prophetic Dream."

Liszt, "Es war ein König in Thule," ballad for voice and piano, arr. for voice and orch., 1874.

Dargomïzhsky, *Nochevala tuchka zolotaya* [The golden cloud has slept], vocal trio with piano, arr. for vocal trio and orch., 1876(?).

Glinka, "S nebesi uslïshi" [From the heavens hearken], vocal quartet, text underlaid by Tchaikovsky (1877).

Bortnyansky, *Polnoe sobranie dukhovno-muzïkal'nïkh sochineniy* [The Complete Sacred Music Works], in 10 volumes (June–Oct. 1881) [96, 499–501; 309 I 382; 423, 742–49, 854–58].

Glinka, *A Life for the Tsar,* final chorus, arranged and retexted for presentation during the coronation festivities of Alexander III (Feb. 1883). First performance, Moscow, 10 May 1883 [96, 488–89; 309 I 383; 423, 760].

Opus 61: Mozart, 4 pieces called Suite no. 4 (*Mozartiana*): Gigue (K. 574), Minuet (K. 355), *Ave verum corpus* (K. 618, possibly arr. from a keyboard version by F. Liszt), Theme and 10 Variations on a Theme by Gluck from *La recontre imprévue* (K. 455), arranged and orchestrated 1887. First performance, Moscow, 14 Nov. 1887.

Laroche, Overture/Fantasia in D, orchestrated 1888 [309 I 383–84; 423, 749–51].

Mozart, *Idomeneo,* dances, Chaconne (fragment) and Gavotte, edited before Oct. 1889.

S. Menter (and F. Liszt), *Ungarische Zigeunerweisen* [Hungarian Gypsy Songs; Hungarian Rhapsody], for piano, arranged, orchestrated, and edited Sept.–Oct. 1892 [428; 423, 752–53].

XI. Arrangements and Editions of Folk Songs

Pyat'desyat russkikh narodnïkh pesen [Fifty Russian Folk Songs], arr. pf, 4 hands (1868–1869) [96, 394–96; 309 I 356–61; 423, 705–22].

65 russkikh narodnïkh pesen [65 Russian Folk Songs] for voice and piano, collected and arranged by V. Prokunin, edited by P. Tchaikovsky, before May 1872 [309 I 371–78; 423, 722–23].

Detskie pesni na russkie i malorusskie napevï [Children's Songs on Russian and Ukrainian Melodies], arranged by M. Mamontova, edited by P. Tchaikovsky. First volume (24 songs), before Apr. 1872; second volume (19 songs), unpublished during Tchaikovsky's lifetime [96, 487–88; 309 I 365–70; 423, 723–25].

Poddelki pod russkuyu pesn' [Imitations of Russian Songs], sketches of themes (1884?) [309 I 406–7].

To ne veter vetku klonit [It is not the wind that bows the branches]. Piano arrangement of the folk song (June 1893) [96, 420–21; 309 I 385].

XII. Writings (Excluding juvenilia [309 I 457–60; 423, 841–42], programs for instrumental works, song texts, and opera librettos [423, 829])

An autobiographical account and a poem (1851), reported to his parents [v 22–23], lost.

Istoriya literaturï nashego klassa [The History of the Literature of Our Class], essay for *Uchilishchnïy vestnik* [School Herald] of the School of Jurisprudence (1854). Reported by Modest Tchaikovsky [1997 I 88], lost.

Raz kogda-to v svete belom [Once upon a time in the wide world], a verse (1855) quoted in part by Modest Tchaikovsky [1997 I 88, n. 2].

Sevodnya ya za chashkoy kofe [Today I, over a cup of coffee], poem addressed to his sister Sasha (9 June 1861) [v 64].

Vozradusya, velikaya Tat'yana [Rejoice, great Tatyana], poem addressed to Tatyana Davïdova in a letter to Sasha Davïdova dated 23 Oct. 1861 [v 70].

Pust' kak veshnyaya prokhlada [Let it be as spring's coolness], a poem addressed to Vera Davïdova (Aug. 1865) [309 I 461; 423, 824].

Notebooks outlining four courses in harmony: "A Course in Harmony" (for students of instruments), "Harmony, Course I" (the first half of a two-year sequence), "Program for a Harmony Course, Given in the 1869–1870 Academic Year," and "A Course in Harmony" (for the passing of a full course in an obligatory harmony class) (1869–1872?) [423, 798–99].

Humorous couplets and short verses contained within letters addressed to Ivan Klimenko (1869–1872, 1877) [309 I 460–62; 423, 825–26].

Rukovodstvo k prakticheskomu izucheniyu garmonii [Guide to the Practical Study of Harmony] (1871).

Pis'mo v redaktsiyu *Golosa* [Letter to the editor of *The Voice*], *Sanktpeterburgskiya vedomosti* [St. Petersburg News], 1/13 Mar. 1873.

"Betkhoven i ego vremya" [Beethoven and His Time], *Grazhdanin* [Citizen], 1873, nos. 7, 8, 11, 12 [79].

"*Zhizn' za Tsarya* na milanskoi stsene" [*A Life for the Tsar* on the Milan Stage], *Russkiya vedomosti* [Russian News], 25 May/6 June 1874.

Kratkiy uchebnik garmonii, prisposoblyonnïy k chteniyu dukhovno-muzïkal'nïkh sochineniy v Rossii [A Short Manual of Harmony, Adapted to the Study of Sacred-Music Works in Russia] (1875).

Vï odeyalo bednoy Bishke svyazali lovoyu rukoy [You wrapped a blanket around poor Bishka with your deft hand], poem about Tchaikovsky's dog in an album of Maria Golovina (20 Oct. 1875).

Vopl' bol'nogo duraka k Fife [A sick fool's howl to Fifi], a poem of the (fever-stricken) Tchaikovsky to Maria Kiseleva (spring 1876) [vi 36].

Verses for Tatyana Davïdova's name-day (by 6 Sept. 1877).

Landïshi [Lilies-of-the-Valley], a poem (1878) [vii 544–45].

Open letter to E. Colonne, published in the *Gazette musicale,* Paris, 16 Mar. 1879 [viii 136–37].

Kogda bumazhnik tvoy, chakhotkoyu srazhennï [When your wallet is shrunk with emptiness], poem for Tatyana Davïdova's 15th birthday (6 Sept. 1880) [ix 260–61].

Khotel segodnya bït' u vas [I wanted to be with you today], poem for Anna Maslova's birthday (13 Dec. 1880) [ix 330].

"Pis'mo k izdatelyu: Poslednie dni zhizni N. G. Rubinshteyna" [Letter to the editor: The Last Days of the Life of N. G. Rubinstein], *Moskovskie vedomosti* [Moscow News], 23 Mar. 1881, p. 3 [x 65–67].

Letter to the editor of *Signale für die Musikalische Welt,* Oct. 1881. Tchaikovsky is responding to being wrongly identified as the translator of Mozart's *Don Giovanni,* who was harshly criticized in this journal.

Original foreword to *All-Night Vigil,* op. 52 (Naples, 8/20 Mar. 1882) [CW 63, 273–74].

Poem about beetles (12 June 1882) [D&Y 696].

Letter to the editor of *Gaulois,* Paris, 23 May 1883, p. 4. Tchaikovsky attempts to quell the rumor that Anton Rubinstein refused to write a cantata for the coronation of Alexander III [xii 163–64].

Notes made in the margins of Rimsky-Korsakov's harmony textbook (Dec. 1884–Apr. 1885) [iii-a 226–49; 423, 843].

Devitsï Sashen'ka i Lenochka khoteli [Misses Sashenka and Lenochka Wanted], poem to Alexandra Jurgenson and Elena Tolstaya (6 Mar. 1886) [xiii 295].

Letter to the editor of V. V. Bessel's journal, *Muzïkal'noe obozrenie* [Music Review], 24 Dec. 1886, p. 111 [xiii 545–46]. Tchaikovsky is disputing that Eduard Nápravnik does not want to stage *Evgeniy Onegin* on the imperial stage.

Klimenka [To Klimenko], poem (13 Sept. 1887) [xiv 214].

Notes on A. G. Poluektov's *The Arrangement of Churchly Songs,* before Oct. 1887 [423, 819–20]. At the request of the director of the Synodal School in Moscow, Tchaikovsky looked over Poluektov's manuscript in connection with its publication by Jurgenson.

Testimonial to the singer Aline Fride, anticipating her performance in a concert with Tchaikovsky in Berlin (28 Jan./9 Feb. 1888) [xiv 619].

Ne znal ya, lyubeznaya Anna [I did not know, sweet Anna], lines addressed to Anna Merkling, 1 July 1888 [xiv 475].

Autobiography, written at the request of Otto Neitzel, published in German translation (from Tchaikovsky's French) in *Nord und Süd* 54 (July 1890): 66–71 (written summer 1889) [309 I 442; 423, 820]. English translation: 309 I 523–28.

V tebe ko vlasti net stremlen'ya [In you there is no striving for power], lines addressed to Sergey Taneyev, apparently on his departure from the directorship of the Moscow Conservatory (between 7 and 9 Oct. 1889) [xv-a 196; 423, 828].

Testimonial (in French) to the Edison phonograph after a demonstration of the machine in Moscow (14 Oct. 1889) [309 I 443; 423, 820; xv-a 227].

Letter to the editor of *Novoe vremya* [New Time], opposing any celebration of the 25th anniversary of his musical activity (4 Nov. 1890) [xv-b 286].

"Wagner and His Music," *Morning Journal* (New York), 3 May 1891. Rpt. 84, 329–30; English in 439, 71–72.

Testimonial for the Colombo company from Naples, recommending it to the Moscow public (5 July 1891) [423, 821–22; xvi-a 310].

Bestalannomu stikhopleta [To a clueless rhymester], poem for the Maslov family (10 Apr. 1892) [xvi-b 74; 423, 829].

Essay on the C clef, written in response to a request by Vladimir Pogozhev (before 11 Oct. 1892) [309 I 443; 423, 821].

Letter to the editor of *Figaro,* disapproving the publication of A. Maurel's article "Un voyage musical en Russie" (29 Dec. 1892/10 Jan. 1893) [423, 823; xvi-b 216–18].

Contributions to the *Slovar' russkago yazïka* [Dictionary of the Russian Language] (1891–beginning of 1893) [423, 845]. Tchaikovsky edited the proofs of articles from the letter *v* to the letter *dya* (second and third volumes) and wrote an entry on Demestvenny chant [iii-a 253], which was apparently heavily edited by the time it was published after his death.

Letter to the editor of *Russkie vedomosti* [Russian News], approving Georgy Konyus's composition "From a Child's Life" (26 Feb. 1893) [xvii 48–49]. The letter was not published, but passed from Modest to K.R. to the emperor, whereupon Konyus was granted a subsidy.

"Avtobiograficheskoye opisaniye puteshestviya za granitsu v 1888 godu" [Autobiographical Description of a Journey Abroad in 1888], *Russkiy vestnik* [Russian Messenger] 2 (1894): 165–203.

Muzïkal'nïe fel'etonï i zametki Petra Il'icha Chaykovskago (1868–1876 g.): S prilozheniem portreta, avtobiograficheskago opisaniya puteshestviya zagranitsu v 1888 godu i predisloviya G. A. Larosha [Musical Feuilletons and Notes of Pyotr Ilyich Tchaikovsky (1868–1876): With a Supplement of a Portrait, the Autobiographical Account of the Journey Abroad in 1888, and a Foreword by H. A. Laroche] (Moscow, 1898) [83; 309 I 433–42; 423, 799–817]. English translation: 278.

Dnevniki P. I. Chaykovskogo [Diaries of P. I. Tchaikovsky]. Ed. Ip[polit] I[l'ich] Chaykovskiy (Moscow, 1923; rpt. St. Petersburg, 1993).

"Dnevnik no. 2: 1881 goda" [Diary no. 2: 1881] [80].

Muzïkal'no-kriticheskie stat'i [Musico-Critical Articles] (Moscow, 1953).

XIII. Notebooks and Sketches

18 notebooks of various descriptions and contents (including musical sketches but also much data extraneous to music), dating from about 1876–1893 [309 I 467–70; 423, 848–52].

8 notebooks with sketches [423, 852–53].

17 drafts and notes on separate sheets [423, 846–48]. Some are relatable to his compositions.

XIV. Translations

F.-A. Gevaert, *Traité général d'instrumentation* (summer 1865).

Scribe, *Les Huguenots,* Urbain's cavatina "Une dame noble et sage" (before 5 June 1868).

Schumann, *Musikalische Haus- und Lebensregeln für junge Musiker* (before 20 July 1868).

Schumann, *Vorwort zu Opus 3* (before 8 Feb. 1869).

J. C. Lobe, *Katechismus der Musik* (by 8 Nov. 1869).

Translations into Russian from German texts used by A. Rubinstein [423, 832–38].

12 persische Lieder, op. 34 (F. von Bodenstedt, after Mirza Shafi) (before 21 Dec. 1869)

4 songs, op. 32, nos. 1 and 6, and op. 33, nos. 2 and 4 (1870–1871?)

6 romances, op. 72 (1870–1871?)

6 romances, op. 76 (1871?)
3 songs, op. 83, nos. 1, 5, and 9 (1871?)

Mozart/da Ponte, *Le nozze di Figaro* (1875). Published by Jurgenson in 1884.

Translation from Italian of five texts used by Glinka (1877) [423, 838–40].
Mio ben, ricordati
Ho perduto il mio tesoro
Mi sento il cor traffigere
Pur nel sonno
Tu sei figlia

Molitva [Prayer], text underlay of Glinka's vocal quartet (1877); Tchaikovsky may have been author of the text.

XV. Interviews and Speeches

Address made at the celebratory dinner on the occasion of the opening of the Moscow Conservatory, 1 Sept. 1866. Published in the newspaper *Sovremennaya letopis'* [Contemporary Chronicle], 4 Sept. 1866, pp. 2–4.

Address made at a celebratory dinner in honor of Hector Berlioz's visit to Moscow (Dec. 1867), lost.

Address made at a celebratory dinner in Prague, given in honor of Tchaikovsky's visit, on 7/19 Feb. 1888. Published in the newspaper *Narodni Listy* [National Leaflet], 8/20 Feb. 1888.

"Tschaikowsky on Music in America," *New York Herald,* 17 May 1891. Rpt. 439, 139–42.

"U P. I. Chaykovskago" [With P. I. Tchaikovsky], *Novosti dnya* [News of the Day], 13/25 Apr. 1892. Rpt. *Sovetskaya muzïka* 5 (1965): 30–34. English translation: 306, 199–202.

"Beseda s Chaikovskom v noyabre 1892 g. v Peterburge" [A Conversation with Tchaikovsky in November 1892 in Petersburg], *Peterburgskaya zhizn'* [Petersburg Life], 12/24 Nov. 1892. Rpt. 84, 367–73. English translation: 306, 202–8.

"U avtora 'Iolantï'" [With the Composer of *Iolanta*], *Peterburgskaya gazeta,* 6/18 Dec. 1892. Rpt. *Sovetskaya muzïka* 5 (1965): 34–35. English translation: 306, 208–10.

"U P. I. Chaykovskago" [With P. I. Tchaikovsky], *Odesskiy listok* [Odessa Leaflet], 19 Jan. 1893.

"Pamyati P. I. Chaykovskago" [In Memory of P. I. Tchaikovsky], *Odesskie novosti* [Odessa News], 27 Oct. 1893. An interview with an Odessa reporter, published after Tchaikovsky's death.

"Chaykovskiy ob Odesse" [Tchaikovsky on Odessa], *Odesskiy listok* [Odessa Leaflet], 28 Oct. 1893. A conversation with Lev Kupernik of the Odessa branch of the Russian Musical Society.

 APPENDIX C 

Personalia

N.B. The following names are cited alphabetically in strict transliteration; informal spellings may be used in the elaborations.

Al'brekht [Albrecht], Karl [Konstantin] Karlovich (1836–1893). Teacher, authority on choral singing, inspector of the Moscow Conservatory (1866–1889), and Tchaikovsky's close friend, for whom he composed a short chorus entitled "Spring," published in special choral notation; thought lost; its rediscovery was reported in 1993 [425, 293–95]. Later, Tchaikovsky brokered Albrecht's retirement from the Moscow Conservatory.

Alekseeva (née Assier), Ekaterina Andreevna (1805–1882). Sister of Pyotr's mother. An amateur contralto, she tutored Pyotr in singing during his years at the School of Jurisprudence.

Al'tani [Altani], Ippolit Karlovich (1846–1919). Opera conductor at Kiev and Moscow (chief conductor at the Moscow Bolshoy Theater, 1882–1906). He conducted numerous first performances of Tchaikovsky's operas in Moscow; his indisposition made possible Tchaikovsky's vocational debut as a conductor at the first performance of *Cherevichki* (January 1887), for which he coached the composer in the rudiments of that art.

Apukhtin, Aleksey Nikolaevich "Lel" (1840–1893). Russian poet, Tchaikovsky's close, lifelong friend from the School of Jurisprudence; an uncloseted homosexual who may have helped to shape Tchaikovsky's response to public mores about homosexuality. Tchaikovsky set several of his poems as songs and was approached by the Grand Duke Konstantin with a proposal to set Apukhtin's "Requiem" in 1893, shortly before Tchaikovsky's death.

Artôt (Padilla by marriage), Désirée (1835–1907). Belgian mezzo-soprano, trained under Pauline Viardot-Garcia, who performed in Moscow in the 1860s and 1870s. For a time in 1868, she and Tchaikovsky apparently contemplated marriage; they revived their friendship 20 years later in Berlin. Tchaikovsky wrote the op. 65 songs for her.

Assier [Chaykovskaya], Aleksandra Andreevna (1813–1854). Tchaikovsky's mother.

Assier, Hendrikh [André] Mikhaylovich (c. 1778–after 1830). Tchaikovsky's maternal grandfather; a porcelain maker from Prussia who in Russia worked as a customs official and a teacher at the Mining Institute [368; 370].

Auer, Leopol'd Semenovich (1845–1937). Russian violinist, conductor, and pedagogue; professor at the St. Petersburg Conservatory (1868–1917) [19].

Aus der Ohe, Adèle (1864–1937). German pianist who played Tchaikovsky's First Piano Concerto under the composer's baton in the United States and St. Petersburg.

Ave-Lallemant, Johann Friedrich Theodor (1806–1890). One of the founders and directors of the Hamburg Philharmonic Society and a supporter of Tchaikovsky's conducting activities in Hamburg; dedicatee of Tchaikovsky's Fifth Symphony.

Bakhmetev, Nikolay Ivanovich (1807–1891). Director of the Imperial Court Chapel; subject of a lawsuit over the publication of Pyotr's *Liturgy,* op. 41.

Balakirev, Miliy Alekseevich (1837–1910). Important Russian composer, pianist, and conductor; leader of the so-called Mighty Handful of nationalist musicians and co-founder of the Free School of Music in St. Petersburg. He encouraged the composition of Tchaikovsky's *Romeo and Juliet* overture/fantasia and the *Manfred* Symphony.

Barbier, Jules (1825–1901). French dramatist and librettist, from whose play on Joan of Arc Tchaikovsky borrowed for parts of the libretto of his opera *The Maid of Orleans.*

Begichev, Vladimir Petrovich (1838–1891). Dramatist; husband of Mariya Shilovskaya; head of repertoire of the Moscow Imperial Theaters from 1864; director of the Moscow Imperial Theaters (1881–1882); commissioned *Swan Lake.*

Bélard. Family of hotel proprietors in Paris, with whom Tchaikovsky coordinated communications and business arrangements with the foster parents of his grandnephew Georges-Léon.

Belyaev [Belaïeff], Mitrofan Petrovich (1836–1904). Organizer of chamber and orchestral concerts in St. Petersburg; founder of a music publishing company of the same name in Leipzig. Tchaikovsky was the recipient of composition prizes from Belaïeff.

Benardaki, Mariya Pavlovna (née Lebroque) (d. 1913). Singer; graduate of the St. Petersburg Conservatory; later, a high society hostess of a Tchaikovsky concert in Paris.

Berberova, Nina [Antonina?] Nikolaevna (1901–1993). The first biographer of Tchaikovsky to consider the realities of his intimate life.

Berger, Francesco (1834–1919). Pianist, composer, organizer of Tchaikovsky's conducting concerts in London.

Bernard, Nikolay Matveevich (1844–1905). Music publisher in St. Petersburg who commissioned *The Seasons* and other works from Tchaikovsky for his music journal, *Nouvelliste.*

Bertenson, Lev Bernadovich (1850–1929). Physician in St. Petersburg who headed the team of doctors treating Tchaikovsky's last illness; brother of Vasiliy.

Bertenson, Vasiliy [Basile] Bernardovich (1853–1933). Physician in St. Petersburg who attended Tchaikovsky's last illness; brother of Lev.

Bessel', Vasiliy Vasil'evich (1843–1907). Violist, critic, and music publisher of some of Tchaikovsky's early works.

Blinov, Nikolay Orestovich (1929–1988). Microbiologist who investigated the causes of Tchaikovsky's death [44].

Block, Julius H. (1858–1934). Thomas Edison's representative in Russia; responsible for the only extant recording of Tchaikovsky's voice [45; 392; 413].

Blumenfel'd, Feliks Mikhaylovich (1863–1931). Pianist, conductor, and composer; a teacher (from 1885), then professor of the St. Petersburg Conservatory (1897–1905) and the Petrograd Conservatory (1911–1918).

Blumenfel'd, Stanislav Mikhaylovich (1850–1897). Pianist; director of a music school in Kiev; father of Tatyana Davïdova's son Georges-Léon.

Bochechkarov, Nikolay L'vovich (d. 1879). A friend of the composer.

Bogatïrev [Bogatïryov], Semen Semenovich [Semyon Semyonovich] (1890–1961). Music theorist and composer, professor of the Moscow Conservatory. He restored Tchaikovsky's Symphony in E-flat (Symphony no. 7) and was involved in the restoration of the original version of the Second Symphony.

Bortnyanskiy, Dmitriy Stepanovich (1751–1825). Russian composer of sacred music in the Italian manner. Tchaikovsky labored over a new edition of his sacred concertos.

Brandukov, Anatoliy Andreevich (1859–1930). Russian and Soviet cellist, conductor, and composer; professor of the Moscow Conservatory (1921–1930). A companion of Tchaikovsky in the late 1880s in his visits to Paris, where he performed Tchaikovsky's music.

Brodskiy, Adol'f Davïdovich (1851–1929). Violinist and teacher; professor of the Moscow Conservatory (1875–1879), Leipzig Conservatory (1882–1893), and College of Music in Manchester (from 1893); played the first performances of Tchaikovsky's Violin Concerto in Vienna and Moscow.

Bryullova (née Meyer), Alina Ivanovna (1849–1932). Mother of Nikolay Germanovich Konradi, Modest Tchaikovsky's deaf mute student.

Bülow, Hans von (1830–1894). German pianist and conductor; advocate of Wagner and Brahms. Declared Tchaikovsky's importance in German newspapers, performed his music (notably, the premiere of the First Piano Concerto), and lobbied for his music in Germany.

Carnegie, Andrew (1835–1919). American steel manufacturer and philanthropist who financed Tchaikovsky's visit to the United States in 1891.

Čech, Adolf (1841–1903). Czech conductor; principal conductor of the National Theater in Prague (1874–1900); conducted first Czech performances of *The Maid of Orleans,* act II of *Swan Lake, Evgeniy Onegin,* and *The Queen of Spades.*

Chayka, Fyodor Afanas'evich [in some sources, Afanasiy Chaykovskiy]. One of Pyotr's paternal great-grandfathers; a soldier; father of Pyotr Fyodorovich Chaykovskiy.

Chaykovskaya (née Milyukova), Antonina Ivanovna (1848–1917). Tchaikovsky's wife.

Chaykovskaya (née von Berens), Elizaveta Petrovna (d. 1880). Tchaikovsky's aunt, mother of Anna Merkling.

Chaykovskaya (Popova by marriage), Evdokiya Petrovna (b. 1780). Tchaikovsky's aunt, mother of Anastasiya Vasil'evna Popova, known in the Tchaikovsky family as "Sestritsa."

Chaykovskaya (née Denis'eva), Ol'ga Sergeevna (d. 1919 or 1920). Tchaikovsky's sister-in-law, wife of his older brother Nikolay Tchaikovsky.

Chaykovskaya (née Konshina), Praskov'ya Vladimirovna (1864–1956). Wife of Pyotr's brother Anatoly.

Chaykovskaya (Ol'khovskaya by marriage), Zinaida Il'inichna (1829–1878). Tchaikovsky's half-sister by his father's first marriage.

Chaykovskiy, Anatoliy [Anatoly] Il'ich ("Tolya," "Tolichka," "Anatosha") (1850–1915). Pyotr's younger brother, twin of Modest; dedicatee of the Six Romances, op. 38. Jurist who attempted to secure Pyotr's divorce and whose appointment as procurator in Tiflis brought Pyotr south to the Caucasus; later, a vice governor in Revel (now Tallinn) and in Nizhnïy-Novgorod and a senator.

Chaykovskiy, Georgiy Nikolaevich [Georges-Léon] (1883–1940). Tatyana Davïdova's son, adopted by Nikolay Il'ich Tchaikovsky and his wife, Olga.

Chaykovskiy, Il'ya Petrovich (1795–1880). Tchaikovsky's father; a mining engineer in the towns of Votkinsk and Alapaevsk; later, director of the Technological Institute in St. Petersburg [164].

Chaykovskiy, Ippolit Il'ich "Polya" (1843–1927). Tchaikovsky's younger brother; a maritime officer (later, major general of the admiralty); editor of the composer's diaries (1923).

Chaykovskiy, Modest Il'ich "Modya" (1850–1916). Pyotr's younger brother, twin of Anatoly; dedicatee of the piano pieces, op. 40. Pyotr's first comprehensive biographer, first director of the Tchaikovsky Home-Museum at

Klin, and an important figure in Russian letters; a playwright and librettist, particularly of *The Queen of Spades* and *Iolanta.*

Chaykovskiy, Nikolay Il'ich (1838–1911). Tchaikovsky's elder brother, a mining engineer and railroad administrator; adoptive father of Tatyana Davïdova's child Georges-Léon.

Chaykovskiy, Pyotr Fyodorovich (1745–1818). Tchaikovsky's paternal grandfather.

Chaykovskiy, Pyotr Petrovich (1788–1871). Tchaikovsky's paternal uncle. From the end of 1854 to the autumn of 1857, Pyotr Petrovich's family and Tchaikovsky's family lived together.

Cui. See Kyui.

Dahlhaus, Carl (1928–1989). German musicologist, editor, and theorist.

Damrosch, Walter (1862–1950). American composer and conductor; Tchaikovsky's advocate in the United States; encouraged his visit to New York to conduct at the opening of the (Carnegie) Music Hall in 1891.

Dannreuther, Edward (1844–1905). British pianist who suggested improvements in Tchaikovsky's First Piano Concerto.

Davïdov [Davydov], Karl Yul'evich (1838–1889). Cellist, composer, and conductor; director of the St. Petersburg Conservatory (1876–1886). Davïdov supplied Tchaikovsky with the libretto that the composer adapted for *Mazepa.*

Davïdov, Lev Vasil'evich (1837–1896). Son of the Decembrist Vasily Davïdov; husband of Pyotr's sister Aleksandra; supervisor of family estates at Kamenka and Verbovka in the Ukraine.

Davïdov, Vladimir L'vovich "Bob" (1872–1906). Tchaikovsky's nephew, dedicatee of *The Children's Album,* op. 39, and the Sixth Symphony, op. 74. In his later years, Pyotr developed a strong affection for Davïdov and made him a major beneficiary of his will [371].

Davïdov, Yuriy L'vovich (1876–1965). Tchaikovsky's nephew; agronomist; curator of the Tchaikovsky Home-Museum at Klin (1945–1962). Some of his memoirs of Tchaikovsky, written decades after the fact, have been discredited.

Davïdova [Chaykovskaya], Aleksandra Il'inichna "Sasha" (1842–1891). Tchaikovsky's sister, wife of Lev Davïdov, matriarch of the Davïdov estate at Kamenka.

Davïdova, Tatyana L'vovna "Tanya" (1861–1887). Tchaikovsky's niece, daughter of his sister Aleksandra and Lev Davïdov.

Davïdova [Butakova by marriage], Vera Vasil'evna (1848–1923). Sister of Tchaikovsky's brother-in-law Lev Davïdov; apparently, the object of Pyotr's affections at Hapsal in the summer of 1867; dedicatee of the *Souvenir de Hapsal,* op. 2.

de Lazari [stage surname Konstantinov], Konstantin Nikolaevich (1838–1903). Singer and dramatic actor in the theaters of Moscow and St. Petersburg.

Détroyat, Pierre Léonce (1829–1898). French journalist and opera librettist; developed various opera topics for Tchaikovsky to compose for Paris, principally *La courtisane; ou, Sadia.*

Diémer, Louis (1843–1919). French pianist and pedagogue; friend of Tchaikovsky and advocate of his music in Paris.

Donaurov, Sergey Ivanovich (1838–1897). Friend of Tchaikovsky in the 1870s; author, translator, official censor of dramatic works.

Door, Anton (1833–1919). Pianist and professor at the Moscow Conservatory in Tchaikovsky's early years; settled later in Vienna.

Drigo, Riccardo (1846–1930). Italian composer and conductor; principal conductor of the Imperial Ballet in St. Petersburg (1886–1920).

Dürbach, Fanny (1822–1895). Tchaikovsky's first governess (1844–1848), who preserved the written compositions of Tchaikovsky the child and was a principal source of anecdotes about his early life [72; 100; 228; 232].

Erdmannsdörfer, Max (1848–1905). Nikolay Rubinstein's successor as conductor of the Moscow branch of the Russian Musical Society. Conducted many first performances of Tchaikovsky's orchestral works [37].

Fedorov, Pavel Stepanovich (1803–1879). Russian dramatist; head of repertoire in the St. Petersburg Imperial Theaters (1853–1879). Tchaikovsky composed music (lost) for one of his plays.

Fet (Shenshin), Afanasiy Afanas'evich (1820–1892). Celebrated Russian poet, whose verses provided a number of song texts for Tchaikovsky.

Figner (née Mey), Medeya Ivanovna (1859–1952). Soprano; artist of the Maryinsky Theater in St. Petersburg (1887–1912); wife of Nikolay Figner; created the roles of Lise in *The Queen of Spades* and the title role in *Iolanta.*

Figner, Nikolay Nikolaevich (1857–1918). Russian tenor; artist of the Maryinsky Theater in St. Petersburg (1887–1897); director of the opera company at the Narodnïy Dom in St. Petersburg (1910–1915); husband of Medea Figner. He created the roles of Hermann in *The Queen of Spades* and Vaudémont in *Iolanta.*

Fitingof-Shel' [Fitinhof-Schell], (Baron) Boris Aleksandrovich (1829–1901). Composer and memoirist; claimed that Tchaikovsky consulted him on how to compose ballet music [122].

Fitzenhagen, Karl Friedrich Wilhelm (1848–1890). German cellist; professor of the Moscow Conservatory from 1870; radically revised Tchaikovsky's *Variations on a Rococo Theme,* of which he is dedicatee.

Flerov [Flyorov], Sergey Vasil'evich (1841–1901). Journalist and music critic called "Ignotus." Provided Tchaikovsky with a translation of Hoffmann's "The Nutcracker and the Mouse-King" in Rome in 1882.

Galler, Konstantin Petrovich (1845–1888). Music critic, composer, collector of folk songs.

Gallet, Louis Marie Alexandre (1835–1898). French writer; librettist of *Sadia,* Tchaikovsky's unrealized opera for Paris.

Gerard, Vladimir Nikolaevich (1839–1903). Tchaikovsky's classmate at the School of Jurisprudence, later an important jurist; he delivered an oration at Tchaikovsky's funeral.

Gerke, Anton Avgustovich (1812–1870). Russian pianist and professor at the St. Petersburg Conservatory (1862–1870), where he taught Pyotr.

Gerke, Avgust Antonovich (1844–1917). Pianist; member of the direction of the Russian Musical Society in St. Petersburg; according to the court-of-honor theory, complicit in Tchaikovsky's death for supplying him with poison.

Gleason, Frederick Grant (1848–1903). American organist, composer, and teacher; in the 1880s, critic for the *Chicago Tribune.* Approached Tchaikovsky to conduct at the World's Columbian Exhibition in Chicago in 1894.

Golitsïn, (Prince) Aleksey Vasil'evich (1832–1901). A friend of Pyotr; owner of Trostinets, the estate where Pyotr translated Gevaert's *Traité général d'instrumentation* and composed op. 76, the overture to *The Storm,* in the summer of 1864.

Gubert [Hubert], Nikolay Al'bertovich (1840–1888). Pyotr's schoolmate at the St. Petersburg Conservatory; later, his colleague and director of the Moscow Conservatory (1881–1883).

Guitry, Lucien-Germain (1860–1925). Actor of the French drama company of the Mikhaylovsky Theater in St. Petersburg. Tchaikovsky wrote the incidental music to *Hamlet* for him.

Halíř, Karel [Halir, Carl] (1859–1909). Czech violinist; soloist to Tchaikovsky's conducting on tour.

Hanslick, Eduard (1825–1904). Czech-born music critic, active primarily in Vienna. He heaped notorious epithets on Tchaikovsky's early music.

Hubert, Nikolay. *See Gubert, Nikolay Al'bertovich.*

Ippolitov-Ivanov, Mikhail Mikhaylovich (1859–1935). Composer and conductor, active in Tiflis (Tbilsi) before moving to Moscow, where he became professor (from 1893) then director (from 1905) of the Moscow Conservatory [165].

Ivanov, Lev Ivanovich (1834–1901). Russian dancer and balletmaster (from 1885) in the St. Petersburg Imperial Theaters. Ivanov prepared the dances for *Mazepa* and restaged act II of *Swan Lake* for a performance in Tchaikovsky's memory in 1894.

Jacobi, Nikolay Borisovich (1839–1902). Jurist and public prosecutor who allegedly instigated the court of honor against Tchaikovsky.

Jurgenson. See Yurgenson.

Kashkin, Nikolay Dmitrievich (1839–1920). Tchaikovsky's friend; a professor of theory and music history at the Moscow Conservatory (1866–1908); an important music critic and advocate of Tchaikovsky's music; a chronicler of musical life in Moscow, including reminiscences of Pyotr published in 1896 and 1920. Those of 1920 are the sole source of some colorful anecdotes whose accuracy has been called into question [142; 437].

Keiser, Mariya Karlovna (d. 1831). First wife of Ilya Petrovich Chaykovskiy. Mother of Zinaida Chaykovskaya (later, Ol'khovskaya by marriage), Pyotr's half sister.

Kireyev, Sergey Aleksandrovich (1845–1888). A student at the School of Jurisprudence for whom Pyotr admitted a strong if not lasting affection.

Klimenko, Ivan Alexandrovich (1841–1914). Architect; a friend of Pyotr from the early 1860s in St. Petersburg. Klimenko was among the first to recognize Tchaikovsky's greatness as a composer; he left anecdotal, humorous recollections of Pyotr [199; 200; 201].

Klindworth, Karl (1830–1916). German pianist, conductor, and composer; professor at the Moscow Conservatory (1868–1884). Together with Hans von Bülow, Klindworth is largely responsible for the dissemination of Tchaikovsky's music in Germany.

Kondrat'ev [Kondratiev], Nikolay Dmitrievich (1832–1887). Friend of Pyotr; landowner whose estate, Nizï, in the Kharkov region Tchaikovsky visited regularly in the 1870s. Tchaikovsky traveled across Asia and Europe to attend Kondratiev during his final illness in 1887.

Konradi, Nikolay Germanovich (1868–1923). Deaf mute student of Modest Tchaikovsky, for whom, early in Modest's tutelage, Pyotr conceived a powerful affection, possibly contributing, in the autumn of 1876, to his resolve to marry.

Kotek [Kotik], Iosif Iosifovich (1855–1885), on rare occasion referred to by the first name Eduard. Violinist; graduate of the Moscow Conservatory; object of Pyotr's special affection around the time of his marriage. Kotek was present during and involved in the composition of Tchaikovsky's Violin Concerto.

K.R. See Romanov, Konstantin Konstantinovich.

Kramer, H. Pseudonym by which Tchaikovsky occasionally signed himself.

Kündinger, Rudolf Vasil'evich (1832–1913). German-born pianist and pedagogue who lived in Russia from 1850; gave Pyotr piano lessons and took him to orchestral concerts in 1855–1858.

Kyui [Cui], Tsezar' [César] Antonovich (1835–1918). Russian composer and critic; member of the Mighty Handful; by training, a professor of fortification. Pyotr's persistent adversary among critics.

Larosh [Laroche], German [Hermann] Avgustovich (1845–1904). Pyotr's friend from his days at the St. Petersburg Conservatory, though the friendship could be tempestuous; an important critic (disdainful of program music); contributed great insights into Pyotr's music and the occasional negative assessment of it; sometime professor at the Moscow and St. Petersburg conservatories; wrote about Pyotr's years at the St. Petersburg Conservatory in Modest Tchaikovsky's biography of Pyotr [38; 70; 103; 184].

Laub, Ferdinand (1832–1875). Czech violinist and pedagogue; professor of the Moscow Conservatory (1866–1874). Tchaikovsky's Third String Quartet is dedicated to Laub's memory.

Laube, Heinrich Wilhelm Julius (1841–1910). German conductor, notably in Hamburg; conducted Tchaikovsky's music with his own orchestra at concerts at the Pavlovsk Railway Station near St. Petersburg (1888–1891).

Lavrovskaya, Elizaveta Andreevna [Princess Tserteleva by marriage] (1845–1919). Russian contralto who sang in Moscow and St. Petersburg (1868–1891); suggested to Tchaikovsky that he write an opera on the story of Pushkin's *Evgeniy Onegin.*

Lomakin, Gavriil Yakimovich (1812–1885). Russian choral conductor, composer, and pedagogue; with Mily Balakirev founded the Free Music School in St. Petersburg. Pyotr studied with him at the School of Jurisprudence.

Mackar, Felix (1837–1903). Founder of a music publishing firm in Paris, who bought from Jurgenson the rights to sell Tchaikovsky's works in France and Belgium. An important advocate of Tchaikovsky's music in Paris.

Mamanov, Nikolay N. One of the physicians attending Tchaikovsky during his final illness.

Meck, Nadezhda Filaretovna von (1831–1894). Wealthy, somewhat eccentric widow of a railroad magnate who became Tchaikovsky's patron and with whom he conducted an extensive and revealing correspondence (1876–1890), arguably the most important in his life.

Menter, Sophie (1846–1918). German pianist; student of Liszt; professor of the St. Petersburg Conservatory (1883–1887); friend of Tchaikovsky. Tchaikovsky orchestrated her (possibly Liszt's) "Hungarian Gypsy Songs" in 1892.

Merkling (née Chaykovskaya), Anna Petrovna "Anya" (1830–1911). Pyotr's first cousin and confidante; daughter of Pyotr Petrovich Tchaikovsky and his wife Elizaveta Petrovna; Merkling was an important correspondent outside the immediate family.

Meshcherskiy, (Prince) Vladimir Petrovich (1839–1911). Writer and publisher; editor of the newspaper *Grazhdanin* (Citizen); friend of Pyotr from the School of Jurisprudence.

Mighty Handful. The corporate identity of five Russian nationalist composers (hence their other nickname, "The Five") in the 1860s: Mily Balakirev (the leader), César Cui, Modest Musorgsky, Alexander Borodin, and Nikolay Rimsky-Korsakov.

Nápravnik, Eduard Francevič (1839–1916). Composer and celebrated conductor of the St. Petersburg branch of the Russian Musical Society (1869–1891) and other concerts and of opera in the St. Petersburg Imperial Theaters (1869–1916). He conducted many first performances of Tchaikovsky's music and was the dedicatee of *The Maid of Orleans.* Tchaikovsky regularly accepted Nápravnik's advice concerning the practical revision of operas [191; 268].

Nápravnik, Vladimir Eduardovich (1869–1948). Son of Eduard; secretary to the direction of the Russian Musical Society; an important correspondent of Tchaikovsky in the composer's later years.

Ol'khovskiy, Viktor Ivanovich. Poet, correspondent, and librettist of the 14-year-old Pyotr's project for an opera, *Hyperbole.*

Orlova (née Shneyerson), Aleksandra Anatol'ievna (b. 1911). Musicologist; publicized outside Russia the theory of Tchaikovsky's death by suicide.

Ostrovskiy, Aleksandr Nikolaevich (1823–1886). Celebrated Russian dramatist, with whom Pyotr collaborated in Moscow, notably on the opera *The Voevoda* and the play *The Snow Maiden.*

Pachulski, Genrikh [Pakul'skiy, Genrikh Al'bertovich] (1859–1921). Pianist and composer, professor of the Moscow Conservatory. Brother of Wladislaw Pachulski.

Pachulski, Wladislaw [Pakul'skiy, Vladislav Al'bertovich] (d. 1919). Son of a forester on Nadezhda von Meck's estate; later, her house violinist and son-in-law. At Meck's request, Tchaikovsky critiqued his compositions; he relayed messages to Tchaikovsky about Meck after the formal cessation of their correspondence.

Pal'chikova, Mariya Markovna (d. 1888). Tchaikovsky's first music teacher.

Palechek, Iosif Iosifovich [Osip Osipovich] (1842–1915). Bass singer; *régisseur;* leader of the opera chorus of the Maryinsky Theater, St. Petersburg. He prepared detailed production synopses of some of Tchaikovsky's operas, which were used as the bases for stagings outside St. Petersburg.

Pavlovskaya, Emilia Karlovna (1856–1935). Soprano of the Russian Imperial Theaters who created various roles in Tchaikovsky's operas; his correspondent.

Petipa, Marius Ivanovich (1818–1910). Dancer and choreographer; balletmaster (from 1862) and first balletmaster (from 1870) of the St. Petersburg Imperial Theaters. Collaborated with Tchaikovsky on *The Sleeping Beauty.*

Petrova, Anastasiya Petrovna (1824–1893). Pyotr's second childhood governess (1849–1850), who readied him for the entrance examinations to the preparatory division of the School of Jurisprudence. Dedicatee of Pyotr's first surviving composition, the "Anastasia Waltz" (1854) [440; 441].

Piccioli, Luigi (1812–1868). Teacher of singing in St. Petersburg who tutored Pyotr in Italian language and opera in the later 1850s.

Pogozhev, Vladimir Petrovich (1851–1935). Military officer and jurist; official of the direction of the Imperial Theaters (from 1881); involved with the production of Tchaikovsky's theater works in St. Petersburg.

Pollini, Bernhard (1838–1897). Impresario; conductor of an opera theater in Hamburg; from 1890, held rights in German-speaking countries to several of Tchaikovsky's stage works.

Popova, Anastasiya Vasil'evna "Sestritsa" (1807–1894). Daughter of Pyotr's father's sister. She lived with the Tchaikovsky family at Votkinsk and Alapaevsk and, later, with Sasha and Lev Davïdov at Kamenka.

Posokhova, Anastasiya Stepanovna (b. 1756 or 1760). Pyotr's paternal grandmother; wife of Pyotr Fyodorovich Tchaikovsky and the daughter of a *voevoda,* a garrison supervisor in the town of Kungera in the Perm region.

Pryanishnikov, Ippolit Petrovich (1847–1921). Baritone (the first Lionel in *The Maid of Orleans,* the first Mazepa in St. Petersburg); *régisseur;* pedagogue; opera impresario (mostly in Kiev) for whom Tchaikovsky conducted opera in Moscow in April 1892 [290; 317].

Rachinskiy, Sergey Aleksandrovich (1836–1902). Professor of botany at Moscow University; proposed the epigraph that served as a program for Tchaikovsky's *Fatum;* and suggested opera subjects to him.

Rahter, Daniel Fedorovich (1828–1891). Tchaikovsky's publisher in Hamburg; owner of the music firm A. Bittner in St. Petersburg [224].

Razumovskiy, (Father) Dmitriy Vasil'evich (1818–1889). Orthodox priest who performed Tchaikovsky's marriage ceremony and who later assisted him in matters of church singing; Pyotr's colleague at the Moscow Conservatory and an important scholar in his own right [162].

Reno, Morris. President of the Music Hall Company of New York, he was involved with Tchaikovsky's invitations to conduct in the United States.

Romanov, (Grand Duke) Konstantin Konstantinovich (1858–1916). Poet who signed himself "K.R." and provided texts for Tchaikovsky's op. 63 songs; an important correspondent of the composer on the aesthetics of poetry and the setting of words to music [244].

Romanov, (Grand Duke) Konstantin Nikolaevich (1827–1892). President of the Russian Musical Society; father of the Grand Duke Konstantin Konstantinovich; dedicatee of Tchaikovsky's opera *The Oprichnik* and the Third String Quartet.

Rubinshteyn [Rubinstein], Anton Grigor'evich (1829–1894). Eminent pianist and composer; brother of Nikolay; founder and first director of the Russian Musical Society in St. Petersburg and the St. Petersburg Conservatory; Pyotr's principal composition teacher [25; 26].

Rubinshteyn [Rubinstein], Nikolay Grigor'evich (1835–1881). Russian pianist, conductor, and pedagogue; brother of Anton; founder and first director of the Moscow Conservatory; responsible for many first performances of Tchaikovsky's works. He is the "great artist" memorialized in the dedication of Tchaikovsky's Piano Trio, op. 50 [27; 134; 179; 180; 185; 186].

Sack. See Zak.

Safonov, Vasiliy Il'ich (1852–1918). Pianist, conductor, professor, then director (1889–1905) of the Moscow Conservatory. Quarreled with Tchaikovsky over the appointment of Anatoly Brandukov as professor of cello after the death of Wilhelm Fitzenhagen; they were ultimately reconciled. Safonov conducted the read-through of Tchaikovsky's Sixth Symphony at the Moscow Conservatory before the composer conducted the first public performance in St. Petersburg.

Samarin, Ivan Vasil'evich (1817–1885). Russian actor, dramatist, and pedagogue. He produced the first staging of *Evgeniy Onegin* with students of the Moscow Conservatory and devised Onegin's closing lines in the opera.

Sapel'nikov, Vasiliy L'vovich (1868–1940). Russian pianist; student of Sophie Menter, who made concert tours with Tchaikovsky as conductor.

Shenshin, Dmitri Semenovich (1828–1897). Major-general; one of Tchaikovsky's creditors in Moscow.

Shilovskaya (née Verderezhskaya), Mariya Vasil'evna (1830–1879). Singer; wife of Vladimir Begichev (after her first marriage to Stepan Shilovsky); hostess of a Moscow salon that Pyotr frequented in his early years there. He was tutor to her sons, Vladimir and Konstantin Shilovsky.

Shilovskiy, Konstantin Stepanovich (1849–1893). Actor, poet, musician; brother of Vladimir; assisted Tchaikovsky in the formulation of the libretto of *Evgeniy Onegin.*

Shilovskiy, Vladimir Stepanovich [Count Vasil'ev-Shilovskiy] (1852–1893). Pyotr's sometime student, with whom he developed a long and occasionally tempestuous friendship; brother of Konstantin. Shilovsky composed the Entr'acte before act II of Tchaikovsky's *The Oprichnik.*

Shlïkov, Aleksandr Aleksandrovich [also known as Pyotr Fedorovich Simonov and as Bol'kov]. Attorney for and, later, common-law husband of Tchaikovsky's wife, Antonina.

Shobert [Schobert] (née Assier), Elizaveta Andreevna (b. 1823). Half sister of Pyotr's mother. She lived with the Tchaikovsky family for a time in Alapaevsk (1849–1852) and they with her in St. Petersburg in 1858 after Pyotr's father lost his capital in a bad investment.

Shpazhinskaya (née Porokhontseva), Yuliya Petrovna (d. 1919). Pianist, aspiring writer. Wife of Ippolit Shpazhinsky.

Shpazhinskiy, Ippolit Vasil'evich (1848–1917). Dramatist. Librettist of Tchaikovsky's opera *The Enchantress.*

Sieger, Friedrich. German writer on music and critic, director of the Frankfurt Museum Society, which sponsored concerts.

Siloti [Ziloti], Aleksandr Il'ich (1863–1945). Pianist, conductor, professor of the Moscow Conservatory. Tchaikovsky conferred with Siloti on various editorial matters, controversially on the first two piano concertos; he arranged *The Sleeping Beauty* for two hands [251].

Sinopov, P. Pseudonym by which Tchaikovsky occasionally signed himself.

Sofronov, Aleksey Ivanovich "Alyosha" (1859–1925). Pyotr's principal servant and the arranger of his domestic affairs from 1871, especially the preparation of the composer's homes in later life; beneficiary of Pyotr's will; brother of Mikhail. After Pyotr's death, Sofronov sold to Modest Tchaikovsky and Bob Davïdov the house at Klin, which became the composer's Home-Museum.

Sofronov, Mikhail Ivanovich (1848–1932). Brother of Aleksey; Pyotr's house servant for a time in the 1870s.

Sollogub, (Count) Vladimir Aleksandrovich (1814–1882). Russian writer and dramatist; author of the libretto Tchaikovsky set in the opera *Undine* (1869).

Solov'ev [Solovyov], Nikolay Feopemptovich (1846–1916). Composer; professor of the St. Petersburg Conservatory; critic generally ill disposed toward Tchaikovsky's music.

Stasov, Vladimir Vasil'evich (1824–1906). Art expert, publicist, critic, defender of the Mighty Handful.

Steinbok-Fermor, Aleksandr Vladimirovich. According to the court-of-honor theory of Tchaikovsky's death, the object of the composer's affections, which triggered the events leading to his suicide.

Strauss, Johann, Jr. (1825–1899). Austrian composer (the so-called Waltz King) who conducted at the Pavlovsk Railway Station near St. Petersburg from 1856 to 1865; conducted the first known public performance of an orchestral work by Tchaikovsky, the "Characteristic Dances," which was later revised and included in the opera *The Voevoda.*

Taffanel, Paul Claude (1844–1908). French flautist; conductor of the Paris Conservatory Concerts (1890–1893) and at the Opéra (1892–1908); appeared in Moscow as a flautist at Tchaikovsky's invitation.

Taneev [Taneyev], Sergey Ivanovich (1856–1915). Student and, later, professor and director of the Moscow Conservatory (1885–1889); pianist and composer; Tchaikovsky's close friend. He prepared a number of Tchaikovsky's compositions for posthumous publication, including a duet from *Romeo and Juliet* (music based on the overture/fantasia), the Andante and Finale for Piano and Orchestra, and several smaller works.

Tarnavich, (Father) Aleksandr Danilovich (1843–1923). Village priest at Kamenka, from whom Pyotr sought information about the text of the *All-Night Vigil.*

Tchaikovskaya. See Chaykovskaya.

Tchaikovsky. See Chaykovskiy.

Tkachenko, Leontiy Grigor'evich (1857–1921). Mentally disturbed young man whom Tchaikovsky assisted (unsuccessfully) to develop an artistic career.

Tolstoy, Aleksey Konstantinovich (1817–1875). Russian poet and dramatist; provided the largest number of song texts of any poet whom Tchaikovsky set.

Tolstoy, (Count) Lev [Leo] Nikolaevich (1828–1910). Outstanding Russian novelist and writer, whom Tchaikovsky met in 1876 and engaged in a brief correspondence.

Vakar, Modest Alekseyevich. Friend of Ilya Petrovich Tchaikovsky who housed Pyotr as a student in his first years of school in St. Petersburg.

Vakar, Nikolay Modestovich (d. 1850). Son of Modest Vakar, whose death from scarlet fever may have been attributable to the 10-year-old Pyotr as a carrier of the illness into the Vakar home.

Vakar, Platon Alekseyevich (1826–1899). An important jurist in the Russian government; brother of Modest Vakar.

Val'ts [Valts, Waltz], Karl Fedorovich (1846–1929). Machinist and decorator of the Moscow Bolshoy and Maly theaters; occasional librettist of opera and ballet [402].

Verinovskiy, Ivan Aleksandrovich "Bomba" (d. 1886). Artillery officer for whom Pyotr developed strong feelings on his trip to Tiflis in 1886; Verinovsky committed suicide soon after Tchaikovsky's departure.

Viardot [Viardot-Garcia], Michelle Ferdinande Pauline (1821–1910). Eminent French mezzo-soprano, teacher of singing, and composer; trained under her father, Manuel Garcia, Liszt, and Reicha; sister of Maria Malibran. Tchaikovsky studied the autograph of *Don Giovanni* in her home in Paris.

Voitov, Aleksandr (d. 1966). Numismatist at the Russian Museum in Leningrad; unofficial historian of the School of Jurisprudence, who conveyed the court-of-honor theory of Tchaikovsky's death between generations, from Nikolay Jacobi's widow to the Soviet musicologist Alexandra Orlova.

Vsevolozhskiy, Ivan Aleksandrovich (1835–1909). Director of the Imperial Theaters (1881–1899), who commissioned operas and ballets from Tchaikovsky.

Wolff, Hermann (1845–1902). Founder of an artists' agency in Berlin (1881); helped arrange Tchaikovsky's tours abroad.

Yurgenson [Jurgenson], Pyotr Ivanovich (1836–1903). Founder of the music publishing company of that name, based in Moscow; Tchaikovsky's principal publisher.

Zak [Sack], Eduard (1854–1873). Student of Tchaikovsky at the Moscow Conservatory, toward whom the composer exhibited strong feelings and whose early suicide he lamented.

Zaremba, Nikolay Ivanovich (1821–1879). Music theorist and composer; Pyotr's teacher at the St. Petersburg Conservatory, of which he was later director.

Zet, Yuliy Ivanovich. Pianist and impresario; Tchaikovsky's agent; involved with arranging his foreign tours.

Zverev, Nikolay Sergeevich (1832–1893). Tchaikovsky's colleague at the Moscow Conservatory; professor of piano who taught (among others) Sergey Rachmaninov.

 APPENDIX D 

Select Bibliography

1. Abraham, Gerald, ed. *Tchaikovsky: A Symposium*. London: Lindsay Drummond, 1945.
2. Abraham, Gerald. "Tchaikovsky's First Opera." In *Festschrift Karl Gustav Fellerer zum Sechzigsten Geburtstag am 7: Jul 1962*. Regensburg: Gustav Bosse, 1962, pp. 12–18.
3. Adorno, Thedor W. *Quasi una Fantasia: Essays on Modern Music*. Tr. Rodney Livingstone. London: Verso, 1994.
4. Afanas'ev, A[leksandr] N[ikolaevich]. *Poeticheskie vozzreniya Slavyan na prirodu* [The Slavonic People's Poetical Views of Nature]. 3 vols. Moscow: Sovremennïy pisatel', 1995.
5. Alekseev, A[leksandr] D[mitrievich]. *Russkaya fortep'yannaya muzïka konets XIX—nachalo XX veka* [Russian Piano Music, End of the 19th–Beginning of the 20th Centuries]. Moscow: Nauka, 1969.
6. Alekseev, N[ikolay] A[lekseevich], comp. *Chaikovskiy i zarubezhnïe muzïkantï: Izbrannïe pis'ma inostrannïkh korrespondentov* [Tchaikovsky and Foreign Musicians: Selected Letters of Foreign Correspondents]. Leningrad: Muzïka, 1970.
7. Alekseeva, E. N., and Pribigina, G. A., comps. *Vospominaniya o Moskovskoy Konservatorii* [Recollections of the Moscow Conservatory]. Ed. N[adezhda] V[asil'evna] Tumanina. Moscow: Muzïka, 1966.
8. Al'shvang, A[rnol'd Aleksandrovich]. *Opït analiza tvorchestva P. I. Chaykovskogo* [An Attempt at Analysis of P. I. Tchaikovsky's Work]. Moscow: State Music Publisher, 1951.
9. Al'shvang, A[rnol'd Aleksandrovich]. *P. I. Chaikovskiy*, 3rd ed. Moscow: Muzïka, 1970.
10. Al'shvang, A[rnol'd Aleksandrovich]. "Romansï Chaykovskogo" [Tchaikovsky's Songs]. *Sovetskaya muzïka* 9–10 (1939): 100–122; 1 (1940): 14–27.
11. Al'zutskiy, I. Ya. *Kritika muzïka i libretto operï "Pikovaya dama" P. I. Chaykovskago i M. I. Chaykovskago* [Critique of the Music and Libretto of the Opera "The Queen of Spades" by P. I. Tchaikovsky and M. I. Tchaikovsky]. St. Petersburg: Printed Art, 1910.

12. Amfiteatrova-Levitskaya, A. N. "Perviy spektakl' 'Evgeniya Onegina'" [The First Performance of "Evgeniy Onegin"]. In *Chaykovskiy i teatr* [Tchaikovsky and Theater: Articles and Materials]. Ed. A. I. Shaverdyan. Moscow: Iskusstvo, 1940, pp. 140–46.
13. Anshakov, B[oris Yakovlevich]. *Brat'ya Chaykovskie: Ocherk* [The Tchaikovsky Brothers: An Essay]. Izhevsk: Udmurtiya, 1981.
14. Anshakov, B[oris] Ya[kovlevich]. *Dom Muzey P. I. Chaykovskogo v Votkinske* [The Home Museum of P. I. Tchaikovsky in Votkinsk]. Izhevsk: Udmurtiya, 1978.
15. Anshakov, B[oris Yakovlevich], and Polina Efimovna Vaydman, comps. *P. I. Chaykovskiy i russkaya literatura* [P. I. Tchaikovsky and Russian Literature]. Izhevsk: Udmurtiya, 1980.
16. Anshakov, B[oris Yakovlevich], and Polina Efimovna Vaydman, eds. *P. I. Chaikovskiy i Ural* [P. I. Tchaikovsky and the Urals]. Izhevsk: Udmurtiya, 1983.
17. Anshakov, Boris Yakovlevich, Galina Ivanovna Belonovich, and Moris Shlemovich Bonfel'd, eds. *Teatr v zhizni i tvorchestve P. I. Chaykovskogo* [Theater in the Life and Work of P. I. Tchaikovsky]. Izhevsk: Udmurtiya, 1985.
18. Aranovskiy, M. G. "Nakhodki i oshibki tvorcheskoy intuitii (Iz rukopisnogo arkhiva P. I. Chaykovskogo" [Finds and Errors of Creative Intuition (from P. I. Tchaikovsky's Manuscript Archive)]. In *P. I. Chaykovskiy: K 100-letiyu so dnya smerti (1893–1993): Materialï nauchnoy konferentsii* [P. I. Tchaikovsky: On the 100th Anniversary of His Death (1893–1993): Materials of a Scholarly Conference]. Moscow: Moscow State Conservatory Named for P. I. Tchaikovsky, 1995, pp. 31–39.
19. Auer, Leopold. *My Long Life in Music.* New York: Stokes, 1923.
20. Auerbakh, L. *Trio Chaykovskogo "Pamyati velikogo khudozhnika": Putevoditel'* [Tchaikovsky's Trio "To the Memory of a Great Artist": A Guide]. Moscow: Muzïka, 1977.
21. Av'erino, N[ikolay] K[onstantinovich]. "Moi vospominaniya o P. I. Chaikovskom" [My Recollections of P. I. Tchaikovsky]. *Vozrozhdenie "La renaissance": Literaturno-politicheskiya tetradi* [The Renaissance: Literary-Political Notebooks] 16 (July–August 1951): 97–106.
22. Balakirev, Miliy Alekseevich. *Perepiska M. A. Balakireva s P. I. Chaykovskim* [Correspondence of M. A. Balakirev with P. I. Tchaikovsky]. St. Petersburg: Tsimmerman, 1912.
23. Balakirev, M[iliy] A[lekseevich]. *Perepiska s notoizdatel'stvom P. Yurgensona* [Correspondence with the Music Publisher P. Jurgenson]. Ed. V. A. Kiselev and A. S. Lyapunov. Moscow: State Music Publisher, 1958.
24. [Balakirev, M. A., ed.]. *Sbornik russkikh narodnïkh pesen sostavlennïy M. Balakirevïm* [Collection of Russian Folk Songs Compiled by M. Balakirev]. St. Petersburg: Iogansen, [1866].
25. Baremboym, L[ev] A[ronovich], comp. and ed. *A. G. Rubinshteyn: Literaturnoe nasledie v trekh tomakh* [A. G. Rubinstein: Literary Heritage in Three Volumes]. Moscow: Muzïka, 1983–1986.
26. Barenboym, L[ev Aronovich]. *Anton Grigor'evich Rubinshteyn: Zhizn', artisticheskiy put', tvorchestvo, muzïkal'no-obshchestvennaya deyatel'nost'* [Anton Grigorevich Rubinstein: Life, Artistic Path, Oeuvre, Musico-Societal Activity]. 2 vols. Leningrad: State Music Publisher, 1957–1962.
27. Barenboym, L[ev Aronovich]. *Nikolay Grigor'evich Rubinshteyn: Istoriya zhizni i deyatel'nosti* [Nikolay Grigorevich Rubinstein: The Story of His Life and Activity]. Moscow: Muzïka, 1982.
28. Barsova, Inna. "Mahler—ein 'Schuler' Čajkovskijs?" *Čajkovskij-Studien* 1 (1995): 51–56.
29. Barsova, Inna. "'Samïe pateticheskie kompozitorï evropeyskoy muzïki': Chaykovskiy i Maler" ["The Most Passionate Composers of European Music": Tchaikovsky and Mahler]. *Sovetskaya muzïka* 6 (1990): 125–32.
30. Bartlett, Rosamund. "Tchaikovsky and Wagner: A Reassessment." In *Tchaikovsky and His Contemporaries: A Centennial Symposium.* Ed. Alexandar Mihailovic. Westport, CT: Greenwood, 1999, pp. 95–116.
31. Baskin, V. S. *Russkie kompozitorï: P. I. Chaykovskiy (Ocherk ego deyatel'nosti)* [Russian Composers: P. I. Tchaikovsky (A Study of His Activity)]. St. Petersburg: Marks, 1895.

32. Belonoviè, Galina. "Čajkovskijs letzter Wohnsitz und das Museum in Klin." *Čajkovskij-Studien* 1 (1995): 57–62.
33. Benoit, Camille. "Bibliographie musicale: Oeuvres de P. Tchaikowsky." *Revue et gazette musicale,* 17 June 1877, pp. 188–89; 24 June 1877, pp. 196–97.
34. Benua [Benois], Aleksandr [Nikolaevich]. *Moi vospominaniya* [My Recollections]. 2 vols. Ed. D. S. Likhachev. Moscow: Nauka, 1980.
35. Berberova, Nina. *Chaykovskiy,* 2nd ed. St. Petersburg: Limbus, 1997.
36. Berberova, Nina, Malcolm Brown, and Simon Karlinsky. "Tchaikovsky's 'Suicide' Reconsidered: A Rebuttal." *High Fidelity,* August 1981, pp. 49, 85.
37. Berčenko, Roman. "Max Erdmannsdörfer und Čajkovskij." *Tschaikowsky-Gesellschaft Mitteilungen* 13 (2006): 199–208.
38. Bernandt, Gr. "Larosh—neskol'ko shtrikhov k portretu" [Laroche—Some Features of His Portrait]. *Sovetskaya muzïka* 1 (1975): 110–15.
39. Bertenson V[asilii] B[ernardovich]. "Za tridtsat' let (Listki iz vospominaniy)" [After Thirty Years (Leaves from Reminiscences)]. *Istoricheskiy vestnik* [Historical Messenger] 128 (April–June 1912): 437–51; 129 (July–September 1912): 96–110, 505–16.
40. Bessel', V[asiliy]. "Iz moikh vospominaniy o P. Chaykovskom. 'Oprichnik.'" *Novoe vremya* [New Time] 7404 (7 October 1896): 2.
41. Bessel', V[asiliy]. "Moi vospominaniya o P. I. Chaykovskom." *Ezheognik Imperatorskikh Teatrov* [Yearbook of the Imperial Theaters], *1896–1897,* suppl. 1, pp. 19–43.
42. Bessel', Vasiliy. "Moi vospominaniya ob Antone Grigor'eviche Rubinsteyne (1829–1894)" [My Recollections of Anton Grigor'evich Rubinstein (1829–1894)]. *Russkaya starina* [Russian Antiquity] (May 1898): 315–74.
43. Bessel', V[asiliy]. "Neskol'ko slov po povodu vozobnovleniya 'Oprichnika' P. Chaykovskago na stsene Mariinskago teatra *(Iz moikh vospominaniy o Chaikovskom)*" [Some Words apropos the Revival of "The Oprichnik" by P. Tchaikovsky on the Stage of the Maryinsky Theater *(From My Recollections of Tchaikovsky)*]. *Russkaya muzïkal'naya gazeta* 12 (1897): cols. 1717–20.
44. Blinov, N[ikolay] O[restovich]. *Poslednyaya bolezn' i smert' P. I. Chaykovskogo* [P. I. Tchaikovsky's Last Illness and Death]. Moscow: Muzïka, 1994. [n.b. Bound/published with V. S. Sokolov, *Do i posle tragedii.*]
45. Block, Julius H. *Mortals and Immortals: Edison, Nikisch, Tchaikofsky [sic], Tolstoy: Episodes under Three Tzars.* N.p., n.d.
46. Blok, V. "Na puti k 'Pateticheskom'" [On the Road to the "Pathétique"]. *Sovetskaya Muzïka* 9 (1970): 78–80.
47. Bobéth, Marek. "Čajkovskij und das *Mächtige Häuflein.*" *Čajkovskij-Studien* 1 (1995): 63–85.
48. Bobéth, Marek. "Petr Il'ič Čajkovskij und Hans von Bülow." *Čajkovskij-Studien* 3 (1998): 355–66.
49. Bogatïrev, Semon S., ed. *P. Chaykovskiy, Simfoniya Es-Dur: Vosstanovlenie, instrumentovka i redaksiya S. Bogatïreva: Partitura* [P. Tchaikovsky, Symphony in E-flat Major: Restoration, Orchestration and Edition by S. Bogatyrev: Score]. Moscow: State Music Publisher, 1961.
50. Bonfel'd, M[oris] Sh[lemovich]. "Chaykovskiy v Peterburgskoy kritike: Pervoe desyatiletie tvorchestva (1865–1875)" [Tchaikovsky in Petersburg Criticism: The First Decade of His Work (1865–1875)]. In *Chaykovskiy: Novïe dokumentï i materialï* [Tchaikovsky: New Documents and Materials]. St. Petersburg: Compozitor Publishing House, 2003, pp. 56–65.
51. Bonfel'd, M[oris] Sh[lemovich]. "Problema dvuyazïchiya v opere P. I. Chaykovskogo 'Pikovaya dama'" [The Problem of Dual-Language in P. I. Tchaikovsky's Opera "The Queen of Spades"]. In *P. I. Chayikovskiy i russkaya literatura* [P. I. Tchaikovsky and Russian Literature]. Ed. T. A. Pozdeeva. Izhevsk: Udmurtiya, 1980, pp. 178–88.
52. Botstein, Leon. "Music as the Language of Psychological Realism: Tchaikovsky and Russian Art." In *Tchaikovsky and His World.* Ed. Leslie Kearney. Princeton, NJ: Princeton University Press, 1998, pp. 99–144.

53. Braun, Lucinde. "Čajkovskijs *Pikovaja dama* und der Historismus—Anmerkungen zu Tamara Skvirskajas Aufsatz." *Tschaikowsky-Gesellschaft Mitteilungen* 12 (2005): 186–90.
54. Braun, Lucinde. "Das 'pezzo concertato' in Čajkovskijs Opern." *Tschaikowsky-Gesellschaft Mitteilungen* 6 (March 1999): 17–26.
55. Braun, Lucinde. "Die Familie Acier in Dresden—Dokumente aus dem Sächsischen Hauptstaatsarchiv." *Tschaikowsky-Gesellschaft Mitteilungen* 11 (2004): 55–72.
56. Braun, Lucinde. *Studien zur russischen Oper im späten 19 Jahrhundert. Čajkovskij-Studien* 4 (1999).
57. Brezhneva, I.V. "Rukopisnïe materialï o Chaykovskom v biblioteke Moskovskoy konservatorii" [Manuscript Materials about Tchaikovsky in the Library of the Moscow Conservatory]. In *P. I. Chaykovskiy: Zabïtoe i novoe: Issledovaniya; materialï i dokumentï k biografii; vospominaniya sovremennikov; iz fotoarkhiva* [P. I. Tchaikovsky: Forgotten and New: Researches; Materials and Documents Relating to Biography; Recollections of Contemporaries; from the Photo Archive]. Comp. P. E. Vaydman and G. I. Belonovich. Moscow: Ministry of Culture of the Moscow Region and the P. I. Tchaikovsky State Home-Museum, 2003, pp. 337–34.
58. Brown, David. *Tchaikovsky Remembered.* London: Faber and Faber, 1993; Portland, OR: Amadeus, 1994.
59. Brown, David. *Tchaikovsky: The Crisis Years 1874–1878.* London: Gollancz, 1982.
60. Brown, David. *Tchaikovsky: The Early Years 1840–1874.* New York: Norton, 1978.
61. Brown, Malcolm Hamrick, ed. *A Collection of Russian Folk Songs by Nikolai Lvov and Ivan Prach.* Ann Arbor, MI: UMI Research Press, 1987.
62. Brown, Malcolm Hamrick. "Tchaikovsky and His Music in Anglo-American Criticism, 1890s–1950s." In *Tchaikovsky and His Contemporaries: A Centennial Symposium.* Ed. Alexandar Mihailovic. Westport, CT: Greenwood, 1999, pp. 61–73.
63. Budyakovskiy, A. "Russkiy natsional'nïy geniy" [Russian National Genius]. *Sovetskaya muzïka* 5–6 (1940): 8–17.
64. Bullard, Truman. "Tchaikovsky's *Eugene Onegin:* Tatiana and Lensky, the Third Couple." In *Tchaikovsky and His Contemporaries: A Centennial Symposium.* Ed. Alexandar Mihailovic. Westport, CT: Greenwood, 1999, pp. 157–65.
65. Bülow, Hans v[on]. "Musikalisches aus Italien, II." *Allgemeine Zeitung* [Augsburg], 1 June 1874, p. 2351.
66. Byalik, M. G. "Chaykovskiy i Shuman" [Tchaikovsky and Schumann]. *P. I. Chaykovskiy: Nasledie* [P. I. Tchaikovsky: Heritage] 2 (2000): 160–72.
67. Challis, Natalia. "An Appreciation of 'Eugene Onegin.'" In *Eugene Onegin: Pyotr Tchaikovsky.* English National Opera/Royal Opera Guide no. 38. Ed. Nicholas John. London: John Calder; New York: Riverrun Press, 1988, pp. 37–46.
68. Chaykovskaya, Antonina. "Vospominaniya vdovï P. I. Chaikovskago" [Recollections of P. I. Tchaikovsky's Widow]. *Russkaya muzïkal'naya gazeta* 42 (1913): cols. 915–27.
69. *Chaykovskiy i teatr* [Tchaikovsky and Theater: Articles and Materials]. Ed. A. A. Shaverdyan. Moscow: Iskusstvo, 1940.
70. Chaykovskiy, M[odest Il'ich]. "German Avgustovich Larosh. 13 maya 1845–7 oktyabrya 1904." In G. A. Larosh [Laroche], *Sobranie muzïkal'no-kriticheskikh statey* [Collection of Musico-Critical Articles], vol. 1. Moscow: Kusherov, 1913, pp. v–xxv.
71. Chaykovskiy, M[odest] I[l'ich]. "[Iz semeynïkh vospominaniy]" [From Family Recollections]. In *P. I. Chaikovskiy: Zabïtoe i novoe: Vospominaniya sovremennikov, novïe materialï i dokumentï* [P. I. Tchaikovsky: Forgotten and New: Recollections of Contemporaries, New Materials and Documents]. Comp. P. E. Vaydman and G. I. Belonovich. Moscow: Ministry of Culture of the Moscow Region and the P. I. Tchaikovsky State Home-Museum, 1995, pp. 18–63.
72. Chaykovskiy, M[odest] I[l'ich]. "M-elle Fanny Durbach." In *P. I. Chaykovskiy: Zabïtoe i novoe: Vospominaniya sovremennikov, novïe materialï i dokumentï* [P. I. Tchaikovsky: Forgotten and

New: Recollections of Contemporaries, New Materials and Documents]. Comp. P. E. Vaydman and G. I. Belonovich. Moscow: Ministry of Culture of the Moscow Region and the P. I. Tchaikovsky State Home-Museum, 1995, pp. 154–58.

73. [Chaykovskiy, Modest Il'ich]. *Pikovaya dama: Opera v 3-kh deystviyakh i 7 kartinakh (po syuzhet A. S. Pushkina): Muzïka P. Chaykovskago. Tekst Modesta Chaykovskago* [The Queen of Spades: Opera in 3 Acts and 7 Scenes (after the Story by A. S. Pushkin): Music by P. Tchaikovsky. Text by Modest Tchaikovsky] [libretto]. Moscow: Music Press of P. Jurgenson, 1890.

74. [Chaykovskiy, Modest Il'ich]. *Pikovaya dama: Opera v trekh deystviyakh i semi kartinakh: Muzïka P. Chaykovskago. Soderzhanie zaimstvovano iz povesti A. S. Pushkina. Deystvie proiskhodit v kontse XVIII v. v Peterburge* [The Queen of Spades: Opera in Three Acts and Seven Scenes: Music by P. Tchaikovsky. The Story Borrowed from the Tale by A. S. Pushkin. The Action Takes Place at the End of the 18th Century in Petersburg] [synopsis of the action of the opera]. St. Petersburg: Typographer of the Imperial St. Petersburg Theaters (Department of Crown Affairs), 1890.

75. Chaykovskiy, Modest [Il'ich]. *Zhizn' Petra Il'icha Chaykovskogo: Po dokumentam, khranyashchimsya v arkhive v Klinu* [The Life of Pyotr Ilyich Tchaikovsky: According to Documents, Preserved in the Archive at Klin], 2nd ed. 3 vols. Moscow: Jurgenson, 1901–1903.

76. Chaykovskiy, M[odest Il'ich]. *Zhizn' Petra Il'icha Chaykovskogo (Po dokumentam, khranyashchimsya v arkhive v Klinu) v 3-kh tomakh* [The Life of Pyotr Ilyich Tchaikovsky (According to Documents, Preserved in the Archive at Klin) in 3 Volumes]. Moscow: Algoritm, 1997 [= reprint of no. 75].

77. *Chaykovskiy na moskovskoy stsene; pervïe postanovki v godï ego zhizni* [Tchaikovsky on the Moscow Stage: First Performances during His Life]. Moscow: Iskusstvo, 1940.

78. [Chaykovskiy, Petr Il'ich]. *Avtografï P. I. Chaykovskogo v arkhive Doma-Muzeya v Klinu: Spravochnik* [Autographs of P. I. Tchaikovsky in the Archive of the House-Museum at Klin: A Handbook]. Comp. K. Yu Davïdova, E. M. Orlova, and G. R. Freyndling. Ed. Z. B. Korotkova-Leviton. Moscow: State Music Publisher, 1950.

79. Chaykovskiy, P[etr Il'ich]. "Betkhoven i ego vremya" [Beethoven and His Time]. *Grazhdanin* [Citizen] 7 (12 February 1873): 211–16; 8 (19 February 1873): 245–49; 11 (12 March 1873): 356–58; 12 (19 March 1873): 386–93. Reprinted in CW, *Literary Works and Correspondence,* vol. III-Ь, pp. 487–520; partly translated with commentary by Alexander Komarov in *Beethoven Journal* 26, no. 1 (Summer 2006): 12–19.

80. Chaykovskiy, P[etr] I[l'ich], and V. V. Protopopov, preparer. "Dnevnik no. 2: 1881 goda" [Diary no. 2: 1881]. In *P. I. Chaykovskiy: Zabïtoe i novoe: Issledovaniya; materialï i dokumentï k biografii; vospominaniya sovremennikov; iz fotoarkhiva* [P. I. Tchaikovsky: Forgotten and New: Researches; Materials and Documents Relating to Biography; Recollections of Contemporaries; from the Photo Archive]. Comp. P. E. Vaydman and G. I. Belonovich. Moscow: Ministry of Culture of the Moscow Region and the P. I. Tchaikovsky State Home-Museum, 2003, pp. 296–301.

81. Chaykovskiy, P[etr Il'ich]. *Dnevniki P. I. Chaykovskogo* [Diaries of P. I. Tchaikovsky]. Ed. Ip[polit] I[l'ich] Chaykovskiy. Moscow: State Publishers, Music Sector, 1923. Rpt. St. Petersburg: EGO Publishers and Reindeer Publishers, 1993.

82. Chaykovskiy, P[etr] I[l'ich]. *Kuznets Vakula: Opera* [Vakula the Smith: Opera] [edition for piano and voices]. Moscow: Jurgenson, [1876].

83. [Chaykovskiy, Petr Il'ich]. *Muzïkal'nïe fel'etonï i zametki Petra Il'icha Chaykovskago (1868–1876 g.): S prilozheniem portreta, avtobiograficheskago opisaniya puteshestviya zagranitsu v 1888 godu i predisloviya G.A. Larosha* [Musical Feuilletons and Notes of Pyotr Ilyich Tchaikovsky (1868–1876): With a Supplement of a Portrait, the Autobiographical Account of the Journey Abroad in 1888, and a Foreword by H. A. Laroche]. Moscow: Yakovlev, 1898.

84. Chaykovskiy, P[etr] I[l'ich]. *Muzïkal'no-kriticheskie stat'i* [Musico-Critical Articles]. Moscow: State Music Publisher, 1953.

85. Chaykovskiy, Petr Il'ich. *Novoe polnoe sobranie sochineniy* [New Collected Works]. Moscow and Mainz, 1993–.
86. Chaykovskiy, P[etr] I[l'ich]. *Perepiska s N. F. fon Mekk* [Correspondence with N. F. von Meck]. Ed. V. A Zhdanov and N. T. Zhegin. 3 vols. Moscow: Academia, 1934–1936.
87. Chaykovskiy, P[etr] I[l'ich]. *Perepiska s P. I. Yurgensonom* [Correspondence with P. I. Jurgenson]. Ed. V. A. Zhdanov. 2 vols. Moscow: Muzgiz, 1938; Moscow: State Music Publisher, 1952.
88. Chaykovskiy, P[yotr] I[l'ich]. *Pis'ma k rodnïm* [Letters to Relatives]: vol. 1, *1850–1879*. Ed. V. A. Zhdanov. [Moscow]: State Music Publisher, 1940.
89. Chaykovskiy, P[etr] I[l'ich]. *Polnoe sobranie sochineniy* [Collected Works]. Moscow: State Music Publisher/"Muzïka", 1940–1990 [abbreviated throughout text as CW].
90. Chaykovskiy, P[yotr] I[l'ich]. *Polnoe sobranie sochineniy: Literaturnïe proizvedeniya i perepiska* (Complete Works: Literary Works and Correspondence). 17 vols. [vols. 1 and 4 never published]. Moscow: State Music Publisher/"Muzïka", 1953–1981.
91. Coppola, Catherine. "The Elusive Fantasy: Genre, Form, and Program in Tchaikovsky's *Francesca da Rimini.*" *19th Century Music* 22, no. 2 (Fall 1998): 169–89.
92. Dammann, Susanne. "An Examination of Problem History in Tchaikovsky's Fourth Symphony." Tr. Alice Dampman Humel. In *Tchaikovsky and His World.* Ed. Leslie Kearney. Princeton, NJ: Princeton University Press, 1998, pp. 197–215.
93. Dammann, Susanne. *Gattung und Einzelwerk im symphonischen Frühwerk Čajkovskijs.* Stuttgart: M&P, 1996.
94. Dan'ko, L. G., and T[amara] Z. Skvirskaya, comps. and eds. *Peterburskiy muzïkal'nïy arkhiv: Sbornik statey i materialov* [St. Petersburg Musical Archives: Collection of Articles and Materials], vol. 1. St. Petersburg: Kanon, 1997.
95. Davïdov, Yu[riy] L['vovich]. *Zapiski o P. I. Chaykovskom* [Memoirs about P. I. Tchaikovsky]. Moscow: State Music Publisher, 1962.
96. Davïdova, K. Yu., V. V. Protopopov, and N. V. Tumanina, eds. *Muzïkal'noe nasledie Chaykovskogo: Iz istorii ego proizvedeniy* [Tchaikovsky's Musical Legacy: From the History of His Works]. Moscow: Academy of Sciences of the USSR, 1958.
97. Davïdova, K. [Yu.]. "Problemï epistolyarii" [Epistolary Problems]. *Sovetskaya muzïka* 6 (1986): 87–88.
98. Davydoff, Alexander. *Russian Sketches: Memoirs.* Tenafly, NJ: Hermitage, 1984.
99. De Lazari, K. "Vospominaniya o Petre Il'iche Chaykovskom" [Recollections of Pyotr Ilyich Tchaikovsky]. *Rossiya* [Russia] 388 (25 May 1900); 393 (31 May 1900); 405 (12 June 1900); and 441 (18 July 1900). [English translation in 306, 82–94.]
100. Delines, M. "Une institutrice française." *Le temps,* 23 November 1896, p. 2.
101. Demidov, A[leksandr Pavlovich]. *Lebedinoe ozero* [Swan Lake]. Moscow: Iskusstvo, 1985.
102. Demyanova, O. A. "50 russkikh narodnïkh pesen v obrabotke Chaykovskogo" [Tchaikovsky's Arrangement of 50 Russian Folk Songs]. *Soobshcheniya Instituta Istorii Iskusstv* [Reports of the Institute of the History of the Arts] 15 (1959): 88–116.
103. Dianova, L. "'Avtobiografiya' G. A. Larosha (materialï k biografii i portreta uchenogo)" [G. A. Laroche's "Autobiography" (Materials for the Biography and a Portrait of the Scholar)]. In *P. I. Chaykovskiy: Issledovaniya i materialï* [P. I. Tchaikovsky: Researches and Materials]. Comp. S. V. Frolov. St. Petersburg: Kanon, 1997, pp. 76–101.
104. Dickens, Charles. *Christmas Stories from "Household Words" & "All the Year Round."* London: Chapman & Hall, and Henry Frowde, n.d.
105. Dobrovol'skaya, G[alina] N[ikolaevna]. *Shchelkunchik* [The Nutcracker]. St. Petersburg: MOL, 1996.
106. Dolskaya, Olga, ed. *Vasily Titov and the Russian Baroque: Selected Choral Works.* Madison, CT: Musica Russica, 1995.
107. Dolzhanskiy, A[leksandr Naumovich]. *Simfonicheskaya muzïka Chaykovskogo: Izbrannïe proizvedeniya* [Tchaikovsky's Symphonic Music: Selected Works]. Moscow: Muzïka, 1965.

108. Dombaev, G[rigoriy Savel'evich]. *Tvorchestvo P. I. Chaykovskogo* [The Works of P. I. Tchaikovsky]. Moscow: State Music Publisher, 1958.

109. Dulova, E[katerina Nikolaevna]. *Baletï P. I. Chaykovskogo i zhanrovaya stilistika baletnoy muzïki XIX veka* [P. I. Tchaikovsky's Ballets and the Stylistics of Genre of Ballet Music of the 19th Century]. Leningrad: Leningrad State Conservatory Named for N. A. Rimsky-Korsakov, 1989.

110. Dulova, E[katerina] N[ikolaevna]. "*Spyashchaya krasavitsa* P. I. Chaykovskogo i tipologicheskie osobennosti skazochnogo baletnogo syuzheta XIX veka" [P. I. Tchaikovsky's *The Sleeping Beauty* and the Typological Particulars of the Fairytale Ballet Story in the 19th Century]. *P. I. Chaykovskiy: Nasledie* [P. I. Tchaikovsky: Heritage] 2 (2000): 125–59.

111. Dulova, E[katerina] N[ikolaevna]. "'Spyashchaya krasavitsa': Tekstologicheskie problemï izucheniya" ["The Sleeping Beauty": Textological Problems in Its Study]. In *P. I. Chaykovskiy: Zabïtoe i novoe: Issledovaniya; materialï i dokumentï k biografii; vospominaniya sovremennikov; iz fotoarkhiva* [P. I. Tchaikovsky: Forgotten and New: Researches; Materials and Documents Relating to Biography; Recollections of Contemporaries; from the Photo Archive]. Comp. P. E. Vaydman and G. I. Belonovich. Moscow: Ministry of Culture of the Moscow Region and the P. I. Tchaikovsky State Home-Museum, 2003, pp. 182–93.

112. Dulova, E[katerina] N[ikolaevna]. "'Vvidu osobenno vïdayushchikhsya kachestv muzïki . . .': Otgoloski Peterburgskoy prem'erï 'Spyashchey krasavitsï.' (Neizvestnïe arkhivnïe materialï)" ["In View of the Particularly Outstanding Qualities of the Music . . .": Echoes of the Petersburg Premiere of "The Sleeping Beauty" (Unknown Archival Materials)]. In *Chaykovskiy: Novïe dokumentï i materialï* [Tchaikovsky: New Documents and Materials]. St. Petersburg: Compozitor Publishing House, 2003, pp. 243–51.

113. Dunaeva, N. L. "Pedagog Peterburgskoy Konservatorii—V. I. Presnyakov (1877–1956)" [V. I. Presnyakov—Pedagogue of the Petersburg Conservatory]. In *Peterburgskiy muzïkal'nïy arkhiv: Sbornik statey i materialov* [St. Petersburg Musical Archives: Collection of Articles and Materials], vol. 3. Ed. F. V. Panchenko and R. Z. Skvirskaya. St. Petersburg: Scientific Music Library of the St. Petersburg State Conservatory, 1999, pp. 113–20.

114. Efimovskaya, E. "O dramaturgicheskom znachenii dueta 'Slïkhali l' vï' v opere P. I. Chaykovskogo 'Evgeniy Onegin'" [On the Dramaturgical Significance of the Duet "Did you hear" in P. I. Tchaikovsky's Opera "Eugene Onegin"]. In *P. I. Chaykovskiy: Issledovaniya i materialï: Sbornik studencheskikh rabot* [P. I. Tchaikovsky: Researches and Materials: A Collection of Student Works]. Comp. S. V. Frolov. St. Petersburg: Kanon, 1997, pp. 12–19.

115. Engel', Yu. "Rukopisi Chaikovskago" [Tchaikovsky's Manuscripts]. *Muzïkal'nïy sovremennik* [Musical Contemporary] 20 (1916): 3–5.

116. Ermolaeva, T. N. "Eskizï Simfonii 'Manfred' i Uvertyurï-fantazii 'Gamlet' Chaykovskogo kak istochnik izucheniya tvorcheskogo protsessa" [Sketches of Tchaikovsky's "Manfred" Symphony and Overture/Fantasia "Hamlet" as a Source for Studying Compositional Process]. In *Chaykovskiy: Novïe dokumentï i materialï* [Tchaikovsky: New Documents and Materials]. St. Petersburg: Compozitor Publishing House, 2003, pp. 155–60.

117. Ermolaeva, T. N. "Biblioteka Kamsko-Votkinskogo zavoda i literaturnïe interesï sem'i Chaykovskikh" [The Library of the Kamsko-Votkinsk Factory and the Literary Interests of the Tchaikovsky Family]. In *P. I. Chaykovskiy: Zabïtoe i novoe: Issledovaniya; materialï i dokumentï k biografii; vospominaniya sovremennikov; iz fotoarkhiva* [P. I. Tchaikovsky: Forgotten and New: Researches; Materials and Documents Relating to Biography; Recollections of Contemporaries; from the Photo Archive]. Comp. P. E. Vaydman and G. I. Belonovich. Moscow: Ministry of Culture of the Moscow Region and the P. I. Tchaikovsky State Home-Museum, 2003, pp. 246–52.

118. Evseev, S[ergey] V[asil'evich]. *Narodnïe pesni v obrabotke P. I. Chaykovskogo* [Folk Songs in P. I. Tchaikovsky's Arrangement]. Moscow: Muzïka, 1973.

119. Feddersen, Peter. *Tschaikowsky in Hamburg: Eine Dokumentation. Čajkovskij-Studien* 8 (2006).

120. Fédorov, V. "Čajkovskij et la France (A propos de quelque letters de Čajkovskij à Félix Mackar)." *Revue de musicologie* 54, no. 1 (1968): 16–95.
121. Findeizen, Nik[olay]. "P. I. Chaykovskiy v 1877–84 gg" [P. I. Tchaikovsky in the Years 1877–1884]. *Russkaya muzïkal'naya gazeta* 26–27 (1902): cols. 641–51; 28–29 (1902): cols. 686–88; 30–31 (1902): cols. 720–25; 34–35 (1902): cols. 779–86; 39 (1902): cols. 897–901.
122. Fitingof-Shel', B. A. [Baron]. "Al'bom avtografov, XVIII. Petr Il'ich Chaykovskiy" [Album of Autographs, XVIII: Pyotr Il'ich Tchaikovsky]. *Moskovskiya vedomosti* [Moscow News], 5 January 1899, p. 3.
123. Friskin, James. "The Text of Tchaikovsky's B flat Minor Concerto." *Music & Letters* 50 (1969): 246–51.
124. Frolov, S. V. "O kontseptsii finala Chetvertoy simfonii Chaykovskogo" [On the Conception of the Finale of Tchaikovsky's Fourth Symphony]. In *P. I. Chaykovskiy: K 100-letiyu so dnya smerti (1893–1993): Materialï nauchnoy konferentsii* [P. I. Tchaikovsky: On the Hundredth Anniversary of His Death (1893–1993): Materials of a Scholarly Conference]. Moscow: Moscow State Conservatory Named for P. I. Tchaikovsky, 1995, pp. 64–73.
125. Frolov, S. V., comp. *P. I. Chaykovskiy: Issledovaniya i materialï* [P. I. Tchaikovsky: Researches and Materials]. St. Petersburg: Kanon, 1997.
126. Frolov, S. V. "Traurno-Elegicheskiy intonatsionnïy kompleks v pervoy kartine operï 'Evgeniy Onegin'" [The Funereal-Elegiac Intonational Complex in the First Scene of "Evgeniy Onegin"]. In *P. I. Chaykovskiy: Zabïtoe i novoe: Issledovaniya; materialï i dokumentï k biografii; vospominaniya sovremennikov; iz fotoarkhiva* [P. I. Tchaikovsky: Forgotten and New: Researches; Materials and Documents Relating to Biography; Recollections of Contemporaries; from the Photo Archive]. Comp. P. E. Vaydman and G. I. Belonovich. Moscow: Ministry of Culture of the Moscow Region and the P. I. Tchaikovsky State Home-Museum, 2003, pp. 114–25.
127. Frolova, M. "Chaykovskiy i Shuman" [Tchaikovsky and Schumann]. In *Chaykovskiy: Voprosï istorii i teorii* [Tchaikovsky: Questions of History and Theory]. Moscow: Moscow State Conservatory Named for P. I. Tchaikovsky, 1991, pp. 54–64.
128. Frumkis, T. "Kantata P. I. Chaykovskogo 'Moskva': (Ne)sluchaynïy tekst v (ne)sluchaynom kontekste" [P. I. Tchaikovsky's Cantata "Moscow": The (Non-)accidental Text in Its (Non-)accidental Context]. In *Moskva i moskovskiy tekst russkoy kul'turï* [Moscow and the Moscow Text of Russian Culture]. Ed. G. S. Knabe. Moscow: Russian State Institute for the Humanities, 1998, pp. 119–36.
129. Frumkis, Tat'jana. "Zu deutschen Vorbildern von Čajkovskijs Harmonielehre." *Čajkovskij-Studien* 1 (1995): 111–26.
130. Gaevskiy, E. I. "P. I. Chaykovskiy i Master S. Penn" [P. I. Tchaikovsky and Master S. Penn]. In *P. I. Chaykovskiy i Ural* [P. I. Tchaikovsky and the Urals]. Comp. B. Ya. Anshakov and P. E. Vaydman. Izhevsk: Udmurtiya, 1983, pp. 33–39.
131. Gangelin, Aleksandr. *Chetvertaya simfoniya Chaykovskago v stikhakh* [The Fourth Symphony of Tchaikovsky in Verses]. St. Petersburg: Sheval'e, 1911.
132. Garden, Edward. *Tchaikovsky.* London: Dent, and New York: Octagon, 1973.
133. Genika, Rost[islav Vladimirovich]. "Fortepiannoe tvorchestvo P. I. Chaykovskovo" [P. I. Tchaikovsky's Piano Music]. *Russkaya muzïkal'naya gazeta* 1 (1908): cols. 9–15; 2 (1908): cols. 33–40; 5 (1908): cols. 120–25; 7 (1908): cols. 187–92; 11 (1908): cols. 257–60; 12 (1908): cols. 289–94; 13 (1908): cols. 329–33; 43 (1908): cols. 935–44; 44 (1908): cols. 961–67; 45 (1908): cols. 995–96; 47 (1908): cols. 1049–55; 50 (1908): cols. 1174–77.
134. Genika, Rost[islav Vladimirovich]. "Iz konservatorskikh vospominaniy (1871–79) (N. G. Rubinshteyn i Chaykovskiy)" [From Recollections of the Conservatory (1871–1879) (N. G. Rubinstein and Tchaikovsky)]. *Russkaya muzïkal'naya gazeta* 36–37 (1916): cols. 637–50; 40 (1916): cols. 690–95; 42 (1916): cols. 756–62; 43 (1916): cols. 799–807; 44 (1916): cols. 809–25; 47 (1916): cols. 889–95; 49 (1916): cols. 1137–45; 51–52 (1916): cols. 938–48. Partial reprint in no. 316, 71–76.

135. Gerashko, L.V. "Avtografï Chaykovskogo v sobranii Pushkinskogo doma" [Tchaikovsky Autographs in the Collection of Pushkin House]. In *Chaykovskiy: Novïe dokumentï i materialï* [Tchaikovsky: New Documents and Materials]. St. Petersburg: Compozitor Publishing House, 2003, pp. 66–80.
136. Gershovskiy, E. "Chaykovskiy v Departamente Yustitsii" [Tchaikovsky in the Department of Justice]. *Sovetskaya muzïka* 1 (1959): 83–88.
137. Glaab, Wolfgang. "Čajkovskijs vier Tage in Frankfurt am Main. Eine Station seiner Konzertreise 1889." *Tschaikowsky-Gesellschaft Mitteilungen* 9 (2002): 34–75.
138. Glebov, Igor' [= Boris Asaf'ev]. *Anton Grigor'evich Rubinshteyn v ego muzïkal'noy deyatel'nosti i otzïvakh sovremennikov 1829–1929)* [Anton Grigoryevich Rubinstein in His Musical Activity and the Reports of Contemporaries (1829–1929)]. Moscow: State Pusblisher, Music Sector, 1929.
139. Glebov, Igor' [= Boris Asaf'ev]. *Chaykovskiy* [on the inner title page: *Instrumental'noe tvorchestvo Chaykovskogo* (Tchaikovsky's Instrumental Compositions)]. St. Petersburg: State Philharmonia, 1922.
140. Glebov, Igor' [= Boris Asaf'ev]. *Chaykovskiy: Opït kharakteristiki* [Tchaikovsky: An Attempt at Characteristics]. Petersburg: Svetozar, 1923.
141. Glebov, Igor' [= Boris Asaf'ev], ed. *Chaykovskiy: Vospominaniya i pis'ma* [Tchaikovsky: Recollections and Letters]. Leningrad: State Academic Philharmonia, 1924.
142. Glebov, Igor' [= Boris Asaf'ev], ed. *Proshloe russkoy muzïki: Materialï i issledovaniya* [The Past of Russian Music: Materials and Research]: vol. 1, *P. I. Tchaikovsky.* Petrograd: Ogni, 1920.
143. Glumov, A[leksandr Nikolaevich]. *Muzïka v russkom dramaticheskom teatre* [Music in Russian Dramatic Theater]. Moscow: State Music Publisher, 1955.
144. Glushchenko, G[eorgiy Semenovich]. *N. D. Kashkin.* Moscow: Muzïka, 1974.
145. "Golosa iz Klinskogo doma: Pis'ma, dokumentï" [Voices from the House at Klin: Letters, Documents]. *Sovetskaya muzïka* 6 (1990): 91–98 [reminiscences of Tchaikovsky].
146. Golovinskiy, G. "Chaykovskiy—muzïkal'nïy kritik" [Tchaikovsky as Music Critic]. *Sovetskaya muzïka* 8 (1950): 81–86.
147. Gorodilina, V. B. "Domashnïe predstavleniya v sem'e Chaykovskikh" [Domestic Performances in the Tchaikovsky Family]. In *Teatr v zhizni i tvorchestve P. I. Chaykovskogo* [Theater in the Life and Work of P. I. Tchaikovsky]. Ed. N. N. Sin'kovskaya. Izhevsk: Udmurtiya, 1985, pp. 12–16.
148. Gorodilina, V. B. "Posvyashchaetsya Anastasii Petrovoy" [Dedicated to Anastasia Petrova]. In *P. I. Chaykovskiy i Ural* [P. I. Tchaikovsky and the Urals]. Ed. Boris Yakovlevich Anshakov and Polina Efimovna Vaydman. Izhevsk: Udmurtiya, 1983, pp. 39–44.
149. Gozenpud, A[bram Akimovich]. *Russkiy opernïy teatr XIX veka 1873–1889* [Russian Opera Theater of the 19th Century 1873–1889]. Leningrad: Muzïka, 1973.
150. Grönke, Kadja. "Čajkovskij und die Brüder Anton und Nikolaj Rubinštejn." *Tschaikowsky-Gesellschaft Mitteilungen* 13 (2006): 17–36.
151. Grönke, Kadja. "Čajkovskijs Oper *Čarodejka—Die Bezaubernde.*" *Tschaikowsky-Gesellschaft Mitteilungen* 13 (2006): 144–54.
152. Grönke, Kadja. "Čajkovskijs Einakter *Iolanta:* Verwandlung durch Liebe." *Tschaikowsky-Gesellschaft Mitteilungen* 5 (March 1998): 17–25.
153. Grönke, Kadja. *Frauenschicksale in Čajkovskijs Puškin-Opern: Aspekte einer Werke-Einheit. Čajkovskij-Studien* 5 (2002).
154. Grönke, Kadia, comp. "Genealogische Tafeln Čajkovskij/Assier, Miljukov, Davydov, fon-Mekk." *Čajkovskij-Studien* 3 (1998): 367–78.
155. Grönke, Kadja. "Mehr Schatten als Licht: Čajkovskij und seine *16 Lieder für Kinder* op. 54 (1883)." *Tschaikowsky-Gesellschaft Mitteilungen* 10 (2003): 127–53.
156. Grönke, Kadja. "On the Role of Gremin: Tchaikovsky's *Eugene Onegin.*" Tr. Alice Dampman Humel. In *Tchaikovsky and His World.* Ed. Leslie Kearney. Princeton, NJ: Princeton University Press, 1998, pp. 220–33.

157. Grönke, Kadja. "'Und ich sagte dir nichts'? Čajkovskijs *Sechs Romanzen* op. 73 (1893)." *Tschaikowsky-Gesellschaft Mitteilungen* 12 (2005): 191–212.
158. Gusman, Boris. "Chaykovskiy v Moskve 1865–1877" [Tchaikovsky in Moscow 1865–1877]. *Sovetskaya muzïka* 5 (1939): 48–65.
159. Gusman, B[oris]. "Etyud k biografii P. I. Chaykovskogo" [Study in P. I. Tchaikovsky's Biography]. *Sovetskaya muzïka* 1 (1939): 60–71.
160. Holden, Anthony. "Čajkovskij's Death: Cholera or Suicide?" *Čajkovskij-Studien* 1 (1995): 141–53.
161. Holden, Anthony. *Tchaikovsky: A Biography*. New York: Random House, 1995.
162. *Hymnology: Papers of [a] Musicological Congress, "Rev. Dimitry Razumovsky's ad memoriam" (on the Occasion of the 130th Anniversary of the Moscow Conservatory) September 3–8, 1996*. 2 vols. Moscow: Moscow State Conservatory/Kompozitor Publishing House, 2000.
163. [Hyperbole]. "Opera 'Giperbola': Dva pis'ma P. I. Chaykovskogo" [The Opera "Hyperbole": Two Letters of P. I. Tchaikovsky]. *Vechernyaya Moskva* [Evening Moscow], 22 August 1936, p. 3.
164. *Ilya Petrovich Chaykovskiy: Zhizn' i deyatel'nost': Materialï k 180-letiyu so dnya rozhdeniya* [Ilya Petrovich Tchaikovsky: Life and Activity: Materials Marking the 180th Anniversary of His Birth]. Izhevsk: Udmurtiya, 1976.
165. Ippolitov-Ivanov, M[ikhail] M[ikhaylovich]. *50 let russkoy muzïki v moikh vospominaniyakh* [50 Years of Russian Music in My Recollections]. Moscow: State Music Publisher, 1934.
166. Ito, Keiko. "Der liturgische Gesang in Čajkovskijs Festouvertüre '1812' op. 49." *Tschaikowsky-Gesellschaft Mitteilungen* 10 (2003): 154–60.
167. Ivanchenko, G. I. "Traditsii A. S. Pushkina v opere P. I. Chaykovskogo 'Pikovaya dama'" [A. S. Pushkin's Traditions in P. I. Tchaikovsky's Opera "The Queen of Spades"]. In *P. I. Chaykovskiy i russkaya literatura* [P. I. Tchaikovsky and Russian Literature]. Ed. T. A. Pozdeeva. Izhevsk: Udmurtiya, 1980, pp. 144–54.
168. "Iz nasledstva P. I. Chaikovskago" [From P. I. Tchaikovsky's Legacy]. *Novoe vremya* [New Time], 20 March 1916, p. 6.
169. Jackson, Timothy L. "Aspects of Sexuality and Structure in the Later Symphonies of Tchaikovsky." *Music Analysis* 14, no. 1 (March 1995): 3–25.
170. Jackson, Timothy L. *Tchaikovsky, Symphony no. 6 (Pathétique)*. Cambridge: Cambridge University Press, 1999.
171. Janés, Alfonsina. "*Die Jungfrau von Orleans*: Čajkovskij und Schiller." *Tschaikowsky-Gesellschaft Mitteilungen* 13 (2006): 131–43.
172. Kalinichenko. N. N. "Traditsii zhanra 'zhivïkh kartin' v tvorchestve Chaykovskogo" [Traditions of the Genre of 'Tableaux Vivants' in Tchaikovsky's Work]. In *P. I. Chaykovskiy: Zabïtoe i novoe: Issledovaniya; materialï i dokumentï k biografii; vospominaniya sovremennikov; iz fotoarkhiva* [P. I. Tchaikovsky: Forgotten and New: Researches; Materials and Documents Relating to Biography; Recollections of Contemporaries; from the Photo Archive]. Comp. P. E. Vaydman and G. I. Belonovich. Moscow: Ministry of Culture of the Moscow Region and the P. I. Tchaikovsky State Home-Museum, 2003, pp. 206–8.
173. Karlinsky, Simon. "Should We Retire Tchaikovsky?" *Christopher Street* 11, no. 3 [Issue 123], pp. 16–21.
174. Kashkin, N[ikolay Dmitrievich]. "Iolanta: Opera v odnom deistvii: Tekst M. I. Chaykovskago. Muz. P. I. Chaykovskago" [Iolanthe: Opera in One Act: Text by M. I. Tchaikovsky. Mus[ic] by P. I. Tchaikovsky]. *Teatral'nïy, muzykal'nïy i khudozhestvennïy zhurnal "Artist"* [Theatrical, Musical and Artistic Journal "Artist"] 32 (December 1893): 110–14.
175. Kashkin, N[ikolay Dmitrievich]. "Iz vospominaniy o P. I. Chaykovskom" [From Recollections about P. I. Tchaikovsky]. In *Proshloe russkoy muzïki: Materialï i issledovaniya I: P. I. Chaykovskiy* [The Past of Russian Music: Materials and Researches I: P. I. Tchaikovsky]. Ed. Boris Asaf'ev. St. Petersburg: Ogni, 1920, pp. 99–132.

176. Kashkin, N[ikolay Dmitrievich]. "Muzïkal'noe obozrenie" [Music Review (of the 1889–1890 concert season in Moscow)]. *Russkoe obozrenie* [Russian Review] 2 (April 1890): 800–809.
177. Kashkin, N[ikolay Dmitrievich]. "Muzïkal'noe obozrenie" [Music Review (of the first performance of *The Queen of Spades*)]. *Russkoe obozrenie* [Russian Review] 2 (December 1890): 780–93.
178. Kashkin, N. D., and G. A. Larosh [Laroche]. *Na pamyat' o P. I. Chaykovskom: Stat'i G. A. Larosha i N. D. Kashkina s portretom* [In Memory of P. I. Tchaikovsky: Articles by G. A. Laroche and N. D. Kashkin; with a Photograph]. Moscow: Elizaveta Gerbek, 1894.
179. Kashkin, N[ikolay Dmitrievich]. "Nikolay Grigor'evich Rubinshteyn i ego rol' v muzïkal'nom razvitii Moskvï (Muzïkal'no-istoricheskie ocherki)" [Nikolay Grigorievich Rubinstein and His Role in Moscow's Musical Development. (Musico-Historical Essays)]. *Moskovskie vedomosti* [Moscow News], 15 November 1898; 9 December 1898. Continued in no. 185, below.
180. K[ashkin] N[ikolay Dmitrievich]. "Nikolay Grigor'evich Rubinstein (1881–11 March 1906)." *Moskovskie vedomosti* [Moscow News], 10 March 1906, p. 3.
181. Kashkin, N[ikolay Dmitrievich]. "P. I. Chaykovskiy i ego biografiya" [P. I. Tchaikovsky and His Biography]. *Moskovskiya vedomosti* [Moscow News], 11 January 1902; 14 May 1902; 11 June 1902; 20 August 1902; 16 March 1903; 27 June 1903.
182. K[ashk]in, N[ikolay Dmitrievch]. "Pervoe predstavlenie operï P. I. Chaykovskago 'Iolanta' na stsene Mariinskago teatra, v Peterburge, 6-go dekabrya 1892 g" [The First Performance of P. I. Tchaikovsky's Opera "Iolanthe" on the Stage of the Maryinsky Theater in St. Petersburg, 6 December 1892]. *Russkiya vedomosti* [Russian News], 12 December 1892, p. 3.
183. Kashkin, N[ikolay Dmitrievich]. "Pikovaya dama: Opera v trekh deystviyakh i semi kartinakh: Syuzhet zaimstvovan iz povesti Pushkina. Muzïka P. I. Chaykovskago. Tekst M. I. Chaykovskago" [The Queen of Spades: Opera in Three Acts and Seven Scenes: Story Borrowed from the Story by Pushkin. Music by P. I. Tchaikovsky. Text by M. I. Tchaikovsky]. *Artist* 12 (January 1891): 171–78.
184. Kashkin, N[ikolay Dmitrievich]. "Vospominaniya o G. A. Laroshe" [Recollections of G. A. Laroche]. In G. A. Larosh [Laroche], *Sobranie muzïkal'no-kriticheskikh statey* [Collection of Musico-Critical Articles], vol. 1. Moscow: Kushnerev, 1913, pp. xxvi–xlii.
185. Kashkin, N[ikolay Dmitrievich]. "Vospominaniya o N. G. Rubinshteyne" [Recollections of N. G. Rubinstein]. *Moskovskiya vedomosti* [Moscow News], 22 January 1899; 12 February 1899; 18 June 1899; 23 June 1899; 20 July 1899; 6 August 1899; 18 August 1899; 25 August 1899; 1 October 1899; 6 June 1900; 26 July 1900; 16 August 1900.
186. Kashkin, N[ikolay Dmitrievich]. "Vospominaniya o Nikolae Grigor'eviche Rubinshteyne" [Recollections of Nikolay Grigor'evich Rubinstein]. *Russkoe obozrenie* [Russian Review] 47 (September–October 1897): 151–69; 49 (January–February 1898): 328–38.
187. Kashkin, N[ikolay Dmitrievich]. *Vospominaniya o P. I. Chaykovskom* [Recollections of P. I. Tchaikovsky]. Moscow: Jurgenson, 1896.
188. Kashkin, N[ikolay Dmitrievich]. "Ya. P. Polonskiy i P. I. Chaykovskiy kak avtorï odnogo obshchago proizvedeniya" [Ya. P. Polonsky and P. I. Tchaikovsky as Authors of a Single Joint Work]. *Moskovskiya vedomosti* [Moscow News], 23 November 1898.
189. Kearney, Leslie, ed. *Tchaikovsky and His World.* Princeton, NJ: Princeton University Press, 1998.
190. Kearney, Leslie. "Tchaikovsky Androgyne: *The Maid of Orleans.*" In *Tchaikovsky and His World.* Ed. Leslie Kearney. Princeton, NJ: Princeton University Press, 1998, pp. 239–76.
191. Keldïsh, Yu[riy] V., ed. *E. F. Napravnik: Avtobiograficheskie, tvorcheskie materialï, dokumentï, pis'ma* [E. F. Napravnik: Autobiographical, Creative Materials, Documents, Letters]. Leningrad: State Music Publisher, 1959.

192. Keldïsh, Yuriy. "Simfonism Chaykovskogo i evolyutsiya simfonicheskogo mïshleniya v XIX veke" [Tchaikovsky's Symphonism and the Evolution of Symphonic Thought in the 19th Century]. *Sovetskaya muzïka* 12 (1990): 92–101.
193. Keldïsh, Yu[riy] V. "Uvertyura-fantaziya 'Romeo i Dzhul'etta' i ee rol' v stanovlenii simfonizma Chaykovskogo" [The Overture/Fantasia "Romeo and Juliet" and Its Role in the Formation of Tchaikovsky's Symphonism]. In *P. I. Chaikovskiy: K 100-letiyu so dnya smerti (1893–1993): Materialï nauchnoy konferentsii* [P. I. Tchaikovsky: On the Hundredth Anniversary of His Death (1893–1993): Materials of a Scholarly Conference]. Moscow: Moscow State Conservatory Named for P. I. Tchaikovsky, 1995, pp. 24–30.
194. Kenfield, Warren Goeffrey. *The Programme for Tchaikovsky's Fifth Symphony: "Elegy on the Death of a Brother in Battle."* Norfolk, CT: Egler, 1970.
195. Khokhlov, Yu[riy Nikolaevich]. *Orkestrovïe syuitï Chaykovskogo* [Tchaikovsky's Orchestral Suites]. Moscow: State Music Publisher, 1961.
196. Khokhlov, Yuriy [Nikolaevich]. "Pyata Betkhovena i Chetvertaya Chaykovskovo" [Beethoven's Fifth and Tchaikovsky's Fourth]. *Muzïkal'naya akademiya* 4 (1993): 211–12.
197. Kindermann, Jürgen. "Unterhaltungs und Gebrauchsmusik in 19. Jahrhundert. Ein musikwissenschaftliches Symposium in Colberg." *Die Musikforschung* 19 (1966): 176–79.
198. Kiselev, V. "Poslednyaya instrumentovka" [The Last Orchestration]. *Sovetskaya muzïka* 11 (1968): 116–17.
199. Klimenko, I[van] A[leksandrovich]. *Moi vospominaniya o Petre Il'iche Chaikovskom* [My Recollections of P. I. Tchaikovsky]. Ryazan: Lyubomudrov, 1908.
200. Klimenko, I[van] A[leksandrovich]. "Moi vospominaniya o Petre Il'iche Chaykovskom." Publikatsiya P. E. Vaydman [My Recollections of P. I. Tchaikovsky. Publication of P. E. Vaydman]. In *P. I. Chaikovskiy: Zabïtoe i novoe: Vospominaniya sovremennikov, novïe materialï i dokumentï* [P. I. Tchaikovsky: Forgotten and New: Recollections of Contemporaries, New Materials and Documents]. Comp. P. E. Vaydman and G. I. Belonovich. Moscow: Ministry of Culture of the Moscow Region and the P. I. Tchaikovsky State Home-Museum, 1995, pp. 64–92.
201. Klimenko, T[at'yana] I[vanovna]. "Vospominaniya ob ottse" [Recollections of My Father]. In *P. I. Chaykovskiy: Zabïtoe i novoe: Vospominaniya sovremennikov, novïe materialï i dokumentï* [P. I. Tchaikovsky: Forgotten and New: Recollections of Contemporaries, New Materials and Documents]. Comp. P. E. Vaydman and G. I. Belonovich. Moscow: Ministry of Culture of the Moscow Region and the P. I. Tchaikovsky State Home-Museum, 1995, pp. 159–60.
202. Klimovitskiy, A[rkadiy] I. "Dirizherskie pometï Chaykovskogo v partiture devyatoy simfonii Betkhovena" [Tchaikovsky's Conductor's Notes in the Score of Beethoven's Ninth Symphony]. In *Chaykovskiy: Novïe dokumentï i materialï* [Tchaikovsky: New Documents and Materials]. St. Petersburg: Compozitor Publishing House, 2003, pp. 170–90.
203. Klimovitskiy, Arkadiy. "Neizvestnïe stranitsï epistolyariya Chaykovskogo" [Unknown Pages from Tchaikovsky's Letters]. *Sovetskaya muzïka* 6 (1990): 99–103.
204. Klimovitskiy, A[rkadiy] I. "Nekotorïe kul'turno-istoricheskie paradoksï bïtovaniya tvorcheskogo naslediya Chaykovskogo v Rossii (K probleme: Chaykovskiy na poroge XX veka)" [Some Cultural-Historical Paradoxes of the State of Tchaikovsky's Heritage in Russia (On the Problem: Tchaikovsky on the Threshold of the 20th Century)]. *P. I. Chaykovskiy: Nasledie* [P. I. Tchaikovsky: Heritage] 2 (2000): 6–48.
205. Klimovitskiy, Arkadiy. "Otzvuki russkogo sentimentalizma v pushkinskikh operakh Chaykovskogo" [Echos of Russian Sentimentalism in Tchaikovsky's Pushkin Operas]. *Muzïkal'naya akademiya* 1 (1995): 167–78.
206. Klimovitskiy, A[rkadiy] I. "'Pikovaya dama' Chaykovskogo: kul'turnïe pamyat' i kul'turnie predchuvstviya" [Tchaikovsky's "The Queen of Spades": Cultural Memory and Cultural Premonition]. In *Russia–Europe: Contacts between Musical Cultures.* Ed. Elena Khodorkovskaia. St. Petersburg, 1994, pp. 221–74.

207. Klimovitsky [= Klimovitskiy], Arkadii. "Tchaikovsky and the Russian 'Silver Age.'" Tr. Alice Dampman Humel. In *Tchaikovsky and His World*. Ed. Leslie Kearney. Princeton, NJ: Princeton University Press, 1998, 319–30.

208. Klimovitskiy, A[rkadiy]. "Zametki o shestoy simfonii Chaykovskogo (K probleme: Chaykovskiy na poroge XX veka)" [Notes on Tchaikovsky's Sixth Symphony (On the Problem: Tchaikovsky at the Threshold of the Twentieth Century)]. In *Problemï muzïkal'nogo romantisma* [Problems of Musical Romanticism]. Ed. A. L. Porfir'eva. Leningrad: Leningrad State Institute of Theater, Music and Cinematography Named for N. K. Cherkasov, 1987, pp. 109–29.

209. Kluge, Rolf-Dieter. "Čajkovskij und die literarische Kultur Rußlands." *Čajkovskij-Studien* 1 (1995): 165–75.

210. Kogan, Marina. "Rodoslovnaya" [Genealogy]. *Sovetskaya muzïka* 6 (1990): 83–90.

211. Kohlhase, Thomas, comp. *"An Tschaikowsky scheiden sich die Geister": Textzeugnisse der Čajkovskij-Rezeption 1866–2004*. *Čajkovskij-Studien* 10 (2006).

212. Kohlhase, Thomas. "Autobiographie in Tönen? Über Čajkovskijs späte Sinfonien." *Tschaikowsky-Gesellschaft Mitteilungen* 15 (2008): 76–90.

213. Kohlhase, Thomas. "Bisher unbekannte Briefe P. I. Čajkovskijs." *Tschaikowsky-Gesellschaft Mitteilungen* 7 (2000): 12–41.

214. Kohlhase, Thomas. "Čajkovskij als Dirigent." *Tschaikowsky-Gesellschaft Mitteilungen* 7 (2000): 62–90.

215. Kohlhase, Thomas, comp. "Čajkovskij und die Internationale Ausstellung für Musik- und Theaterwesen Wien 1892—samt Auszügen aus ihrem 'Russland'-Katalog." *Tschaikowsky-Gesellschaft Mitteilungen* 14 (2007): 79–97.

216. K[ohlhase], Th[omas]. "Čajkovskij und die *Union Internationale des Compositeurs*—ein bisher unbekannter Brief Čajkovskijs von 1884." *Tschaikowsky-Gesellschaft Mitteilungen* 4 (March 1997): 8–18.

217. Kohlhase, Thomas. "Čajkovskijs Bearbeitungen eigener Werke: Ein Überblick." *Tschaikowsky-Gesellschaft Mitteilungen* 10 (2003): 170–222.

218. Kohlhase, Thomas. "Čajkovskijs Briefwechsel mit Dr. Friedrich Sieger (Direktor der Frankfurter Museumsgesellschaft) und ein bisher unbekannter Brief vom 6./18. Januar 1891." *Tschaikowsky-Gesellschaft Mitteilungen* 5 (March 1998): 4–16.

219. Kohlhase, Thomas. "Čajkovskijs Kammermusik." *Tschaikowsky-Gesellschaft Mitteilungen* 12 (2005): 3–70.

220. Kohlhase, Thomas. "Čajkovskijs nicht erhaltener Trauermarsch über Motive seiner Oper 'Opričnik'—eine von drei Auftragsarbeiten für Nadežda F. fon Mekk aus dem Jahre 1877." *Tschaikowsky-Gesellschaft Mitteilungen* 10 (2003): 161–69.

221. Kohlhase, Thomas, comp. "Čajkovskijs Wagner-Rezeption: Daten und Texte." *Čajkovskiy-Studien* 3 (1998): 299–325.

222. Kohlhase, Thomas. "'Daran hindert mich mein Gesundheitszustand': Ein bisher unbekannter Brief Čajkovskijs, San Remo, 23. XII. 1877/4. I. 1878, mit seiner Absage an den russischen Generalkonsul in Paris, als russischer Musikdelegierter bei der Pariser Weltausstellung 1878 zu fungieren." *Tschaikowsky-Gesellschaft Mitteilungen* 11 (2004): 19–34.

223. Kohlhase, Thomas, comp. "'Daß ich mein Leben der Musik geweiht habe, verdanke ich Mozart': Dokumente zu Čajkovskijs Mozart-Rezeption." *Tschaikowsky-Gesellschaft Mitteilungen* 12 (2005): 85–122.

224. Kohlhase, Thomas, ed. and commentator, and Peter Feddersen, collaborator. "Der Briefwechsel des Hamburger Verlegers Daniel Rahter mit P. I. Čajkovskij 1887–1891." *Tschaikowsky-Gesellschaft Mitteilungen* 8 (2001): 47–122.

225. Kohlhase, Thomas, comp. "Der 'Gott Zebaoth' der Musik: Dokumente zu Čajkovskijs Beethoven-Rezeption." *Tschaikowsky-Gesellschaft Mitteilungen* 12 (2005): 123–46.

226. Kohlhase, Thomas. "Editionsprobleme der *Neuen Čajkovskij-Gesamtausgabe* am Beispiel der 6. Sinfonie." *Čajkovskij-Studien* 1 (1995): 177–86.

227. Kohlhase, Thomas. "Kritischer Bericht zu Band 69b der Neuen Čajkovskij-Gesamtausgabe (NČE): *Grand Sonate* op. 37 und *Kinderalbum* op. 39." *Čajkovskij-Studien* 3 (1998): 439–533.
228. K[ohlhase], Th[omas]. "Nachtrag zu: Fanny Durbachs Briefe an Čajkovskij von 1892 und 1893 und sein Besuch bei ihr in Montbéliard." *Tschaikowsky-Gesellschaft Mitteilungen* 12 (2005): 213–18.
229. Kohlhase, Thomas, comp. "Neue Čajkovskij-Funde." *Tschaikowsky-Gesellschaft Mitteilungen* 6 (March 1999): 2–16.
230. Kohlhase, Thomas, comp. "'Paris vaut bien une messe!' Bisher unbekannte Briefe, Notenautogaphe und andere Čajkovskij-Funde." *Čajkovskij-Studien* 3 (1998): 163–298.
231. [Kohlhase, T.]. *Pjotr Iljitsch Tschaikowsky Sinfonie Nr. 6. Einführung und Analyse von Thomas Kohlhase* [Goldman Schott miniature score]. Munich: Wilhelm Goldmann; Mainz: B. Schott's Söhne, 1983.
232. Kohlhase, Thomas. "'Que Dieu soit béni de ce que je puis encore vous aimer comme autrefois': Fanny Durbachs Briefe an Čajkovskij von 1892 und 1893 und sein Besuch bei ihr in Montbéliard." *Tschaikowsky-Gesellschaft Mitteilungen* 11 (2004): 93–141.
233. Kohlhase, Thomas, comp. "Schlagworte, Tendenzen und Texte zur frühen Čajkovskij-Rezeption in Deutschland und Österreich." *Čajkovskij-Studien* 3 (1998): 327–54.
234. Kohlhase, Thomas, preparer. "'Sind Sie einverstanden?' Ein bisher unbekannter Brief Čajikovskijs an die Pianisten Sophie Menter, Klin, 19.[/31.] VII. [1893]." *Tschaikowsky-Gesellschaft Mitteilungen* 11 (2004): 50–54.
235. Kohlhase, Thomas, preparer. "Zwei neu aufgetauchte Briefe Čajkovskijs von 1876/77 und 1879." *Tschaikowsky-Gesellschaft Mitteilungen* 15 (2008): 3–19.
236. Komarov, A[lekxandr] V[iktorovich]. "'Betkhoven i ego vremya': Istoriya odnogo unikal'nogo literaturnogo sochineniya Chaykovskogo" ["Beethoven and His Time": The History of One Unique Literary Work by Tchaikovsky]. In *P. I. Chaykovskiy: Zabïtoe i novoe: Issledovaniya; materialï i dokumentï k biografii; vospominaniya sovremennikov; iz fotoarkhiva* [P. I. Tchaikovsky: Forgotten and New: Researches; Materials and Documents Relating to Biography; Recollections of Contemporaries; from the Photo Archive]. Comp. P. E. Vaydman and G. I. Belonovich. Moscow: Ministry of Culture of the Moscow Region and the P. I. Tchaikovsky State Home-Museum, 2003, pp. 150–61.
237. Komarov, Alexander [= Komarov, Aleksandr Viktorovich]. "Chaykovskiy, Dostoevskii, and Beethoven: Chaykovskiy's 1873 Russian Edition of Excerpts from Thayer's *Ludwig van Beethoven's Leben.*" *Beethoven Journal* 26, no. 1 (Summer 2006): 12–19.
238. Komarov, A[leksandr] V[iktorovich]. "Rukopisnïe partii sochineniy Chaykovskogo kak istochniki teksta i materialï k istorii proizvedeniy" [Manuscript (Orchestral): Parts of Tchaikovsky's Works as Sources of the Text and Materials for the History of the Works]. In *Chaykovskiy: Novïe dokumentï i materialï* [Tchaikovsky: New Documents and Materials]. St. Petersburg: Compozitor Publishing House, 2003, pp. 124–41.
239. Komarov, Aleksandr Viktorovich. *Vosstanovlenie proizvedeniy P. I. Chaykovskogo v istorii russkoy muzïkal'noy tekstologii* . . . [The Restoration of P. I. Tchaikovsky's Works in the History of Russian Musical Textology . . .]. Moscow, 2007.
240. Konstantinova, M[arina Evgen'evna]. *Spyashchaya krasavitsa* [The Sleeping Beauty]. Moscow: Iskusstvo, 1990.
241. Konyus, Yu[liy] E[duardovich]. "Vospominaniya o moikh vstrechakh s Petrom Il'ichom i o prebïvanii moem v Klinu" [Recollections of My Meetings with Pyotr Il'ich, and about My Visit to Klin]. In *P. I. Chaykovskiy: Zabïtoe i novoe: Issledovaniya; materialï i dokumentï k biografii; vospominaniya sovremennikov; iz fotoarkhiva* [P. I. Tchaikovsky: Forgotten and New: Researches; Materials and Documents Relating to Biography; Recollections of Contemporaries; from the Photo Archive]. Comp. P. E. Vaydman and G. I. Belonovich. Moscow: Ministry of Culture of the Moscow Region and the P. I. Tchaikovsky State Home-Museum, 2003, pp. 363–73.

242. Korabel'nikova, L. "Pis'ma k Chaykovskom: Dialog s epokhoy" [Letters to Tchaikovsky: Dialogue with the Epoch]. *Sovetskaya muzïka* 6 (1990): 103–14.

243. *K. P. Pobedonostsev i ego korrespondentï: Pis'ma i zapiski* [K. P. Pobedonostsev and His Correspondents: Letters and Notes]. Moscow: Gosudarstvennoe Izdatel'stvo, 1923.

244. K. R. [= Konstantin Romanov]. *Izbrannaya perepiska* [Selected Correspondence]. Comp. L. I. Kuz'mina. St. Petersburg: Russian Academy of Sciences, Institute of Russian Literature (Pushkin House), 1999.

245. Krasinskaya, L[iya Emmanuilovna]. *Opernaya melodika P. I. Chaykovskovo: K voprosu o vzaimodeystvii melodii i rechevoy intonatsii: Isslevovanie* [P. I. Tchaikovsky's Opera Melodics: On the Question of the Interrelation of Melody and Speech Intonation: A Study]. Leningrad: Muzïka, 1986.

246. Kraus, Joseph C. "Analysis and Influence: A Comparison of Rhythmic Structures in the Instrumental Music of Schumann and Tchaikovsky." In *Tchaikovsky and His Contemporaries: A Centennial Symposium*. Ed. Alexandar Mihailovic. Westport, CT: Greenwood, 1999, pp. 117–27.

247. Kraus, Joseph C. "Tchaikovsky." In *The Nineteenth-Century Symphony*. Ed. D. Kern Holoman. New York: Schirmer, 1997, pp. 299–326.

248. Kremlev, Yu. "Printsipï simfonicheskogo razvitiya u Chaykovskogo" [Principles of Symphonic Development in Tchaikovsky]. *Sovetskaya muzïka* 5–6 (1940): 18–34.

249. Kunin, I[osif Filippovich]. "Chaykovskiy i Iogann Shtraus" [Tchaikovsky and Johann Strauss]. *Sovetskaya muzïka* 8 (1965): 157.

250. Kunin, I[osif] F[ilippovich], ed. and comp. *P. I. Chaykovskiy ob opere i balete: Izbrannïe otrïvki iz pisem i statey* [P. I. Tchaikovsky on Opera and Ballet: Selected Excerpts from Letters and Articles], 2nd ed. Moscow: State Music Publisher, 1960.

251. Kutateladze, L. M. *Aleksandr Il'ich Ziloti 1863–1945: Vospominaniya i pis'ma* [Alexander Ilyich Siloti 1863–1945: Recollections and Letters]. Ed. L[ev] N[ikolaevich] Raaben. Leningrad: State Music Publisher, 1963.

252. Kuznetsov, K. E., ed. *Istoriya russkoy muzïki . . . v issledovaniyakh i materialakh* [The History of Russian Music . . . in Researches and Materials], vol. 1. Moscow: State Publisher, Music Sector, 1924.

253. Lakond, Wladimir, tr. *The Diaries of Tchaikovsky*. New York: Norton, 1945.

254. Langston, Brett. "'I will not alter a single note': New Information on the History of Čajkovskij's First Piano Concerto." *Tschaikowsky-Gesellschaft Mitteilungen* 15 (2008): 63–75.

255. Larosh [Laroche], G[erman] A[vgustovich]. *Izbrannïe stat'i v pyati vïpuskakh* [Selected Articles in Five Issues], 5 vols. Leningrad: Muzïka, 1974–1978.

256. Larosh [Laroche], G[erman] A[vgustovich]. *Sobranie muzïkal'no-kriticheskikh statey* [Collected Musico-Critical Articles], vol. 1. With an introductory article by M. I. Tchaikovsky and recollections of N. D. Kashkin. Moscow: Kushnerev, 1913.

257. Lavrishcheva, T[at'yana] I[l'inichna]. "Romansï i detskie pesni P. I. Chaykovskogo na stikhi A. N. Pleshcheeva" [Romances and Children's Songs by P. I. Tchaikovsky on Verses of A. N. Pleshcheyev]. In *P. I. Chaykovskiy i russkaya literatura* [P. I. Tchaikovsky and Russian Literature]. Ed. T. A. Pozdeeva. Izhevsk: Udmurtiya, 1980, pp. 100–111.

258. Lebedeva, I. G., ed. *P. I. Chaykovskiy: K 100-letiyu so dnya smerti (1893–1993): Materialï nauchnoy konferentsii* [P. I. Tchaikovsky: On the 100th Anniversary of His Death (1893–1993): Materials of a Scholarly Conference]. Moscow: Moscow State Conservatory Named for P. I. Tchaikovsky, 1995.

259. Leighton, Lauren G. "Gematria in 'The Queen of Spades': A Decembrist Puzzle." *Slavic and East European Journal* 21, no. 4 (Winter 1977): 455–69.

260. Leighton, Lauren G. "Numbers and Numerology in 'The Queen of Spades.'" *Canadian Slavonic Papers* 19, no. 4 (December 1977): 417–43.

261. Levando. P. P. "K voprosu o 'dukhovnom' i 'svetskom' v khorovoy muzïke P. Chaykovskogo" [On the Question of "Sacred" and "Secular" in P. Tchaikovsky's Choral Music]. *P. I. Chaykovskiy: Nasledie* [P. I. Tchaikovsky: Heritage] 1 (2000): 100–111.
262. Linke, Ulrich. "Verfahren der Zyklusbildung in Čajkovskijs späten Romanzen." *Tschaikowsky-Gesellschaft Mitteilungen* 15 (2008): 91–133.
263. Lobanova, Marina. "Drei, Sieben, As. Zu der Oper 'Pique Dame' von Pjotr Ilyitsch Čajkovskij." *Die Musikforschung* 49, no. 3 (July–September 1996): 275–86.
264. M., D. "Oprichnik (opera P. I. Chaykovskago)." *Vsemirnaya illyustratsiya* 13, no. 283 (1 June 1874): 366–67.
265. Mann, Alfred. "Tchaikovsky as Teacher." In *Music and Civilization: Essays in Honor of Paul Henry Lang.* Ed. Edmond Strainchamps and Maria Rike Maniates in collaboration with Christopher Hatch. New York: Norton, 1984, pp. 279–96.
266. Meck, Nadezhda von, and Pyotr Ilich Tchaikovsky. *"To my best friend": Correspondence between Tchaikovsky and Nadezhda von Meck 1876–1878.* Tr. Galina von Meck. Ed. Edward Garden and Nigel Gotteri. Oxford: Clarendon, 1993.
267. Mihailovic, Alexandar, ed. *Tchaikovsky and His Contemporaries: A Centennial Symposium.* Westport, CT: Greenwood, 1999.
268. Mikheeva, L[yudmila] V[ikent'eva]. *Eduard Frantsevich Napravnik.* Moscow: Muzïka, 1985.
269. Morosan, Vladimir. "A Stranger in a Strange Land: Tchaikovsky as a Composer of Church Music." In *Tchaikovsky and His Contemporaries: A Centennial Symposium.* Ed. Alexandar Mihailovic. Westport, CT: Greenwood, 1999, pp. 197–225.
270. Morosan, Vladimir. *Choral Performance in Pre-Revolutionary Russia.* Ann Arbor, MI: UMI Research Press, 1986.
271. Morosan, Vladimir, ed. *One Thousand Years of Russian Church Music 988–1988.* Washington, DC: Musica Russica, 1991.
272. Morosan, Vladimir. "The Sacred Choral Works of Peter Tchaikovsky." In *Peter Tchaikovsky: The Complete Sacred Choral Works.* Ed. Vladimir Morosan. Madison, CT: Musica Russica, 1996, pp. lxxxiii–cxix.
273. Morrison, Simon. *Russian Opera and the Symbolist Movement.* Berkeley: University of California Press, 2002.
274. Müller, Claudia. "'Mein Arbeitssystem is ganz und gar das eines Handwerkers': Anmerkungen zu Čajkovskijs Schaffensweise." *Tschaikowsky-Gesellschaft Mitteilungen* 5 (March 1998): 26–46.
275. "Muzïkal'noe obozrenie" [Music Review]. *Nuvellist* [*Nouvelliste*] 1 (1893): 1–3.
276. Myaskovskiy, N. Ya. "Chaykovskiy i Betkhoven" [Tchaikovsky and Beethoven]. In *Iz istorii sovetskoy Betkhovenianï* [From the History of Soviet Beethoveniana]. Ed. N. L. Fishman. Moscow: Soviet Composer, 1972, pp. 35–39.
277. Nemirovskaya, A. "Vïrazitel'noe znachenie zhanrovïkh splavov i transformatsii v simfoniyakh Chaykovskogo" [The Expressive Significance of Genre Fusion and Transformation in Tchaikovsky's Symphonies]. In *P. I. Chaykovskiy: Voprosï istorii i stilya (k 150-letiyu so dnya rozhdeniya): Sbornik trudov: Vïpusk 108* [P. I. Tchaikovsky: Questions of History and Style (on the 150th Anniversary of His Birth): Collection of Works: Issue 108]. Ed. and comp. M[argarita] E[duardovna] Rittikh. Moscow: State Musico-Pedagogical Institute Named for the Gnesins, 1989, pp. 115–34.
278. Newmarch, Rosa [Harriet Jeaffreson]. *Tchaikovsky: His Life and Works with Extracts from His Writings, and the Diary of His Tour Abroad in 1888.* New York: John Lane, the Bodley Head, 1900. Rpt. St. Clair Shores, MI: Scholarly Press, 1970.
279. Niebuhr, Ulrich. "Der Einfluß Anton Rubinsteins auf die Klavierkonzert Peter Tschaikovskys." *Die Musikforschung* 27 (1974): 412–34.
280. Nikitin, K. N. "Ob odnom khore P. I. Chaykovskogo, schitavshemsya uteryannïm" [On a Chorus by P. I. Tchaikovsky Considered Lost]. In *P. I. Chaykovskiy: Zabïtoe i novoe: Vospom-*

inaniya sovremennikov, novïe materialï i dokumentï [P. I. Tchaikovsky: Forgotten and New: Recollections of Contemporaries, New Materials and Documents]. Comp. P. E. Vaydman and G. I. Belonovich. Moscow: Ministry of Culture of the Moscow Region and the P. I. Tchaikovsky State Home-Museum, 1995, pp. 136–44.

281. Nikolaev, A[leksandr Aleksandrovich]. *Fortep'yannoe nasledie Chaykovskogo* [Tchaikovsky's Piano Legacy], 2nd ed. Moscow: State Music Publisher, 1958.

282. Nikolaeva, N[adezhda Sergeevna]. *Simfonii P. I. Chaykovskogo ot "Zimnikh grez" k "Pateticheskoy"* [P. I. Tchaikovsky's Symphonies from "Winter Dreams" to the "Pathétique"]. Moscow: State Music Publisher, 1958.

283. Norris, Gerald. *Stanford, the Cambridge Jubilee, and Tchaikovsky.* London: David & Charles, 1980.

284. Onnoré, I[rina] I[vanovna]. "Odinnadtsat' let v teatre (Iz vospominaniy artisticheskoy zhizni Irinï Ivanovnï Onnore, bïvshey pevitsï Imperatorskago Moskovskago teatra, nïne professora peniya v Peterburge)" [Eleven Years in the Theater (from Recollections of the Artistic Life of Irina Ivanovna Onnoré, Former Singer of the Imperial Moscow Theater, Presently a Professor of Singing in Petersburg)]. *Russkaya starina* [Russian Antiquity] 141 (January–March 1910): 95–108, 543–54; 149 (January–March 1912): 160–72, 316–26.

285. Orlova, Aleksandra [Anatol'evna]. *Chaykovskiy bez retushi* [Tchaikovsky without Retouching]. New York: Slovo-Word, 2001.

286. Orlova, Alexandra [Anatol'evna]. "Tchaikovsky: The Last Chapter." *Music & Letters* 62 (1981): 125–45.

287. Orlova, E[lena Mikhailovna]. *Romansï Chaykovskogo* [Tchaikovsky's Songs]. Moscow: State Music Publisher, 1948.

288. Pavlov-Arbenin, A. B. "Bibliograficheskiy ukazatel': Po stranitsam zhurnala *Sovetskaya muzïka* (1933–1991)—*Muzïkal'naya akademiya* (1992–1995)" [Bibliographic Index: According to the Pages of the Journal *Sovetskaya muzïka* (1933–1991)—*Muzïkal'naya akademiya* (1992–1995)]. *P. I. Chaykovskiy: Nasledie* [P. I. Tchaikovsky: Heritage] 1 (2000): 198–216.

289. Pavlova-Arbenina, L. A. "V izdatel'stve P. I. Yurgensona (K istorii prizhiznennïkh izdaniy operï Chaykovskogo 'Evgeniy Onegin'" [In P. I. Jurgenson's Publishing House (On the History of the Editions of Tchaikovsky's Opera "Evgeniy Onegin" during His Lifetime)]. In *Chaykovskiy: Novïe dokumentï i materialï* [Tchaikovsky: New Documents and Materials]. St. Petersburg: Compozitor Publishing House, 2003, pp. 161–69.

290. Pergament, El. "Neotsenimaya pomoshch" [Inestimable Assistance]. *Sovetskaya muzïka* 7 (1980): 94–99.

291. Petrov, S. B. "Modest Chaykovskiy v Simbirske" [Modest Tchaikovsky in Simbirsk]. *Simbirskiy vestnik* [Simbirsk Messenger] 1 (1993): 51–58.

292. Pfann, Walter. "'Hat er es denn beschlossen . . .': Anmerkungen zu einem neuen Verständnis von Čajkovskijs 'Symphonie Pathétique.'" *Die Musikforschung* 51, no. 2 (1998): 191–209.

293. *Pikovaya dama: Opera. Muzïka P. I. Chaykovskogo. K sorokapyatiletiyu so dnya pervoy postanovki na stsene bibsh. Mariinskogo teatra 1890–1935* [The Queen of Spades: Opera. Music by P. I. Tchaikovsky. On the Forty-Fifth Anniversary of the First Production on the Stage of the Maryinsky Theater, 1890–1935]. Leningrad: Leningrad State Academic Theater of Opera and Ballet, 1935.

294. *P. I. Chaykovskiy S. I. Taneev: Pis'ma* [P. I. Tchaikovsky–S. I. Taneyev: Letters]. Ed. V. A. Zhdanov. [Moscow:] Goskul'tprosvetizdat, 1951.

295. "P. I. Tschaikowskys *Russischer Tanz* im Bellini-Album 1885." *Tschaikowsky-Gesellschaft Mitteilungen* 3 (March 1996): 20–25.

296. Platte, Nathan. "'Your tale, sir, would cure deafness': The Problem of Program in Tchaikovsky's *The Tempest.*" Unpublished term paper, University of Michigan, Ann Arbor, 2005.

297. Pleshcheev, A[leksandr Alekseevich]. *Moe vremya* [My Time]. Paris, n.p., n.d.

298. Poberezhnaya, G. I. "'Masonskiy sled' v tvorchestve Chaykovskogo" [The "Masonic Trace" in Tchaikovsky's Works]. In *P. I. Chaykovskiy: Zabïtoe i novoe: Issledovaniya; materialï i dokumentï k biografii; vospominaniya sovremennikov; iz fotoarkhiva* [P. I. Tchaikovsky: Forgotten and New: Researches; Materials and Documents Relating to Biography; Recollections of Contemporaries; from the Photo Archive]. Comp. P. E. Vaydman and G. I. Belonovich. Moscow: Ministry of Culture of the Moscow Region and the P. I. Tchaikovsky State Home-Museum, 2003, pp. 99–113.
299. Polonskiy, Ya[kov] P[etrovich]. *Vakula Kuznets: Libretto dlya operï: Zaimstvovano iz povesti N. V. Gogolya "Noch' pered Rozhdestvom"* [Vakula the Smith: Libretto for the Opera: Borrowed from N.V. Gogol's story "Christmas Eve"]. St. Petersburg: Typographer of the II Section of H[is] I[mperial] M[ajesty's] Chancery, 1871.
300. Polovtsov, A.V. *P. I. Chaykovskiy kak pisatel'* [P. I. Tchaikovsky as Writer]. Moscow: Typographer of the University, 1903.
301. Popov, S. "Novoe o zabïtïkh muzïkal'nïkh proizvedeniyakh P. I. Chaykovskogo" [New Information about Forgotten Works of P. I. Tchaikovsky]. *Sovetskaya muzïka* 6 (November–December 1933): 102–4.
302. P[opo]v, S. "Pervaya opera Chaykovskogo" [Tchaikovsky's First Opera]. *Kul'tura teatra* [Culture of the Theater] 5 (1921): 27–32.
303. Poznansky, Alexander. "Modest Čajkovskij: In His Brother's Shadow." *Čajkovskij-Studien* 1 (1995): 233–46.
304. Poznanskiy, A[lexander] N. [= Poznansky, Alexander]. "Pis'ma Chaykovskogo v Yel'skom Universitete (SShA)" [Letters of Tchaikovsky at Yale University (USA)]. In *Chaykovskiy: Novïe dokumentï i materialï* [Tchaikovsky: New Documents and Materials]. St. Petersburg: Compozitor Publishing House, 2003, pp. 81–99.
305. Poznansky, Alexander. *Tchaikovsky: The Quest for the Inner Man.* New York: Schirmer, 1991.
306. Poznansky, Alexander, ed. and comp. *Tchaikovsky through Others' Eyes.* Tr. Ralph C. Burr and Robert Bird. Bloomington: Indiana University Press, 1999.
307. Poznansky, Alexander. *Tchaikovsky's Last Days: A Documentary Study.* Oxford: Clarendon, 1996.
308. Poznansky, Alexander. "Tchaikovsky's Suicide: Myth and Reality: A Documentary Study." *19th Century Music* 11, no. 3 (Spring 1988): 199–220.
309. Poznansky, Alexander, and Brett Langston. *The Tchaikovsky Handbook: A Guide to the Man and His Music.* 2 vols. Bloomington: Indiana University Press, 2002.
310. Poznansky, Alexander. "The Tchaikovsky Myths: A Critical Reassessment." In *Tchaikovsky and His Contemporaries: A Centennial Symposium.* Ed. Alexandar Mihailovic. Westport, CT: Greenwood, 1999, pp. 75–91.
311. Poznansky, Alexander. "Unknown Tchaikovsky: A Reconstruction of Previously Censored Letters to His Brothers (1875–1879)." In *Tchaikovsky and His World.* Ed. Leslie Kearney. Princeton, NJ: Princeton University Press, 1998, pp. 55–96.
312. Pribegina, Galina [Alekseevna], ed. *P. I. Chaykovskiy: Shestaya simfoniya: Pateticheskaya: Partitura. Faksimile* [P. I. Tchaikovsky: Sixth Symphony: Pathétique: Score. Facsimile]. Moscow: Muzïka, 1970.
313. Proleeva, V. I. "K istorii rodoslovnoy Chaykovskikh" [On the History of the Genealogy of the Tchaikovskys]. In *Il'ya Petrovich Chaykovskiy: Zhizn' i deyatel'nost': Materialï k 180-letiyu so dnya rozhdeniya* [Ilya Petrovich Tchaikovsky: Life and Work: Materials Marking the 180th Anniversary of His Birth]. Compiled by A. Ya. Anshakov. Izhevsk: Udmurtiya, 1976, pp. 8–14.
314. Protopopov, V[ladimir Vasil'evich], and N[adezhda] Tumanina. *Opernoe tvorchestvo Chaykovskogo* [Tchaikovsky's Operatic Works]. Moscow: Academy of Sciences of the USSR, 1957.
315. Protopopov, Vl[adimir] V[asil'evich], ed. *Vospominaniya o P. I. Chaykovskom* [Recollections about P. I. Tchaikovsky]. Moscow: State Music Publisher, 1962.

316. Protopopov, V[ladimir] V[asil'evich], ed. *Vospominaniya o P. I. Chaykovskom* [Recollections about P. I. Tchaikovsky], 2nd ed. Moscow: Muzïka, 1973.
317. Pryanishnikov, I[ppolit Petrovich]. "P. I. Chaykovskiy—kak dirizher (Pis'mo k izdatelyu)" [P. I. Tchaikovsky—as Conductor (Letter to the Editor)]. *Russkaya muzïkal'naya gazeta* 9 (1896): cols. 1001–8.
318. Pushkareva, N. G., and G. I. Samartseva, comps. *P. I. Chaykovskiy i Udmurtiya: Sbornik dokumentov* [P. I. Tchaikovsky and Udmurtia: A Collection of Documents]. Izhevsk: Udmurtiya, 2001.
319. Rabinovich, B. I. "Moskva i narodnaya pesnya v tvorchestve Chaykovskogo" [Moscow and Folk Song in the Work of Tchaikovsky]. In *P. I. Chaykovskiy: Zabïtoe i novoe: Issledovaniya; materialï i dokumentï k biografii; vospominaniya sovremennikov; iz fotoarkhiva* [P. I. Tchaikovsky: Forgotten and New: Researches; Materials and Documents Relating to Biography; Recollections of Contemporaries; from the Photo Archive]. Comp. P. E. Vaydman and G. I. Belonovich. Moscow: Ministry of Culture of the Moscow Region and the P. I. Tchaikovsky State Home-Museum, 2003, pp. 67–74.
320. Rabinovich, B. I., ed. and comp. *P. I. Chaykovskiy i narodnaya pesnya* [P. I. Tchaikovsky and Folk Song]. Moscow: State Music Publisher, 1963. German translation, with additional sources on the topic by Imgard Wille, in *Tschaikowsky-Gesellschaft Mitteilungen* 8 (2001): 123–90.
321. Rakhmanova, Marina. "Ogromnoe i eshcho edva tronutoye pole deyatel'nosti" [An Immense and Hardly Touched Field of Activity]. *Sovetskaya muzïka* 6 (1990): 67–74.
322. Riman, G. [= Riemann, H.]. *P. Chaykovskiy: VI-ya Simfoniya (H-moll) (Symphonie pathétique, op. 74): Tematicheskaya paz'yasnenie soderzhanie* [P. Tchaikovsky: VI Symphony (B-minor) (*Pathétique* Symphony, op. 74): Thematic Interpretation of Its Content]. Tr. B. Yu. Moscow: Jurgenson, 1912.
323. Rimskiy-Korsakov, M[ikhail] N[ikolaevich], and P. E. Vaydman, preparer. "Zapis' o Chaykovskom" [A Note about P. I. Tchaikovsky]. In *P. I. Chaykovskiy: Zabïtoe i novoe: Issledovaniya; materialï i dokumentï k biografii; vospominaniya sovremennikov; iz fotoarkhiva* [P. I. Tchaikovsky: Forgotten and New: Researches; Materials and Documents Relating to Biography; Recollections of Contemporaries; from the Photo Archive]. Comp. P. E. Vaydman and G. I. Belonovich. Moscow: Ministry of Culture of the Moscow Region and the P. I. Tchaikovsky State Home-Museum, 2003, pp. 355–62.
324. Rimskiy-Korsakov, N[ikolay] A[ndreevich]. *Letopis' moey muzïkal'noy zhizni* [The Chronicle of My Musical Life], 8th ed. Moscow: Muzïka, 1980.
325. Ritter, Rüdiger. "Musik als Mittel zur Reflexion bei Čajkovskij." *Tschaikowsky-Gesellschaft Mitteilungen* 11 (2004): 159–80.
326. Rittikh, M[argarita] E[duardovna]. "Iz istorii vesenney skazki 'Snegurochka' A. N. Ostrovskogo—P. I. Chaykovskogo" [From the History of the Springtime Tale "The Snow Maiden" by A. N. Ostrovsky and P. I. Tchaikovsky]. In *Teatr v zhizni i tvorchestve P. I. Chaykovskogo* [Theater in the Life and Work of P. I. Tchaikovsky]. Ed. N[atal'ya] N[ikolaevna] Sin'kovskaya. Izhevsk: Udmurtiya, 1985, pp. 40–53.
327. Rogozina, A. A. "Dialog vremen: K istorii odnoy nesostoyavsheysya poezdki Chaykovskogo" [Dialogue of the Times: On the History of a Trip Tchaikovsky Did Not Make]. In *P. I. Chaykovskiy: Zabïtoe i novoe: Issledovaniya; materialï i dokumentï k biografii; vospominaniya sovremennikov; iz fotoarkhiva* [P. I. Tchaikovsky: Forgotten and New: Researches; Materials and Documents Relating to Biography; Recollections of Contemporaries; from the Photo Archive]. Comp. P. E. Vaydman and G. I. Belonovich. Moscow: Ministry of Culture of the Moscow Region and the P. I. Tchaikovsky State Home-Museum, 2003, pp. 253–58.
328. Rosen, Nathan. "The Magic Cards in *The Queen of Spades*." *Slavic and East European Journal* 19, no. 3 (Autumn 1975): 255–75.

329. Rossiev, P. A. "Artisticheskiy kruzhok v Moskve (1865–1883)" [The Artistic Circle in Moscow (1865–1883)]. *Istoricheskiy vestnik* [Historical Messenger] 128 (April–June 1912): 482–98; 129 (July–September 1912): 111–36.
330. Rozanova, Yu[liya] A[ndreyevna], comp. and ed. *Chaykovskiy: K 150-letiyu so dnya rozhdeniya: Voprosï istorii, teorii i ispolnitel'stva* [Tchaikovsky: On the 150th Anniversary of His Birth: Questions of History, Theory and Performance]. Moscow: Moscow State Conservatory Named for P. I. Tchaikovsky, 1990.
331. Rozanova, Yu[liya] A[ndreyevna], comp. and ed. *Chaykovskiy: Voprosï istorii i teorii* [Tchaikovsky: Questions of History and Theory]. Moscow: Moscow State Conservatory Named for P. I. Tchaikovsky, 1991.
332. Rozanova, Yu[liya Andreevna]. *Simfonicheskie printsipï baletov Chaykovskogo: Issledovanie* [Symphonic Principles of Tchaikovsky's Ballets: An Investigation]. Moscow: Muzïka, 1976.
333. Rozanova, Yu[ilya Andreyevna]. "Sozdavaya novuyu Letopis' zhizni i tvorchestva Chaykovskogo" [Producing a New Chronicle of the Life and Work of Tchaikovsky]. In *Chaykovskiy: K 150-letiyu so dnya rozhdeniya: Voprosï istorii, teorii i ispolnitel'stva* [Tchaikovsky: On the 150th Anniversary of His Birth: Questions of History, Theory and Performance]. Moscow: Moscow State Conservatory Named for P. I. Tchaikovsky, 1990, pp. 4–17.
334. Rubcova, Valentina. "Čajkovskij und die russische Kultur seiner Zeit." *Čajkovskij-Studien* 1 (1995): 247–52.
335. Rubets, A[leksandr] I[vanovich]. "Vospominaniya prof. A. I. Rubtsa o pervïkh godakh peterburgskoy konservatorii" [Recollections of Prof. A. I Rubets about the First Years of the Petersburg Conservatory]. *Novoe vremya* [New Time], 7 May 1912, p. 4; 21 May 1912, p. 3; 4 June 1912, p. 4; 11 June 1912, p. 4; 25 June 1912, p. 4; 6 August 1912, p. 3; 27 August 1912, p. 4; 3 September 1912, p. 3; 10 September 1912, p. 4; 24 September 1912, p. 4; 19 November 1912, p. 5; 26 November 1912, p. 4.
336. Rukavishnikov, N. "Pushkin v biblioteke P. I. Chaykovskogo" [Pushkin in P. I. Tchaikovsky's Library]. *Sovetskaya muzïka* 1 (1937): 60–81.
337. Rukavishnikov, N. "Vstrechi Chaykovskogo s Dezire Arto" [Tchaikovsky's Meetings with Désirée Artôt]. *Sovetskaya muzïka* 9 (1937): 43–54.
338. S., K. P. "P. I. Chaykovskiy i moskovskiy sinodal'nïy khor" [P. I. Tchaikovsky and the Moscow Synodal Choir]. *Moskovskiya vedomosti* [Moscow News], 19 February 1902, p. 4.
339. Said, Edward W. *On Late Style: Music and Literature against the Grain.* New York: Pantheon, 2006.
340. Savelova, I. I. "Iz istorii formisoveniya zamïsla baleta P. I. Chaykovskogo 'Shchelkunchik'" [From the History of the Formulation of the Concept of P. I. Tchaikovsky's Ballet "The Nutcracker"]. In *Teatr v zhizni i tvorchestva P. I. Chaykovskogo* [Theater in the Life and Works of P. I. Tchaikovsky]. Ed. N. N. Sin'kovskaya. Izhevsk: Udmurtiya, 1985, pp. 76–88.
341. Schwarz, K. Robert. "Classical Music: Composers' Closets Open for All to See." *New York Times,* 19 June 1994, sec. 2, pp. H-1, 24.
342. Seibert, D[onald] C. "The Tchaikovsky Fifth: Symphony without a Program." *Music Review* 51 (1991): 1, 36–45.
343. Shemanin, M., comp. "Literatura o P. I. Chaykovskom za 17 let (1917–34)" [Literature about Tchaikovsky for 17 Years (1917–1934)]. *Muzïkal'noe nasledstvo* 1 (1935): 76–93.
344. Shokhman, Gennadiy. "Vzglyad s drugikh beregov" [The View from Other Shores]. *Sovetskaya muzïka* 6 (1990): 134–41.
345. Shol'p, A[leksandra Evgen'evna]. *"Evgeniy Onegin" Chaykovskogo: Ocherki* [Tchaikovsky's "Eugene Onegin": Essays]. Leningrad: Muzïka, 1982.
346. Šubert, Fr. Ad. *Dìjiny Národního Divadla v Praze 1883–1900: S nìkterými pamìtmi, vzpominkami a doklady.* [Prague:] Unie, 1908.
347. Sidel'nikov, Leonid [Sergeevich], and Galina Pribegina. *25 Days in America: For the Centenary of Peter Tchaikovsky's Concert Tour.* Moscow: Muzïka, 1991.

348. Sin'kovskaya, N. N. "Iz tvorcheskoy istorii *Val'sa-skertso* dlya skripki s orkestrom op. 34 Chaykovskogo" [From the History of the Composition of the *Valse-Scherzo* for Violin and Orchestra, op. 34, by Tchaikovsky]. *P. I. Chaykovskiy: Nasledie* [P. I. Tchaikovsky: Heritage] 1 (2000): 67–76.
349. Sin'kovskaya, N. "Neizvestnaya stranitsa" [An Unknown Page]. *Sovetskaya muzïka* 6 (1986): 81–86 [an interpolated aria Tchaikovsky wrote for the part of Prince Vyazminsky in *The Oprichnik*].
350. Sizko, G. S. "Chaykovskiy i Pravoslavie: Nablyudeniya i zametki" [Tchaikovsky and Orthodoxy: Observations and Notes]. In *P. I. Chaykovskiy: Zabïtoe i novoe: Issledovaniya; materialï i dokumentï k biografii; vospominaniya sovremennikov; iz fotoarkhiva* [P. I. Tchaikovsky: Forgotten and New: Researches; Materials and Documents Relating to Biography; Recollections of Contemporaries; from the Photo Archive]. Comp. P. E. Vaydman and G. I. Belonovich. Moscow: Ministry of Culture of the Moscow Region and the P. I. Tchaikovsky State Home-Museum, 2003, pp. 167–74.
351. Skal'kovskiy, K[onstantin Apollonovich]. *V teatral'nom mire: Nablyudeniya, vospominaniya i razsuzhdeniya* [In the Theater World: Observations, Recollections and Debates]. St. Petersburg: Suvorin, 1899.
352. Skvirskaya, T[amara] Z. "Avtografï P. I. Chaykovskogo v Otdele rukopisey Peterburgskoy konservatorii" [Autographs of P. I. Tchaikovsky in the Manuscript Division of the Petersburg Conservatory]. In *Peterburgskiy Muzïkal'nïy Arkhiv: Sbornik statey i materialov* [St. Petersburg Musical Archives: Collection of Articles and Materials], vol. 1. St. Petersburg: Kanon, 1997, pp. 117–22.
353. Skvirskaya, T[amara] Z. "'Dragotsennost' P. A. Vakara' (Ob odnom avtografe P. I Chaykovskogo)" ["P. A. Vakar's Treasure" (On One Autograph of P. I. Tchaikovsiky)]. In *Peterburgskiy Muzïkal'nïy Arkhiv: Sbornik statey i materialov* [St. Petersburg Musical Archives: Collection of Articles and Materials], vol. 2. St. Petersburg: Kanon, 1998, pp. 144–49.
354. Skvirskaya, Tamara Z. "K istorii sozdaniya operï 'Pikovaya dama' (O nekotorïkh istochnikakh XVIII veka, ispol'zovannïkh librettistom i kompozitorom" [On the History of the Creation of the Opera "The Queen of Spades" (about Certain 18th-Century Sources Used by the Librettist and Composer)]. In *Chaykovskiy: Novïe dokumentï i materialï* [Tchaikovsky: New Documents and Materials]. St. Petersburg: Compozitor Publishing House, 2003, pp. 191–229.
355. Skvirskaya, T[amara] Z. "Materialï k rodoslovnoy Chaykovskogo po materinskoy linii" [Materials for Tchaikovsky's Genealogy on His Mother's Side]. In *P. I. Chaykovskiy: Zabïtoe i novoe: Issledovaniya; materialï i dokumentï k biografii; vospominaniya sovremennikov; iz fotoarkhiva* [P. I. Tchaikovsky: Forgotten and New: Researches; Materials and Documents Relating to Biography; Recollections of Contemporaries; from the Photo Archive]. Comp. P. E. Vaydman and G. I. Belonovich. Moscow: Ministry of Culture of the Moscow Region and the P. I. Tchaikovsky State Home-Museum, 2003, pp. 224–35.
356. Skvirskaya, T[amara] Z. "Neizvestnïe pis'ma Chaykovskogo: Iz fondov Russiyskoy natsional'noy biblioteki" [Unknown Letters of Tchaikovsky: From the Archives of the Russian National Library]. In *P. I. Chaykovskiy: Zabïtoe i novoe: Issledovaniya; materialï i dokumentï k biografii; vospominaniya sovremennikov; iz fotoarkhiva* [P. I. Tchaikovsky: Forgotten and New: Researches; Materials and Documents Relating to Biography; Recollections of Contemporaries; from the Photo Archive]. Comp. P. E. Vaydman and G. I. Belonovich. Moscow: Ministry of Culture of the Moscow Region and the P. I. Tchaikovsky State Home-Museum, 2003, pp. 312–19.
357. Skvirskaya, T[amara] Z., et al., eds. *Peterburgskiy muzïkal'nïy arkhiv: Sbornik statey i materialov* [St. Petersburg Musical Archives: Collection of Articles and Materials], vol. 2. St. Petersburg: Kanon, 1998.
358. Skvirskaya, Tamara Z., ed. *Peterburgskiy muzïkal'nïy arkhiv: Sbornik statey i materialov* [St. Petersburg Musical Archives: Collection of Articles and Materials], vol. 3. St. Petersburg: Scientific Music Library of the St. Petersburg State Conservatory, 1999.

359. Skvirskaya, Tamara Z. "Pis'mo Chaykovskogo k P. L. Peterssenu" [A Letter of Tchaikovsky to P. L. Peterssen]. In *Chaykovskiy: Novïe dokumentï i materialï* [Tchaikovsky: New Documents and Materials]. St. Petersburg: Compozitor Publishing House, 2003, pp. 118–23.
360. Skvortsova, I. A. "'Iolanta' na moskovskoy stsene" ["Iolanta" on the Moscow Stage]. In *P. I. Chaykovskiy: Zabïtoe i Novoe: Issledovaniya; materialï i dokumentï k biografii; vospominaniya sovremennikov; iz fotoarkhiva* [P. I. Tchaikovsky: Forgotten and New: Researches; Materials and Documents Relating to Biography; Recollections of Contemporaries; from the Photo Archive]. Comp. P. E. Vaydman and G. I. Belonovich. Moscow: Ministry of Culture of the Moscow Region and the P. I. Tchaikovsky State Home-Museum, 2003, pp. 194–200.
361. Skvortsova, I. "'Shchelkunchik': Problemï pozdnego stilya" ["The Nutcracker": Problems of Late Style]. In *Chaykovskiy: Voprosï istorii i teorii* [Tchaikovsky: Questions of History and Theory]. Moscow: Moscow State Conservatory Named for P. I. Tchaikovsky, 1991, pp. 38–54.
362. Slonimskiy, Yu[riy Iosifovich]. *P. I. Chaykovskiy i baletnïy teatr ego vremeni* [P. I. Tchaikovsky and the Ballet Theater of His Time]. Moscow: State Music Publisher, 1956.
363. "Sobïtiya dvukh dney: Khronika po soobshcheniyam peterburgskikh gazet i svidetel'stvam sovremennikov, 25 oktyabrya 1893 goda" [The Events of Two Days: Chronicle of Communications of Petersburg Newspapers and Contemporary Witnesses, 25 October 1893]. *Sovetskaya muzïka* 6 (1990): 117–23.
364. Sokolov, N. "Kapel'meyster russkoy operï" [Kapellmeister of the Russian Opera]. *Sovetskaya muzïka* 11 (1971): 158–60.
365. Sokolov, V[aleriy Solomonovich]. *Antonina Chaykovskaya: Istoriya zabïtoi zhizni* [Antonina Tchaikovskaya: The Story of a Forgotten Life]. Moscow: Muzïka, 1994.
366. Sokolov, Valerij [= Valeriy Solomonovich Sokolov]. "Čajkovskijs Tod." *Čajkovskij-Studien* 1 (1995): 259–80.
367. Sokolov, V[aleriy] S[olomonovich]. *Do i posle tragedii* [Before and After the Tragedy]. Moscow: Muzïka, 1994. [NB Bound/published with N. O. Blinov, *Poslednyaya bolezn' i smert' P. I. Chaykovskogo.*]
368. Sokolov, V[aleriy] S[olomonovich]. "Peterburgskie 'taynï' v rodoslovnoy i biografii Chaykovskogo" [Petersburg 'Secrets' in Tchaikovsky's Genealogy and Biography]. In *P. I. Chaykovskiy: Zabïtoe i novoe: Issledovaniya; materialï i dokumentï k biografii; vospominaniya sovremennikov; iz fotoarkhiva* [P. I. Tchaikovsky: Forgotten and New: Researches; Materials and Documents Relating to Biography; Recollections of Contemporaries; from the Photo Archive]. Comp. P. E. Vaydman and G. I. Belonovich. Moscow: Ministry of Culture of the Moscow Region and the P. I. Tchaikovsky State Home-Museum, 2003, pp. 236–45.
369. Sokolov, V[aleriy] S[olomonovich]. "Pis'ma P. I. Chaykovskogo bez kupyur" [P. I. Tchaikovsky's Letters without Cuts]. In *P. I. Chaykovskiy: Zabïtoe i novoe: Vospominaniya sovremennikov, novïe materialï i dokumentï* [P. I. Tchaikovsky. Forgotten and New: Recollections of Contemporaries, New Materials and Documents]. Comp. P. E. Vaydman and G. I. Belonovich. Moscow: Ministry of Culture of the Moscow Region and the P. I. Tchaikovsky State Home-Museum, 1995, pp. 118–34.
370. Sokolov, V[aleriy] S[olomonovich]. "Rodoslovnaya Chaykovskogo: Novïe imena" [Tchaikovsky's Genealogy: New Names]. In *Chaykovskiy: Novïe dokumentï i materialï* [Tchaikovsky: New Documents and Materials]. St. Petersburg: Compozitor Publishing House, 2003, pp. 7–33.
371. Sokolov, V[aleriy] S[olomonovich]. "Zhizn' i smert' Vladimira L'vovicha Davïdova (Materialï k biografii Chaykovskogo)" [The Life and Death of Vladimir L'vovich Davïdov (Materials for Tchaikovsky's Biography)]. In *Chaykovskiy: Novïe dokumentï i materialï* [Tchaikovsky: New Documents and Materials]. St. Petersburg: Compozitor Publishing House, 2003, pp. 252–90.
372. Sokolova, T[atyana Ivanovna]. *"Francheska da Rimini": Simfonicheskaya fantaziya Chaykovskogo* ["Francesca da Rimini": Symphonic Fantasia by Tchaikovsky]. Moscow: Muzïka, 1964.

373. Solovtsov, An[atoliy Aleksandrovich]. *Pikovaya dama P. I. Chaykovskogo* [The Queen of Spades by P. I. Tchaikovsky], 2nd ed. Moscow: State Music Publisher, 1954.
374. Sorokina, E. G., Yu[liya] A[ndreyevna] Rozanova, A. I. Kandinskiy, and I. A. Skvortsova, eds. and comps. *P. I. Chaykovskiy: K 100-letiyu so dnya smerti (1893–1993): Materialï nauchnoy konferentsiya* [P. I. Tchaikovsky: On the Hundredth Anniversary of His Death (1893–1993): Materials of a Scholarly Conference]. Moscow: Moscow State Conservatory Named for P. I. Tchaikovsky, 1995.
375. Stark, E. A., et al. *P. I. Chaykovskiy na stsene Teatra Operï i Baleta imeni S. M. Kirova (b. Mariinskiy)* [P. I. Tchaikovsky on the Stage of the Theater of Opera and Ballet Named for S. M. Kirov (Formerly the Maryinsky)]. Leningrad: Leningrad State Order of Lenin Academic Theater of Opera and Ballet Named for S. M. Kirov, 1941.
376. Swartz, Anne. "The Intrigue of Love and Illusion in Tchaikovsky's *The Oprichnik*." In *Tchaikovsky and His Contemporaries: A Centennial Symposium*. Ed. Alexandar Mihailovic. Westport, CT: Greenwood, 1999, pp. 147–54.
377. Sylvester, Richard D. *Tchaikovsky's Complete Songs: A Companion with Texts and Translations.* Bloomington: Indiana University Press, 2002.
378. *Systematisches Verzeichnis der Werke von Pjotr Iljitsch Tschaikowsky: Ein Handbuch für die Musikpraxis.* Ed. Tschaikowsky-Studio Institut International. Hamburg: Sikorski, [c. 1973].
379. Tambovskaya, N. A. "Illyuziya prostotï: Nekotorïe intonatsionno-poeticheskie osobennosti operï 'Iolanta'" [Illusions of Simplicity: Some Intonational-Poetical Particulars of the Opera "Iolanta"]. In *P. I. Chaykovskiy: Zabïtoe i novoe: Issledovaniya; materialï i dokumentï k biografii; vospominaniya sovremennikov; iz fotoarkhiva* [P. I. Tchaikovsky: Forgotten and New: Researches; Materials and Documents Relating to Biography; Recollections of Contemporaries; from the Photo Archive]. Comp. P. E. Vaydman and G. I. Belonovich. Moscow: Ministry of Culture of the Moscow Region and the P. I. Tchaikovsky State Home-Museum, 2003, pp. 126–38.
380. Taruskin, Richard. "Tchaikovsky: A New View—A Centennial Essay." In *Tchaikovsky and His Contemporaries: A Centennial Symposium.* Ed. Alexandar Mihailovic. Westport, CT: Greenwood, 1999, pp. 17–60.
381. Taruskin, Richard. *Defining Russia Musically: Historical and Hermeneutical Essays.* Princeton, NJ: Princeton University Press, 1997.
382. Taruskin, Richard. "'The Present in the Past': Russian Opera and Russian Historiography, ca. 1870." In *Russian and Soviet Music: Essays for Boris Schwarz.* Ed. Malcolm Hamrick Brown. Ann Arbor, MI: UMI Research Press, 1984, pp. 77–146.
383. Taylor, Philip. *Gogolian Interludes: Gogol's Story "Christmas Eve" as the Subject of the Operas by Tchaikovsky and Rimsky-Korsakov.* London: Collets, 1984.
384. Taylor, Philip, ed. *The Oprichnik.* London: Collets, 1980.
385. Tchaikovsky, Mme. Anatol. "Recollections of Tchaikovsky." *Music and Letters* 21, no. 2 (April 1940): 103–9.
386. Tchaikovsky, Modeste. *The Life & Letters of Peter Ilich Tchaikovsky.* Edited from the Russian, with an introduction, by Rosa Newmarch. London: John Lane, 1905. Rpt. in 2 vols., New York: Vienna House, 1973.
387. Tchaikovsky, [Pyotr Il'ich]. *Moscow—Coronation Cantata for Alexander III; Ode to Joy; "K radosti" Cantata; Dmitri the Imposter—Incidental Music* [sound recording]. Citadel CTD 88138 (P) 1999.
388. Tchaikovsky, Pyotr Il'yich. *Opričnik* [sound recording sponsored by the Teatro Lirico di Cagliari Fondazione]. Dynamic CDS 430/1-3.
389. Tchaikovsky, [Peter Ilyich]. *Secular Choruses* [sound recording]. Russian Season RUS 288 156 [compact disc] (P) 1998.
390. Tchaikovsky, Peter Ilyich. *Symphony no. 6 in B Minor ("Pathetique"), opus 74: Undine (Fragments from the Unfinished Opera).* Original Master Recording. Mobile Fidelity Sound Lab–Melodiya MFCD 892 (c) (P) 1959, 1963.

391. Tchaikovsky, Peter [Il'ich]. *The Complete Sacred Choral Works.* Ed. Vladimir Morosan. Madison, CT: Musica Russica, 1996.
392. Tchaikovsky, Pjotr I. *The 4 Piano Concertos: Bohemian Melodies.* Unabridged Original Versions [sound recording]. 3 vols. Koch Schwann 3-6489-2 (P) (c) 1998. [n.b. The last track on vol. 3 is a transfer of an Edison cylinder with Tchaikovsky's voice.]
393. Tchaikovsky, P[yotr Il'ich]. *Vremena goda* [The Seasons for Piano]. Facsimile. Ed. Elena Orlova. Moscow: Muzïka, 1978.
394. Tcherkashina, Marina. "Tchaikovsky—*The Maid of Orleans:* The Problem of the Genre and the Specific Treatment of the Subject." *International Journal of Musicology* 3 (1994): 175–85.
395. Tikhonova, I. E. "Cherta khorovogo pis'ma P. I. Chaykovskogo (na primere svetskikh khorov a capella)" [Features of P. I. Tchaikovsky's Choral Style (Based on the Secular a Capella Choruses]. *P. I. Chaykovskiy: Nasledie* [P. I. Tchaikovsky: Heritage] 1 (2000): 113–38.
396. Timofeev, Gr. *P. I. Chaykovskiy v roli muzïkal'nago kritika* [P. I. Tchaikovsky in the Role of Music Critic]. Separate issue from the *Russkaya muzïkal'naya gazeta* of 1899. N.p.: Rossiya, n.d.
397. Tschaikowskaja, Antonina. "Sich selbst nannte er 'Ein Mischung aus Kind und Greis' (die Erinnerungen der Witwe Tschaikowskys aus dem Jahre 1893)." *Tschaikowsky-Gesellschaft Mitteilungen* 1 (March 1994): 17–27.
398. Tschaikowsky, P. "Danse russe (Mai 1878)" [as published in the *Album per pianoforte alla memoria di Vicenzo Bellini* (Milan, 1885)]. *Tschaikowsky-Gesellschaft Mitteilungen* 3 (March 1996): 20–25.
399. Tumanina, N[adezhda Vasil'evna]. *Chaykovskiy: Put' k masterstvu 1840–1877* [Tchaikovsky: The Path to Mastery, 1840–1877]. Moscow: Academy of Sciences of the USSR, 1962.
400. Tumanina, N[adezhda Vasil'evna]. [*P. I. Chaykovskiy*]*: Velikiy master, 1878–1893* [Great Master, 1878–1893]. Moscow: Nauka, 1968.
401. "V. V. Stasov i P. I. Chaykovskiy: Neizdannïya pis'ma, s predisloviem i primechaniyami V. Karenina" [V. V. Stasov and P. I. Tchaikovsky: Unpublished Letters, with a Foreword and Notes by V. Karenin]. *Russkaya mïsl'* [Russian Thought] 13, no. 3 (1909): 93–149.
402. Val'ts, Karl Fedorovich. *Shest'desyat pyat' let v teatre* [Sixty-Five Years in the Theater]. Leningrad: Academia, 1928.
403. Vasil'ev, Yu. V. "Etapï tvorcheskoy rabotï P. I. Chaykovskogo nad proizvedeniyami 1890-kh godov" [Stages in P. I. Tchaikovsky's Creative Work on Compositions of the 1890s]. *P. I. Chaykovskiy: Nasledie* [P. I. Tchaikovsky: Heritage] 2 (2000): 81–124.
404. Vasil'ev, Yu. "K rukopisyam 'Pikovoy damï'" [On the Manuscripts of "The Queen of Spades"]. *Sovetskaya muzïka* 7 (1980): 99–103.
405. Vasil'ev, Yu. V. "O printsipakh atributsii nekotorïkh nabroskov P. I. Chaykovskogo" [On Principles of Attribution of Several of P. I. Tchaikovsky's Sketches]. *P. I. Chaykovskiy: Nasledie* [P. I. Tchaikovsky: Heritage] 1 (2000): 21–66.
406. Vaydman, P[olina] E[fimovna], preparer. "Attestat (A. M. Assiera)" [Testimonial (A. M. Assier)]. In *P. I. Chaykovskiy: Zabïtoe i novoe: Vospominaniya sovremennikov, novïe materialï i dokumentï* [P. I. Tchaikovsky: Forgotten and New: Recollections of Contemporaries, New Materials and Documents]. Comp. P. E. Vaydman and G. I. Belonovich. Moscow: Ministry of Culture of the Moscow Region and the P. I. Tchaikovsky State Home-Museum, 1995, pp. 151–53.
407. Vaydman, P[olina] E[fimovna]. "Biografii Chaykovskogo v otechestvennoy muzïkal'noy istoriografii XIX–XX vekov" [Biographies of Tchaikovsky in the Homeland's Musical Historiography of the 19th and 20th Centuries]. In *Chaykovskiy: Novïe dokumentï i materialï* [Tchaikovsky: New Documents and Materials]. St. Petersburg: Compozitor Publishing House, 2003, pp. 34–55.
408. Vaydman, P[olina] E[fimovna]. "Biografiya khudozhnika: Zhizn' i proizvedeniya (Po materialam k biografii P. I. Chaykovskogo)" [Biography of an Artist: The Life and the Works (on Materials for P. I. Tchaikovsky's Biography)]. In *Peterburgskiy muzïkal'nïy arkhiv: Sbornik*

statey i materialov [St. Petersburg Musical Archives: Collection of Articles and Materials], vol. 3. Ed. F.V. Panchenko and R. Z. Skvirskaya. St. Petersburg: Scientific Music Library of the St. Petersburg State Conservatory, 1999, pp. 173–80.

409. Vaydman, P[olina] E[fimovna]. "Chaykovskiy i ego biografii: Ot veka XIX k XXI" [Tchaikovsky and His Biography: From the 19th Century to the 21st]. In *P. I. Chaykovskiy: Zabïtoe i novoe: Issledovaniya; materialï i dokumentï k biografii; vospominaniya sovremennikov; iz fotoarkhiva* [P. I. Tchaikovsky: Forgotten and New: Researches; Materials and Documents Relating to Biography; Recollections of Contemporaries; from the Photo Archive]. Comp. P. E. Vaydman and G. I. Belonovich. Moscow: Ministry of Culture of the Moscow Region and the P. I. Tchaikovsky State Home-Museum, 2003, pp. 11–48.

410. Vaydman, P[olina] E[fimovna]. "Esli b sud'ba ne tolknula menya v Moskvu" [If Destiny Had Not Pushed Me to Moscow]. In *P. I. Chaykovskiy: Zabïtoe i novoe: Issledovaniya; materialï i dokumentï k biografii; vospominaniya sovremennikov; iz fotoarkhiva* [P. I. Tchaikovsky: Forgotten and New: Researches; Materials and Documents Relating to Biography; Recollections of Contemporaries; from the Photo Archive]. Comp. P. E. Vaydman and G. I. Belonovich. Moscow: Ministry of Culture of the Moscow Region and the P. I. Tchaikovsky State Home-Museum, 2003, pp. 50–60.

411. Vaydman, P[olina] E[fimovna]. "Klavir 'Pikovoy damï' s mizanstsenami O. O. Palacheka (K stsenicheskoy istorii operï)" [The Piano-Vocal Score of "The Queen of Spades" with the Mise-en-Scène of O. O. Palachek (on the Stage History of the Opera)]. In *Chaykovskiy: Novïe dokumentï i materialï* [Tchaikovsky: New Documents and Materials]. St. Petersburg: Compozitor Publishing House, 2003, pp. 230–42.

412. [Vaydman, Polina Efimovna]. "Listï iz Al'boma" [Leaves from an Album]. *Muzïkal'naya zhizn'* [Musical Life] 20 (October 1986): 9, 14.

413. Vaydman, P[olina] E[fimovna]. "Mï slïshali golos Chaykovskogo . . . " [We Heard Tchaikovsky's Voice . . .]. In *P. I. Chaykovskiy: Zabïtoe i novoe: Issledovaniya; materialï i dokumentï k biografii; vospominaniya sovremennikov; iz fotoarkhiva* [P. I. Tchaikovsky: Forgotten and New: Researches; Materials and Documents Relating to Biography; Recollections of Contemporaries; from the Photo Archive]. Comp. P. E. Vaydman and G. I. Belonovich. Moscow: Ministry of Culture of the Moscow Region and the P. I. Tchaikovsky State Home-Museum, 2003, pp. 393–97.

414. Vaydman, Polina [Efimovna]. "Nachalo: Novïe materialï iz arkhiva P. I. Chaykovskogo" [The Beginning: New Materials from the Archive of P. I. Tchaikovsky]. *Nashe nasledie* [Our Heritage] 2 (1990): 19–22.

415. Vaydman, P[olina] E[fimovna]. "Otkrïvaya novogo Chaykovskogo" [Discovering the New Tchaikovsky]. In *P. I. Chaykovskiy: Zabïtoe i novoe: Vospominaniya sovremennikov, novïe materialï i dokumentï* [P. I. Tchaikovsky: Forgotten and new: Recollections of Contemporaries, New Materials and Documents]. Comp. P. E. Vaydman and G. I. Belonovich. Moscow: Ministry of Culture of the Moscow Region and the P. I. Tchaikovsky State Home-Museum, 1995, pp. 7–15.

416. Vaydman, P[olina] E[fimovna], K[seniya] Yu[revna] Davïdova, and I. G. Sokolinskaya, comps. *Petr Il'ich Chaykovskiy.* Ed. E[lena] M[ikhailovna] Orlova. Tr. [into German] by Christof Rüger. Moscow: Muzïka, and Leipzig: VEB Deutscher Verlag für Musik, 1978.

417. Vaydman, P[olina] E[fimovna]. "P. I. Chaykovskiy: Novïe stranitsï biografii: Po materialam rukopisey uchenicheskikh rabot kompozitora" [P. I. Tchaikovsky: New Pages of Biography: After Materials of Manuscripts of the Composer's Student Works]. In *Peterburgskiy Muzïkal'nïy Archiv: Sbornik statey i materialov* [St. Petersburg Musical Archives: Collection of Articles and Materials], vol. 2. St. Petersburg: Kanon, 1998, pp. 134–43.

418. Vaydman, P[olina] E[fimovna], and G[alina] I. Belonovich, comps. *P. I. Chaykovskiy: Zabïtoe i novoe: Issledovaniya; materialï i dokumentï k biografii; vospominaniya sovremennikov; iz fotoarkhiva* [P. I. Tchaikovsky: Forgotten and New: Researches; Materials and Documents Relating to Biography; Recollections of Contemporaries; from the Photo Archive].

Moscow: Ministry of Culture of the Moscow Region and the P. I. Tchaikovsky State Home-Museum, 2003.

419. Vaydman, P[olina] E[fimovna], and G[alina] I. Belonovich, comps. *P. I. Chaykovskiy: Zabïtoe i novoe: Vospominaniya sovremennikov, novïe materialï i dokumentï* [P. I. Tchaikovsky: Forgotten and New: Recollections of Contemporaries, New Materials and Documents]. Moscow: Ministry of Culture of the Moscow Region and the P. I. Tchaikovsky State Home-Museum, 1995.
420. Vaydman, P[olina] E[fimovna]. "Rabota P. I. Chaykovskogo nad rukopis'yu libretto operï 'Pikovaya dama'" [P. I. Tchaikovsky's Work on the Manuscript Libretto of the Opera "The Queen of Spades"]. In *P. I. Chaykovskiy i russkaya literatura* [P. I. Tchaikovsky and Russian Literature]. Ed. T. A. Pozdeeva. Izhevsk: Udmurtiya, 1980, pp. 155–77.
421. Vaydman, P[olina] E[fimovna], preparer. "Rod Chaykovskikh k 1894 g." [The Tchaikovsky Family in 1894]. In *P. I. Chaykovskiy: Zabïtoe i novoe: Vospominaniya sovremennikov, novïe materialï i dokumentï* [P. I. Tchaikovsky: Forgotten and New: Recollections of Contemporaries, New Materials and Documents]. Comp. P. E. Vaydman and G. I. Belonovich. Moscow: Ministry of Culture of the Moscow Region and the P. I. Tchaikovsky State Home-Museum, 1995, pp. 146–47.
422. Vaydman, P[olina] E[fimovna]. "Slovo Chaykovskogo v rukopisyakh ego instrumental'nïkh proizvedeniy" [Tchaikovsky's Word in the Manuscripts of His Instrumental Works]. In *Chaykovskiy: Novïe dokumentï i materialï* [Tchaikovsky: New Documents and Materials]. St. Petersburg: Compozitor Publishing House, 2003, pp. 142–54.
423. Vajdman [=Vaydman], Polina, Ljudmila Korabelnikova [Korabel'nikova], and Valentina Rubcova [Rubtsova], eds. *Thematic and Bibliographical Catalogue of P. I. Čajkovskij's Works.* Moscow: Muzïka, 2003.
424. Vaydman, P[olina] E[fimovna]. *Tvorcheskiy arkhiv P. I. Chaykovskogo* [P. I. Tchaikovsky's Creative Archive]. Moscow: Muzïka, 1988.
425. Vajdman [=Vaydman], Polina. "Unbekannter Čajkovskij—Entwürfe zu nicht ausgeführten Kompositionen." *Čajkovskij-Studien* 1 (1993): 281–97.
426. Vaydman, P[olina Efimovna]. "Zamïslï 1887–1888 godov" [Conceptions of 1887–1888]. *Sovetskaya muzïka* 7 (1980): 84–90.
427. Vaydman, P[olina] E[fimovna], preparer. "Zapiski kadeta Gornogo kadetskogo korpusa I. P. Ch." [Notes of I. P. Ch., Cadet of the Mining Cadets Corps]. In *P. I. Chaykovskiy: Zabïtoe i novoe: Vospominaniya sovremennikov, novïe materialï i dokumentï* [P. I. Tchaikovsky: Forgotten and New: Recollections of Contemporaries, New Materials and Documents]. Comp. P. E. Vaydman and G. I. Belonovich. Moscow: Ministry of Culture of the Moscow Region and the P. I. Tchaikovsky State Home-Museum, 1995, pp. 148–50.
428. Vinocour, Lev. "Liszt–Menter–Čajkovskij: Zur Geschichte des Konzertstücks 'Ungarische Zigeunerweisen.'" *Tschaikowsky-Gesellschaft Mitteliungen* 13 (2006): 37–130.
429. Vinogradov, V[iktor] V[ladimirovich]. "Stil' 'Pikovoy damï.'" *Vremennik pushkinskoy komissii* [Annals of the Pushkin Commission] 1 (1936): 74–147.
430. Weber, Harry B. "*Pikovaya dama:* A Case for Freemasonry in Russian Literature." *Slavic and East European Journal* 12, no. 4 (Winter 1968): 435–47.
431. Wiley, Roland John. *Tchaikovsky's Ballets.* Oxford: Clarendon, 1985.
432. Wiley, Roland John. "Tchaikovsky's 'Eugene Onegin.'" In *Eugene Onegin: Pyotr Tchaikovsky.* English National Opera/Royal Opera Guide no. 38, ed. Nicholas John. London: John Calder, and New York: Riverrun Press, 1988, pp. 17–36.
433. Wille, Imgard, tr., and Thomas Kohlhase, ed. "Čajkovskijs Kindheit und Jugend—nach Briefen und Erinnerungen." *Tschaikowsky-Gesellschaft Mitteilungen* 11 (2004): 73–92.
434. Yakovlev, Vas[iliy Vasil'evich]. "Chaykovskiy v moskovskikh teatrakh: Pervïe postanovki v Moskve ego muzïkal'no-stsenicheskikh proizvedeniy" [Tchaikovsky in the Moscow Theaters: The First Productions in Moscow of His Works for the Musical Stage]. In *Chaykovskiy*

na moskovskoy stsene: Pervïe postanovki v godï ego zhizni [Tchaikovsky on the Moscow Stage: First Performances during His Life]. Moscow: Iskusstvo, 1940, pp. 5–244.

435. Yakovlev, V[asiliy], E. E. Zaydenshnur, V. Kiselev, A. Orlova, and N. Shemanin, eds. *Dni i godï P. I. Chaykovskogo: Letopis' zhizni i tvorchestva* [The Days and Years of P. I. Tchaikovsky: A Chronicle of His Life and Work]. Moscow: Muzgiz, 1940.
436. Yakovlev, Vas[iliy Vasil'evich]. *Izbrannïe trudï* [Selected Works]: vol. 1, *P. I. Tchaikovsky.* Moscow: Muzïka, 1964.
437. Yakovlev, Vas[iliy Vasil'evich]. *N. D. Kashkin.* Moscow: State Music Publisher, 1950.
438. Yampol'skiy, I. "Neopublikovannïe rukopisi 'Variatsiy na temu rokoko' Chaykovskovo" [Unpublished Manuscripts of Tchaikovsky's "Variations on a Rococo Theme"]. *Sovetskaya muzïka*[3rd Collection of Articles (Moscow and Leningrad: Muzgiz], 1945): 32–44.
439. Yoffe, Elkhonon. *Tchaikovsky in America: The Composer's Visit in 1891.* New York: Oxford University Press, 1986.
440. Zagornïy, N. N. "Pervoe sochinenie P. I. Chaykovskogo" [P. I. Tchaikovsky's First Composition]. *Muzïkal'noe nasledstvo* [Musical Heritage] 1 (1962): 463–64, 587–91.
441. Zaitsev, Pavel. "Yunosheskoe proizvedenie P. I. Chaykovskago" [A Youthful Work of P. I. Tchaikovsky]. *Den'* [Day], 21 October 1913, suppl.
442. Zajaczkowski, Henry. *An Introduction to Tchaikovsky's Operas.* Westport, CT: Praeger, 2005.
443. Zajaczkowski, Henry. "On Čajkovskij's Psychopathology and Its Relationship with His Creativity." *Čajkovskij-Studien* 1 (1995): 307–28.
444. Zakharova, O[l'ga I]. "Religioznïe vzglyadï Chaykovskogo" [Tchaikovsky's Religious Views]. In *P. I. Chaykovskiy: Zabïtoe i novoe: Issledovaniya; materialï i dokumentï k biografii; vospominaniya sovremennikov; iz fotoarkhiva* [P. I. Tchaikovsky: Forgotten and New: Researches; Materials and Documents Relating to Biography; Recollections of Contemporaries; from the Photo Archive]. Comp. P. E. Vaydman and G. I. Belonovich. Moscow: Ministry of Culture of the Moscow Region and the P. I. Tchaikovsky State Home-Museum, 2003, pp. 162–66.
445. Zakharova, Ol'ga [I.]. "Chaykovskiy chitaet Bibliyu" [Tchaikovsky Reads the Bible]. *Nashe nasledie* [Our Heritage] 2 (1990): 22–24.
446. Zemcovskij, Izalij [= Zemtsovskiy, Izaliy]. "Čajkovskij and the European Melosphere: A Case of Cantilena-Narration." *Čajkovskij-Studien* 1 (1995): 329–35.
447. Zemtsovskiy, I[zaliy Iosifovich]. *Po sledam vesnyanki iz fortepiannogo kontserta P. Chaykovskogo* [In the Footsteps of the Spring Song from P. Tchaikovsky's Piano Concerto]. Leningrad: Muzïka, 1987.
448. Zenkin, K. V. "Poslednïy fortepiannïy opus Chaykovskogo" [Tchaikovsky's Last Piano Opus]. In *P. I. Chaykovskiy: Zabïtoe i novoe: Issledovaniya; materialï i dokumentï k biografii; vospominaniya sovremennikov; iz fotoarkhiva* [P. I. Tchaikovsky: Forgotten and New: Researches; Materials and Documents Relating to Biography; Recollections of Contemporaries; from the Photo Archive]. Comp. P. E. Vaydman and G. I. Belonovich. Moscow: Ministry of Culture of the Moscow Region and the P. I. Tchaikovsky State Home-Museum, 2003, pp. 93–98.
449. Zhitomirskiy, D[aniel' Vladimirovich]. "O simfonizme Chaykovskogo" [On Tchaikovsky's Symphonism]. *Sovetskaya muzïka* 6 (1933): 50–65.
450. Zhitomirskiy, D[aniel' Vladimirovich]. "Rannyaya redaktsiya 'Zimnikh grez'" [The Early Redaction of "Winter Dreams"]. *Sovetskaya muzïka* 5 (1950): 65–66.
451. Zhukova, N. G. "Materialï po istorii Peterburgskoy konservatorii v Fonde Russkogo muzïkal'nogo obshchestva v TsGIA Peterburga" (Materials Relating to the History of the Petersburg Conservatory in the Archive of the Russian Musical Society at the State Historical Archive in Petersburg]. In *Peterburgskiy muzïkal'nïy arkhiv: Sbornik statey i materialov* [St. Petersburg Musical Archives: Collection of Articles and Materials], vol. 1. Ed. L. G. Dan'ko and T. Z. Skvirskaya. St. Petersburg: Kanon, 1997, pp. 34–38.

Index

The main entries for Russian surnames observe strict transliteration; informal spellings may be used elsewhere.